Criminal Justice

CRIMINAL JUSTICE

Volume 1

Abortion—Fingerprint identification

Edited by
Phyllis B. Gerstenfeld
California State University, Stanislaus
Department of Criminal Justice

Salem Press, Inc.
Pasadena, California   Hackensack, New Jersey

Editor in Chief: Dawn P. Dawson

Editorial Director: Christina J. Moose   *Editorial Assistant:* Dana Garey
Project Editor: R. Kent Rasmussen   *Photo Editor:* Cynthia Beres
Production Editor: Joyce I. Buchea   *Acquisitions Editor:* Mark Rehn
Manuscript Editor: Elizabeth Ferry Slocum   *Graphics and Design:* James Hutson
Assistant Editor: Andrea Miller   *Layout:* William Zimmerman

Cover photo: Brand-X Pictures/Bill Fritsch

Library of Congress Cataloging-in-Publication Data

Criminal justice / edited by Phyllis B. Gerstenfeld.
    p. cm.
Includes bibliographical references and index.
ISBN-10: 1-58765-218-8 (set : alk. paper)
ISBN-13: 978-1-58765-218-9 (13-digit set : alk. paper)
ISBN-10: 1-58765-219-6 (vol. 1 : alk. paper)
ISBN-13: 978-1-58765-219-6 (vol. 1 : alk. paper)
1. Criminal law—United States—Encyclopedias. 2. Criminal justice, Administration of—United States—Encyclopedias. 3. Crime—United States—Encyclopedias. 4. Criminal procedure—United States—Encyclopedias. I. Gerstenfeld, Phyllis B.

KF9214.5.C75 2006
345.75'05—dc22

2005017803

First Printing

Contents

Contents

Publisher's Note

Criminal Justice is a new Salem Press reference set designed to cover the most important aspects of criminal justice in the United States—from individual types of crimes through broad issues of law enforcement, prosecution, and punishment of wrongdoers.

Designed to meet the needs of lay readers and students from middle school level and up, this three-volume set contains 625 alphabetically arranged articles that are designed to answer the types of questions that readers are most likely to bring. Since many questions arise from readers' exposure to the popular media, special attention is given throughout the set to relationships between the realities of criminal justice and depictions of the subject in films, television, fiction, and the news media. The set carries this emphasis still further in special essays and numerous sidebars on films, television, literature, and the media that point out the connections between media depictions of criminal justice and reality.

Subject coverage

The core issues of criminal justice may be approached through a variety of perspectives, which criminal justice scholars have dubbed the "six C's":

✓ *Criminals:* Who they are, what types of crimes they commit, what motivates them, the impact of their criminal activities on society, and the cost to them of their criminal activities. *Criminal Justice* has nearly 40 core articles on specific categories of crime—ranging from animal abuse and arson to vandalism and white-collar crime. Each of these articles includes profiles of perpetrators of these crimes and summarizes what typically becomes of them. The set also has another 40 articles on issues pertaining to criminal defendants.

✓ *Codes:* The framework of American law and significant individual pieces of legislation. In addition to 20 articles on specific codes and categories of law, *Criminal Justice* has 30 articles on individual laws and many other articles on aspects of law, as well as an index to laws.

✓ *Constitutions:* The content of the nation's foundation documents, their interpretation, and their impact on modern criminal justice. The U.S. Constitution may be said to be the bedrock of the criminal justice system, as all legislation, court decisions, law-enforcement practices, and corrections ultimately rest on constitutional law, as it is interpreted by the courts, and particularly the U.S. Supreme Court. In addition to its many essays on aspects of constitutional law, *Criminal Justice* contains more than 60 articles on Supreme Court rulings that relate to criminal law. The appendix section in volume 3 also contains an Index to Court Cases offering page references to more than 250 court cases.

✓ *Cops:* The varieties of municipal, state, and federal law-enforcement agencies and the relationships among them, as well as their investigative work, specific functions, and arrests and other procedures. *Criminal Justice* has more than 160 articles on policing, law-enforcement agencies, and other aspects of law enforcement.

✓ *Courts:* The structures of the federal and state court systems; relationships among the courts, attorneys, judges, and officers of the courts; and trial procedures. These subjects are covered in about 140 *Criminal Justice* articles.

✓ *Corrections:* Sentencing, capital and other punishments, prison systems, prison conditions, and parole and pardons are covered in about 69 articles, including 11 on capital punishment and 20 on prisons and alternative forms of incarceration.

Other broad subjects covered in *Criminal Justice* include business and commerce (11 articles), drugs (12), juvenile justice (20), the media (13), military justice (4), rights issues (26), traffic law (11), victims (12), and aspects of international justice (10). The last subject includes articles on the Canadian and Mexican justice systems, deportation and extradition, Interpol and other international law-enforcement organizations, and such international tribunals as the World Court.

Organization and Format

The 625 articles in *Criminal Justice* are arranged alphabetically to enable readers to go directly to the topics in which they are interested. Moreover, since readers often do not know which topics they should consult first, the set offers several other features to help readers find the information they need. Volume 3 contains a detailed general subject index and separate indexes to court cases, laws, and personages. It also lists essay topics under 72 different subject categories, ranging from "Appeals," "Arrest and arraignment," and "Arson" to "White-collar crime," "Witnesses," and "Women's issues." Finally, a list of cross-references to other articles follows every essay to help guide readers to the most closely related articles.

Individual articles offer helpful top matter that highlights the most important aspects of each topic. The top matter of all articles provides concise definitions, summaries of the subjects' significance, and identification of key criminal justice issues. The top matter in articles on individual laws, court cases, events, government agencies, organizations, and individual persons also provides dates and places, as relevant.

Criminal Justice is illustrated with nearly 250 photographs, 11 maps, 81 graphs, charts, and tables, and 141 textual sidebars. Other features in the set include two general indexes and 13 appendices in volume 3. In addition to the 4 special indexes already described, the appendix section includes a bibliography of basic works on criminal justice; a glossary; tables summarizing U.S. crime rates; graphs summarizing modern trends in crime rates; summaries of the U.S. Supreme Court decisions most important to criminal justice; summaries of the positions that all Supreme Court justices have taken on criminal justice; an annotated list of famous trials in U.S. history; an annotated list of representative television shows with criminal justice themes, a time line; and an extensive list of criminal justice sites on the World Wide Web.

Acknowledgments

Although *Criminal Justice* is a new reference work, about one-quarter of its 625 articles are taken from Salem's *American Justice* (1996) and *Magill's Legal Guide* (1999). However, articles from those works pertain mostly to legal terminology and other subjects that are relatively unchanging. Topics demanding attention to up-to-date developments in the field of criminal justice, most notably in forensics and crime scene investigation (CSI), are the subjects of entirely new articles.

The editors of Salem Press would like to thank the nearly 300 scholars who wrote essays for *Criminal Justice*. They bring a wide range of expertise from the academic world and the criminal justice professions. We also particularly wish to thank the project's editor, Professor Phyllis B. Gerstenfeld of California State University, Stanislaus, for her many and varied contributions to this project.

Contributors

Richard Adler
University of Michigan, Dearborn

Jennifer R. Albright
Washington State University

Mahalley D. Allen
University of Kansas

W. Dene Eddings Andrews
Indiana State University

Frank Andritzky
Concordia University

Michael L. Arter
*Indiana University of
Pennsylvania*

Betty Attaway-Fink
*Southeastern Louisiana
University*

Mary Welek Atwell
Radford University

Douglas E. Baker
Welch, Wulff & Childers

Thomas E. Baker
University of Scranton

Rachel Bandy
University of Colorado at Boulder

Michael L. Barrett
Ashland University

Charles A. Bartocci
Independent Scholar

Paul Albert Bateman
*Southwestern University School
of Law*

Kimberly J. Belvedere
*Southwestern University School
of Law*

Alvin K. Benson
Utah Valley State College

T. J. Berard
Kent State University

Milton Berman
University of Rochester

Joseph M. Bessette
Claremont McKenna College

Denis Binder
Western New England College

Heidi Jo Blair-Esteves
Wayne State College

William P. Bloss
The Citadel

David Blurton
University of Alaska, Fairbanks

Steve D. Boilard
Independent Scholar

Olivia Boler
Independent Scholar

Denise Paquette Boots
University of South Florida

Bernadette Lynn Bosky
Independent Scholar

William Bourns
*California State University,
Stanislaus*

Peggy C. Bowen
Alvernia College

Timothy M. Bray
University of Texas at Dallas

Pauline K. Brennan
University of Nebraska at Omaha

Thomas W. Buchanan
Ancilla Domini College

Fred Buchstein
John Carroll University

Kevin G. Buckler
*University of Texas at
Brownsville and Texas
Southmost College*

Michael H. Burchett
Limestone College

Alison S. Burke
Independent Scholar

Ann Burnett
North Dakota State University

William H. Burnside
John Brown University

Johnny C. Burris
*Nova Southeastern University
Shepard Broad Law Center*

Edmund J. Campion
University of Tennessee

D. Scott Canevit
*University of Wisconsin,
Milwaukee*

Joel M. Caplan
University of Pennsylvania

Amy I. Cass
University of Delaware

Tammy L. Castle
*Indiana University of
Pennsylvania*

Gilbert T. Cave
Lakeland Community College

Jan M. Chaiken
LINC

Marcia R. Chaiken
LINC

David R. Champion
Slippery Rock University

Frederick B. Chary
Indiana University Northwest

Maxwell O. Chibundu
*University of Maryland School
of Law*

Thomas Clarkin
University of Texas

Scot Clifford
Jett & Laquer

Douglas Clouatre
Mid-Plains Community College

Susan Coleman
West Texas A&M University

William H. Coogan
University of Southern Maine

Allison M. Cotton
Prairie View A&M University

Michael Coulter
Grove City College

Michael J. Coyle
Arizona State University

Randall Coyne
University of Oklahoma Law School

Michael A. Cretacci
State University of New York at Brockport

Sara Criscitelli
Independent Scholar

Mark Anthony Cubillos
Northeastern University

Harry R. Dammer
University of Scranton

Jennifer Davis
University of Dayton

Elizabeth Quinn DeValve
Fayetteville State University

Michael J. DeValve
University of North Carolina Fayetteville State University

Thomas E. DeWolfe
Hampden-Sydney College

Gordon Neal Diem
ADVANCE Education and Development Institute

Ronna F. Dillon
Southern Illinois University

Donald R. Dixon
California State University, Sacramento

Duane L. Dobbert
Florida Gulf Coast University

Mary Dodge
University of Colorado at Denver

Kimberly D. Dodson
Lincoln Memorial University

Pamela Donovan
Bloomsburg University

Philip A. Dynia
Loyola University

C. Randall Eastep
Brevard Community College

Christine Ivie Edge
Indiana University

Preston Elrod
Eastern Kentucky University

Ayn Embar-Seddon
Tiffin University

Patricia E. Erickson
Canisius College

Erin J. Farley
University of Delaware

Yvette Farmer
California State University, Sacramento

John W. Fiero
University of Southwestern Louisiana

Gerald P. Fisher
Georgia College and State University

Dale L. Flesher
University of Mississippi

David R. Forde
University of Memphis

Katherine A. Fowler
Independent Scholar

Carl J. Franklin
Southern Utah University

Carol Franks
Portland State University

Raymond Frey
Centenary College

Gennifer Furst
College of New Jersey

Karen Garner
University of Texas at Austin

Gilbert Geis
University of California, Irvine

Phyllis B. Gerstenfeld
California State University, Stanislaus

Jennifer C. Gibbs
University of Maryland

Camille Gibson
Prairie View A&M University

James N. Gilbert
University of Nebraska at Kearney

Jen Girgen
Florida State University

Marc Goldstein
Independent Scholar

Kuroki M. Gonzalzles
Independent Scholar

Robert F. Gorman
Texas State University

William Crawford Green
Morehead State University

Peter Gregware
New Mexico State University

Timothy Griffin
University of Nevada, Reno

Gwendolyn Griffith
Willamette University College of Law

Michael Haas
University of Hawaii

Michael Hackett
California Command College

Timothy L. Hall
University of Mississippi

Roger D. Haney
Murray State University

Edgar J. Hartung
Alvernia College

Sterling Harwood
San Jose State University

Karen L. Hayslett-McCall
University of Texas at Dallas

Michelle R. Hecht
Indiana University

Peter B. Heller
Manhattan College

Pati K. Hendrickson
Tarleton State University

Diane Andrews Henningfeld
Adrian College

Stuart Henry
Wayne State University

Steve Hewitt
University of Birmingham

Wendy L. Hicks
Loyola University

Christopher M. Hill
Supreme Court of Florida

Arthur D. Hlavaty
Independent Scholar

Kenneth M. Holland
University of Memphis

Jerry W. Hollingsworth
McMurry University

Kimberley M. Holloway
King College

Eric Howard
Independent Scholar

John C. Hughes
St. Michael's College

Robert Jacobs
Central Washington University

Jenephyr James
*Indiana University of
    Pennsylvania*

Dwight Jensen
Marshall University

Charles L. Johnson
Washington State University

Edward Johnson
University of New Orleans

Scott P. Johnson
Frostburg State University

David M. Jones
University of Wisconsin, Oshkosh

Charles L. Kammer
College of Wooster

Tracie L. Keesee
University of Denver

George F. Kermis
Independent Scholar

John C. Kilburn, Jr.
*Eastern Connecticut State
    University*

Paul M. Klenowski
*Indiana University of
    Pennsylvania*

Kim Kochanek
*University of Michigan,
    Ann Arbor*

David B. Kopel
Independence Institute

Laurie M. Kubicek
*California State University,
    Sacramento*

Melvin Kulbicki
York College of Pennsylvania

Karen F. Lahm
Capital University

Eugene Larson
Los Angeles Pierce College

Daria T. LaTorre
Alvernia College

Abraham D. Lavender
Florida International University

Michele Leavitt
North Shore Community College

Jenifer A. Lee
*Indiana University of
    Pennsylvania*

Margaret E. Leigey
University of Delaware

Thomas Tandy Lewis
*Anoka Ramsey Community
    College*

Scott O. Lilienfeld
Emory University

Michael A. Livingston
Rutgers-Camden School of Law

William C. Lowe
Mount St. Clare College

Anthony J. Luongo III
Temple University

Arthur J. Lurigio
Loyola University

Donna Echols Mabus
PLATO Associates

Richard D. McAnulty
*University of North Carolina,
    Charlotte*

Elizabeth H. McConnell
Charleston Southern University

Jerome McKean
Ball State University

Thomas C. Mackey
University of Louisville

Jean Sinclair McKnight
*Southern Illinois University
School of Law*

Samuel C. McQuade III
Rochester Institute of Technology

Richard L. McWhorter
Prairie View A&M University

Stacy L. Mallicoat
*California State University,
Fullerton*

Stephen L. Mallory
*University of Southern
Mississippi*

Bill Manikas
Gaston College

Michael E. Meagher
University of Missouri, Rolla

Kevin Meehan
*California State University,
Fullerton*

Joseph A. Melusky
Saint Francis College

Eric W. Metchik
Salem State College

Diane P. Michelfelder
Utah State University

J. Mitchell Miller
University of South Carolina

Damon Mitchell
*Central Connecticut State
University*

Robert D. Mitchell
*California State University,
Northridge*

William V. Moore
College of Charleston

Mario F. Morelli
Western Illinois University

Debra L. Murphy
Huston-Tillotson College

Lisa Landis Murphy
University of South Florida

Jerry Murtagh
Fort Valley State College

Stephen L. Muzzatti
Ryerson University

David L. Myers
*Indiana University of
Pennsylvania*

Jerome L. Neapolitan
*Tennessee Technological
University*

Elizabeth M. McGhee Nelson
Christian Brothers University

Dale K. Nesbary
Oakland University

Jana Nestlerode
West Chester University

James J. Nolan III
West Virginia University

Charles H. O'Brien
Western Illinois University

Holona L. Ochs
University of Kansas

Emmanuel C. Onyeozili
*University of Maryland Eastern
Shore*

Sharon K. O'Roke
Independent Scholar

Douglas A. Orr
Washington State University

Lisa Paddock
Independent Scholar

John M. Paitakes
Seton Hall University

Carolyn Palmer-Johnson
*Southern Illinois University,
Carbondale*

Michael J. Palmiotto
Wichita State University

Bernadette Jones Palombo
*Louisiana State University,
Shreveport*

Gordon A. Parker
University of Michigan, Dearborn

Allan D. Pass
*National Behavioral Science
Consultants*

Darryl Paulson
University of South Florida

Bruce G. Peabody
University of Texas at Austin

Carrie A. Pettus
University of Kansas

Wayne J. Pitts
University of Memphis

Christina Polsenberg
Michigan State University

Frank J. Prerost
Midwestern University

Maureen Puffer-Rothenberg
Valdosta State University

Neil Quisenberry
McKendree College

Robert J. Ramsey
Indiana University East

Jennifer Ret
Independent Scholar

Betty Richardson
*Southern Illinois University,
Edwardsville*

Edward A. Riedinger
Ohio State University Libraries

Janice G. Rienerth
Appalachian State University

Mark W. Rizzo
*National Gang Crime Research
Center*

Thomas J. Roach
Purdue University, Calumet

Monica L. P. Robbers
Marymount University

Cliff Roberson
Washburn University

Gina M. Robertiello
Seton Hall University

Robert Rogers
Middle Tennessee State University

Carol A. Rolf
Rivier College

Dawn Rothe
Western Michigan University

Kelly Rothenberg
Independent Scholar

Michelle R. Royle
Northern Arizona University

Robert Rubinson
University of Baltimore School of Law

Joseph R. Rudolph, Jr.
Towson University

Michael L. Rustad
Suffolk University Law School

Frank A. Salamone
Iona College

Lawrence M. Salinger
Arkansas State University

Tulsi B. Saral
University of Houston, Clear Lake

Kurt M. Saunders
California State University, Northridge

Sean J. Savage
Saint Mary's College

Daniel C. Scavone
University of Southern Indiana

Amie R. Scheidegger
Charleston Southern University

Heidi V. Schumacher
University of Colorado at Boulder

Brion Sever
Monmouth University

Elizabeth Algren Shaw
Kitchen, Deery & Barnhouse

Taylor Shaw
ADVANCE Education and Development Institute

Theodore Shields
Charleston Southern University

William L. Shulman
Middle Tennessee State University

R. Baird Shuman
University of Illinois at Urbana-Champaign

David M. Siegel
New England School of Law

Donald C. Simmons, Jr.
Mississippi Humanities Council

Donna Addkison Simmons
Troy State University

Vic Sims
Southern Oregon University

Sanford S. Singer
Independent Scholar

Cary Stacy Smith
Mississippi State University

Christopher E. Smith
Michigan State University

Nick Smith
University of New Hampshire

Roger Smith
Independent Scholar

David R. Sobel
Provosty, Sadler & deLaunay

Robert Sobel
Hofstra University

Raymond L. Sparks
California State University, Bakersfield

Steven Stack
Wayne State University

Benjamin Steiner
University of Cincinnati

Barry M. Stentiford
Grambling State University

Joan C. Stevenson
Western Washington University

Robert Stewart
California Maritime Academy

Leslie Stricker
Independent Scholar

David Struckhoff
Loyola University

Susan A. Stussy
Independent Scholar

Hung-En Sung
Columbia University

Susan M. Taylor
Indiana University at South Bend

Victoria M. Time
Old Dominion University

Leslie V. Tischauser
Prairie State College

Kimberly Tobin
Westfield State College

Paul B. Trescott
Southern Illinois University

Emily I. Troshynski
University of Florida

Lawrence C. Trostle
University of Alaska, Anchorage

Sheryl L. Van Horne
Radford University

Diane C. Van Noord
Independent Scholar

Holly E. Ventura
University of South Carolina

Theodore M. Vestal
Oklahoma State University

Kathryn Vincent
University of Maryland

Lydia Voigt
Loyola University

Linda Volonino
Canisius College

Courtney A. Waid
Florida State University

John C. Watkins, Jr.
University of Alabama

T. Steuart Watson
Miami University

Donald A. Watt
Dakota Wesleyan University

William L. Waugh, Jr.
Georgia State University

Marcia J. Weiss
Point Park University

Ashton Wesley Welch
Creighton University

Robert R. Wiggins
Cedarville College

LaVerne McQuiller Williams
Rochester Institute of Technology

Lisa A. Williams
*John Jay College of Criminal
Justice*

Ryan K. Williams
*University of Illinois at
Springfield*

Tonya Y. Willingham
Prairie View A&M University

Thomas Winter
University of Cincinnati

Clifton K. Yearley
*State University of New York at
Buffalo*

Jay Zumbrun
*Baltimore City Community
College*

Complete List of Contents

Volume I

Volume II

Volume III

Introduction to Criminal Justice

The criminal justice system affects the lives of all of us every day—often in ways of which we are unaware.

That statement may surprise some. After all, most of us are not going to be arrested today, nor are we likely to become victims of crime. Indeed, most people give the role of criminal justice in our own lives little thought. Nevertheless, the criminal justice system has a very real impact on each of us every day.

The great influence of the criminal justice system should actually not be surprising. Although criminal justice has changed dramatically over the centuries, it is one of the oldest types of formal societal structures, predating such things as organized health care and public education by many centuries. In the modern United States, criminal justice is also one of the largest and most complex systems, with numerous agencies at local, state, and federal levels.

Criminal justice has also captured a great deal of the popular imagination. Its themes are frequently represented in films, books, plays, and songs, and television programming is filled with shows depicting real and imaginary criminal justice-related stories. Most newspapers splash crime stories across their front pages nearly every day, and television and radio news is filled with crime stories.

Nevertheless, despite the size and importance of the criminal justice system, despite its prominence in the media, and despite its tremendous impact on our lives, most people know little about it. Moreover, much of what they think they know is tainted by myths and misconceptions. Misunderstandings and lack of knowledge about criminal justice can lead us to make faulty decisions in our daily lives; it can also shape misguided decisions on the part of policymakers. Happily, comprehensive reference works about the criminal justice system, such as this one, can help readers to make better and more informed choices about their own lives and about society in general.

What Is the Criminal Justice System?

One reason the average person knows so little about the criminal justice system may be its enormous complexity. The criminal justice system can generally be defined as encompassing public and private agencies and initiatives that seek to define, prevent, prosecute, and punish criminal behavior. Of the system's many components, the most prominent are criminal laws, courts, police forces, and corrections. Criminal justice also exists at many levels, including city, county, state, federal, and international. Moreover, the workings of the criminal justice system vary a great deal from place to place and have evolved radically over time.

Those who wish to study the criminal justice system may feel overwhelmed by the range of approaches that are taken to explain and improve it. While criminal justice is now an academic discipline in its own right, the study of criminal justice connects to a broad variety of fields, including anthropology, biology, business, chemistry, economics, education, history, law, political science, psychology, public administration, social work, and sociology. Because of the breadth and complexity of the criminal justice system, not even those who make its study their profession can honestly claim a full understanding of all its facets.

Paying for Criminal Justice

In 2001, the most recent year for which full data are available, local, state, and federal governments spent more than $167 billion on components of the criminal justice system. At $5.7 billion per year, the budget for the state of California's Department of Corrections—which oversaw about 300,000 inmates and parolees—surpassed the budget of the University of California system, with more than 200,000 students; the budget of the California State University, with more than 300,000 students; and the budget of the state's community college system, with more than 1 million students. In 2005, the state's total expenditures for public safety—which includes corrections, state police, and other departments—approached $11 billion, and that figure does not even include the billions of dollars spent on local police forces, jails, courts, prosecutors, public defenders, offender treatment programs, and other components of the justice system.

Significant portions of the local and state budgets of every state go toward criminal justice, and every dollar spent on criminal justice is a dollar that cannot be spent on education, health care, environmental protection, or other vital services. The resources poured into criminal justice affect everyone by helping to ensure that classrooms remain overcrowded, streets are poorly maintained, libraries are sparsely equipped, and taxes are too high.

The money spent by government on criminal justice is only a small part of the costs of crime. It has been estimated that every year, crime costs Americans more than $100 billion in tangible losses and more than $400 billion more in pain, suffering, and other intangible costs. Crime raises the costs of insurance, health care, and retail goods.

Offenders and Victims

The criminal justice system also affects all of us because eventually almost everyone becomes a victim of crime. Moreover, nearly everyone becomes an offender.

Contrary to popular perceptions, crime rates in the United States have actually been going down since the mid-1990's. Nonetheless, crime is hardly a rare occurrence. In 2003, there were more than 24 million crime victimizations in the United States. The crimes behind these victimizations ranged from minor thefts to rape and murder. Scarcely any segment of society is immune to victimization, but teenagers, young adults, African Americans, and residents of urban areas are particularly likely to experience crime.

One need not be a direct victim of crime to be affected by its occurrence. When we hear about people being attacked near our schools and workplaces, we are likely to become fearful. When we hear about neighbors' homes being burglarized, we are likely to take extra security precautions in our own homes.

Happily, most of the crimes occurring in the United States are not violent. In 2003, about 78 percent of the crimes reported in the National Crime Victimization Survey were property crimes. However, despite their nonviolence, even minor property crimes can have major impacts on their victims' lives. Any student who has ever had

a laptop computer or a backpack containing a semester's accumulation of books and notes stolen can attest to this.

The chances are excellent that all of us will become victims of crime at some point in our lives. Moreover, each of us is also likely to become an offender. Most of us will never commit serious or violent crimes, but it is common for people to commit more moderate crimes, such as drinking while underage, petty shoplifting, fighting, and fudging on our taxes. In a survey made in 2003, more than 70 percent of the high school seniors polled admitted to having consumed alcohol during the previous twelve months, and 46 percent of the respondents admitted having used illegal drugs at least once in their lives. Furthermore, most of us perpetrate minor offenses, such as driving over speed limits and jaywalking on an almost daily basis.

Most of the time, people are not caught and punished for the crimes they commit. Therefore, our formal contact with the criminal justice system as victims or offenders tends to be minimal. Nevertheless, the system still shapes our behavior and the behavior of others.

How Criminal Justice Shapes Our Behavior

Every day we each make many choices, both large and small, that are shaped by the criminal justice system and our perceptions of that system. For example, we may decide how fast we drive our cars. We wonder if we have left any valuables in our cars and whether we have locked our cars properly. We choose what neighborhoods we live in, how and where we spend our recreation time, and where we allow our children to spend theirs. All of these decisions are influenced, at least in part, by the criminal justice system.

However, it is not only individuals whose behavior is affected by criminal justice. Corporate scandals, such as those at Enron, Tyco, and WorldCom, remind us that corporations, too, can be tempted to violate the law—sometimes on a scale even the most corrupt individuals can only dream of. Corporate crime affects not only the companies' employees and shareholders, but also members of the public at large. For example, in early 2005, a grand jury issued an indictment charging executives of a mining company with knowingly exposing people in Montana to cancer-causing asbestos fibers that may have killed nearly two hundred people, made another twelve hundred people seriously ill, and required the federal Environmental Protection Agency to spend more than $55 million to clean up the contamination.

As we remove our belts and shoes and permit strangers to examine our possessions at airports; as we press our feet to our car accelerators; as we contemplate the safety of the food we eat, the air we breathe, and the water we drink, we can surely realize that criminal justice shapes our decisions and the decisions of those around us.

Criminal Justice and the Media

If there is one aspect of our daily lives in which the impact of criminal justice is unmistakably clear, it is the media. How pervasive is the influence of criminal justice in the media? Television provides one answer. During the last week of January, 2005, nine of the twenty highest-rated television programs in the United States had some aspect of criminal justice as their primary themes. Of the remaining eleven programs, four featured criminal justice topics prominently, and one (*Everybody Loves Raymond*) had a major character who is a police officer. Films provide another answer. Of the ten top-grossing films of 2004, three featured unconventional crime-fighters (*Spiderman 2*, *The Incredibles*, and *Harry Potter and the Prisoner of Azkaban*) and a fourth featured a former Central Intelligence Agency (CIA) assassin (*The Bourne Supremacy*). Even the sixth-rated light comedy *Meet the Fockers* had a major character who is a former CIA agent and had a scene involving a confrontation with police. Among the twenty all-time favorite films of users of the Internet Movie Database, eleven have crime or criminal justice as central themes (*The Godfather* and *The Shawshank Redemption* are the highest rated), and two more concern warfare.

Crime features widely in books as well. Five of the top ten titles on an early 2005 *New York Times* list of best-selling hardcover fiction and nine of the ten best-selling titles in paperback fiction have to do with criminal justice. Some cities have bookstores that sell nothing but mystery fiction.

Whether we get our news from television, read it in newspapers or on the World Wide Web, or hear it on the radio, we are constantly exposed to stories related to criminal justice. In fact, criminal justice is likely the most widely reported subject in the news; it accounts for as much as 28 percent of print news coverage and 20 percent of television news.

Those for whom the Internet is the media outlet of choice find countless Web sites dedicated to all aspects of crime and justice. Recent Google searches yielded nearly 15 million hits for the phrase "criminal justice," more than 84 million hits for "crime," and more than 92 million hits for "police." Those who spend a great deal of time online also risk becoming victims of Internet crime—as unwilling recipients of illegal spam and computer viruses, victims of identity theft and malevolent hacking, and the sly advances of sexual predators.

Although criminal justice themes do not appear as much in music as they do in other forms of media, it is nevertheless not difficult to find songs about crime and justice. Centuries before Gangsta Rap was born, folk songs lamented murders, celebrated outlaws and whores, and warned about sheriffs and prisons.

Few themes hold as much appeal to the popular imagination as criminal justice. In fact, an entire academic journal devoted to this very topic is called *The Journal of Criminal Justice and Popular Culture*. Unfortunately, media depictions of criminal justice tend to focus on the sensational, rather than the commonplace. They oversimplify and appeal to the public's fears and desires. Despite the fact that it is nearly impossible to be exposed to the media without being exposed to criminal justice, it might be argued that this exposure actually does more to enhance myths and misconceptions about criminal justice than it does to educate the public about its realities.

The Criminal Justice Paradox

Criminal justice absorbs a significant portion of governmental spending, it touches virtually everyone as both victims and offenders, it shapes the behaviors of individuals and organizations, and it pervades all aspects of the media and popular culture. Criminal justice is a popular major on many college campuses, and the components of the system itself are major sources of employment. Nevertheless, most Americans, young and old, have only a vague concept of how the system operates, and what they think they know about it is often wrong. Several factors contribute to this lack of knowledge: artificial depictions of criminal justice by the media, the vast size and complexity of the criminal justice system, and the speed with which the system undergoes changes and innovations.

If people are uninformed or misinformed about criminal justice, they may make poor choices in their daily lives, and also may create or support poor policy decisions. A reference set such as the present one is valuable because it provides concise and easily understood explanations about all the major topics in criminal justice today. It also provides references for exploring particular subjects in more detail. This set will be an important tool for those who wish to educate themselves about a system that has such a broad and profound influence upon their lives, and for those who wish to make more informed choices.

Phyllis B. Gerstenfeld

Criminal Justice

A

Abortion

Definition: Voluntary early termination of a pregnancy

Criminal justice issues: Homicide; medical and health issues; privacy; women's issues

Significance: Fierce controversy has raged over the questions of whether abortions are acts of homicide and whether decisions to procure abortions should be legal rights guaranteed to women.

Before the nineteenth century, abortions were performed by midwives, herbalists, and rogue doctors and were widely available in the United States. Practitioners even freely advertised their services in newspapers. Eventually, however, the medical profession launched a drive to outlaw abortion in an effort to upgrade patient care and to monopolize it. By 1900, abortion had been rendered illegal throughout the United States, except when performed by a medical doctors in cases in which pregnancies threatened mothers' lives.

Since the U.S. Supreme Court's *Roe v. Wade* ruling in 1973, abortions during the first months of pregnancy have been legally permissible. However, intense public disputes have centered on the moral and criminal justice legitimacy of this doctrine.

Because of their secretive nature, the number of illegal abortions that were performed in the past remains uncertain. A leading authority on the subject observed that he knew of no other instance in which there had been as much disregard for the law as in the case of illegal abortions. Crime statisticians have pointed out that if all women who had illegal abortions were counted in tallies of criminal behavior, the crime rate for women might ex-

ceed that of men, and generalizations about criminal tendencies by gender would have to be revised.

Roe v. Wade

The Supreme Court's *Roe v. Wade* decision legalized abortions during the first trimester of pregnancy and in later stages when a woman's health is at risk. The right to privacy lay at the heart of the Court's decision. Though not explicitly mentioned in the U.S. Constitution, privacy had earlier been invoked in the Supreme Court's *Griswold v. Connecticut* decision (1965) to invalidate a Connecticut law that prohibited the use of contraceptives. The Supreme Court's 7-2 majority in *Roe v. Wade* offered three principles to support its ruling: the protection of life, safeguarding of health, and the preservation of standards in the practice of medicine.

Various forces contributed to the decriminalization of abortion. The vigor of the feminist movement played a large part, particularly as increasing numbers of women were moving into the

President George W. Bush signing the Unborn Victims of Violence Act on April 1, 2004. *(AP/Wide World Photos)*

workforce. Fears of overpopulation also underlay the drive for legalizing abortion. The introduction of birth-control pills, which allowed a greater degree of interference with conception than ever before, served to call into question the inviolability of the birth process. In addition, the illegality of many acts in which participation of involved parties was voluntary—such as homosexuality, gambling, and recreational drug use—were being challenged during this period.

The Antiabortion Crusade

Roe v. Wade produced a strong countermovement among persons who believe that any abortion constitutes criminal homicide. During the early years of the twenty-first century, abortion stood high on the list of criminal justice issues that divided Americans. In the political arena, nominees for judicial positions typically have had to field questions concerning how they might rule if abortion cases were to come before them. The ways in which they respond often determine whether their appointments are confirmed.

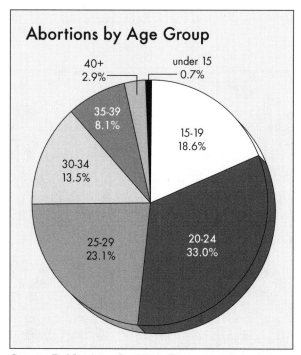

Abortions by Age Group

- 40+ 2.9%
- under 15 0.7%
- 35-39 8.1%
- 15-19 18.6%
- 30-34 13.5%
- 25-29 23.1%
- 20-24 33.0%

Source: Public Agenda, 2004. Figures are based on an estimated total of 1,313,300 abortions in the United States in 2000.

Opposition to abortion is based on the theological doctrine of "ensoulment," a concept that refers to the moment when an embryo or fetus becomes a human being with a God-given right to life. In 1859, Pope Pius IX promulgated the doctrine of "immediate ensoulment," declaring that life begins when a sperm unites with an egg and that artificially ending the gestation process constitutes murder. This position was emphatically restated by Pope John Paul II in 1995, when he condemned abortion as the deliberate killing of innocent human beings and therefore a crime that no human law could legitimate. The stand of the Roman Catholic Church on abortion typically is echoed by fundamentalist religious groups. On the other hand, Jewish theology teaches that a fetus becomes human at the moment some part of its body comes into external view—a position also held by some Protestant groups.

Attitudes toward abortion become more complicated when pregnancy is the result of rape. Those who define themselves as "pro-life" generally insist that regardless of how a fetus is conceived, the mother is morally obligated to bear the child. On the other side, those who call themselves "pro-choice" challenge this position. They ask questions, such as this: If a thirteen-year-old girl were an impregnated rape victim, should she be required to give birth or should she be allowed to have the fetus aborted? Pro-choice advocates favor the latter position.

Twenty-first Century Developments

Since 1973, inroads have been made into *Roe v. Wade* by a series of legislative enactments and court decisions that have outlawed aspects of unrestricted access to abortion. In 1989, for example, the U.S. Supreme Court upheld a Missouri statute that prohibited the use of public facilities, such as municipally owned hospitals, to perform abortions, except when necessary to save a woman's life. Three years later, the Court decided, by a 5-4 vote, to uphold a Pennsylvania law requiring women seeking abortions to listen to a lecture or watch a film about fetal development and then wait one full day before undergoing the procedure.

In 2003, Congress passed what it labeled the Partial-Birth Abortion Act, which designated as criminal offenders any persons who destroy fe-

Pro-Abortion Rights Marchers in 2004

On April 25, 2004, an estimated 800,000 pro-choice activists gathered in Washington, D.C.'s National Mall to protest the abortion policies of President George W. Bush's administration. The marchers charged that reproductive liberties were being eroded in the United States and that the Bush administration's foreign polices were endangering women around the globe. Marchers chanted and carried signs with slogans such as "It's Your Choice, Not Theirs!" and "My Body Is Not Public Property!" Francis Kissling of the Catholics for a Free Choice organization addressed her comments directly to legislators when she stated "You will hear our pro-choice voices ringing in your ears until such time that you permit all women to make our own reproductive choices." During the last previous major pro-abortion march in Washington in 1992, an estimated 500,000 people participated.

tuses that have been partially extracted from their mothers' bodies. The now-outlawed procedure generally was employed after about twenty weeks of pregnancy. Its performance was made a felony carrying possible prison sentences of not more than two years and fines of not more than $25,000.

The Unborn Victims of Violence Act, passed by Congress in 2004, was tied to the killing of Laci Peterson of Modesto, California, who was pregnant at the time of her murder. That act makes it a crime to injure or kill a fetus during an act of violence that violates federal law. It need not be proven that an offender is aware that the woman is pregnant. The response to the act was predictably partisan. Pro-life advocates maintained that women who lose their babies to attackers will no longer be told that they have lost nothing. Pro-choice proponents denounced the act as part of a broader strategy to define fetuses as human beings.

By 2004, thirty-three U.S. states required minors to obtain parental consent before they could have legal abortions. However, the U.S. Supreme Court declared that minors must have the option of seeking a court order authorizing an abortion. However, it has been argued that appearing in court to testify in such a private and intimate matter can be so intimidating that some girls might instead choose illegal or self-inflicted abortions or bear children that they cannot properly

care for. Those who favor parental notification maintain that underage girls are not sufficiently mature to make decisions as vital as whether to have abortions. Furthermore, they argue, minors who obtain parental consent before having abortions can transform what might be a lonely and frightening experience into a more comfortable experience.

Those taking a contrary position say that parents sometimes are part of the problem and not the desired solution to it. When the pregnancy is the result of sexual assault within the family, parental involvement in the abortion decision may not be a sound idea.

The application of parental notification laws is illustrated by a criminal case involving a woman who drove a thirteen-year-old Pennsylvania girl to New York, which had no notification law, for the girl to have an abortion without informing the girl's mother. The woman was fined $500 and sentenced to 150 hours of community service. Her eighteen-year-old stepson, who had impregnated the girl, was convicted of statutory rape for having sexual intercourse with an underage female partner.

Some research has shown that legalized abortion may reduce future juvenile delinquency and crime rates by reducing the numbers of unwanted children who come into the world, as such children have a disproportionate tendency to get into legal trouble. Studies have also shown that the numbers of adopted children—another high crime-risk group—dropped from about 9 percent of all births before 1973 to 4 percent in the decade following the *Roe v. Wade* decision.

Gilbert Geis

Further Reading

Baird, Robert M., and Stuart E. Rosenbaum, eds. *The Ethics of Abortion: Pro-Life v. Pro-Choice.* Amherst, N.Y.: Prometheus, 2001. Reasoned appraisal of the conflicting views of the pro-life and pro-choice sides in the abortion debate.

Gay, Kathlyn. *Abortion: Understanding the Debate.* Berkeley Heights, N.J.: Enslow Publishers, 2004. Contemporary analysis of the competing positions in regard to what the writers maintain should be the moral and legal status of abortion.

Hull, N. E. H., and Peter Charles Huffer. *Roe v. Wade: The Abortion Rights Controversy in American History*. Lawrence: University of Kansas Press, 2001. Attempt to locate the *Roe v. Wade* decision in the context of broader social changes in American society.

Messer, Ellen, and Kathryn May. *Back Room: Voices from the Illegal Abortion Era*. New York: St. Martin's Press, 1988. Examination of illegal abortions prior to the court ruling in *Roe v. Wade*.

Williams, Mary E., ed. *Abortion: Opposing Viewpoints*. San Diego: Greenhaven Press, 2002. Collection of twenty-six articles setting forth conflicting positions on subjects such as the morality and safety of abortion, the abortion drug RU-486, and rape and abortion.

See also *Bowers v. Hardwick*; Murder and homicide; Privacy rights; Rape and sex offenses; Sex discrimination; Statutory rape.

Accomplices and accessories

Definition: Any help, encouragement, or advice that facilitates the commission of crimes

Criminal justice issues: Law codes; legal terms and principles

Significance: The doctrine of complicity explains circumstances under which those who associate with criminal ventures incur liability for the wrongful acts of others before, during, and after crimes are committed.

In common-law tradition, people who acted before crimes were committed were known as "accessories before the fact." Those who acted during commission of the crimes were considered "principals in the second"; those who carried out the actual crimes were considered "principals in the first"; and those who aided after the crimes were committed were called "accessories after the fact." Most modern U.S. statutes have merged these classifications into three categories: People who carry out the crimes are "principals"; those who act before and during the crimes are "accomplices"; and those who act after the fact are "accessories."

The *actus reus* of accomplices constitutes any acts that assist or encourage commission of crimes. In essence, any affirmative acts that enhance the commission of a crime constitute the guilty act in complicity. These acts may comprise, but are not limited to, serving as getaway drivers, acting as lookouts, providing weapons or know-how, and luring victims to the perpetrators. A person's mere presence at a crime scene or flight from a crime scene does not in itself constitute accomplice liability unless there is a legal duty to act. Words that tacitly approve and reinforce the criminal venture may constitute the guilty act in complicity.

Although there is some disagreement in the justice system as to whether the *mens rea* of accomplices constitute recklessness and negligence, there is consensus on the view that accomplices should possess the specific intent to commit acts that satisfy aiding and abetting someone to commit a crime. In *United States v. Peoni* (1938), U.S. circuit court judge Learned Hand noted that a person must associate with the criminal enterprise and actively "participate in it" in an effort to help "make it succeed." Further, besides the intended crime, the guilty intent may be imputed as well for crimes that accomplices could have reasonably foreseen may result from their aiding and abetting one crime.

To incur liability following crimes, most states require that accessories know that the crimes have been committed, that those persons whom accessories assist have committed the crimes, and that the accessories themselves have rendered aid so that the perpetrators could elude justice. Liability for accessories is usually less severe than that for accomplices, and it is based on acts such as providing safe haven, destroying evidence, or assisting in escape.

Victoria M. Time

Further Reading

Dix, E. G., and M. M. Sharlot. *Criminal Law*. 4th ed. Belmont, Calif.: Wadsworth, 1998.

Gardner, T. J. *Criminal Law: Principles and*

Cases. 4th ed. St. Paul, Minn.: West Publishing, 1989.

Reid, Sue Titus. *Criminal Justice.* 6th ed. Cincinnati: Atomic Dog Publishing, 2001.

Samaha, J. *Criminal Law.* 8th ed. Belmont, Calif.: Thomson/Wadsworth, 2004.

Schmalleger, F. *Criminal Law Today.* Upper Saddle River, N.J.: Prentice-Hall, 1999.

See also Conspiracy; Crime; Criminal law; Inchoate crimes; Outlaws of the Old West; Principals (criminal); Solicitation to commit a crime; *Tison v. Arizona.*

Acquittal

Definition: Formal legal certification of the innocence of a defendant who has been charged with a crime

Criminal justice issues: Convictions; trial procedures; verdicts

Significance: Acquittals automatically follow determinations through legal processes that defendants are innocent of the crimes for which they are tried.

An acquittal can result when the jury finds a defendant not guilty, when a judge determines that there is insufficient evidence in a case, or by dismissal of indictments by the court. Once an accused person has been acquitted of crimes, that person may not be lawfully prosecuted a second time for the same crime. If such prosecution were to take place, it would place the defendant in double jeopardy of losing life, liberty, or property, which is in violation of common law and of the U.S. Constitution and state constitutions.

Typically, protection against double jeopardy extends to any prosecution associated with the same act or acts. For example, if an individual has been acquitted of a charge of using a weapon to commit murder, the defendant cannot be retried for any assault committed on the alleged victim. However, when a trial is terminated because of a procedural defect, the defendant is not protected by the rule against double jeopardy. Thus, the defendant can be prosecuted again on the same charge or on related charges. In most states, no degree of procedural error on the part of the state can justify acquittal of a suspect whose conviction is sure based on the evidence. In addition, no evidence can be excluded for reasons of procedural error provided that the procedural error does not affect the confidence that can be safely vested in the evidence.

A motion for a judgment of acquittal can be made prior to submission of the case to the jury, at the close of all the evidence presented before the jury, or after the jury has been discharged. If the evidence is insufficient to produce a conviction, the defendant or the court may request a judgment for acquittal before the case is turned over to the jury. If a motion for judgment of acquittal is made at the close of all the evidence, the court can choose to reserve a decision on the motion, submit the case to the jury, and decide on the acquittal either before or after the jury returns a verdict. After the jury returns a verdict of guilty or is discharged without having returned a

The moment defendants are acquitted, they are cast free of the criminal justice system and cannot be tried again on the same criminal charges. *(Brand-X Pictures)*

verdict, a motion for judgment of acquittal may be made or renewed within a specified time frame (usually fourteen days) after the jury is discharged. In order to make a motion for judgment of acquittal after the jury has rendered its verdict, it is not necessary that a motion was made prior to the submission of the case to the jury.

Alvin K. Benson

Further Reading

Abramson, Jeffery. *We, the Jury: The Jury System and the Ideal of Democracy.* Cambridge, Mass.: Harvard University Press, 1994.

Del Carmen, Rolando V. *Criminal Procedure: Law and Practice.* 6th ed. Belmont, Calif.: Thomson/Wadsworth, 2004.

Emanuel, S. L. *Criminal Procedure.* Aspen, Colo.: Aspen Publishing, 2003.

See also Convictions; Criminal law; Dismissals; Double jeopardy; Principals (criminal); Trials; Verdicts.

Adultery

Definition: Sexual relations between a married person and someone other than that person's spouse

Criminal justice issues: Morality and public order; sex offenses; women's issues

Significance: Definitions, conditions, and penalties for adultery vary significantly from one state to another and frequently undergo modification.

U.S. federal law has never defined adultery as criminal behavior. However, recognizing that adultery is common despite guilt, shame, and social pressures against it, thirty states and the District of Columbia provide for either criminal or civil penalties. Nineteen states and the District of Columbia treat it as a misdemeanor, five states treat it as a felony, and six states provide for forfeiture of property.

If a married person has sexual relations with an unmarried person, some states apply the adultery law only to the married person, while other states also apply the law to the unmarried partner. Some states require that only one sexual act take place, while other states require habitual relations, cohabitation, or open adultery. In some states the government can bring charges, while in others charges can be brought only by the spouse of the married partner. In actuality, criminal charges are rarely applied. In ten states adultery is grounds only for divorce with no civil or criminal penalties. One state prohibits adultery but provides no penalties. Nine states have no adultery statutes.

Despite the lack or diversity of criminal or civil penalties, adultery is almost universally recognized in the United States as grounds for divorce. Before the common acceptance of divorce in the United States and the expansion of legal grounds to obtain it, which began in the 1960's, and especially before no-fault divorces were allowed, married couples sometimes faked extramarital affairs in order to establish grounds for divorce. Consequently, several states specifically ruled out extramarital sexual relations as grounds for divorce.

Since the 1960's research has suggested that adultery might simply reflect diversity in values rather than a marital problem and that adultery is not a major factor causing divorce. Because of this view, less punitive actions have been taken against married people who engage in adultery. Proof of adultery frequently has been a factor in child-custody decisions and in property settlements, with the partner who engages in adultery usually being at a disadvantage in both cases. As divorce has become more common and as attitudes toward sexuality have become more flexible, the issue of adultery has become less important in child-custody and property-settlement decisions. Although it has continued to be important in some child-custody cases, there has been a trend toward emphasizing child welfare rather than parents' adultery. Scientific and social changes have also affected attitudes toward adultery. For example, while deoxyribonucleic acid (DNA) testing has been used by women to prove paternity in child-support cases, it has also become acceptable for husbands to test the paternity of their children when they suspect their wives of adultery. Incidences of adultery have increased among both husbands and wives, fostering less punitive legal and civil responses.

Abraham D. Lavender

Further Reading

Boylan, Brian Richard. *Infidelity*. Englewood Cliffs, N.J.: Prentice-Hall, 1971.

Brown, Emily M. *Patterns of Infidelity and Their Treatment*. 2d ed. Philadelphia: Brunner-Routledge, 2001.

Caprio, Frank S. *Marital Infidelity*. New York: Citadel Press, 1953.

Levitt, Shelley. "Why Men Cheat." *New Woman* 20 (October, 1990): 74.

See also Bigamy and polygamy; Crimes of passion; Domestic violence; Mann Act; Pornography; Rape and sex offenses.

Aggravating circumstances

Definition: Circumstances relating to violations of law that increase the severity of sentences

Criminal justice issues: Punishment; sentencing; violent crime

Significance: The circumstances that surround the commission of crimes can influence the severity of the penalties. Whereas mitigating circumstances can reduce the penalties, aggravating circumstances can increase them.

All crimes are surrounded by facts that must be proven before defendants can be found guilty of crimes. These are called attendant circumstances. When the attendant circumstances increase the severity of the act, they are known as aggravating.

After defendants are found guilty of crimes, judges usually have some discretion in imposing sentences. When such judicial discretion is allowed, prosecutors are apt to bring up whatever factual circumstances may influence the judges to award harsher sentences. Aggravating circumstances often grow out of the ways in which crimes are committed. Sometimes, however, laws themselves specify what constitute aggravating circumstances, such as the use of lethal weapons in commission of crimes.

Many kinds of behavior can be defined as aggravating. Examples include causing serious bodily injury, torturing victims, lying in wait to commit crimes, and using deadly or dangerous weapons. Specific behaviors that might influence sentencing vary among states and are found in the state statutes. When it can be proven that these circumstances have occurred, sentences are generally increased. Some states permit limited judicial discretion, however, and require judges to follow mandatory sentencing guidelines. These guidelines also generally include sentencing ranges based on presumptive, aggravating, and mitigating circumstances.

Janice G. Rienerth

Further Reading

Garner, Bryan A., ed. *Black's Law Dictionary*. 8th ed. St. Paul, Minn.: Thomson/West, 2004.

Wood, J. D., and Linda Picard, eds. *Dictionary of Law*. Springfield, Mass.: Merriam-Webster, 1996.

See also Bifurcated trials; Branch Davidian raid; *Coker v. Georgia*; Convictions; Defenses to crime; Mitigating circumstances; Self-defense.

AIDS

Definition: Acquired immunodeficiency syndrome, a sexually transmitted disease that is conveyed by the human immunodeficiency virus, better known as HIV

Criminal justice issues: Homicide; medical and health issues; morality and public order; sex offenses

Significance: Punishing those who knowingly expose others to HIV infection without their consent poses many legal and social challenges.

Criminalizing the act of intentionally exposing others to HIV infections without their consent involves complex legal issues. AIDS is caused by the human immunodeficiency virus, which is transmitted through blood-to-blood contact or body fluids. It destroys the body's defense mechanism (T-cells) and shortens life spans. The term HIV/AIDS is used to encompass the entire spec-

An HIV "Predator"

In one well-known case that began in 1997, a HIV-carrier named Nushawn Williams infected at least thirteen young women and teenagers with the virus after he was told that he was HIV-positive and was counseled. He denied believing that he was HIV-positive or having harmful intentions. Since HIV has a lengthy disease course, none of the women he infected died, and he thus could not be charged with murder or manslaughter.

When disregard for the serious risks that a behavior poses to other people can be shown, reckless endangerment charges can be made. That was the charge to which Williams eventually pled guilty, along with statutory rape. He was sentenced to four to eighteen years in prison. His full story is told in Thomas C. Shevory's *Notorious H.I.V.: The Media Spectacle of Nushawn Williams* (Minneapolis: University of Minnesota Press, 2004).

trum of the disease, from a patient's testing positive for HIV, without symptoms, to contracting the full-blown disease, AIDS. Persons infected with HIV can infect others, even if they do not have AIDS themselves.

Intentionally transmitting or exposing other persons to HIV without their knowledge and consent can result in criminal charges ranging from reckless endangerment to homicidal intent. Prosecution and sentencing for such offenses vary among the U.S. states. Among the points of difference are such questions as whether knowledge of one's HIV infection is enough to constitute "intent," what transmission modes of the virus can be considered criminal, and whether condom use in sexual intercourse reduces the culpability of carriers. Among the modes of HIV transmission that have been the bases of prosecution are sexual relations with partners; donating infected body fluids, tissues, or organs; rape; child abuse; prostitution; sharing hypodermic needles used for drugs; spitting; biting; and throwing infected fluids.

If purposefulness of conduct to expose other people to HIV can be shown, levels of prosecution can be elevated to assault. HIV assault may be considered either aggravated—an interpretation that would classify HIV as a deadly weapon—or even attempted murder, if it can be shown that offenders use their bodies as weapons intentionally to expose others to HIV.

The early twenty-first century has seen an ongoing debate over question surrounding whether HIV exposure should be criminalized because it victimizes other persons or because it poses a serious public health threat. The latter argument is especially controversial, and there has been virtually no public support for it. Extending prosecution into drug and sex subcultures generally has raised complex issues. Because drug and sex subcultures by their very nature entail the participants' awareness of certain risks, consent may be considered implicit.

Harm reduction and public health proponents argue that extending prosecution into these subcultures would serve only to drive the illicit behaviors farther underground and thereby increase the spread of HIV. Harm-reduction proponents support a strategy of promoting education, treatment, testing and counseling, and sterile-needle exchange for drug users. There is additional concern that prosecution at this level would further stigmatize, and promote discrimination against, HIV carriers.

Debra L. Murphy

Further Reading

Baldwin, Peter. *Disease and Democracy: The State Faces AIDS in the Industrialized World.* Berkeley: University of California Press, 2005.

Jackson, M. H. "The Criminalization of HIV." In *AIDS Agenda: Emerging Issues in Civil Rights*, edited by N. D. Hunter and W. B. Rubenstein. New York: New Press, 1992.

Orcutt, James D., and David R. Rudy, eds. *Drugs, Alcohol, and Social Problems.* Lanham, Md.: Rowman & Littlefield, 2003.

See also Commercialized vice; Prison health care; Prison violence; Rape and sex offenses.

Alcohol use and abuse

Definition: Consumption and overconsumption of alcoholic beverages

Criminal justice issues: Domestic violence; medical and health issues; substance abuse; violent crime

Significance: A long and well-established relationship exists between alcohol and criminal justice. A primary reason for this is the fact that criminal offenders often commit their crimes under the influence of alcohol they consume. However, while there is a consistent pattern of association between alcohol abuse and crime, most people who consume alcohol do not commit crimes, so any notion that the use of alcohol itself causes crime remains to be proven.

Concern about alcohol use and criminal activity can be traced back to the early nineteenth century. By the 1850's, middle-class Americans viewed individuals who engaged in alcohol use and abuse as sinners who were weak in resisting temptation. The temperance movement reflected this attitude by calling for total abstinence and the elimination of liquor traffic. That sentiment gained popularity that resulted in an amendment to the U.S. Constitution that launched Prohibition in 1919. However, the nation as a whole remained divided on this issue, and Prohibition encouraged unlawful behavior, created a black market for alcohol beverages, and fostered organized crime. The demand for alcohol was so strong through the Prohibition years that the Eighteenth Amendment was repealed in 1933.

Repeal of Prohibition did not end the association between alcohol and crime. Instead it led to the implementation of regulations governing the consump-

tion of alcoholic beverages, which resulted in alcohol-specific crimes. Such crimes include drunken driving, public drunkenness, underage drinking, and unlicensed production of alcoholic beverages. Other ways in which crimes are associated with alcohol include engaging in illegal behaviors, such as theft and burglary, to obtain alcohol; engaging in unlawful behaviors, such as disorderly conduct, because of the effects alcohol consumption; and violating laws that regulate the use and distribution of alcohol.

Alcohol and Crime

Relationships between alcohol and criminal justice remain steady in the twenty-first century, despite reductions in certain alcohol-specific crimes. For example, the numbers of offenses related to drunk driving, driving under the influence (DUI), and driving while intoxicated (DWI), have gone down. Arrests for driving under the influence peaked during the early 1980's, with almost 2 million arrests per year and have since shown a downward trend for every age group.

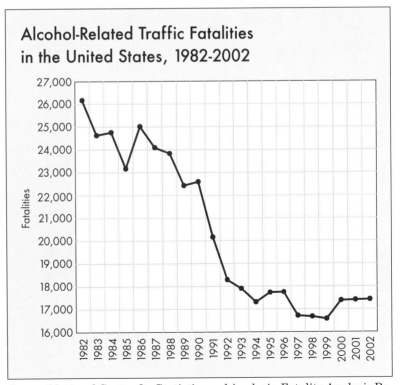

Alcohol-Related Traffic Fatalities in the United States, 1982-2002

Source: National Center for Statistics and Analysis. Fatality Analysis Reporting System (NARS), 2002.

Alcohol-related traffic fatalities and rates of intoxication in fatal accidents have also gone down for every age group.

Several studies have examined relationships between alcohol and crime victimization. One trend is clear: People who drink alcohol are more vulnerable to becoming victims of crime than nondrinkers. In New York homicide cases, for example, both victims and perpetrators are frequently under the influence of alcohol at the time of the offenses. Although targets of crime may often drink alcoholic beverages before being victimized, millions of victims each year perceive that the offenders are drinking at the moments of their crimes. Alcohol use is also frequently linked with violent encounters among intimate partners. In fact, a majority of domestic violence cases involve the use of alcohol, which also increases the likelihood of injuries being associated with domestic disputes.

A number of studies have also examined alcohol use among criminal justice populations, which include probationers, jail residents, and prison inmates. Respondents in these studies report that nearly 38 percent (or more than 2 million offenders) were drinking at the time that they committed their offenses. Virtually all prison inmates report that they have used alcohol during their lifetime, and the average age at the time of their first consumption of alcohol is fourteen. This is consistent with information about serious violent offenders who often report alcohol use to the point of intoxication. There is also evidence to suggest that the most serious violent offenders are using alcohol in combination with other drugs.

Mandatory Sentencing Policies

The implementation of mandatory sentencing policies has resulted in increasing numbers of inmates with substance abuse issues. Repeat drug offenders who have been incarcerated without the opportunity to participate in substance-abuse treatment programs demonstrate that punishment alone does not deter them from future alcohol-related crimes. Corrections officials realize the importance of establishing substance-abuse treatment programs, which contribute to low recidivism rates for released offenders. Despite the recognized importance of substance-abuse treatment in prisons, the demand for such programs still outweighs the number of programs available to inmates.

During the first years of the twenty-first century, patterns of association between alcohol and criminal justice were expected to remain stable. Moreover, even though there have been reductions in alcohol-specific crimes, such as drunk driving, such crimes remain common. In addition, some problems have grown more common, such as the use of alcohol in combination with other drugs and the commission of crimes.

Yvette Farmer

Further Reading

Brecklin, Leanne. "The Role of Perpetrator Alcohol Use in the Inquiry Outcomes of Intimate Assaults." *Journal of Family Violence* 17, no. 3 (2002): 185-197.

Greenfeld, Lawrence. *Alcohol and Crime: An Analysis of National Data on the Prevalence of Alcohol Involvement in Crime.* Washington, D.C.: Bureau of Justice Statistics, 1998.

Greenfeld, Lawrence, and Maureen Henneberg. "Victim and Offender Self-Reports of Alcohol Involvement in Crime." *Alcohol Research and Health* 25, no. 1 (2001): 1-31.

Leukefeld, Carl, et al. "Alcohol and Drug Use Among Rural and Urban Incarcerated Substance Abusers." *International Journal of Offender Therapy and Comparative Criminology* 46, no. 6 (2002): 715-728.

Logan, T. K., Robert Walker, Michele Staton, and Carl Leukefeld. "Substance Use and Intimate Violence Among Incarcerated Males." *Journal of Family Violence* 16, no. 2 (2001): 93-114.

Tardiff, Kenneth, et al. "A Study of Drug Abuse and Other Causes of Homicide in New York." *Journal of Criminal Justice* 30, no. 4 (2002): 317-325.

Valle, Stephen, and Dennis Humphrey. "American Prisons as Alcohol and Drug Treatment Centers: A Twenty-Year Reflection, 1980 to 2000." *Alcoholism Treatment Quarterly* 20, nos. 3/4 (2002): 83-106.

See also Antismoking laws; Blue laws; Crime; Criminals; Drug courts; Drugs and law enforcement; Gangsters of the Prohibition era; Mothers

Against Drunk Driving; Psychopathy; Sobriety testing; Status offenses; Traffic law; Traffic schools.

Alvarez-Machain, United States v.

The Case: U.S. Supreme Court ruling on extradition

Date: Decided on June 15, 1992

Criminal justice issues: International law; kidnapping

Significance: In this ruling, the Supreme Court held that nothing in the extradition treaty between the United States and Mexico and nothing in general international law prohibited the trial of a defendant whose arrest was the result of a forcible abduction from Mexico.

Humberto Alvarez-Machain, a physician and a citizen of Mexico, was believed by the U.S. Drug Enforcement Administration (DEA) to have been partly responsible for the torture and murder of a DEA agent. Alvarez-Machain was indicted by a federal court for kidnapping and murder. After U.S. negotiations with Mexico for his extradition failed, he was forcibly abducted from his office in Guadalajara, flown to the United States, and arrested on arrival. His abductors, though not employees of the federal government, had been solicited by the DEA and promised a reward.

When Alvarez-Machain was brought to trial, he moved to dismiss the indictment because his arrest had been illegal. The district court judge found that although the Drug Enforcement Administration did not directly participate in the kidnapping, it was responsible for it. The indictment was dismissed on the grounds that the extradition treaty between the United States and Mexico had been violated by the illegal arrest. The court of appeals upheld the district court, arguing that the abduction violated the purpose of the extradition treaty. The government appealed to the Supreme Court.

Justice William Rehnquist wrote the opinion for a 6-3 majority. He held that the complicity of the U.S. government in Alvarez-Machain's abduction did not nullify the indictment. The case turned on a narrow question: Does the extradition treaty between the United States and Mexico provide the only means by which a defendant can legally be brought from one of the two countries to the other? As the majority saw the case, the extradition treaty does not establish an exclusive means of bringing potential defendants from Mexico to the United States. It does not specifically exclude kidnapping or unlawful arrest. Therefore the illegality of U.S. actions in Mexico did not affect the validity of the indictment. The case was remanded to the lower courts so that Alvarez-Machain's trial could go forward.

Justice John Paul Stevens wrote a strong dissenting opinion in which he argued that the extradition processes set out in the treaty are designed to provide an orderly means of dealing with cross-border crimes. The dissent argued that by substituting kidnapping for extradition, the United States had violated the treaty. Stevens also argued that the decision would encourage the government to engage in additional acts of international lawlessness.

Although the decision cleared the way for Alvarez-Machain to be put on trial in the United States, Mexican protests about U.S. violation of Mexican sovereignty resulted in an executive decision to return Alvarez-Machain to Mexico. He was repatriated within a few months of the Court's decision.

Robert Jacobs

Further Reading

Blakesley, Christopher L. *Terrorism, Drugs, International Law, and the Protection of Human Liberty.* Ardley-on-Hudson, N.Y.: Transnational, 1992.

Cassese, Antonio. *International Criminal Law.* New York: Oxford University Press, 2003.

See also Arrest; Drug Enforcement Administration; Extradition; Mexican justice system.

Amicus curiae briefs

Definition: Also known as "friend of the court" briefs, statements in favor of one of the sides in legal disputes

Criminal justice issues: Legal terms and principles; trial procedures

Significance: An *amicus* brief need not take one side of a case exclusively. The purpose of these briefs is to assist judges. One can assist the judge most by pointing out the strengths and weaknesses of both sides of a case.

Judges have the power to summon advisers to their aid. This power has led to the use of "friend of the court" briefs, known in Latin as *amicus curiae* briefs. Modern judges can, if they wish, call in advisers and ask for written or oral advice, but it has become much more common for friends of the court to nominate themselves. Nevertheless, as one needs the permission of the judge to be an *amicus curiae*, the first paper to be filed is likely a petition to be admitted as an *amicus*.

Amici (the plural form) must follow certain rules. For example, they are not supposed to bring new issues into the case—that is a right reserved to the parties. *Amici* must comment only on the issues raised by the parties. *Amici* work in two general ways. In some cases they simply file briefs expounding their theories and argue that a certain action should or should not be taken. In others their work is coordinated by one or the other party. For example, it is common in such cases for the parties to stick to fairly conservative lines of argument in their briefs, arguing according to precedents and case law, while the novel arguments that might help them are presented by *amici*. In this way, a party does not offend the judge by raising unusual arguments, but the judge still hears these arguments and, if interested, can respond to them. Judges may give *amicus curiae* briefs as much or as little attention as they think they deserve. They can read them at length several times or glance at their titles and toss them aside.

Amicus curiae briefs are best if the cases cited are recent—not more than ten years old in most cases, and preferably not more than five years old. They are most effective if they have been carefully "shepardized," or, checked against *Shephard's Citations* to ensure that the cases cited are still considered valid law or to point out how they differ from those that are valid law.

Dwight Jensen

Further Reading

Emanuel, S. L. *Criminal Procedure*. Aspen, Colo.: Aspen Publishing, 2003.

Schiller, N. *Criminal Procedure for the Criminal Justice Professional*. Eagan, Minn.: West Publishing, 2001.

See also Judges; Solicitor general of the United States; Vehicle checkpoints.

Amnesty

Definition: General pardon made by government to persons who have been convicted of crimes

Criminal justice issues: Convictions; immunity; pardons and parole

Significance: Often based on political considerations, the granting of amnesty is often controversial.

Amnesty is a government action that grants immunity from prosecution to an identified group of people for a specified criminal offense. The term is derived from the Greek word meaning "oblivion," which is appropriate, because amnesty involves the "forgetting" of an offense. Although accused individuals do not have to exchange information or testimony to receive amnesty, they are expected to abide by all laws in the future. In some cases grants of amnesty are conditional, requiring a loyalty oath or community service. The difference between amnesties and pardons is not well defined, but amnesties are typically granted to persons before prosecution has taken place, while pardons are usually granted to persons after their trial and conviction.

In the United States the power to grant amnesty usually resides in the chief executive. Governors usually possess the power to grant amnesties for violations of state law. At the federal

The Vietnam War generated unprecedented levels of public protest. Many young men who opposed the war refused to serve in the armed services, and some fled to Canada to avoid the draft. After the United States pulled out of the war, the federal government faced the problem of how to deal with tens of thousands of draft evaders. President Gerald Ford resolved the matter by declaring a general amnesty. *(Library of Congress)*

level, both the president and Congress can grant amnesties. The president's authority derives from Article II, section 2 of the U.S. Constitution, which gives the president the "Power to grant Reprieves and Pardons for Offenses against the United States, except in cases of Impeachment." Congress may grant amnesties under the terms of the "necessary and proper" clause found in Article I, Section 8 of the Constitution. The U.S. Congress does not have the power to limit or place conditions on any presidential amnesties.

Presidents have generally granted amnesties in situations involving actions undertaken in protest against government policies. In 1795 President George Washington granted amnesty to participants in the Whiskey Rebellion, which was essentially a revolt against excise taxes. In 1865 President Andrew Johnson offered most ex-Confederates amnesty if they agreed to take a loyalty oath to the Union. These examples reveal

the intent behind most amnesties: to end divisive conflicts within American society in order to achieve reconciliation and domestic tranquillity.

President Gerald R. Ford's 1974 decision to offer amnesty to individuals who had refused to serve in the Vietnam War illustrated both the confusion surrounding the meaning of the term "amnesty" and the political calculations involved in granting it. As late as March, 1974, Ford declared that draft evaders had to be tried in the nation's courts. However, upon succeeding President Richard M. Nixon as president the following August, Ford was advised by his cabinet officers that an amnesty program would speed the nation's recovery from the war. In addition, the American public would regard Ford as a conciliator, which would improve his political standing. Later that same month, Ford announced that draft evaders would have the opportunity to earn their reentry into American society. He called his proposal clemency rather than amnesty on the grounds that draft evaders would be required to perform some form of alternative nonmilitary service to the nation. Ford's action, commonly regarded as an example of conditional amnesty, was intended to appease Americans who opposed the unconditional pardon of persons who refused to perform military service during the Vietnam War.

Thomas Clarkin

Further Reading

Gioglio, Gerald. *Days of Decision: An Oral History of Conscientious Objectors in the Military During the Vietnam War*. Trenton, N.J.: Broken Rifle Press, 1989.

Levi, Margaret. *Consent, Dissent, and Patriotism*. New York: Cambridge University Press, 1997.

Moore, Kathleen Dean. *Pardons: Justice, Mercy and the Public Interest*. New York: Oxford University Press, 1989.

See also Appellate process; Attica prison riot; Clemency; Pardons.

Animal abuse

Definition: Socially unacceptable behavior that inflicts pain and suffering on animals

Criminal justice issues: Deviancy; domestic violence; medical and health issues; vandalism

Significance: Animal abuse is a common crime that causes its victims much suffering and death. Many offenders are at risk to commit violent acts against human beings. The crime of animal abuse presents a unique set of problems for criminal justice practitioners. Consequently, most animal abuse is not reported, investigated, prosecuted, or punished.

Defining animal abuse, or cruelty to animals, is a challenge. Because laws protecting animals vary from state to state, no single legal definition of animal abuse exists. Generally, animal abuse is seen as acts or omissions that inflict unnecessary

Indications That Animals Are Being Treated Cruelly

✓ untreated tick or flea infestations
✓ body wounds
✓ patches of missing hair
✓ extreme thinness—a sign of starvation
✓ limping
✓ persons in the act of striking or otherwise physically abusing animals
✓ dogs that are frequently left alone without food or water, often chained up in yards
✓ dogs that are kept outside without shelter in extreme weather conditions
✓ animals that cower in fear or behave aggressively when approached by their owners

Source: American Society for the Prevention of Cruelty to Animals (http://www.aspca.org/site).

pain and suffering on animals and that occur outside the realm of socially acceptable behavior. Although animal research, certain animal agriculture practices, hunting, fishing, trapping, pest control, and the use of animals in rodeos, zoos, and circuses may cause animals to suffer, because these behaviors are generally socially condoned, they are not usually considered animal abuse. However, not all observers agree that these latter behaviors should be socially condoned.

Intentional abuse occurs when a person knowingly tortures, maims, or kills an animal, or knowingly deprives an animal of food, water, shelter, socialization, or veterinary care. Neglect—acts of omission—occurs when people who do not intend to cause harm fail to provide animals with proper food, water, shelter, attention, or veterinary care. Unique forms of animal abuse include animal fighting and "hoarding." The latter practice is the accumulation of tens, or even hundreds, of animals within places such as human residences and usually failing to provide adequate standards of nutrition, sanitation, and veterinary care.

Attempts to Control Animal Abuse

The first American law protecting animals was passed in 1641 by the Puritans of the Massachusetts Bay Colony. However, the first postcolonial anticruelty law was not enacted until 1821, when Maine's state legislature made it illegal to beat horses or cattle cruelly. By 1913, every state and the District of Columbia had enacted anticruelty statutes. However, these laws were rarely enforced until the formation of societies for the prevention of cruelty to animals. Such societies were often granted powers to enforce the anticruelty laws. The first such organization was the American Society for the Prevention of Cruelty to Animals, formed in New York in 1866 by Henry Bergh.

The late twentieth century saw a new trend to strengthen laws making animal abuse a crime. In 1998, only twenty states had felony animal-cruelty laws. By 2004, that number had doubled.

Prevalence

Unlike other violent crimes, animal abuse is not tracked in centralized national crime reporting systems. It is thus impossible accurately to estimate the number of animals who are victims of abuse or the number of people who inflict such abuse. Estimates of the prevalence of animal cruelty are usually obtained from the data derived from studies done by researchers. In addition, several nonprofit organizations maintain databases of animal-abuse cases and compile statistics based on cases known to them. These sources suggest that animal abuse is an often occurring and widespread problem. However, more research is needed before the true incidence and prevalence of animal abuse can be known. However, it is known that the perpetrators of most types of animal abuse are more likely to be male than female. On the other hand, women appear to be more likely than men to commit hoarding-type abuses.

Animal Abuse and Violence Against People

Since the mid-1970's, numerous studies in psychology, sociology, and criminology have demonstrated that persons who abuse animals are often—although not always—also dangerous to other people. Serial killers, mass murderers, sexual homicide perpetrators, serial rapists, and arsonists often have childhood histories of animal abuse. Perpetrators of more common forms of violence, such as child abuse, spouse abuse, and elder abuse, also tend to be abusive toward animals.

Animal abuse has also been identified as a "red flag" that may help identify youthful offenders at risk for perpetrating violence against people. For example, in 1997, a sixteen-year-old boy in Mississippi killed his mother and then went on a shooting spree at his high school, where he killed two fellow students and wounded seven others. Several months earlier, a neighbor had witnessed the boy torture and kill his own pet dog.

Animal abuse, like any other form of violence, may be prompted by a number of motives. One person may abuse an animal in the process of disciplining or training it. Other motives may include shocking or offending others; retaliating against animals or their owners for real or imagined offenses; expressing power through animals, such as by training them to be aggressive;

Animal control officers in Connecticut removing a dog from a home whose owner was running an unlicensed kennel in mid-2004. The owner was charged with nineteen counts of animal cruelty for keeping nineteen dogs confined within his modest home. *(AP/Wide World Photos)*

and simply enjoying the suffering that the abused animals experience. Children who abuse animals may be succumbing to peer pressure, satisfying their curiosity, imitating cruelty they have seen others commit, or reacting to their own experiences of being abused.

Investigation

Investigating animal abuse can be difficult. Because the animal victims cannot speak for themselves, most animal abuse is not reported. To investigate animal-abuse crimes more efficiently, Florida's Broward County Sheriff's Office formed an Animal Cruelty Investigation Unit in 1982—the first such unit of its kind in a law-enforcement agency in the United States.

In some states, investigation of animal abuse is the responsibility of regular law-enforcement agencies. In others, animal control agencies and humane societies may also investigate claims of abuse; they may also have the power to intervene, take custody of abused animals, make arrests, and even carry weapons.

Investigation, prosecution, and punishment of animal abuse are regarded as low priorities in the U.S. criminal justice system. Laws penalizing animal abuse are often ambiguous or only misdemeanor-level offenses. Moreover, law-enforcement agencies may have limited resources to enforce animal-protection laws, and some law-enforcement officers, prosecutors, and judges may not regard animal abuse as a serious crime.

Prosecutors may be reluctant to charge offenders with the commission of animal-abuse crimes, especially if the offenses are merely misdemeanors. For example, in 1996, prosecutors in one state filed criminal charges in only 2 percent of cases in which animal abuse was alleged. However, this situation may change as more states enact felony cruelty laws and more criminal justice practitioners become aware of connections between cruelty to animals and violence against people.

Most anticruelty laws make animal abuse misdemeanor offenses, and most offenders who are convicted receive only light sentences. However, at least forty-one states and the District of Columbia have enacted statutes making certain forms of more serious animal abuse felony-level crimes with increased punishment. A notable ex-

---

Statistics on Animal Abuse

Founded in October, 2001, Pet-Abuse.com is a registered nonprofit organization based in Southern California that is dedicated to helping to prevent animal abuse through the collection and dissemination of information. The organization maintains an elaborate Web site (www.pet-abuse.com) that provides general information on animal cruelty, pet adoption, and other subjects and detailed and frequently updated statistics on animal abuse in the United States. Visitors to the Web site can search for statistics under a variety of headings: regions, types of animals, types of abuse, and types of abuser.

Additional information on animal abuse can be found on the Web site of the Humane Society of the United States at www.hsus.org/firststrike.

---

ample of changing state attitudes toward animal abuse occurred in Wisconsin in 1998, when a state court sentenced a convicted pedophile and prior animal abuser to ten years in prison for the torture and killing of five cats. This was the longest animal-cruelty sentence ever awarded in U.S. history.

Like most crimes, animal abuse is often punished by periods of probation, restitution, community service, fines, and imprisonment. In addition, convicted offenders may be required to forfeit their own animals or reimburse expenses for the care of seized animals. They may also be prohibited from keeping animals in the future. In some jurisdictions, offenders may also be required to undergo counseling or other forms of intervention.

Jen Girgen

Further Reading

Animals and Their Legal Rights: A Survey of American Laws from 1641 to 1990. 4th ed. Washington, D.C.: Animal Welfare Institute, 1990. Comprehensive examination of laws relating to animals. Includes discussions about the evolution of anticruelty laws, and animal protective organizations and law-enforcement agencies.

Ascione, Frank R. *Animal Abuse and Youth Violence.* Washington, D.C.: U.S. Department of

Justice, 2001. Report on psychiatric, psychological, and criminological research linking animal abuse—especially that perpetrated by children and adolescents—to violence against people.

Ascione, Frank R., and Phil Arkow, eds. *Child Abuse, Domestic Violence, and Animal Abuse: Linking the Circles of Compassion for Prevention and Intervention*. West Lafayette, Ind.: Purdue University Press, 1999. Essays based on the firsthand experience of professionals working to prevent, investigate, and prosecute the abuse of animals and vulnerable people.

Ascione, Frank R., and Randall Lockwood. "Cruelty to Animals: Changing Psychological, Social, and Legislative Perspectives." In *State of the Animals 2001*, edited by D. J. Salem and A. N. Rowan. Washington, D.C.: Humane Society Press, 2001. Thorough examination of what is currently known—and not known—about animal abuse. Emphasizes the need for more research.

Lockwood, Randall, and Frank R. Ascione, eds. *Cruelty to Animals and Interpersonal Violence: Readings in Research and Application*. West Lafayette, Ind.: Purdue University Press, 1998. Interdisciplinary collection of historical, philosophical, and research articles exploring the relationship between violence against animals and violence against people.

Merz-Perez, Linda, and Kathleen M. Heide. *Animal Cruelty: Pathway to Violence Against People*. Walnut Creek, Calif.: AltaMira Press, 2004. Study of the animal cruelty-human violence link. Includes a critical review of previous research, and an examination of three theoretical explanations for the relationship.

Mitchell, Angela. *Animal FAQs: An Encyclopedia of Animal Abuse*. Leicester, England: Troubadour Publishing, 2003. Reference guide with facts, figures, and more than 300 definitions of terms related to the abuse of animals.

See also Child abuse and molestation; Community service; Cultural defense; Domestic violence; Fines; Restitution; Statutes.

Annotated codes

Definition: Compilations of statutory laws organized by topics
Criminal justice issues: Law codes; legal terms and principles
Significance: Orderly compilations of laws, together with citations to court opinions interpreting these laws, are crucial legal research tools.

Legislative bodies at the national, state, and local levels regularly enact laws. Examples of lawmaking bodies include the U.S. Congress, state legislatures, and city councils. When legislative bodies pass laws, these enactments take their place among previously enacted laws. However, the collection of laws passed over a period of time can eventually become a bewildering assortment of legal prescriptions on a variety of topics, since legislative bodies pass new laws regularly and also amend and repeal old ones.

To bring order to this potentially confusing array of laws, federal, state, and local governments routinely incorporate legislative enactments into codes. These codes are orderly compilations of existing laws arranged by topic. For example, laws passed by the U.S. Congress are included in the United States Code.

In a code, legislative acts that amend previously existing laws appear with that law, and the various enactments still in force are generally arranged by subject matter. For example, laws on the protection of the environment appear in one place while laws on deportation appear in another. A code also reflects the repeal of laws by legislative bodies.

Once a legislative body passes a law, the work of interpreting it falls to the courts. Federal and state appellate courts routinely publish their decisions, including the decisions they render with respect to legislative enactments. These published decisions guide subsequent courts that may be called upon to interpret the same laws, since courts generally attempt to make their decisions harmonize with previously decided cases, which are called precedents. The respect for precedent is a standard feature of the U.S. legal system and is generally referred to as the doctrine of *stare decisis*, which literally means, "let the decision stand." According to this legal doctrine, a court should, whenever possible, seek to make rulings consistent with the rulings by previous courts on the same subject. Thus, to understand a legislative enactment, one must generally have access not only to the text of the enactment but also to court opinions that have interpreted it.

Annotated codes assist lawyers and judges in conducting research on specific laws. These codes include not only the text of laws but also a brief description of cases and of other legal authorities that have interpreted the law. These descriptions themselves are arranged topically, thus assisting researchers in finding cases that discuss the particular legal issues of interest to them. In addition, laws in annotated codes generally include cross-references to related laws in the same general field. For federal laws, the most widely consulted reference edition is the *United States Code Annotated* (St. Paul, Minn.: West Publishing). Furthermore, the laws of each state are published in annotated codes.

Timothy L. Hall

Further Reading

Dubber, Markus Dirk. *Criminal Law: Model Penal Code*. New York: Foundation Press, 2002.

Federal Criminal Code and Rules. St. Paul, Minn.: West Group Publishing, 2003.

Livingston, E. *A System of Penal Law for the United States of America: Consisting of a Code of Crimes and Punishments, a Code of Procedure in Criminal Cases, a Code of Prison Discipline, and a Book of Definitions*. New York: William S. Hein, 2000.

See also Counterfeiting; Model Penal Code; United States Code; United States Statutes at Large.

Anti-Racketeering Act of 1934

The Law: Federal legislation enacted to protect trade and commerce from interference by criminal threats of violence or coercion
Date: Became law May 18, 1934
Criminal justice issues: Federal law; organized crime

Significance: The Anti-Racketeering Act was the first federal law enacted to fight the control that organized crime was suspected of holding over local communities.

During the 1920's and 1930's, there was a significant increase in gangster activity and organized crime in the United States. Groups of criminals used bribery, extortion, threats, and violence to manipulate and control political officials, judges, and police officers and to harass local businesses. These groups were suspected of controlling gambling, prostitution, and the sale of illegal alcohol. Local authorities felt helpless in their fight to end criminally controlled rackets.

The 1934 Anti-Racketeering Act was proposed by Assistant Attorney General Joseph B. Keenan. Keenan, who testified before the Senate Judiciary Subcommittee on March 2, 1934, asserted that federal authorities needed an antiracketeering law to help fight organized crime. Racketeers were debilitating legitimate businesses and communities. To fight back, local authorities needed assistance from the federal government. The Anti-Racketeering Act was one of six changes in the criminal justice code recommended by Keenan to aid the Department of Justice in its goal to put every gangster, racketeer, and kidnapper out of business and into jail.

The Anti-Racketeering Act was one of several crime-fighting bills submitted to Congress by Senator Hy Ashurst of Arizona and Senator Royal Copeland of New York. Reflecting the recommendations made by Keenan, these bills aimed to reduce crime in the United States by increasing the powers of the federal government to assist local communities. The crime bills were vigorously supported by President Franklin D. Roosevelt. The House of Representatives quickly approved all six bills on May 5, 1934, and the Senate passed them on May 15. Numerous criminals were subsequently arrested and convicted under the Anti-Racketeering Act.

Under the Anti-Racketeering Act, racketeering was defined as any act or threat of violence committed to divert or interfere with interstate commerce and any actual or intended attempts at extortion in connection with interstate commerce transactions. Racketeering included any acts or coercions used to force an individual or business to join or not to join any organization or to buy or not to buy goods. It included any acts of violence to individuals in connection with such activities. Those convicted of racketeering would receive a maximum of ninety-nine years in prison and a fine commensurate with the profits derived from racketeering transactions.

The Anti-Racketeering Act remained unchanged until 1946, when Congress passed the Hobbs Act. The Hobbs Act placed previously exempted illegal labor-union activity within the reach of federal prosecutors. In 1970, Congress passed the Racketeer Influenced and Corrupt Organizations Act (RICO), which increased penalties for those convicted of racketeering and permitted the seizure of assets acquired or used at the time of the criminal activity.

Leslie Stricker

Further Reading

Cressey, Donald R. *Theft of the Nation: The Structure and Operations of Organized Crime in America*. New York: Harper & Row, 1969.

After New York City imposed a ban on smoking in bars, restaurants, and public buildings, a new sight emerged throughout the city: clusters of smokers on public sidewalks, which suddenly became major sources of secondary smoke to pedestrians. *(AP/Wide World Photos)*

Lyman, Michael D., and Gary W. Potter. *Organized Crime*. 3d ed. Upper Saddle River, N.J.: Prentice-Hall, 2000.

See also Blackmail and extortion; Hobbs Act; Mafia; Motor vehicle theft; Organized crime; Organized Crime Control Act; Political corruption; Witness protection programs.

Antismoking laws

Definition: State and municipal ordinances that prohibit smoking in designated places, such as restaurants, public buildings, and private office buildings

Criminal justice issues: Law codes; medical and health issues; victimless crime

Significance: Laws that restrict smoking have extended the authority of government entities to regulate when and where people can engage in what is otherwise a legal behavior and have extended the reach of the government to regulate the policies and practices of private businesses.

During the early twenty-first century, the number of municipal and county jurisdictions passing antismoking ordinances steadily increased. The ordinances prohibit smoking in public places such as government buildings, restaurants, and even bars. The primary rationale behind such legislation is public health. Political sponsors and advocates of antismoking legislation frequently cite significant health-related issues that are correlated with secondhand smoke as the justification for antismoking legislation.

However, opponents of antismoking legislation have frequently cited what they call the rights of the smokers themselves, as well as the rights of private business owners to make decisions about what constitutes permissible behavior within their own establishments. In addition, business owners who oppose antismoking laws frequently argue that such bans will cost them the business of smokers who choose not to visit their establishments.

While the issue continues to be intensely debated, it is clear that the trend toward antismoking legislation is gaining strength. Such legislation has been passed in what many would regard as highly unlikely places. In 2004, for example, a smoking ban was passed in Lexington-Fayette County, Kentucky—in the center of a major tobacco-producing region. After lengthy delays because of legal challenges to the ban, it took effect in April, 2004, after Kentucky's supreme court ruled that it was within the province of local authorities to establish smoking bans and that doing so did not preempt state law.

The Lexington-Fayette County ban prohibited smoking in all areas open to the public, including restaurants and bars, with the exceptions of dwellings and designated motel and hotel rooms, tobacco warehouses, nonenclosed public spaces, rooms and halls used for private social activities that are not open to the public, and nonprofit private organizations.

While much is understood about the intense and ongoing political debates between advocates and opponents of antismoking legislation, less is known about the impact of the smoking bans themselves. The findings of such research as has been done are mixed. Some studies have indicated no effects in terms of the prevalence of smoking, while other studies have observed reductions in smoking behavior. A 2004 study in Massachusetts found that in areas with the strongest restrictions on smoking in public places, both adults and juveniles report perceiving a lower social acceptability of smoking. In addition, juveniles reported observing less adult smoking.

Some research has also addressed compliance-related issues. A 1996 study found that many of the concerns of opponents of smoking bans about such matters as enforcement problems, negative reactions of customers, and effects on business were unrealized fifteen months after the bans took effect. Research has also reported that employee and patron compliance with California's Smoke-Free Workplace law improved between 1998 and 2002. Therefore, while antismoking ban

legislation continues to be controversial, there is evidence of its having positive community-based effects.

Kevin G. Buckler

Further Reading

Hudson, D. *Smoking Bans*. Philadelphia: Chelsea House Publishers, 2004.

Jacobson, P. D. *Tobacco Control Laws: Implementation and Enforcement*. Santa Monica, Calif.: Rand, 1997.

Rabin, R. L., and S. D. Sugarman, eds. *Smoking Policy: Law, Politics, and Culture*. New York: Oxford University Press, 1993.

Schaler, J. A., and M. E. Schaler, eds. *Smoking: Who Has the Right?* Amherst, N.Y.: Prometheus Books, 1998.

Weber, M. D., et al. "Long-Term Compliance with California's Smoke-Free Workplace Law Among Bars and Restaurants in Los Angeles County." *Tobacco Control* 12, no. 3 (2003): 269-273.

See also Alcohol use and abuse; Contributing to delinquency of minors; Drug legalization debate; *New Jersey v. T.L.O.*; Public-order offenses; Regulatory crime; School violence; Victimless crimes.

Antiterrorism and Effective Death Penalty Act

The Law: Federal law expanding federal law-enforcement powers to counter terrorism and restrict appeals for those convicted of capital crimes

Date: Signed into law on April 24, 1996

Criminal justice issues: Capital punishment; federal law; terrorism

Significance: The Antiterrorism and Effective Death Penalty Act granted the federal government new powers in fighting terrorism and significantly restricted post-conviction appeals brought by death-row inmates in federal court.

Following the 1993 bombing of the World Trade Center and the 1995 Oklahoma City bombing,

New York City police and firefighters examining the crater made by a terrorist bomb that exploded in a subterranean level of the World Trade Center on February 26, 1993. (AP/Wide World Photos)

the federal government was under increasing pressure to respond to terrorism taking place on American soil. At the same time, condemned inmates who filed *habeas corpus* petitions to have their convictions reviewed were extending their time on death row by years, at cost to taxpayers. The Antiterrorism and Effective Death Penalty Act (AEDPA) was a response to these two situations.

The new law empowered the federal government to deny visas to people identified as belonging to terrorist groups and to deport legal resident aliens by expanding the definition of crimes that result in deportation and by eliminating judicial review of deportation orders. An important provision of the law is the authority of the federal government to designate a group as a foreign terrorist organization (FTO), allowing the group's assets to be seized and limiting their fund-raising ability in the United States. Also, the law banned

the provision of support to countries that aid terrorist groups, granted Americans the ability to sue foreign countries in federal court for terrorism aimed at Americans abroad, and declared acts of participation in terrorism in the United States to be federal crimes.

The AEDPA was also designed to limit federal *habeas corpus* petitions filed by state inmates convicted of capital crimes, in an effort to prevent frivolous lawsuits. It accomplished this by requiring all inmates to exhaust their state-level appeals before filing a petition in federal court and limited the time inmates had to file a federal petition to one year after exhausting their state appeals. Also, federal petitions were effectively limited to one by requiring any successive petitions be reviewed for merit by a panel of three federal judges before being considered.

Gennifer Furst

Further Reading

Chang, Nancy. *Silencing Political Dissent*. New York: Seven Stories Press, 2002. Argues that antiterrorism policies, including the Patriot Act, threaten civil liberties and may lead to excessive executive power.

Dempsey, James X., and David Cole. *Terrorism and the Constitution: Sacrificing Civil Liberties in the Name of National Security*. 2d ed. Washington, D.C.: First Amendment Foundation, 2002. This book covers national security concerns, the law and legislation, and terrorism in the United States. Includes bibliography.

Latzer, Barry. *Death Penalty Cases*. 2d ed. Boston: Butterworth-Heinemann, 2002. Contains excerpts of U.S. Supreme Court death-penalty cases as well as statistical data on capital punishment and selected death-penalty statutes.

See also Attorney general of the United States; Capital punishment; Cruel and unusual punishment; Espionage; *Habeas corpus*; International law; Terrorism.

Antitrust law

Definition: Laws that provide for civil and criminal penalties against businesses that act or conspire unreasonably to limit competition in the marketplace

Criminal justice issues: Business and financial crime; political issues; white-collar crime

Significance: Federal antitrust laws have protected competition and benefited consumers by prohibiting business practices that result in artificially higher prices and lower-quality goods and services.

Competitive markets are more efficient and benefit consumers more than markets that are dominated by one or few firms. Markets in which firms compete vigorously with one another tend to produce lower prices and better quality and a larger variety of goods or services. The main purpose of the antitrust laws is to protect competition. If anticompetitive behavior is left unchecked, new firms may be discouraged from entering the market, innovations may be suppressed, and consumers may have to pay higher prices while having less choice. For these reasons, and to demonstrate its commitment to a competitive economy, Congress decided in 1890 to enact the Sherman Antitrust Act. To the present day, that law remains the principal federal antitrust law.

Federal Prohibitions

The first section of the Sherman Act forbids all contracts, combinations, and conspiracies among businesses that unreasonably restrain interstate trade. Such contracts include agreements among competitors to fix prices, restrict output, rig bids, and allocate customers among themselves. These actions are often called per se offenses because, once proved, they are automatically deemed to be illegal and no evidence that defendants might offer to justify their conduct will be allowed.

Price-fixing occurs when two or more firms agree that they will set prices at a certain amount or that they will not sell below a certain set price. Price-fixing occurs indirectly when firms agree to limit or reduce the amount of goods produced. This has the effect of reducing the supply of goods available to consumers and thereby drives up prices. Bid-rigging occurs when two or more firms agree not to bid against each other to supply goods or services to local, state, or federal government agencies, or when they agree in advance on the level of their individual bids as a means of predetermining the winner of the bidding process and thus ensure the winner of being able to charge a higher price than might result if the bidding were fair. Market allocation occurs when firms agree to divide up their markets by territory, product line, or some other means. This practice ensures that each firm will dominate its own share of the market and be able to charge higher prices than it would if it had to compete with other firms.

The second section of the Sherman Antitrust Act makes it a crime to monopolize any part of interstate commerce. An illegal monopoly results when a firm becomes the only supplier of a good or service not because its goods or services are superior to others, but because it has acted to suppress competition in its market. However, it is not a monopolization violation if a firm's vigorous competition, superior goods or services, or lower

The United States v. Microsoft Case

In only twenty-five years, the Microsoft Corporation grew from a tiny start-up company to become the world's largest software developer. This growth was due mostly to the company's Windows operating system, which gained a near monopoly in the personal computer business by the early 1990's. At the same time, however, the company's Internet Explorer software trailed the rival Internet browser, Netscape Navigator, badly. Microsoft campaigned to overtake Netscape by attaching Explorer to its Windows software, while threatening to cancel contracts with Internet access providers and other software developers unless they made Explorer their default browser.

In July, 1994, the U.S. Department of Justice and nineteen U.S. states filed a civil antitrust suit against Microsoft. The government argued that Microsoft had leveraged its monopoly position in the market for operating systems designed to run on Intel-compatible computers to gain a monopoly position in the Internet browser market. The government charged that Microsoft had used anticompetitive business practices to maintain a monopoly in the operating systems market with licensing and software developer agreements containing anticompetitive terms. It also charged Microsoft with attempting to monopolize the Internet browser market by unlawfully bundling its Explorer browser with its Windows operating system and entering into exclusive dealing agreements with software vendors and Internet access providers.

In the complex case that followed, a federal district court held that Microsoft violated section 1 of the Sherman Antitrust Act by unlawfully tying sales of its operating system to its browser. The court also held that Microsoft monopolized the market for Intel-compatible personal computer operating systems and attempted to monopolize the browser market in violation of section 2 of the Sherman Act.

Microsoft chairman Bill Gates responding to the April, 2000, court ruling that his company had violated the Sherman Antitrust Act. *(AP/Wide World Photos)*

However, the court also held that Microsoft's exclusive dealing agreements were not unlawful because there was no evidence that the agreements had decreased use of alternative browsers.

After Microsoft appealed, a federal court of appeals agreed that its exclusive dealing agreements did not violate the Sherman Act. The appellate court upheld the district court's ruling that Microsoft had monopolized the operating systems market; however, it reversed the lower court's decision that Microsoft had violated the Sherman Act by attempting to monopolize the browser market because it had not been proven that Microsoft was likely to succeed in doing so. Likewise, the court of appeals reversed the district court's holding that Microsoft had violated the Sherman Act by tying sales of Windows to distribution of the Explorer browser. On this charge, the appellate court remanded the case back to the district court to collect further evidence.

After the case was returned to the district court, Microsoft entered into a settlement agreement to resolve the case. Under the resulting agreement, Microsoft was obligated to allow computer manufacturers to add icons for competitors' browsers, use uniform licensing agreements when dealing with software developers, and provide technical information to Internet access providers and competing software vendors so that their programs would work with the Windows operating system.

The U.S. Department of Justice usually files criminal actions only in clear-cut antitrust cases involving intentional violations, such as price-fixing—which was not one of the charges brought against Microsoft. Also, by bringing a civil, rather than a criminal, action against Microsoft, the government did not have to prove its case beyond a reasonable doubt. The lower standard of proof required in the civil action made it easier for the government to win its case.

Landmarks in Antitrust History

Date	Action	Significance
1890	Sherman Antitrust Act	Banned every "contract, combination . . . or conspiracy" in restraint of trade or commerce.
1898	*United States v. Addyston Pipe and Steel Co.*	U.S. Supreme Court decision ruling an agreement to set prices to be illegal because it gave the parties power to set unreasonable prices.
1904	*Northern Securities v. United States*	Supreme Court ruling against holding companies that control stock of competing companies.
1911	*Standard Oil Co. v. United States*	Supreme Court order to break up Standard Oil.
1911	*United States v. American Tobacco Co.*	Supreme Court order to break up American Tobacco Co. Along with the Standard Oil case, this ruling established the "rule of reason" approach to antitrust prosecution.
1914	Clayton Antitrust Act	Federal law specifying actions subject to antitrust prosecution.
1914	Federal Trade Commission Act	Law establishing the Federal Trade Commission as an administrative agency to police "unfair methods of competition."
1920	*United States v. U.S. Steel Corp.*	Supreme Court ruling holding that size alone, in the absence of abuse of power, does not make a monopoly illegal.
1921	*American Column and Lumber Co. v. United States*	Supreme Court ruling holding that competitors can be convicted if they discuss prices and later set identical prices, even if no agreement to do so is reached.
1936	Robinson-Patman Act	Federal law specifying the types of price discrimination that are illegal.
1936	*International Business Machines Corp. v. United States*	Supreme Court ruling establishing conditions under which it is illegal to tie the sale of one product to the sale of another.
1937	Miller-Tydings Act	Federal law exempting manufacturers and retailers from prosecution for agreeing to set minimum prices if the states in which they operate allow such agreements.

prices attract sales away from its less efficient competitors and lead them to exit the market.

Finally, a statute known as the Robinson-Patman Act of 1936 prohibits any price discrimination that does not reflect a real need to compete with a rival's lower price. While this law provides misdemeanor criminal sanctions for a firm that intentionally eliminates or attempts to eliminate competition by selling at "unreasonably low prices" by general price discrimination or by geographical price discrimination, criminal prosecutions are rarely brought.

Enforcement

Public enforcement of the antitrust laws is the responsibility of the Antitrust Division of the

Date	Action	Significance
1938	Wheeler-Lea Act	Federal law strengthening enforcement powers of the Federal Trade Commission.
1945	*United States v. Aluminum Co. of America*	Supreme Court ruling ordering the breakup of Alcoa, ruling that a monopoly is illegal even if not accompanied by an abuse of power.
1948	*Federal Trade Commission v. Cement Institute*	Supreme Court ruling holding that agreements by producers to base prices on manufacturing costs plus transportation from a given location (base-point pricing) are illegal.
1950	Celler-Kefauver Anti-merger Act	Federal law clarifying the Clayton Antitrust Act, making it enforceable against mergers accomplished by sales of assets in addition to those accomplished by sales of stock.
1967	*Federal Trade Commission v. Procter & Gamble Co.*	Supreme Court ruling forcing Procter & Gamble to divest itself of Clorox because P&G's market power would allow Clorox to dominate the bleach market.
1976	Antitrust Improvements Act	Federal law allowing state attorney generals to sue on behalf of state residents.
1976	*United States v. American Telephone and Telegraph Co.*	Supreme Court ruling holding that even though a company is subject to regulation it remains subject to antitrust prosecution.
1984	Divestiture of AT&T	Following on the Supreme Court's 1976 decision, the breakup of AT&T into seven smaller companies introduced a new era in telecommunications.
1994	Microsoft Corporation antitrust suit	U.S. Department of Justice and nineteen states file civil antitrust suit against Microsoft for illegally leveraging its monopoly position in computer operating systems.
1998	Exxon-Mobil merger	Merger forms the world's largest oil company, following more than a decade of oil-company mergers that are tolerated by the federal government because of the need to compete against foreign oil companies.
2000	Microsoft ruling	Federal court rules that Microsoft Corporation is a monopoly.

U.S. Department of Justice and the Federal Trade Commission. State attorneys general and private citizens may also bring civil antitrust suits. However, it is exclusively the federal Department of Justice that files criminal charges under the Sherman Antitrust Act. In all Sherman Antitrust Act cases, it is necessary to prove that two or more entities have formed a combination or conspiracy; that the combination or conspiracy produces, or potentially produces, an unreasonable restraint of trade or commerce; and that the restrained trade or commerce is interstate in nature. In a criminal prosecution, however, the Justice Department must also prove beyond a reasonable doubt that the defendants intended to restrain commerce and acted with knowledge of the probable consequences of their actions.

Violations of the Sherman Antitrust Act are punished as criminal felonies. Individual violators can be fined up to $350,000 and sentenced to up to three years in prison for each offense. Corporate violators can be fined up to $10 million for each offense. Under some circumstances, the fines may be doubled. During the late 1990's and the first years of the twenty-first century, the Department of Justice reported it had successfully brought criminal prosecutions against firms in the soft drink, motion picture, trash-hauling, road-building, electrical contracting, and other industries involving hundreds of millions of dollars in business.

The Justice Department also has an amnesty program known as the Corporate Lenience Policy. This amnesty program, which allows for a reduction in criminal fines and can even allow for immunity from prosecution, applies to all corporate officers, directors, or employees. Immunity is automatically granted if the defendant self-reports its illegal conduct to the Justice Department and meets certain other conditions. In addition, the Justice Department has the discretion to grant immunity to any defendant in exchange for full cooperation in an investigation.

Kurt M. Saunders

Further Reading

Cefrey, Holly. *The Sherman Antitrust Act: Getting Big Business Under Control*. New York: Rosen Publishing Group, 2004. Discusses the history and purposes of the Sherman Antitrust Act.

Gellhorn, Ernest, and William E. Kovacic. *Antitrust Law and Economics in a Nutshell*. St. Paul, Minn.: West Publishing, 1994. Provides a concise overview of the federal antitrust laws and related economic principles.

Hovenkamp, Herbert. *Federal Antitrust Policy: The Law of Competition and Its Practice*. 2d ed. St. Paul, Minn.: West Publishing, 1999. Detailed treatment of federal antitrust enforcement.

Shenefield, John H., and Irwin M. Stelzer. *The Antitrust Laws: A Primer*. 2d ed. Washington, D.C.: AEI Press, 1996. Brief and understandable summary of the principal antitrust statutes.

Sullivan, E. Thomas, and Jeffrey L. Harrison. *Understanding Antitrust and Its Economic Implications*. 3d ed. New York: Matthew Bender, 1998. Reviews the scope and economic rationale of the U.S. antitrust laws.

See also Attorney general of the United States; Consumer fraud; Corporate scandals; Criminal prosecution; Hobbs Act; Regulatory crime; Sherman Antitrust Act; White-collar crime.

Appellate process

Definition: Process through which higher courts review the decisions of subordinate courts

Criminal justice issues: Appeals; courts; defendants

Significance: The appellate process provides checks on the criminal justice system by ensuring that errors do not adversely affect the fairness of trial processes and the rights of defendants.

The United States has a dual court system, made up of state and federal courts. Each of these two systems encompasses two or three "tiers," or levels, of courts. The lowest level is made up of trial courts, which hear evidence and reach decisions based upon that evidence. The next tier, or tiers, is made up of appellate courts. These courts do not hear evidence but review the records of what has taken place in the trial courts. Some states have two appellate tiers, consisting of an intermediate appellate court and a court of "last resort." In other states, there are only two tiers: the trial courts and the courts of last resort.

The federal court system has three tiers, but few cases ever proceed to the highest federal court—the U.S. Supreme Court. There are also some situations in which the Supreme Court hears appeals from state courts of last resort.

Appellate courts do not automatically review every case handled by trial courts and assume jurisdiction over only cases that are appealed to them by aggrieved parties. There are usually fairly stringent time limits for making appeals, and it is common for appellate courts to require

---

A Hollywood Reversal

Considering the legal expertise behind the making of film *Reversal of Fortune* (1990), it is surprising how inaccurately the film depicts the appellate process. The film is based on Harvard law professor Alan Dershowitz's book about the real-life murder case of Claus von Bulow, who was convicted of assault with intent to murder his wife.

In the film, Dershowitz (played by Ron Silver) represents von Bulow (Jeremy Irons) after von Bulow's wife (Glenn Close) dies under suspicious circumstances and von Bulow is convicted. Dershowitz assembles a team of students to help him appeal von Bulow's case. They eventually locate new evidence that is favorable to von Bulow and persuade an appeals court to consider this evidence. The appeals court subsequently reverses von Bulow's conviction and orders him to be tried again. At the new trial, he is acquitted of all charges.

The film errs badly in having the new evidence taken directly to the appeals court. Appellate courts do not consider new evidence and use it as a basis for overturning prior verdicts. A lawyer who uncovers new evidence favorable to a client would first approach the trial court and ask to have the evidence considered and, possibly, have a new trial ordered. If the trial court unreasonably refuses to consider the evidence, then an appeals court might be asked to overturn its decision. However, the appeals court would never be the initial forum in which the new evidence is presented, as is depicted in *Reversal of Fortune*.

Timothy L. Hall

---

bers—as does the U.S. Supreme Court. Judges who serve on appellate courts of last resort are usually called "justices," as are the members of the U.S. Supreme Court.

After an appeal is heard, one member of a panel is usually assigned to write an opinion representing the majority position of the panel. Sometimes the panel cannot reach a unanimous decision, and members who disagree write opinions known as dissents.

In reviewing lower-court decisions for error, appellate courts usually limit their reviews to errors that are brought to the attention of the trial courts, through either objections or some sorts of motions. This process is known as preserving an error, or making a record. If an error is not properly preserved, the appellate court reviews a case only if it raises a matter of fundamental importance or if it has actually caused prejudice to the complaining party.

that appeals be brought within thirty days of the decisions being appealed. However, after the appellate court is given notice that an appeal has been filed, it may take several months for the record to be assembled at the trial court level and forwarded to the appellate court for review. Assembling the record often requires that court reporters transcribe testimony taken at the trial, which can be time-consuming. After the records are delivered to the appellate court, the parties prepare briefs containing their arguments and the applicable law. Sometimes the parties are asked to argue their cases in person before the appellate court so that the court can ask questions about the issues.

Unlike trial courts, which are usually presided over by lone judges, appellate courts usually have panels of judges. In court systems with two appellate levels, panels of the intermediate courts are small—usually only three or five judges, while the courts of last resort typically have nine mem-

Appellate Court Decisions

Appellate courts issue their decisions in documents called opinions or memorandum decisions. Written decision of the courts include reasons for the decisions and the facts on which the decisions are based. At the conclusion of an opinion, the court explains whether it agrees with the trial court's decision or believes that the trial court has made some type of error. When the court's opinion agrees with that of the trial court, the opinion states, "affirmed." If the opinion disagrees with that of the trial court, it may state, "reversed" or "reversed and remanded." When as case is reversed or remanded, the court explains why it thinks the original decision was wrong and instructs the trial court to modify its result or rehear the case.

Appellate courts follow a doctrine known as *stare decisis*, which requires courts to adhere to their own prior decisions and those of the courts above it. This principle lends certainty and predictability to the law and provides a framework for the decision-making processes of individual judges. Although judges may be otherwise swayed by the equities of particular cases, they are bound to follow prior law—or "precedent"—in reaching their decisions. Occasionally, courts decide to depart from their prior decisions and "overrule" them. From that moment, the new decisions govern.

The U.S. Supreme Court is the highest court in the federal system but does not always hear appeals from the intermediate federal courts, known as courts of appeal. Only a small class of federal cases are automatically entitled to appeals to the Supreme Court. The remainder are only heard if they present particularly novel or important issues. This discretionary type of appeal is known as *certiorari* appeal. The Supreme Court also has the authority to hear *certiorari* appeals of state court decisions when they are state courts of last resort and they raise issues of federal constitutional law. It is estimated that the

Supreme Court hears only about 3 percent of the cases for which *certiorari* appeals are sought.

Sharon K. O'Roke

Further Reading

Chapper, Joy. *Understanding Reversible Error in Criminal Appeals*. Williamsburg, Va.: The Center, 1989. Primer written by the chief deputy clerk for the Court of Appeals for the District of Columbia.

Coffin, Frank M. *On Appeal: Courts, Lawyering, and Judging*. New York: W. W. Norton, 1994. Judge's inside view of the appellate process in the U.S. Court of Appeals for the First Circuit. Coffin tells exactly how his court processes appeals, from receipt of the briefs, through oral argument, and on to final decisions.

Greenberg, Ellen. *The Supreme Court Explained*. New York: W. W. Norton, 1997. The basics of the Supreme Court, including the process and rules in clear terms. Tracks the flow of cases through the Court.

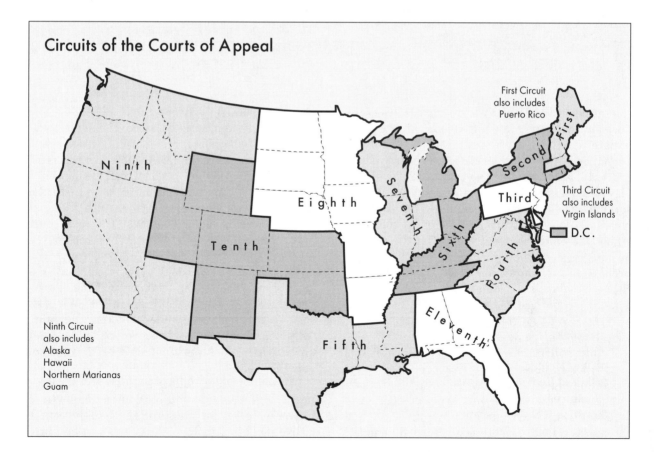

Circuits of the Courts of Appeal

First Circuit also includes Puerto Rico

Third Circuit also includes Virgin Islands

D.C.

Ninth Circuit also includes Alaska Hawaii Northern Marianas Guam

Ninth / Eighth / Seventh / Sixth / Fifth / Fourth / Third / Second / First / Tenth / Eleventh

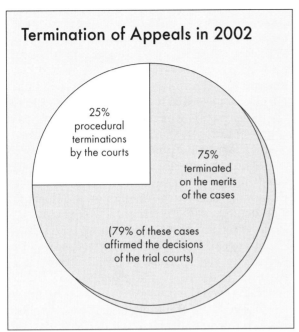

Termination of Appeals in 2002

25% procedural terminations by the courts

75% terminated on the merits of the cases

(79% of these cases affirmed the decisions of the trial courts)

Source: U.S. Bureau of Justice Statistics, 2005. Figures reflect termination of 11,695 appeals by U.S. Courts of Appeal in 2002.

Wasserman, David T. *A Sword for the Convicted: Representing Indigent Defendants on Appeal.* Westport, Conn.: Greenwood Press, 1990. Study of indigent criminal appellate representation in the United States, using New York City as a research model.

See also Amnesty; *Certiorari*; Criminal justice system; Criminal procedure; False convictions; *Habeas corpus*; Harmless error; Judicial review; Judicial system, U.S.; Miscarriage of justice; Opinions; Reversible error; Scottsboro cases; *Stare decisis*; Suspended sentences.

Argersinger v. Hamlin

The Case: U.S. Supreme Court ruling on right to counsel

Date: Decided on June 12, 1972

Criminal justice issues: Defendants; trial procedures

Significance: Defendants have the right to counsel at criminal trials whenever they may be imprisoned for any offense, whether it be classified as a felony or misdemeanor.

The police arrested Jon Richard Argersinger for carrying a concealed weapon. The potential punishment was up to six months in jail and/or a fine of one thousand dollars. Being indigent, Argersinger was unable to afford counsel. He was convicted and sentenced to serve ninety days in jail. At that time the Florida courts did not provide counsel, except for nonpetty offenses punishable by more than six months in jail. In a *habeas corpus* petition to the Florida Supreme Court, Argersinger argued that because he was poor and had not been provided with counsel, the charge against him could not effectively be defended. The Florida appellate court rejected the claim, and the U.S. Supreme Court agreed to hear the case.

In a unanimous decision, the Court ruled that the right to counsel applied not only to state defendants charged with felonies but also in all trials of persons for offenses serious enough to warrant a jail sentence. Prior to *Argersinger*, some doubt had existed as to whether the constitutional right to appointed counsel applied to any misdemeanor prosecutions. In *Gideon v. Wainwright* (1963), the Court had established a right to counsel only in felony prosecutions.

The Court in *Argersinger* held *Gideon* to be applicable to all misdemeanor defendants who could be sentenced to a jail term. The Court rejected the state's contention that the Sixth Amendment's right to counsel should not apply to petty offenses even when a jail sentence might be imposed. Nothing in the history of the right to counsel, the Court said, suggested a retraction of that right in petty offenses; conversely, the common law previously did require that counsel be provided.

The problems associated with petty offenses often require the expertise of counsel. The legal questions involved in a misdemeanor trial, or in a guilty plea, are not necessarily less complex simply because the jail sentence would not exceed six months. Indeed, petty misdemeanors may create a special need for counsel because the great volume of such cases may provide a tendency for speedy dispositions regardless of the fairness of the results.

Since the defendant had been sentenced to jail, the Court found it unnecessary to rule on the defendant's right to appointed counsel where "a loss of liberty was not involved." The opinion laid the foundation for distinguishing between cases involving sentences of imprisonment and those in which only fines are imposed. The Court noted the special qualities of imprisonment, "for however short a time," including its possible serious repercussions affecting the defendant's career and reputation.

Argersinger v. Hamlin established that, under the Sixth and Fourteenth Amendments to the U.S. Constitution, without a knowing and intelligent waiver, no person may be imprisoned for any offense, whether classified as petty, misdemeanor, or felony, unless represented by counsel at trial.

Susan M. Taylor

Further Reading

Smith, Christopher E. *Courts and the Poor*. Chicago: Nelson-Hall, 1991.

Taylor, John B. *Right to Counsel and Privilege Against Self-Incrimination: Rights and Liberties Under the Law*. Santa Barbara, Calif.: ABC-Clio, 2004.

Tomkovicz, James J. *The Right to the Assistance of Counsel: A Reference Guide to the United States Constitution*. Westport, Conn.: Greenwood Press, 2002.

See also *Brown v. Mississippi*; Counsel, right to; Criminal procedure; Felonies; *Gideon v. Wainwright*; *Powell v. Alabama*; Public defenders.

Arizona v. Fulminante

The Case: U.S. Supreme Court ruling on confessions

Date: Decided on March 26, 1991

Criminal justice issues: Confessions; convictions; trial procedures

Significance: The Supreme Court ruled that coerced confessions wrongly admitted as evidence cannot be subjected to "harmless error" analysis and might not be grounds for automatic invalidation of criminal convictions.

In 1983, Oreste C. Fulminante, incarcerated in a federal prison for an unrelated crime, confessed to another inmate, a paid informant for the Federal Bureau of Investigation, that he had raped and murdered his eleven-year-old stepdaughter. He also confessed to a woman who later married the informant. The next year, when tried for first-degree murder in the Superior Court, Maricopa County, Arizona, Fulminante sought to have his confessions suppressed on grounds that they violated his due process rights guaranteed by the Fifth and Fourteenth Amendments. The motion was denied, and Fulminante was convicted of first-degree murder and sentenced to death.

On appeal, Fulminante's conviction was first upheld by the Arizona Supreme Court; later, however, under reconsideration, that same court ordered a retrial on the grounds that the "harmless error" basis of admitting Fulminante's confession was inapplicable because the first confession was coerced.

On *certiorari*, the U.S. Supreme Court upheld the ruling of the Arizona Supreme Court. It confirmed that Fulminante's first confession had been coerced and that admission of his confession was not harmless under the specific circumstances. Yet part of the majority opinion, argued by Chief Justice William H. Rehnquist, advanced the 5-4 majority's conclusion that in a state criminal trial an involuntary confession admitted in violation of the Fourteenth Amendment's due process clause is, in fact, subject to harmless-error analysis. This opinion was rooted in a distinction made between due process violations and "trial error," holding that the admission of an involuntary confession does not transcend the criminal trial process and that it is similar in kind and degree to other evidence admitted in court. It noted, too, that confessions secured in violation of *Massiah v. United States* (1964) and *Miranda v. Arizona* (1966) had already been subject to harmless-error analysis.

Justice Byron R. White, vigorously dissenting, argued that the admission of a coerced confession in a criminal trial violated the defendant's constitutional rights and should not be subject to harmless-error analysis, and, further, that no sufficient reason had been presented for departing from the Supreme Court's time-honored "rule of automatic reversal" in coerced-confession cases.

According to that rule, if a coerced, involuntary confession was erroneously admitted in criminal proceedings, any conviction had to be overturned regardless of how much other evidence of guilt supported it.

In effect, the Supreme Court's *Fulminante* decision overturned earlier decisions such as that rendered in *Chapman v. California* (1967), one of the last cases prior to *Fulminante* upholding the rule of automatic reversal. This departure from that rule raised questions whether admission of a coerced confession as evidence must always be interpreted as a violation of a defendant's constitutional rights or of those protected by the rulings in the *Massiah* and *Miranda* decisions. The finding has been criticized for eroding those rights.

John W. Fiero

Further Reading

Dressler, Joshua. *Understanding Criminal Procedure*. 3d ed. New York: LexisNexis, 2002.

Inbau, Fred, John Reid, Joseph Buckley, and Brian Jayne. *Criminal Interrogations and Confessions*. 4th ed. Boston: Jones and Bartlett, 2001.

Lassiter, G. Daniel, ed. *Interrogations, Confessions, and Entrapment*. New York: Kluwer Academic/Plenum, 2004.

Mirfield, Timothy. *Silence, Confessions, and Improperly Obtained Evidence*. Oxford, England: Clarendon Press, 1997.

See also *Brown v. Mississippi*; Due process of law; *Escobedo v. Illinois*; Harmless error; *Miranda v. Arizona*.

Arraignment

Definition: First stage of the criminal trial process, when defendants are formally informed of the charges brought against them and are expected to respond by entering pleas

Criminal justice issues: Arrest and arraignment; legal terms and principles; pleas

Significance: To meet their Sixth Amendment burden of providing due process to defendants, courts are required formally to arraign defendants before trying them.

After criminal defendants are arrested, their first appearances in court are arraignments. The Federal Rules of Criminal Procedure specify that at the arraignment hearings, defendants are read in open court the formal criminal complaints against them. These complains should outline the crimes of which the defendants stand accused. Defendants are then required to enter a plea to the charges. If the defendants are without attorneys, they may request the opportunity to secure them. If they cannot afford attorneys, they may request that the court appoint attorneys for them.

If the defendants wish to wait to enter pleas because they have not yet consulted with attorneys or if they refuse to enter pleas, the judges may enter pleas of "not guilty" on their behalf. Defendants may also enter preemptory pleas, which explain why the trials cannot legally go forward. When defendants plead not guilty, trial dates may be set at the arraignments.

Defendants have the right to be present at their own arraignments. They also have the constitutional right to be arraigned within twenty-four to forty-eight hours after they are arrested. If they are arrested without previously issued warrants, they have the right to be arraigned within forty-eight hours to allow time for judicial determinations of probable cause for their arrests. Failures to follow any of these procedures or rules may be considered violations of the defendants' Sixth Amendment rights under the U.S. Constitution.

Rachel Bandy

Further Reading

Federal Criminal Code and Rules. St. Paul, Minn.: West Publishing, 2003.

Loewy, Arnold H., and Arthur B. LaFrance. *Criminal Procedure: Arrest and Investigation*. Cincinnati: Anderson Publishing, 1996.

See also Arrest; Bail system; Competency to stand trial; Counsel, right to; Criminal procedure; Due process of law; Hearings; Manhattan Bail Project; Misdemeanors; *Nolo contendere*; Plea bargaining; Pleas; Preliminary hearings; Resisting arrest.

Arrest

Definition: Taking into custody of legal authority of persons who are to be charged with criminal offenses

Criminal justice issues: Arrest and arraignment; confessions; defendants; interrogation

Significance: The main process through which people enter the criminal justice system, arrests may be made by law-enforcement officers or private citizens who take other persons into custody in the manner authorized by law.

The function of the administration of justice in the United States is to control crime, a process performed by agents and agencies of government with assigned jobs and territorial jurisdiction. The U.S. Constitution requires that every person be afforded due process of law through a program of judicial review that preserves the dignity of individuals and guards against the misuse of governmental power. Police officers have the basic obligation of apprehending criminals, and they share a role with prosecutors in investigating crime. The work of the police and prosecutors is reviewed by officers of the court, who judicially review the circumstances of arrests, the legality of evidence-gathering techniques, and the substance and form of the accusatory pleading.

When a crime is committed, an investigation begins to focus on those suspected of involvement. If persons are caught in the act of committing crimes or if an accumulation of evidence leads the police to believe that probable cause exists that persons have been involved, they seek an arrest warrant and arrest, book, and detain (incarcerate) the suspects. Safeguards built into the Constitution guard the rights of accused persons throughout the judicial process. Administration of justice procedures must ensure these rights at each step of adjudication. Arrest does not mean guilt; a person is presumed innocent until proven guilty through a confession of guilt or a decision by a judge or jury based on the preponderance of evidence.

Types of Laws

A crime is an act committed or omitted in violation of a law forbidding or commanding it and punishable, upon conviction, by death, imprisonment, fine, removal from office, or disqualification from holding any office of honor, trust, or profit. Crimes are divided into three groups: felonies, misdemeanors, and infractions. To guide police officers in the use of proper arrest techniques, the laws of each state specifically designate the more serious crimes as felonies (for example, murder, rape, assault, and fraud). Crimes not classified as felonies are either misdemeanors, which are punishable by imprisonment or fine (or both), or infractions, which are minor offenses not punishable by imprisonment. Law in the United States is wholly statutory—no act is unlawful unless at the time of its commission a valid written law (statute or ordinance) is in force that defines such an act as a crime and sets a penalty for its commission or omission.

Civil (tort) law deals with noncriminal offenses that are handled by civil rather than criminal courts. Civil offenses are not considered to be offenses against the state or the general welfare of society at large, even though they may cause suffering, harm, or injury to a person or persons. Therefore, the civil courts do not defend the interests of society but rather function as arbitrators between particular individuals. Car accident cases and some child-protection cases are examples of civil court matters. Criminal law, by contrast, imposes punishments on persons on behalf of the state for acts deemed harmful to social interests. Some acts end up in both civil and criminal courts. For example, rape violates criminal law and constitutes a wrong done to an individual. A civil court can award damages (usually monetary) for injury, and criminal courts can impose punishments (such as prison or probation) for the same act.

Arrest Statutes and Agencies

An arrest is the process of taking an accused person into physical custody through booking and detention procedures. The prevention, detection, and suppression of crime; the arrest and prosecution of persons charged with offenses; and the imprisonment, supervision, and rehabilitation of convicted offenders are major concerns faced by federal, state, and local government. These public safety responsibilities are assigned to six primary functional areas within the criminal justice system: police protection, prosecution, criminal court systems, probation services, prisons and other institutions, and parole supervision.

Each state has its own statutes delegating the power of arrest within its jurisdiction, with some variance in peripheral areas but with basic harmony in core areas. California's Penal Code clearly and concisely delineates the rights and limitations in this important area of criminal justice and is generally illustrative of the law of arrest in other states.

Police officers, prosecutors, court personnel, and other agents of criminal justice, along with statute and case law, provide the raw material for law enforcement in the United States. Basic procedures are established by the separation-of-powers doctrine, which compartmentalizes the duties of the executive, legislative, and judicial branches of government. Other aspects of this compartmentalization are the dual system of federal and state courts and federalism.

The police, prosecutors, and court magistrates form the main arresting team. The major role of the police is a dual one: law enforcement and the maintenance of order. Police departments are divided into two main groups: patrol and investigation. Part of the work of the police consists in arresting persons suspected of breaking laws. Prosecutors play the key role in law enforcement in the United States. Prosecutors decide whether to prosecute, to accept a plea of guilty to a lesser charge, or to drop a case for lack of evidence. Crime detection and the arrest of offenders by the police can be upgraded or downgraded by prosecutors and their staff.

The authority of prosecutors to exercise discretion in the performance of their duties is traditionally recognized, whereas the authority of the police to use discretion exists but has been questioned. The public acceptance of prosecutors as decision makers in criminal

justice probably derives from the general belief that they are ordinarily better educated than police officers, are more conscious of public response to their decisions inasmuch as they are elected officials directly responsible to the voters, and have broader perspectives on the allocation of available resources to achieve public order and safety.

Arrest Procedures

All modern police units offer training programs in the prompt recognition of suspicious places, people, and circumstances. If alleged perpetrators are not arrested at the time of criminal acts, police forces operate through established procedures to reconstruct criminal incidents and investigate the crimes. This involves working with victims to single out the persons legally responsible for contributing to the crimes. Generally, prior to an arrest, a judge issues a warrant. Once an arrest occurs, the incident is open to review by a judicial officer (judge), before whom the police are legally required to arraign prisoners promptly.

Suspects can be questioned by investigators without being arrested. In this case, suspects are

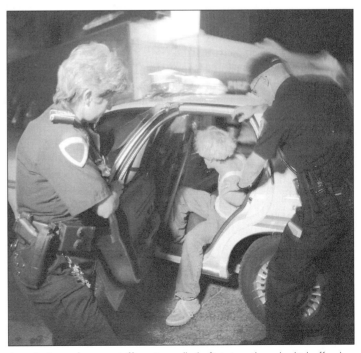

Arrest by law-enforcement officers is usually the first stage through which offenders enter the criminal justice system. *(Brand-X Pictures)*

free to discontinue the questioning and leave. Once the officers investigating a crime have enough physical or circumstantial evidence on a particular suspect and they or the prosecutor begin to question the suspect, questioning is no longer neutral. In *Miranda v. Arizona* (1966), the U.S. Supreme Court stated that an investigation is no longer neutral when "custodial interrogation" takes place—that is, when "questioning initiated by law-enforcement officers after a person has been taken into custody or otherwise deprived of his freedom of action in any significant way" occurs. This transpires when suspects are no longer free to leave. At that point, suspects need the protection of legal counsel, friends, or relatives.

In most cases, a warrant for arrest must be obtained from a court officer, usually a magistrate (the judge or justice of a trial court, including inferior courts, but sometimes restricted to "courts of record") who reviews the circumstances of the arrest prior to any summary action and either approves or disapproves the proposed arrest. A warrant of arrest may be issued when a complaint is filed with a magistrate and the magistrate, after a hearing, independently and on the basis of evidence is satisfied that the offense complained of has been committed, that the information given is from a reliable and credible source, and that there are reasonable grounds to believe that the person to be arrested has committed the specific offense.

An arrest is made by arresting officers or other persons, who are supposed to give adequate notice to the persons to be arrested. Such notice should include the intention to arrest, the cause of the arrest, and the authority to make it, except when the arresting persons have reasonable cause to believe that the suspects are engaged in the criminal acts or they must pursue the suspects immediately after the commission of the crimes. Adequate notice also includes informing persons to be arrested of the charges against them whenever they request such information. If the offense for which an arrest is being made is a felony, the arrest may be made on any day and at any time of the day or night. If the offense is a misdemeanor, the arrest cannot be made at night unless it takes place under the direction of a magistrate and is authorized on the warrant or unless

the offense is committed in the presence of the arresting officer.

Private citizens may arrest others for public offenses committed or attempted in their presence, they may arrest a felon although the felony was not committed in their presence, and they may arrest a person when a felony has been committed and they have reasonable cause to believe that the person to be arrested has committed it. However, if a crime has not been committed, such arresting persons are subject to legal action for false arrest.

Any person making an arrest may take from the arrested person all offensive weapons and deliver them to the arraigning magistrate. Breaking and entering a building to make an arrest may be necessary but is under the "reasonable and prudent man" purview (the test of whether a just, fair, sensible man with ordinary wisdom, carefulness, and sound judgment would do the same under similar circumstances). As a reasonable and prudent person, an officer acting in good faith may omit the demand for entrance and explanation of purpose if the delay would permit the destruction of evidence or its hiding, if the officer is threatened with attack by the person to be arrested, or if delay may allow the suspect to escape. Caution is necessary whenever regular procedures are not used during an arrest, because any incriminating evidence discovered may be excluded from evidence at trial if the arrest is ruled unlawful.

Booking and Detention

In most jurisdictions the rules of police procedure require that peace officers bring arrested persons to a central point (usually a city or county jail) in order to search them, record the details of arrest (booking), and incarcerate them. The search must be conducted under the supervision of the law-enforcement officer assigned to the booking office, who is usually a superior officer, and involves a thorough bodily examination, including the removal of clothing and the possible examination of body crevices such as mouth, underarms, and anus. Male officers search men and female officers search women. A record is made of all evidence taken from prisoners and the evidence itself is appropriately marked and safeguarded. Receipts are prepared of all articles of value taken from prisoners, and copies of these receipts are delivered to the prisoners by the booking officer at the time of booking.

Booking procedures may vary slightly across the country, but certain rules are in general use by all police forces. The specific laws violated must be established and entered in the official arrest records. These records must include the names of victims, the times and places of the crimes charged and of the arrests, enough of the circumstances of the case to establish probable cause for the arrests, and the essential elements of the crimes charged. Prisoners' fingerprints and photographs must be taken. When prisoners' identities are established, checks are made with the records division to determine if they have outstanding warrants for other crimes and to establish if they have past criminal records.

The arresting officers inform prisoners of their right to remain silent, warning them that anything they say is likely to be used in court against them, and inform them of their right to speak to an attorney prior to making any statements. This information is entered in the arrest records. Prisoners are informed of the approximate time and date of arraignment (a court appearance at which they are informed of the charges against them and they enter a plea), the name of the court and its location, the law about bail, and the rules of the detention jail. Prisoners are then placed in cells, permitted release on bail (if applicable), sent to a hospital (if required), or released as otherwise provided by law.

Suspect Rights

Prosecutors in California recommend that the police use a simple and uniform statement during the arrest process to warn prisoners of their

Total Arrests in the United States in 2002

	Arrests (1,000)		
Serious crimes	Male	Female	Total
Murder and nonnegligent manslaughter	9.6	1.2	10.8
Forcible rape	21.2	0.3	21.5
Robbery	75.3	8.5	83.8
Aggravated assault	285.0	72.6	357.6
Burglary	189.5	28.8	218.3
Larceny/theft	563.3	329.2	892.5
Motor vehicle theft	95.6	18.8	114.4
Arson	10.7	1.9	12.6
Subtotals	250.2	461.3	1,711.5
All other nonserious crimes			
Other assaults	749.3	235.9	985.2
Forgery and counterfeiting	53.2	35.3	88.5
Fraud	140.7	117.5	258.2
Receiving stolen property	79.4	17.3	96.7
Weapons possession	114.7	10.1	124.8
Prostitution and commercialized vice	21.8	41.3	63.1
Other sex offenses (not including rape)	65.4	5.9	71.3
Drug-abuse violations	977.1	214.3	1,191.4
Offenses against family and children	76.9	25.3	102.2
Driving under the influence	881.6	185.6	1,067.2
Subtotals	3,160.1	888.5	4,048.6
Minor offenses	3,637.0	1,055.0	4,692.0
Totals	7,047.3	2,404.8	10,452.1

Source: Federal Bureau of Investigation, *Crime in the United States.*

rights when they face custodial interrogation, so that officers can testify on the witness stand about the advice they gave to arrested persons. In California arrested persons have the right (except where physically impossible) to make at least two telephone calls from the booking office during the period extending from immediately after booking to not more than three hours after arrest. However, the number of calls and the time frame vary from state to state. These calls are made at prisoners' expense and in the presence of a public officer or employee. Any public officer or employee who deprives an arrested person of the right to such communications is guilty of a misdemeanor.

After they are arrested, prisoners or their relatives may request to see an attorney entitled to practice in the courts of record. Any responsible officer who willfully refuses or neglects to allow such an attorney to visit a prisoner is guilty of a misdemeanor, and any responsible officer who refuses to allow an attorney to visit the prisoner when proper application is made is liable for a monetary fine.

Peace officers in California may release from custody prisoners who are arrested without a warrant if they are satisfied that no grounds for making a criminal complaint exist. A record of such arrests must note that the prisoners have been released and that their arrests have been deemed to be detentions. Prisoners arrested without a warrant may also be released from custody if the offenses with which they are charged are not considered a threat to society or its members. If arrested persons are charged with misdemeanors only and have signed an agreement to appear in court or before a magistrate at a designated place and time, they may also be released.

When prisoners are not subject to release in accordance with an established schedule of bail or they cannot post bail, they must be taken without unnecessary delay to the nearest or most accessible magistrate in the county in which the offense is triable if they are in a condition to make a court appearance—that is, if they are not drunk, unconscious, ill, or mentally incompetent. The stricture against unnecessary delay stipulates a period of no longer than two days after the arrest, excluding Sundays and holidays. However, when the two days prescribed expire at a time when the court in which the magistrate is sitting is not in session, the time for the original arraignment of the prisoner is extended to include the duration of the next regular court session on the judicial day immediately following. The period of permissible delay usually is described as two court (working) days. Upon prisoners' arraignment before examining magistrates and the filing of complaints, cases are placed before the court for review of police action since the time of the criminal act.

Carolyn Palmer-Johnson

Further Reading

Del Carmen, Rolando V. *Briefs of Leading Cases in Law Enforcement*. Cincinnati: Anderson Publishing, 1997. Examines legal issues surrounding the practice and structure of law enforcement.

Friedman, Lawrence M. *American Law: An Introduction*. New York: W. W. Norton, 1988. Good general treatment of American law that discusses confessions and the *Miranda* rules.

Geller, William, and Hans Toch, eds. *Police Violence: Understanding and Controlling Police Abuse of Force*. New Haven, Conn.: Yale University Press, 1996. Collection of fifteen substantial articles on the improper use of force by the police.

Inbau, Fred E., and John E. Reid. *Criminal Interrogation and Confessions*. Baltimore: Williams & Wilkins, 1962. An older text, but still useful in explaining the overall process of arrests.

LaFave, Wayne R. *Arrest: The Decision to Take a Suspect into Custody*. Boston: Little, Brown, 1965. Explains differences in police and prosecutorial discretion.

Walker, Samuel. *The Police in America*. 2d ed. New York: McGraw-Hill, 1992. General overview of police work.

Weston, Paul B., and Kenneth M. Wells. *The Administration of Justice*. 2d ed. Englewood Cliffs, N.J.: Prentice-Hall, 1973. Covers the role of criminal justice officials.

See also Arraignment; Arrest warrants; Bail system; Booking; Citations; Criminal history record information; Extradition; Jurisdiction of courts; Miranda rights; Nonviolent resistance; Presumption of innocence; Preventive detention; Probable cause; Reasonable force; Stop and frisk; Suspects.

Arrest warrants

Definition: Official documents signed by judges or magistrates authorizing law-enforcement officers to arrest the persons whom the documents name

Criminal justice issues: Arrest and arraignment; judges; probation and pretrial release

Significance: Arrest warrants authorize police officers to arrest named persons. To obtain warrants, police officers usually submit affidavits to the judges or magistrates in the appropriate jurisdictions.

Arrest warrants typically specify the crimes that the arrestees are alleged to have committed and may direct the manner in which the arrests are to be made. Bail also may be specified. Bench warrants are arrest warrants for previous failures to appear in court.

All lawful arrests comply with the Fourth Amendment to the U.S. Constitution. The amendment guarantees the right of people to be secure in their homes "against unreasonable searches and seizures" and states that warrants are not to be issued without "probable cause, supported by Oath or affirmation, and particularly describing the place to be searched, and the persons or things to be seized." Arrests are a form of seizure—a seizure of the body. Consequently, the Fourth Amendment applies both to searches and seizures of property, as well as to arrests of persons.

In its 1980 *Payton v. New York* decision, the U.S. Supreme Court ruled that arresting officers must secure arrest warrants before entering dwellings to arrest suspects in nonemergency situations. In emergency situations, arrest warrants may not be necessary to enter suspects' dwellings. No requirement derives from the Fourth Amendment that a warrantless arrest take place only upon probable cause. However, judges have applied the amendment's requirement of probable cause to warrantless arrests as well as arrests under warrants, as a matter of interpretation.

A warrantless arrest typically may be made when a crime is committed in a police officer's presence, or when an officer has probable cause to believe that a suspect has committed a felony and does not need to enter the suspect's dwelling to execute the arrest. Probable cause is the key issue in the arrest process in both warrant and warrantless arrests. To establish probable cause, police officers must be able to delineate factual circumstances indicating that suspects have committed specified crimes. Although police officers provide information regarding the existence of probable cause, magistrates make the determination of probable cause. Whether an arrest is made with a warrant or is a warrantless arrest, it must always be reasonable.

Ronna F. Dillon

Further Reading

Emanuel, S. L. *Criminal Procedure*. Aspen, Colo.: Aspen Publishing, 2003.

Langbein, J. H. *The Origins of Adversary Criminal Trial*. Oxford, England: Oxford University Press, 2003.

Livingston, E. *A System of Penal Law for the United States of America: Consisting of a Code of Crimes and Punishments, a Code of Procedure in Criminal Cases, a Code of Prison Discipline, and a Book of Definitions*. New York: William S. Hein, 2000.

Schiller, N. *Criminal Procedure for the Criminal Justice Professional*. Eagan, Minn.: West Publishing, 2001.

See also Arrest; Bench warrants; Citations; Criminal justice system; Marshals Service, U.S.; Special weapons and tactics teams (SWAT); *Wilson v. Arkansas*.

Arson

Definition: Deliberate setting of fire to structures, vehicles, or personal property

Criminal justice issues: Fraud; technology; vandalism

Significance: The evolution of the concept of arson from its common-law origins of the burning of a dwelling of another to a crime involving burning of any person's property reflects a change in public policy as a result of insurance fraud and the perceived need to protect all property from malicious destruction through burning and related activities.

Before statutory law existed, courts defined arson at common law as a crime against habitation. For an act to be considered arson, five elements had to be present: intent or malice on the part of the arsonist; an actual burning; the burning had to be of a dwelling or surrounding structures; the burned property had to belong to someone other than the arsonist; and the action had to occur during nighttime. Under modern statutory law, which varies among state and federal jurisdictions, legislative bodies and courts have broadened the definition of arson to encompass *all* acts that result in the intentional burning of any person's property at any time.

Arson Definition Expanded

Usually the *mens rea* or intent for arson is malicious and willful conduct, that is, the intentional desire to cause harm. Some jurisdictions require a specific intent to defraud by burning a structure, vehicle, or personal property. Others include in the definition of intent risky behavior that has a strong likelihood of leading to property destruction. Under early twenty-first century law, not only intentionally set fires, but also explosions or similar acts that destroy property—even when no fires are involved—may constitute the intent for arson.

Reasons for committing arson are varied and include pyromaniacs, that is, vandals who set fires for emotional excitement; people who set fires for purposes of revenge or sabotage; people who hope to collect insurance settlements or commit tax fraud; and people who set fires to conceal other crimes, such as murder.

At common law the definition of arson required the actual burning or charring of some part of a building or structure. Now, scorching, smoking, and discoloration are sufficient evidence to support arson convictions. Some state statutes even include criminal liability for impeding firefighting efforts or refusing to help extinguish fires. In addition, under modern statutes the properties that are burned are no longer limited to dwellings. They may also include structures, vehicles, other personal property, and other real property—such as forests or agricultural crops—whether they belong to other people or to the arsonists. Because of the various degrees of arson found in most statutes, acts of arson may now take place at any time of the day or night.

History

Arson is an ancient property crime because it relates to one of the basic human needs—shelter or habitation. Arson was a crime in common law because it threatened the need of community members to feel secure in their homes and other buildings in communities. At common law arsonists had to burn dwellings in the possession of, or occupied by, others, as the belief was that people

Fire in Fiction

Don Winslow's *California Fire and Life* (1999) is a skillfully constructed novel about an insurance claims adjuster whose uncovering of an arson fire draws him into ever-deepening intrigue. Taking its title from a fictional insurance company, the story provides a fascinating inside look at arson investigation that draws on Winslow's own long real-life experience in that field.

Another novel by an experienced arson investigator is John L. Orr's *Points of Origin: Playing with Fire* (2001). This story about a serial arsonist draws on the author's experience as a city fire captain and arson investigator.

would not intentionally burn the houses in which they themselves lived. However, wives could be charged with arson for burning their husbands' property. In two early English cases, a tenant was found guilty of arson for burning a house that he occupied but did not own, and a prisoner was found guilty of arson for setting fire to the building in which he was confined so that he could escape.

After homeowner insurance became available, arson laws began to change, and increasing numbers of people were charged with intentionally burning their own dwellings for purposes of defrauding insurers and collecting the insurance proceeds. Municipalities also became proactive by limiting the use of wood in construction of buildings to reduce the number of natural and deliberately set fires, which often destroyed entire blocks of buildings in overcrowded cities.

In common law, arson was considered a felony, and it continues to be classified as a felony in most modern jurisdictions. However, many statutes provide several degrees of arson and malicious burning, some of which are classified as misdemeanors. Under old English common law, the penalty for arson was death. Today, no jurisdiction employs the penalty of death for arson, unless it is coupled with a homicide, which will bring a felony murder charge.

Prevalence

The Uniform Crime Reporting (UCR) Program of the Federal Bureau of Investigation (FBI) for 2003 showed a decline in the number of reported arson cases and arrests nationwide with a 28.5 percent drop in arson arrests from 1994 to 2003. Smaller cities of 10,000 or fewer inhabitants showed the greatest decrease in reported cases since 2002, although they still had the highest arson arrest rates. Based on data in the UCR, there was a nationwide average of 5.6 arson arrests per 100,000 persons in 2003. Single family residential structures suffered the highest rate of arson in 2003, while average monetary damages were highest for industrial and manufacturing structures. The majority of arson offenses are committed by white boys and men, with an almost equal division of arrests between adults and juveniles under the age of majority, which usually is considered to be eighteen years.

The National Fire Protection Association estimates that arson may actually be on the increase because statistics are based only on provable facts and not estimates. In addition, the UCR Program relies on only the data that are reported, and arson data are not reported uniformly by all law-enforcement agencies in the United States. In the future, the continuous improvement of forensic science, technology, and methods of investigating fire scenes should result in improved reporting of statistics related to the crime of arson.

Investigations

Many modern municipal fire departments include specially trained arson investigation units, which are typically made up of firefighters, expert fire examiners, forensic scientists, and law-enforcement officers. Members of such units act as detectives in investigating suspicious fires and gathering evidence that is used in prosecution of arson cases. To ensure that evidence is properly

Arson investigators of the federal Bureau of Alcohol, Tobacco and Firearms (ATF) sifting through the ashes of a burned-out Baptist church in Mississippi in mid-1996. The mid-1990's saw an epidemic of arson burnings of African American churches throughout the South, and the federal government created the National Church Arson Task Force to investigate and control the problem. The task force drew on the services of state and local law-enforcement agencies and the Federal Bureau of Investigation and the ATF. (AP/Wide World Photos)

obtained and preserved, many prosecutors become involved in the early stages of such investigations.

Technological advances and modern forensics enable investigators to solve past and present cases of suspicious fires more readily than in the past. Before investigation begins, however, the fire scenes must be made secure by ensuring that the fires are out and that no structures are likely to collapse during the investigations. However, arson investigation is often made more difficult by the fact that evidence is not always preserved by the first responders to fire scenes. Moreover, chemical evidence is not always readily detectible; it may also be volatile and evaporate quickly.

Once fire scenes are secure, investigators conduct "cause and origin" investigations. First, they determine the seats of the fires; then, they look for evidence that the fires have been deliberately set. Investigators search through fire debris and use new technologies, such as those able to detect odorless accelerants, to determine the sources of the fires. The goal of arson investigators is to reconstruct fire scenes and provide adequate evidence to show that the fires are not accidental.

Prosecution and Punishment

Prosecutor in arson cases must prove that fires have been set deliberately. Much of the evidence to prove intent in arson cases is highly technical and thus not always understood by juries. If mistakes are made during a fire investigation and proper protocols are not followed, the prosecution may be unable to provide adequate scientific evidence to prove that the fire was arson.

Many courts request evidence of motive, especially in cases involving insurance fraud or covering up other crimes. Eye witnesses to arson are rare, so evidence in such cases is largely circumstantial. This fact makes it more difficult to prove that a fire has been set beyond a reasonable doubt—which is the standard for obtaining guilty verdicts.

The forms of arson carrying the severest penalties are instances in which human life may be at stake—which is usually the case in arson fires set in inhabited dwellings at night. In addition, in any arson case in which a person is killed, the penalty is high in most jurisdictions. Moreover, such cases may lead to arrests and convictions for

felony murder, or murder with aggravated circumstances, and result in death sentences.

Carol A. Rolf

Further Reading

Cosgrove, Bill. *Accident or Arson?* Bethel, Conn.: Rutledge Books, 2001. Story of an actual fire scene through initial report to final investigation.

DeHaan, John D., and Paul Leland Kirk. *Kirk's Fire Investigation.* 5th ed. Upper Saddle River, N.J.: Prentice Hall, 2002. Textbook that discusses various types of fires, new petroleum products, documentation, and case analyses.

Faith, Nicholas. *Blaze: The Forensics of Fire.* New York: St. Martin's Press, 2000. Useful information on modern improvements in forensic science, technology, and behavioral patterns in solving the crime of arson.

Icove, David J., and John D. DeHaan. *Combating Arson-For-Profit: Advanced Techniques for Investigators.* Upper Saddle River, N.J.: Prentice Hall, 2003. Up-to-date text on the modern means employed to investigate arson.

Micheels, Peter A., ed. *Heat: Fire C.S.I. and the War on Arson and Murder.* New York: Adrenaline Classics, 2003. Collection of first-person accounts of arson by professional fire marshals.

Wambaugh, Joseph. *Fire Lover: A True Story.* New York: Avon Books, 2002. True story about the investigation and conviction of an arsonist by a best-selling novelist and former Los Angeles police officer.

See also Attempt to commit a crime; Bombs and explosives; Bureau of Alcohol, Tobacco, Firearms and Explosives; Common law; Crime scene investigation; Criminal law; Federal Bureau of Investigation; Federal Crimes Act; Felonies; Model Penal Code; Uniform Crime Reports.

Assault and battery

Definition: Physically harming other persons or putting them in fear of being harmed

Criminal justice issues: Domestic violence; violent crime

Significance: Assault and battery are the most

common violent crimes in the United States. In criminal law, assault and battery represent two separate actions that are more often referred to simply as assault. This general term includes simple and aggravated assault, and can refer to offenses that are either attempted or completed.

Assault and battery are generally used to refer to both threats and the actual carrying out of inflicting harm on other persons. The term "assault" applies to the act of threatening or intimidating others, while the term "battery" applies to the actual infliction of physical harm, through punches, slaps, kicks, stabbings, or other contacts that are delivered with the intent of causing harm or death to the victims. Assaults are unlawful offers of violence against others, with the reasonable capability to carry out the acts. Battery is the actual and intentional infliction of the violence resulting in injury—regardless of the seriousness of the injury. "Assault and battery" therefore refers to the coupling of these two offenses: the threat and the delivery of unlawful force.

The federal criminal justice system and many state systems use the general term assault to refer to both the unlawful offer or threat of harm and the actual delivery of illegal force against the victim. From the criminal law standpoint, then, no actual attack needs to occur for a charge of assault to be brought against a person.

Assaults may be simple or aggravated, depending upon the level of violence and other factors. Simple assault, as defined by the Federal Bureau of Investigation's Uniform Crime Reports (UCR), refers to the offenses in which no weapons are used and the victims' sustained injuries are comparatively minor. Examples of assault under this definition include slapping and punching in which no serious injury is sustained by the victims, or shaking one's fist at another person and placing that person in fear of being hurt.

Aggravated assault, according to the UCR, is characterized by the intentional attempted, threatened, or delivered infliction of serious harm upon another person. In addition, other federal reporting systems specify that the use of a dangerous weapon in an assault is sufficient to characterize an offense as aggravated, regardless of whether a victim sustains an injury.

Therefore, the mere act of threatening a person with a gun constitutes aggravated assault.

Unarmed attacks in which a victim sustains severe bodily injuries, such as broken bones or teeth or loss of consciousness, may also be categorized as aggravated assault. In addition, some states have declared that all assaults against persons of specified status, such as police or corrections officers, are to be considered aggravated, even if such attacks would otherwise be considered simple assaults.

In both types of assault, victims need not be placed in actual peril for offenses to be committed. The key issue is whether the victims have a reasonable fear of being injured. Under this principle, pointing a toy gun that appears to be real at someone is aggravated assault, even though the victim is never in actual danger.

History

Statutes against unwarranted violence have existed in human societies as long as there has been written law. Recorded laws dating back earlier than 2000 B.C.E., such as the code of the Babylonian king Hammurabi, set limits on human actions and asserted the principle that the strong shall not injure the weak. Ancient Roman law described assault and other acts that modern societies would regard as criminal offenses as instead civil "wrongs," or torts, and offenses were resolved by payments of monetary compensation to victims' families.

In early medieval England, self-governing tribes enforced their own laws and punishments for criminal activities, but in the twelfth century, crimes of violence were declared to be against the king's peace and became punishable by the state.

While this principle of the state assuming responsibility for the protection of its citizens against crimes of violence still exists today, it has only been fairly recently that some types of assault have been recognized as crimes and have been subject to punishment. For example, although rape has long been recognized as a crime, in early history, the law ignored rape victims who lacked social status and tended to treat the husbands and fathers of female rape victims as the true victims of the crime.

Similarly, acts that should have been prosecuted as criminal assaults committed against

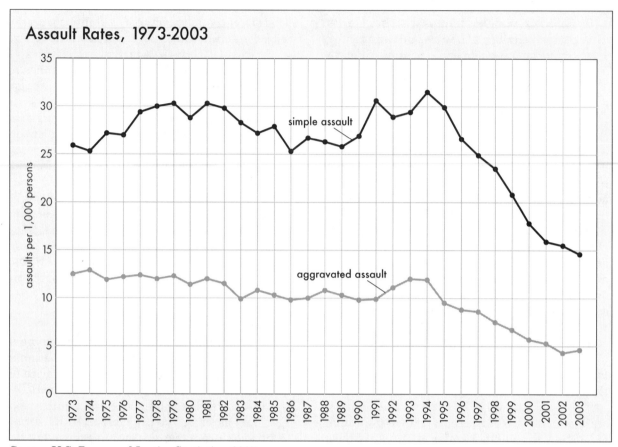

Assault Rates, 1973-2003

Source: U.S. Bureau of Justice Statistics, 2005.

slaves in pre-Civil War America were ignored. The victims were considered to be the property of their masters and therefore received negligible legal protection. The extent to which assault laws have protected people has thus varied over time.

Prevalence

The prevalence of assaults in the modern United States is difficult to estimate because of the many unreported offenses that occur, especially sexual and domestic assaults. However, studies have indicated that aggravated assault and simple assault rates have declined since 1994. Estimates of aggravated assault cases in the year 2002 range from 753,330 to 894,438 incidents. Aggravated assaults accounted for almost 63 percent of all violent crimes for that year. The National Crime Victimization Survey (NCVS) estimates that 2,456,660 simple assaults occurred in 2002; the figure is equivalent to 2.2 percent of U.S. households.

Although the prevalence of assault and battery crimes appear still to be declining during the first years of the twenty-first century, protection of people from interpersonal violence remains a fundamental responsibility of the criminal justice system, especially when addressing emerging issues of social concern, such as intimate partner violence and sexual assault.

Investigation

The effective investigation, prosecution and punishment of assault and battery hinge upon establishment of the elements of the crime by investigators and upon the ability of prosecutors to demonstrate those elements in courts of law. Punishments can range from fines or probation for some types of simple assault to several years in prison for aggravated assault.

In general, simple assaults refer to unlawful threatening behavior or to physical attacks that result in minor injuries, such as cuts and bruises. An important element of this crime in cases in which no actual physical attack occurs is that victims are placed in reasonable fear of being injured. Aggravated assault can be charged when offenders unlawfully use dangerous weapons, such as guns, to threaten or actually harm victims, or when victims sustain severe injuries, such as broken bones or teeth, deep lacerations, internal bleeding, maiming or other serious harm.

Investigating assault requires careful documentation by law-enforcement officers to establish the elements of the crime. In general, when no physical attacks occur, prosecutors must prove that the victims have been placed in reasonable fear for their safety and that the offenders unlawfully and intentionally offered threats.

In cases involving physical attacks, there must be careful recording of all evidence that establishes intent and injury. For example, investigators photograph victims to record all sustained injuries and counsel the victim to seek medical treatment so that medical records documenting the extent of the injuries can be obtained. Suspects should also be photographed in order to record any injuries on the knuckles, hands, elbows, or any other body parts that may demonstrate that those parts were used in attacks. Investigators should also take detailed statements from the victims, witnesses, and suspects (if the Fifth Amendment is not invoked) that may provide evidence of the offenders' threatening language and actions so that intent can be established.

When victims resist their attackers, physical evidence that may help establishing the suspects' identities may be collected from under the victims' fingernails, from blood spatters at the scene, from the victims' clothing, from bite marks on the victims, and from hair and fiber analysis. When weapons are used, every attempt must be made to locate them and subject them to analysis for fingerprints, DNA, and other trace evidence.

Victims of sexual assault should always be counseled not to bathe, shower, douche, or discard any items of clothing until after investigators have inspected them for possible evidence. Rape victims should be urged to seek medical at-

tention and to have rape examinations performed. Officers investigating assault cases should canvass the scenes for witnesses and record any evidence of intent and action.

Prosecuting Assault and Battery Cases

Successful prosecution of assault depends on how thoroughly the elements of assault are established by law enforcement. In cases involving attempted assault, prosecutors have to establish that the victims have been put in fear for their physical safety. That can usually be established by witness and victim statements, among other evidence. It does not matter whether the threats are real or not; it is only the reasonableness of the victims' fear that matters. For example, if an offender points a realistic toy gun at the victim, then aggravated assault can be established, even if the offender cannot carry out the threat.

Prosecutors must also establish intent. For example, if a defendant has harmed another person by accidentally tripping and colliding with someone who then banged his head into a wall, then no assault has been committed, despite the victim's injury. Intent to threaten or harm is a key element in prosecuting assault cases.

Prosecutors make important decisions in deciding whether to charge offenders with simple or aggravated assault. This is sometimes a clear choice due to the nature of the injuries sustained by the victims or due to the use or nonuse of deadly weapons. However, the decision can also be difficult when it requires determining the degree of injuries. Prosecutors rely on medical documentation in making decisions of that nature.

Punishment

Depending upon the severity of the assault, sentences can range from fines to probation to several years in prison. There has been some recent controversy about the levels of punishment that are most appropriate for violent assaults. Some recent legislation has proposed stiffer sentences for aggravated assaults that result in permanent disfigurement or disability in victims. Federal assault guidelines provide for tougher penalties in cases in which the assaults involve more than minimal planning, when life-threatening or permanent bodily injuries occur, when deadly weapons are involved, when firearms are discharged, and other aggravating circumstances.

David R. Champion

Further Reading

Ammerman, Robert T., and Michel Hersen, eds. *Case Studies in Family Violence*. New York: Plenum Press, 2000. Scholarly essays on legal, medical, social, and psychological issues involved in domestic violence.

Brewer, James D. *The Danger from Strangers: Confronting the Threat of Assault*. New York: Insight Books, 1994. Guidebook by a personal-security expert offering advice on how to avoid and protect oneself from assault. Contains a wealth of anecdotal material collected from assault victims.

Dalton, Clare, and Elizabeth M. Schneider. *Battered Women and the Law*. New York: Foundation Press, 2001. Casebook by two feminist law professors that examines violence against women in intimate relationships and how it shapes law.

Harries, Keith D. *Serious Violence: Patterns of Homicide and Assault in America*. 2d ed. Springfield, Ill.: Charles C Thomas, 1997. Comprehensive study of violent crime in the United States, addressing the subject from a variety of perspectives.

See also Criminal law; Felonies; Lesser-included offenses; Nonlethal weapons; Police brutality; Rape and sex offenses; School violence; Self-defense; Victimology.

Asset forfeiture

Definition: Government seizure of personal property derived from, or connected to, criminal activity

Criminal justice issues: Federal law; search and seizure; substance abuse

Significance: Asset forfeiture serves the goals of U.S. drug law-enforcement strategy as a significant financial resource.

While the practice of asset forfeiture has a long history dating back to the seizure of pirate ships in colonial America and the widespread acquisition of Confederate property during the Civil War, its modern use almost exclusively refers to drug law enforcement. Asset forfeiture was an important feature of the Reagan administration's War on Drugs that was legitimized by the Anti-Drug Abuse Act of 1988. Policymakers hoped that asset forfeiture would help stem the tide of the illicit drug problem in the United States. Theoretically, forfeiture augments the nature of drug enforcement strategy through serving as a fine levied against the proceeds of crime, removing the working capital of drug operations, and bringing partial penalty against drug lords otherwise not susceptible to sanction.

Asset forfeiture is a curious feature within the American criminal justice system in that forfeiture proceedings typically occur in civil, not criminal, courts, as *in rem* actions. Forfeiture hearings in the civil legal arena greatly advantage the state, which must meet only a preponderance of evidence versus beyond the reasonable-doubt standard of proof. Oddly, it is the property in question, and not the accused, that is at issue in civil forfeiture deliberations. In fact, property associated with crime may be forfeited in the absence of any arrest. Law enforcement, then, seizes questionable property, and forfeiture transpires in the court system. Once property transfers to the state, it may be put to use in law-enforcement operations or auctioned, with proceeds split between the seizing agency and other components of local, state, and federal government according to state law.

Forfeiture practices have become one of the most controversial components of the American criminal justice system, raising civil liberty and law enforcement over-reach issues. The controversy primarily arises from the financial incentive of selecting and prioritizing cases wherein forfeiture-derived revenue is high, but more traditional drug enforcement objectives—such as the apprehension of offenders and the eradication of illicit substances—are low. Through proactive policing strategies like reverse sting operations, drug units can be almost assured of generating income through seizures as suspects arrive at undercover "take-down" meetings with predetermined amounts of cash in hopes of purchasing wholesale quantities of various illicit drugs. Seemingly appropriate, a growing body of research suggests that far too often the recipients of police attention are corruptible but not necessarily culpable if not for encouragement from sworn officers and confidential informants, which adheres to the spirit, if not the legal definition, of entrapment.

Forfeiture victims, academic scrutiny, and social activist organizations such as Forfeiture Endangers American Rights (FEAR) have successfully lobbied forfeiture reforms featured in the 2000 Civil Asset Forfeiture Reform Act. The Forfeiture Reform Act provides protection for the innocent owners of questionable property and bolsters the applicability of the constitutional principle of proportionality to prevent home, automobile, and bank account seizures associated with only minor offenses. Forfeiture monies enable law enforcement generally, and drug enforcement particularly, to realize greater autonomy and are touted as tax relief from public support of the drug war.

J. Mitchell Miller

Further Reading

Miller, J. M., and L. H. Selva. "Law Enforcement's Double-edged Sword: An Assessment of Asset Forfeiture Programs." *Justice Quarterly* 11 (1994): 313-335.

United States Department of Justice. *Civil Asset Forfeiture Reform Act of 2000 (CAFRA: Pub. L. no. 106-185, 114 Stat. 202)*. Washington, D.C.: Author, 2000.

Williams, H. E. *Asset Forfeiture: A Law Enforcement Perspective*. Springfield, Ill.: Charles C Thomas, 2002.

See also Drugs and law enforcement; Marshals Service, U.S.; Organized crime; Racketeer Influenced and Corrupt Organizations Act.

Attempt to commit a crime

Definition: Act that includes the intent or purpose to commit a crime, overt acts in pursuit of that intent, and failure to complete the intended crime

Criminal justice issues: Crime prevention; legal terms and principles

Significance: Statutes banning attempted crimes are designed to deter dangerous behavior and potentially dangerous persons; however, criminal law consistently imposes lesser penalties on attempted crimes than on completed crimes.

Criminal law punishes both complete and uncompleted crimes. Uncompleted crimes, also called inchoate crimes, include attempt, conspiracy, and solicitation. Of the three, those who attempt to commit crimes get punished most severely.

As failures to achieve designated goals, attempts require specific intent and conscious efforts to achieve those goals that ultimately are not realized. Criminal law punishes those who attempt to commit crimes to deter persons who have manifested "dangerous conduct" from continuing with their criminal pursuits. The first component of an attempt to commit a crime is intent: One must purposely want to commit a crime. In *People v. Terry* (1984), the U.S. Supreme Court held that "one cannot attempt to commit a crime which one does not intend to commit."

The second component of an attempt to commit a crime is acts. An unlawful attempt requires its actor to take steps that exceed mere preparations to commit the crime. As people cannot be punished simply for harboring evil thoughts, the law requires that some significant steps be taken toward acting on the unlawful intent. State laws vary as to how many steps distinguish preparations from attempts. While the majority of states and the Model Penal Code require that "substantial steps" be taken toward completing the intended crime, some statutes specify merely "some steps." Most states classify activities such as purchasing weapons to use in crimes as preparations, not attempts. However, if the weapons or other devices of crime are actually taken to crime scenes, those actions may fulfill the substantial steps requirement of attempt.

A variety of defenses are used by people charged with attempting to commit crimes. For example, they may claim abandonment, arguing that they voluntarily renounced their intent to commit crimes. For such a defense to work, the accused persons must demonstrate that their abandonment was both voluntary and complete; it should not have been prompted by extraneous or outside factors, such as other persons walking in on the crime scenes. Postponing the intended crimes or transferring an intended crime to another target does not constitute abandonment.

A second defense is impossibility. However, only legal, not factual, impossibilities constitute a defense to attempt a crime. An act constitutes a legal impossibility if it is not defined by law as a crime. Keeping with the principle of legality, there cannot be a punishment. Factual impossibility is not a defense to attempt because but for some extraneous factor unknown to the actor that prevents the crime from happening, the crime would have been completed.

Victoria M. Time

Further Reading

Dix, E. G., and M. M. Sharlot. *Criminal Law.* 4th ed. Belmont, Calif.: Wadsworth, 1998.

Reid, Sue Titus. *Criminal Justice.* 6th ed. Cincinnati: Atomic Dog Publishing, 2001.

Samaha, J. *Criminal Law.* 8th ed. Belmont, Calif.: Thomson/Wadsworth, 2004.

Schmalleger, F. *Criminal Law Today.* Upper Saddle River, N.J.: Prentice-Hall, 1999.

See also Arson; Conspiracy; Criminal intent; Criminal law; Criminal liability; Inchoate crimes; Pickpocketing; Solicitation to commit a crime.

Attica prison riot

The Event: Large-scale uprising of inmates of a New York State prison
Date: September 9-13, 1971
Place: Attica Correctional Facility, Attica, New York

"Attempts" vs. "Preparations"

American courts generally apply four tests to establish that the actions of an accused person constitute an illegal attempt to commit a crime and are not merely preparations.

No.	Principle	Test
1	Substantial steps	Have sufficient measures been taken to confirm the intent of the accused?
2	Physical proximity doctrine	How close in time, space, and actions was the accused to completing the intended crime?
3	Equivocality approach	Do acts taken by the accused leave no doubt as to the crime the accused intended to commit?
4	Probable desistance approach	How probable is it that the crime would have been committed, had the accused not been interrupted by an intervening person or event?

Criminal justice issues: Police powers; punishment
Significance: More than a thousand inmates in this maximum security prison, angry over prison conditions, took control of four of the five prison blocks and held forty hostages.

The unrest that became the Attica prison riot had been building for months prior to the outbreak of hostilities. A report of the New York Committee on Crime and Correction in January of 1971 warned of possible prison violence at Attica. In June, a number of prisoners drafted a petition asking for better food and medicine and for better training for the guards, among other demands. The new correctional commissioner, Russell Oswald, began to move forward on the demands, and in early September he outlined a series of reforms intended to address the problems identified by the prisoners. He asked that the prison population give him more time to put these changes into effect.

On Wednesday, September 8, however, two inmates were placed in solitary confinement for fighting. The next morning just before 9 A.M. twelve hundred prisoners rioted, overpowering the unarmed guards. During this initial breakout, twenty-eight guards were seized, along with eleven civilian employees. Quickly the hostages were herded to cell block D, which would become the prisoner stronghold for the next four days. Throughout the confrontation, Oswald played an active part, but the prisoners demanded and received a group of fifteen observers/negotiators consisting of people who were sympathetic to their cause. Since the committee had no real power to change any of the conditions, the demands had to be taken to Oswald and Prison Superintendent Vincent Mancusi.

Amnesty for all misdeeds was in every list of demands that was made. By Saturday, September 11, the inmates had a list of twenty-eight demands, including things such as wages, health care, education, food, and recreation. Commissioner Oswald agreed to support all the reforms he had the power to implement, except for two:

amnesty and the ouster of Mancusi. Saturday evening things worsened when prison guard William Quinn died of injuries sustained during the initial uprising. There was now no chance of amnesty.

The Police Move In

At 9:46 A.M. on Sunday, under the cover of tear gas and rifle and shotgun fire, two hundred state police officers quickly subdued the prisoners. In what was the bloodiest confrontation in United States prison history, thirty inmates were killed outright, with another two hundred injured. Nine of the thirty-nine hostages were also killed by state police gunfire. A total of forty-two people died. Many of the reforms that the prisoners wanted were reasonable, and except for positions taken by some of the more extreme members of

Inmates of the Attica state prison negotiating with New York's state prison commissioner, Russell Oswald (lower left), during the midst of their 1971 riot. (AP/Wide World Photos)

the convict leadership, the bloodbath might have been avoided. There was also some evidence that prison authorities had invented stories about harsh treatment of hostages in order to gain support for the Sunday police attack.

The battle lasted only four minutes, but the impact was felt through the entire correctional system. The public attention generated by the riot and deaths focused on the inhumane conditions that had existed at the prison. Food, hygiene, and medical care in prisons have generally been improved since 1971, and recreational and educational opportunities have been provided to many inmates. In 1974, a civil suit claiming civil rights violations and "cruel and unusual punishment" at the time the authorities retook the prison was filed by 1,281 Attica inmates. They sought $2.8 billion in damages. It took eighteen years for the case to come to trial. In 1992, a jury ruled that the constitutional rights of the inmates had been violated but exonerated three of the four former prison officials named in the suit, holding liable only Karl Pfeil, a deputy warden.

Charles A. Bartocci

Further Reading

Selke, W. A. *Prisons in Crisis*. Bloomington: Indiana University Press, 1993.

Useem, Bert, and Peter Kimball. *States of Siege: U.S. Prison Riots, 1971-1986*. Reprint. New York: Oxford University Press, 1991.

Wicker, Tom. *A Time to Die: The Attica Prison Revolt*. Reprint. Lincoln: University of Nebraska Press, 1994.

See also Cruel and unusual punishment; Neighborhood watch programs; New Mexico state penitentiary riot; Prison and jail systems; Prison overcrowding; Prison violence; Punishment.

Attorney ethics

Definition: Ethical rules and norms under which attorneys are expected to operate

Criminal justice issues: Attorneys; professional standards

Significance: Defense attorneys and prosecutors largely control the presentation of evi-

dence in criminal proceedings, as well as the conduct of plea bargaining. Thus, the ethics of how they perform these functions are critical to the criminal justice system.

Attorneys in criminal proceedings are both officers of the court and zealous advocates. These obligations may conflict, generating difficult ethical dilemmas that attorneys must resolve. As prosecutors and defense lawyers play distinct roles in the criminal justice system, ethical obligations differ between the two.

Ethical Obligations of Prosecutors

Prosecutors, as representatives of the state or the people, operate under specific ethical constraints. In general terms, a prosecutor must act to further the public interest. As a result, a prosecutor is not only an advocate but also an agent of justice. It is often said that the role of a prosecutor is to see that justice is done, not to obtain convictions. Thus, prosecutors are ethically bound to protect the rights of accused persons.

Even prior to pressing formal charges, prosecutors must make reasonable efforts to ensure that a suspect is appropriately advised of the right to counsel. The prosecutor must not seek to have an unrepresented suspect waive pretrial rights. While prosecutors have discretion about when and if to press charges, such power—usually nonreviewable by the courts—must be exercised with extreme care and fairness. In legal terms, prosecutors can bring charges only when there is probable cause to do so. Moreover, given that defense attorneys are not present at grand jury proceedings, prosecutors must present evidence in such proceedings without generating subjective bias against a defendant.

Once charges have been filed, prosecutors must operate under more rigorous ethical constraints than defense attorneys. Foremost among these constraints are constitutional, statutory, and ethical requirements mandating that prosecutors disclose to defendants all information or evidence that tends to negate a defendant's guilt or mitigate an offense. This duty usually extends to sentencing. A failure to make appropriate disclosures may be grounds for the defendant to appeal a conviction.

While all attorneys must adhere to some limitations in extrajudicial statements about a case, prosecutors tend to be subject to the greatest scrutiny in this regard. It is unethical for prosecutors to make extrajudicial statements that will prejudice observers or heighten public condemnation of an accused.

Ethical Obligations of Defense Attorneys

Like prosecutors, defense attorneys are officers of the court. In contrast, however, the primary role of a defense counselor is to advocate zealously on behalf of a client. There tend to be fewer ethical constraints upon the performance of defense counselors than on that of prosecutors.

Nonetheless, several ethical issues are particularly applicable to criminal defense attorneys. While all lawyers, including prosecutors, must adhere to rules regarding conflicts of interest, it is nearly always unethical for an attorney to represent more than one criminal defendant in the same matter because the risks of conflicts between or among codefendants are so grave. Moreover, ethical rules prohibit attorneys from establishing contingent fee arrangements in criminal cases because of the corrupting influence that such fees could have on the administration of criminal justice. This rule, although well established, has sometimes been the subject of criticism.

Finally, ethical rules prohibit the sale of media or literary rights by a client to an attorney prior to the conclusion of the representation. The reason for this prohibition is that an attorney's interest in generating publicity or going to trial in order to increase the value of such rights might conflict with a client's interests in, for example, a speedy plea bargain.

Apart from these specific rules, two other ethical issues are of paramount importance when considering criminal defense counsel. First, defense attorneys have an obligation to zealously represent their clients, even those clients whom the attorney believes to be guilty. This principle has several justifications. A primary one is that defense attorneys have a role to play in administering justice and that role does not extend to the power to determine guilt or innocence—a power vested solely in judges and juries.

The Problem of Perjury

Perhaps the most celebrated ethical issue confronting criminal defense counsel is the so-called

---

Unethical Movie Attorneys

In director Richard Marquand's film *Jagged Edge* (1985), a lawyer (Glenn Close) defending a husband (Jeff Bridges) accused of murdering his wife begins an affair with her client. After her client is acquitted, the lawyer discovers evidence of his guilt and confronts him. When he attempts to kill her, she defends herself and shoots him dead. Despite its melodrama, the film realistically illustrates the adverse effect on attorneys' professional performances when they have affairs with their clients. Although such affairs are seldom specifically prohibited by the ethics rules for attorneys, lawyers can find themselves reprimanded, suspended from the practice of law, or even disbarred when such affairs cause them to provide inadequate representation to their clients.

In director Martin Scorsese's 1991 film *Cape Fear*, a remake of a 1962 film, an ex-convict played by Robert De Niro sets out to terrorize and exact revenge upon his former attorney (Nick Nolte) for having not adequately represented him. He claims that the attorney concealed evidence that might have saved him from going to prison. At first, the attorney tries to use the law to protect his family, but when the law proves to be—in the words of one character—"slow and suspicious," he hires a private investigator to protect him. The investigator, in turn, hires thugs to beat up the ex-con. After this plan fails, the attorney eventually fights hand-to-hand against the ex-con to protect his family.

Cape Fear poses intelligent questions about the nature of attorney obligations to clients. However, in dealing with the ethical difficulties into which its attorney lands after agreeing to the hiring of thugs to beat up his nemesis, the film strays from reality. Moreover, contrary to a suggestion made in the film, the American Bar Association does not grant attorneys the right to practice law or disbar attorneys who behave badly. Instead, each state has a bar association responsible for such matters.

Timothy L. Hall

client perjury problem. This issue arises when a criminal defense attorney knows that a client intends to commit perjury or already has committed perjury. Criminal defense attorneys, like all attorneys, cannot knowingly offer false evidence and are obligated to correct the record when they later learn that a piece of evidence presented was false.

Some courts and jurisdictions have modified this principle in the criminal context in light of constitutional protections afforded an accused. What is or is not ethical in such circumstances varies and remains subject to vigorous debate. Some of the answers that have been proposed include having an attorney seek withdrawal from representation, mandating that an attorney refuse to elicit perjured testimony and, if necessary and if the client continues to insist on the perjury, disclose the proposed perjury to the court or to the prosecution, allowing a client to present perjured testimony in narrative form or permitting an attorney to elicit the testimony as an attorney normally would. Virtually all authorities agree, however, that as an initial matter, an attorney is ethically bound to try to dissuade a client from committing perjury.

Robert Rubinson

Further Reading

ABA Standards for Criminal Justice: Prosecution and Defense Function. 3d ed. Washington, D.C.: American Bar Association, 1993. A widely influential set of standards that some jurisdictions have adopted as law.

Freedman, Monroe H., and Abbe Smith. *Understanding Lawyers' Ethics*. 3d ed. Newark, N.J.: LexisNexis, 2004. A compact treatment of lawyer's ethics, including chapters on prosecutors' ethics and the client perjury problem.

Hall, John Wesley, Jr. *Professional Responsibility of the Criminal Lawyer*. 2d ed. Deerfield, Ill.: Clark Boardman Callaghan, 1996. A detailed examination of the full range of ethical issues surrounding legal representation in criminal proceedings.

Wolfram, Charles. *Modern Legal Ethics*. St. Paul, Minn.: West, 1986. A treatise on legal ethics that addresses ethical obligations of prosecutors and defense attorneys in some detail.

See also *Brady v. United States*; Celebrity trial attorneys; Counsel, right to; Cross-examination; Defense attorneys; District attorneys; Effective counsel; Moral turpitude; National District Attorneys Association; Paralegals; Police ethics; Public defenders; Trial publicity.

Attorney general of the United States

Definition: Cabinet-level head of the U.S. Department of Justice and chief federal law-enforcement officer

Criminal justice issues: Federal law; law-enforcement organization; political issues

Significance: As the chief law-enforcement officer in the United States, the attorney general occupies a position of unique influence on the criminal justice system.

The attorney general of the United States is appointed by the president of the United States and confirmed by a majority vote in the U.S. Senate. As leader of the Justice Department, the attorney general is a member of the president's cabinet but is the only cabinet position not called a "secretary." The Office of the Attorney general represents the United States in legal cases and counsels the president and other executive officials on various legal issues. The attorney general represents the U.S. government before the U.S. Supreme Court in important cases; however, the U.S. solicitor general is the Justice Department representative who usually argues cases when the United States is party to legal disputes.

History of the Office

In 1789, the newly formed U.S. Congress passed the Judiciary Act, which created the basic structure of the federal court system. The same legislation also created the position of attorney general, which was originally conceived as a part-time position for only one person. The position was not initially a cabinet-office rank, but President George Washington requested that his attorney general be present at all cabinet meetings because legal issues were frequently discussed.

Over the years, the attorney general's office grew into a vast bureaucracy that employed a large number of private attorneys and legal assistants. From 1790 until 1819, both the Congress and the presidents received legal advice from attorneys general. However, in 1819, the attorney general's role as legal counsel for Congress ended because the workload of the position had increased dramatically. In 1870, Congress created the Department of Justice as an official cabinet position within the executive branch and the attorney general assumed leadership of the cabinet post, but the office's duties and responsibilities did not change in any material way.

As the head of the Department of Justice, the attorney general's office controls a variety of operating agencies within the executive branch such as the Bureau of Alcohol, Tobacco, Firearms, and Explosives; the Drug Enforcement Administration; the Federal Bureau of Investigation; and the Bureau of Justice Statistics. In 2004, the department had an operating budget of $23 billion and employed more than 112,000 people.

John Ashcroft and the War on Terror

In 2002, President George W. Bush nominated John Ashcroft to be his attorney general. In the aftermath of the terrorist attacks of September 11, 2001, Ashcroft directed the Justice Department to focus upon providing security for Americans by preventing further terrorist attacks within the United States. Ashcroft was given more power and discretion as the leading law-enforcement officer in the United States to pursue an aggressive antiterrorism agenda. Ashcroft assisted in obstructing the plans of international terrorists, dismantled terrorist groups in a number of American cities, and arrested hundreds of persons suspected of terrorist-related activities.

The Patriot Act passed in late 2001 increased the powers of the attorney general to investigate suspected terrorists by using various types of surveillance. The attorney general can now use roving wiretaps against terrorist suspects

U.S. attorney general John Ashcroft during an inspection of the damage done to the Pentagon building by a hijacked airliner that was flown into it by terrorists on September 11, 2001. As the head of the U.S. Department of Justice, Ashcroft bore ultimate responsibility for the government's investigation of the terrorist attacks. *(AP/Wide World Photos)*

who switch locations and communication devices in attempts to deceive law-enforcement officials. Law-enforcement officers under the attorney general can also employ search warrants in more flexible ways to prevent suspected terrorists from being tipped off about investigations. The attorney general also can access personal information and monitor computer activity on the Internet by accessing electronic mail and chat rooms more easily under the powers given to the office under the Patriot Act. The Patriot Act has also made penalties more severe for terrorists and their allies.

The actions of Ashcroft caused considerable controversy because many civil libertarians are concerned that, as attorney general, he was given so much power that there has been a narrowing of freedom and liberty for Americans. After Bush was reelected in November, 2004, Ashcroft resigned, and Bush replaced him with Alberto R. Gonzales, who was sworn in on February 3, 2005. A former justice of the supreme court of Texas, President Bush's home state, Gonzales became the first Hispanic attorney general of the United States.

Scott P. Johnson

Further Reading

Ashcroft, John, and Gary Thomas. *On My Honor: The Beliefs That Shape My Life.* Nashville, Tenn.: Thomas Nelson, 2001. This book reveals Attorney General Ashcroft's personal beliefs on various issues related to the criminal justice system.

Clayton, Cornell C. *The Politics of Justice: The Attorney General and the Making of Legal Policy.* Armonk, N.Y.: M. E. Sharpe, 1992. Scholarly examination of the role of the attorney general in the shaping of national legal policies.

Dash, Samuel. *The Intruders: Unreasonable Searches and Seizures from King John to John Ashcroft.* New Brunswick, N.J.: Rutgers University Press, 2004. Historical overview of violations of the Fourth Amendment guarantee against unreasonable searches and seizures and the danger of the recently passed Patriot Act.

Kleindienst, Richard. *Justice: The Memoirs of Attorney General Richard Kleindienst.* Ottawa, Ill.: Jameson Books, 1985. Autobiography of the attorney general appointed by President Richard Nixon in 1973. Kleindienst was forced to resign along with other members of the Nixon administration during the Watergate scandal in 1974, after it was revealed that he had lied during the Senate hearings on his confirmation.

See also Attorneys, U.S.; Attorneys general, state; Criminal prosecution; Deportation; Drug Enforcement Administration; Federal Bureau of Investigation; Homeland Security Department; Immigration and Naturalization Service; Interpol; Justice Department, U.S.; Marshals Service, U.S.; National Institute of Justice; Patriot Act; Solicitor general of the United States.

Attorneys, U.S.

Definition: Federal government attorneys practice law on behalf of the U.S. government

Criminal justice issues: Attorneys; federal law

Significance: Practicing in a wide number of legal areas, U.S. attorneys represent both the federal government and the interests of all American citizens.

The Department of Justice is, in effect, the law firm for the federal government. U.S. attorneys work under the authority of the U.S. attorney general. They are appointed directly by the president of the United States, with advice and consent of the Senate, as required by Article II of the U.S. Constitution.

The primary job of U.S. attorneys is to conduct criminal prosecutions involving violations of federal law, to represent the interests of the United

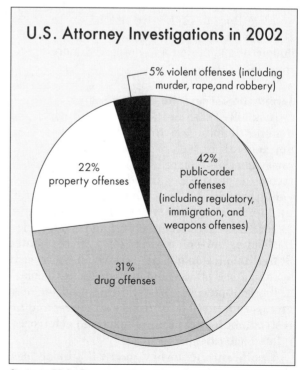

U.S. Attorney Investigations in 2002

- 5% violent offenses (including murder, rape, and robbery)
- 42% public-order offenses (including regulatory, immigration, and weapons offenses)
- 22% property offenses
- 31% drug offenses

Source: U.S. Bureau of Justice Statistics, 2005. Percentages are estimates based on 124,335 investigations opened in 2002. Approximately 73 percent of investigations were referred for prosecution.

States—either as plaintiff or defendant—in all civil suits to which the United States is named as a party. The attorneys also render legal advice on questions posed by the president and members of the various government departments.

In 2005, the Justice Department's ninety-three U.S. attorneys were based in offices across the country. The attorneys are supported by a staff of assistant U.S. attorneys, who conduct most of the day-to-day legal work. U.S. attorneys have a large variety of resources available to them, and there is a high amount of communication and interaction among the divisions in which they work. The Justice Department's litigation divisions include Antitrust, Civil, Civil Rights, Criminal, Environment and Natural Resources, and Taxes.

Kimberly J. Belvedere

Further Reading

Johns, Margaret, and Rex R. Perschbacher. *The United States Legal System: An Introduction*. Durham, N.C.: Carolina Academic Press, 2002.

Sander, R. H., and E. D. Williams. "Why Are There So Many Lawyers? Perspectives of a Turbulent Market." *Law and Sociological Inquiry* 14 (1989): 478.

See also Attorneys general, state; Attorney general of the United States; Death-row attorneys; Federal Crimes Act; Justice Department, U.S.; Marshals Service, U.S.; President, U.S.; Public prosecutors; Treason.

Attorneys general, state

Definition: Chief legal officers of the states, who serve as counselors for state government agencies, legislatures, and the citizenry

Criminal justice issues: Law-enforcement organization; prosecution

Significance: Attorneys general provide legal advice and legal representation for state agencies and the public on diverse matters such as drug abuse, the environment, business regulation, and criminal appeals.

New York State attorney general Eliot Spitzer at a December, 2003, news conference, in which he announced that he had filed lawsuits against a spam ring responsible for sending billions of illegal electronic-mail messages. *(AP/Wide World Photos)*

The development of state attorneys general in the United States can be traced to England. The king of England had specially designated lawyers to represent his legal interests. The attorney general of England served as legal adviser to the king and all government departments and was responsible for all litigation. During the American colonial era, the attorney general provided legal advice to the king and governance over the colonies. After the revolution, American officials adapted the English version of the office of attorney general to govern their own legal interests. Constitutional provisions were enacted to create the office of the attorney general to have jurisdiction of legal affairs of the federal government. As the new nation grew, the states also adopted the office of attorney general, and many had constitutional provisions for the office.

Attorneys general are popularly elected in

forty-three states, appointed by the governors in five states and six jurisdictions, appointed by the state supreme court in Tennessee, and selected by the state legislature in Maine. New legislation and conceptions of the office have significantly expanded the powers and duties of the state attorneys general. There is much diversity in the role of the attorney general from state to state.

In response to needs identified by governors and legislatures, attorneys general have become active in areas of consumer protection, antitrust law, toxic waste, child-support enforcement, organized crime, and many other areas. The most common duties of the attorney general involve controlling litigation concerning the state, serving as chief legal officer, writing opinions that clarify law, acting as public advocate, enforcing criminal law, and investigating issues of public interest.

Public advocacy is a growing field for attorneys general in nearly all states. In addition to providing legal service in such areas as consumer protection and child-support enforcement, relatively new areas of concern for states' chief legal officers include utility regulation and advocacy regarding the provision of services to crime victims. These new areas of interest put attorneys general in the position of being the initiator of legal action, or plaintiff, which is a role reversal that provides a new opportunity to implement and interpret public policy. One of the most important functions of the state attorney general is writing opinions. Opinions clarify law for the executive and legislative branches. Attorneys general use their opinions to identify legislative oversight that is in need of correction and to resolve issues that are not likely to be solved through litigation.

Donna Echols Mabus

Further Reading

National Association of Attorneys General, Committee on the Office of Attorney General. *Powers, Duties, and Operations of State Attorneys General*. Raleigh, N.C.: Author, 1977.

Ross, Lynne M., ed. *State Attorneys General: Powers and Responsibilities*. Washington, D.C.: Bureau of National Affairs, 1990.

See also Attorney general of the United States; Attorneys, U.S.; District attorneys; Public prosecutors.

Atwater v. City of Lago Vista

The Case: U.S. Supreme Court decision on warrantless arrests for minor criminal offenses

Date: Decided on April 24, 2001

Criminal justice issues: Police powers; search and seizure

Significance: The case ratified routine arrests for minor crimes punishable only by a fine.

In 1997, Gail Atwater was driving her three-year-old son and five-year-old daughter home from soccer practice. Officer Barton Turek of the City of Lago Vista police stopped Atwater because neither she nor the children were wearing seat belts, a violation of Texas law with a maximum fine of $50. Turek approached the car and began yelling at Atwater that she was going to jail.

Instead of following the common practice of issuing a citation, Turek arrested Atwater, handcuffed her, and transported her to the police station. There the booking officers took a "mug shot" and had her empty her pockets and remove her shoes, jewelry, and eyeglasses. She was placed alone in a jail cell for approximately an hour before appearing in front of a magistrate and posting a $310 bond. Eventually, she pleaded no contest to the seatbelt violations and paid the fines. She then filed a lawsuit against the city and Turek under the federal Civil Rights Act, claiming that her right to be free from unreasonable seizure had been violated.

In a 5-4 decision, the U.S. Supreme Court deemed the custodial arrest constitutional even though the justices thought the officer at best "exercis[ed] extremely poor judgment." The Court rejected Atwater's contention that the common law, at the time of the adoption of the Fourth Amendment, generally prohibited warrantless arrests for minor crimes unless special circumstances such as violence or a demonstrable threat existed. The Court also declined to establish a rule prohibiting routine warrantless arrests for fine-only offenses on the grounds that officers might not have the time or knowledge to make the distinction among the fine-only crimes and others. Instead, the Court focused on Turek's probable cause that Atwater committed a crime in his presence and that Texas law permitted such arrests.

Justice Sandra Day O'Connor, writing for the dissent, recognized that "significant qualitative differences" exist between a traffic stop and a full custodial arrest, a much greater infringement on a person's liberty and privacy interests. In weighing the competing interests of the state in enforcing traffic laws against the invasion of the individual's rights, she found arrests for fine-only offenses should be unreasonable unless special circumstances exist.

Atwater v. City of Lago Vista (2001) was immediately criticized by commentators from across the political spectrum. Even those who usually advocate stronger police powers were dismayed by this expansion of police discretion to permit someone to be jailed for a fine-only offense.

Susan Coleman

Further Reading

Katz, Jason. "*Atwater v. City of Lago Vista*: Buckle Up or Get Locked Up." *Akron Law Review* 491 (2003).

Milloy, Ross E. "Public Lives: For Seat-Belt Violator, a Jam, a Jail, and Unmoved Justices." *The New York Times*, April 28, 2001.

Osborne, Jonathan, and Bob Dart. "Lago Vista Mom Loses in High Court." *Austin American-Statesman*, April 25, 2001.

See also Arrest; Police powers; *Terry v. Ohio*; Traffic law.

Auburn system

Identification: Prison-design plan developed and implemented during the penitentiary movement of the early nineteenth century
Date: Begun in 1822
Place: Auburn, New York
Criminal justice issues: Prisons; rehabilitation
Significance: The Auburn system of prison design was the architectural plan for the first large-scale prison built to maximize the re-

habilitation and the labor potential of incarcerated offenders, while reducing construction and operating costs. Even though this model of incarceration was the key mechanism implemented to reform offenders during the penitentiary movement, it has been noted, even since its inception, for pervasive offender abuse and overcrowding.

At the turn of the nineteenth century, American prison reformers embraced the ideals and promises of the penitentiary. In essence, the penitentiary's purpose was to rehabilitate the offender through silent reflection and penance. Initially, penitentiary design followed the model of the Pennsylvania system plan, wherein individual offenders were housed in solitary cells at all times. However, that system was too expensive to build and manage, as considerable land was needed to erect the large structures, and exceptional numbers of qualified staff were required for inmate surveillance and control. The Auburn system was thus developed and implemented to counter the negative reality of the Pennsylvania system design.

The Auburn system penitentiary called for offenders to sleep in small, individual cells, yet dine and work silently in common areas. Hence, this design and its inherent regimes were often referred to as the congregate system. The first two penitentiaries built according to this plan were New York's Auburn and Sing Sing prisons, both which opened during the 1820's.

Cells in Auburn-style facilities were positioned back-to-back and stacked in tiers within hollow buildings. The ideal of the Auburn-style prison was maximization of the rehabilitation and labor potential of offenders. This ideal of the Auburn design was so widely embraced, it influenced prison construction throughout the United States during the remainder of the nineteenth and the early twentieth centuries. In fact, Sing Sing prison remains in use today.

Auburn-style facilities were often built to be large, foreboding structures, in the hope that the very essence of the prisons would serve as a deterrent to potential offenders. Nevertheless, penologists have questioned the rehabilitative and deterrent value of the Auburn system design, as offender recidivism, unsanitary conditions, and corporal punishment have been the reality in many facilities built according to the design plan of the Auburn system.

Courtney A. Waid

Further Reading

Blomberg, Thomas G., and Karol Lucken. *American Penology*. New York: Aldine de Gruyter, 2000.

Johnston, Norman. *The Human Cage: A Brief History of Prison Architecture*. New York: Walker, 1973.

Waid, Courtney A., and Carl B. Clements. "Correctional Facility Design: Past, Present and Future." *Corrections Compendium* 26, no. 11 (2001).

See also Bureau of Prisons; Corporal punishment; Criminal justice system; Incapacitation; Prison and jail systems; Prison industries; Prison overcrowding; Punishment; Rehabilitation; Rosenberg espionage case; Solitary confinement.

Automobile searches

Definition: Lawful searches by police of vehicles and seizure of evidence discovered therein

Criminal justice issues: Police powers; search and seizure

Significance: Police frequently have occasion to stop vehicles and conduct searches because automobiles are the most common form of conveyance in the United States.

Because of the proliferation of vehicles on U.S. roads and highways, police often encounter situations in which they must conduct searches of automobiles for criminal evidence. Since 1925, the courts have permitted law-enforcement officers to search automobiles without search warrants. This practice is allowed as an "automobile exception" to the warrant requirement of the Fourth Amendment to the U.S. Constitution. In *Carroll v. United States* (1925), the U.S. Supreme Court ruled that because of the "mobility" of motor vehicles, police could conduct searches without search warrants.

The Court established two requirements for conducting warrantless searches of automobiles. First, officers must have probable cause to believe that the vehicles contain evidence or contraband related to crimes. Second, the mobility of automobiles makes it impractical for police to hold them until they can obtain search warrants. Therefore, the Court permits police to search motor vehicles with or without search warrants if they have probable cause.

Other rationales used by the courts to permit automobile searches include the reduced privacy expectation citizens have when traveling in cars, compared with when they are in their homes. Moreover, many of the articles subject to search in vehicles may be in plain view of the police. Warrantless automobile searches can be as extensive as those conducted with warrants, under the conditions established in the *Carroll* decision.

Scope of Automobile Searches

Automobile searches fall into two categories—searches of vehicle contents and inventory searches of vehicles. The courts have expanded police automobile search authority to include motor vehicles, containers, and passengers. These rules enable the police to search passenger compartments of automobiles if they have legal reason to believe that they may contain evidence or illegal goods. Searches can be expanded to include entire vehicles and all accessible unlocked containers when probable cause is present. In fact, if the police have probable cause to believe that a specific container in an automobile contains a weapon or evidence of crime, they are allowed to search it even when they lack probable cause to search the entire vehicle. Beyond the vehicle contents, the police may search the personal effects of the occupants if they believe weapons or evidence are present.

Police are allowed to search passenger compartments and surrounding areas within the reach of occupants of the vehicles whom they arrest. Although they are permitted to conduct searches for weapons or evidence, such searches must be conducted at the same times as the arrests of the occupants. If police officers lawfully stop or approach a vehicle, they may peer inside it and seize any article they readily identify as illegal, so long as it is in their visual "plain view."

Automobile searches can also be conducted when the drivers or owners voluntarily give consent, verbally or in writing. Ordinarily, consent searches allow the police look in areas of the vehicle, including containers, that are accessible and unlocked.

Other circumstances may permit limited searches of passenger compartments of vehicles and passengers within their immediate reach. To ensure the safety of the officers, the police may order occupants to exit vehicles so they can conduct limited outer clothing touch-searches of them and areas within their reach when reasonable suspicion exists that the occupants may be armed with weapons. If the officers have probable cause to believe that occupants may be hiding weapons or evidence, they may also search the occupants' personal effects.

A Utah police officer searches a van whose owner was charged with possession of marijuana and drug paraphernalia and with driving with an open container of alcohol, as a backup police officer and the van's owner and passengers look on. *(AP/Wide World Photos)*

Limited warrantless searches of vehicles may also be performed when vehicles have been involved in accidents or have been subjected to vandalism. Abandoned vehicles seized in public places that are believed to contain contraband can also be searched in a similar manner.

Automobile Inventory Searches

The second category of permissible automobile search is vehicle inventory searches. This type of search is designed to protect vehicle owners' personal effects at the time the police impound their vehicles. Vehicles may be impounded for several reasons. For example, police may have towed automobiles involved in the commission of criminal offenses that may contain evidence, They may also have vehicles that impede traffic or that are abandoned towed. However, the courts have also stated that police officers should take care to reduce the chances of theft of personal articles within the towed vehicles. They should also take care to reduce reasons for suspecting that the police themselves have removed items from cars. Vehicle inventory searches were devised to en-

able the police to document articles found in passenger compartments and trunks of automobiles.

Another situation in which vehicle inventories are permissible arises when police arrest drivers for offenses and impound their vehicles. In *South Dakota v. Opperman* (1976), the Supreme Court established the automobile inventory search doctrine by ruling that police may inventory personal effects found in impounded automobiles, so long as the items are accessible without the use of force—such as might be required to open a locked storage box. The courts have also stated that valid inventory searches must follow established departmental procedures using standardized practices. The scope of inventory searches is restricted to documenting accessible items found in cars and cannot be used as a pretext to conduct extensive searches of vehicles.

Although the U.S. Supreme Court has established many guidelines for automobile searches, state court rulings and individual department policies may affect the manner in which the police conduct vehicle searches. Indeed, local rules and policies in some jurisdictions may be even more restrictive than the practices allowed by the federal courts.

William P. Bloss

Further Reading

Del Carmen, Rolando V. *Criminal Procedure: Law and Practice*. 6th ed. Belmont, Calif.: Thomson/Wadsworth, 2004. Comprehensive and readable review of criminal procedure, including constitutional rights, that covers each stage of criminal procedure, with special attention given to Supreme Court cases. Includes detailed discussions of search and seizure legal doctrines.

Holtz, Larry. *Contemporary Criminal Procedure*. 8th ed. Longwood, Fla.: Gould Publications, 2004. Another comprehensive and up-to-date textbook on criminal procedures.

LaFave, W. R. *Search and Seizure: A Treatise on the Fourth Amendment*. 3d ed. St Paul, Minn.: West Publishing, 1995. Comprehensive overview of search and seizure.

McWhirter, Darien A. *Search, Seizure, and Privacy*. Phoenix, Ariz.: Oryx Press, 1994. Written to make subjects such as search and seizure and the exclusionary rule interesting for high school and undergraduate college students.

See also Bill of Rights, U.S.; *Chimel v. California*; Consent searches; Constitution, U.S.; Fourth Amendment; *Knowles v. Iowa*; Plain view doctrine; Probable cause; Search and seizure; Stop and frisk; *Terry v. Ohio*; Vehicle checkpoints; *Whren v. United States*.

Autopsies

Definition: Medical examination of a dead body in order to learn the cause of death

Criminal justice issues: Evidence and forensics; investigation; medical and health issues; technology

Significance: Through examination, medical examiners and investigators can learn how someone died, how that kind of death might be prevented in the future, and if the death in question was caused by criminal means.

An autopsy, or postmortem examination, is a way of learning how a person died. The first autopsies were performed by and for medical students, but eventually it became clear that autopsies could also be used to determine if a person's death was a result of natural causes. If homicide is discovered to be the cause of death, then the results of the autopsy are used in coordination with other evidence to attempt to bring the murderer to justice.

Autopsies are performed in hospitals, medical schools, and forensics laboratories. While training to become doctors, medical students perform autopsies to familiarize themselves with parts of the body—both healthy and unhealthy. When an autopsy is performed at a hospital, it is usually at the request of the family or other legal guardian of the deceased who wants to know how the death came about. Mitigating circumstances regarding the care that person received while alive can sometimes be determined by the autopsy. If it is shown that reasonable steps to keep a patient alive were not taken, then legal action may be sought. A coroner has to decide whether the death of the body found at a crime scene was natural or not. Many times, the only way to find out is by performing an autopsy.

Performing an Autopsy

Before a legal autopsy begins, permission to perform it must be obtained. This permission is usually granted by a family member. If there are no known surviving relatives, a friend may give permission, or a brief period of time may be allowed for a relative search to be performed. If the person in question was enlisted in the military at the time of death, an autopsy may be ordered by the appropriate military commander. Religion also plays a factor: Autopsies are permitted by some faiths, while the doctrines of others may object to the procedure.

An autopsy can range from examination of a single organ removed for further study (a selective autopsy) to dissection of the entire body, one organ at a time (a complete autopsy). The latter is almost always done for a medicolegal/forensic investigation. After the body is placed upon the autopsy table (sometimes with the help of a diener, or attendant), a detailed external examination is made in order to record the body's height, weight, any visible markings such as tattoos or scars, injuries, and any other trace evidence that can be found. These details can help with a forensic investigation, and if the body is that of an unknown person, they may help with identification.

Once external examination has been completed, an internal examination begins. A standard autopsy starts with a Y- or U-shaped incision cut into the torso, from the shoulders to the pubic bone. The medical examiner or pathologist then proceeds to remove every organ from the neck, chest, abdominal cavity, and skull. If further information is needed, organs are sent to a laboratory for analysis, which may include microbiological (testing for infections), histology (whether the body's organs and tissues have changed), and toxicology (testing for drugs, poisons, or medications). At every step of the autopsy, a detailed record is kept so that it may be referred to later. After the autopsy is completed, the incisions are sutured shut so that the body can be given to a mortuary in preparation for funeral services.

History of Autopsies

The term autopsy comes from *autopsia*, a Greek word meaning "to see with one's own eyes." Around 3000 B.C.E., the Egyptians practiced mummification—removing organs through tiny slits in the body so that the body itself remained whole—and the Greek Hirophilus broke religious taboos by dissecting bodies to learn how the inner organs worked. By around 150 B.C.E., autopsy results had legal parameters in the Roman Empire. Giovanni Battista Morgagni wrote *The Seats and Causes of Diseases Investigated by Anatomy* in 1769, the first exhaustive written work on pathology.

The nineteenth century Austrian anatomy professor Karl Rokitansky is regarded as the founder of the modern autopsy. Rokitansky personally performed or supervised more than 100,000 autopsies and was also one of the world's first pathologists. Under his leadership, all autopsies were carried out equally so that every part of the body in question could be studied exactly the same way.

The Decline of Autopsies

Even though autopsies help both medical doctors and criminal investigators gain invaluable information, their use is on the decline. Since the 1950's, the number of procedures performed has decreased as the public has become resistant to the idea of autopsies. Pathologists are also overworked on other lab jobs such as biopsies, and interest has fallen in autopsy-based research.

Magnetic resonance imaging (MRI) machines also play a part in the decline of autopsies: Because they are noninvasive, people are more comfortable in accepting MRI autopsies, and sometimes MRIs do find things that traditional autopsies miss. Also, full-body autopsies are slowly being removed from medical university curricula because many students and teachers feel the time is better used to study other topics.

Kelly Rothenberg

Further Reading

Baden, Michael, M.D., and Marion Roach. *Dead Reckoning: The New Science of Catching Killers*. New York: Simon & Schuster, 2001. Detailed chapter describing a forensic autopsy.

Blanche, Tony, and Brad Schreiber. *Death in Paradise: An Illustrated History of the Los Angeles County Department of Coroner*. New York: Four Walls Eight Windows, 2001. Details and examples of autopsies done in one of the largest coroner offices in the United States.

Burton, Julian L., and Guy N. Rutty. *The Hospital Autopsy*. New York: Oxford University Press, 2001. History and legal chapters about autopsies.

Roach, Mary. *Stiff: The Curious Lives of Human Cadavers*. New York: W. H. Norton, 2003. Chapter about medical students performing autopsies.

See also Cold cases; Coroners; Forensic entomology; Forensics; Inquests; Medical examiners; Toxicology; Trace evidence.

B

Background checks

Definition: Searches undertaken to verify the identifies of, and information about, individuals

Criminal justice issues: Investigation; privacy; terrorism

Significance: Sometimes known as record checks or criminal history checks, background checks are available to local, state, and federal law-enforcement agencies and members of the general public. The primary goal of the checks is to validate information concerning the persons being investigated.

Since the United States has undergone dangerous terrorist attacks, emphasis on safety and security has dramatically increased. In fact, many jobs in the public and private sectors now require background checks. In some instances, background checks are made to determine if there are any indications of corruption or blackmail by organized crime or foreign governments. Employers are also concerned about the possibility of job applicants providing false or inflated information in their resumes, so many employees require that such information by verified through background checks.

People applying for positions involving major corporate or government responsibility, or who are in positions of trust are required to undergo background checks. Examples of those who might undergo background checks include employees of financial institutions; law-enforcement officers on the local, state, national, and international levels; military personnel who handle sensitive and classified information; people in high-risk positions, such as White House staff members; candidates for court offices; and scientists working on classified projects.

Background checks are often made by employers to ascertain whether prospective employees have any troublesome facts about their lives that they wish to hide and that may make them security risks as employees. At an entirely different level, parents might require background checks for prospective nannies. Such checks might uncover information about a prospective employee's history of abusive behavior. Background checks are also used by volunteer organizations to reduce their liability, especially in organizations whose volunteers work with youth.

The most thorough types of background checks are usually made by private investigators who are contracted by major businesses, police departments, the Federal Bureau of Investigation, the military, and other government agencies. The information they gather is more extensive than that gathered for employees who do not represent possible security risks, such as child-care workers or volunteers.

Background checks can be long, involved, and complicated processes of acquiring as much information as possible about people. The details that background checks cover may range from verification of applicants' Social Security numbers to complete and thorough investigations of their histories and acquaintances. Information may be acquired from such sources as school records, criminal records, motor vehicle records, credit records, drug tests, and bankruptcies. Informa-

---

Rights of the Subjects of Background Checks

It is generally up to the person who will become the subject of a background check to allow or disallow the investigation. Potential and current employers cannot conduct background checks without the subjects' written authorization. Those who refuse to allow background checks may be eliminated from consideration for job openings and possibly even lose the jobs they currently have. However, anyone who authorizes a background check has the right to see the results of the investigation and also has the right to dispute the findings if they appear to be incorrect.

tion from sex-offender lists, worker's compensation claims, and property ownership may also be searched. In addition, character references are also sometimes investigated; past employers and coworkers are contacted, and neighbors are interviewed to provide information about the ethics and morals of the people being investigated.

Peggy C. Bowen

Further Reading

Butler, Teresa, et al. *Background Checks and Investigations of Applicants and Employees: Four Steps to Basic Compliance with Federal and State Laws.* San Francisco: Littler Mendelson, 2002.

Dickinson, Philip D. *Hiring Smart: How to Conduct Background Checks.* Brentwood, Tenn.: M. Lee Smith Publishers, 1997.

See also Blackmail and extortion; Consumer fraud; Criminal history record information; Criminal records; Gun laws; Immunity from prosecution; Moral turpitude; Tax evasion.

Bail system

Definition: System that allows individuals accused of criminal offenses to be released prior to their court appearances by securing funds to ensure their appearances in court

Criminal justice issues: Arrest and arraignment; defendants; probation and pretrial release

Significance: This highly debated practice has been criticized for discriminating against poor and minority arrestees; it has also been criticized for the practice of preventive detention, which uses exorbitant bail to keep accused offenders from committing crimes while awaiting trial.

The United States bail system operates on the premise that some individuals can be released prior to their appointed court date by leaving an amount of money with the court. Individuals are expected to return for their subsequent court appearance to have the amount of bail returned to them. Many argue that this practice discrimi-

nates against poor arrestees who cannot afford a monetary bail and thus must remain incarcerated while awaiting trial.

Tradition in English Law

The bail system in the United States is rooted in the traditional court systems of England. In feudal England (prior to the Battle of Hastings in 1066), law was dispensed by judges who would travel from county to county. Sheriffs would typically keep accused offenders in local jails with the promise to turn the offender in when the judge returned. As the number of offenders increased and jail space became limited, offenders were occasionally entrusted to the custody of a friend or relative who would ensure their appearance. In some cases, these individuals were required to sign a bond promising a specific sum of money to the king if the accused failed to appear when the judge next visited the area.

Over time (and eventually in the American colonies), the practice of having an individual step forward for an accused was replaced by the use of financial security, or monetary bail. In exchange for freedom prior to trial, the accused would deposit a certain amount of money with the court, which would be returned following appearance. Even before the colonization of America it was recognized that the practice discriminates against individuals who cannot afford to leave a monetary bail. Arrestees who could not afford to leave bail were frequently incarcerated until their appearance at trial, a time period that could encompass years. Thus, the first formal regulations governing the use of bail were written in England in the year 1275. These statutes set forth specific conditions under which bail could be imposed, defining which crimes were "bailable" and which were not. That is, they specified for which crimes bail must be denied and the accused must be incarcerated prior to trial. Laws forbidding excessive bail eventually appeared in England, but not until they were included in the English Bill of Rights in 1688.

History of the American Bail System

Like the English system, early Americans also protected against excessive bail. The Eighth Amendment to the U.S. Constitution begins with the phrase, "Excessive bail shall not be required."

The meaning of this phrase, however, has not been successfully decided by the U.S. Supreme Court. For example, does excessive bail refer to the defendant's ability to pay, or does it relate to the seriousness of the crime committed? In addition, is there a constitutional right to bail?

The Judiciary Act of 1789 gave offenders a right to bail unless arrested for a capital offense. For a capital offense, maximum penalties can consist of life imprisonment or death. Assuming that these offenders may be likely to flee, considering the severity of punishment, bail is typically denied. Thus, every defendant in a noncapital case was guaranteed to receive bail. The appropriate amount of bail was not discussed in the Judiciary Act of 1789.

A recommended or appropriate amount of bail was not dealt with in the United States until 1951, when the Supreme Court, in *Stack v. Boyle*, decided that bail must be of sufficient amount to ensure the defendant's appearance at trial. In other words, the amount of bail must be enough to assure the defendant's appearance, but it cannot be more than that amount, or else it would be considered excessive. The vagueness of this decision has left many experts speculating about the appropriate amount of bail.

Bail Reform

During the 1960's, it became apparent that the United States bail system was not operating as it was designed. Judges were accused of having an excessive amount of discretion in setting amounts for bail. In addition, judges were responsible for setting bail based on which defendants were at high risk for flight and which were not. These decisions were supposed to be based on criminal characteristics, such as the seriousness of the crime committed and prior appearance history. It became clear, however, that among the factors taken into account in the assessment of flight risk were race and sex. Thus, judges' decisions were discriminatory against certain racial groups and against male offenders.

Another form of discrimination emerged in the practice of pretrial detention. Although the primary purpose of bail is to assure a defendant's appearance at trial, there is another purpose. Preventive detention is the practice of holding arrestees prior to trial so that they cannot commit crimes during the time between their arrests and court appearances. If a defendant is deemed to be a danger to the community during the pretrial period, a high amount of bail might be set in order to keep the arrestee locked up. Judges are responsible for making the determination regarding the "dangerousness" of an offender. Again, it was found that these decisions were influenced by noncriminal characteristics such as sex and race. Thus, the type of discrimination that appeared when assessing risk of flight also occurred when judges attempted to assess how likely an offender was to commit a crime while awaiting trial.

In the face of these problems, the first bail reform movement developed. Beginning during the early 1960's, bail came to the forefront as a serious problem within the criminal justice system. The Bail Reform Act of 1966 was an attempt to limit judicial discretion and remove discrimination from the bail process. There were two important developments that came from the Bail Reform Act of 1966. First, judges were expected to release all defendants on their own recognizance unless the judge had some good reason to set bail. In other words, the judge had to have solid grounds for setting bail. Second, "pretrial service agencies" were created to collect information about defendants, thus allowing the judge to have more—and more correct—information about each defendant.

Although preventive detention was a reality in the bail system, there were no laws in the United States stating that it was legal. The second bail reform movement occurred during the early 1970's, and it focused on the issue of legalizing preventive detention. In 1970, the District of Columbia enacted a law that authorized the detention of arrestees without bail if they were deemed a danger to the community. This was the first statute to set standards for the detention of arrestees for preventive reasons.

The issue of preventive detention was not a legal one until the year 1984. In this year, the United States bail system was a central focus of the Comprehensive Crime Control Act of 1984. The Bail Reform Act of 1984 legitimated two federal judicial practices that were informally used before 1984. First, this act gave judges the power to assess defendants on their level of "dangerousness" to the community if released. It gave federal judges the legal right to use preventive detention. While the District of Columbia had its own provisions for preventive detention in 1970, it was not until 1984 that federal judges were given that right. Second, judges were given the right to deny bail in certain circumstances. Traditionally, bail was denied to offenders arrested for capital crimes; the Bail Reform Act of 1984 permitted judges to deny bail to those offenders who were judged to be at extremely high risk for nonappearance. Most notable in this group of offenders were drug traffickers, who were usually able to make extremely high bail and then flee the country.

The Bail Reform Act of 1984 was challenged in 1987, when *United States v. Salerno* was heard before the Supreme Court. This case challenged the idea of preventive detention, arguing that incarcerating alleged offenders violates their right to due process of law. Opponents of preventive detention argue that incarcerating offenders because of *potential* threat violates the presumption of innocence to which every arrestee is entitled. The Supreme Court did not agree with Salerno and upheld the judicial right to preventive detention. As long as judges have convincing evidence that the offender is likely to commit a crime while awaiting trial, they may set bail at a level higher than the typical amount.

Types of Bail

Judges must make a decision for every offender regarding the likelihood that the offender will appear for trial. They take several factors into account in making this decision, usually including prior arrest record, whether the defendant has appeared at previous hearings, stable family ties, and steady employment. After judges weigh these factors, they make a determination about how likely the defendant is to appear at trial. If offenders are classified as good risks—

Actor Robert Blake (right) with his attorney at a bail hearing in October, 2002, after he was arrested for the murder of his wife. After initially being denied bail, Blake was released the following March, when he posted one million dollars in bail. Judges base the amounts they set for bail on such factors as the defendant's financial resources, the possibility of the defendant's attempting to flee prosecution, and the possibility of the defendant's committing additional crimes. In Blake's case, the possibility of his fleeing from prosecution was almost nil because his fame would have made it difficult for him to hide and because his personal financial resources were limited. *(AP/Wide World Photos)*

that is, if they are likely to appear for trial—they are typically released on their own recognizance. Release on recognizance (ROR) allows offenders to remain free before trial with the expectation that they will appear at the appropriate time.

Not all offenders are judged as good risks for appearance. For those expected to be bad risks, or those who are unlikely to appear at trial, some type of bail is usually required. While bail itself involves leaving some type of financial security with the court, the type of security can vary. The most obvious type of bail is typically called a cash bond, and this occurs when the defendant turns over money in the exact amount of bail to the court. Money is not the only type of bail that a defendant can leave with the court. In some cases, a defendant can post a property bond instead, which entails leaving property (personal possessions) with the court to ensure appearance. If the defendant does not appear for the next court appearance, all money and property are forfeited to the court.

Courts are aware that not everyone has the financial ability to post the exact amount of bail or to put up a substantial amount of property. For these individuals, a deposit bond is available. In a deposit bond, the accused offender deposits only a portion of the full bail amount to the court. If the defendant fails to appear, the deposit is kept by the court. If the defendant appears for trial, the majority of the bond is returned, with a small percentage kept by the court to cover court costs.

Finally, the most common type of bail is a surety bond. In this arrangement, a third party (not the court nor defendant) promises the court that if the defendant does not appear, they will turn over the amount of bail to the court. In exchange for this service, the defendant pays a fee to the third party. Usually, this third party is a bailbondsman.

Bailbondsmen

When defendants are required to pay bail prior to release, they may enlist the aid of a bailbondsman in securing funds. Bondsmen are independent businessmen who loan bail money to defendants with only a small amount of cash used as a fee. Bondsmen typically require 10 percent of the amount of bail for the fee. They use part of this fee to purchase a surety bond from an insurance company, which actually pays the bail if the defendant does not appear. In addition, bondsmen usually require some collateral as assurance that the defendant will not default on the loan. Many bond businesses also serve as pawn shops in their spare time, selling the collateral left by those who jump bail. Not all defendants will qualify for a bondsman's services. If defendants have a prior history of jumping bail, they will most likely be denied the bondsman's service.

Even those defendants judged as good risks for the bondsman's service sometimes jump bail. When a defendant fails to appear for trial after securing a bondsman, the bailbondsman has legal authority to retrieve the defendant. The bondsman hires individuals referred to as "bounty hunters" or "skip tracers," people who search for those who jump bail. These skip tracers have vir-

tually unlimited discretion in apprehending the defendant. Unlike state and local police officers, skip tracers are allowed to cross state lines to retrieve individuals who jump bail and are allowed to enter a residence without an arrest warrant.

A major criticism of the bailbondsman trade is the ease with which corruption can flourish. Officers of the court, for example, are sometimes paid by bondsmen to refer defendants to their offices. These officers are typically given kickbacks for each defendant referred to the bondsmen. Judges are not immune from inappropriate behavior—some judges may set unreasonably high bail so that defendants are forced to utilize the bondsman's services. In return for these "referrals," judges are paid by the bondsman. Finally, the bondsman trade also discriminates against indigent offenders, as most poor people cannot afford the fees.

Trends and Statistics

Approximately half of all defendants are held prior to trial, according to 1991 statistics. This figure includes individuals who do not make bail (44 percent of all defendants) and those who are held without bail (9 percent of all defendants). Only about 18 percent are released on their own recognizance. The amount of bail also varies across individuals and is usually dependent on the seriousness of the crime committed and prior criminal record. Property offenders are likely to receive lower bail (under $2,500), while violent offenders are more likely to receive high bail (sometimes over $20,000).

Of those who are released prior to trial, about one-fourth fail to appear for trial. Drug offenders are most likely to jump bail, and public order offenders are most likely to appear for trial. There also appears to be a relationship between the type of bond and rates of appearance. For example, offenders who are released on their own recognizance and offenders who leave a deposit bond have the highest rates of failure to appear. Offenders who use a bondsman are most likely to appear at their appointed court date.

Christina Polsenberg

Further Reading

Bureau of Justice Statistics. *Sourcebook of Criminal Justice Statistics.* Washington, D.C.: U.S.

Government Printing Office. Annual compilation of information on released and detained defendants

Flemming, Roy B. *Punishment Before Trial: An Organizational Perspective of Felony Bail Processes*. New York: Longman, 1982. Summarizes the felony bail process.

Goldfarb, Ronald. *Ransom: A Critique of the American Bail System*. New York: Harper & Row, 1965. Provides a general review and history of the American and English bail systems.

Thomas, Wayne H., Jr. *Bail Reform in America*. Berkeley: University of California Press, 1976. Provides an overview of bail reform in the United States.

Walker, Samuel. *Taming the System: The Control of Discretion in Criminal Justice, 1950-1990*. New York: Oxford University Press, 1993. Broad review of bail reform.

See also Arraignment; Arrest; Bench warrants; Bill of Rights, U.S.; Booking; Bounty hunters; Criminal procedure; Criminal prosecution; Discretion; Due process of law; Manhattan Bail Project; Preventive detention; Speedy trial right; Suspects.

Bailiffs

Definition: Minor court official charged with duties designed to keep order in the courtroom

Criminal justice issues: Courts; trial procedures

Significance: Bailiffs have primary responsibility for maintaining security and order within courtrooms and ensuring that courtroom procedures are followed.

The term "bailiff" has been used since the Middle Ages to designate an administrative official of the courts. Although contemporary bailiffs have fewer duties and less power than their medieval counterparts, they nonetheless serve an important function in courtroom operations. A bailiff is usually a deputy sheriff with police authority whose main jurisdiction is the courtroom. The duties of the bailiff can be divided into two major categories: courtroom management and process serving.

Bailiffs are responsible for a host of courtroom duties. They provide security for the court, including searches before hearings to ensure there are no weapons present; they evict unruly spectators from the courtroom; they escort judges into courtrooms. They are also responsible for transporting defendants to court. Once there, they must control and guard defendants. Further, it is the bailiff who provides defendants with food. Bailiffs also ensure that the people in the court room act with decorum. For example, it is the bailiff who announces the entry of the judge and requests all present to stand. Bailiffs are responsible for the smooth running of court procedures by handling the docket—the order in which cases are heard.

An important function of bailiffs is the protection of the jury.

A court bailiff (rear) stands by as a judge (seated) views a videotape concerning an illegal high-stakes poker game played in the Tallahassee, Florida, home of professional football player Corey Fuller (left). *(AP/Wide World Photos)*

Bailiffs escort juries in and out of the courtroom. Sometimes juries must be kept isolated during a trial so that they are not influenced by others outside the court. This procedure is called "sequestering." When a jury is sequestered, it is the responsibility of the bailiff to guard jurors and to arrange their food, lodging, and transportation.

The second major category of a bailiff's duties is process serving. In Louisiana, for example, bailiffs may be responsible for typing and serving subpoenas and other papers ordered by the court. In Ohio, bailiffs serve papers that include, among other things, criminal warrants, garnishment, and judgment executions. By so doing, the bailiff helps to enforce judgments made by the court.

Requirements for becoming a bailiff vary from state to state. Generally, a bailiff must be at least twenty-one years old, be a citizen of the United States, and have at least a high school diploma or the equivalent. Some states require additional training. In Missouri, for example, bailiffs who have not been certified as peace officers in other capacities must undertake sixty hours of basic training in a state-certified training course.

There are a number of skills bailiffs must have in order to do their jobs well. Some of these include typing, handling paperwork efficiently, knowing courtroom procedures, operating alarm systems, and having familiarity with the jails from which they transport prisoners. In addition, some states set minimal physical requirements for bailiffs. That is, bailiffs must be able to lift at least thirty pounds, sit and stand for long periods, and have good eyesight.

Diane Andrews Henningfeld

Further Reading

Meyer, J. F., and D. R. Grant. *The Courts in Our Criminal Justice System*. Upper Saddle River, N.J.: Prentice-Hall, 2003.

Neubauer, D. W. *America's Courts and the Criminal Justice System*. 7th ed. Belmont, Calif.: Wadsworth, 2002.

See also Criminal justice system; Jury sequestration; Marshals Service, U.S.; September 11, 2001, attacks.

Bank robbery

Definition: Theft of money from banking institutions

Criminal justice issues: Business and financial crime; media; robbery, theft and burglary

Significance: The crime of bank robbery and notorious bank robbers have often been glamorized in the media, but bank robbery is frequently violent and most robbers are captured quickly.

Of all the criminals who practice their craft in the United States, bank robbers have been the most glamorized. Books and movies have portrayed them as folk heroes. The public's fascination with bank robberies has been linked to the negative view of banks and the robber's arguments that they were only stealing from the rich. Despite the folk-hero status given to famous bank robbers, bank robbers are violent criminals who use threats or violence to steal money from banks and their customers. During the nineteenth century, some of the most famous bank-robbing gangs were also among the most murderous. These included the Dalton gang and Jesse James's gang, who robbed banks in the Old West and were tracked down by locals.

Twentieth Century Bank Robbers

Some of the best-known bank robbers of the early twentieth century include Bonnie Parker and Clyde Barrow, who stole comparatively small sums of money and killed nearly a dozen people until they themselves were gunned down by law-enforcement officers in 1934. The popularity of bank robbers peaked during the Depression years of the 1930's, when banks were known mainly for foreclosing on farmers and members of the middle class. For some people, bank robbers represented the oppressed striking back at the banks for taking people's land. During that period, some of the most colorful bank robbers became heroes to the public but were nevertheless dangerous criminals. Their popularity can be seen in the catchy nicknames given to them, such as "Baby Face" Nelson, Charles "Pretty Boy" Floyd, and George "Machine Gun" Kelly. This was also the era of John Dillinger, whose violent death was romanticized by the media.

During the 1940's one of the most celebrated bank robbers was Willie Sutton, who is credited with the famous line that he robbed banks because "that was where the money was." Sutton used his acting skills and ability to create disguises to gain entry into banks, usually before they opened. He dressed as postal employees, government workers, and even a police officer. He also changed his hairstyle, facial appearance, and accent to confuse bank employees. Throughout his criminal career, Sutton held a regular job, under an assumed name. He was different from his 1930's predecessors in that his robberies were nonviolent; no one was ever killed or injured during one of his heists.

During the mid-twentieth century, bank robbers and their crimes became more notorious because of the role of the Federal Bureau of Investigation (FBI) in tracking and attempting to arrest them. J. Edgar Hoover, the head of the FBI, used his ten-most-wanted list to call attention to notorious bank robbers and get the public involved in their capture. Every famous bank robber of that era was eventually captured or killed. Their demise brought the end of what might be called the golden era of bank heists.

Modern Bank Heists

After the 1940's, bank heists became more difficult as banks enhanced their security. The federal government's involvement in tracking and arresting bank robbers made the crime ever more dangerous for robbers. Bank robbers responded by changing their tactics. Their new techniques included taking bank employees hostage in their own homes and then forcing them to open their banks during off-hours. In the late twentieth century, the advent of electronic banking over telephone lines and the Internet opened another avenue for heists. Instead of carrying guns or charging into banks and demanding money, the new breed of bank robbers resembled embezzlers, siphoning funds out of banks without anyone noticing the money was gone until it was too late. When the robbers hid their tracks, the banks might not even know they were robbed until after the robbers were safely away. However, after a series of such robberies, banks and law enforcement became wiser and started using computer technology against the robbers and making heists more difficult.

Meanwhile, as the FBI improved at tracking down robbers and banks improved methods of preventing robberies, the number of bank robberies in the United States declined during the 1980's and 1990's. However, one of the most dangerous and daring heists occurred in February, 1997, when two men robbed a Bank of America branch in Southern California. When the robbers were confronted by dozens of police, they initiated what became a running gun battle. Outfitted with protective body armor, the robbers withstood direct hits while blasting away with even greater firepower than that used by the police. Both men

---

Films Glamorizing Bank Robbers

The Internet Movie Database (IMDb.com) lists hundreds of films about bank robberies. The films listed below are comparatively well-known titles that may be fairly said to glamorize bank robbers.

1961	*One-Eyed Jacks*
1967	*Bonnie and Clyde*
1968	*The Thomas Crown Affair*
1969	*Butch Cassidy and the Sundance Kid*
1969	*One Hundred Rifles*
1969	*Take the Money and Run*
1969	*The Wild Bunch*
1970	*Bloody Mama*
1972	*The Getaway*
1973	*Dillinger*
1973	*Thieves Like Us*
1975	*Dog Day Afternoon*
1975	*W. W. and the Dixie Dancekings*
1980	*The Long Riders*
1986	*Wisdom*
1989	*Three Fugitives*
1991	*Harley Davidson and the Marlboro Man*
1991	*Point Break*
1994	*Lightning Jack*
1996	*Public Enemies*
1997	*The James Gang*
1998	*The Newton Boys*
2001	*Bandits*
2002	*Riders*
2004	*Catch That Kid*

were eventually killed, but the incident left law-enforcement officials across the nation afraid that future bank heists would be performed by similarly dangerous robbers who could outshoot police and thus escape with the money.

Types of Banks Heists

Bank robberies are committed by both amateur and professional criminals and came be either well-planned heists or spur-of-the-moment robberies. The motive behind virtually all bank heists is to obtain money; however, the uses to which the money is put differ from robbery to robbery. For example, amateurs sometimes rob banks to pay their outstanding household bills. Professionals may also rob banks to pay their bills, but many steal from banks in order to live luxurious lifestyles they could not otherwise afford. Some rob banks to advance political causes.

Amateurs and professionals typically differ in their approaches to their heists. Many amateurs conduct their robberies peacefully, with the use of weapons; their crimes are usually isolated events, in which the robbers are concerned mostly with escaping with their money as quickly as possible. By contrast, professionals generally concentrate on obtaining as much money as possible, and their crimes are usually part of strings of heists using the same methods. Bank heists conducted for political purposes tend to be the most violent, as they usually involve weapons and robbers who are willing to kill to get the money they seek.

Robbers who work alone typically initiate their robberies by handing notes to tellers that demand money. This approach tends to be quick and nonviolent but yields small returns for the robbers. Professional robbers often seize control of the banks and use weapons to compel bank employees to hand over money. While this form of

A Modern Celebrity Bank Robber

The 1960's and 1970's did not see bank robbers like those who had been celebrated in earlier periods; however, bank robbery did produce one celebrity whose name was famous before she became a thief: Patricia Hearst, heir to a newspaper fortune, who was kidnapped from her Northern California apartment in February, 1974. She was not seen again in public until the following April, when she took part in a bank robbery staged by members of the Symbionese Liberation Army. Over the next two years, Hearst was in the midst of a crime spree conducted by members of the group that led to several deaths, more bank heists, and a shoot-out with police. After she was captured and put on trial, Hearst claimed that she had been an unwilling part of the group, having been brainwashed while she was kidnapped. A California jury did not buy her defense, however, and she was convicted and sent to prison.

Surveillance camera image of Patricia Hearst, apparently carrying a gun, during a robbery of a San Francisco bank in April, 1974. (AP/Wide World Photos)

robbery generally produces larger takes, it is also more likely to end in violence, particularly when bank employees or customers do not follow the robbers' instructions perfectly.

Bank robbers sometimes employ diversions that help them to escape. For example, some robbers telephone police to report false bombs threats in other locations. As police rush to those locations to investigate the threats, the robbers complete their bank heists and escape before police can redirect their efforts from the fake crimes to the real ones. Some bank robbers take advantage of visits by high-ranking dignitaries to cities. Such visits often tie up the protective services of local police, giving bank robbers opportunities to commit their crimes when police response is likely to be delayed. Sometimes, however, the robbers outsmart themselves. For example, a gang of robbers once cleverly timed their heist to take advantage of a visit of the president of the United States to Chicago. However, they made the mistake of hitting a bank located next to the building in which the president was speaking, thus bringing down on themselves large numbers of both local police and Secret Service agents.

Prevention and Investigation

During the 1990's, the FBI and other law-enforcement agencies were able to concentrate many of their resources on crimes such as bank robbery. However, after the terrorist attacks of September 11, 2001, many law-enforcement resources have been diverted to investigating suspected terrorists. Apparently, for this reason, after 2001, bank robberies were again on the rise.

Banks and law enforcement work together to develop new techniques and technologies to prevent bank robberies or make it easier to capture and prosecute bank robbers. One of the first defenses against robberies was the development of armored bank vaults, which federal law now requires banks to use to prevent criminals who break into banks after hours from gaining access to the money and other valuables. Modern vaults are protected by several feet of concrete or steel. The difficulty of penetrating vaults moves most robbers to rob banks when they are open for business—which is a much more hazardous undertaking for the thieves.

Another early defense against bank robberies was the use of armed guards; however, they gen-

Bank robbery investigations have a high rate of successful identifications of perpetrators, largely because of the efficiency of bank surveillance cameras in capturing images of robbers at work—such as this man videotaped in the act of passing a note to a teller in a Manhattan bank in late 2003. *(AP/Wide World Photos)*

erally proved ineffective, so banks shifted their protective efforts to improved technology. Bank-prevention devices include alarm systems, video cameras for surveillance, tracking devices, and automatically locking entry and exit doors. Some of these devices are used to prevent robberies, while others aid police in tracking down thieves who succeed in getting away with the banks' money.

Tellers at all banks have switches to silent alarm systems within their reach. The alarms are hidden from bank robbers but can be easily activated by employees. Once activated, the alarms alert police that robberies are in progress and give them a head start in tracking robbers as the latter leave the scenes of their crimes. At the same time, trained tellers try to delay handing over money to give the police more time to arrive on the scene. When police do not arrive while robberies are in progress, banks have the means of identifying the robbers using security cameras. Such cameras take pictures of robbers' faces, but professional thieves generally wear masks or wide-brimmed hats to obscure their faces. Some banks have taken to using closed-circuit cameras that send their pictures directly to police stations, alerting them of robberies in progress and allowing trained police to witness the crimes and the robbers.

Banks also use tracking devices, the best known of which are dye packs. When tellers load money into bags for robbers, they try to insert dye packs that are designed explode after they leave the banks. The explosions spread brightly colored dyes over both the stolen money and the robbers, making apprehension and identification easier. Banks also try to insert sophisticated tracking devices among stolen money. These devices emit signals that police can use to track down the robbers. Part of the stolen money itself can also serve as a tracking device. Banks provide tellers with packs of marked money whose serial numbers are recorded. When thieves take the marked money, police distribute the serial numbers to local businesses, which contact the police when the stolen bills are used at the business.

Some banks have special entrances with devices that detect firearms. When the devices sense guns, they automatically lock the banks' in-ner doors, preventing persons with guns from entering.

Most of these defenses require the quick thinking and action of bank employees. Banks utilize training sessions including fake robberies carried out by the police. These teach employees how to handle bank robberies without getting themselves killed or injured, while increasing the changes of catching the thieves. When robbers are not immediately captured, the police use wanted posters, television programs, and the Internet to solicit public help in identifying and locating the suspects.

Bank robbers are occasionally successful at stealing large amounts of money and escaping. When that happens, law-enforcement agencies generally must wait for the robbers to perform additional crimes. The more robberies that criminals commit, the more likely it is that they will make mistakes and be captured.

Investigation

During the nineteenth century, bank robberies were purely local concerns, as no federal law-enforcement agencies were designed to combat such crimes. As the numbers of bank robberies increased, the federal government became involved indirectly. For example, a 1919 federal law made it a crime to drive getaway cars across state lines. When bank robbers broke this law during their escapes, the federal government was authorized to become involved. The rise in crime during the 1920's and early 1930's prompted Congress to consider making bank robbery a federal offense. Finally, in 1934, Congress enacted a law making bank robbery a federal crime, and it gave the FBI primary responsibility for tracking down bank robbers.

While local police are the first on the scene at bank robberies and frequently capture bank robbers, the federal government is responsible for prosecuting them. Bank robbery is a serious felony under federal law. Robbers who perform heists at several banks, steal tens of thousands of dollars, or use or threaten to use weapons can be incarcerated for more than ten years. The more additions to the crime, the longer the punishment.

Douglas Clouatre

Further Reading

De Simone, Donald. *I Rob Banks, That's Where the Money Is*. New York: SPI Books, 1992. Describes the career of bank robber Willy Sutton, his various heists, and his escapes from prison.

Kirchner, L. R. *Robbing Banks: An American History 1839-1999*. New York: DeCapo Press, 2000. This book discusses bank robbery and how it differs from other types of crimes, while highlighting some of the best-known bank robbers in history.

Newton, Michael. *The Encyclopedia of Robberies, Heists and Capers*. New York: Checkmark Books, 2002. Quick reference book describing some of the great bank robberies and other robberies that have occurred through history.

Pinkerton, Allan. *Banks: Robbers and the Detectives*. New York: Fredonia Books, 2002. The autobiography of the founder of the Pinkerton Detective Agency, this book discusses how Pinkerton and his agency tracked down bank robbers when the federal government could not.

Rehder, William J., and Gordon Dillow. *Where the Money Is: True Tales from the Bank Robbery Capital of the World*. New York: W. W. Norton, 2003. Written by a former FBI agent, this book details how he investigated bank robberies and includes stories about some modern heists and thieves.

Swierczynski, Duane. *This Here's a Stick Up: The Big Bad Book of American Bank Robbery*. Indianapolis: Alpha Books, 2003. Fast-paced book that highlights some of the famous bank robbers and heists in U.S. history and discusses in detail how criminals rob banks and the investigation techniques and methods used by banks to prevent bank robberies or capture bank robbers.

See also Bribery; Chain of custody; Cybercrime; Embezzlement; Federal Bureau of Investigation; Hoover, J. Edgar; Outlaws of the Old West; Robbery; Symbionese Liberation Army.

Barker v. Wingo

The Case: U.S. Supreme Court ruling on speedy trials
Date: Decided on June 22, 1972
Criminal justice issues: Constitutional protections; probation and pretrial release; trial procedures
Significance: In this case for the first time, the Supreme Court gave substantive content to the Constitution's guarantee of a speedy trial.

In 1958 Silas Manning and Willie Barker were arrested for the murder of an elderly Kentucky couple. Kentucky had a stronger case against Manning, and the state decided to try him first. If Manning were convicted, then he could be required to testify against Barker. Kentucky sought and obtained the first of what would be sixteen continuances of Barker's trial.

Meanwhile, the prosecution had great difficulty in getting a conviction against Manning. The first trial ended in a hung jury, and a second trial, at which Manning was convicted, was annulled because of the admission of illegally seized evidence. Barker finally objected to additional delay when the state requested a twelfth continuance. Even after Manning's conviction—after a third trial—became final, the Kentucky court granted a further continuance because of the illness of the former sheriff, who had been the investigating officer in the case. Barker finally came to trial in 1963, more than five years after his arrest. During ten months of that period he had been held in jail. He moved to dismiss the charge on the ground that his right to a speedy trial had been violated. After several unsuccessful appeals, Barker asked the U.S. Supreme Court to review his claim.

In an opinion for a unanimous Supreme Court, Justice Lewis F. Powell, Jr., held that Barker's right to a speedy trial had indeed been violated. Justice Powell pointed out that the notion of a "speedy" trial is slippery because there is no clearly definable standard. The circumstances of each case are likely to determine whether any postponements are reasonable. Powell saw two possible alternatives. The first would be to set a rigid time period and to apply it to every case. This the Court rejected because it would amount to law making, a function reserved to the legislature. The second alternative would be to restrict the speedy trial right to defendants who demand it. Justice Powell rejected that solution because it would amount to waiving constitutional rights except for those who ask for them. That would be inconsistent with the Court's general approach to constitutional liberties.

The Court adopted a "balancing test" in which the conduct of both the prosecution and the defendant is considered. This approach requires courts to approach speedy trial issues on an *ad hoc* basis, but once the defendant has asserted the right to a speedy trial, the state must move forward expeditiously. Among the factors that courts must consider are the reasons for any delays, the strength and frequency of the defendant's objections, if any, and the length of any pretrial incarceration defendants have suffered.

The *Barker v. Wingo* balancing test did not prove satisfactory in practice, and the federal government and many states passed statutes to establish rigid time limits for trial. Typically, if no continuances are at the defendant's request, trial must proceed within ninety to one hundred days or the charges against the defendant must be dismissed with prejudice.

Robert Jacobs

Further Reading

Garcia, Alfredo. *The Sixth Amendment in Modern American Jurisprudence*. Westport, Conn.: Greenwood Press, 1992.

Lewis, Thomas T., ed. *The Bill of Rights*. 2 vols. Pasadena, Calif.: Salem Press, 2002.

See also Bill of Rights, U.S.; Criminal procedure; Speedy trial right.

Batson v. Kentucky

The Case: U.S. Supreme Court decision on juries
Date: Decided on April 3, 1986
Criminal justice issues: Civil rights and liberties; juries

Significance: This Supreme Court ruling held that the equal protection clause of the Fourteenth Amendment forbids prosecutors from using peremptory challenges to remove potential jurors because of their race.

On the surface, *Batson v. Kentucky* was one of a long string of Supreme Court efforts to eliminate discrimination from the U.S. judicial system. It departed from the Court's 1965 holding in *Swain v. Alabama*, in which the Court first considered the use of the peremptory challenge for discriminatory purposes.

In *Swain*, when asked whether the equal protection clause of the Fourteenth Amendment prevented the total exclusion of African Americans from juries, the Court declared that the "presumption in any particular case must be that the prosecutor is using the State's challenges to obtain a fair and impartial jury. . . . [even if] all Negroes were removed because they were Negroes." To overcome the presumption, the Court ruled, a defendant would have to demonstrate that the state followed a consistent pattern of discrimination in "case after case."

Swain prevailed until 1986. Challengers were unable to meet the standards of systematic exclusion established in the decision. State and federal courts alike refused to countenance presentation of evidence from only cases that involved black defendants. Over the repeated objections of Justice Thurgood Marshall, the Supreme Court waited to allow "states to serve as laboratories in which the issue receives further study before it is addressed by this Court" again. Marshall called the experimentation cruel, noting that "there is no point in taking elaborate steps to ensure Negroes are included in venires [pools of prospective jurors] simply so they can be struck because of their race by a prosecutor's use of peremptory challenges."

The reconsideration came in *Batson v. Kentucky*. Batson's counsel asked the Court:

In a criminal case, does a state trial court err when, over the objection of a black defendant, it swears an all-white jury constituted only after the prosecutor had exercised four of his six peremptory challenges to strike all of the black veniremen from the panel in violation of constitutional provisions guaranteeing the defendant an impartial jury and a jury composed of persons representing a fair cross section of the community?

James Kirkland Batson had been charged with burglary and the receipt of stolen goods. The prosecutor used four of his six peremptory challenges to create, in his words, an "all-white jury." The defense counsel's motion to discharge the panel before it was sworn in on grounds that the panel did not represent a cross-section of the community and that to use it would be a denial of equal protection was denied by the trial judge. Tried and convicted, Batson appealed to the Kentucky Supreme Court, which upheld the conviction in 1984, based on the *Swain* doctrine. The U.S. Supreme Court disagreed. Reversing the conviction, it held that the impaneling of the jury resulted in a denial of equal protection. It ruled that when objection is lodged against an alleged racially discriminatory use of the peremptory challenge, the trial court must examine the validity of the claim.

Thus, for the first time, a federal court agreed that attorneys can be forced to explain their reasons for invoking peremptory challenges. In the process, the Court created a second category of peremptory challenges: those that must be explained.

Ashton Wesley Welch

Further Reading

Barak, Gregg, Jeanne M. Flavin, and Paul S. Leighton. *Class, Race, Gender and Crime: Social Realities of Justice in America*. Los Angeles: Roxbury, 2002. Broad overviews of justice issues.

Jonakait, Randolph N. *The American Jury System*. New Haven, Conn.: Yale University Press, 2003.

Schwartz, Victor E., et al. *Safeguarding the Right to a Representative Jury: The Need for Improved Jury Service Laws*. Washington, D.C.: National Legal Center for the Public Interest, 2003.

See also Equal protection under the law; Jury duty; Jury system.

Battered child and battered wife syndromes

Definition: Condition of sufferers of family violence who have undergone physical abuse that leaves them with both physical and psychological trauma

Criminal justice issues: Domestic violence; medical and health issues; violent crime; women's issues

Significance: The terms battered child syndrome and battered wife syndrome have brought to public attention the prevalence of family violence and the need to enact new laws to protect children and women. In addition, the terms are important in the criminal prosecution and defense of child abuse and domestic violence cases.

Although family violence is not a new problem in the United States, the criminal prosecution of family members who physically or sexually abuse relatives is a relatively recent development. Medical and social science research during the 1960's and 1970's documented the unique kinds of injuries, both physical and psychological, that are suffered when family members are the abusers. The researchers who identified and brought to public attention battered child syndrome and battered wife syndrome helped increase public awareness of family violence and helped change criminal justice policy concerning prosecution of such cases. In addition, recognition of the psychological trauma associated with such victimization, led to the development of controversial criminal defenses that attempt to utilize battered child syndrome and battered wife syndrome as justifications for victims killing their abusers.

Battered Child Syndrome

Battered child syndrome is the condition suffered by children who have undergone physical abuse that has left them with both physical and psychological trauma. Dr. Henry C. Kempe and his associates coined the term in a landmark article published in the *Journal of the American Medical Association* in 1962. Kempe presented the group's findings in a nationwide survey of hospitals that documented 302 cases of battered child syndrome during one year in which thirty-three battered children had died and eighty-five had suffered permanent brain injury.

In analyzing the data from the study, Kempe found that the studied cases shared certain characteristics. First, battered child syndrome usually occurred to children younger than the age of three. Second, noticeable discrepancies usually appeared between the medical findings and the parents' explanations of how their children's injuries occurred. Third, histories of previous injuries in many children revealed various stages of healing that indicated that people were intentionally injuring the children. Kempe's research received a great deal of public attention and was

---

"Discipline" vs. "Abuse"

Public perceptions of what constitutes discipline and what constitutes abuse have changed considerably in recent decades. During the early 1970's, it was a rare parent who did not use spanking as a form of discipline, and whipping children with belts was not uncommon. Today, many American parents wonder whether it is ever appropriate to spank their children. State laws governing the types of physical punishment parents may impose have changed considerably, and some parents have been arrested for hitting or slapping their own children.

Some actions that were once considered legitimate forms of parental discipline are now criminal actions, and many people believe that states have gone too far in interfering with the legitimate attempts of parents to discipline. Children—particularly adolescents—have become aware of how their parents' hands are literally tied in some states when it comes to matters of discipline. Many adolescents have manipulated the legal system to get their own way by charging abuse when none may have occurred or by using the threat of calling child protective services to control their parents. At the other extreme, however, are parents who regard actions such as severely beating their children with belts and straps—clearly abusive actions—as "discipline."

Ayn Embar-Seddon
Allan D. Pass

---

the impetus for drafting a federal child-abuse reporting statute.

All U.S. states now have child abuse laws mandating that certain caretakers such as physicians, nurses, and teachers report cases of suspected child abuse. While Kempe focused on using physiological data to identify battered child syndrome, later researchers have tended to focus on examining psychological data to identify emotional effects suffered by children with the syndrome. These data include hyper-vigilance, helplessness, and posttraumatic stress disorder.

Courts have recognized the importance of battered child syndrome in prosecuting cases of child abuse. Prosecutors use battered child syndrome particularly in cases in which a child's death results from abuse and in which very young children sustain serious injuries. In the latter cases, the children are not able to testify about their abuse, so prosecutors must rely upon expert witnesses. The experts testify about previous injuries suffered by the children, even though there may be no direct proof that their battered children's parents have caused their injuries. In its 1991 *Estelle v. McGuire* ruling, the U.S. Supreme Court evaluated the use of evidence of battered child syndrome and held that in battered child cases it was constitutional for courts to admit as evidence prior injuries of children, even without proof that the defendants caused the prior injuries.

Although courts frequently use battered child syndrome to prove the intent to commit child abuse, they rarely permit its use in situations in which children kill their parents and then try to use battered child syndrome as their defense. Such cases typically involve adolescent children or adults who make claims about the long-term psychological effects of past parental abuse on them. While experts may be able to testify about the psychological effects of battered child syndrome, most courts reject it as a defense because it departs too much from traditional self-defense theory.

Battered Wife Syndrome

Battered wife, or battered woman, syndrome is a set of psychological and behavioral symptoms exhibited by victims of severe, long-term domestic abuse. The term is associated with the pioneer

Types of Violent Acts by Intimate Partners

rape and sexual assault
6%

robbery
9%

aggravated assault
17%

simple assault
68%

Source: U.S. Bureau of Justice Statistics, *Intimate Partner Violence*, 2003. Percentages are based on 691,710 incidents between intimate partners in the United States in 2001. Intimate partners include current and former spouses and current and former boyfriends and girlfriends.

research of Dr. Lenore Walker who introduced the term in her 1979 book, *The Battered Woman*. While Walker's definition of the syndrome encompasses any woman who has been the victim of physical, sexual, or psychological abuse by her partner, not all battered women develop battered woman syndrome. The syndrome applies only to a woman who has been the victim at least twice of physical, sexual, or serious psychological abuse by a man with whom she has an intimate relationship. Walker's research advances a psychological theory of the process of victimization of battered women. Her theory explains why even after prolonged spousal abuse, battered women lack the psychological ability to leave their abusive relationships.

Walker defined battered woman syndrome as comprising two distinct components: a cycle of violence and learned helplessness. The term cycle of violence refers to a three-part repetitive pattern of interaction between batterers and their

victim that consists of gradual periods of tension building—expressed in verbal and psychological abuse—followed by acute battering incidents, and concluding with calm, loving respites, during which the batterers apologize for their behavior. Walker identified this third phase as the one that most victimizes women psychologically because the cycles of violence almost inevitably recur. Battered women become increasingly demoralized as they realize that their abusive partners have again fooled them into believing that they will change.

The second component of Walker's theory, learned helplessness, explains the psychological paralysis that prevents some women from leaving their abusers. Walker argued that learned helplessness occurs in domestic violence situations when the battered women cannot ensure their own safety because—regardless of their own behavior—they face their partners' unpredictable abusive behavior. Believing that there is no way for them to prevent the violence, battered women simply give up and accept the abuse. In some cases, battered women resort to violence themselves and kill their partners to free themselves from further abuse.

Criminal courts in all fifty U.S. states permit the introduction of expert testimony on battered woman syndrome. Often this occurs in the context of murder trials in which women homicide defendants claim to have been battered women and argue that they have acted in self-defense. In many cases, objective evidence is lacking that meets traditional standards for self-defense, namely fear of imminent death or serious injury at the time of the homicide. Therefore, the mental states or beliefs of the battered women are considered in evaluating self-defense claims. Expert witnesses testify about battered woman syndrome and the psychological states of the defendants at the time of their homicides to assist juries in determining whether the defendants have acted out of reasonable beliefs that they were in imminent danger of death or great bodily harm.

Patricia E. Erickson

Further Reading

Crosson-Tower, Cynthia. *Understanding Child Abuse and Neglect*. 5th ed. Boston: Allyn & Bacon, 2001. Textbook covering all aspects of

Minnesotans demonstrating outside the state capitol in May, 2003, in protest of proposed cuts in state funding for domestic abuse programs. Members of the Minnesota Coalition for Battered Women and the Domestic Violence Legislative Alliance hold cutouts representing individual victims of domestic violence in the state. *(AP/Wide World Photos)*

child maltreatment, from symptoms and signs to parental motivations, and the role of the social service system.

Giardino, Angelo P., and Eileen Giardino. *Recognition of Child Abuse for the Mandated Reporter*. 3d ed. St. Louis: G. W. Medical Publishing, 2001. Guide for school teachers, nurses, social workers, day-care workers, law-enforcement officers, and others who work with children that explains what they must do to fulfill their responsibilities as "mandated reporters." Written by specialists in several different disciplines.

Monteleone, James A. *A Parent's and Teacher's Handbook on Identifying and Preventing Child Abuse*. St. Louis: G. W. Medical Publishing, 1998. Handbook by a medical doctor explaining to general readers how to identify signs of abuse. Attention is paid to all situations in which child abuse may occur. Offers

practical advice on what steps to take to combat abuse. Well illustrated.

Raphael, Jody. *Saving Bernice: Battered Women, Welfare and Poverty*. Boston: Northeastern University Press, 2000. Moving study of one woman's long struggle to free herself from domestic violence and poverty.

Wallace, Harvey. *Family Violence: Legal, Medical and Social Perspectives*. 3d ed. Boston: Allyn & Bacon, 2001. Introductory study of domestic violence that explores contemporary controversies in the field. Individual chapters cover such subjects as ritualistic abuse, gay and lesbian abuse, and victims' rights.

See also Arrest warrants; Child abuse and molestation; Criminal intent; Criminals; Cultural defense; Defenses to crime; Domestic violence; Excuses and justifications; Pornography, child; Self-defense; Victimology.

Bench warrants

Definition: Documents issued by judges demanding that specific defendants be arrested and brought before the court without unneeded delay

Criminal justice issues: Judges; probation and pretrial release; trial procedures

Significance: The increasing frequency with which defendants skip their scheduled court dates has serious implications for future policy on pretrial release and bail.

Defendants released prior to trial do not always appear in court as mandated. Consequently, a judge issues a bench warrant, or *capias*, to retrieve them. Unlike an arrest warrant, which is requested by police officials and based on probable cause, a bench warrant is issued solely on failure to appear at a required legal proceeding. Leading to custody for the defendant, a bench warrant has other ramifications: Bail is forfeited, and the defendant is subject to a separate charge of bond jumping, which incurs additional penalties.

A 2000 Bureau of Justice Statistics study of the seventy-five largest U.S. jurisdictions reports that bench warrants for failure to appear were issued for 22 percent of released defendants. This percentage remained relatively stable from 1990 to 2004. Statistical data on bench warrants, however, should be read with caution. Percentages can vary greatly from study to study depending upon how the researcher defines "failure to appear." For example, during the early 1970's, Detroit's courts were under pressure to keep pretrial release to a minimum, thus a defendant only a minute late was said to be skipping. On the other hand, a city hoping to expand pretrial release may be more liberal, allowing a day or two for defendants to report before issuing a bench warrant.

Defendants who fail to appear do not always do so intentionally. In fact, failure-to-appear rates are strongly associated with court practices. A large percentage of defendants miss court dates because they are not given clear notice of when to appear next. In some jurisdictions, notification is simply an oral statement at the end of a proceeding. Considering the noise and confusion in the courtroom, as well as the strangeness of legal proceedings themselves, it seems logical that a defendant would fail to appear under these circumstances. Further, considering that defendants are often transients and courts keep only the last known address, delivery by mail of notices to appear may also be ineffective. Last, the court's consistent and lengthy delays seem to increase failure-to-appear rates.

Amy I. Cass

Further Reading

Clarke, Stevens, Jean Freeman, and Gary Koch. *The Effectiveness of Bail Systems: An Analysis of Failure to Appear in Court and Rearrest While on Bail*. Chapel Hill, N.C.: Institute of Government, University of Carolina, 1976.

Eskridge, Chris. *Pre-trial Release Programming: Issues and Trends*. New York: Clark Boardman, 1983.

Goldkamp, John, Michael Gottfredson, Peter Jones, and Doris Weiland. *Personal Liberty and Community Safety: Pre-trial Release in the Criminal Court*. New York: Plenum Press, 1995.

See also Arrest warrants; Bail system; Bounty hunters; Fourth Amendment; Marshals Service, U.S.; No-knock warrants; Plain view doctrine; Search warrants.

Bifurcated trials

Definition: Proceedings in which two or more separate hearings or trials are held on different issues of the same cases

Criminal justice issues: Legal terms and principles; trial procedures

Significance: Bifurcated trials are often employed in complicated criminal cases to ensure efficiency and due process.

Frequently utilized in civil cases, the bifurcated trial process is also applied to criminal cases that require judges or juries to rule on certain issues before other issues are addressed. For example, a case in which a criminal defendant claims insanity or diminished capacity is typically decided by bifurcated trials. The guilt or innocence of the defendant is determined in the first phase, and the defendant's sanity is determined and sentence or treatment is imposed in the second phase. In cases involving juries, separate juries are often convened at each stage of the trial process.

Bifurcated trials are most frequently employed in capital murder cases and other cases in which defendants are eligible for the death penalty. During the 1970's, many states passed laws providing for bifurcated capital murder trials after the U.S. Supreme Court mandated that states wishing to impose the death penalty must enact procedural reforms to ensure higher standards of due process for capital defendants. A bifurcated capital murder trial consists of a guilt phase in which a jury decides whether the defendant is guilty and a penalty phase in which a judge or jury determines whether the convicted defendant is to be sentenced to death or to a lesser penalty, usually life without possibility of parole. The penalty phase allows judges and juries to evaluate evidence of aggravating or mitigating circumstances connected with the crime and to hear testimony from victims.

Michael H. Burchett

Further Reading

Bedau, Hugo A. *The Death Penalty in America: Current Controversies*. New York: Oxford University Press, 1997.

Roberts, Albert R., ed. *Critical Issues in Crime and Justice*. Thousand Oaks, Calif.: Sage, 2003.

See also Aggravating circumstances; Capital punishment; Death qualification; Diminished capacity; Due process of law; *Gregg v. Georgia*; Insanity defense; Mitigating circumstances; Sentencing; Trials.

Bigamy and polygamy

Definition: Condition of having more than one spouse at the same time

Criminal justice issues: Sex offenses; victimless crime

Significance: Both bigamy and polygamy are illegal practices in the United States, but

neither is regularly prosecuted. The legal ramifications of bigamy include possible felony convictions for fraud resulting in imprisonment for no less than two and no more than seven years.

Both bigamy and polygamy are defined as having more than one spouse. Bigamy is the crime of one person's knowingly taking a second spouse through a fraudulent marriage, while that person's first marriage remains legally binding. By contrast, polygamy is the practice of having more than one spouse, or love partner, with the knowledge and consent of all the partners, even though only one marriage is legally binding. In legal terms, then, the key distinction between bigamy and polygamy is that the deceit inherent in the former is absent in the latter.

Anyone who willfully and knowingly enters into a second marriage before a prior marriage has been legally terminated by divorce, annulment, or death of the first spouse commits the crime of bigamy. It is not bigamy, however, for people to remarry after their spouses have been missing for a specific number of years—usually seven—and are not known to be alive. If a first spouse reappears, proof must be offered that there was a false report of death or that there has been no knowledge of the first spouse's existence for a specified period of time. When this proof is accepted, laws in most states do not consider such remarriages bigamous. In some states, a remarried person may choose between their two spouses, and one of the marriages must be annulled.

During the mid-to-late nineteenth century, polygamy was a commonly accepted and publicly taught practice among Mormons—members of the recently established Church of Jesus Christ of Latter-day Saints, who built their church in what was then the federal territory of Utah. In 1862, the U.S. Congress formally made polygamous marriages illegal in federal territories. Although Mormons believed that their religious-based practice of what they called "plural marriage" was protected under the U.S. Constitution, its practice was used to delay Utah's admittance to the Union as a state until 1896. Because anti-polygamy legislation stripped members of the church of their rights as citizens and permitted

"Bigamy" vs. "Polygamy"

Bigamy and polygamy are two of a variety of English terms for multiple marriage, and both words have ancient roots. Bigamy, which is generally understood to be the practice of having *two* (and only two) spouses, derives from Latin *bi-* for "two" and *-gamia* for "marriage." Polygamy, which is the word generally used for plural marriages involving more than two spouses, incorporates the Greek *poly* for "many." Other terms include "polygyny," the condition of having multiple wives. It derives from Greek *poly* for "many" and *gynē* for "woman" (as in "gynecology"). By contrast, "polyandry," the practice of having multiple husbands, is from a Greek—by way of Latin—word for "man."

government seizure of church property, the church ordered the official discontinuance of this practice in 1890.

In the early twenty-first century, many communities in the United States continue practicing polygamy, which they believe to be constitutionally protected under the principles of religious freedom, the right to privacy and separation of church and state. These issues represent the focal point for legal challenges regarding polygamy, and since it also has been perceived as a victimless crime, courts have continued to look the other way. However, several recent incidents in Utah have brought polygamy back to the courts' attention. In one, a sixteen-year-old girl was severely beaten by her father when she refused to marry her uncle. In another, a group of former polygamist wives formed the Tapestry Against Polygamy, and the *Salt Lake Tribune* ran a series of investigative exposés that documented reliance on welfare benefits, forced marriages, incest, pedophilia, and abuse.

Bernadette Jones Palombo

Further Reading

Harriss, John, ed. *The Family: A Social History of the Twentieth Century.* New York: Oxford University Press, 1991.

Henslin, James M., ed. *Marriage and Family in a Changing Society.* 3d ed. New York: Free Press, 1989.

Holmes, Stephen T., and Ronald M. Holmes. *Sex Crimes: Patterns and Behavior.* 2d ed. Thousand Oaks, Calif.: Sage Publications, 2002.

Wietzman, Lenore J. *The Marriage Contract: Spouses, Lovers, and the Law.* New York: Free Press, 1981.

Yalom, Marilyn. *A History of the Wife.* New York: HarperCollins, 2001.

See also Adultery; Fraud.

Bill of attainder

Definition: Legislative act that assigns a penalty to a person or group of people
Criminal justice issues: Legal terms and principles; punishment
Significance: Bills of attainder are prohibited by the U.S. Constitution because they are believed to treat people unfairly and because they would undermine rule of law.

A bill of attainder is an act of a legislative body that assigns a penalty to a specific person or group of people. A prohibition on assigning penalties in this manner was included in the U.S. Constitution because its framers considered such acts to be abuses of power by the legislative body.

Bills of attainder, which assigned the death penalty, and bills of pains and penalties, which assigned lesser penalties, were passed by the British parliament from 1321 to 1798. Both penalties have generally been known as bills of attainder. They were rarely used in the fourteenth and fifteenth centuries but were widely used in the seventeenth and eighteenth centuries against political enemies of Parliament and the monarchy.

During the American Revolution, bills of attainder were used both by the British parliament against those supporting the revolution and by the new state legislatures against those loyal to the British government.

After the American Revolution, framers of the Constitution agreed that bills of attainder undermined the rule of law by having a legislative body engage in a judicial act. This violated the principle of the separation of powers and therefore was included in Article I of the Constitution in 1787.

Michael Coulter

Further Reading

Anastaplo, George. *The Constitution of 1787: A Commentary*. Baltimore: Johns Hopkins University Press, 1989.

Rehnquist, William. *The Supreme Court*. New York: Alfred A. Knopf, 2001.

See also Bill of Rights, U.S.; Constitution, U.S.; *Hurtado v. California*; Judicial review; Justice; Statutes.

Bill of particulars

Definition: Detailed document itemizing charges against a defendant

Criminal justice issues: Defendants; prosecution; trial procedures

Significance: Defense attorneys file motions to obtain bills of particulars for their clients so they will know all the details of the charges against their clients and be better prepared to organize their defenses.

A bill of particulars amplifies the charging document, which can be a complaint, information, or indictment, depending on the jurisdiction. Charging documents typically contain minimal information. In such cases, defense attorneys file formal motions for, or informally request—depending on the jurisdiction—bills of particulars. The prosecution must then give the defense documents providing additional details about the charges listed in the complaints.

A bill of particulars is essential to defendants in cases in which multiple offenses, or multiple counts of the same offense, are charged, as the information they contain prevents later surprises and thereby helps ensure fair trials. For example, a sexual assault offense occurring over a period of years may be generally charged as a continuing course of conduct. A defendant against such a charge should request a bill of particulars to learn the specific dates, times, and places of the alleged offenses.

Defendants who have detailed information of the charges against them can intelligently prepare their defenses against the charges. While having the same general purpose as discovery—requested by either the prosecution or the defense, used to produce evidence that will be used at a trial—a bill of particulars differs from discovery in that it is not designed to produce evidence that will be used at a trial.

Jennifer C. Gibbs

Further Reading

Emanuel, S. L. *Criminal Procedure*. Aspen, Colo.: Aspen Publishing, 2003.

Garner, Bryan A., ed. *Black's Law Dictionary*. 8th ed. St. Paul, Minn.: Thomson/West, 2004.

Schiller, N. *Criminal Procedure for the Criminal Justice Professional*. Eagan, Minn.: West Publishing, 2001.

See also Criminal procedure; Indictment; Information; United States Statutes at Large.

Bill of Rights, U.S.

The Law: First ten amendments to the U.S. Constitution

Date: Ratified in December, 1791

Criminal justice issues: Civil rights and liberties; constitutional protections; federal law

Significance: The rights and liberties spelled out in the U.S. Bill of Rights are an integral part of the Constitution and as such are guaranteed to everyone, including those accused of crimes. In fact, significant portions of several amendments protect the rights of defendants in criminal cases. The Bill of Rights originally applied only to the federal government; however, through the Fourteenth Amendment, all the protections relevant to defendants now apply also to states.

Beset by the ever-present threat of violent crime, frightened citizens wish to feel safe and therefore look with favor on rigid enforcement of criminal laws. At the same time, however, citizens must recognize that the rights and freedoms they enjoy as American citizens extend to those accused of crimes. Most of the basic constitutional protections that criminal defendants enjoy derive from the U.S. Bill of Rights, which in 1791 added the first ten amendments to the U.S. Constitution, which had been ratified two years earlier.

In criminal justice, the most important provisions of the Bill of Rights can be found in the Fourth, Fifth, Sixth, and Eighth Amendments. Under the due process clause of the Fourteenth Amendment, which was ratified in 1868, all those provisions now apply equally to both state and federal criminal prosecutions.

The Fourth Amendment

The Fourth Amendment offers protection against unreasonable searches and seizures. It was framed in response to the English practices that permitted government authorities to search anywhere, anytime, and for any reason. The U.S. Constitution requires search warrants describing with particularity the areas to be searched and the things to be seized before searches can be conducted. This protection protects victims from having to relinquish their privacy completely. Moreover, if other incidental evidence is found during the course of lawful searches, it can be included in trials only when the police can show that there was a good-faith effort to conform with the Fourth Amendment.

In case law, the Supreme Court has held that the Fourth Amendment extends to every place or every thing in which an individual may have a reasonable expectation of privacy. In addition to private residents, among the types of places protected are hotel rooms, garages, offices, automobiles, sealed letters, suitcases, and other closed containers. On the other hand, the Supreme Court has also held that the Fourth Amendment protections do not extend to abandoned or discarded property or open fields. Courts have collectively determined that personal privacy is not protected in such public objects as the sound of a person's voice, the paint on the outside of a car, or bank records.

The Supreme Court has recognized exceptions to the warrant requirement and has regarded probable cause as a precondition of valid searches. Although "probable cause" has never been precisely defined, rulings in court cases have indicated that for searches to be valid, police officers

James Madison, who later became the fourth president, is credited with principal authorship of the Bill of Rights. *(White House Historical Society)*

must have good reasons to believe that they will produce evidence of crimes. Under federal law, officers are required to knock and announce their arrival at the places they intend to search in order to reduce the potential for violence and protect the privacy rights of occupants.

Warrantless searches are authorized in circumstances that require immediate action; however, they must nonetheless conform to the reasonableness requirement. Other types of permissible warrantless searches include searches incidental to lawful arrests, searches based on consent, searches undertaken when officers are in hot pursuit of fleeing suspects, searches in situations in which evidence is evanescent and may disappear if too much time lapses before warrants are obtained (e.g., blood under fingernails or dried semen), and emergency searches. Automobile searches are fraught with rules and exceptions.

One of the most controversial forms of police searches, stop and frisk searches are limited searches that occur when police officers confront suspicious persons in efforts to prevent crimes from occurring. Pat-down searches to look for weapons are permissible on the basis of reasonable suspicion. When pat-down searches reveal contraband or other evidence of crimes, the evidence found is admissible at trial. While suspects are being detained during pat-downs, computer searches can be performed to determine if they are wanted for crimes elsewhere.

The Fifth Amendment

The Fifth Amendment protects suspects' rights by guaranteeing that accused persons can-

not be forced to confess. It stipulates the right against self-incrimination and provides that all persons accused of serious crimes are to have their cases reviewed by grand juries. The Fifth Amendment also prohibits double jeopardy, which means that criminal defendants cannot be tried twice for the same offense. This protection does not preclude separate actions in state and federal courts or civil and criminal actions growing out of the same set of facts. For example, after former football star O. J. Simpson was acquitted on criminal charges of murder, he was convicted on civil charges of wrongful death on the same set

---

The U.S. Bill of Rights

Portions of the amendments that are most relevant to criminal justice are underlined.

1. Congress shall make no law respecting an establishment of religion, or prohibiting the free exercise thereof; or abridging the freedom of speech, or of the press, or the right of the people peaceably to assemble, and to petition the Government for a redress of grievances.

2. A well regulated Militia, being necessary to the security of a free State, the right of the people to keep and bear Arms, shall not be infringed.

3. No Soldier shall, in time of peace be quartered in any house, without the consent of the Owner, nor in time of war, but in a manner to be prescribed by law.

4. The right of the people to be secure in their persons, houses, papers, and effects, against unreasonable searches and seizures, shall not be violated, and no Warrants shall issue, but upon probable cause, supported by Oath or affirmation, and particularly describing the place to be searched, and the persons or things to be seized.

5. No person shall be held to answer for a capital, or otherwise infamous crime, unless on a presentment or indictment of a Grand Jury, except in cases arising in the land or naval forces, or in the Militia, when in actual service in time of War or public danger; nor shall any person be subject for the same offence to be twice put in jeopardy of life or limb, nor shall be compelled in any criminal case to be a witness against him-

self, nor be deprived of life, liberty, or property, without due process of law; nor shall private property be taken for public use without just compensation.

6. In all criminal prosecutions, the accused shall enjoy the right to a speedy and public trial, by an impartial jury of the State and district wherein the crime shall have been committed; which district shall have been previously ascertained by law, and to be informed of the nature and cause of the accusation; to be confronted with the witnesses against him; to have compulsory process for obtaining witnesses in his favor, and to have the assistance of counsel for his defence.

7. In Suits at common law, where the value in controversy shall exceed twenty dollars, the right of trial by jury shall be preserved, and no fact tried by a jury shall be otherwise re-examined in any Court of the United States, than according to the rules of the common law.

8. Excessive bail shall not be required, nor excessive fines imposed, nor cruel and unusual punishments inflicted.

9. The enumeration in the Constitution, of certain rights, shall not be construed to deny or disparage others retained by the people.

10. The powers not delegated to the United States by the Constitution, nor prohibited by it to the States, are reserved to the States respectively, or to the people.

of facts. Criminal defendants can, however, be re-tried in cases that end in mistrials or hung juries.

The so-called Miranda warnings that arresting officers read to criminal suspects have become such a staple in the vocabulary of law enforcement and popular culture that the process has come to be called "mirandizing." Arresting officers must inform suspects of their Fifth Amendment right to remain silent to avoid self-incrimination, remind them of their right to seek legal counsel before answering any questions, and also advise them that any incriminating statements they make can and will be used against them in a court of law.

No one can be tortured or coerced into giving a confession. In order for a confession to be valid, therefore, suspects must be advised of their rights and it must also be determined that they did not waive their rights voluntarily. Moreover, if it is determined that rights have been waived, the waiver must be knowing and intelligent, and the suspects must understand their rights. Several exceptions exist. The Omnibus Crime Control and Safe Streets Act of 1968 provides that voluntary confessions can be used in federal courts, even when they are given by suspects who are not informed of their rights. There is also a "public safety" exception, holding that Fifth Amendment rights are not violated when police do not mirandize suspects prior to asking them for weapons in an effort to protect officers and other people in the vicinity where arrests take place.

The Sixth Amendment

The Sixth Amendment deals with the nature of criminal trials, which must be speedy and public and be conducted before impartial juries. Accused persons must also be informed of the crimes for which they are being tried, be able to confront witnesses brought against them, and have the assistance of counsel. The guarantee of the right to speedy and public trials relieves defendants of anxiety about the long-term consequences of their incarceration while they await trial, and it also satisfies society's interest in the prompt disposition of justice.

The public nature of trials is guaranteed as a result of distrust of secret government activities that British colonists experienced before the Revolutionary War. It also enhances community par-ticipation in law enforcement. Public trials permit citizens to receive notice of actions taken against them, and the public nature of trials extends to every stage, including jury selection, communication among judges and juries, and the judges' jury instructions.

Sometimes trials take place as closed proceedings. This happens when judges determine that the subject matter of trials is sensitive, as in rape cases; when witnesses are too shy and introverted to testify publicly; and when it is necessary to protect the identities of undercover agents. In such situations, the courts have the power to exclude members of the public from attending. A controversial question exists as to whether members of the media should be allowed to attend the proceedings.

The Sixth Amendment right to confront witnesses helps ensure that witnesses testify truthfully. Witnesses must swear oaths, they are subject to cross-examination, and judges and juries can assess their credibility by observing their demeanor as they testify. The confrontation right includes right of defendants be present during the course of the trial.

It should be noted that criminal defendants, unlike civil defendants, have a Fifth Amendment right not to testify in their own behalf if they do not wish to do so. Moreover, if they choose not to testify, the prosecution may not comment on that decision. In trials, defendants often waive that privilege when they wish to explain their own versions of the facts. Additionally, the prosecution must prove their guilt beyond a reasonable doubt for conviction. Throughout the legal system, moreover, notions of fundamental fairness exist in the form of due process of law. In both the civil and criminal systems, defendants must receive notices of the proceedings against them as well as opportunities to come forward and be heard before impartial, detached, and neutral tribunals.

The Eighth Amendment

The Eighth Amendment prohibits the imposition of excessive bail for those indicted of crimes and also forbids cruel and unusual punishment of convicted defendants. Cruel and unusual punishment is any punishment that is considered grossly disproportionate to the offenses for which defendants are convicted. These provisions were included in the Bill of Rights because its framers were aware of the history of torture that characterized criminal punishment in pre-Revolutionary times.

Following convictions and guilty pleas, judges decide punishments based on broad legislative sentencing guidelines. Parties sentenced may challenge the constitutionality of their sentences as "cruel and unusual punishment" or a violation of the equal protection clause of the Fourteenth Amendment due to alleged disparity in sentencing. While defendants may appeal verdicts when they are convicted, the prosecution cannot appeal verdicts when they lose cases. The Fifth Amendment's double jeopardy clause specifically prohibits appealing acquittals.

Incorporation Doctrine

Ratification of the Fourteenth Amendment in 1868 established a legal basis for extending Bill of Rights protections to the states in a process known as the incorporation doctrine. However, actual incorporation of the protections did not come until much later. During the twentieth century, the selective incorporation process applied most of the essential provisions of the Bill of Rights to the states under the Fourteenth Amendment's due process clause.

Marcia J. Weiss

Further Reading

Amar, Akhil Reed. *The Constitution and Criminal Procedure: First Principles*. New Haven, Conn.: Yale University Press, 1997. Constitutional scholar's examination of basic constitutional criminal guarantees through a close analysis of text, history, structure, and precedent. Amar addresses readers with legal backgrounds but also targets an audience of policymakers and citizens seeking to understand this area of law.

Barker, Lucius J., et al. *Civil Liberties and the Constitution*. 8th ed. Upper Saddle River, N.J.: Prentice-Hall, 1999. College textbook containing edited cases and clear explanations of central principles. The commentaries alone provide thorough overviews of the subject.

Campbell, Andrea. *Rights of the Accused*. Philadelphia: Chelsea House, 2001. Overview of the constitutional protections in the Bill of Rights through detailed discussion of landmark Supreme Court cases and their histories, as well as fundamental principles. Well written and easily understood.

Samaha, Joel. *Criminal Procedure*. 6th ed. Belmont, Calif.: Wadsworth, 2004. College textbook integrating edited cases and principles with clear explanations.

Schmalleger, Frank. *Criminal Justice, A Brief Introduction*. 2d ed. Upper Saddle River, N.J.: Prentice-Hall, 1997. College textbook containing concise coverage of major components of the criminal justice system.

Stephens, Otis H., Jr., and John M. Scheb II. *American Civil Liberties*. Belmont, Calif.: West/Wadsworth, 1999. College textbook containing edited cases and thorough explanations illustrating important principles.

See also Arrest; Bail system; Bill of attainder; Burden of proof; Constitution, U.S.; Corporal punishment; Counsel, right to; Criminal procedure; Cruel and unusual punishment; Defendants; Due process of law; Equal protection under the law; Exclusionary rule; Fifth Amendment; Freedom of assembly and association; *Habeas corpus*; Incorporation doctrine; Magna Carta; Miranda rights; Patriot Act; Privacy rights; Probable cause; Right to bear arms; Search and seizure; Self-incrimination, privilege against; Speedy trial right; Supreme Court, U.S.

Bivens v. Six Unknown Named Agents

The Case: U.S. Supreme Court ruling on search and seizure

Date: Decided on June 21, 1971

Criminal justice issues: Constitutional protections; search and seizure

Significance: This case established that, under certain conditions, plaintiffs have the right to claim civil damages when federal officials violate the Fourth Amendment protection against unreasonable search and seizure

The plaintiff in this case filed a civil action against federal employees of the Federal Bureau of Narcotics who had entered his house, searched it, and arrested him for possession of narcotics. He alleged that the entry and search had been without probable cause and was therefore in violation of the Fourth Amendment of the U.S. Constitution. He sought $15,000 in damages from each federal official.

The lower courts denied him relief on the ground that in the absence of a federal statute giving him the right to sue federal officials for violation of his constitutional rights, he could not sue the federal officials in a federal court for monetary relief. The Supreme Court disagreed. In his opinion for the Court, Justice William J. Brennan held that federal law permitted the plaintiff to bring the action. He reserved the question of whether the action might nevertheless be defeated by a claim of immunity by the officials.

Justice Brennan reasoned that the Fourth Amendment "guarantees to citizens of the United States the absolute right to be free from unreasonable searches and seizures carried out by virtue of federal authority" and that, "where federally protected rights have been invaded, it has been the rule from the beginning that courts will be alert to adjust their remedies so as to grant the necessary relief." He saw no reason to depart from this rule simply because there was no specific congressional authorization of the suit or because the plaintiff might have been able to bring an action under state law for the invasion of his privacy.

Dissenting opinions argued against the decision on the grounds that it invaded Congress' prerogative to define the rights of persons to sue in federal courts, that it would result in an avalanche of unmeritorious claims against federal officials, and that, like the exclusionary rule in criminal prosecutions, it would hamper the capacity of law-enforcement officers to carry out their duties because they would be fearful of direct personal liability for violation of the Fourth Amendment.

Bivens established that federal courts may, at least in some circumstances, hear and adjudicate civil actions for monetary damages against federal officials predicated on violation of constitutional rights even though Congress has not explicitly created the right to sue. It therefore raises questions regarding the distribution of lawmaking (or "right-creating") power between the judicial and the legislative branches of the federal government. The issue, generally referred to as the "implication of a private right of action," continues to be a difficult and challenging one for the courts: When should the courts find that the existence of a federal law (a statute, a constitutional provision, a treaty, or even a prior decision) gives a plaintiff a right to seek damages for violation of the law? Despite *Bivens* and numerous other cases since, the Supreme Court has failed to give a clear and concise answer to the question and has proceeded on a case-by-case basis.

Maxwell O. Chibundu

Further Reading

Dash, Samuel. *The Intruders: Unreasonable Searches and Seizures from King John to John Ashcroft.* New Brunswick, N.J.: Rutgers University Press, 2004.

Del Carmen, Rolando V. *Criminal Procedure: Law and Practice.* 6th ed. Belmont, Calif.: Thomson/Wadsworth, 2004.

LaFave, W. R. *Search and Seizure: A Treatise on the Fourth Amendment.* 3d ed. St. Paul, Minn.: West Publishing, 1995.

McWhirter, Darien A. *Search, Seizure, and Privacy.* Phoenix, Ariz.: Oryx Press, 1994.

See also Evidence, rules of; Probable cause; Search and seizure.

Blackmail and extortion

Definition: Crimes associated with the unlawful coercive extraction of money or other gain from victims by threatening harm or instilling fear

Criminal justice issues: Business and financial crime; white-collar crime; terrorism

Significance: Blackmail and extortion are predatory and coercive criminal acts that take a variety of forms, all of which use coercion to extract money or property from their victims. The emergence of extortion and blackmail in related acts such as cyber-crime and international terrorism represent ongoing threats to all levels of government and corporate entities, individual political or celebrity figures, as well as private citizens.

Blackmail and extortion are both crimes in which offenders extract payments—in money or property—from their victims through some criminal means, such as threatening the victims with harm, harm to the their loved ones, damaging accusations, or revelations of detrimental information. A 1952 case involved a group of offenders who baited men into homosexual situations and actions and then coerced payments from their victims by threatening to expose them as homosexuals at a time when such revelations could have ruined the victims' lives.

Definitions

Blackmail and extortion are usually regarded as felonies. Extortion is considered to be a more general crime than blackmail and includes the unlawful demand for money that is not legitimately due, often by an officer or other persons in official capacities. Extortion can involve any type of intimidation or threat against victims or those close to the victims. Extortion that is based upon direct threats of physical harm to victims is considered robbery. The threats of harm or violence can be either explicit or implicit.

Extortion also refers to the abuse of official power, in which public officers misuse their official status or authority to take property or money unlawfully. The criminal means and the attainment of money or property are both elements of the crimes.

Blackmail is regarded as a particular type of extortion, in which victims are threatened with the release of damaging or embarrassing revelations that are likely to harm the victims' reputations. Ransom and bribery are also often considered to fall under the definition of extortion.

The Federal Bureau of Investigation's Uniform Crime Reports (UCR) do not include a specific category for extortion or blackmail. However, the National Incident-Based Reporting System defines these crimes as the unlawful attainment of "money, property, or any other thing of value, either tangible or intangible, through the use or threat of force, misuse of authority, threat of criminal prosecution, threat of destruction of reputation or social standing, or through other coercive means."

Historical Background

Extortion and blackmail have probably been around as long as humans have lived together in societies. Because extortion and blackmail are driven by the abuse of authority, coercion, threats, and illicitly deriving material gain, some form of extortion or blackmail has most likely always attended human society. The books of Matthew and Corinthians in the Bible both allude to Pharisees and tax collectors who use their status to extort money from the people.

During the Middle Ages, church officials were often charged with extortive acts. The Sicilian Mafia grew out of an organized extortion system that supported local chieftains, providing protection for and settling disputes for villagers in return for payments. Some Sicilian-Italian extortionists transferred their practices to the United States when they emigrated from the Old World. Known as the Black Hand, these loosely organized criminals threatened their fellow Italian immigrants with violence if the victims did not pay for protection.

In the modern United States, extortion and blackmail continue to be linked with various forms of white-collar crimes, larceny, robbery, and other related offenses. Extortion and blackmail continue to play a part in organized criminal activities as well as corporate, bureaucratic, and other white-collar criminal actions.

The Sin of Extortion in the Bible

Know ye not that the unrighteous shall not inherit the kingdom of God? Be not deceived: neither fornicators, nor idolaters, nor adulterers, nor effeminate, nor abusers of themselves with mankind,

Nor thieves, nor covetous, nor drunkards, nor revilers, nor extortioners, shall inherit the kingdom of God.

1 Corinthians 6:9-10

The reluctance of victims to report extortion attempts makes tracking extortion data difficult. Extortion and blackmail can take many forms: from local protection rackets to single blackmailers with damaging photos to organized rings of corrupt police officers. Extortion and blackmail represent crimes of opportunity and abuse of power or advantage. Victims of blackmail and extortion are sometimes forced to continue making payments well beyond the extortionist's initial demands, as the offenders prey on their victims over the course of years.

In additional to traditional extortion shakedowns, organized shake-down efforts, and official abuse, another emerging threat relates to cybercrime. Corporations and individuals whose vital and personal information is stolen by hackers represent a new direction for this age-old crime. Computer hackers who gain access to and then hold particular damaging or sensitive items of information for ransom are a recent type of criminal to engage in extortion and blackmail. Extortion and blackmail are also used as tools by terrorists who threaten violence and murder if their demands are not met. The use of videotaped and Internet-disseminated threats by terrorist factions represents a disturbing new trend for this venerable criminal activity.

Prevalence

Because extortion and blackmail do not have their own UCR criteria, they are often layered into other white-collar crimes, as well as robbery and larceny. Reliable data for the national aggregate incidence of these crimes are scarce. However, sources indicate the rate of blackmail and extortion is growing, due to the growth of cybercrime.

Extortion and blackmail are global threats, and governments, corporations, political figures and private individuals are all potentially vulnerable. When these crimes are folded into other crimes, such as kidnapping, assault, and murder, it becomes easier to understand the threat that they pose—not only to individual citizens but also to national and international stability. Because these crimes are based on coercion and fear, as well as the use of damaging information, opportunities to engage in them are limited only by the imaginations of the offenders.

Investigation

The investigation, prosecution and punishment of blackmail and extortion are hampered by the wide-ranging nature of these crimes. Investigation and prosecution of blackmailers and extorters can be hampered by the victims' fears. Victims of these crimes may face violent retribution by the offenders, personal or professional embarrassment, or criminal prosecution for their own illicit activities. Furthermore, corporate victims of extortion might face having to make hard choices between giving in to extortionist demands and risking having proprietary or embarrassing information exposed, damaging their financial status and their public reputations. For all these reasons, victims tend to be reluctant to report the crimes and may not cooperate fully with the investigators.

Extortion victims may range from the owners of neighborhood businesses forced to pay protection money to gangs to avoid having their businesses burned to the ground to international companies making hush payments to keep embarrassing or incriminating information from being made public. In both types of cases, the reluctance of victims to report the crimes or cooperate fully with law enforcement can obstruct the investigative process.

When perpetrators are government officials who are committing extortion under color of authority—such as police officers or prosecutors who abuse their powers for financial gain—victims may be especially wary of pursuing criminal investigations. They may fear that they will not be believed or that their cases will be ignored by authorities.

Prosecution

As in any criminal investigation and prosecution, the elements of blackmail and extortion crimes must be substantiated and eventually proved. These elements include not only the forced payment of property or money, but also proof that the offenders have used criminal means to collect the payments. In cases involving threatened violence, this element can be investigated and proved in a straightforward manner. A pizza shop owner who pays for protection to avoid being beaten or killed, or to keep from having his store ransacked and burned is clearly being extorted. By contrast, a corporation that hides its extortion payments as "settlements" or as business expenses to avoid exposing sensitive or proprietary information represents a greater challenge for investigators. Because extortion and blackmail can take so many forms, from subtle and implicit to overtly threatening, investigators must demonstrate that offenders have indeed used criminal means to extract payments from their victims.

Finally, the crimes of extortion and blackmail are often packaged into other criminal acts, such as robbery, bribery, assault, embezzlement, cybercrime, abuse of authority, and racketeering. Therefore, inquiries into one of these other related offenses may lead to charges of extortion and blackmail that might not be apparent at the beginning of an investigation. Conversely, officials investigating homicides or aggravated assaults must remain open to the possibility that the victims of these offenses might have been perpetrating blackmail or extortion themselves.

Organized extortion, such as that traditionally practiced by the Mafia, can also fall under the Racketeer Influenced and Corrupt Organizations (RICO) Act, introducing federal jurisdiction into cases that may originate in state or local investigations.

Punishment

Blackmail and extortion are considered either felonies or misdemeanors, depending upon whether violence is threatened or used in commission of the crimes, the amounts of payments sought, and other factors. Federal sentencing guidelines set forth criteria on the different types of extortion, including extortion by means of false accusation, by threats of kidnapping or murder, by sending threatening letters, or by verbal threats.

Extortion attempts for payment amounts of five hundred dollars or less are considered to be misdemeanors under federal guidelines. Punishments under these statutes range from six months confinement for misdemeanor extortion by state or local officer (less than five hundred dollars) up to ten years for extortion offenses exceeding five hundred dollars that also involve written or verbal threats. When extortion is tied to other charges such as assault, kidnapping, ar-

son, bribery, or murder, the other offenses also carry their own punishments.

Successful investigation and punishment of blackmail and extortion depend upon the ability of the investigator and the prosecution not only to establish the legal elements of those crimes, but also to integrate other offenses that are packaged with them.

David R. Champion

Further Reading

Chin, Ko-Lin. *Chinatown Gangs: Extortion, Enterprise, and Ethnicity.* New York: Oxford University Press, 1996. Study of extortion practiced by Chinese gangs in major cities.

Katz, L. *Ill-Gotten Gains: Evasion, Blackmail, Fraud, and Kindred Puzzles of the Law.* Chicago: University of Chicago Press, 1996. Broad study of extortion, fraud, and other related crimes.

McChesney, F. S. *Money for Nothing: Politicians, Rent Extraction, and Political Extortion.* Cambridge, Mass.: Harvard University Press, 1997. Scholarly study that examines the role of extortion in political crimes.

Verton, Dan. *Black Ice: The Invisible Threat of Cyber-Terrorism.* Emeryville, Calif.: McGraw-Hill, 2003. Examination of the dangers of cyber-terrorist attacks on American computer networks.

See also Anti-Racketeering Act of 1934; Background checks; Duress; Hobbs Act; Mafia; Police corruption; Political corruption; Racketeer Influenced and Corrupt Organizations Act.

Blended sentences

Definition: Types of sentences in which judges simultaneously impose both juvenile and adult sanctions on juvenile offenders

Criminal justice issues: Convictions; juvenile justice; sentencing

Significance: A relatively new form of sentencing, blended sentences allow juvenile courts to impose penalties on youthful offenders that can move them directly into the adult correctional system when they reach the age of maturity.

Trends indicating increases in violent juvenile crimes such as aggravated assault and robbery captured the attention of the criminal justice system during the late 1990's and the first years of the twenty-first century. In response to those trends, about one-half of state legislatures have enacted blended sentencing (also called "blended jurisdiction") statutes directed at the growing numbers of serious youthful offenders. Blended-sentencing laws allow courts to impose either juvenile or adult correctional sanctions, or a combination of the two, on violent juvenile offenders whose cases are adjudicated in juvenile courts or convicted in criminal courts.

Major justifications for the use of blended sentencing include making juveniles who commit serious or violent crimes more accountable for their actions and promoting the rehabilitation of young criminals. In the matter of choosing whether to invoke blended sentencing, most statutes direct courts to consider three significant criteria: the seriousness of the offenses and need to protect communities; the maturity of the juvenile offenders; and the amenability of the offenders to treatment and rehabilitation while in the juvenile justice system.

Juvenile offenders who are given blended sentences are adjudicated as delinquents and sentenced as adults at the same time, for the same offenses. However, their adult sentences are suspended through the time they spend completing the conditions of their juvenile sentences. When they reach the age at which they pass from the juvenile justice system to the adult justice system, the courts can decide whether to impose what remains of the adult sentences that have hitherto been suspended.

Pati K. Hendrickson

Further Reading

Champion, Dean John. *The Juvenile Justice System: Delinquency, Processing, and the Law*. 4th ed. Upper Saddle River, N.J.: Prentice-Hall, 2003.

Clarke, E. E. "A Case for Reinventing Juvenile Transfer." *Juvenile and Family Court Journal* 47, no. 1 (1996): 3-21.

Cox, Steven M., John J. Conrad, and Jennifer M. Allen. *Juvenile Justice: A Guide to Theory and Practice*. 5th ed. New York: McGraw Hill, 2003.

See also Indeterminate sentencing; Juvenile waivers to adult courts; Restitution.

Bloodstains

Definition: Type of biological evidence found at crime scenes that can be used to establish whether crimes have occurred, reconstruct events leading up to crimes, and solve the crimes themselves

Criminal justice issues: Evidence and forensics; investigation; violent crime

Significance: Bloodstains can be used by forensic scientists to determine if crimes have occurred in such situations as differentiating between a suicide and murder. They can also help identify perpetrators of crimes by allowing forensic scientists to reconstruct sequences of events and match DNA samples.

Before deoxyribonucleic acid (DNA) technology become widespread in law enforcement, bloodstain evidence was of only limited use to investigators, who used it mainly to match basic blood types. Blood-typing helped but generally served to narrow lists of possible suspects only slightly because of the small number of unique blood types carried by human beings. Now, with the prolific use of DNA technology, bloodstains are invaluable resources for solving crimes. By using swabs to collect small samples of blood left at crime scenes, detectives and forensic scientists can analyze their DNA and compare the results with the DNA of any suspects they take into custody.

In addition, spatter patterns of blood found at crime scenes help forensic scientists and detectives reconstruct what happens between victims and offenders. Blood drops and spatters often reveal what weapons were used, in what fashion, and in what order. For example, the amount of

A Telltale Stain

In an episode of the cable television series *Monk* that aired in early 2005, the automobile in which Adrian Monk (Tony Shalhoub) is riding on a California highway is stopped by a traffic tie-up caused by a multivehicle accident in which a Volkswagen Beetle driver has died. The first highway patrolman on the scene concludes that the accident was caused by the Volkswagen driver's speeding, but Monk quickly notices several details that make him suspect—correctly—that the driver was murdered *before* the accident occurred. One of those details is a small, fresh bloodstain on the *outside* of the passenger-seat window—a location that the blood could not have reached from inside the car.

bleeding from puncture wounds made while victims' hearts are still beating is much greater than the bleeding that occurs when the same wounds are made after victims are already dead.

When blood traces are not apparent to the naked eye, scientists use special chemicals to test for their presence. Such chemicals can reveal the presence of blood after perpetrators try to wash away all traces with strong detergents or even bleach. One such chemical, called Luminol, emits light when it comes in contact with blood and can detect bloodstains diluted up to ten thousand times. Luminol is especially useful in forensic work because it does not interfere with DNA testing or destroy potentially valuable evidence that may be needed later. Other analyses, such as precipitin tests, can determine whether bloodstains are of human or animal origin.

Jenephyr James

Further Reading

Genge, Ngaire E. *The Forensic Casebook: The Science of Crime Scene Investigation*. New York: Ballantine, 2002.

Lee, Henry C., and Frank Tirnady. *Blood Evidence: How DNA Is Revolutionizing the Way We Solve Crimes*. Cambridge, Mass.: Perseus, 2003.

Saferstein, Richard. *Criminalistics: An Introduction to Forensic Science*. 7th ed. Upper Saddle River, N.J.: Prentice-Hall, 2001.

See also Cold cases; Crime labs; Crime scene investigation; DNA testing; Forensic entomology; Forensics; Latent evidence; Simpson trials; Toxicology; Trace evidence.

Blue laws

Definition: State and local regulations banning certain activities, particularly on Sundays

Criminal justice issues: Law codes; morality and public order; victimless crime

Significance: Sunday closing laws originated for religious reasons, and the U.S. Supreme Court has held them constitutional; nevertheless, in most areas blue laws have little significance in the twenty-first century.

The origin of the term "blue laws" is uncertain; it may refer to the color of the paper on which colonial New Haven, Connecticut, printed its laws. During the early colonial period the Puritans established their civil government as an outgrowth of their religious convictions. Many of their laws had the purpose of enforcing moral behavior; it was for moral and religious reasons that they restricted or required certain activities, especially on Sundays. As the Christian Sabbath, Sunday was to be a day of rest in compliance with the Fourth Commandment: "Remember the Sabbath day and keep it holy . . . you shall not do any work."

In addition to regulations against work, there were prohibitions against selling liquor and against such activities as dancing, card playing, cooking, traveling, public sports, and smoking. In the early 1600's, Virginia (not a Puritan colony) passed a law requiring church attendance on Sunday.

Blue laws restricting activities ranging from general labor to retail sales to clam digging have remained on the books in many states and localities, although in most areas they gradually fell into disuse in the twentieth century. Blue laws have been challenged in the courts, and in two cases in 1961 (the first was *McGowan v. Maryland*) the U.S. Supreme Court upheld the constitutionality of blue laws. The Court held that a blue law requiring businesses to close on Sundays did not violate the freedom of religion clause of the First Amendment, saying that the state has a legitimate interest in designating a day of rest for its citizens. Nevertheless, since the 1960's blue laws have been a relatively minor issue. In some areas they have been repealed; in others they are still on the books but are ignored.

Christopher E. Kent

Further Reading

Laband, David N., and Deborah Hendry Hein-buch. *Blue Laws: The History, Economics, and Politics of Sunday-Closing Laws*. Lexington, Mass.: Lexington Books, 1987.

Myers, Gustavus. *Ye Olden Blue Laws*. New York: Century Co., 1921.

Wallenstein, Peter. *Blue Laws and Black Codes: Conflict, Courts, and Change in Twentieth-Century Virginia*. Charlottesville: University of Virginia Press, 2004.

See also Alcohol use and abuse; Common law; Drunk driving; Mothers Against Drunk Driving; Prohibition; Religious sects and cults.

Bombs and explosives

Definition: Devices that employ combustion, usually within enclosed spaces, to detonate with considerable destructive force

Criminal justice issues: Evidence and forensics; terrorism; violent crime

Significance: Although explosives have been used since ancient times, in modern law enforcement they are becoming increasingly popular and deadly tools of criminals and terrorists.

Bombs and explosives present law enforcement with numerous difficulties. The primary difficulty is the fear that such weapons—whether

A major safety advance in bomb detection is the use of robots to search vehicles. *(AP/Wide World Photos)*

detonated or not—can generate in the public. The fact that mass hysteria alone may cause more damage than an actual bomb makes bombs a weapon of choice of terrorists. Another difficulty is that when these devices are detonated, the force of their blasts has a tendency to scatter and break evidence down into small pieces.

Crime scenes in bomb and explosives investigations extend not only to the furthest reaches of wherever debris from the explosions is thrown but even beyond. An extreme example is the explosion of the space shuttle *Columbia*, which disintegrated over Texas while reentering the atmosphere in January, 2003. Debris from the shuttle's explosion was scattered over hundreds of thousands of square miles, creating an investigation scene of unprecedented proportions. A similar disaster on a somewhat smaller scale that was an actual crime event was the terrorist bombing of Pan Am Flight 103 over Lockerbie, Scotland, in December, 1988. Not only did that jetliner explode at a considerable height, the explosion occurred over water. The resulting investigation called for the specialized services of divers in addition to the usual forensic team. Some types of explosives degrade in water but others suffer little damage. The shuttle and airliner disasters were unusual, but almost all bomb and explosive incidents pose special problems in controlling crime scenes and preserving evidence.

Collecting and Preserving Evidence

At all explosion crime scenes, systematic and controlled approaches to the collection, preservation, and processing of evidence are essential. Crime scene searches should begin at the most distant points at which debris is found and progress inward, toward the origins of the explosions.

Explosive investigations are similar in many ways to arson investigations. In both cases, investigators begin by locating the origins of the fires or explosions. In explosive investigations, the origins of the explosions are frequently marked by craters—the "blast seats"—in which large amounts of explosive residue are generally found. All debris, soil, and surfaces in these areas should be given special attention during the collection phase, and as much material as possible should be sent to labs for analysis. These areas may also contain unexploded, or partially burned,

particles that may contain fingerprints, fibers, or hairs that can be linked to the perpetrators.

Investigations should focus on locating as much as possible of the ignition devices and their containers, including wires, tapes, electric switches, timing devices, and batteries. These, too, may reveal fingerprints, fibers, hairs, and other particles that can be used to link suspects to the crime scenes.

Evidence collected in both arson and explosives investigations are also packaged and handled in similar manners. After other sorts of wet evidence—such as blood and semen—are allowed to air-dry, they are packaged in breathable containers. By contrast, arson and explosive evidence, which often contains residues that require laboratory analysis, must be packaged in airtight plastic containers. It is important that these containers not allow the escape of vapors, which may be the only indication of what sorts of accelerants or explosives have been used. As with other forms of evidence, these containers should be appropriately marked and chain of custody should be observed.

Types of Explosives

Explosives are typically classified according to their origins, which may be commercial, military, or improvised. A significant proportion of explosive investigations involve explosives that are improvised, that is, made from ordinary materials available to almost everyone, such as chemical fertilizers. Explosives are also classified according to the speed with which their compounds explode—either high or low. High explosives burn at rates of up to 20,000 feet per second and are said to "detonate." Low explosives burn at rates under 1,200 feet per second and are said to "deflagrate." Low explosives are stable under normal atmospheric conditions and burn only when ignited in the open. However, they can explode violently if they are ignited when they are confined.

A variety of tests are performed to determine the chemical makeup of residue found at explosion scenes. For example, chemical color tests are used to identify explosive residue. A device called the gas chromatograph provides the most reliable method to determine the chemical makeup of flammable residues in laboratories. Samples of

The Dangers of "Dirty Bombs"

There has been considerable discussion about the possibility of terrorists using so-called "dirty bombs" to carry out their missions. There has also been a debate over the amount of destruction that such bombs might cause. A dirty bomb is not a nuclear device, but a traditional bomb packaged with radioactive material. Such devices are comparatively easy to construct, requiring only small amounts of stolen radioactive material. When they explode, they release dangerous radiation, along with the damage that normal bombs of the same sizes cause. Through 2005, no dirty bomb had ever been successfully deployed. In any case, most experts agree that dirty bombs would actually cause only slightly more damage and loss of life than the same bombs would without radioactive material. However, the fear that dirty bombs engender is their greatest power.

substances found at explosion scenes are injected into the chromatograph, which then creates a chemical profile of the substance that can be compared to known substances.

Investigations of explosion sites themselves can present significant safety concerns. Scenes of explosions sometimes still have unexploded devices or remnants of devices that present a hazard to investigators. Moreover, bombers often set two or more bombs to explode at the same sites, timing the second devices so that they explode at times when help is likely to have arrived on the site of the first explosions. All explosive investigation scenes should therefore be approached as though yet-to-be-exploded devices still remain at the scenes.

Ayn Embar-Seddon
Allan D. Pass

Further Reading

Brodie, Thomas G. *Bombs and Bombings: A Handbook to Protection, Security, Disposal, and Investigation for Industry, Police and Fire Departments.* 3d ed. Springfield, Ill.: C. C. Thomas, 2005. Third edition of an industry handbook on explosives that was first published in 1972.

Kelly, Jack. *Gunpowder: Alchemy, Bombards, and Pyrotechnics: The History of the Explosive That Changed the World.* New York: Basic Books, 2004. Popular study of the development and impact of gunpowder in world history. Emphasis is on firearm weaponry, but much of the material is relevant to other types of explosives.

Mello, Michael. *The United States of America Versus Theodore John Kaczynski: Ethics, Power, and the Invention of the Unabomber.* New York: Context Books, 1999. Description of the Kaczynski case by an attorney who assisted in Kaczynski's appeal.

See also Arson; Bureau of Alcohol, Tobacco, Firearms and Explosives; Circumstantial evidence; Crime scene investigation; Firearms; MOVE bombing; Police dogs; Skyjacking; Terrorism; Unabomber.

Booking

Definition: Police administrative procedure following arrest, during which suspects are identified and official records of arrests are made

Criminal justice issues: Arrest and arraignment; probation and pretrial release

Significance: Booking records a suspect's official entry (or reentry) into the criminal justice system and moves the suspect from the jurisdiction of the police department to that of the courts.

Booking is one of many criminal procedures that suspects undergo following arrest. Police make an official record of arrest when a suspect is booked. This usually occurs at a police station or central booking facility and is managed by the arresting officer or booking personnel. Booking methods are guided by departmental Standard Operating Procedures and vary among law-enforcement agencies.

During booking, all suspects are searched, fingerprinted, and photographed. Evidence is documented, and reports are begun. Positive identification is made by cross-checking the suspects'

Booking and the Miranda Warning

Before questioning arrestees in custody, law-enforcement officers read them their Miranda rights:

> You have the right to remain silent. If you give up the right to remain silent, anything you say can and will be used against you in a court of law. You have the right to an attorney. If you desire an attorney and cannot afford one, an attorney will be obtained for you before police questioning.

Miranda warnings are not needed prior to asking general booking questions. Arrestees are required by law to disclose their identities, and police may detain them until their identities can reliably be established. Some states, however, require that juvenile detainees automatically be read their Miranda rights, whether they are questioned or not.

Social Security numbers, driver's license numbers, and dates of birth, and their photographs may also be checked against those stored in various databases. Other law-enforcement agencies are then contacted to determine whether the suspects have outstanding warrants, often using the National Crime Information Center (NCIC), a computerized database of criminal justice information. Arrest reports list this information as well as the dates, times, locations, and circumstances of arrests. Separate uniform incident reports contain narratives describing the arrests and information pertinent to the crimes committed and offenses charged.

The entire booking process generally takes between one and two hours. If a maximum of forty-eight hours has elapsed, a person must either be charged with a crime or released. If charged, the defendant will be given a complaint summons. This document states the charges and the time and place to appear in court. Those arrested and booked for serious offenses or those eligible for bail but lacking financial resources must remain at a jail or holding facility until their initial appearance. People arrested for minor offenses are generally released on their own recognizance when booking is complete. The procedural treatment of defendants throughout the booking pro-

cess is subject to judicial review. A suspect is booked pursuant to the commission of a crime, investigation, and arrest. Following booking, defendants move to the jurisdiction of the courts for their initial appearance before a magistrate.

Joel M. Caplan

Further Reading

Cole, Simon A. *Suspect Identities: A History of Fingerprinting and Criminal Identification.* Cambridge, Mass.: Harvard University Press, 2001. Discusses human identification techniques since the seventeenth century.

Feld, Bary C. *Cases and Materials on Juvenile Justice Administration.* St. Paul, Minn.: West Publishing, 2000. Compilation of court cases, statutes, and articles on juvenile administrative procedures in the United States.

See also Arrest; Bail system; Computer information systems; Criminal procedure; Criminal records; Fingerprint identification; *Miranda v. Arizona*; National Crime Information Center; Police lineups; Suspects.

Boot camps

Definition: Alternative form of incarceration using rigid discipline modeled on military training camps

Criminal justice issues: Juvenile justice; prisons; punishment

Significance: The United States incarcerates a higher proportion of juveniles and young adults than most of the nations of the world. The resulting high costs and overcrowding, with few positive rehabilitation benefits, have created a need for more cost-effective programs that reduce recidivism rates. It was initially hoped that boot camps would meet these goals; however, they have failed to fulfill their promise.

Boot camps—or, as they are also known, shock incarceration programs—were first established during the 1980's in response to rising crime rates, overcrowding in prisons, and high recidivism rates. The camps were intended to be an intermediate sanction between long-term institutionalization and immediate supervised release. While boot camp programs were originally designed for adults, the juvenile justice system has also adopted them. Some boot camps are financed and run by state governments, while others are privately owned and operated. Private boot camps often operate with little regulation. The great majority of boot camps are for male prisoners only, but a few have included female prisoners, and some have been designed exclusively for female prisoners.

Shock Incarceration

The types of programs known as "boot camps" vary considerably. The military "basic training" aspect of boot camps is what distinguishes them from other correction programs. These camps are referred as "shock incarceration" because they offer short, stressful experiences that are intended to encourage reform by the offenders. The first-generation boot camps emphasized military discipline, physical training, and hard physical work. Second-generation camps placed more emphasis on rehabilitation by adding such components as alcohol and drug treatment and social skills counseling. By the early twentieth century, some boot camps—particularly those for juveniles—were placing greater emphasis on educational and vocational skills than on military components, while still providing similar structure and discipline.

Adult boot camp programs are generally designed for younger, nonviolent offenders with first felony convictions. However, some camps have age limits as high as forty years. Juvenile boot camps are also generally restricted to nonviolent, first-time offenders. Lengths of stay are generally from three to six months in adult boot camps and from one to three months in juvenile camps. Adults are placed in boot camps though criminal courts. State courts also send juveniles to state-run boot camps, but juveniles are also sent to private boot camps by other courts and parents.

Oklahoma and Georgia were the first states to implement boot camp programs during the early 1980's. Other states followed in rapidly increasing numbers during the late 1980's and early 1990's. However, during the mid-1990's, both the numbers and daily populations of boot camps started decreasing, and that trend has continued through the first half decade of the twenty-first century. The state of Texas, formerly a leading state in boot camps, provides one example. By August, 2004, officials in Texas had shut down or converted six of the state's seven boot camps that had been created during the 1990's. Georgia, Colorado, North Dakota, and Arizona have all ended their programs, and Florida and California have both scaled back their programs.

Inmates of Minnesota's Challenge Incarceration Program at Willow River lining up for inspection in early 2005. In return for enduring six months of rigorous military-type training and drug treatment programs, nonviolent offenders in the Minnesota boot camp have the opportunity to have their prison sentences reduced by as much as six years. *(AP/Wide World Photos)*

Decline of Boot Camp Programs

The two most prominent reasons for the decline of boot camps are research findings indicating that the camps have failed to achieve their goals and widespread reports of abuses, deaths, and lawsuits. In 2003, the National Institute of Justice concluded a summary of research done on boot camps over a ten-year period. That study analysis found that while boot camps did have positive effects on the attitudes, perceptions, behaviors, and skills of inmates in the programs, the programs did not result in reduced recidivism, with limited exceptions. Similarly, a study in 2003 by the Texas Department of Criminal Justice found that people in drug treatment or employment-training programs were less likely to be recidivists than those who were sent to boot camps. The National Institute of Justice study, as well as other research, indicates that boot camps cost somewhat less than prison or juvenile training schools, resulting in modest reductions in correctional costs. They can also contribute to small reductions in prison and training school populations.

Numerous reports of abuses, deaths, and suicides at both juvenile and adult boot camps across the country have also contributed to their decline, both because they have outraged people and because they have resulted in expensive lawsuits. Notorious examples include a 2000 case involving a fourteen-year-old girl who died from heat exhaustion in a South Dakota boot camp, where she was placed for shoplifting, after her drill instructors decided that her complaints were merely malingering. In 2001, a sixteen-year-old in Arizona died after being punished for discipline violations. By 2003, at least thirty-six juveniles had died in boot camps.

Financial risks may have as much to do with the reduction in use of boot camps as abuses and deaths. Courts have ordered many states and private corrections corporations to pay large amounts in punitive damages. For example, a class-action suit in Maryland led to a court order for the state to pay four million dollars to juveniles abused at its boot camps from 1996 to 1999. The largest such award was in Texas in 2003, when a Tarrant County jury ordered the Correctional Services Corporation to pay the parents of a juvenile named Bryan Alexander $5.1 million in punitive damages and $35 million in actual damages for their son's death and suffering and their mental anguish. The boy had died at the Mansfield boot camp run by the Correctional Services Corporation, which is based in Florida.

The Future of Boot Camps

It is generally believed that if boot camps are to have a future in either the adult or juvenile justice system, they must be better regulated and be more successful in reducing recidivism. Moreover, the National Institute of Justice study and other smaller research studies indicate that if boot camps are to be more successful in the future there should be a standard boot camp model that includes therapeutic programs as well as discipline, with more emphasis on re-entry into the community and post-release supervision and assistance.

Jerome L. Neapolitan

Further Reading

Allen, Harry E., Clifford E. Simonsen, and Edward J. Latessa. *Corrections in America: An Introduction.* 10th ed. Upper Saddle River, N.J.: Pearson Education, 2004. An introductory discussion of the history of corrections, sentencing, incarceration, alternatives to confinement, types of offenders under correctional supervision, and reintegration.

Champion, Dean John. *The Juvenile Justice System: Delinquency, Processing, and the Law.* 4th ed. Upper Saddle River, N.J.: Prentice-Hall, 2003. Broad overview of delinquency and the stages through which offenders are processed in the juvenile justice system.

Kempinen, C., and M. Kurlychek. "An Outcome Evaluation of Pennsylvania's Boot Camp: Does Rehabilitative Programming Within a Disciplinary Setting Reduce Recidivism?" *Crime and Delinquency* 49 (2003): 581-602. Critical examination of the effects of one state's boot camps on inmates.

MacKenzie, D. L., and G. S. Armstrong. *Correctional Boot Camps: Military Basic Training or a Model for Corrections?* Thousand Oaks, Calif.: Sage Publications, 2004. Broad examination of the boot camp system.

Parent, D. *Correctional Boot Camps: Lessons from a Decade of Research.* Washington, D.C.: U.S.

Department of Justice, National Institute of Justice, 2003. Report from the National Institute of Justice's ten-year study of boot camps.

See also Chain gangs; Forestry camps; Juvenile justice system; Prison and jail systems; Prison overcrowding; Recidivism; Rehabilitation; Sentencing; Work camps.

Border patrols

Definition: Units of the federal agency that oversees the 8,000 miles of coastal and land boundaries of the United States

Criminal justice issues: International law; law-enforcement organization; terrorism

Significance: As a federal law-enforcement body under the aegis of the Department of Homeland Security, the U.S. Customs and Border Protection agency is responsible for controlling the entry of both people and substances into the United States.

The Customs and Border Protection (CBP) is one of the busiest law-enforcement agencies in the United States. On March 1, 2003, the Department of Homeland Security unified border personnel working in the immigration, customs, agriculture, and border patrol divisions under one agency. Formerly known as the U.S. Border Patrol under the Immigration and Naturalization Service, the border patrol was originally founded in 1924 after Congress passed strict limitations on legal immigration. With only several hundred agents on horseback, there were challenges in patrolling all the areas between inspection stations in the United States. Over the next eighty years, the border patrols evolved into a technologically advanced and increasingly sophisticated workforce with nearly ten thousand uniformed agents.

During the early twenty-first century, the CBP still maintained its primary mission to prevent the illegal entry of goods and immigrants into the United States. This duty, undertaken in cooperation with numerous other local and state law-enforcement agencies across the United States, resulted in approximately twelve million arrests between 1994 and 2004. This monumental task requires scrutiny from the land, air, and sea of more than 6,000 miles of international boundaries with Canada and Mexico and another 2,000 miles of coastal waters. Agents from twenty-one sectors across the United States work in all weather conditions and terrains, twenty-four hours a day, 365 days a year.

Twenty-first Century Priorities

During the 1980's and 1990's, Congress reacted to the increased flow of illegal immigrants and drugs across U.S. borders by providing for a significant increase in the number of agents and better technology to apprehend contraband and aliens. Drug seizures then became a major focus, with more than 18,500 pounds of cocaine and 1.1 million pounds of marijuana seized in 2001 alone by border patrol agents. Resources of equipment and personnel have typically been concentrated across the U.S.-Mexico border, where the majority of illegal entries have occurred. These initiatives in areas such as San Diego, California, resulted in illegal crossings decreasing by more

---

Selection and Training of Border Patrol Agents

To become Customs and Border Protection agents, applicants must pass language and achievement tests, undergo federal background checks and thorough physical examinations, and complete personal interviews. Upon acceptance of their applications, agent trainees must successfully complete a rigorous nineteen-week program of study at a Federal Law Enforcement Training Center in Glynco, Georgia, or Charleston, South Carolina. Trainees must maintain 70 percent averages in their coursework, which involves physical training, firearms, driving, Spanish language, border patrol operations, immigration, criminal and statutory law, and other topics. They are also cross-trained in the areas of customs, money laundering, copyrights, patents, and smuggling of drugs and other contraband under various titles of the United States Code. After reporting to their assigned duty stations, trainees receive post-academy instruction and field training for an additional twelve months.

than 70 percent during the late 1990's. Similar strategic plans to concentrate resources have been implemented in Arizona, New Mexico, and Texas under the National Border Patrol Strategy. These activities have not occurred without controversy, as pro-immigration advocates and human rights groups have protested the arrest and return of detainees to their home countries.

In reaction to criticism of the border patrol's inability to render aid to illegal aliens in remote and isolated areas, the CBP began the Border Safety Initiative in 1998, in joint cooperation with Mexican authorities. This plan seeks to reduce injuries and deaths along the border between the United States and Mexico by sharing intelligence, conducting joint search-and-rescue training, and posting signs that warn of the dangers of unauthorized border crossings. By reducing dangerous crossings, rescuing aliens in trouble, identifying casualties, and tracking and recording data collected from this initiative, the CBP aims to make national borders safer and to reduce fatalities.

Immigration policies continue to be a considerable source of debate nationally, as some illegal immigrants are given asylum and others are deported back to their home countries. Laws passed by several presidential administrations have allowed for illegal immigrants to attain citizenship. These laws have been applauded by advocates of various immigrant populations and denounced by others who back strict enforcement of immigration laws across the United States.

The most serious concern of the modern CBP since the terrorist attacks of September 11, 2001, involves intercepting terrorists who may be attempting to enter the United States, possibly with weapons of mass destruction. With the increased focus on homeland security, border defense and law enforcement has again become a hot topic on Capital Hill. The use of advanced military equipment such as the unmanned drone aircraft in mid-2004 in the American Southwest and other developments offer the CBP new tools to stop the flow of illegal persons and goods into the United States. Increased funding and enforcement proposals were likely to continue as terrorism prevention and the protection of its borders were considered a vital link in the safety of the United States.

Denise Paquette Boots

Further Reading

Byrd, Bobby, and Susannah M. Byrd, eds. *The Late Great Mexican Border: Reports from a Disappearing Line*. El Paso, Tex.: Cinco Puntos Press, 1996. Sixteen essays that chronicle life on the U.S./Mexico border and the issues and influences that are part of this landscape.

Crosthwaite, Luis Humberto, John William Byrd, and Bobby Byrd, eds. *Puro Border: Dispatches, Snapshots and Graffiti from La Frontera*. El Paso, Tex.: Cinco Puntos Press, 2003. This collage of illustrations and writings attempts to portray the various cultural and geographical considerations of those people who live on the line. Considers how the destitute of Mexico are ignored and forgotten.

Krauss, Erich. *On the Line: Inside the U.S. Border Patrol*. New York: Kensington, 2004. A former border patrol agent details the five-month basic training regimen all agents must undergo and follows them into the field to give the reader a sense of how smugglers and drug dealers challenge these agents who work on the line every day.

Moore, Alvin Edward. *Border Patrol*. Santa Fe, N.Mex.: Sunstone Press, 1991. Based on actual incidents, this fictional work describes a world of smugglers and illegal aliens and the dangerous nature of working on the U.S./Mexico border.

Nevin, Joseph. *Operation Gatekeeper: The Rise of the "Illegal Alien" and the Making of the U.S.-Mexico Boundary*. New York: Routledge, 2002. Details the federal government's *Operation Gatekeeper*, which in the 1990's targeted the San Diego-Tijuana border in efforts to stop illegal immigration. The author argues that this assault on immigration did not effectively reduce illegal immigration and served to inflame anti-Hispanic racism in the United States.

Urrea, Luis Alberto. *The Devil's Highway: A True Story*. New York: Little, Brown, 2004. Graphic, true story describes the harrowing journey of twenty-six Mexican men who attempted to enter the Arizona desert. The author argues that U.S. immigration policies are inhumane.

Urrea, Luis Alberto, and John Lueders-Booth. *Across the Wire: Life and Hard Times on the*

Mexican Border. New York: Doubleday, 1992. The author describes his interactions with Mexicans who live on the border and the deplorable living conditions that many of them endure.

Williams, Mary E., ed. *Immigration: Opposing Viewpoints*. San Diego: Greenhaven Press, 2004. Various social, political and legal viewpoints are given by experts and observers familiar with immigration into the United States.

See also Drugs and law enforcement; Homeland Security Department; Illegal aliens; Immigration and Naturalization Service; Law enforcement; Mexican justice system; September 11, 2001, attacks; Vehicle checkpoints.

Boston police strike

The Event: Two-week work stoppage by the majority of Boston's uniformed police officers

Date: September 9-22, 1919

Place: Boston, Massachusetts

Criminal justice issues: Law-enforcement organization; police powers

Significance: This strike raised the question of how to balance public safety and the right of police officers to unionize, bargain collectively, and strike for economic justice.

The Boston police strike lasted from September 9 to September 22, 1919. Of the city's 1,544 policemen, 1,117 went on strike. Immediately after the policemen walked out, acts of violence broke out in the South End area of Boston. On September 11, Governor Calvin Coolidge brought in the state guard, which quickly established control over the city. On September 22, the police gave in, ending the strike, and the recruiting of new policemen began. None of the striking policemen was allowed to return to duty.

The Boston police strike was only one of many labor disturbances in 1919. During World War I, inflation had driven prices up, while unions had gained government backing for the right to organize and bargain collectively in exchange for wage concessions. In 1919, 4 million workers, or 22 percent of the workforce, engaged in strikes. In Boston, telephone operators and transit workers had gone on strike and succeeded before the policemen walked out.

Work conditions for policemen in Boston had deteriorated significantly over the decades. Their pay scale dated back to 1898, while prices had gone up 79 percent, city government had increased their obligations, promotion regulations were arbitrary, and the quality of police facilities was generally poor. When Mayor Andrew J. Peters and Police Commissioner Edwin Upton Curtis responded hesitatingly to the policemen's demands, offering only a two-hundred-dollar annual increase, they decided to organize and affiliate themselves with the American Federation of Labor (AFL). The Boston Police Union was part of a larger movement: By August of 1919, the police forces of thirty-seven large cities had unionized and affiliated themselves with the AFL. Commissioner Curtis suspended the nineteen policemen who had been elected officers of the new union, among them union president John F. McInnes. The bad pay and work conditions, along with the city officials' hostile response to their demands, convinced the policemen to strike: They voted 1,134 to 2 for the walkout.

From the perspective of the city officials, the policemen, by joining the AFL, had entered a conflict of interest. City government argued that policemen were officers of the state, bound to the impartial enforcement of the law. Any affiliation, then, with an outside group that represents only a part of the population would compromise police officers in the exercise of their duty. The policemen, on the other hand, could point to pay and work conditions that undermined their ability to carry out their mission effectively.

For police unions, the Boston strike had important consequences. Most police unions remained and remain independent. Those that are affiliated with the AFL-CIO carry a no-strike rule in their charters. The Boston policemen eventually reorganized as the Boston Police Patrolmen's Association in 1965. In 1968, the police officers arbitrated a labor contract with the city of Boston.

Thomas Winter

Further Reading

Russell, Francis. *A City in Terror: The 1919 Boston Police Strike.* New York: Penguin Books, 1977.

Wells, Donna M. *Boston Police Department.* Mount Pleasant, S.C.: Arcadia, 2003.

See also National Guard; Police.

Bounty hunters

Definition: Bounty hunters—also known as bail-enforcement agents or bail agents—who track bail skippers, defendants who flee after bail-bond companies post their bail

Criminal justice issues: Defendants; investigation; probation and pretrial release

Significance: In some ways, bail agents enjoy wider latitude in their enforcement powers than sworn law-enforcement officers. In addition, many bail-bond agencies have reported increasingly widespread problems with bail skippers.

To many people, the term bounty hunter evokes romantic visions of the Old West, with murderous men on horseback trailing escaped cattle rustlers across desolate deserts. In the modern world, however, bail-enforcement agents are professional investigators who work for private bail-bond companies that earn their incomes by charging interest on bail payments that they make for defendants who cannot afford to post bail themselves. When defendants appear for bail hearings, judges usually impose specific monetary amounts that they must post with the courts to ensure that they will return to appear in court for their trials. Defendants who fail to appear in court may forfeit the bail that they post.

Defendants who cannot post bail from their own resources engage

bond companies, to whom they typically pay nonrefundable fees of about 10 percent of the total bail. For example, a defendant who must post five thousand dollars pays a bond company five hundred dollars to post the full amount. When defendants flee the jurisdiction after companies post their bail, the companies send licensed bounty hunters to track them down and deliver them to the courts, which then have the defendants incarcerated. Licensed bail-enforcement agents are legally empowered to arrest bail skippers and take them into custody.

Bounty hunters work for the bail companies and are hired to locate and apprehend those who flee the jurisdiction. Although they are legally empowered to arrest fugitives, they are not necessarily bound by the same restrictions imposed on sworn police officers. For example, they can forcibly enter fugitives' residences without search warrants and are not required to have extradition documents to take into custody defendants who flee from one state to another. Bounty hunters have this latter power because bail applicants sign extradition waivers when they apply for their bail. In some states, bail enforcers

Duane "Dog" Chapman (left), his half brother, and his son holding a news conference in Los Angeles in July, 2003. The three bounty hunters were credited with tracking down a fugitive rapist who had fled to Mexico but were themselves held on misdemeanor charges of deprivation of liberty. *(AP/Wide World Photos)*

are required to register with local police before apprehending bail skippers in the local jurisdictions. Bounty hunters who fail to comply with state and local regulations can be charged with kidnapping, assault, or other offenses.

The wide powers afforded to bounty hunters are a matter of controversy in legal circles. Some jurists argue that bail enforcers are granted too much leeway to carry out their missions. Others argue that bounty hunters cannot do their jobs effectively if they are bound by the same legal restrictions as sworn law-enforcement officers.

Complaints about bounty hunters also relate to another controversial issue. Some people in the justice system complain that many bail-bond agencies make poor decisions choosing to whom to grant bonds. By posting bail for untrustworthy defendants, they place greater demands on the services of bounty hunters and the courts. Moreover, these critics contend that too many defendants are skipping on their bail and are not being tracked down. Despite such criticisms, bounty hunters remain integral elements of the criminal justice system and represent examples of how private and governmental interests intersect in modern society.

David R. Champion

Further Reading

Burton, Bob. *Bail Enforcer: The Advanced Bounty Hunter*. New York: Paladin Press, 1990.

_____. *Bounty Hunter*. New York: Paladin Press, 1984.

Devine, F. E. *Commercial Bail Bonding: A Comparison of Common Law Alternatives*. New York: Praeger, 1991.

See also Bail system; Bench warrants; Criminal justice system; Manhattan Bail Project; Police corruption; Vigilantism.

Bowers v. Hardwick

The Case: U.S. Supreme Court decision on the right to privacy
Date: Decided on June 30, 1986
Criminal justice issues: Civil rights and liberties; privacy; sex offenses

Significance: In upholding a Georgia sodomy law criminalizing homosexual relations, this Supreme Court decision also upheld similar laws in other states until the Court reversed itself seventeen years later.

In August, 1982, Michael Hardwick was arrested in his home while having intimate sexual relations with another man. Although charged with violating Georgia's sodomy law, Hardwick was never prosecuted. The local district attorney wanted additional evidence and information before bringing charges against him.

Claiming that Georgia's law interfered with his ability to live as a gay man in his community without the fear of arrest in his own home, Hardwick filed suit in a U.S. federal court seeking judicial relief. The local district court rejected his case, saying that because the state of Georgia had not prosecuted him, there was no basis for his lawsuit in a federal court. In 1985, a federal appeals court reversed the district court decision, agreeing that Hardwick's right to privacy had been violated. Drawing on precedents established in several Supreme Court decisions on privacy rights, including *Roe v. Wade* (1973) and *Griswold v. Connecticut* (1965), the appeals court ruled that Hardwick's right to privacy had been compromised because the behavior had occurred within Hardwick's home, where he had a reasonable expectation of privacy.

Despite Hardwick's victory at the appellate level, the case moved forward to the U.S. Supreme Court for a final decision. The Supreme Court reversed the lower court's ruling, stating that the individual states have the right to regulate behavior that they deem contrary to the public interest. Noting that laws against sodomy had existed since the English Reformation and that homosexual activity was antithetical to the Judeo-Christian foundation of the United States, the Court ruled that there is no constitutional guarantee of privacy granted to homosexuals.

Following the Supreme Court's *Bowers v. Hardwick* ruling, the status of the sodomy laws in the states became a potent political force. Some states removed sodomy laws from their statutes. Other states retained their sodomy laws but rarely enforced them. In 2003, the Supreme Court reversed itself and declared that sodomy laws, such as the one in Georgia, were unconstitutional. Ironically, Georgia's own high court had already ruled a few years earlier that the state could no longer enforce its sodomy laws.

Michael E. Meagher

Further Reading

Ball, Carlos A. *The Morality of Gay Rights: An Exploration in Political Philosophy.* New York: Routledge, 2003.

Phelan, Shane. *Sexual Strangers: Gays, Lesbians, and Dilemmas of Citizenship.* Philadelphia: Temple University Press, 2001.

Richards, David A. J. *Identity and the Case for Gay Rights.* Chicago: University of Chicago Press, 1999.

See also Abortion; Commercialized vice; Hate crime; Privacy rights.

Brady v. United States

The Case: U.S. Supreme Court ruling on plea bargaining

Date: Decided on May 4, 1970

Criminal justice issues: Attorneys; defendants; pleas

Significance: In this decision the Supreme Court first acknowledged the validity of plea bargaining, asserting that it offered a "mutuality of advantage" for both the defendant and the state.

In 1959, Robert M. Brady, a defendant in a kidnapping case that involved the death of the victim, changed a plea of innocent to guilty when a codefendant in the case pleaded guilty and became available as a witness against him. Before admitting the new plea, the judge twice asked Brady if his plea was voluntary. Brady was convicted, but in 1967 he sought a reversal of his conviction in the U.S. District Court for the District of New Mexico, arguing that his guilty plea had not been voluntary. The petitioner argued that the death-penalty provisions of the Federal Kidnapping Act had coerced his plea. The district court denied Brady relief, upholding the constitutionality of the federal statute and arguing that

Brady changed his plea because of his codefendant's confession. The Court of Appeals for the Tenth Circuit affirmed the lower court's finding.

On *certiorari*, the U.S. Supreme Court concurred. In the various opinions issued by the Court, it was argued that an earlier case, *United States v. Jackson* (1968), which struck down the section of the Federal Kidnapping Act under which Brady had originally been tried, did not mandate that every guilty plea previously entered under the statute be deemed invalid, even when the threat of death was a consideration. It was further argued that a guilty plea was not a violation of the Fifth Amendment protection against self-incrimination when it was entered to ensure a lesser penalty than the maximum provided for by a criminal statute. It was also noted that the Fifth Amendment did not bar prosecutors or judges from accepting pleas of guilty to lesser, reduced, or selected charges in order to secure milder penalties. Brady's guilty plea was held to have been made voluntarily, despite the fact that it was influenced by the death-penalty provision of the statute that *United States v. Jackson* later declared unconstitutional.

The formal recognition of plea bargaining as a valid procedure for obtaining criminal convictions was very important because plea bargaining has been widely used in the United States, despite the fact that there is no statutory or constitutional basis for it. In fact, almost four-fifths of all convictions in serious state and federal criminal cases are obtained through guilty pleas made to secure either reduced charges or milder punishments. Although the procedure has its critics, it is a practical way of speeding up justice and clearing court dockets. It also mitigates against long pretrial imprisonment and anxiety and protects the public from the criminal activities of habitual offenders who would be free on bail for indefinite periods.

John W. Fiero

Further Reading

Fisher, George. *Plea Bargaining's Triumph: A History of Plea Bargaining in America.* Stanford, Calif.: Stanford University Press, 2003.

Rosett, Arthur I. *Justice by Consent: Plea Bargains in the American Courthouse.* New York: Lippincott, 1976.

Vogel, Mary E. *Coercion to Compromise: Social Conflict and the Emergence of Plea Bargaining, 1830-1920*. Rev. ed. New York: Oxford University Press, 2005.

See also Attorney ethics; Kidnapping; Plea bargaining; *Rummel v. Estelle*; *Santobello v. New York*; Self-incrimination, privilege against.

Branch Davidian raid

The Event: Raid by federal law-enforcement officers and state national guard troops on the compound of the Branch Davidian religious sect, followed by a fifty-one-day siege that ended with an attack in which the compound burned down and most of its members were killed

Date: February 28, 1993-April 19, 1993

Place: near Waco, Texas

Criminal justice issues: Federal law; government misconduct; police powers

Significance: The government raids on the Branch Davidian compound were widely criticized for their excessive use of force and exercise of poor judgment, giving rise to a public debate about the proper use of government force and questions of religious freedom.

The Branch Davidians are a splinter group from the Seventh-day Adventist Church whose Waco, Texas, group formed during the mid-1930's. During the 1980's, the group fell under the leadership of a man named Vernon Wayne Howell, who was better known as David Koresh. Claiming to have heard divine voices speaking to him, Howell redefined the rules of his sect to make all its women members—including one child—his wives. Around the same time, rumors of sexual

The Branch Davidian compound going up in flames on April 19, 1993. *(AP/Wide World Photos)*

abuse of members within the compound reached the outside world, and evidence appeared indicating that the sect was amassing an arsenal of heavy firearms.

On February 28, 1993, seventy-six agents of the Bureau of Alcohol, Tobacco and Firearms (ATF), with the assistance of helicopters and troops from the Texas and Alabama National Guards, attempted to raid the Branch Davidian compound, using a warrant alleging that the Davidians were illegally manufacturing machine guns. The raid was intended to be a surprise; however, even after it was clear that the element of surprise had been lost, the raiders proceeded. In the shoot-out that followed, four ATF agents and six members of the Branch Davidians were killed.

The Federal Bureau of Investigation (FBI) then took charge of the operation and began a siege that lasted fifty-one days. The siege ended when the FBI used tanks to break down the compound's main building and sprayed powerful CS tear gas into the compound. Some sect members died from CS poisoning, and many others died in a fire that may have been set by members themselves to fulfill Howell's apocalyptic vision. The few members who survived the raid fled the burning compound.

In a criminal trial that followed later, several members of the Branch Davidians were acquitted of homicide in the original ATF raid but were convicted of manslaughter. They received substantially longer prison sentences than are usually given out in manslaughter convictions because the judge in their case found that machine guns were involved. In *Castillo v. United States* (2000), the U.S. Supreme Court ruled that when a person is sentenced to extra years for using machine guns in a crime, their use of the guns must be presented to the jury, and the jury must make a finding about the use of machine guns.

David B. Kopel

Further Reading

Davis, Derek, and Barry Hankins, eds. *New Religious Movements and Religious Liberty in America*. Waco, Tex.: Baylor University Press, 2002.

Hardy, David T., and Rex Kimball. *This Is Not an Assault*. New York: Xlibris, 2001.

Kopel, David B., and Paul H. Blackman. *No More Wacos: What's Wrong with Federal Law Enforcement and How to Fix It*. Amherst, N.Y.: Prometheus Books, 1997.

Reavis, Dick J. *The Ashes of Waco: An Investigation*. Syracuse, N.Y.: Syracuse University Press, 1998.

Reebel, Patrick A., ed. *Federal Bureau of Investigation: Current Issues and Background*. New York: Nova Science, 2002. Includes a chapter on the Branch Davidians.

See also Aggravating circumstances; Attorney general of the United States; Bureau of Alcohol, Tobacco, Firearms and Explosives; Deadly force; Federal Bureau of Investigation; Firearms; Manslaughter; Police brutality; Resisting arrest; Statutory rape.

Breach of the peace

Definition: Disorderly behavior that disrupts the tranquillity or security of other individuals

Criminal justice issues: Constitutional protections; morality and public order; punishment

Significance: The preservation of public peace is a basic goal of the U.S. Constitution.

Breach of the peace covers crimes that cause disruption of the peace or infringe on the security of individual citizens or communities. Other terms commonly associated with breach of the peace are disorderly conduct, disorderly behavior, and disturbance of the peace. Individuals can be arrested for breach of the peace for a wide variety of reasons. Offenses classified as breach of the peace include riots, harassment, unlawful assembly, forcible entry, open obscenity, obstruction of the flow of traffic, unlawful discharge of firearms, public fighting, aggressive begging, use of abusive or threatening language, and public drunkenness. Since it is a rather flexible charge that is often implicit in the commission of most crimes, breach of the peace has sometimes been used as a catch-all offense when no alternative charge is available.

Breach of the peace is punishable as a misdemeanor. Article 1 of the U.S. Constitution provides all members of the U.S. Congress with congressional immunity while Congress is in session, meaning that Congress members cannot be arrested for any unlawful offense while going to and from sessions or while in session, except for cases that involve breach of the peace, felony, or treason. In the case of *Edwards v. South Carolina* in 1963, the U.S. Supreme Court ruled that a subjective, unsupported fear of a breach of the peace was never grounds for suppressing any freedoms guaranteed by the First Amendment of the Constitution.

Alvin K. Benson

Further Reading

Garner, Bryan A., ed. *Black's Law Dictionary*. 8th ed. St. Paul, Minn.: Thomson/West, 2004.

Garner, Bryan A., David W. Schultz, Lance A. Cooper, and Stephen W. Kotara, eds. *A Handbook of Basic Law Terms*. St. Paul, Minn.: West Publishing, 1999.

Vile, John R. *A Companion to the United States Constitution and Its Amendments*. 3d ed. Westport, Conn.: Praeger, 2001.

See also Citizen's arrests; Disorderly conduct; Loitering; Misdemeanors; Public-order offenses; Resisting arrest; Stalking; Vagrancy laws; Victimless crimes.

Bribery

Definition: Illegal offering of money, goods, or favors, and acceptance of such offers—especially by public officials—for the purpose of influencing an official's actions

Criminal justice issues: Business and financial crime; government misconduct; morality and public order

Significance: Bribery is a crime in which parties give and receive items or services of value in exchange for favors, usually having to do with public administration. This crime leads to many forms of corporate and governmental corruption that erode public trust in business and government.

Bribery dates back at least as far as biblical times, when it was regarded as a punishable offense to attempt to influence judges with gifts or promises of gifts. Because the judges were viewed as representing God, acts of bribery were considered to be sins against the divine. As society evolved through history, the crime of bribery was included in various European common-law doctrines. England, for example, included offenses such as bribery in its law to establish and maintain the integrity of acts conducted by public officials. Other acts that were made illegal in order to enhance the honesty of public officials included perjury, obstruction of justice, and resisting arrest.

To understand bribery fully, the common-law definition adopted in England must be referenced to explain the crime in its original context. During medieval times, bribery was criminalized to punish only those persons whose actions were intended to influence wrongfully public officials who were part of the criminal justice system. During that period, bribery was deemed a misdemeanor offense. As common law evolved, the scope of bribery legislation changed to include anyone who either gave or received anything of value for the purpose of influencing any public official's legal duty. Then, as now, both givers and receivers of bribes were regarded as equally guilty.

Forms of Bribery

Criminal acts of bribery can take place in many different ways. The common-law definition dealt specifically with those individuals who tried to bribe public officials. Today, the scope of bribery has widened to include not only public officials but also employees working in any capacity for these officials, as well as commercial acts of bribery and sports bribery. Examples of bribery include bribing legislators to vote particular ways on issues, bribing judges to make rulings in favor of known criminal offenders, and bribing members of government to secure business contracts for companies. Some forms of bribery may even take the form of charitable gifts or endowments in exchange for political or businesses favors.

Commercial bribery encompasses illegal business practices in which purchasing agents are given bribes in return for guaranteeing business transactions. Money, services, and political favors are a few of the most common types of bribes offered in acts of commercial bribery. Sports bribery laws make it a criminal offense to offer anything of value to participants or officials in amateur and professional athletic events. The purpose of such bribes is to alter the athletes' performances or to influence officials to alter their rulings.

Bribes can take the form of either tangible or intangible items or promises. Examples of tangible bribes include money, secured contracts, sexual favors, and illegal use of government or company property. Intangible bribes mainly include future promises to complete certain predetermined tasks or duties that favor the parties who are acting in the capacity of the givers. Examples of intangible bribes include stock or bond options.

Dave Johnson (right), with his wife, arriving at the federal courthouse in Salt Lake City, Utah, in October, 2003, where Johnson was being tried in one of the most-publicized bribery cases in modern American history. The federal government brought fifteen felony charges against Johnson and Tom Welch (not pictured), the chief officers of the committee that brought the 2002 Winter Olympic Games to Salt Lake City. The men were charged with fifty-seven counts of bribery in connection with deals they made to get members of the International Olympic Committee to award the games to Salt Lake. However, a judge eventually threw out the case because he found no evidence of criminal intent in the men's actions. (AP/Wide World Photos)

Prevalence

As with other types of white-collar crime, there is a paucity of statistics that can offer a true picture of the extent of bribery. The true prevalence and scope of the crime can only be estimated by using the Federal Bureau of Investigation's National Incident-Based Reporting System (NIBRS). According to NIBRS officials, bribery as a white-collar offense has a higher proportion of individual victims than other property and white-collar offenses. Compared to other white-collar offenses, bribery tends to have the fewest reported incidents—an average of fewer than 200 cases per year from the late 1990's through 2004. However, this statistic may be misleading, as measurement and recording errors are always a possibility in quantitative research. It should also be noted that only about 4,000 of the 19,000 law-enforcement agencies in the United States report their crime statistics.

Of the average 200 yearly incidents reported in recent years, there has been a 94-percent success rate in prosecutions. However, this figure is only an estimate. To gauge the true prevalence of bribery more accurately, more research needs to be done.

Investigation

Bribery is an intricate and sometimes complicated crime to prove. It takes a concerted effort on the part of experienced investigators and prosecutors to mount strong cases against both givers and receivers of bribes. All parties are equally culpable; however, the mere offering of a bribe that is not accepted may also constitute a crime by itself. Investigating bribery takes many hours of evidence gathering, interviewing witnesses, and corroborating facts.

Most local, state, and federal law-enforcement agencies are empowered to investigate and arrest parties involved in bribery. Investigators at all levels must work with prosecutors to ensure that the evidence of the crime is in order before arrests and convictions can be sought. This is difficult at local levels because many departments' resources are spread thin.

To compound this problem, few local investigators are familiar with the techniques for investigating and establishing cases against white-collar offenders who engage in crimes such as bribery. Federal investigators, on the other hand, have more resources including manpower, technical investigative skills, and finances to combat bribery.

Prosecution

The main component of bribery is the illegal offer or agreement to give or do something in exchange for favors. Prosecutors must not only prove that defendants have the criminal intent to carry out their bribes but also provide evidence regarding the actual offers, agreements, or requests and acceptances of things of value. The main obstacle for prosecution of most bribery cases is the matter of intent. This is the most difficult element of the crime to prove because there must be concrete evidence that the transactions or attempted transactions have in fact taken place. Savvy criminals who are familiar with bribery laws often make their bribes in the form of gifts or endowments to reduce the possibilities of being detected.

Federal bribery statutes tend to focus on government officers and support employees, along with public witnesses and jurors who are testifying in federal cases. State bribery laws vary and usually offer only general definitions of the crime. However, many states are now broadening the parameters of their bribery laws to include new categories of perpetrators and illegal conduct.

Punishment

Under common law, punishments for bribery tended to be less harsh than they are today. In fact, bribery was considered merely a misdemeanor offense, so most punishments involved little or no time in prison. Now, however, bribery is considered a felony offense by both state and federal governments.

Federal and state authorities offer stiff criminal penalties for engaging in bribery. Most states and the federal government offer either imprisonment, probation, fines, or combinations of all three sanctions. Depending on the size of their bribes, convicted felons generally receive prison sentences, hefty fines, and some form of supervised probation. Average prison sentences for persons convicted of bribery are sixteen to nineteen months, but federal and state sentences may be as high as ten years. Moreover, both givers and receivers of bribes may be found criminally liable, and both are likely to receive the same sentences.

The first years of the twenty-first century have seen increasing numbers of white-collar crimes in the United States. For some government officials, however, bribery is the price of doing business. The federal government and the governments of most states have prescribed stiff penalties for persons convicted of bribery. This notable increase in punishment offers a decisive indication that both state and federal authorities regard bribery as a serious crime, harmful to the integrity of society as a whole.

Paul M. Klenowski

Further Reading

Blintliff, Russell L. *Complete Manual of White Collar Crime Detection and Prevention*. Englewood Cliffs, N.J.: Prentice-Hall, 1993. Offers a detailed look at the different forms of white collar crimes including bribery. Detection, investigation, and prevention measures are outlined in great detail.

Heftel, Cecil. *End Legalized Bribery: An Ex-Congressman's Proposal to Clean Up Congress*. Washington, D.C.: Seven Locks Press, 1998. Impassioned case by a former five-term congressman for eliminating the corruption of Congress by corporate influence buyers.

Reiman, Jeffrey. *The Rich Get Richer and the Poor Get Prison: Ideology, Crime, and Criminal Justice*. Boston: Allyn and Bacon, 2004. Critical assessment of the failure to control white-collar crime.

Scheb, John M., and John M. Scheb II. *Criminal Law*. Belmont, Calif.: Wadsworth Publishing, 1999. General criminal law text that offers a fascinating historical examination of crimes such as bribery. Covers the evolution of English common law into today's modern law.

Simon, David R. *Elite Deviance*. Boston: Allyn and Bacon, 2002. Penetrating and unbiased view of white-collar crime in general. Bribery is explained and many real life examples are offered throughout.

Vincke, François, Fritz Heimann, and Ron Katz, eds. *Fighting Bribery: A Corporate Practices Manual*. Paris: ICC, 1999. Practical handbook for businesses published by the International Chamber of Commerce.

See also Bank robbery; Corporate scandals; Federal Crimes Act.

Brinks bank robbery

The Event: Robbery of 2.7 million dollars in cash, checks, and securities from a Boston bank
Date: January 17, 1950
Place: Boston, Massachusetts
Criminal justice issues: Business and financial crime; organized crime; robbery, theft, and burglary
Significance: One of the most sensational and celebrated crimes of the twentieth century, the Brinks robbery is notable for both its size and the meticulousness with which it was carried out.

The largest bank robbery in American history at its time, the Brinks bank robbery was the culmination of a criminal scheme that required more than two years of elaborate preparation. Preparations included breaking into the bank several times prior to the main robbery, changing locks to key doors, and conducting a series of exacting rehearsals. On the evening of the robbery, the bandits, all career criminals, crept into the building at 7:30 P.M., passed through several locked doors to the bank's counting room, and bound and gagged five surprised employees present. They left the building with approximately $1.2 million in cash and $1.5 million in money orders and securities.

The bandits' initial plans to hide their loot and stay out of view until the relevant statute of limitations expired were derailed when one of the robbers, Joseph "Specs" O'Keefe, complained that he had been cheated by his partners and demanded more money. Concerned that he would reveal the crime to authorities, the rest of the gang hired an assassin to kill him. O'Keefe was wounded in a dramatic street shootout but survived and subsequently confessed to police.

In 1956, eight of the robbers received life sentences as a result of O'Keefe's testimony. Numerous other accessories to the crime received shorter sentences. A large portion of the money and securities recovered had decomposed or was otherwise damaged, and more than $1 million in cash was never recovered. The government spent approximately $29 million to arrest, try, and convict all parties to the crime.

Michael H. Burchett

Further Reading
Kirchner, L. R. *Robbing Banks: An American History, 1831-1999*. Cambridge, Mass.: Da Capo Press, 2000.
Sifakis, Carl. *Strange Crimes and Criminals*. New York: Facts On File, 2001.

See also Bank robbery; Corporate scandals; Federal Crimes Act.

Brown v. Mississippi

The Case: U.S. Supreme Court ruling on coerced confessions
Date: Decided on February 17, 1936
Criminal justice issues: Confessions; constitutional protections; defendants
Significance: This was one of the first cases in which the U.S. Supreme Court held that a state's criminal process had deprived the defendant of due process of law under the Fourteenth Amendment; it paved the way for later cases requiring states to exclude coerced confessions and to provide humane and fair procedures for defendants.

Brown and his two codefendants were tried and convicted of murder in Mississippi in 1934. Confessions had been obtained from them by deputy sheriffs and jailers by means of torture. They were repeatedly hanged until nearly dead and then flogged unmercifully with a leather strap with buckles on it. After initially denying their guilt they confessed, adjusting or changing their statements until these had been provided in the exact form demanded by the deputies. After being allowed to recuperate for a day, they were put through the farce of repeating these confessions to witnesses. On the basis of the confessions alone, the defendants were convicted of murder and condemned to death. Although the deputies and others who had participated in the whippings freely admitted to the fact on the witness stand, the trial judge and later the Mississippi Supreme Court refused to reverse the convictions. The defendants appealed to the U.S. Supreme Court.

Under the Fourteenth Amendment, states are forbidden to "deprive any person of life, liberty, or property without due process of law." At that time this clause had been interpreted to mean that states had to provide a fundamentally fair procedure in criminal cases. Although they could establish their own court policies, the policies could not "offend some principle of liberty and justice so rooted in the traditions of conscience of our people as to be ranked as fundamental." Under this rule the Supreme Court reversed Brown's conviction.

Chief Justice Charles Evans Hughes, writing for a unanimous Court, held that Mississippi could not substitute the rack and torture chamber for the witness stand. The defendants had been deprived of a fundamental aspect of due process of law. Hughes gave short shrift to Mississippi's argument that Brown's counsel had made a technical procedural error in not asking more clearly to have the confessions suppressed: "The duty of maintaining constitutional rights of a person on trial for his life rises above mere rules of procedure."

Brown v. Mississippi was the first case in which the Supreme Court held that a coerced confession was inadmissible in a state criminal trial. It mirrored *Weeks v. United States* (1914), in which the same rule had been applied to federal trials. In the three decades that followed *Brown*, the rule was broadened to include more and more forms of coercion. This line of cases culminated in 1966 when, in *Miranda v. Arizona*, the Court decided that no confession obtained once a defendant is in custody is admissible unless the defendant has been fully informed of his constitutional rights.

Robert Jacobs

Further Reading

Inbau, Fred, John Reid, Joseph Buckley, and Brian Jayne. *Criminal Interrogations and Confessions.* 4th ed. Boston: Jones and Bartlett, 2001.
Lassiter, G. Daniel, ed. *Interrogations, Confessions, and Entrapment.* New York: Kluwer Academic/Plenum, 2004.
Mirfield, Timothy. *Silence, Confessions, and Improperly Obtained Evidence.* Oxford, England: Clarendon Press, 1997.

See also *Argersinger v. Hamlin*; *Arizona v. Fulminante*; Criminal procedure; Due process of law.

Burden of proof

Definition: Responsibility of prosecutors to present evidence to persuade the fact-finder
Criminal justice issues: Legal terms and principles; prosecution; trial procedures
Significance: Gathering facts and presenting them as evidence are essential components of criminal procedure; convictions for crime require enough facts to add up to proof beyond a reasonable doubt.

The concept of burden of proof encompasses two types of burdens: the burden of production and the burden of persuasion. Although similar, each has different distinctions. In criminal cases, the prosecution bears the burden of production; it must offer sufficient evidence to support a claim. If the prosecution does not proceed with its initial presentation of evidence supporting an action, the case will not move forward, and the judge has authority to terminate the proceedings. Moreover, if the prosecution does not offer sufficient evidence to support its allegations, the defense will request a directed verdict, asking the judge to end the case with a verdict in its favor because the party with the burden of production has failed to meet that burden. If the motion is granted, the case ends. If a motion is denied, the case continues.

The burden of production is met in various ways: presenting physical evidence, introducing exhibits, and presenting witnesses to testify about events related to cases. In criminal cases, the U.S. Constitution requires that the government (prosecution) present proof that defendants have committed crimes. Judges determine whether the parties have met their burden of production. Generally, the burden of production remains with the prosecution and does not shift in criminal cases. However, when defendants raise defenses that require proof such as insanity, the burden of production shifts.

Burden of Persuasion

The burden of persuasion requires presentation of evidence that will convince juries that certain parties should prevail. Juries, not judges, make those determinations. Juries must measure the facts that they find from the evidence according to three standards of proof. First is the preponderance, or weight, of the evidence in which plaintiffs must tip the scales, indicating that there is more credible or convincing evidence on one side than on the other (used in civil cases only). The second is clear and convincing evidence (also used in some civil cases) that attains a higher standard of proof than preponderance of the evidence. The third and highest standard is proof beyond a reasonable doubt, which is required in all criminal cases.

The government bears the burden of providing to juries evidence that is of sufficient quality to demonstrate high probability of guilt. It should be noted that this burden of proof does not require "proof beyond *any* doubt," but rather, "proof beyond a *reasonable* doubt." In mathematical terms, this standard might equate to a 90-95 percent certainty on the part of juries that defendants are guilty of the crimes with which they are charged. Defendants in criminal cases are

presumed to be innocent until proven guilty, and every element of the charges must be proved beyond a reasonable doubt.

There are instances in which the same set of facts give rise to two different lawsuits, criminal and civil. In such situations, the burdens of proof are different and the results may also differ. For example, in the O. J. Simpson murder case of the mid-1990's, Simpson was found not guilty in his criminal murder trial but was found liable for wrongful death in a civil case, which had a less stringent burden of proof.

Marcia J. Weiss

Further Reading

Pellicciotti, Joseph M. *Handbook of Basic Trial Evidence: A College Introduction*. Bristol, Ind.: Wyndham Hall Press, 1992.

Stopp, Margaret T. *Evidence Law in the Trial Process*. Albany, N.Y.: West/Delmar, 1999.

See also Bill of Rights, U.S.; Convictions; Jury system; Reasonable doubt; Simpson trials; Standards of proof; Trials.

Bureau of Alcohol, Tobacco, Firearms and Explosives

Identification: Federal agency that enforces federal laws involving firearms, moonshine liquor, untaxed cigarettes, and explosives

Date: Established as the Alcohol Prohibition Unit in 1919

Criminal justice issues: Federal law; law-enforcement organization; substance abuse

Significance: Originally created to enforce the federal prohibition on alcohol, the Bureau of Alcohol, Tobacco, Firearms and Explosives (ATF) has undergone many changes during its history and is now the main federal agency responsible for the enforcement of gun-control laws. It has many other responsibilities, but its involvement in gun-law enforcement has made it one of the most controversial federal law-enforcement agencies.

The Bureau of Alcohol, Tobacco, Firearms and Explosives began in 1919 as the Alcohol Prohibition Unit in the Bureau of Internal Revenue (which later became the Internal Revenue Service). It was soon moved to the Department of Justice and was renamed the Bureau of Prohibition. Under that name, it enforced federal laws against the consumption or manufacture of alcohol. After Prohibition was repealed in 1933, the bureau was returned to the Treasury Department's Bureau of Internal Revenue. At first called the Alcohol Tax Unit, it was renamed the Alcohol and Tobacco Tax Division (ATTD).

Federal laws required that alcohol producers and tobacco sellers pay special excise taxes. Some citizens, particularly in the South, produced "moonshine" liquor without paying the necessary taxes and sold their homemade liquor in states or localities where alcohol was illegal. Through the 1960's, the ATTD's main law-enforcement responsibility was pursuit of illegal liquor stills, especially in southeastern states. The ATTD also regulated the lawful commerce of alcohol, acting as the administrative agency to enforce alcohol production and sales by legitimate companies, pursuant to the federal Alcohol Administration Act of 1935.

The U.S. Constitution does not explicitly grant the federal government any law-enforcement powers, except in a few discrete areas, such as piracy and counterfeiting. That is why it was necessary to add the Eighteenth Amendment to the Constitution in 1919 to empower the federal government to enforce prohibition. In 1934, when Congress wanted to impose federal controls on the possession of machine guns, it used its taxing power. The National Firearms Act that Congress passed that same year required that owners of machine guns—and certain other firearms—pay a federal tax and register their guns with the federal government. The latter requirement was ostensibly enacted for tax purposes but was actually a method by which the federal government gave itself control over firearms ownership. The ATTD was given responsibility for enforcing this new tax law.

Expanding Jurisdiction

As national crime rates rose during the 1960's, Congress passed new federal crime laws. The U.S. Supreme Court's increasingly expansive interpretations of Congress's power to regulate interstate commerce provided the basis for new laws enacted on the theory that local crime affects interstate commerce. In 1968, Congress passed the Gun Control Act, which provided detailed regulations for the retail sale of firearms and prohibited large classes of people from buying guns. The following year, the ATTD was renamed the Alcohol, Tobacco and Firearms Division (ATFD) and given responsibility for enforcing the new Gun Control Act.

In 1970, Congress passed the Explosives Control Act. The ATFD and the Federal Bureau of Investigation (FBI) shared responsibility for enforcing this law's criminal law provisions, but the ATFD took sole responsibility for regulating the lawful production and sale of explosives. Two years later, the ATFD was removed from the Internal Revenue Service. Renamed the Bureau of Alcohol, Tobacco and Firearms (ATF), it became an autonomous law-enforcement agency within the Treasury Department, along with that department's Secret Service and Bureau of Customs.

Gun Enforcement Controversy

The ATF's enforcement of the new gun laws was controversial from the start. Many gun owners—as well as groups such as the National Rifle Association, Gun Owners of America, and Second Amendment Foundation—contended that ATF tactics were unconstitutional and illegitimate. They claimed that the agency often seized guns and refused to return them, even when there was no legal basis for doing so. Critics of the agency also charged that ATF agents entrapped many innocent people into committing technical violations of federal laws, and that the agency frequently abused its search and seizure powers.

The ATF denied the charges, but a unanimous 1982 report of the U.S. Senate Subcommittee on the Constitution provided a scathing denunciation of ATF tactics. In 1986, Congress passed, by large margins in both the House and the Senate, the Firearms Owners' Protection Act (FOPA). This new law significantly revised the Gun Con-

trol Act of 1968, provided more precise definitions of what was covered by federal law, reduced
some technical violations of gun laws to misdemeanors, and set limits on the ATF's search and
seizure powers.

Expanding Operations

In 1975, the ATF began to take on arson cases
under the theory that the accelerants used by arsonists constituted explosives. Later, the federal
explosives law was amended to encompass arson,
thus making ATF's jurisdiction over arson more
legally secure.

During the late 1980's and early 1990's, as the
federal war on drugs became a major national issue, the ATF created "Special Response Teams"
to conduct violent and high-profile raids into
homes that ATF alleged were occupied by drug
dealers in possession of illegal firearms. During
that period, the bureau began styling itself as

"ATF," rather than "BATF," to mimic the three-
letter acronyms of the Federal Bureau of Investigation (FBI) and Drug Enforcement Agency
(DEA).

In early 1993, an ATF raid on the compound of
the Branch Davidian religious cult outside Waco,
Texas, went disastrously wrong. Four ATF
agents and several civilians were killed, and the
ATF's decision-making about the raid was widely
criticized. The bureau's image was further tar-
nished by a congressional investigation of the
case of Randy Weaver.

Weaver and his family were white separatists
who lived in Ruby Ridge, Idaho. In 1989, an informant working for an ATF agent entrapped Randy
Weaver into selling him two shotguns (a legal
act) and then sawing off their barrels to shorten
them (an illegal act). The case eventually led to
an FBI siege of Weaver's cabin in 1992 and the fatal shooting of Weaver's wife. Weaver himself

A special agent of the Bureau of Alcohol, Tobacco, Firearms and Explosives addressing a news conference in December 2003, about the bureau's recent raids on Los Angeles County hangouts of outlaw motorcycle gangs, from which the weapons on display and other evidence were
seized. (AP/Wide World Photos)

was tried and acquitted for the original firearms sale charge in 1993.

The Waco and Weaver cases, allegations of racial and sex discrimination within the ATF, and other serious management problems, appeared to put the bureau's existence in jeopardy, especially when committees in both houses of Congress held hearings to investigate the bureau in 1995. However, the bureau survived, and afterward avoided major negative publicity. The bureau continues to be criticized by gun-rights groups for its unduly severe enforcement of federal gun laws, while simultaneously receiving criticism from anti-gun groups for excessive timidity in its enforcement of the same laws.

Reorganization

As part of a federal law-enforcement reorganization following the September 11, 2001, terrorist attacks on the United States, the ATF was renamed the Bureau of Alcohol, Tobacco, Firearms, and Explosives and was transferred from the Treasury Department to the Justice Department—where, ironically, its Prohibition ancestor had been transferred decades before. Despite its name change, the bureau retained "ATF" as its official acronym.

In 2004, Congress enacted legislation that restricted the release—except for law-enforcement purposes—of ATF records identifying lawful gun buyers. The new law also restricted the release of the "trace" records used by the ATF to track the sale and ownership of individual firearms. Requests for such information are usually made by local law-enforcement agencies that find guns that may have been used in crimes or guns that have been stolen. Supporters of the new federal legislation argued that law-abiding gun owners, as well as nonowners who may be mentioned in trace reports—such as witnesses to crimes—should have their privacy rights protected. Critics responded that the law interfered with the ability of the public to learn important information about gun ownership and gun-law enforcement.

David B. Kopel

Further Reading

Hardy, David. *The B.A.T.F.'s War on Civil Liberties*. Bellevue, Wash.: Second Amendment Foundation, 1979. Collection and analysis of stories of alleged enforcement abuse by an attorney who played a major role in the drafting of the Firearms Owners' Protection Act.

Holmes, Bill. *Entrapment: The BATF in Action*. El Dorado, Ark.: Desert Publications, 1998. Another critical study of the ATF that covers more recent allegations of abuse.

Moore, James A. *Very Special Agents: The Inside Story of America's Most Controversial Law Enforcement Agency—the Bureau of Alcohol, Tobacco, and Firearms*. Champaign: University of Illinois Press, 2001. Vigorous defense of the bureau, written by a former special agent.

United States Government. *Twenty-first Century Guide to the U.S. Bureau of Alcohol, Tobacco, and Firearms*. Washington, D.C.: Progressive Management, 2002. Compact disc containing more than 21,000 pages of ATF documents on every aspect of ATF work.

Vizzard, William J. *In the Cross Fire: A Political History of the Bureau of Alcohol, Tobacco and Firearms*. Boulder, Colo.: Lynne Rienner, 1997. Well-informed history by a retired ATF supervisor and agent.

See also Arson; Attorney general of the United States; Bombs and explosives; Branch Davidian raid; Entrapment; Firearms; Gun laws; Justice Department, U.S.; Organized crime; Regulatory crime; Right to bear arms.

Bureau of Justice Statistics

Definition: Branch of the U.S. Department of Justice that collects and disseminates statistical information about crime, criminals, victims, and the operations of the American justice system

Criminal justice issues: Crime statistics; professional standards

Significance: Timely and accurate information about crime is needed for decision-making at all levels of government.

The Bureau of Justice Statistics (BJS) assembles and analyzes data that were originally collected by municipal, county, state, and federal justice agencies. These data, along with information from BJS surveys, are used to prepare publications and data files on topics such as criminal victimization, law enforcement, prosecution and adjudication of crimes, jails and prisons, and capital punishment. BJS publications and data files are freely available on the World Wide Web at www .ojp.usdoj.gov/bjs/. The Web site also helps those who are unfamiliar with the justice system to find key facts in charts and tables or get answers to questions from the BJS staff.

As a member of the Interagency Council on Statistical Policy, which includes the major federal statistics agencies such as the Census Bureau, BJS establishes national standards for data collection, terminology, statistical methods, data quality, and keeping statistics independent from political influence.

National collection of statistical data about crime and justice was originally recommended by the President's Crime Commission in 1965 and was initially housed in the Census Bureau. The Census Bureau continues to administer BJS principal data collection activity, the National Crime Victimization Survey (NCVS). Crime statistics from the NCVS include some crimes not counted in the FBI's Uniform Crime Reports, which are prepared from police records. BJS also administers funds for states to improve their crime statistics keeping and criminal history records.

Jan M. Chaiken

Further Reading

Committee on National Statistics. *Principles and Practices for a Federal Statistical Agency*. Washington, D.C.: National Academy Press, 2001.

Federal Bureau of Investigation. "The Nation's Two Crime Measures." *Crime in the United States, 2002*. Washington, D.C.: U.S. Department of Justice, 2003.

See also Attorney general of the United States; Criminal history record information; Federal Bureau of Investigation; National Crime Victimization Survey; President's Commission on Law Enforcement and Administration of Justice; Sex offender registries; Uniform Crime Reports.

Bureau of Prisons

Identification: Federal agency responsible for incarceration of prisoners convicted in federal courts
Date: Created in 1930
Criminal justice issues: Federal law; prisons; punishment
Significance: The creation of the U.S. Bureau of Prisons to oversee the confining of criminals convicted in federal courts reflected the general expansion of federal criminal law and the growing role of federal law-enforcement agencies.

The first two federal prisons were opened in Leavenworth, Kansas, and Atlanta, Georgia, in 1905. Before that time, persons convicted of federal crimes were confined either in a facility on a military reservation or in a state or local corrections facility. Prohibition and the expansion of federal powers to combat organized crime in the 1920's and 1930's increased federal responsibilities for law enforcement and created a need for a separate federal prison system. In 1930, the Bureau of Prisons was created to administer the expanding federal corrections programs and a growing network of prison facilities. High-profile federal law-enforcement agencies, particularly the Federal Bureau of Investigation under J. Edgar Hoover's leadership, focused attention on violent crime, and new prisons were built. Alcatraz, perhaps the best known of the maximum-security facilities, was opened in 1934 and held some of the most notorious U.S. criminals until its closing in 1963.

The Bureau of Prisons, a unit of the U.S. Department of Justice, is divided into six geographical regions that have a significant amount of autonomy. The directors of the regions also serve on the executive staff of the bureau and provide national coordination of the agency's programs. The organization of the bureau includes the executive office of the director, with a general counsel and an internal affairs section. There are also divisions for administration, correctional programs (with responsibility for managing the facilities), health services, human resource management, program review, community corrections and detention, and information, policy, and public affairs. The Bureau of Prisons is also responsible for UNICOR, a public corporation and the successor to Federal Prisons Industries, founded in 1934, which provides employment and training for inmates. It produces goods and services ranging from furniture to electronics to data entry. The Bureau of Prisons also operates the National Institute of Corrections, which supports state and local corrections agencies and operates the National Academy of Corrections, an information center, and the National Jail Center. The institute has a budget separate from that of the Bureau of Prisons.

The Bureau of Prisons began to experience problems in the 1980's and 1990's because of the age of its facilities, the need for increased capacity, and the increasing costs of corrections programs. In particular, prison overcrowding, the need to accommodate a wide variety of inmate populations, and increasing costs of treating drug abuse problems and addressing health problems related to acquired immunodeficiency syndrome (AIDS) have taxed the agency. The lack of strong political constituencies in the corrections profession and the increasing unwillingness of Congress to expand funding for federal programs are making it difficult to address the growing problems, even though the need for additional resources and new programs has been noted in numerous U.S. General Accounting Office reports. The Bureau of Prisons is also facing challenges in the form of recommendations for privatization of its facilities, and it has been targeted periodically by Congress for elimination.

William L. Waugh, Jr.

Further Reading

Alarid, Leanne, and Paul Cromwell. *Correctional Perspectives: Views from Academics, Practitioners, and Prisoners*. Los Angeles, Calif.: Roxbury, 2002.

Elsner, Alan. *Gates of Injustice: The Crisis in America's Prisons*. Upper Saddle River, N.J.: Financial Times/Prentice-Hall, 2004.

Herman, P. G., ed. *The American Prison System*. New York: H. W. Wilson, 2001.

Johnson, R. *Hard Time: Understanding and Reforming the Prison*. 3d ed. Belmont, Calif.: Wadsworth, 2002.

See also Auburn system; Criminal justice education; Forestry camps; Model Penal Code; New Mexico state penitentiary riot; Parole; Prison and jail systems; Prison escapes; Prison industries; Rehabilitation; Work camps.

Burglary

Definition: Unlawful entry into a building with the intent to commit an underlying crime

Criminal justice issues: Robbery, theft, and burglary; vandalism

Significance: Burglary often involves the invasion of a person's home and, as such, undermines the security a home is thought to provide. In the early English common law, the notion that one's home is inviolate was established, and its unlawful invasion with the intent to commit further criminal acts is viewed as a particularly serious offense.

Burglary is often characterized as a crime against habitation, and the essence of the crime, as it developed through the common law, is the violation of one's security associated with the home. A home is expected to be a place in which the occupant can escape from the outside world and feel safe. The burglary of a home strips its occupants of that sense of security. Consistent with that concept, elements for the crime of burglary traditionally included breaking and entering into a dwelling, at night, with the intent to commit a felony crime once inside the home.

Definitions Through History

The concept of burglary in the United States has evolved over time into a broader definition that is no longer limited to the invasion of homes, having been expanded to encompass invasions of all buildings. In fact, in many jurisdictions a building is defined, for purposes of the burglary statute, as including motor vehicles or vessels.

Additionally, modern burglary statutes have extended their reach by eliminating the common-law element that the invasion occur at night, and in many jurisdictions the intended underlying crime no longer need be a felony; the intent to commit malicious mischief or vandalism once inside the building will often suffice as the intent to commit an underlying crime.

Similarly, the breaking and entering elements have been broadened generally to encompass any unlawful entry. Thus, it is not necessary for an offender to gain entrance through some means of force; a charge of burglary only requires that the offender entered the building without authorization or license to do so. However, the conversion to "unlawful entering" does not allow for the burglary of commercial establishments during business hours, even if the offender surreptitiously enters the building. The offender, like the remainder of the public, has a license to enter the building during business hours. For the purposes of burglary statutes, the entire business establishment is characterized as one unit, and even rooms designated for "authorized personnel only" are considered open to the public during business hours. An exception to this general rule is when separate property interests are involved with the separate rooms of a commercial building (such as multiple lessees operating individual businesses within their respective rooms of a building).

While the dwelling element of common-law burglary has been broadened to include buildings in general, the concern with the violation of the security provided by the home has been retained.

The fact that a building is a dwelling is frequently considered an aggravating factor, raising the degree and seriousness of the crime. In determining if a building is a dwelling, whether or not individuals routinely sleep in the building is a key factor. Consistent with the treatment of an entire building as a unit, if the predominant characteristic of a building is that of a dwelling, then every component of the building assumes the dwelling classification. Consequently, attached garages are characterized as dwellings.

The actual use of a building as a home is critical to a building being characterized as a dwelling. When a home is under construction it is not considered a dwelling for burglary purposes. However, once the new home has been occupied, it retains its dwelling character even when subsequently vacant.

Similar to the retention of the dwelling element as an aggravating factor, the nighttime element of common-law burglary has been retained in many jurisdictions as another aggravating factor. In such jurisdictions, nighttime is frequently defined not by the physical presence of the sun but rather by there not being sufficient light to recognize a person's face—a definition emphasizing the feelings of vulnerability associated with the crime of burglary.

Prevalence

In 2000, crime statistics indicated that burglary was second in occurrence only to the crime of theft. In that year, more than 1.5 billion burglaries occurred in the United States. For the unlawful entry of a building to constitute a burglary, the offender must have committed the entry with the intent to commit a second or underlying crime. The most common underlying crime, indeed the crime most people associate with burglary, is theft. Also closely associated with burglary is the crime of robbery. Whenever a burglary is committed while occupants are inside the building, there exists a fair potential for the burglary to evolve into a robbery when the occupants realize an intruder has entered the building.

One of the key elements of a burglary is the use of force to gain entry to the place that is being robbed. *(Brand-X Pictures)*

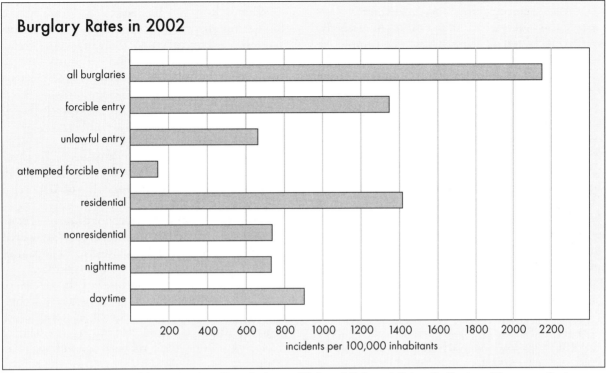

Burglary Rates in 2002

Category	incidents per 100,000 inhabitants
all burglaries	~2150
forcible entry	~1346
unlawful entry	~660
attempted forcible entry	~150
residential	~1420
nonresidential	~730
nighttime	~720
daytime	~880

incidents per 100,000 inhabitants

Source: Federal Bureau of Investigation, *Population-at-Risk and Selected Crime Indicators*. Figures reflect aggregate statistics on reported burglaries in the United States in 2002. For example, in that year there were 1,346 forcible-entry offenses for every 100,000 people. Note that many categories overlap.

Criminologists studying the times and locations of burglary occurrences have found that burglaries tend to occur in clusters. British researchers have shown that residences within 400 meters of a burgled home (particularly those on the same side of the street) have an increased risk of being burgled for up to two months after the initial incident. Research in England has also documented a significant decrease in burglaries. Among other reasons posited for the decline is the demise of the professional burglar, leaving the field primarily to amateurs with no special expertise and often with drug addictions. Concurrently, the value of loot typically taken from homes (such as stereo systems and other electronics) has decreased significantly. While expensive television sets, traditionally popular targets for burglars, have retained their value, they have become physically so large that their removal is problematic. Consequently, it appears that economics, at least in England, partially determines the prevalence of burglary.

Investigation

The crime of burglary is unusual in that it requires that offenders possess intent to commit a second crime upon entering their targeted buildings. Consequently, investigators and prosecutors must be able to provide evidence of that secondary intent in order to convict a person of burglary.

The tendency for burglaries to occur in time and space clusters results in law enforcement benefiting from thorough analysis of burglary scenes to reveal the modus operandi (repeated patterns of behavior exhibited in committing crimes) of the burglar. Such information enables better prediction of which nearby buildings will be victimized next, and if a professional burglar is involved, the information may lead authorities to a particular suspect.

Prosecution

In prosecuting burglaries, two issues appear to surface regularly. The first is whether the prosecution can establish that the defendant possessed the requisite intent to commit an underlying crime. When a burglary has been completed, the intent to commit an underlying crime at the time of entry into the building is inferred from the commission of the underlying crime. However, when the burglary is interrupted prior to the commission of the underlying crime, the prosecution must be able to establish some evidence from which the defendant's intent to commit an underlying crime can be inferred. With the broadening of burglary statutes to include crimes other than felonies, the task of prosecutors has been facilitated. Courts have allowed an inference to be drawn that defendants intend some kind of mischief when unlawfully entering a building; consequently, the offender intended to commit a malicious mischief or vandalism category of crime.

If a burglary is interrupted, a second issue may be whether the defendant actually entered the building. For the purposes of burglary, offenders have entered a building when any parts of their bodies has passed into the building. Additionally, courts have concluded that the introduction into the building of tools associated with the commission of the underlying crime, not merely used to break into the building, satisfies the entry element for burglary.

Punishment

Burglary is considered a serious offense and is punished as a felony. The characterization as a serious crime is based upon two factors. First is the notion that a burglary is an extreme violation of a person's security. Second is the fact that burglaries have a significant potential for evolving into robberies, resulting in physical harm to people. With the broadening of the scope of burglary under modern criminal statutes, the violation of one's security is not as significant when burglaries involve commercial buildings. However, the potential for a burglary to evolve into a robbery is not diminished.

When a burglary has been committed, the offender may be prosecuted and punished for two crimes, the burglary and the underlying crime. This does not represent double jeopardy because the focus of burglary is distinct from the focus of the underlying crimes.

David Blurton

Further Reading

"The Decline of the English Burglary." *The Economist*, May 5, 2004. Discusses possible factors that have led to a decrease in the occurrence of burglaries in England.

Dix, George E., and M. Michael Sharlot. *Criminal Law*. 4th ed. Belmont, Calif.: Wadsworth, 1999. A general text on substantive criminal law, including a segment on burglary.

Rosenfield, Richard. "The Case of the Unsolved Crime Decline." *Scientific American*, February, 2004. Discusses theories set forth to explain unprecedented decline in the United States of homicides, robberies, and burglaries during the 1990's.

Samaha, Joel. *Criminal Law*. 7th ed. Belmont, Calif.: Wadsworth, 2002. A general substantive criminal law text discussing burglary among other topics.

"Time Bandits." *The Economist*, May 8, 2004. A discussion of the tendency of burglaries to occur in clusters and the development of a new crime mapping technique.

Tseloni, Andromachi, K. Wittebrood, G. Farrell, and K. Pease. "Burglary Victimization in England and Wales, the United States, and the Netherlands: A Cross-National Comparative Test of Routine Activities and Lifestyle Theories." *British Journal of Criminology*, Winter, 2004. Examines activities of burglary victims, seeking causal relationships.

See also Aggravating circumstances; Common law; Criminal law; Criminal prosecution; Fingerprint identification; Model Penal Code; Robbery; Theft; Trespass; Vandalism.

C

Cable and satellite television signal theft

Definition: Pilfering of pay-television signals to obtain free programming

Criminal justice issues: Fraud; robbery, theft, and burglary; technology

Significance: In addition to harming paying customers by not sharing in the costs of pay-television services, using low-quality cable and satellite equipment contributes to electronic signal outflow that can disrupt emergency communication systems for firefighters, ambulances, and police.

While many Americans consider telecommunication theft to be a victimless crime, the practice actually harms paying subscribers by driving up rates to generate the revenue needed to cover signal loss and disruption caused by the low-quality equipment used by signal thieves. A National Cable Television Association survey has shown that cable and satellite television companies lose approximately $5.1 billion annually to signal theft.

There are three main types of signal theft: active, premium, and passive. Active theft takes place when people intentionally make illegal connections to receive cable or satellite signals. Premium theft occurs when subscribers to basic services use descramblers or black boxes to obtain premium or pay-per-view channels for free. The third type, passive theft, happens when people not paying for service fail to notify the service providers that there are active connections in their homes and thereby receive programming free of charge.

The Cable Communications Policy Act of 1984 originally prohibited the unauthorized use of cable and satellite signals. Persons who are aware of unauthorized use of the signals are considered guilty as well, unless they report perpetrators to the proper authorities. (Most companies have on-line forms for this purpose.) Sentences in cable theft cases have ranged from probation to sixteen years in prison, while fines have ranged from several hundred dollars to almost $3 million.

Kathryn Vincent

Further Reading

Ciciora, Walter. *Modern Cable Television Technology: Video, Voice and Data Communications.* 2d ed. San Francisco: Morgan Kaufmann, 2004.

Paglin, Max D. *The Communications Act: A Legislative History of the Major Amendments, 1934-1996.* Silver Spring, Md.: Pike & Fischer, 1999.

Paradise, Paul R. *Trademark Counterfeiting, Product Piracy, and the Billion Dollar Threat to the U.S. Economy.* Westport, Conn.: Quorum Books, 1999.

See also Consumer fraud; Cybercrime; Fraud; Telephone fraud; Theft.

California v. Greenwood

The Case: U.S. Supreme Court decision on warrantless searches

Date: Decided on May 16, 1988

Criminal justice issue: Search and seizure

Significance: This case expanded the ability of all levels of law-enforcement bodies to conduct searches, without judicial warrants, for things in which persons are considered to have no "reasonable expectation of privacy"—such as garbage left out for collection.

In 1984, police in Laguna Beach, California, received information that a man named Billy Greenwood was selling drugs out of his home. However, there was not sufficient evidence for the police to obtain a warrant to search Greenwood's home. Consequently, the police asked the local trash collection company to turn over to them garbage that they collected from Green-wood's house.

Greenwood was in the habit of leaving his gar-bage in opaque plastic bags at the curbside in front of his house. When officers searched the bags that had been collected at this house, they found evidence of illegal drug use. Citing that evidence, they obtained a warrant to search Greenwood's house, in which they found hard ev-idence of drug trafficking and then arrested Greenwood. While Greenwood was out on bail, of-ficers searched his garbage again, found more in-criminating evidence, obtained a second search warrant, and eventually arrested Greenwood on additional charges.

During Greenwood's ensuing criminal trial, the court found that the searches of his trash bags without a warrant were illegal. Without the evidence obtained from the trash, there would have been no probable cause to obtain the search warrants. Therefore, under what is known as the "fruit of the poisonous tree" doctrine, the war-rants were invalid, and the charges against Greenwood were dropped. The state of California then appealed the decision to a higher court but lost. The state's own supreme court did not agree to hear the case, but the U.S. Supreme Court did because the case touched on an issue of broad na-tional importance.

In previous cases, the Supreme Court had held that the Fourth Amendment to the U.S. Consti-tution requires police to obtain search warrants when subjects of their investigations have a "rea-sonable expectation of privacy" in the places or items to be searched. In *Katz v. United States* (1967), for example, the Court had held that a person had a reasonable expectation of privacy in the content of a phone conversation he had con-ducted in a public phone booth.

In the *Greenwood* case, the defendant argued that he had a reasonable expectation of privacy in the contents of his trash bags. Although the opaque bags were placed on a public street, Greenwood argued that he did not suppose that anyone was likely to inspect the contents of those bags. He assumed that, as always, his trash would be picked up by the trash company and mingled with that of his neighbors. However, a majority of justices on the Supreme Court ruled that while Greenwood might have expected that

his garbage was private, that was not a *rea-sonable* expectation, as anyone—"animals, chil-dren, scavengers, [or] snoops"—could have gone through the contents of his trash bags after he placed them on the curb. The Court's ruling in his case, therefore, narrowed the range of searches for which law-enforcement officers had to obtain search warrants, thereby making it easier to col-lect evidence.

Phyllis B. Gerstenfeld

Further Reading
Kennedy, Caroline, and Ellen Alderman. *The Right to Privacy*. New York: Vintage, 1997.
Sykes, Charles. *The End of Privacy: The Attack on Personal Rights at Home, at Work, On-Line, and in Court*. New York: St. Martin's Griffin, 2000.

See also Bill of Rights, U.S.; Fourth Amendment; Plain view doctrine; Search and seizure.

Campus police

Definition: Law-enforcement departments based on college and university campuses
Criminal justice issues: Law-enforcement or-ganization; police powers
Significance: Long little more than campus custodians, campus security forces began evolving into modern police forces during the 1960's and now play important roles in law enforcement.

Campus police forces trace their origins back to 1894, when Yale University administrators hired two New Haven, Connecticut, police officers to patrol university grounds. Those first two cam-pus officers were hired simply as campus "watch-men," and their duties included patrolling the university grounds and watching for fire, water, or other damage.

Over the next half-century, as other universi-ties throughout the United States followed Yale's example, the campus "watchman" system pre-dominated. Most officers hired by university and college administrators had no formal law-enforcement experience and were typically people who had retired from other occupations. Rarely performing any true police or law-enforcement functions, they acted in a custodial capacity for their campuses.

A subtle transformation in the established watchman system occurred in campus policing in the 1930's and 1940's. During the late 1930's, campus watchmen were increasingly entrusted with additional duties, including some with true law-enforcement functions, as well as the enforcement of campus rules. However, while these quasi-police officers were still used primarily as campus custodians, they had the added responsibility of campus social control.

Emergence of Modern Campus Police

Modern campus police forces finally began to emerge during the 1950's, as American colleges and universities were entering an era of unprecedented growth in both student enrollments and campus sizes. During that period, university and college administrators began acknowledging the need for the full-time presence of law-enforcement officers on their campuses. Many chose to hire retired municipal police officers to act as campus security officers.

These newly hired campus security officers began the transformation of campus watchmen to full-fledged security officers and, finally, campus police officers. In an effort to become more professional and autonomous, campus security officers generally broke away from the traditional affiliations with physical plants and affiliated with upper administrations. However, despite the administrative and organizational changes occurring in campus policing during the 1950's, the primary duties of the officers remained custodial. They had no more power to police the behavior of students and campus visitors than any other ordinary citizen.

Until the 1960's, the legal doctrine of *in loco parentis* (in place of parents) guided the relations of campus security officers and students. This doctrinal basis created many unforeseen problems for campus security as well as administrations. Campus security officers might legally be able to detain troublesome outside visitors to their campuses, but enrolled students who caused problems were generally referred to campus administrators for disciplinary action. Moreover, campus security officers had to refer cases involving faculty or staff to local municipal police.

The last major shift in campus policing occurred during the era of campus social unrest of the 1960's. As student protests became increasingly unruly, college and university administrators were forced to admit that they had to create more efficient mechanisms to deal with the growing problem of campus strife. In conjunction with previously hired campus security officers, college administrators utilized the existing model of municipal law enforcement. As a result campus police started reorganizing along the lines of traditional paramilitary police hierarchies, complete with badges, police uniforms, and firearms.

Modern campus police have witnessed increases in the size of most departments, as college and university enrollments have grown. By the year 2005, 680 different institutions had their own campus police departments. These departments had an average of twenty-one full-time employees, including twelve sworn officers. Duties of campus police officers in the twenty-first century include routine patrols, building lockup, personal-safety escorts, and alarm monitoring.

As a result of decades of growth and professionalization, campus police forces have evolved from campus custodians and watchmen to the modern campus police forces seen on today's college and university campuses. As educational requirements for recruits have grown more rigorous, campus police have become increasingly similar to municipal law-enforcement agencies, and campus police work is now becoming an important law-enforcement career choice.

Wendy L. Hicks

Further Reading

Fisher, Bonnie, and John J. Sloan. *Campus Crime: Legal, Social, and Policy Perspectives.* Springfield, Ill.: Charles C Thomas, 1997.

Powell, John, Michael Pander, and Robert Nielsen. *Campus Security and Law Enforcement.* 2d ed. St. Louis, Mo.: Butterworth-Heinemann, 1994.

Rengert, George F. *Campus Security: Situational Crime Prevention in High-Density Environ-*

ments. Monsey, N.Y.: Willow Tree Publishing, 2001.

See also Community-oriented policing; Date rape; Law enforcement; Police; Private police and guards; School violence.

Canadian justice system

Criminal justice issues: International law; law-enforcement organization

Significance: As a neighbor of the United States and one with which the United States shares a long border, Canada is a nation whose criminal justice system is of great importance to many Americans.

A democratic federation comprising ten provinces and three territories, Canada occupies the northern half of North America. Most of Canada's 32 million people reside in urban areas, and the vast majority live within one hundred miles of the U.S. border. North of this band of settlement, geographic conditions grow increasingly harsh, and the population is sparse in most areas. Canada's land mass of about 3,855,081 square miles makes it the second largest country in the world. However, its population is only about the same size as that of the state of California, which is one-twenty-fifth its size.

The first inhabitants of Canada were Indians and Inuits (Eskimos). European involvement in Canada began in 1497, when the Italian navigator John Cabot landed on the Atlantic coast of North America and claimed it for England. Four decades later, France began claiming parts of North America and introducing its own settlers. European ownership of Canada was settled by the Seven Years War, whose 1763 treaty gave Great Britain control of the region. Most of the European settlers were of French and English descent, a fact that left Canada with a dual cultural heritage. The right of Canada to self-government was recognized in 1849. In 1867 Canada became a fully self-governing dominion within the British Empire. Canada is now fully independent but still recognizes British monarchs as its titular heads of state.

Legal Tradition

Canada's modern criminal justice system grew out of two distinct traditions: Roman law and English common law. The common legal tradition is based upon the tenants of Roman civil law and was put into practice in England by William the Conqueror in 1066. With this system, law was originally defined through immemorial custom. Judges, as did everyone else in the community, knew what behavior was acceptable. The common law is unique in that it cannot be found in any written codes or legislation; it exists only in past judicial decisions. This makes it flexible for an evolving society.

The tradition of civil law is quite different. Crime in the civil legal tradition is defined through codification. Questions as to what constitutes criminal acts are relatively simple. By contrast, civil law has been associated with a "civil code," containing almost all private law. Unlike common-law courts, courts in civil-law systems look first to the codes and only then refer to previous court decisions for consistency. Other than in the province Quebec, whose civil law was codified on the model of France, Canada's criminal and private law has its basis in English common and statutory law.

Canada indigenous peoples had their own sets of laws and customs. Aboriginal rights and treaty rights are protected under Canada's modern constitution. Aboriginal rights are those relating to the historical occupancy and use of the land by Aboriginal peoples, and treaty rights are those set out in treaties entered into between the British crown and individual groups of Aboriginal people.

Government

Like the United States, Canada is a federal system. The nation as a whole is governed by Parliament, which is led by a prime minister. The prime minister is the head of the government, and the monarch of Great Britain is the head of state. The British monarchs appoint governor generals to represent them in Canada's parliament. Like the U.S. Congress, parliament is divided into two chambers, the Senate and the House of Commons. All members of the Senate are appointed; members of the House of Commons are elected. In contrast to the U.S. system of government, members of parliament are not elected to fixed terms. Elections can be held whenever the party in power calls them. Also in contrast to the American political system, elected members of the Canadian House of Commons follow strict party discipline and have difficulty voting against the party line. Members of the prime minister's party who vote against their own party's legislation may be expelled from the party.

In addition to the national parliament in the capital city of Ottawa, every province and territory has its own legislature to make local laws. Whenever the national parliament or provincial legislatures pass laws, the new laws take the place of common law dealing with the same matters. Because of the complexity of modern society, more laws are made today than ever before. To solve this problem, parliament and provincial legislatures often pass general laws delegating authority to make more specific laws called regulations. Regulations serve to carry out the purposes of or expand on the general laws.

Like the United States, Canada operates under the rule of law, which means that everyone is subject to the same laws. No one, no matter how important or powerful, is above the law. Also like the United States, but unlike Britain, Canada has a written constitution. Its constitution does not contain any information on prime ministerial qualifications, methods of election or removal, or most of the prime minister's powers.

Moreover, none of these matters is addressed in any act of parliament, aside from the provision of the prime minster's salary, pension, and residence. Every other aspect of the office is a matter of convention. In fact, there is not even a law requiring prime ministers, or any other ministers, to have seats in parliament. The fact that all ministers do have seats in parliament is simply a custom.

Police

Canada has a decentralized police system, whose forces are divided among provincial, municipal, and federal units. The Royal Canadian Mounted Police (RCMP) is the national police service and an agency of the Ministry of Public Safety and Emergency Preparedness Canada. Its primary responsibilities include enforcing federal statutes and executive orders, providing protective services, policing airports and government buildings, and policing remote regions. The RCMP sometimes works with municipal and provincial forces. The RCMP is the only policing agency serving the Yukon and Northwest Territories, which combined account for more than one-third of Canada's entire territory—a region larger than all of Mexico.

Municipal police forces have jurisdiction over the most heavily populated areas and comprise city, village, county, and township police forces. By law, the provinces must financially support municipal police forces. Police services can be contracted out on the municipal level as well. For example, some cities and towns contract for the services of their provincial police or of the RCMP, which provides provincial police services in eight provinces.

In cases in which the RCMP is contracted to provide police services to a municipality, its local unit is accountable to the municipal chief executive. The contracting system is highly cost effective, for both the provinces and the municipalities. Provincial policing is largely decentralized. In 2005, Ontario and Quebec were currently the only provinces that operated their own provincial police. Generally, the duties of provincial police cover those areas not already covered by municipal police forces, although there are continuous exchanges of information among the provincial and local agencies.

Canada's solicitor general is accountable to parliament for the operation of four ministry agencies: the Royal Canadian Mounted Police, the Correctional Service, the National Parole Board, and the Canadian Security Intelligence Service. The Canadian Security Intelligence Service (CSIS) is a government agency dedicated to protecting the national security interests of Canada. It has a mandate to collect, analyze, and retain information or intelligence on activities that may on reasonable grounds be suspected of constituting threats to Canada's security. The CSIS can also provide security assessments to all federal departments and agencies, with the exception of the RCMP.

Courts

Canada's criminal courts are adversarial common-law courts, which are divided among four levels. Provincial courts handle the great majority of cases that come into the system. These cases are mainly the less serious and nonviolent crimes. Second are the provincial and territorial superior courts, which handle more serious crimes and also take appeals from provincial court judgments. At the same level, but responsible for different issues, are the federal trial division courts. The next level contains the provincial courts of appeal and the federal court of appeal. The highest level is occupied by the Supreme Court of Canada.

Constitutional authority for Canada's judicial system is divided between the federal and provincial governments. The provincial governments have jurisdiction over the administration of justice within their own territories, but the federal government has the exclusive authority to appoint and support the judges of the superior courts based in the provinces. Parliament also has the authority to establish a general court of appeal and courts for the better administration of the laws of Canada. Parliament created the Supreme Court of Canada, the federal courts, and the tax courts. In addition, parliament has exclusive authority over procedures in courts of criminal jurisdiction. Federal authority for criminal law and procedures ensures reasonable and consistent treatment of criminal behavior across the country.

Criminal trials in Canada are similar to those

in the United States. The prosecution has the burden of proving that the accused are guilty beyond a reasonable doubt. Also, if any evidence introduced in trials is obtained in ways that violate the defendants' rights, such as unreasonable search and seizures, judges may refuse to admit it.

Canadian trial judges have discretionary power to pass sentences, regardless of whether juries are present. However, for certain offenses, the judges' discretion may be limited by maximum, minimum, and fixed penalties provided under statute. When imposing sentences, judges refer to the principle "justice must always be tempered with mercy" for direction; it is a sentiment not often heard in American courts.

A method of keeping cases out of the courts is to utilize alternative dispute resolution (ADR). ADR allows people to settle their differences through means such as mediation and arbitration. The courts themselves often make use of ADR. However, for serious or violent crimes, or when mediation or arbitration is rejected, the formal court system remains indispensable.

Sentencing and Corrections

Prison sentences are generally regarded as a last resort in sentencing. Except in cases of capital and other serious crimes, it is unusual for first-time offenders to be incarcerated. The majority of offenders serve four or five probationary terms before they are given their first prison sentences. The primary goal of Canadian corrections is to reintegrate offenders into the community, through guidance, supervision, and training. Some inmates with sentences of ninety days or less are given intermittent sentences in which they serve their prison time on the weekends. After completing at least one-sixth of their sentences, federal and provincial inmates can be released on full or day parole.

The Mandatory Release Program is a federal program in which prison inmates who complete two-thirds of their sentences with good behavior are released into the community but remain under correctional authority until their time warrants expire. Although they are accountable to parole officers, they are technically not "on parole," as no parole boards make decisions concerning their release. Their parole officers serve

mainly as resources for the released inmates, helping them to find housing and employment and acting as counselors, rather than as wardens.

An innovative corrections program is the Land Program, in which offenders in the Northwest Territories are often placed. This plan is designed to accommodate members of hunter-gatherer cultures, which are still prevalent among the Aboriginal peoples of those regions. Inmates in the Land Program are allowed to carry firearms to hunt caribou, which provide meat for the hunters, their families, and their communities. The guards who oversee inmates in this program are not armed. Despite the ostensibly dangerous situation, no incidents of escapes or violence occurred during the first fifteen years after the program began in 1990.

Parliament abolished Canada's death penalty in 1976. The maximum sentence for first-degree murder convictions is called "Life-25"—life imprisonment with the first chance of parole set at twenty-five years.

International Cooperation

The United States and Canada have long-standing agreements on law-enforcement cooperation that include treaties on extradition and mutual legal assistance. Both countries participate in the Cross-Border Crime Forum. A logical approach to law enforcement and border cooperation ensures an effective and efficient way to target cross-border crime, including attempts by transnational criminal organizations to move arms, drugs, and human cargo across the border.

Canada's Transfer of Offenders Act (1978) allows for the prison transfer and exchange of Canadian and foreign offenders to their home countries. Canada has prison transfer agreements with the United States, Mexico, most of the nations of Western Europe, and several other nations.

Not only has Canada abolished capital punishment, it refuses to extradite most prisoners wanted for capital offenses to other countries without first obtaining assurances that they will not be executed. This prohibition extends to the United States, which is one of the few industrialized nations that still has capital punishment. In 1999, the Supreme Court of Canada ruled unanimously that a Canadian teenager and his friend could not be extradited to the state of Washington for a triple-murder case unless the state first assured Canada that the accused would not be executed.

Heidi V. Schumacher

Further Reading

Brown, Desmond H. *The Birth of a Criminal Code: The Evolution of Canada's Justice System*. Toronto: University of Toronto Press, 1995. Brown documents the evolution of the Canadian Criminal Code, largely through legislative initiatives that laid the foundation of the Canadian justice system and marked its departure from the legal traditions of England.

Dekeseredy, Walter S. *Women, Crime, and the Canadian Criminal Justice System*. Cincinnati: Anderson Publishing, 1999. Examination of the nature and extent of female crime in Canada and the justice system's response to it. Special attention is given to the relationship between women victims of crime who become offenders.

Ebbe, Obi N. Ignatius. *Comparative and International Criminal Justice Systems: Policing, Judiciary, and Corrections*. 2d ed. Boston: Butterworth-Heinemann, 2000. Study of criminal justice systems in Africa, Asia, the Middle East, Europe, and North and South America, specifically covering police, judiciary, and corrections systems. The contributors examine these diverse justice systems and seek to isolate the philosophies motivating criminal justice in countries with low crime rates.

Gerlach, Neil. *The Genetic Imaginary: DNA in the Canadian Criminal Justice System*. Toronto: University of Toronto Press, 2004. DNA testing and banking have become institutionalized in the Canadian criminal justice system, and this book critically examines the social, legal, and criminal justice origins and effects of the practices. Gerlach attempts to clarify why Canadians have accepted DNA technology with barely a ripple of public outcry.

Reichel, Philip L. *Comparative Criminal Justice Systems: A Topical Approach*. 3d ed. Upper Saddle River, N.J.: Prentice Hall, 2002. Offers a look at how criminal justice is practiced throughout the world. This book delves into the difference between police, corrections, and courts around the world.

Roberts, Julian V., Loretta J. Stalans, David Indermaur, and Mike Hough. *Penal Populism and Public Opinion: Lessons from Five Countries (Studies in Crime and Public Policy)*. New York: Oxford University Press, 2002. Although criminal justice systems vary greatly around the world, there has been a rise in the practice of severe punishment at a time when public opinion has played a pivotal role in sentencing policy and reforms. Startling commonalities exist among the five countries studied—Great Britain, the United States, Canada, Australia, and New Zealand.

Rounds, Delbert L. *International Criminal Justice: Issues in Global Perspective*. Upper Saddle River, N.J.: Allyn & Bacon, 1999. Examination of some of the world's most pressing issues in the field. Chapters cover such issues as drugs and policy, domestic violence, nuclear proliferation, money laundering, policing, juvenile delinquency, correctional systems, capital punishment, and gun-control policy.

See also Criminal justice in U.S. history; Extradition; International Association of Chiefs of Police; International law; Interpol; Mexican justice system; Royal Canadian Mounted Police; World Court.

Capital punishment

Definition: Execution of defendants convicted of capital crimes

Criminal justice issues: Capital punishment; punishment

Significance: Capital punishment has been one of the most debated topics in criminal justice policy in the United States, which at the beginning of the twenty-first century was one of the few remaining Western democracies still to employ the death penalty.

While the use of capital punishment as a criminal justice policy has been substantially reduced or eliminated in many countries around the world,

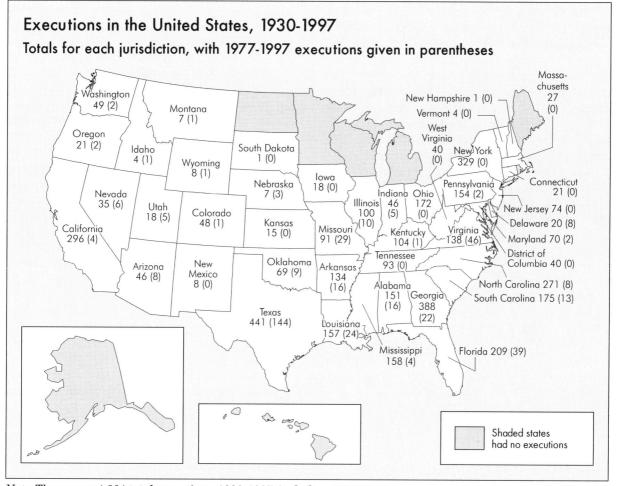

Executions in the United States, 1930-1997

Totals for each jurisdiction, with 1977-1997 executions given in parentheses

Washington 49 (2)
Montana 7 (1)
Oregon 21 (2)
Idaho 4 (1)
Wyoming 8 (1)
South Dakota 1 (0)
Iowa 18 (0)
Nevada 35 (6)
Utah 18 (5)
Colorado 48 (1)
Nebraska 7 (3)
California 296 (4)
Kansas 15 (0)
Missouri 91 (29)
Arizona 46 (8)
New Mexico 8 (0)
Oklahoma 69 (9)
Arkansas 134 (16)
Texas 441 (144)
Louisiana 157 (24)
Mississippi 158 (4)
Alabama 151 (16)
Georgia 388 (22)
Tennessee 93 (0)
Kentucky 104 (1)
Illinois 100 (10)
Indiana 46 (5)
Ohio 172 (0)
Virginia 138 (46)
Florida 209 (39)
North Carolina 271 (8)
South Carolina 175 (13)
West Virginia 40 (0)
New Hampshire 1 (0)
Vermont 4 (0)
New York 329 (0)
Pennsylvania 154 (2)
Massachusetts 27 (0)
Connecticut 21 (0)
New Jersey 74 (0)
Delaware 20 (8)
Maryland 70 (2)
District of Columbia 40 (0)

Shaded states had no executions

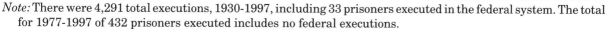

Note: There were 4,291 total executions, 1930-1997, including 33 prisoners executed in the federal system. The total for 1977-1997 of 432 prisoners executed includes no federal executions.

Source: U.S. Department of Justice, Bureau of Justice Statistics, *Capital Punishment 1997* (December, 1998).

the death penalty continues to be utilized as the ultimate punishment for criminal behavior.

Between 1608 and the year 2004, the number of people legally executed in what is now the United States has been estimated to be between 20,000 and 22,500. From January, 1977, to July, 2004, alone, 921 executions were carried out in the United States. By the end of 2004, more than 3,400 convicted felons were being held on death rows across the United States. By that time, thirty-eight states, the federal government, and the U.S. military had laws permitting the use of capital punishment. Although a small portion of states account for the majority of executions, seven of the jurisdictions—including the U.S.

military—conducted no executions at all between 1972 and 2003. Of the thirty-eight states with the death penalty, all but three also permit the sentencing of offenders to life in prison without the possibility of parole.

Although the specific circumstances of death-eligible cases vary from jurisdiction to jurisdiction, few states now authorize the use of capital punishment for offenses other than murder. At the federal level, the death penalty can be sought in aggravated murder cases, as well as in four offenses that may not involve homicide: treason, espionage, large-scale drug trafficking, and attempted murder of officers, witnesses, or jurors in cases involving continuing criminal enterprises.

The majority of capital cases involve adult male offenders, but a small percentage involve women and juvenile offenders. Women represent a small percentage of death-row inmates and felons who are actually executed. Throughout the twentieth century and the first years of the twenty-first century, women accounted for only forty-nine executions in the United States. Only ten women were executed between 1976 and 2004, and forty-nine women awaited execution in 2004.

Also representing a small proportion of the death-row population and number of executions are juvenile offenders. Twenty-two executions of offenders who committed their crimes when they were under the age of eighteen account for less than 2 percent of all executions carried out between 1976 and 2004. In 2004, seventy-two offenders on death rows in twelve states were considered juvenile offenders. Nineteen of the thirty-eight states with death-penalty laws permitted the execution of juvenile offenders, but only seven states carried out such sentences between 1976 and 2004.

Capital Punishment in History

The history of capital punishment in America dates back to early colonial times. Early settlers were influenced by their British counterparts, whose laws mandated the death penalty for more than 150 separate crimes. While the laws on

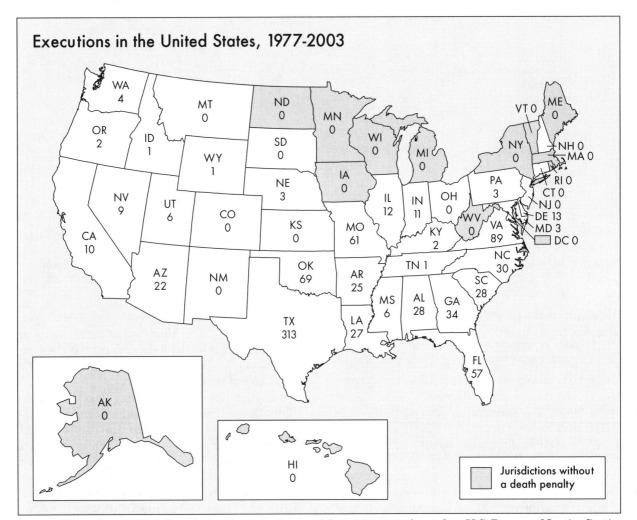

Executions in the United States, 1977-2003

State	Executions
WA	4
MT	0
ND	0
MN	0
VT	0
ME	0
OR	2
ID	1
SD	0
WI	0
MI	0
NY	0
NH	0
MA	0
WY	1
NE	3
IA	0
PA	3
RI	0
NV	9
UT	6
CO	0
IL	12
IN	11
OH	0
CT	0
NJ	0
DE	13
CA	10
KS	0
MO	61
KY	2
WV	0
VA	89
MD	3
DC	0
AZ	22
NM	0
OK	69
AR	25
TN	1
NC	30
MS	6
AL	28
GA	34
SC	28
TX	313
LA	27
FL	57
AK	0
HI	0

Jurisdictions without a death penalty

Source: Through 1978, U.S. Law Enforcement Assistance Administration; thereafter, U.S. Bureau of Justice Statistics, *Capital Punishment*, annual.

Marchers in Missouri's capital city protesting an impending execution in March, 1999. One of the many arguments made against capital punishment is that violence should not be used to punish violence. *(AP/Wide World Photos)*

death sentencing varied from colony to colony, its practice was dramatically reduced in comparison to Britain. Massachusetts had one of the strictest laws on the books, with twelve crimes that were considered "death-eligible."

In contrast, colonies dominated by Quakers were more lenient in their use of executions. They restricted the death penalty to cases of treason and murder. However, decisions to execute sparingly were not made solely for philosophical reasons, but because of the colonies' need for able-bodied workers.

The number of executions in the United States increased significantly during the nineteenth century. However, the rate of executions reached its peak during the 1930's, when more than sixteen hundred people were put to death in the country.

Methods of Execution

Just as the policies on capital punishment have evolved from colonial times, so, too, have the methods by which executions are carried out. Early methods, such as burning at the stake and beheading, have since been ruled as unconstitutional on the grounds that they violate the Eighth Amendment's protection against cruel and unusual punishment. Death by hanging is the only early method that has stood the test of time; it has been responsible for the greatest number of executions. A few U.S. states still permit hanging, but methods such as electrocution, firing squads, and lethal gas are now either rarely used or have been declared unconstitutional.

By the early twenty-first century, lethal injection had become the primary method of execution in most states with death penalties. It was created in an effort to provide a more humane and socially acceptable method of execution. Lethal injections generally use three drugs: sodium thiopental sedates the convicted felon; pancuronium bromide provides a total muscle relaxant; and potassium chloride induces cardiac arrest, which results in death.

Opposition to Capital Punishment

As executions surged during the nineteenth century, an anti-death-penalty movement also began to develop. During that period, several changes were made to the policies and practices of capital punishment that abolitionists viewed as progress toward its elimination in the United States. First, states began to change the processes by which death sentences were handed down. Up until that time, all the states utilized mandatory death sentencing for specific offenses. That practice changed in 1838, when Tennessee became the first state to change its capital sentencing policy to allow discretion in sentencing. The modern U.S. Supreme Court has declared mandatory death sentences as unconstitutional.

The second nineteenth century change came when several states limited the number of offenses that were considered death-eligible. Southern states expanded the use of capital punishment for slaves, but the majority of states limited its use to crimes of murder and treason. In 1846, Michigan became the first state to abolish the death penalty for all crimes, with the exception of treason.

A third change was the transformation of executions from public to private events. Previously, hangings had traditionally been held in public squares in order to deter criminal activity, and religious readings and prayers provided a foundation for the occasions. However, public executions often created public disorder as a result of public drunkenness, botched executions, and rioting. In 1834, Pennsylvania became the first state to remove executions from public view. The last public execution in the United States was conducted in 1937. Now, public attendance at executions is limited to small numbers of citizens. Access by journalists is also limited, and legal efforts to televise executions to the public have failed.

In addition to policy changes that limited the use of capital punishment, several states began to abandon the practice in its entirety during the late nineteenth and early twentieth centuries. In 1852, Rhode Island became the first state to eliminate the use of the death penalty for all crimes. Since then, several states have abolished the death penalty, only to reinstate it at later dates in response to political or public pressures. In 2005, twelve states, the District of Columbia, and

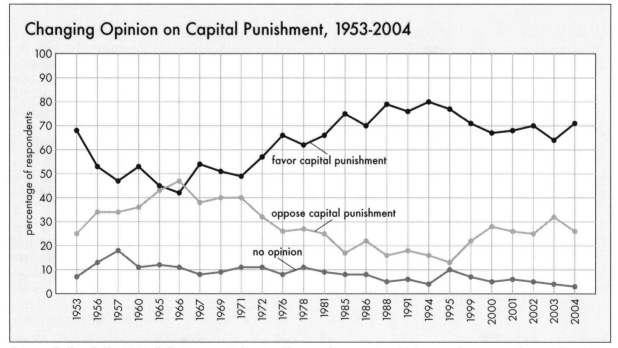

Source: Gallup Polls, 2004. Polls were not taken in all years. In years in which more than one poll was taken, data are entered from the latest polls.

Puerto Rico did not use capital punishment for any crimes.

Supreme Court Decisions

A primary legal issue relating to capital punishment is whether the death penalty violates the Eighth Amendment's protection against cruel and unusual punishment. Before reviewing the constitutionality of the death penalty as a practice, the U.S. Supreme Court addressed the question of how to define cruel and unusual punishment. In 1878, the Court ruled specific forms of torture as unconstitutional in its *Wilkerson v. Utah* decision. That ruling was explicit in specifying what types of execution procedures were cruel and unusual, but the Court's later rulings were less specific.

In *Weems v. United States* (1910), the Court argued that decisions on what constitutes cruel and unusual punishment are not immutable and limited by the beliefs of the framers of the Bill of Rights. Rather, definitions should be subject to interpretation and change. The Court's 1958 *Trop v. Dulles* ruling elaborated on this point, arguing that the definition of cruel and unusual should come from the evolving standards of decency as defined by modern society.

After the *Trop* ruling, measuring the evolving standards of decency led to several changes in death-penalty policy. In 1972, in *Furman v. Georgia*, the Supreme Court overturned state statutes on capital punishment nationwide in a 5-4 vote. The Court found that then-current laws violated the cruel and unusual clause of the Eighth and Fourteenth Amendments. As other justices in the past had debated on the definition of cruel and unusual punishments, so, too, did the *Furman* Court. Justices William J. Brennan and Thurgood Marshall argued that the death penalty itself was inherently cruel and unusual, Justices William O. Douglas, Potter Stewart, and Byron R. White argued that the statutes themselves constituted cruel and unusual punishment as they were arbitrary and were implemented with wide degrees of discretion. With the *Furman* ruling, the death sentences of all the prisoners awaiting execution on death rows throughout the nation were invalidated.

After the Supreme Court's *Furman* decision, legislators looked for ways of ensuring that capital punishment could be administered fairly and equitably, so that the death penalty could be reinstated. Newly written state statutes passed constitutional muster in several 1976 Supreme Court decisions, the most notable of which was *Gregg v. Georgia*. These new Court rulings reopened the floodgates for executions to continue.

The new state laws were designed to set standards for judges and juries in capital cases. First, a bifurcated process was to be conducted for all death-penalty trials, in which the guilt/innocence phases would be separated from the sentencing phases. Second, presentation of information on mitigating and aggravating factors was allowed during the sentencing phases, in which aggravating circumstances had to outweigh the mitigating circumstances before the death penalty could be awarded. Third, all death sentences became subject to automatic reviews by the states' supreme courts. Finally, the states were required periodically to conduct studies of proportionality to determine whether disparities in sentencing were developing.

The conditions outlined in *Gregg* passed the constitutional requirements of the Court in 1976, but the Court's justices continue to argue whether capital punishment itself represents cruel and unusual punishment. Later Court decisions continued to apply the criteria of the evolving standards of decency to limit which offenders may be subjected to capital punishment. In *Penry v. Lynaugh* in 1989, the Court held that the execution of the mentally retarded did not constitute cruel and unusual punishment. However, the Court overturned this decision in 2002 in *Atkins v. Virginia* (2002). In its latter decision, the Court found that a national consensus had developed against the practice of executing the mentally retarded and held that such a practice violates Eighth Amendment protections.

The *Atkins v. Virginia* ruling opened the possibility of other challenges to capital punishment. One example is the execution of juvenile offenders. In 1988, the Court held in *Thompson v. Oklahoma* that offenders under the age of sixteen at the time they commit their crimes are not eligible to receive death sentences. In 2002, four justices voted to hear the case of Kevin Nigel Stanford, who was seventeen at the time of his crime. Their dissenting opinion indicated that not only did

A Mixed Movie Message About Capital Punishment

The 2003 film *The Life of David Gale* makes a curious case against capital punishment. Kevin Spacey plays the title character, a philosophy professor, who is convicted of murder and sentenced to death for killing a woman (Laura Linney) who had participated in anti-death penalty activism with him. Shortly before Gale's scheduled execution, he invites a reporter (Kate Winslet) to hear his story. When the reporter later comes into possession of a videotape showing that the woman's death was a suicide, she tries unsuccessfully to deliver this new evidence to authorities before the professor is executed. Afterward, she discovers that the professor and his alleged victim voluntarily cooperated in the latter's death with the specific intent of having the professor wrongfully executed. The conspirators wanted his wrongful conviction to be discovered too late to stop his execution, hoping that these circumstances would promote public opposition to the death penalty. In other words, both the professor and his alleged victim sacrifice their lives in the cause of ending capital punishment.

The final plot development in *The Life of David Gale* confuses the film's anti-death penalty message. An innocent man is convicted, to be sure, and the possibility of such convictions is a key argument against the death penalty. However, the fact that the innocent man deliberately manipulates the justice system to ensure his own execution makes it difficult to take from the film any clear lesson about the criminal justice system.

Timothy L. Hall

they wish to revisit the issue of the juvenile death penalty, they were prepared to declare it as an unconstitutional practice. The state of Kentucky granted clemency to Stanford and commuted his death sentence to life in prison without the possibility of parole, but the U.S. Supreme Court was still left with the issue of the juvenile death penalty.

In 2003, Missouri's supreme court, drawing largely on the rationale set forth in *Atkins*, declared juvenile executions unconstitutional. The Missouri court referenced public and professional opinion, as well as declining legislative support for capital punishment in its decision. On March 1, 2005, the U.S. Supreme Court upheld the Missouri court ruling in a 5-4 decision. Writing for the majority, Justice Anthony Kennedy stated that to extinguish a juvenile's life before he attains the maturity to understand his own humanity would be cruel and unusual punishment.

Arguments for and Against Capital Punishment

Death-penalty supporters argue that capital punishment should be retained on the basis of retribution and deterrence. Most people who support the death penalty favor it because of the principle of retribution. Retribution is often described by the concept of *lex talionis*, or "an eye for an eye"—a principle holding that punishments must be proportionate responses to crimes. *Lex talionis* is also often associated with the concept of revenge. Retribution is also characterized as just deserts, holding that offenders deserve to be punished for their actions.

Supporters of the death penalty argue that for justice to be served and for order to be restored to the community, society requires the execution of offenders as payment for their crimes. In contrast, death-penalty opponents argue that criminal justice policies should not be based on a retributive position because revenge is an emotional, rather than a reasonable, response. They further argue that the death penalty is a disproportionate response when compared to other sentencing philosophies, as the American system does not rape rapists or steal from thieves.

In contrast to the emotionally laden concept of retribution, deterrence is viewed as a more rational and scientific argument for capital punishment. Proponents are quick to argue that the death penalty provides for both specific and general deterrence. Not only do executions prevent convicted murderers from killing again, but the belief is that if murderers are executed, other potential murderers will think twice before committing murder, for fear of losing their own lives. However, deterrence theory assumes that offenders are thinking individuals who rationally consider the potential consequences of their actions before engaging in them.

Opponents to the death penalty argue that deterrence can be achieved by incarcerating offenders for life without the possibility of parole. Additionally, they argue that if the death penalty were, in fact, an effective deterrent, murder rates would increase when it is abolished and decline when it is restored. However, little empirical research has been done to provide support for general deterrence theory. Proponents counteract this argument by stating that the death penalty as it is currently administered in the United States may not provide a deterrent effect because the average length of time that persons sentenced to death spend awaiting their executions is overly long.

Wrongful Convictions

Between 1973 and 2004, 114 inmates were released from death row after new evidence demonstrated that they had been wrongfully convicted. Their releases seemed to refute arguments presented by supporters of capital punishment that only the guilty are sentenced to death row. In the state of Illinois, thirteen death-row inmates were exonerated between 1977 and 2000, while twelve others were executed. Illinois's Governor George Ryan, previously a strong supporter of the death penalty, expressed concern that the system of handing out death sentences in his state may have allowed executions of the innocent, so he declared a moratorium on executions in 2000. Following a two-year investigation by a commission appointed by Ryan to review capital sentencing procedures, the commission made eighty-five recommendations on the processing of capital cases to ensure a system of fair, equitable, and accurate sentencing. Illinois incorporated some of those recommendations, but many, such as the immediate appointment of counsel, remained to be implemented. Meanwhile, following reviews of Illinois's death-row population, Governor Ryan commuted the sentences of 156 inmates awaiting execution to life in prison without parole.

Proponents of capital punishment disagree with the argument that it is administered in a discriminatory fashion. In 2004, about 46 percent of the prisoners held on death rows were classified as white and 42 percent were black. Similarly, 57 percent of post-*Furman* executions involved white offenders, while 34 percent of executions during the same time period involved black offenders. However, while the majority of inmates and executions have involved white offenders, such statistics do not take into account the proportion of population demographics. Opponents argue that the death penalty is disproportionately applied to African Americans, who constitute only 12 percent of the entire population.

While the role of race in capital punishment sentences remains a subject of debate, a review of post-*Furman* executions provided additional evidence for opponents of capital punishment, as 80 percent of all execution cases involved white murder victims, even though white victims constitute only about 50 percent of all murder victims nationwide. Issues of discrimination are also raised on the variable of class, as poor defendants are unable to obtain the resources to provide an adequate defense

Some critics of capital punishment charge that the death penalty is applied randomly, without concern for legal criteria. While proponents contend that the death penalty is applied in an equitable fashion, opponents disagree. Because the death penalty is actually invoked in only a small number of death-eligible cases, two different offenders who commit similar crimes may receive dramatically different sentences: death versus life imprisonment. Additionally, evidence demonstrates that the death penalty is subject to significant jurisdictional differences, as the majority of post-*Furman* executions have been carried out by southern states. Texas alone accounted for more than one third of all executions between 1972 and 2004.

Conclusion

Even as capital punishment remains a subject of debate, raising issues such as deterrence, retribution, innocence, and discrimination, it remains a component of the American criminal justice system. Questions of who should be executed, for what crimes, and by what methods have been addressed throughout American history and continue to be debated. Recent decisions to limit the application of the death penalty, to declare moratoriums against executions, and to declare the practice in itself as unconstitutional indicate that support for capital punishment may be fading. Regardless of the future of the death penalty, it has sealed its place in history as the ultimate punishment philosophy in criminal justice policy.

Stacy L. Mallicoat

Further Reading

Banner, Stuart. *The Death Penalty: An American History.* Boston, Mass.: Harvard University Press, 2003. Scholarly history of capital punishment in the United States.

Bedau, Hugo Adam, and Paul Cassell. *Debating the Death Penalty: Should America Have Capital Punishment? The Experts on Both Sides Make Their Best Case.* Oxford, England: Oxford University Press, 2003. Collection of essays on a variety of aspects of capital punishment by both supporters and opponents of the death penalty.

Bohm, Robert M. *Deathquest: An Introduction to the Theory and Practice of Capital Punishment in the United States.* Cincinnati: Anderson Publishing, 2003. Introductory text highlighting facts, figures, and arguments on capital punishment in the United States.

Johnson, Robert. *Death Work: A Study of the Modern Execution Process.* Belmont, Calif.: Wadsworth, 1998. Details life on death row for both offenders and the guards who work with them.

Prejean, Helen. *Dead Man Walking: An Eyewitness Account to the Death Penalty in the United States.* New York: Vintage Books, 1993. Narrative story detailing the experience of a Roman Catholic nun who served as a spiritual advisor for death-row inmates in Louisiana.

Radelet, Michael L., Hugo Adam Bedau, and Constance E. Putnam. *In Spite of Innocence: Erroneous Convictions in Capital Cases.* Boston: Northeastern University Press, 1994. Review of wrongful convictions in capital murder cases that discusses how issues in the criminal justice process have led to the incarceration of the innocent.

State of Illinois. *Report of the Former Governor Ryan's Commission on Capital Punishment.* April, 2002. Report issued by the Illinois Commission on Capital Punishment detailing recommendations for improvements to current

death-penalty policy. The entire report can be found on the state's official Web site.

See also Antiterrorism and Effective Death Penalty Act; Bureau of Justice Statistics; *Coker v. Georgia;* Cruel and unusual punishment; Death qualification; Death-row attorneys; Deterrence; Execution, forms of; *Ford v. Wainwright; Furman v. Georgia; Gregg v. Georgia; McCleskey v. Kemp;* Murders, mass and serial; Punishment; Sentencing guidelines, U.S.; Supreme Court, U.S.; Treason.

Capone, Al

Identification: Gangster leader during the Prohibition era

Born: January 17, 1899; Brooklyn, New York

Died: January 25, 1947; Palm Island, Florida

Criminal justice issues: Business and financial crime; organized crime

Al Capone. (*Library of Congress*)

Actors Who Have Played Al Capone on the Screen

Year	Actor	Production
1932	Paul Muni	*Scarface*
1959-1960	Neville Brand	*The Untouchables* (TV series)
1959	Rod Steiger	*Al Capone*
1961	Neville Brand	*The George Raft Story*
1967	Jason Robards	*The St. Valentine's Day Massacre*
1973	Buddy Lester	*Poor Devil* (TV film)
1975	Ben Gazzara	*Capone*
1979	Roberto Malone	*Hot Life of Al Capone*
1981	Robert Costanzo	*Sizzle* (TV film)
1981	Louis Giambalvo	*The Gangster Chronicles* (TV miniseries)
1987	Robert DeNiro	*The Untouchables*
1987	Thomas G. Waites	*The Verne Miller Story*
1990	Eric Roberts	*The Lost Capone* (TV film)
1991	Titus Welliver	*Mobsters*
1992	Bernie Gigliotti	*The Babe*
1993	William Forsythe	*The Untouchables* (TV series)
1995	Kurt Andon	*Kiss of Death*
1995	F. Murray Abraham	*Dillinger and Capone*
1995	F. Murray Abraham	*Baby Face Nelson*
1997	André Lemay	*The Exotic Time Machine*
1999	Paul Campbell	*Third World Cop*
1999	Lou Vani	*Bonanno: A Godfather's Story* (TV film)
2002	Julian Littman	*Al's Lads*

Significance: Perhaps the most notorious American criminal of the twentieth century, Capone remains an icon of the organized crime that flourished during the Prohibition era, and his career provides an object lesson in the difficulties that law-enforcement officials had in building cases against powerful criminals.

Alphonse Capone was born in Brooklyn to Italian immigrant parents. As a youth, he joined a succession of street gangs and ran errands for Johnny Torrio, a powerful local crime boss, while also helping to support his family with legitimate jobs. After his face was badly cut in a knife fight, he acquired the nickname "Scarface," which has become almost as famous as the name "Al Capone."

Capone relocated to Chicago in 1921, the year after the Eighteenth Amendment to the U.S. Constitution prohibited the manufacture and sale of alcoholic beverages. Under Prohibition, new opportunities arose for organized crime, which made large profits by supplying alcohol illegally. Capone soon became Torrio's partner in managing Chicago houses of prostitution, speakeasies that served illegal alcohol, and gambling joints. After Torrio retired in 1924, Capone took over much of Chicago-area organized crime. By the end of the decade, Capone controlled what was probably the largest criminal organization in the United States.

In 1929, Capone moved to Miami. In February of that year, he ordered the killing of rival gangster leader George "Bugs" Moran. Moran himself escaped, but seven of his men were murdered in what became famous as the St. Valentine's Day Massacre. Despite the great amount of publicity that Capone subsequently received, prosecutors were unable to make serious criminal charges stick against him. However, at the urging of President Herbert Hoover, the U.S. Justice Department vigorously began pursuing Capone for bootlegging liquor and tax evasion. Capone's name then headed the Federal Bureau of Investigation's first "Most Wanted" list. His case was symbolic of the government's public battle with organized crime.

Capone was eventually convicted of federal tax evasion and sentenced to eleven years in federal penitentiaries. He began serving his sentence in Atlanta and was later transferred to the notorious federal prison on San Francisco Bay's Alcatraz Island. By the time he was released in 1939, he was in the advanced stages of syphilis, a disease he had contracted as a teenager. He later died quietly in his Florida home.

Phyllis B. Gerstenfeld

Further Reading

Bergreen, Laurence. *Capone: The Man and the Era*. New York: Touchstone Books, 1996.

Kobler, John. *Capone: The Life and World of Al Capone*. New York: Da Capo Press, 2003.

See also Gangsters of the Prohibition era; Organized crime; Prohibition; Saint Valentine's Day Massacre; Tax evasion.

Carjacking

Definition: Theft of vehicles that is committed while the vehicle owners are inside or near the vehicles

Criminal justice issues: Robbery, theft, and burglary; violent crime

Significance: Carjacking evokes a great deal of attention and emotion in people due to the violence or threatened violence that is typically associated with the crime. Carjackers often physically pull owners from their vehicles or force them to remain inside while they make their getaways. When victims of the crime are forced to remain in their vehicles, the crime of kidnapping also applies.

Sensationalist news media treatment of carjacking has placed fear in the hearts of millions of people who regularly drive in congested urban areas. The problem involves an apparent paradox: The more advanced the antitheft technology is on expensive vehicles, the greater the chances are that the owners of those vehicles will become victims of carjacking. The reason is simple: It can be easier for a car thief to steal a vehicle if its owner is in it, or nearby, with the ignition keys that defeat the vehicle's antitheft equipment. Drivers are especially vulnerable to carjacking when they are entering or exiting their vehicles.

In the twenty-first century, personal vehicles are important parts of the lives of many American citizens. The thought that at any time armed criminals can approach drivers and take their vehicles, while pointing guns or other weapons at them, causes much concern and apprehension among the car owners and drivers. While committing their crimes, carjackers also take the opportunity to rob vehicle owners of such personal items as wallets, purses, pocketbooks, and other personal effects.

Tracking the number of carjackings that take place in the United States each year is problematic. The Federal Bureau of Investigation's Uniform Crime Reports (UCR) do not officially track reported carjackings, which are classified as robberies. However, the National Crime Victimization Survey (NCVS), which is compiled by the U.S. Bureau of Justice Statistics, estimated that approximately 49,000 attempted or completed carjackings per year occurred in the early to mid-1990's.

Carjacking obtained notoriety in the United States after media attention was given to a number of incidents in the late 1980's and early 1990's. In one case in Howard County, Maryland, in September of 1992, a mother was placing her small infant in the car seat when two criminals approached her and forcibly took possession of the car with the child in the back seat. Believing that her child was at great risk, the victim attempted to retrieve her child from the car seat while the carjackers were preparing to speed away in her car. During this attempt to free her child, the victim's arm was caught in the seat-belt mechanism and she was dragged several miles to her death. The media focus on this crime and similar violent car thefts resulted in national attention on this ever-increasing problem. Later that year, Congress passed a law making carjacking a federal crime.

Jay Zumbrun

Further Reading

Bureau of Justice Statistics. *Carjackings in the United States, 1992-1996*. Washington, D.C.: U.S. Department of Justice, 1999.

Rand, Michael R. *Carjacking, National Crime Victimization Survey*. Crime Data Brief: U.S. Department of Justice, Office of Justice Programs, Bureau of Justice Statistics, 1994.

Ratledge, Marcus Wayne. *Hot cars! An Inside Look at the Auto Theft Industry*. Boulder, Colo.: Paladin Press, 1982.

See also Kidnapping; Motor vehicle theft; Robbery; Skyjacking; Uniform Crime Reports.

Case law

Definition: Body of past legal decisions that serve as binding authority for judges to issue rulings in cases

Criminal justice issues: Courts; judges; trial procedures

Significance: The use of case law requires judges, in most cases, to craft legal opinions consistent with history and tradition, thus promoting stability and efficiency in the court system.

The U.S. legal system is actually two largely separate systems. One is the federal system, which is composed of district courts at the trial level, circuit courts for appeals, and the U.S. Supreme Court as the highest authority. The second comprises state systems. Each state has different names for the courts within its system, but, at a minimum, every state has trial courts, appellate courts, and a high, or supreme, court.

The primary way in which judges make decisions in all U.S. courts is through the use of case law. Derived from the English common law, case law is a body of prior legal decisions that form the rule of law to be applied to cases before the courts. This concept of using prior decisions to regulate future decisions is more commonly referred to as the doctrine of *stare decisis*, a Latin phrase meaning "to stand by precedent."

A primary purpose of case law is to ensure that judges do not issue rulings based on their own personal opinions. This approach to judicial decision making creates consistency in the legal system and promotes fairness by making sure that people in the same jurisdiction are not treated differently, especially when their cases may be factually similar.

An important limitation to the use of case law is that prior decisions are binding upon courts only when they have been issued by higher courts within the same system. Therefore, a state court decision would not be binding on a federal court. Likewise, a decision made at the trial level in either system would not be binding on an appellate or supreme court within the same system. Decisions that are not binding on courts are known as "persuasive authority." When no binding authority exists on a particular legal question, parties may try using persuasive authority to persuade judges to decide cases in their favor.

Occasionally, past decisions are inconsistent with present societal norms. When this occurs, judges may issue rulings contrary to case law, thus establishing new binding authorities for future courts. A noteworthy historical example of this occurred when slavery was legal in the United States. Early judicial decisions found slavery to be constitutional. Once attitudes changed, the Supreme Court declared slavery unconstitutional, thus overruling its own well-established precedent. Consequently, it can be said that the use of case law in the judicial decision-making process is not absolute.

Kimberly J. Belvedere

Further Reading

Johns, Margaret, and Rex R. Perschbacher. *The United States Legal System: An Introduction*. Durham, N.C.: Carolina Academic Press, 2002.

Rehnquist, William H. *The Supreme Court*. New York: Alfred A. Knopf, 2001.

See also Common law; Discretion; Due process of law; Harmless error; Judges; Judicial review; Opinions; Precedent; *Stare decisis*; Trials.

Cease-and-desist orders

Definition: Order from court or agencies prohibiting certain persons or entities from continuing certain conduct

Criminal justice issues: Courts; judges

Significance: A cease-and-desist order provides a nonstatutory legal remedy to a situation in which one is giving offense but not breaking any specific law.

A cease-and-desist order is a judicial option used to prevent or halt behavior which may not, by itself, be illegal according to statutory law but which could lead to harm if not stopped. The order generally includes a notice of the right to a hearing, and usually there is at least an allegation of a statutory violation, with the appropriate law being cited. Law requires that the order be delivered either through the marshal's office or via registered mail. Tangible evidence of the order's issuance must be stored by a third party, often an attorney.

The issuance of a cease-and-desist order can be beneficial to individuals and to society as a whole. It puts an immediate halt to behavior or activity which could result in measurable harm if the slow-paced justice system were left to move at its usual speed. Such an order could prevent a wrong from occurring for which there is no totally appropriate remedy and no way to satisfy the aggrieved party.

Cease-and-desist orders may also have negative consequences. They have been used to stop reporters or whistle-blowers from exposing corporate wrongs. Issues of jurisdiction sometimes arise, as federal, state, and local judges are capable of issuing the orders. The clarity and uniformity of the various laws impacting the issuance are also questioned at times. Cease-and-desist orders undeniably give courts an effective tool for controlling individual behavior.

Thomas W. Buchanan

Further Reading

Garner, Bryan A., ed. *Black's Law Dictionary.* 8th ed. St. Paul, Minn.: Thomson/West, 2004.

Janosik, Robert J., ed. *Encyclopedia of the American Judicial System.* New York: Scribner, 1987.

See also Judges; Judicial system, U.S.; Jurisdiction of courts; Psychopathy; Restraining orders; Trespass.

Celebrity criminal defendants

Definition: Defendants in criminal proceedings who either are already widely known for unrelated reasons or become famous because of their criminal defenses

Criminal justice issues: Defendants; media

Significance: Although rare, the criminal trials of celebrities garner a great deal of media coverage. These highly publicized trials command great public attention but present distorted and unrealistic pictures of the daily workings of the criminal justice system.

"Celebrity" is by definition a social construct. People are celebrities because the media cover aspects of their lives that are presumably of interest to the general public. Celebrities typically include people who enjoy success in professional sports, entertainment, politics, or business. Celebrity can also be a result of criminal notoriety itself.

Celebrities Who Become Defendants

Celebrities charged with crimes rarely go to trial. Their wealth, power, and influence afford them many privileges, including absence from courtrooms. When they actually do go to trial, however, their cases typically saturate the news. Perhaps the best-known celebrity defendant of modern times to go to trial was former professional football star, actor, and sports commentator O. J. Simpson, who was tried for murdering his former wife and another man.

Other notable defendants have included boxer Mike Tyson who was tried for rape; televangelists Jim and Tammy Faye Bakker, tried for fraud and conspiracy; corporate executive John DeLorean, actor Robert Downey, Jr., and musician Bobby Brown, all of whom were tried for drug possession; Louisiana governor Edwin Edwards and

Ohio congressman James Traficant, Jr., both tried for racketeering; Panama's President Manuel Noriega, tried on drug trafficking charges; home decorating guru Martha Stewart, tried for, among other charges, securities fraud; and basketball superstar Kobe Bryant, who was a criminal defendant in a rape case.

Defendants Who Become Celebrities

Far more numerous than celebrity defendants are "defendant-celebrities"—individuals who, while ordinary in many respects, found themselves celebrated *because* of the media coverage of their crimes and trials. This category includes people who go through most of their lives outside the media spotlight until they become defendants. Their newsworthiness can be attributed to a variety of things. Often, it is due to the heinousness of their alleged crimes or their victimization of public figures, but it may also include elements such as the defendants' relatively privileged social standing, the locations of their alleged crimes, or the rarity or prurience of the crimes.

In many respects, the experiences of such people are dark manifestations of what artist Andy Warhol called everyone's "fifteen minutes of

Notable Celebrity Criminal Defendants

Date	Defendant	Basis of celebrity	Main charges	Outcome
1921	Fatty Arbuckle	film star	rape and manslaughter	acquitted but career was in ruins
1943	Errol Flynn	film star	statutory rape	acquitted
1944	Charles Chaplin	film star	violation of the Mann Act	acquitted
1977	Roman Polanski	film director	statutory rape and sodomy	convicted on plea bargain but fled country before sentencing
1991-1992	Michael Tyson	boxing champion	rape and deviant sexual conduct	convicted and sent to prison
1994-1995	O. J. Simpson	media personality, actor, former football star	double murder	acquitted in criminal case but lost civil case on wrongful death charges
2002	Winona Ryder	film star	shoplifting	convicted
2004	Kobe Bryant	basketball star	rape	criminal case dismissed before trial began; civil case settled out of court
2004	Martha Stewart	media personality and business executive	conspiracy, making false statements, obstruction of justice, and securities fraud	convicted on all counts and sent to federal prison
2004-2005	Jayson Williams	former basketball star	aggravated manslaughter	pending in 2005
2005	Robert Blake	actor	murder	acquitted
2005	Michael Jackson	pop music star	child molestation	acquitted
2005	Phil Spector	pop music producer	murder	pending in 2005

Martha Stewart

One of the most publicized celebrity defendants of the twenty-first century is Martha Stewart, who parlayed her homemaking and fashion skills into a multimillion dollar business empire and became a national icon of style and domesticity. However, her ethical reputation took a severe blow when she was charged with insider trading and other offenses.

In late 2001, the day before the stock of the ImClone company fell sharply because the Federal Drug Administration had refused to approve the company's new anticancer drug, Stewart sold her ImClone shares. Her

Flanked by uniformed officers of the U.S. Marshals Service, Martha Stewart leaves a federal courthouse after being sentenced to prison on July 16, 2004. (AP/Wide World Photos)

timely move gave the appearance of having been improperly influenced by inside information, and the federal government investigated her dealings. In June, 2003, Stewart was indicted, not for insider trading, but for conspiracy, making false statements, obstruction of justice, and securities fraud.

Stewart's indictment occasioned much speculation about the reason for federal interest in a case involving a stock transaction worth less than forty-six thousand dollars—a tiny fraction of Stewart's total assets—when nothing was being done about the multimillion dollar misdeeds of other business leaders. Many claimed that Stewart was singled out for attention because she was a self-made and eminently successful businesswoman and a celebrity. In March, 2004, Stewart and her stockbroker were convicted on all charges. Later sentenced to five months in a federal prison, she began serving her sentence in September, 2004, and was released in March, 2005.

Margaret Duggan

fame." This notorious category of defendants is the most diverse and populous of all celebrity criminal defendants and includes serial killers such as Charles Manson, organized-crime leaders such as John Gotti, high-priced sex-trade workers such as Heidi Fleiss, cold-blooded bombers such as Timothy McVeigh, would-be assassins such as John Hinckley, Jr., celebrity stalkers such as Robert Hoskins, statutory rapists such as schoolteacher Mary Kay LeTourneau, and criminal bankers such as Michael Milken.

Political Dissidence and Celebrity

A final category, "political-celebrity defendants," includes people who, while tried for street crimes, are thought by many to truly have been on trial for their political dissidence. This is to say that their status as criminal defendants has more to do with their controversial political activities than with their involvement in any form of criminal malfeasance. In the opinion of many

scholars, these people are often unfairly persecuted by the criminal justice system. While the relative legal merits, not to mention public opinion, vary greatly from one case to the next, it is interesting to note that while many of these people are actually convicted in courtrooms, history—if not the criminal justice system—eventually exonerates them.

A notable example of a political-celebrity defendant was the young social activist Frank Tannenbaum, who was later to become a distinguished professor at Columbia University and the author of the criminology classic *Crime and the Community* (1938). In 1914, Tannenbaum was tried in New York City for inciting to riot. He was convicted and sentenced to one year in prison and a five-hundred-dollar fine.

Other notables include labor activists and anarchists Nicola Sacco and Bartolomeo Vanzetti, who were tried, convicted, and executed in 1927 for their alleged robbery and murder of a paymaster and security guard in Massachusetts. Also among this group was the philosophy professor, Black Panther leader, and Communist Party member Angela Davis, who was tried for her alleged role in a failed hostage taking in 1970. Native American activist Leonard Peltier received two life sentences for the alleged murders of two Federal Bureau of Investigation agents in South Dakota during a shoot-out in 1975; he subsequently received the International Human Rights Prize. In early 2005, freelance journalist and community activist Mumia Abu-Jamal was still sitting on death row in Pennsylvania for the alleged murder of a Philadelphia police officer in 1981.

Contrary to the mediated images broadcast on television programs, the overwhelming majority of criminal convictions do not result from defendants being found guilty by judges or juries after lengthy trials with highly competent prosecutors, all-star defense teams, and weeks full of complex expert testimony. Unlike celebrity defendants, most criminal defendants do not even see insides of courtrooms for more than a few minutes, when they agree to plea bargains.

Stephen L. Muzzatti

Further Reading

Barak, Gregg, Jeanne M. Flavin, and Paul S. Leighton. *Class, Race, Gender and Crime: Social Realities of Justice in America*. Los Angeles: Roxbury, 2002.

Clehane, Dianem, and Nancy Grace. *Objection! How High-Priced Defense Attorneys, Celebrity Defendants, and a 24/7 Media Have Hijacked Our Criminal Justice System*. New York: Hyperion, 2005.

James, Joy, ed. *Imprisoned Intellectuals: America's Political Prisoners Write on Life, Liberation and Rebellion*. Oxford, England: Rowman & Littlefield, 2003.

Reiman, Jeffrey. *The Rich Get Richer and the Poor Get Prison: Ideology, Class, and Criminal Justice*. 7th ed. Boston: Allyn & Bacon, 2004.

See also Bank robbery; Celebrity trial attorneys; Change of venue; Internal Revenue Service; Shoplifting; Simpson trials; Symbionese Liberation Army; Trial publicity.

Celebrity trial attorneys

Definition: Attorneys whose own fame or notoriety becomes a focus of media attention during their trials

Criminal justice issues: Attorneys; media

Significance: Celebrity lawyers existed long before television. However, television has added a new dimension to the phenomenon, conditioning audiences to perceive televised trials as "stories" that make little effort to weigh evidence fairly. Lawyers' acting tricks are rewarded, and even judges seek celebrity roles. The supporting casts of forensic and color commentators add an air of unreality to the reality.

Celebrity attorneys have long made their presence felt in criminal justice. One of the earliest was Clarence Darrow, who battled intolerance and ignorance in Tennessee's famous Scopes "Monkey Trial" in 1925. Fictional lawyers have also intrigued Americans and helped to attract attention to real-life lawyers. Erle Stanley Gardner's imaginary Perry Mason had a strong role model in Stephen Vincent Benét's dramatized version of the early nineteenth century statesman Daniel Webster, whom he had battle the Devil himself in a courtroom. What has most changed in modern times has been the expansion of television.

Thanks to cable and satellite technology, television now has hundreds of channels to fill with programming, so it is not surprising that many of its hours focus on attorneys, both real and fictional. A turning point for modern celebrity lawyers was former football star O. J. Simpson's 1995 murder trial, which made both its prosecuting and defense attorneys famous. The Courtroom Television Network monitored the Simpson trial, sending out frequent live feeds from the trial to a media pool. The resulting saturation coverage of the Simpson trial changed American perceptions of the criminal justice system, as the trial's lawyers, judge, and the defendant himself all played to the cameras. Even the jurors in the Simpson trial became celebrities after the trial was over. Meanwhile, audiences sat in on the trial, watching live coverage of the whole event,

Some of the Attorneys in the O. J. Simpson Case

Prosecutors

Marcia Clark (1954-): Deputy district attorney and lead prosecutor who in twenty previous murder cases had secured nineteen convictions. During the Simpson trial, the news media played on Clark's physical attractiveness, and her picture often appeared on the covers of tabloid magazines. In early 1997, she resigned from the district attorney's office and received more than four million dollars for her memoirs about the trial, *Without a Doubt* (1997). She also hosted a syndicated television program titled *LadyLaw*.

Christopher A. Darden (1956-): Deputy prosecutor who attracted special media attention because he, like Simpson, was black. After the trial, Darden took a leave of absence from prosecuting to teach in a local law school and published *In Contempt* (1996), a passionate attempt to show why the Simpson verdict was a miscarriage of justice.

Defense attorneys

Robert L. Shapiro (1942-): The lead defense counsel during the early stages of the trial, Shapiro was a well-known Los Angeles defense attorney whose previous celebrity clients included television star Johnny Carson, singer Rod Stewart, athletes Darryl Strawberry and Jose Canseco, parent-murderer Erik Menendez, porn star Linda Lovelace, and attorney F. Lee Bailey. Throughout the Simpson trial, Shapiro held frequent press conferences, but as the defense tactics shifted, he assumed a supporting role and distanced himself from his fellow lawyers.

Johnnie L. Cochran, Jr. (1937-2005): African American defense attorney who displaced Shapiro as lead counsel and is credited with winning Simpson's acquittal by playing the "race card." Cochran came into the trial with a history of defending political activists in high-profile cases, including that of Black Panther leader Geronimo Pratt. After the trial, Cochran was a frequent commentator on television news and talk shows, and he published a memoir, *Journey to Justice* (1996).

F. Lee Bailey (1933-): The most famous of all the lawyers in the Simpson case before it started, Bailey built his career on defenses of such famous clients as Samuel Sheppard, the doctor whose murder conviction inspired the long-running television series *The Fugitive*; Albert

Johnnie Cochran, the lead defense attorney in O. J. Simpson's murder trial, in 1999. *(AP/Wide World Photos)*

DeSalvo, the so-called Boston Strangler; newspaper heiress Patricia Hearst; hotelier Leona Helmsley; and boxer Mike Tyson. He also published several best-selling books, including *The Defense Never Rests* (1971). Like his close friend Shapiro, Bailey held numerous press conferences during the trial; however, he and Shapiro had a falling out over a matter in another trial and Bailey's career later went into a decline.

Alan M. Dershowitz (1938-): Distinguished defense attorney and legal scholar whose earlier celebrity clients included Patricia Hearst, Leona Helmsley, televangelist Jim Bakker, porn star Harry Reems, and *Penthouse* magazine. Although a Jew, Dershowitz was a passionate civil libertarian who defended the right of American Nazis to march in predominantly Jewish Skokie, Illinois, in 1977. His role in the Simpson defense was to prepare for a possible appeal. Afterward, he added *Reasonable Doubts: The O. J. Simpson Case and the Criminal Justice System* (1996) to his long list of publications.

second-guessing lawyers, witnesses, and the judge.

Many lawyers have expressed doubts about television celebrity. They argue that television presents trials not as quests for truth, but as something akin to athletic contests, complete with analysts and color commentators. The presence of television cameras in courtrooms can hamper judges, lawyers, and jurors. Lawyers are particularly prone to being affected by cameras, as they, more so than any other players in trial proceedings, are performers. Trials are not educational processes, say many lawyers. Their purpose is to decide the guilt or innocence of defendants after calm deliberation and careful attention to the arguments.

Celebrity Clients and Celebrity Lawyers

A generally recognized rule is that it takes a celebrity client to make a celebrity lawyer. The Simpson trial was a prototype of this phenomenon; other cases have followed. In 2004-2005, for example, the child-molestation case against singer Michael Jackson helped meet the insatiable demands of twenty-four-hour news channels. Celebrity crimes boost broadcasting ratings.

Attorneys are not the only people who win fame from their participation in high-profile trials. Media commentators also profit from such trials. Talk-show host Larry King is a prime example. During high-profile trials, his general strategy is to gather together a team of lawyers and forensic experts to discuss the cases on his show. These discussions generate endless speculations on legal strategy, the defendants' careers, and anything else that spices up King's show. Media legal experts, in turn, form a subculture and become familiar to audiences as they make the circuit, earning millions of dollars for their instant analyses and boosting television ratings.

Frank A. Salamone

Further Reading

Abramson, Jeffrey, ed. *Postmortem: The O.J. Simpson Case: Justice Confronts Race, Domestic Violence, Lawyers, Money, and the Media.* New York: Basic Books, 1996.

Chiasson, Lloyd, ed. *The Press on Trial: Crimes and Trials as Media Events.* Westport, Conn.: Greenwood Press, 1997.

Clehane, Dianem, and Nancy Grace. *Objection! How High-Priced Defense Attorneys, Celebrity Defendants, and a 24/7 Media Have Hijacked Our Criminal Justice System.* New York: Hyperion, 2005.

Stephen, Andrew. "It All Started with O. J. Simpson. Now, the Twenty-four-Hour News Channels Find That Accusations of Celebrity Crime Boost the Ratings Like Nothing Else, Even War." *New Statesman*, December 1, 2003.

"'We Went Berserk': Live on TV, the O. J. Simpson Trial Spurred the Media to New Levels of Excess." *Columbia Journalism Review* (November/December, 2001).

See also Attorney ethics; Celebrity criminal defendants; Defense attorneys; Print media; Simpson trials; Television news; Trial publicity.

Certiorari

Definition: A writ of *certiorari* is a discretionary procedure employed by appellate courts—including the U.S. Supreme Court—to review lower court decisions

Criminal justice issues: Appeals; constitutional protections; courts; legal terms and principles

Significance: Writs of *certiorari* are the legal mechanisms through which the U.S. Supreme Court accepts almost all cases it decides. The principle gives the Court almost complete discretion in the choice of which cases it hears.

Derived from a Latin word meaning to be "informed," writ of *certiorari* is a legal term that goes back to the early history of English courts. A writ of *certiorari* is a discretionary order issued by an appellate court. When appellate courts want to review decisions of lower courts, they issue writs of *certiorari*. Such writs require the lower courts to deliver their findings to the appeals courts for review. The procedure enables higher courts to review lower court decisions for possible judicial errors that might justify overturning those decisions.

The term *certiorari* is most commonly used in

reference to the process by which the U.S. Supreme Court selects the cases that it reviews. *Certiorari* controls almost all appellate access to the Court. The Supreme Court reviews only the cases that it chooses, which are those that raise the most significant constitutional issues.

In selecting a case for review, four of the Supreme Court's nine justices must agree that it presents an issue that raises a significant constitutional question. After four justices agree (the "rule of four"), the Court issues a writ of *certiorari* to the lower appellate court ordering that its appellate record be brought before the Supreme Court for review. The Supreme Court then reviews the lower court's finding and renders its decision. The Court can dismiss the case, reverse the lower court's decision and send it back for further review or a new trial, or uphold the findings of the lower court.

Lawrence C. Trostle

Further Reading

McGuire, Kevin. *Understanding the U.S. Supreme Court*. New York: McGraw-Hill, 2002.

Wood, Horace G. *A Treatise on the Legal Remedies of Mandamus and Prohibition: Habeas Corpus, Certiorari, and Quo Warranto*. 3d ed. Revised and enlarged by Charles F. Bridge. Littleton, Colo.: Fred B. Rothman, 1997.

See also Appellate process; *Gideon v. Wainwright*; *In forma pauperis*; Supreme Court, U.S.

Chain gangs

Definition: Groups of prisoners who are chained together while performing manual labor outside prisons

Criminal justice issues: Punishment; restorative justice

Significance: Once popular in the American South, chain gangs became criticized as outdated and cruel and eventually fell out of favor in the 1950's. During the mid-1990's, chain gangs made a comeback in some states, leading to much debate over their effectiveness and legitimacy in modern corrections.

Chaining prisoners together is a correctional strategy that has been used when transporting inmates out of a prison for the purpose of performing manual labor. Members are chained together in groups while wearing distinct uniforms identifying them as prisoners. Although the chaining of prisoners provides extra safeguards against prisoner escapes, its popularity may have as much to do with its perceived punitive nature as its deterrent effect.

The origin of chain gangs in the United States is generally traced to the South in the period immediately after the Civil War. With the economy in disarray and adjusting to the loss of slave labor, it became increasingly crucial for the prison systems to be self-providing and to not impede the recovering economic structure. Thus, a lease system developed by which prisoners' labor was offered to businesses. The prisoners often worked on plantations in the southern states, and the leasing idea then spread to a number of western states. The use of chains for work-lease prisoners developed because of the frequency of escape attempts by members of work gangs. Thus, the term "chain gang" was developed for prisoners working on plantations, railroads, highways, and for those who performed other kinds of manual labor.

The lease system had been abolished in all states by 1951, but use of prisoners for manual labor in the South continued for many years afterward until it was finally discontinued. During the mid-1990's, however, chain gangs began to make a small comeback in a few southern and western states. Although the original purpose of chain gangs was largely economic, their renewed use was influenced by a number of other rationales. Included in these justifications were an increased desire to get tough on prisoners, the revival of shaming as a correctional strategy, and a desire to keep prisoners active and avoid the problems associated with idle time.

Much national and international attention has followed the return of chain gangs. Critics claim that chain gangs are inefficient and that their use lacks deterrence value and violates prisoners' protections from cruel and unusual punishment.

Brion Sever

Prisoners from a maximum security Florida prison being led to work on a road in 1995, when Florida reinstituted chain gangs after a nearly fifty-year hiatus. *(AP/Wide World Photos)*

Further Reading

Anderson, J., Laronstine Dyson, and Willie Brooks, Jr. "Alabama Prison Chain Gangs: Reverting to Archaic Punishment to Reduce Crime and Discipline Offenders." *Western Journal of Black Studies* 24 (2000): 9-15.

Burley, L. "History Repeats Itself in the Resurrection of Prisoner Chain Gangs." *Law and Inequality* 15 (1997): 129-130.

Colvin, M. *Penitentiaries, Reformatories, and Chain Gangs: Social Theory and the History of Punishment in the Nineteenth Century.* New York: St. Martin's Press, 1997.

Dodge, T. "State Convict Road Gangs in Alabama." *The Alabama Review* 53 (2000): 243-270.

Reynolds, M. "Back on the Chain Gang." *Corrections Today* 58 (1996): 183.

See also Boot camps; Community service; Cruel and unusual punishment; Prison and jail systems; Prison escapes; Prison guards; Work camps.

Chain of custody

Definition: Procedure which documents the transfer of physical evidence collected at a crime scene from station to station, such as from the preliminary investigation scene to the evidence room, laboratory, and courtroom

Criminal justice issues: Evidence and forensics; investigation; legal terms and principles

Significance: The chain of custody secures and protects the competency of evidence for courtroom presentation and ensures that the evidence remains untainted.

The following hypothetical situation will demonstrate a chain of custody. Police officers arrive at the scene of a bank robbery. During the preliminary investigation, a bank teller discloses information. He provides a bank robbery note from the robber. The note contains the following instructions: "This is a robbery! Follow my instructions and all will go well." The officer carefully collects the document and forwards it to the evidence custodian for storage.

The officer initiates the process by placing his initials and the time and date on the outside of a plastic evidence envelope. This lock-seal envelope will enclose the evidence. An evidence tag and chain-of-custody form are printed on one side of the transmittal envelope.

The investigator records pertinent information before placing the document inside and is careful not to alter the document or place any writing indentation marks on the surface. The reverse side of the envelope is clear plastic, which allows investigators to view the writing without compromising trace evidence or fingerprints. In cases where biological evidence or fluids are involved, envelopes are not appropriate; refrigerator containers are used instead.

Evidence Tag

The evidence tag generally lists the following information: case and control number, date and time, description of the evidence, location, victim/incident, remarks, special handling instructions, test results, and red tags which indicate the presence of blood or other biological fluids that require refrigeration. In addition, red tags indicate the need for special safety precautions. This information may appear on the transmittal envelope or on a white sticker or an attached card.

Chain of Custody Form

The primary purpose of chain-of-custody reports is to identify all handlers by signature. All those who assume authority over the bank robbery note sign to document their handling. The chain-of-custody form also contains the following information: case and control number, receiving agency, location, description, name of person who recovered the evidence, victim's name, name of person who sealed the evidence envelope, name of person who released the evidence, name of person who received the evidence, and purpose of transfer. In this hypothetical investigation, the first person to sign the chain-of-custody form is the bank teller. The investigator's signature is next, followed by those of the evidence custodian and laboratory examiner. The evidence custodian signs the chain-of-custody form, and the investigator signs the form before transporting the evidence to court. The chain-of-custody list is limited to a few handlers and signatures; this prevents gaps or breaks in the chain.

Thomas E. Baker

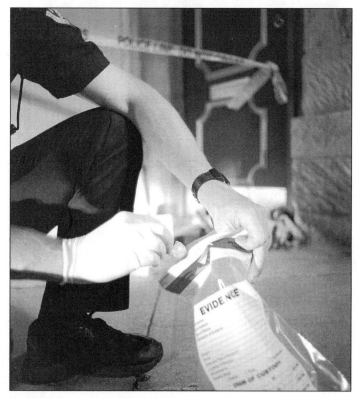

The chain of custody usually begins with evidence being placed in a sealed plastic bag at the scene of a crime. *(Brand-X Pictures)*

Further Reading

Gilbert, James N. *Criminal Investigation*. Upper Saddle River, N.J.: Prentice-Hall, 2001.

Swanson, Charles R., Neil C. Chamelin, and Leonard Territo. *Criminal Investigation*. New York: McGraw-Hill, 2003.

See also Computer forensics; Crime scene investigation; Criminal procedure; Evidence, rules of; Fingerprint identification; Simpson trials; Sobriety testing.

Change of venue

Definition: Relocation of a trial from one jurisdiction to another

Criminal justice issues: Juries; jurisdictions; media; trial procedures

Significance: The importance of impartiality in the court system is demonstrated by court procedures such as change of venue.

A change of venue is a change in the location of a trial. Criminal trials are usually conducted within the jurisdictions in which the crimes being tried take place. Trials can be moved to other jurisdictions because of concerns about jurors being biased because of local media coverage, dangers of violence, or racial prejudice. Initiatives for changing venues are often taken by defense attorneys who ask judges to relocate their trials because they believe different locations will provide more impartial juries for their clients. Prosecutors often object to changing venue because they believe they are more likely to win convictions in the communities in which the crimes take place.

Judges make the decisions to move trials to different parts of the state, due in part to the amount of media attention that cases receive. A judicial decision to change the venue of a trial can impact the outcome of that trial. Moving a trial from its original jurisdiction may locate it in an area where potential jurors are resentful of the media attention it brings to their community. However, choosing not to relocate a high-profile trial can provide the basis for an appeal at the conclusion of the trial.

Jenifer A. Lee

Further Reading

Meyer, J. F., and D. R. Grant. *The Courts in Our Criminal Justice System*. Upper Saddle River, N.J.: Prentice-Hall, 2003.

Neubauer, D. W. *America's Courts and the Criminal Justice System*. 7th ed. Belmont, Calif.: Wadsworth, 2002.

See also Celebrity criminal defendants; Court types; Defendants; Judges; Jurisdiction of courts; King beating case; Presumption of innocence; Trial publicity.

High-Profile Trials Whose Venues Were Changed

Date	Trial	Venue change	Reason
1992	Rodney King beating case	From Los Angeles County to Ventura County, California	Pre-trial publicity and local resentment against the police officers being tried
1996	Oklahoma City bombing defendant Timothy McVeigh	From one part of the federal circuit to another part of the same circuit	Local anger over the bombing
2004	Scott Peterson murder trial	From Stanislaus County to San Mateo County, California	Pre-trial publicity and local bias against Peterson, whose attorney later asked for another change of venue

Chicago Seven trial

The Event: Trial of seven men charged with conspiracy, inciting to riot, and other offenses relating to protest demonstrations at the 1968 Democratic Party National Convention

Date: September, 1969-February, 1970

Place: Chicago, Illinois

Criminal justice issues: Juries; morality and public order; political issues

Significance: One of the most highly publicized trials of its era, the Chicago Seven trial was widely viewed as a political show trial pitting Vietnam War opponents against the established order. However, the trial itself degenerated into such a disorderly affair that the convictions it spent more than a year to reach were eventually overturned because of the court's errors, thereby demonstrating the justice system's success in ensuring that all defendants, regardless of their beliefs or actions, are entitled to fair and impartial trials.

The federal Civil Rights Act of 1968 made it a federal crime to cross state lines for the purpose of inciting a riot. During that same year, several groups announced their intention to protest the Vietnam War and establishment values represented by the Democratic Party at the party's national convention in Chicago. In response, the city of Chicago denied the protesters permission to sleep in the city's Lincoln Park and announced that an eleven P.M. curfew would be enforced. Afterward, numerous confrontations erupted between city police and demonstrators that ultimately resulted in a federal grand jury's indictment of eight demonstrators and eight police officers.

In September, 1969, the trial of the so-called Chicago Eight began. In October, one of the defendants, Black Panther leader Bobby Seale, was ordered bound and gagged in the courtroom by Judge Julius Hoffman because of his repeated outbursts. Seale was later removed from the case and sentenced to four years in prison for contempt of court.

In February, 1970, the remaining seven defendants were acquitted on conspiracy charges, while five—David Dellinger, Rennie Davis, Tom Hayden, Abbie Hoffman, and Jerry Rubin—were found guilty of crossing state lines with the intent of inciting a riot. The final two defendants, John Froines and Lee Weiner, were acquitted on all charges, as were the police officers tried in the case. Each convicted defendant was fined five thousand dollars and sentenced to five years in prison. Judge Hoffman also sentenced all the defendants, as well as their defense attorneys, William Kunstler and Leonard Weinglass, to prison terms on numerous charges of criminal contempt.

The Seventh Circuit Court of Appeals reversed all contempt convictions and the criminal convictions in November, 1972, because of the court's refusal to permit defense attorneys to question prospective jurors about their cultural bias. The appellate court also cited the bias of Judge Hoffman.

William V. Moore

Further Reading

Epstein, Jason. *The Great Conspiracy Trial: An Essay on Law, Liberty and the Constitution.* New York: Random House, 1970.

Schultz, John. *The Chicago Conspiracy Trial.* New introduction by Carl Oglesby. New York: Da Capo Press, 1993.

Walker, Daniel. *Rights in Conflict.* New York: Grosset & Dunlap, 1968.

See also Conspiracy; Contempt of court; Weather Underground.

Child abduction by parents

Definition: Removal from their homes of children under the age of seventeen by family members with the intent of depriving parental access

Criminal justice issues: Domestic violence; kidnapping

Significance: Heightened awareness of the problem of parental abduction of children helps to elicit intervention strategies that may lead to better allocation of law-enforcement resources.

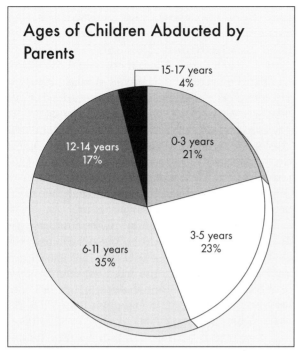

Ages of Children Abducted by Parents

- 15-17 years 4%
- 0-3 years 21%
- 3-5 years 23%
- 6-11 years 35%
- 12-14 years 17%

Source: Office of Justice Programs, Office of Juvenile Justice and Delinquency Prevention, 2002. Figures are based on 203,900 incidents of child abduction in the United States in 1999.

The terms kidnapping and abduction have caused Americans to envision the most heinous of crimes against innocent children. However, the most prevalent forms of child abduction are not the abductions by strangers that are sensationalized in the media but abductions committed by parents or family members. This latter type of abduction became a source of concern during the mid-1980's, at a time when there was a marked increase in the national divorce rate. There is a scarcity of reliable statistical data on parental abduction, partly because definitions of the crime vary from state to state. However, parental abduction is most often defined as the taking and concealment of children in violation of custody orders, with the intent of depriving access to the children by the custodial parents. Because this definition is broad and leaves room for interpretation, a more comprehensive delineation is essential to gain consistency and improve accuracy in reporting mechanisms.

Another factor influencing the disparities in prevalence rates is that parental abduction is one of the most underreported crimes. Custodial parents often cite a variety of justifications for not reporting abductions. Among these justifications are claims that the situations have been resolved by the parents or their lawyers, claims that the parents have known their children's whereabouts all the time and have been confident that their children would not be harmed, fears that harm would come to their children if police were contacted, and lack of confidence that police would intervene.

Almost half of all parental abductions are of children six years old or younger who are abducted during the periods of separation prior to their parents' divorces. The most typical abductors are current husbands or boyfriends in their thirties, who tend to keep the abducted children less than one week. These men usually either fear losing custody of their children prior to divorce decrees, fear that their children are being abused, or wish to use their children as mechanisms of retaliation

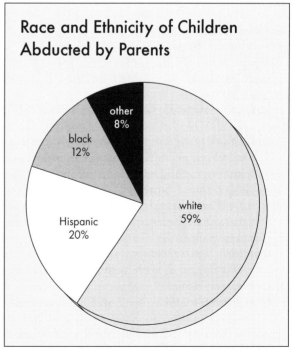

Race and Ethnicity of Children Abducted by Parents

- other 8%
- black 12%
- Hispanic 20%
- white 59%

Source: Office of Justice Programs, Office of Juvenile Justice and Delinquency Prevention, 2002. Figures are based on 200,100 cases of abduction in the United States in 1999. Note that because of rounding down, figures in chart do not add up to 100 percent.

against their former partners. Abduction incidents occur most commonly during school vacation periods, when the children are visiting their noncustodial parents.

Another burgeoning problem is the burden placed upon law enforcement and the subsequent depletion of valuable resources necessary to solve abduction cases. What some parents may consider abduction, others may consider their right to have their own children.

Lisa Landis Murphy

Further Reading

Gunia, M., and J. Vankirk. *No Place That Far: A Story of Parental Abduction*. Philadelphia: Xlibris Corporation, 2001.

Hutchinson, Anne-Marie, and Henry Setright. *International Parental Child Abduction*. 2d ed. Bristol, England: Family Law, 2003.

Sutherland, Patricia. *Perilous Journey: A Mother's International Quest to Rescue Her Children—A True Story*. Far Hills, N.J.: New Horizon Press, 2003.

See also Child abuse and molestation; Kidnapping; Missing persons; Pornography, child.

Child abuse and molestation

Definitions: Child abuse is the intentional infliction of physical, sexual, or emotional trauma on children; molestation is the involvement of minor children by adults in sexual activities, including physical sexual acts and written, pictorial, and verbal communications of a sexual nature

Criminal justice issues: Domestic violence; medical and health issues; sex offenses; women's issues

Significance: Child abuse and child molestation are significant social problems that affect the physical and mental health of more than one million American children every year.

Child abuse and child molestation have been sociologically and legally defined in a variety of ways, and their definitions have changed over time. Child abuse and child molestation can be subsumed under the more general heading of child maltreatment. Child maltreatment includes neglect, child endangerment, emotional and psychological abuse, physical abuse, and sexual abuse. Child neglect is not providing for the needs of a minor child, generally in matters of feeding, sheltering, clothing, educating, or providing for medical needs. For example, neglect cases have come up in the courts that concern parents who have not placed their children in school or have refused to seek medical treatment based on religious beliefs.

Child endangerment occurs when adults who are responsible for the care of children expose the children to potentially or actually dangerous situations. These can range from leaving children unattended in cars while running errands to leaving children home alone for extended periods. Emotional and psychological abuse includes name-calling, belittling, threatening, and terrorizing. Physical abuse includes shaking (including shaken-baby syndrome), hitting, slapping, punching, kicking, beating, striking with objects, stabbing, cutting, burning, and choking. The most severe instances of physical abuse can lead to death.

Sexual abuse includes all forms of sexual contact between minors and adults, from improper touching and fondling to forced vaginal, oral, or anal intercourse. Sexual abuse may also include sexual contact between two minors when a significant age difference exists between them; in some jurisdictions, a difference of three or four years in age constitutes a significant difference. Sexual abuse may also encompass activities such as encouraging minors to watch or to be involved in the making of pornography.

Legal definitions of child abuse, and subtypes of abuse, vary from jurisdiction to jurisdiction and rely upon particular state statutes. In contrast to sociological definitions of abuse that may be vague and open to different interpretations, legal definitions and individual statutes specify exactly what particular abusive behaviors are illegal.

Child Abuse and Molestation in History

Throughout history, human societies have often treated their own children unkindly. Many actions that most Americans would today consider to be abusive have been commonplace throughout the world. For example, infanticide has been common in many parts of the world and still continues in some regions. Especially common is female infanticide and the killing of children with disabilities in developing nations. Some modern and industrialized nations also practice the selective termination of female fetuses and fetuses with disabilities.

Misperceptions of "Stranger Danger"

It is common for parents to talk to their children about "stranger danger," warning them not to take candy from strangers and not to get into cars with strangers. These are certainly good warnings, but it is not strangers that pose the greatest risk to children. Strangers account for a slim minority of the people who harm children. By a wide margin, parents pose the greatest physical danger to their own children. Approximately 75 percent of child-abuse perpetrators are parents. Moreover, sexual abuse is most frequently perpetrated by people whom child victims know very well, often family members.

Because of the high infant mortality rate during the Middle Ages, many children born in that era were not even named until they reached the age of five. Prior to the enactment of compulsory schooling laws during the early twentieth century, education was generally reserved for only wealthy children and was more available to boys than to girls. Before the introduction of child labor laws during the early twentieth century, many children in Europe and North America worked as many as twelve hours a day in factories. Before the era of urban factories, rural children worked equally long hours on farms. In many modern developing nations, young children, especially girls, work as prostitutes to support their families. Children may also be sold to provide money for families. In modern Southeast Asian countries, many children still work in factories for low wages. Even in the United States, many children work without wages and for long hours in businesses owned by their parents.

During the nineteenth century, movements such as the Child-Savers sought to improve the lot of children. However, much of the movement was driven by the need of middle-class white women to control what they saw as unruly and dangerous immigrant children. Rather than improve the conditions in which children lived and labored, the movement often criminalized their actions and placed the children under the control of social services or within the criminal justice system. In 1875, the New York Society for the Prevention of Cruelty to Children was formed.

The first juvenile court system was founded in Chicago in 1899. Prior to that time, children were treated in much the same ways as adults in the legal system. They could be charged with crimes as adults and incarcerated in adult jails and prisons. These conditions naturally created atmospheres ripe for abuse. With the founding of the juvenile court system in Chicago, the American criminal justice system began to see children and their crimes as different from adults and in need of a different response, different treatment, and especially different housing arrangements, away from predatory adults.

Early researchers found a strong correlation between alcohol abuse by parents and abuse of children. The desire to curb violence against children helped fuel the temperance and prohibition movements. Even today, there is a strong correlation between parental abuse of substances and abuse of children. Significant advances in the protection of children were encouraged by the women's movement of the 1960's and 1970's that focused attention on the abuses perpetrated by men in their own homes against women and children.

Prevalence

In criminal justice the "dark figure of crime" is a frequently discussed phrase referring to the fact that, on average, only half the crimes that are committed are brought to the attention of law enforcement. Moreover, certain types of crimes, such as rape, are even less likely to be reported than other crimes. There is also a "dark figure of child abuse," which makes it difficult to estimate the actual prevalence of child abuse and child molestation. The U.S. Department of Health and Human Services Administration for Children and Families has consistently estimated that child-protective services agencies across the country receive more than 50,000 allegations of child maltreatment each week. The Child Abuse Prevention and Treatment Act of 1974 stated that approximately one million children each year were the victims of maltreatment in the United States. By the early twenty-first century, approximately one million cases of child maltreatment reported to child-protective services were substantiated annually.

By far, the most common form of child maltreatment dealt with by child-protective services is neglect. This accounts for about half of the substantiated victims of maltreatment, or approximately 500,000 neglected children each year.

Although neglect is most commonly dealt with by child-protective services, emotional abuse is probably the most prevalent from of abuse. Emotional abuse is so common that it often occurs unnoticed. Many jurisdictions have not enacted specific laws to criminalize emotional abuse, so it is infrequently dealt with through the criminal justice system unless it occurs in conjunction with other forms of abuse that are perceived as being more severe. However, the long-term effects on a young child's psyche of such forms of emotional abuse as being yelled at, belittled, threatened, and terrorized should not be minimized.

Among the factors that increase the likelihood of a child's being victimized are younger age, hav-

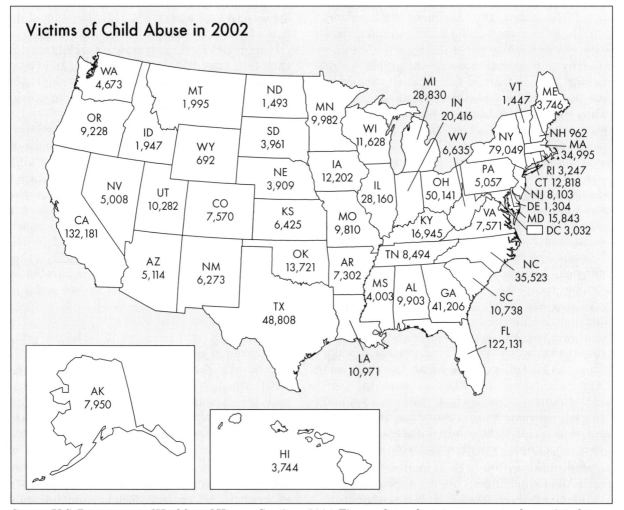

Source: U.S. Department of Health and Human Services, 2004. Figures for each state represent substantiated cases of child maltreatment. Total cases for entire United States in 2002 was 897,168 victims.

ing a disability, alcohol or substance abuse in the home, and having previously come into contact with child-protective services. Younger children are more likely to be victimized and are more likely to die as a result of victimization. The youngest children cannot "tell" anyone of their victimization. Unless injuries are apparent, or incidents of abuse are witnessed by third parties, they often go unnoticed. The younger children are, the greater the risks of abuse that they face. Abuse of children under the age of six is frequently brought to the attention of authorities by medical personnel who may treat victims repeatedly in emergency room settings. The vast differences in size between very young children and adults make younger children more likely than older children to suffer severe harm or death from physical abuse.

Children with disabilities are at increased risk for being abused. This is due to several factors. Their disabilities may interfere with their speech, mobility, or cognition, making these children easier targets for victimization. Often unable even to understand that they are being victimized, children with disabilities may be unable to move away from attacks or unable to tell others about what has occurred. The stress of raising children with disabilities also increases the likelihood of parents treating them in inappropriate or abusive manners.

Parents who abuse alcohol or other substances are more likely to become perpetrators of abuse than parents who do not abuse substances. Individuals who abuse substances are frequently under significant stress themselves. Rather than increase their users' ability to cope with stress, substances have the opposite effect. Abuse of substances also diminishes cognitive reasoning abilities and increases the likelihood of violence. Alcohol and drugs also lower inhibitions.

Many children who come into contact with child-protective services have had prior contact with the agencies. This may indicate that too often child-protective agencies return children to abusive homes for further victimization. Among substantiated victims of child maltreatment, African American children are overrepresented. It is difficult to ascertain whether this can be attributed to higher rates of abuse among this segment of the population, or whether child-protective agencies are more likely to substantiate abuse allegations when the perpetrators are members of minorities.

During the early twenty-first century, annual deaths from child maltreatment were estimated at slightly less than 2 per 100,000 children. In 75 percent of such cases, the victims are under the age of four.

Investigation

The U.S. Congress enacted the federal Child Abuse Prevention and Treatment Act of 1974 to address concerns about alarmingly high rates of child maltreatment. The law provided incentives for states to address this problem in a variety of ways, including research, prosecution, and treatment. The act does two important things. It encourages individuals to report suspected child abuse by providing immunity from prosecution—a protection traditionally granted in the criminal justice system only by judges and prosecutors. The act also mandates the reporting of child maltreatment by certain persons who come into contact with children in their professional capacities.

Two types of investigations may occur into allegations of child abuse or molestation. Child-protective agencies may investigate allegations of abuse and local, state, and federal law-enforcement agencies may conduct investigations. These investigations are usually conducted independently, sometimes with little coordination. Although it may seem sensible for cases in which child-protective agencies have found abuse to be turned over to law enforcement for prosecution, this does not always occur. Generally, abuse allegations are investigated by child-protective services prior to the states considering filing charges against individuals. Investigations by child-protective services begin with the initial contacts with the relevant agencies. About one-third of these initial contacts are not followed up by the agencies; they are either passed on other agencies or dropped because of insufficient information.

Any person may report suspected child abuse, but professionals who work with children—such as teachers, therapists, doctors, and nurses—*must* report suspected abuse to protective agencies. Roughly half of all abuse allegations come

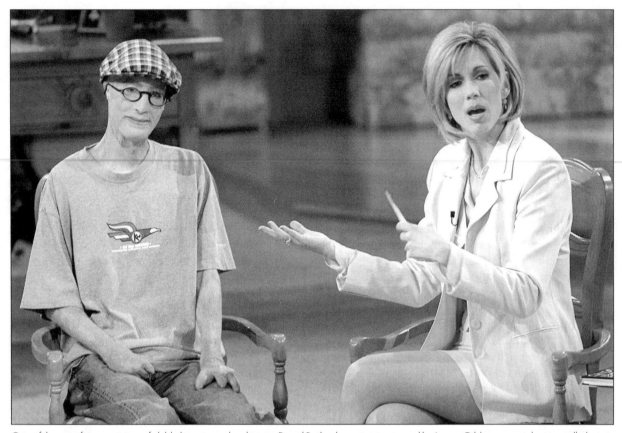

One of the most famous victims of child abuse in modern history, David Rothenberg, is interviewed by Leeza Gibbons on a television talk show in 1996. When Rothenberg was six years old, his father set him on fire to prevent his estranged wife from exercising custody. *(AP/Wide World Photos)*

from professionals. Although these people are mandated to report suspected abuse, even mandated reporters do not report all instances of suspected abuse. Many individuals who are mandated reporters may not be trained to spot possible abuse, or they may not want to report suspected abuse for a variety of reasons. These factors contribute, in part, to the significant underreporting of abuse.

Although there are significant variations in the lengths of time required for investigations to begin, investigations of high-priority cases generally begin within forty-eight hours of the initial contacts with child-protective services. The more severe is the suspected abuse, the quicker is the response. Child-protective service investigations generally include interviewing the children privately in neutral locations such as schools, interviewing parents of the children, and interviewing

the alleged perpetrators. Other individuals involved with the children may be interviewed as necessary.

If instances of abuse have only recently occurred and physical evidence, such as bruises, may be detectable, the children may be taken to medical facilities for examination and documentation of the abuse. Examinations may include photographing bruises or x-raying bones. Under certain circumstances, if a child is believed to be in immediate physical danger, the child may be removed from his or her home and placed into temporary foster care.

Once an investigation is complete, a determination, or disposition, is made as to whether or not abuse has occurred. Although the individual states use a wide variety of terms for these dispositions, the terms generally correspond to the U.S. Department of Health and Human Services

Administration for Children and Families dispositions of "indicated," "substantiated," and "unsubstantiated." Although reports of abuse continue to increase, the percentage of reports that eventually receive dispositions of "unsubstantiated" is rising, totaling about 60 percent of all reports.

Prosecution

Most child-abuse and child molestation cases in the United States are not prosecuted through the criminal justice system. Even those cases in which child-protective agencies have determined that abuse is substantiated are often not criminally prosecuted. This is due to significant differences in goals and standards of proof between child-protective agencies and criminal justice agencies. Moreover, the prioritizing of cases within the criminal justice system for prosecution makes it unlikely that most child-maltreatment cases are prosecuted.

The goals of child-protective agencies and the goals of criminal justice agencies differ greatly. One of the goals of child-protective services is to keep families together. By contrast, a primary goal of the criminal justice system is to punish offenders. Generally, the prosecuting and possible sentencing to jail terms of family members, especially parents, is contradictory to the goal of keeping families together. For child-protective services it is frequently difficult to balance the dual goals of protecting children with keeping families together. In fact, these goals may be irreconcilable, considering the fact that the vast majority of all children who are injured or killed are victimized by their parents within their own homes.

The standards of proof used in the investigation carried out by child-protective services differ substantially from the standards of proof used in criminal courtrooms. There are no specific stan-

dards for what burden of proof a "substantiated" case must reach, but in all criminal cases, the prosecution must prove its case beyond a reasonable doubt. It is difficult for many cases of child abuse and child molestation, even those which child-protective services have found to be substantiated, to reach this high burden of proof.

The standard procedure for deciding which cases brought to the attention of the criminal justice system should be actively prosecuted makes it likely that child-maltreatment cases are "selected out" of the system. Within the criminal justice system, decisions to proceed with cases are made by prosecutors. Cases that are most likely to be prosecuted within the system are those in which complaints are filed within relatively short periods of time after the crimes occur, those for which significant physical evidence exists, and those with credible witnesses.

Normally, only cases of severe child maltreatment are brought to the attention of the criminal

---

False Allegations of Sexual Abuse

Approximately 60 percent of all abuse allegations receive dispositions of "unsubstantiated." A significant portion of these cases are not harmless errors made by well-meaning individuals but knowingly false allegations. While one of the main purposes of the Child Abuse Prevention and Treatment Act of 1974 was to make reporting of suspected abuses easier, it has had the unintended consequence of creating a climate that encourages false allegations. The act provides immunity from prosecution for persons who report alleged abuse. This allows people to report abuse for their own reasons. It also goes against the constitutional right of defendants to face and question their accusers.

Once a child is in contact with the legal system and seen as a victim, the system tends to seek confirmation for that "victim status." Social workers and law-enforcement officers who are well meaning, but untrained in interview techniques that are appropriate for alleged child victims of abuse, often ask leading questions, unintentionally encouraging children to give responses that are consistent with their having been victimized. This can be an important problem in divorce cases. Before the 1980's, mothers were generally awarded custody of their children during divorce proceedings as a matter of course. Since then, as men have sought to assert their rights as parents, custody has become a significant issue during divorce proceedings and frequently for many years afterward. The acrimony that often prevails in divorce cases often leads to false allegations of child abuse when custody is at issue.

justice system. Other cases are handled solely by child-protective agencies. Although the criminal justice system could prosecute cases of child sexual abuse, even they are infrequently prosecuted. Child molestation especially is unlikely to come to light until long after the abusive events occur. Indeed, many victims of molestation do not reveal their experiences to anyone until years afterward. Evidence presents other problems. Generally, only the most severe forms of physical and sexual abuse create physical evidence. However, even this evidence may be lost if the abuse is not reported quickly.

Problems with Child Witnesses

The nature of abuse crimes causes them frequently to be committed either within the privacy of family homes or in situations in which only the victims and perpetrators are present. Victims thus are generally the sole witnesses—apart from the perpetrators—of their own abuse. One of the difficulties that prosecutors face in successfully prosecuting perpetrators of child abuse and child molestation is working with child witnesses. The criminal justice system, correctly or not, has historically viewed child witnesses as less truthful than adult witnesses. Interviewing child witnesses also presents special problems since children are especially susceptible to leading questioning. Moreover, the youngest victims of abuse crimes many not have even learned to speak.

In many instances, the experience of being a witness for the prosecution can be as traumatic for child victims as the actual incidents of victimization they have experienced. However, defendants are guaranteed the right of confronting and questioning their accusers. Officials in the justice system must thus weigh the possibility of further trauma to children against the constitutional rights of the defendants.

Punishment

Responses to child abuse or child molestation are more likely to come from child-protective services agencies than from the criminal justice system. Child-protective services may choose to remove children from their homes, but the services generally do not remove children from homes if they are shown that the children will remain

safe. When children are removed and put into foster care, it is generally for only limited periods of time. It is rare for parental rights to be terminated. Contrary to popular perceptions fueled by media accounts of a few children who have died while in foster homes, children are rarely injured or killed while in foster care.

Criminal justice sanctions against offenders are infrequent. The most common sanction is probation. Prison sentences are rare. By far, the average drug offender receives a much lengthier sentence than the average child abuser or child molester. The child-abuse perpetrators who are least likely to face punishment by the criminal justice system are those offenders who are related to their victims. This is true even though it may be these same offenders who cause the most severe and longest lasting trauma to their victims.

Ayn Embar-Seddon
Allan D. Pass

Further Reading

Barnett, O., and C. Miller-Perrin. *Family Violence Across the Lifespan: An Introduction.* Thousand Oaks, Calif.: Sage Publications, 1997. Examines violence in family contexts and discusses the various forms of child maltreatment. Also discusses date rape, battered women, and elder abuse.

Best, J. *Threatened Children: Rhetoric and Concern About Child-Victims.* Chicago: University of Chicago Press, 1993. Scholarly study of child abuse.

Briere, J., and American Professional Society on the Abuse of Children. *The APSAC Handbook on Child Maltreatment.* Thousand Oaks, Calif.: Sage, 1996. Discusses major types of child abuse along with treatment and legal issues.

Kempe, H., and R. Helfer. *The Battered Child.* 3d ed. Chicago: University of Chicago Press, 1980. Covers a variety of child-abuse topics from history to response of child-protective services and law enforcement, to recognizing abuse, with special emphasis on treatment.

LeRoy, A. *Endangered Children: Dependency, Neglect, and Abuse in American History.* New York: Twayne, 1997. Detailed history of abuse in the United States from early settlement times through the 1990's.

Van Dam, C. *Identifying Child Molesters*. Binghamton, N.Y.: Haworth Press, 2001. Thorough discussion of a variety of topics, including types of molesters, how molesters find their victims, and treatment issues.

See also Animal abuse; Battered child and battered wife syndromes; Child abduction by parents; Domestic violence; Juvenile delinquency; Kidnapping; Pedophilia; Pornography, child; Roman Catholic priests scandal; Sex offender registries; Victimology.

Chimel v. California

The Case: U.S. Supreme Court ruling on warrantless searches

Date: Decided on June 23, 1969

Criminal justice issues: Arrest and arraignment; police powers; search and seizure

Significance: This case was the Supreme Court's most significant pronouncement concerning the permissible extent of a warrantless search of a criminal suspect conducted pursuant to making a lawful arrest.

Ted Chimel, who was suspected of having committed a burglary at a coin shop a month earlier, was arrested at his home, where the police—who had a warrant for his arrest but not one authorizing a search—at the same time conducted a search. Over Chimel's objections, police searched his entire three-bedroom house, seizing some coins found there that were later entered into evidence at Chimel's trial. Chimel was convicted, and his conviction was twice upheld by California state courts before he petitioned the Supreme Court for review, claiming that the warrantless search of his house had been unreasonable and violated the Fourth Amendment.

In overturning Chimel's conviction, the Supreme Court held that police may search only the person of the arrested criminal suspect and the area "within his immediate control" in order to uncover a concealed weapon and prevent the destruction of evidence. In so deciding, the Court overruled two earlier precedents, *Harris v.*

United States (1947) and *United States v. Rabinowitz* (1950), in which a warrantless search was limited only by the nature of what was sought.

As Justice John M. Harlan had stated in *Katz v. United States*, which the Court decided the year before *Chimel* was handed down, "searches conducted outside the judicial process [that is, without a warrant] are per se unreasonable under the Fourth Amendment—subject only to a few specifically established and well-delineated exceptions." One long-standing exception is that permitting a warrantless search that is made incident to a lawful arrest. The justification for this exception is often that the police have not had time to obtain a search warrant, but the open-ended interpretation given the exception by the Harris-Rabinowitz rule gave police tremendous latitude for abuse. In *Chimel*, the offense precipitating the search and the arrest was committed a month before police arrested Chimel, and in the interim Chimel clearly had neither fled nor destroyed all the evidence against him. After obtaining the arrest warrant, police delayed several days before serving it, and they provided no explanation of why there was no time to obtain a search warrant from the court.

In *Weeks v. United States* (1914), the Court made the exclusionary rule, banning introduction at trial of evidence obtained in any unconstitutional fashion, binding on federal courts. Because most crimes are tried at the state level, however, reaction against the exclusionary rule became pronounced only when the Court, led by Chief Justice Earl Warren, extended it to state court proceedings in *Mapp v. Ohio* (1961). The Warren court was accused of coddling criminals, and when Earl Warren retired in 1969, President Richard Nixon, who had made the Warren court a campaign issue in 1968, replaced him with an outspoken critic of the exclusionary rule, Warren Burger.

Lisa Paddock

Further Reading

Bloom, Robert M. *Searches, Seizures, and Warrants*. Westport, Conn.: Praeger, 2003.

Dash, Samuel. *The Intruders: Unreasonable Searches and Seizures from King John to John Ashcroft*. New Brunswick, N.J.: Rutgers University Press, 2004.

LaFave, W. R. *Search and Seizure: A Treatise on the Fourth Amendment.* 3d ed. St. Paul, Minn.: West Publishing, 1995.

McWhirter, Darien A. *Search, Seizure, and Privacy.* Phoenix, Ariz.: Oryx Press, 1994.

See also Automobile searches; Evidence, rules of; Search and seizure.

Circumstantial evidence

Definition: Nondirect evidence from which judges and juries must infer the facts on which they base their verdicts

Criminal justice issues: Evidence and forensics; investigation; witnesses

Significance: Circumstantial evidence is weak material on which to build legal cases, but it is often the only evidence with which both prosecutors and defense attorneys have to work. Most criminal cases, however, are built on combinations of direct and circumstantial evidence.

Circumstantial evidence is, by its nature, less strong than direct evidence. Characteristics of crimes such as fingerprints and eyewitness testimony constitute direct evidence because they can directly link defendants to the crimes with which they are charged. In cases built on direct evidence, prosecutors find it easier to show beyond a reasonable doubt that the accused are guilty.

By contrast, circumstantial evidence does not link defendants to the crimes, leaving judges and jurors to infer what the facts are. Circumstantial evidence is usually based on combinations of facts and circumstances, no one of which necessarily points toward a given suspect, but which together cast suspicion on one or more suspects. In cases based solely on circumstantial evidence, there is less likelihood that juries will reach guilty verdicts because they are left with reasonable doubt. Prosecutors therefore try to build cases primarily upon direct evidence. Even defense attorneys try to build their cases on direct evidence for the same reason—to remove reasonable doubts.

Circumstantial vs. Direct Evidence

If valuable assets were stolen from a company safe that opened without the use of force at a time when no company employees have any business on the premises, evidence for the crime would fall into two categories. Direct evidence might include fingerprints on the safe, trace evidence inside the safe, a videotape of the thief opening the safe made by a surveillance camera, an eyewitness sighting of the thief entering and leaving the premises, or discovery of stolen assets in someone's possession.

If no such evidence were available, investigators would turn their attention more closely to circumstantial evidence. Suspicion might then fall on a company employee who knows the combination to the safe, who shortly after the robbery quits his job and leaves the area, and who cannot account for his whereabouts at the time of the theft. None of those facts would directly link the employee to the crime, but in combination such circumstantial evidence could be used to build a case against him.

Cases based entirely upon circumstantial evidence have lower rates of conviction than those based either entirely on direct evidence or on a combination of direct and circumstantial evidence. Often attorneys on both sides of cases use eyewitness testimony as their primary direct evidence because the only other evidence available to them is circumstantial. By using both types of evidence, both defense attorneys and prosecutors hope to get to the truth of the cases and win favorable verdicts.

Jenephyr James

Further Reading

Meyer, J. F., and D. R. Grant. *The Courts in Our Criminal Justice System.* Upper Saddle River, N.J.: Prentice-Hall, 2003.

Rabe, Gary A., and Dean John Champion. *Criminal Courts: Structure, Process and Issues.* Upper Saddle River, N.J.: Prentice-Hall, 2002.

Skogan, Wesley G., and Kathleen Frydl, eds. *Fairness and Effectiveness in Policing: The Evidence.* Washington, D.C.: National Academies Press, 2003.

See also Bombs and explosives; Document analysis; Embezzlement; Evidence, rules of; Forensics; Latent evidence; Trace evidence; Vicarious liability.

Citations

Definition: Printed documents issued by an officer that serve as an official summons, demanding the presence of the offender at the court on a specified time and date

Criminal justice issues: Arrest and arraignment; traffic law

Significance: Citations are written for the court's administrative purposes: to give an alleged violator notice of a date and time to appear at court, and to contain a law-enforcement officer's notes of the incident at the time the citation is issued.

Citations may be issued by court officials, such as prosecutors, but they are usually issued by law-enforcement officers in conjunction with their daily duties. Citations are usually associated with traffic and parking violations, although they may be written for infractions, misdemeanors, or felonies.

Violators of the law are issued citations in lieu of being taken forthwith before the court, a judge, or a justice of the peace. By signing citations, alleged violators are not admitting guilt to the offenses; rather, they are promising to appear in court at the times and dates specified. By signing citations, alleged violators are, in essence, releasing themselves on their own recognizance. A refusal to sign the citation is not seen by the court as an admission of guilt, but in most jurisdictions failure to sign will result in the arrest of the alleged offender. The failure to sign the citation is thus a failure to acknowledge the mandated court date. The alleged violator is then taken either to a judge or justice of the peace, or if one is not available the violator is held at a local jail facility until a hearing before the court can be arranged. When a citation is written for a parking violation, the offending driver need not sign the citation.

In some misdemeanors and felonies, citations are written and submitted to the prosecutor in conjunction with a report prepared by a law-enforcement officer. In these cases, citations merely serve as an administrative charge-filing reminder. Citations also serve another administrative function for law-enforcement officers and courts: Officers frequently write field notes on citations at the time they are written as a reminder of the circumstances surrounding the citing. Courts recognize such notes, and officers may use them when testifying on the merits of the citation. If such notes exist, the defendant has legal access to view the citation and attendant notes.

Charles L. Johnson

Further Reading

Loewy, Arnold H., and Arthur B. LaFrance. *Criminal Procedure: Arrest and Investigation.* Cincinnati: Anderson Publishing, 1996.

The most common types of citations are those issued to motorists by traffic police. *(Brand-X Pictures)*

Whitcomb, Debra, Bonnie Lewin, and Margaret J. Levine. *Citation Release*. Washington, D.C.: U.S. Department of Justice, National Institute of Justice, 1984.

See also Arrest; Arrest warrants; Court types; Defendants; Jaywalking; Misdemeanors; Plain view doctrine; Speedy trial right; Traffic courts; Traffic law.

Citizen's arrests

Definition: Arrests made without warrants by private citizens, rather than by officers of the law

Criminal justice issue: Arrest and arraignment

Significance: Citizen's arrests allow private citizens to detain criminals either for committing felonies or breaches of the peace; they also allow law-enforcement officials to call for the assistance of citizens in making arrests.

The concept of citizen's arrests has its roots in English common law, formalized in the Statutes of Winchester in 1285. During the first century of United States history, citizen's arrests were abused for individual self-interest, such as bounty hunting, causing most states to restrict citizen-arrest laws in the nineteenth century. Some of these restrictions limited citizen's arrests by making citizens responsible for wrongful arrests and by placing boundaries on ways of getting information that led to arrests. In *Aguilar v. Texas* (1964), for example, restrictions were placed on the use of citizen informers: The informant must be reliable and credible, and the informant's information has to be corroborated. In addition, the resulting arrest must comply with the standards of "probable cause" contained in the Fourth Amendment.

Although citizens in all states may make arrests for both felonies and misdemeanors, usually the arrests involve a breach of peace committed in the presence of the arresting citizen. Other crimes, especially in the case of felonies, need not be committed in the arrester's presence if the ar-

rester has reasonable cause for believing that the person arrested has committed the crime. When a citizen makes an arrest without the assistance of a police officer, the arrester is responsible for turning the arrested person over to an officer of the law as soon as possible. In other instances, a police officer may request the help of a citizen in making an arrest. In these instances, because the private citizen is legally bound to assist the officer, the officer is responsible for the actions of the private citizen assisting in the arrest.

Most arrests made under citizen-arrest laws are not, however, made by private citizens. Most are made by other individuals or groups covered by these laws, including private-security personnel, postal inspectors, bank guards, store employees who detain shoplifters, customs inspectors, private investigators, and state and federal agents. Because not all these groups are registered or licensed, accurate statistics regarding their numbers and their arrests are impossible to obtain.

The degree of physical force that can be used is a critical issue in making a citizen's arrest. State laws vary on the degree of physical force allowable. Deadly force in making a citizen's arrest is generally reserved for situations of protecting other people, and private citizens making such arrests act at their own legal peril in using deadly force. In contrast, when a citizen assists a police officer in making an arrest or in preventing an escape, deadly force may usually be used for self-defense, for the defense of a third party, or at the authorization of a police officer. Because the assisting citizen cannot take time to verify an officer's authority, good-faith assistance is justified, even if the officer misdirects the assisting citizen.

According to Les Johnson, in his book *The Rebirth of Private Policing* (1992), private policing by individual citizens and private groups was increasing during the early 1990's. Even though psychologists and sociologists contend that most citizens avoid intervening in situations of criminal activity, citizens are forming groups such as neighborhood watch groups to lower crimes of theft and personal injury. These groups are especially strong in neighborhoods with high rates of crime and understaffed police forces.

Carol Franks

Further Reading

Abrahams, Ray. *Vigilant Citizens: Vigilantism and the State.* Cambridge, England: Polity Press, 1998.

Johnson, Les. *The Rebirth of Private Policing.* New York: Routledge, 1962.

Loewy, Arnold H., and Arthur B. LaFrance. *Criminal Procedure: Arrest and Investigation.* Cincinnati: Anderson, 1996.

See also Breach of the peace; Criminal law; Criminal procedure; Deadly force; Neighborhood watch programs; Private police and guards; Probable cause; Vigilantism.

Civil disobedience

Definition: A deliberate act of law breaking to protest a law or governmental policy that is regarded as immoral

Criminal justice issues: Civil rights and liberties; morality and public order

Significance: Civil disobedience is an important type of political dissent that goes beyond legal means of protest; it was widely employed by participants in the Civil Rights and anti-Vietnam War movements.

Notable discussions of the conflict between the individual and legal authority are found in Plato's *Apology* and *Crito* and Sophocles' *Antigone.* The classic discussion of civil disobedience, however, is in the essay "Civil Disobedience" by Henry David Thoreau, first presented in a public lecture at Concord, Massachusetts, in January of 1848 under the title, "On the Relation of the Individual to the State." Thoreau defended his refusal to pay the Massachusetts poll tax because of his opposition to government policies, specifically the Mexican War and governmental acceptance of slavery. He contended that the claims of individual conscience were superior to those of the state and should be followed, even if the individual must violate the law and be subject to arrest and imprisonment. Thoreau himself had been arrested for his refusal to pay taxes, and he spent one night in the Concord jail until an anonymous friend made the tax payment owed by Thoreau.

Early in the essay, Thoreau posed the question: "Must the citizen ever for a moment, or in the least degree, resign his conscience to the legislator?" His famous answer was: "I think that we should be men first, and subjects afterward. It is not desirable to cultivate a respect for the law, so much as for the right. The only obligation which I have a right to assume, is to do at any time what I think right." He added the observation that "Law never made men a whit more just; and by means of their respect for it, even the well-disposed are daily made the agents of injustice." For Thoreau, the emphasis is placed on the appeal to individual conscience to justify the breaking of law.

The best-known contemporary manifesto on civil disobedience is Martin Luther King, Jr.'s "Letter from Birmingham Jail," written in April, 1963. King's letter was a response to a public appeal made by eight white Alabama clergymen who urged King and his associates not to engage in mass protests against segregation in Birmingham. Instead they recommended negotiation and dialogue. King in reply insisted that sit-ins, marches, and other forms of nonviolent direct action were a means of creating a crisis and thereby establishing "such creative tensions that a community that has constantly refused to negotiate is forced to confront the issue."

King also addressed the white ministers' criticism of King's readiness to resort to breaking the law, especially when he had urged officials in the South to obey the 1954 Supreme Court decision outlawing racial segregation in public schools. King wrote: "One may well ask, 'How can you advocate breaking some laws and obeying others?' The answer is to be found in the fact that there are two types of laws. There are *just* laws and there are *unjust* laws. I would agree with St. Augustine that 'An unjust law is no law at all.' " According to King, an unjust law is one that is out of harmony with the moral law. He thus offers what is sometimes called a "higher law" defense of civil disobedience, which differs from the appeal to individual conscience made by Thoreau.

Defining Civil Disobedience

In the writings of both Thoreau and King, one characteristic feature of civil disobedience is the deliberate violation of some established law or legal requirement. Civil disobedience is, after all,

Civil rights sit-in demonstration in Washington, D.C., in 1965. Throughout the Civil Rights movement, nonviolent forms of civil disobedience played a constant role. In sit-in demonstrations, protesters often went limp when they were arrested, forcing the arresting officers to carry them away. *(Library of Congress)*

moral belief prompts the illegal act. The revolutionary aims, at least ultimately, at overturning the existing political or legal order, whereas the civil disobedient seeks change within the established system. King captured these points when he affirmed that the civil disobedient must break the law "openly, lovingly . . . , and with a willingness to accept the penalty" and that one who does this "to arouse the conscience of his community over its injustice, is in reality expressing the very highest respect for law."

There is considerable controversy over how precisely to define civil disobedience. The philosopher John Rawls, in his book *A Theory of Justice* (1971), defined civil disobedience as a "public, nonviolent, conscientious yet political act contrary to law usually done with the aim of bringing about a change in the law or policies of government." Rawls regards civil disobedience as breaking the law from motives of conscience (that is, not from self-interest) and also requires that it be nonviolent. Some critics have questioned whether nonviolence should be a defining feature of civil disobedience, suggesting instead that it is a tactical feature of civilly disobedient protest or a factor to be considered in determining whether such a protest is morally justified. Other critics have objected to requiring as part of the definition that acts of civil disobedience be public, with the likelihood of detection and arrest.

Types

Definitions such as that offered by Rawls construe civil disobedience quite narrowly. Thoreau's refusal to pay the poll tax, a pacifist's refusal to submit to military service, and a Jehovah's Witness's refusal to salute the flag are not counted as acts of civil disobedience but instead are classified as cases of "conscientious refusal." Rawls recognizes that his definition is narrower than Thoreau's but favors it because it enables him to call attention to the public and political character of those protests he chooses to label as "civil disobedience," and to relate them to political activity within a constitutional democracy.

Conscientious refusal is not primarily aimed

disobedience, although, as King and others have noted, the law violated may be only a putatively valid law. Especially in American legal contexts, a law may sometimes be challenged in order to test its constitutionality in court. Some have questioned whether such law-testing should be counted as civil disobedience.

Other definitional concerns have been to distinguish civil disobedience from other forms of law-breaking such as "ordinary" criminal activity and revolutionary action. One contrast is in the type of typical motivation; unlike the ordinary criminal, motivated by self-interest or malice, the civil disobedient is often moved by moral or conscientious motivation, in the sense that a at political change and is not made in terms of principles shared by the community. Rawls also excludes from the category of civil disobedience militant acts of resistance and disruption. An example might be animal rights activists breaking into laboratories in order to rescue the animals from experimentation. It is possible to use a more generic definition of civil disobedience, classifying under it such phenomena as conscientious refusal, militant action, and civil disobedience (in its narrow sense).

A commonly drawn distinction is between direct and indirect acts of civil disobedience. The former are acts in which the law objected to is the one violated. A clear example is the sit-ins at segregated lunch counters by civil rights protesters in the 1960's in order to protest segregation laws. They were violating the laws they were protesting. Such direct action is not always possible, since the law or policy regarded as immoral cannot be violated. Indirect acts of civil disobedience are ones in which a law violated is not the one protested. During the late 1950's, Bertrand Russell and the Committee of 100, involved in the Campaign for Nuclear Disarmament, engaged in mass demonstrations involving civil disobedience. They were arrested for violating (morally unobjectionable) trespass law during the demonstrations. In a statement on the subject, "Civil Disobedience and the Threat of Nuclear Warfare," Russell observed: "By means of civil disobedience, a certain kind of publicity becomes possible." The aim of the group was to draw attention to the dangers of nuclear weapons policy, not to protest trespass law.

Some forms of indirect civil disobedience are concerned less with publicity than with interfering with what participants in civil disobedience regard as immoral activity. This is some-

times referred to as "direct action," although that expression is used in other ways as well. Activities associated with "Operation Rescue," a campaign of abortion opponents to shut down abortion clinics in the hope of sparing the lives of the unborn who would have been aborted, constitute an example of direct action.

Justification

One of the most vexing questions is whether and when civil disobedience is morally justified. Thoreau seemed to be of the opinion that he and, presumably, others ought to do what they think is right. Many have taken a polar opposite position to the effect that, in a constitutional democracy at least, deliberately breaking the law is never justified. Others have argued that indirect civil disobedience is never justified. Former Su-

Major Events in the History of Civil Disobedience

1849	Henry David Thoreau publishes "Resistance to Civil Government" (later known as "Civil Disobedience").
1906	Mohandas K. Gandhi urges Indians in South Africa to go to jail rather than accept racist policies, beginning his *satyagraha* campaign.
1919	Gandhi leads nationwide closing of businesses in India to protest discriminatory legislation.
1920-1922	Gandhi leads boycott of courts and councils in India and develops noncooperation strategies.
1928	Gandhi organizes on behalf of indigo workers in Bihar, India, and initiates fasting as a form of *satyagraha*.
1932-1933	Gandhi engages in fasts to protest untouchability.
1942	Gandhi arrested for *satyagraha* activities.
1955	Martin Luther King, Jr., leads boycott of transit company in Montgomery, Alabama.
1956-1960	King leads protest demonstrations throughout the American South.
1963	King leads March on Washington for civil rights.
1965	King leads "Freedom March" from Selma to Montgomery and organizes voter registration drive.
1968	King initiates a "Poor People's Campaign" but is assassinated before it can be carried out.

preme Court justice Abe Fortas, in the widely cited 1968 essay entitled "Concerning Dissent and Civil Disobedience," specifically condemned indirect civil disobedience. Fortas, writing at a time of massive protests in connection with racial discrimination, the military draft, and the Vietnam War, concluded,

> So long as our governments obey the mandate of the Constitution and issue facilities and protection for the powerful expression of individual and mass dissent, the disobedience of laws which are not themselves the target of the protest—the violation of law merely as a technique of demonstration—constitutes an act of rebellion and not merely dissent.

In the background of this issue are large questions about the nature of law, morality, and democratic government. A number of grounds have been offered for a general obligation to obey the law. In Plato's *Crito*, Socrates cites several reasons why he should not escape from jail but should instead submit to the laws of Athens. Among them are gratitude for the protection the law has afforded him as well as an implicit agreement with the state. Another common appeal has been to considerations of fairness—in a democracy, laws and policies are arrived at by procedures in which people can exert their influence.

Finally, others have cited the general value of respect for law and the threat to peaceful and orderly processes of collective decision posed by deliberate law breaking. If individuals are allowed to follow their diverse and sometimes erratic consciences, or if they are permitted to observe "higher laws," which are difficult to verify and to interpret, then the health of the democratic process is seriously jeopardized. On the other hand, many defenders of civil disobedience have held that the obligation to obey the law is not absolute, because even in constitutional democracies the political process may yield morally unacceptable outcomes. Defenders of civil disobedience cite approvingly the nineteenth and twentieth century targets of protest and civil disobedience, including slavery and fugitive slave laws, the denial of suffrage to women, laws supporting segregation and discrimination, the war in Vietnam and the military draft, and nuclear weapons policies.

Few defenders of civil disobedience see its jus-

tification as an issue that lends itself to resolution by a simple and easy formula. Complex factors relating to the type of civil disobedience, the motives and aims of the practitioners, and the circumstances in which it must be carried out must be taken into account. Among the questions that must be answered are: How gravely wrong is the law or policy being protested; what are the motives of those engaging in civil disobedience (that is, whether they are predominantly moral or are heavily mixed with less admirable motives such as fame or greed); what is the likelihood of success; what are the dangers of violence, especially injury to persons; and what is the risk of encouraging or spreading lawlessness and disrespect for law? On this latter point, the distinction between direct and indirect civil disobedience comes into play. Furthermore, significance is also given to the character of civil disobedience—that it is nonviolent, that it is done openly and with an acceptance of the penalty, and that it is done as a last resort, after available political and legal resorts have been exhausted. These are perceived as important in demonstrating that civil disobedience can be, in Rawls's words, "a form of political action within the limits of fidelity to the rule of law."

While civil disobedience may be morally justified, courts and prosecutors have seldom shown any special leniency toward those who have broken the law for reasons of conscience. As noted earlier, in the context of American law, significant constitutional issues are implicated. In particular, there is the issue of whether an apparent illegal act is really that, since the law might subsequently be declared unconstitutional by judicial review. There are also First Amendment concerns, especially the extent to which protests are protected speech. For example, the U.S. Supreme Court has held that burning a draft card is not protected speech (*United States v. O'Brien*, 1968) but that burning an American flag as a political protest is protected speech (*Texas v. Johnson*, 1989).

Mario F. Morelli

Further Reading

Bedau, Hugo. *Civil Disobedience: Theory and Practice*. New York: Pegasus, 1969. One of several excellent collections of essays that include Thoreau's famous essay.

Greenawalt, Kent. *Conflicts of Law and Morality*. New York: Oxford University Press, 1987.

Murphy, Jeffrie, ed. *Civil Disobedience and Violence*. Belmont, Calif.: Wadsworth, 1971.

Singer, Peter. *Democracy and Disobedience*. New York: Oxford University Press, 1974. Scholarly discussion of civil disobedience.

Thoreau, Henry David. *"Walden" and "Civil Disobedience": Complete Texts with Introduction, Historical Contexts, Critical Essays*. Edited by Paul Lauter. Boston: Houghton Mifflin, 2000.

Walzer, Michael. *Obligations: Essays on Disobedience, War and Citizenship*. Cambridge, Mass.: Harvard University Press, 1982. Discussion of the idea that obligation derives from consent and applies it to practical situations, including civil disobedience.

See also Marshals Service, U.S.; Nonviolent resistance; *Texas v. Johnson*; Trespass.

Civilian review boards

Definition: Official groups of citizens that examine the merits of complaints against police officers

Criminal justice issues: Government misconduct; police powers; professional standards

Significance: Civilian review boards have been instituted in various cities as a way to restore public confidence in police departments, some of which had been tainted by corruption scandals and charges of brutality.

One of the greatest potential threats to justice is corruption within law-enforcement organizations. Police corruption has been addressed historically through a variety of mechanisms, including internal affairs divisions, police commissions, political oversight agencies, and special investigatory bodies. Despite these mechanisms, complaints have persisted that charges of police corruption are sometimes ignored by governmental authorities. During the 1960's, experiments were conducted with civilian review boards (CRBs), groups of citizens from the community who would examine complaints against police officers and recommend further action. Police departments strongly opposed the establishment of these boards as a threat to police professionalism and morale. During the 1980's and 1990's, however, enthusiasm for CRBs increased, particularly in larger cities. A series of notorious cases of alleged police abuse of power, particularly against persons belonging to racial minority groups, fueled calls for civilian oversight.

CRBs seldom are empowered to make ultimate determinations on citizen complaints. Instead, their findings and recommendations are passed on to other authorities as well as made available to the general public. CRBs can be seen as a logical complement to the trend toward community-oriented policing, which was gaining popularity at the same time.

Steve D. Boilard

Further Reading

National Research Council. *Fairness and Effectiveness in Policing: The Evidence*. Washington, D.C.: National Academies Press, 2003.

Ostrom, Elinor, R. Parks, and Gordon Whitaker. *Patterns of Metropolitan Policing*. New York: Praeger, 1978.

Prosecuting Police Misconduct: Reflections on the Role of the U.S. Civil Rights Division. New York: Vera Institute of Justice, 1998.

Skolnick, Jerome H., and James J. Fyfe. *Above the Law: Police and Excessive Use of Force*. New York: Free Press, 1993.

See also Community-oriented policing; Deadly force; King beating case; Knapp Commission; Miami riots; Police brutality; Police chiefs; Police corruption; Police ethics; Victim-offender mediation.

Clear and present danger test

Definition: The principle, articulated by Oliver Wendell Holmes, Jr., that political speech is protected unless it creates a "clear and present danger that [it] will bring about the substantive evils that Congress has a right to prevent"

Criminal justice issues: Civil rights and liberties; constitutional protections; espionage and sedition

Significance: This was the first principle used by the Supreme Court to distinguish unprotected from protected political speech; the principle is no longer used to suppress political speech but has been used to prohibit hate speech and disruptive speech.

In 1798, Congress passed the Alien and Sedition Act, which prohibited false, scandalous, and malicious publications against the United States government, the Congress, and the president. The act was particularly designed to punish newspapers which opposed President John Adams and supported Thomas Jefferson. Punishment was a fine of up to two thousand dollars and a jail sentence of up to two years. Similar prohibitions occurred in the Espionage Act of 1917, the Sedition Act of 1918, and the Smith Act of 1940, which were designed to suppress opposition to the war efforts of those times.

The first Supreme Court case to test whether a prosecution for seditious libel constituted a violation of the First Amendment occurred in 1919. Charles Schenck, the general secretary of the Philadelphia Socialist Party, published fifteen thousand leaflets protesting U.S. involvement in World War I. Schenck and several others in the party were convicted of violation of the Espionage Act; the conviction was appealed to the Supreme Court in 1919.

Justice Oliver Wendell Holmes, Jr., wrote the opinion of the Court and formulated the test which could justify suppression of speech. In ordinary times, such pamphlets might be permissible, he wrote, but the character of every act depends upon the circumstances in which it is done. "The most stringent protection of free speech would not protect a man in falsely shouting fire in a theater and causing a panic." "The question in every case," Holmes stated, "is whether the words are used in such circumstances and are of such a nature as to create a clear and present danger that they will bring about the substantive evils that Congress has a right to prevent" (*Schenck v. United States*, 1919).

The principle was used to support the conviction of more than two thousand protesters during World War I in spite of the fact that Justice

Holmes dissented from these later convictions. Later, in *Whitney v. California* (1927), Justice Louis D. Brandeis formulated what was intended to be a more permissive version of the principle. Brandeis wrote that the wide difference between advocacy and incitement, between preparation and attempt, between assembling and conspiracy must be borne in mind.

This is the formulation that was adopted in *Brandenburg v. Ohio* (1969). In this case the Supreme Court overturned a conviction based on the clear and present danger test for the first time. Defendants have not been convicted of seditious libel since.

Roger D. Haney

See also Seditious libel; Smith Act.

Clemency

Definition: Power of an executive authority to pardon convicted criminals and to commute sentences

Criminal justice issues: Appeals; pardons and parole; restorative justice

Significance: Clemency generally serves as a last-ditch effort to secure justice for convicted individuals.

In each of the fifty U.S. states, convicted defendants may appeal their sentences or punishments through a proscribed appeals process. When all steps of the appeals process have been exhausted, the sentences stand unless an executive body grants clemency. In rare instances, clemency may be granted at any step of the legal procedure, even prior to arraignment on charges.

Clemency may take several forms. Pardons nullify punishments and sentences, and all rights of the individual are restored as though no wrongdoing had ever occurred. By contrast, commutation of sentences acts as an exchange of the punishments originally ordered by courts with other sentences, usually sentences that are less severe. For example, a governor may commute a death-penalty sentence to life imprisonment or a ten-year prison sentence to deportation.

Executive bodies may issue clemency in the

Public Opinion on Gubernatorial Clemency Decisions

Responses of people who were asked on what bases state governors usually make decisions about delaying executions or granting clemency.

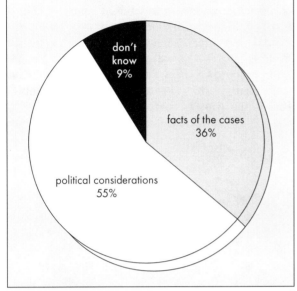

don't know
9%

facts of the cases
36%

political considerations
55%

Source: ABC News.com Poll, June 2000. Poll surveyed 1,004 adults throughout the United States.

form of reprieves from sentences, that is, temporary postponements. Reprieves are most often used for death-penalty cases in which proponents of the convicted inmates seek to keep the inmates from being put to death, while simultaneously hoping to bring forward new evidence that will reverse prior appeals decisions.

Because many states have adopted mandatory sentencing for certain criminal convictions, the courts are occasionally required to impose sentences that seem out of proportion to the crimes, when all facts, exigencies, and personalities are taken into account. The possibility of clemency thus allows for restorative justice in such instances.

Taylor Shaw

Further Reading

Burnett, Cathleen. *Justice Denied: Clemency Appeals in Death Penalty Cases*. Boston: Northeastern University Press, 2002.

Carter, Linda E., and Ellen Krietzberg. *Understanding Capital Punishment Law*. Newark, N.J.: LexisNexis, 2004.

See also Amnesty; Pardons; Parole; Probation, adult; Rehabilitation.

Clerks of the court

Definition: Elected or appointed officer of the court who performs a multitude of legal processing, courtroom, and judicial support duties
Criminal justice issue: Courts
Significance: Acts as the sole custodian of the records of all criminal and civil cases.

Clerks of the court (also referred to as county clerks) are also known as the keepers of the records, as they play a vital role in serving the interests of justice. They are responsible for the maintenance and preservation of all court pleadings for criminal and civil cases. Clerks of the court attend court hearings, motions, and trials in order to log information onto court records. They are responsible for the recording system in the courtroom and transcribing the information onto docket sheets. They maintain the judges' calendars, prepare files for docket, and coordinate the flow of documents necessary for court assignments. During trials, the clerks of the court receive, mark, and assume custody of evidence presented. They also serve as liaisons between judges and a wide variety of agencies throughout the county.

In some states, as determined by a judge, clerks of the court may be afforded limited judicial duties, such as preparing and issuing warrants, subpoenas, and other official documents on behalf of the court. They may also prepare jury pools, swear in witnesses and jurors, file jury charges and verdicts, and record jury service and compensation due jurors. Lastly, clerks of the court may serve as probate judges, becoming responsible for the administration of numerous issues regarding probate estates.

Lisa Landis Murphy

Further Reading

Dileo, A. M., and A. B. Rubin. *Law Clerk Handbook: A Handbook for Federal District and Appellate Court Law Clerks.* Washington, D.C.: Federal Judicial Center, 1977.

Schmalleger, Frank. *Criminal Justice Today: An Introductory Text for the Twenty-first Century.* 8th ed. Upper Saddle River, N.J.: Pearson/Prentice-Hall, 2005.

See also Court types; Criminal justice system; Summonses; Trial transcripts; Trials.

Coast Guard, U.S.

Definition: Federal military service and law-enforcement agency that provides maritime support for the war on terror as part of the Department of Homeland Security

Criminal justice issues: Federal law; military justice; terrorism

Significance: The nation's oldest maritime military service, the U.S. Coast Guard is responsible for protecting coastal boundaries and infrastructure and intercepting illegal drugs, goods, and aliens that are attempting to enter the United States.

The modern-day U.S. Coast Guard is the largest and most advanced maritime law-enforcement agency in the world and has a long and distinguished history as an autonomous military branch. In contrast to other branches of the U.S. military, the Coast Guard has never been part of the Department of Defense. The forerunner of the Coast Guard was established in 1790 as the Revenue Marine. Since then, the service has undergone major changes and restructuring.

In 2003, the Coast Guard became part of the Department of Homeland Security, and since then its primary mission has been to defend more than 95,000 miles of U.S. coastlines, 360 ports, 10,000 miles of interstate riverfronts, and 3.4 million square miles of ocean. This monumental responsibility requires the joint cooperation of local, state, and other federal agencies, as well as the private maritime industry and international entities.

The Coast Guard receives its law-enforcement statutory authority under Title 14 of the United States Code. Historically, the service has had three primary law-enforcement charges. These have included collection of tariffs for imported goods, protection of shipping from piracy on the high seas, and the interception of illegal goods and persons. Of these tasks, the primary goal of the Coast Guard prior to World War II involved the confiscation of material contraband. During the 1960's, however, the service began increasingly to limit the flow of illegal immigration coming from Cuba. After large numbers of Cuban

Coast Guard personnel unloading eight tons of cocaine seized from a Belizean fishing vessel attempting to carry the contraband drug to the United States in early 2001. *(AP/Wide World Photos)*

refugees were intercepted during the early and mid-1960's, the numbers decreased until the landmark Mariel Boatlift of 1980. That massive exodus of 125,000 Cuban refugees to the United States marked the largest Coast Guard peacetime operation to that date.

The 1970's saw a noticeable increase in the role of the Coast Guard in stemming the flow of illicit drugs into the United States. The service's drug-enforcement duties continued to increase into the first years of the twenty-first century, as the service seized large quantities of marijuana, cocaine, and other illicit drugs. Particularly notably were seizures of thirteen tons of marijuana in San Diego in 1984, twenty tons of marijuana in Jamaica in 1987, and 13.5 tons of cocaine from a vessel 1500 miles south of California in 2001.

The Coast Guard also has served in virtually every major military engagement since the founding of the United States. It has assisted U.S. Navy operations with personnel and equipment and has also been assigned special missions. It has a rich and well-documented history of recognized service during the Mexican War, the Spanish-American War, World War I, World War II, the Vietnam War, and the Persian Gulf War of 1991. As part of Operation Iraqi Freedom in early 2003, the Coast Guard continued to support other branches of America's armed services.

Current Day and Beyond

On February 25, 2003, supervision of the Coast Guard was passed from the Department of Transportation to the newly founded Department of Homeland Security. The Homeland Security Act of 2002 lists five specific law-enforcement directives for the Coast Guard. These directives focus on securing ports, waterways, and coastal security; defense readiness and response; drug interdiction; illegal immigrant interdiction; other law-enforcement duties as needed.

In 2004, the Coast Guard employed approximately 39,000 active duty personnel, 8,100 reservists, and some 37,000 civilian auxiliary personnel. On a typical day the Coast Guard boards 138 vessels for law-enforcement checks, performs 450 waterway or port security operations, opens 38 federal cases for law violations, monitors more than 2,500 commercial vessels entering or exiting ports of entry, confiscates 39 pounds of mari-

juana and 324 pounds of cocaine, arrests 15 illegal immigrants, and enforces 103 security zones.

Since the unprecedented loss of life and the disruption of domestic commerce that came with the terrorist attacks of September 11, 2001, the Coast Guard has faced significant challenges as it has defended ports, waterways, and maritime industries. Even before these attacks, however, the Coast Guard had a desperate need to replace its aging and technologically deficient fleet of equipment. The Coast Guard's increased responsibilities have made correcting those shortcomings a major area of concern for adequate domestic security.

To maintain the Coast Guard's state of preparedness and intelligence necessary to prevent and intervene in terrorist threats, a new generation of boats, cutters, fixed-wing aircraft, and helicopters was under development in 2005. This state-of-the-art system, known as the Integrated Deepwater System (IDS), was designed to integrate, link, and network all new equipment assets, both within the Coast Guard and between the Coast Guard and other military and government agencies. The new system promised to be a highly effective, efficient, and intelligent use of resources, equipment, and manpower by establishing a fully integrated communications system. After it is fully implemented, it is expected to provide a modern infrastructure to support the Coast Guard's increasingly complex operations.

Denise Paquette Boots

Further Reading

Beard, Tom, Jose Hanson, and Paul Scotti, eds. *The Coast Guard*. Westport, Conn.: Hugh Lauter Levin, 2004. Containing a foreword by veteran broadcast journalist Walter Cronkite, this illustrated book covers the duty, history, life, and devotion of the Coast Guard and its people through a number of essays and contributors.

Johnson, Robert Erwin. *Guardians of the Sea: History of the U.S. Coast Guard, 1915 to the Present*. Annapolis, Md.: Naval Institute Press, 1987. Comprehensive and detailed account of the history of the Coast Guard from the early twentieth century through the 1980's. It offers explicit accounts of rescues, military operations, and more.

Krietemeyer, George. *The Coast Guardsman's Manual.* 9th ed. Annapolis, Md.: Naval Institute Press, 2000. Designed for members of the Coast Guard, this book offers a thorough overview of Coast Guard history, uniforms, and operations, and is mandatory reading for recruits in boot camp.

Ostrom, Thomas. *The United States Coast Guard: 1790 to the Present.* Oakland, Oreg.: Elderberry Press, 2004. Written for serious scholars of American military and agency history, this book offers an exhaustive history of the Coast Guard.

White, Jonathan R. *Defending the Homeland: Domestic Intelligence Law Enforcement and Security.* Stamford, Conn.: Wadsworth, 2003. Survey of law enforcement in the United States discussing how the criminal justice system has changed since September 11, 2001.

See also Computer information systems; Drugs and law enforcement; Homeland Security Department; Illegal aliens; Law enforcement; Military justice; National Guard; Search and seizure; United States Code.

COINTELPRO

Identification: Secret federal government counterintelligence programs designed to neutralize radical political organizations in the United States

Date: 1956-1971

Criminal justice issues: Constitutional protections; espionage and sedition; political issues

Significance: The utilization of intelligence techniques as part of a criminal investigation is generally considered a legitimate police function. However, the COINTELPRO program's use of counterintelligence techniques to disrupt and repress the ability of groups and individuals to act legally raises both legal and ethical questions in a democratic society.

COINTELPRO was a covert program initiated by the Federal Bureau of Investigation (FBI) to "misdirect, discredit, disrupt and otherwise neu-tralize" specific individuals and groups within the United States. The first program, initiated in 1956, targeted the Communist Party of the USA. During the 1960's, additional programs were created that targeted Groups Seeking Independence for Puerto Rico (1960-1971), the Socialist Workers Party (1961-1971), white hate groups (1964-1971), black nationalist hate groups (1967-1971); and the New Left (1968-1971). White hate groups included the Ku Klux Klan and the American Nazi Party. Black nationalist groups included many civil rights groups as well as organizations such as the Black Panther Party. New Left groups included organizations opposed to the Vietnam War, feminist groups, and student organizations including the Students for a Democratic Society.

COINTELPRO activities were subject to the approval through FBI headquarters in Washington, D.C. Many techniques, some of which were illegal and unethical, were employed to disrupt and discredit the targeted groups and individuals. False statements were issued, correspondence was forged, and anonymous letters and phone calls were widely used. Members of the targeted organizations were subject to break-ins, false arrests, and loss of jobs.

In March, 1971, COINTELPRO operations were publicly exposed after files were stolen from an FBI office in Media, Pennsylvania, and released to the news media. Shortly thereafter, the FBI discontinued COINTELPRO. In November, 1974, the FBI formally apologized for its actions against domestic targets.

William V. Moore

Further Reading

Churchill, Ward, and Jim Vander Wall. *The COINTELPRO Papers: Documents from the FBI's Secret Wars Against Dissent in the United States.* 2d ed. Cambridge, Mass.: South End Press, 2002.

Conner, Frank J. *The Age of Surveillance: The Aims and Methods of America's Political Intelligence System.* New York: Alfred A. Knopf, 1980.

Cunningham, David. *There's Something Happening Here: The New Left, the Klan, and FBI Counterintelligence.* Berkeley: University of California Press, 2004.

Kessler, Ronald. *The Bureau: The Secret History of the FBI*. New York: St. Martin's Press, 2002.

See also Federal Bureau of Investigation; Hoover, J. Edgar; Ku Klux Klan; Patriot Act; Royal Canadian Mounted Police.

Coker v. Georgia

The Case: U.S. Supreme Court ruling on capital punishment

Date: Decided on June 29, 1977

Criminal justice issues: Capital punishment; sex offenses

Significance: In this case, the Supreme Court held that capital punishment for the crime of rape is an excessive and disproportionate penalty, and therefore contrary to the prohibition against cruel and unusual punishments in the Eighth and Fourteenth Amendments.

While serving sentences for murder, rape, kidnapping, and other crimes, Erlich Anthony Coker escaped from a Georgia prison in 1974. That same evening he entered the private home of a couple, tied up the husband in the bathroom, raped the wife, and then forced her to leave with him in the car belonging to the couple. Apprehended by the police, Coker was tried and convicted on charges of rape, armed robbery, and kidnapping. Based on procedures that had been approved by the U.S. Supreme Court in *Gregg v. Georgia* (1976), the jury found Coker guilty of rape with aggravating circumstances and sentenced him to death. After the Georgia Supreme Court upheld the conviction and sentence, the U.S. Supreme Court accepted the case for review.

The Supreme Court limited its review to the single question of whether capital punishment for rape is a cruel and unusual punishment that violates the Eighth and Fourteenth Amendments. Ruling 7 to 2 in the affirmative, the Court reversed Coker's death sentence and remanded the case to the Georgia courts for a new sentencing.

Writing the majority opinion, Justice Byron R. White argued that the sentence of death for the crime of rape is unconstitutional because it is an excessive and disproportionate punishment. As evidence that the public judgment agreed with this conclusion, White pointed to the fact that Georgia was the only state to authorize the death penalty for the rape of an adult woman. Although the crime of rape deserved serious punishment, it was disproportionate to inflict the defendant with a more severe punishment than he inflicted on his victim. Although rape was not equivalent to the unjustifiable taking of a human life, the crime of deliberate murder in Georgia was not a basis for the death penalty except where there were aggravating circumstances. White wrote that it was disproportionate to punish a rapist more severely than a deliberate killer.

As in other cases dealing with capital punishment, the justices expressed a variety of views. Two concurring justices opposed all use of capital punishment, while two dissenters would have allowed it for rape. One justice, Lewis F. Powell, Jr., joined the majority because the rapist did not inflict great brutality or serious injury on the victim.

The *Coker* decision underscored the extent to which the Court had accepted the view that the Eighth Amendment prohibited excessive and disproportionate punishments. It appeared that the Court would not approve the use of the death penalty for any crime other than deliberate murder, but it was not certain how the Court would react to capital punishment for rape with excessive brutality or when the victim sustained serious injury. Some observers noted that *Coker* appeared to indicate that the Court was becoming more reliant upon the doctrine of substantive due process.

Thomas Tandy Lewis

Further Reading

Bohm, Robert M. *Deathquest: An Introduction to the Theory and Practice of Capital Punishment in the United States*. Cincinnati: Anderson Publishing, 2003.

Carter, Linda E., and Ellen Krietzberg. *Understanding Capital Punishment Law*. Newark, N.J.: LexisNexis, 2004.

Latzer, Barry, ed. *Death Penalty Cases: Leading Supreme Court Cases on Capital Punishment*. 2d ed. Burlington, Mass.: Butterworth Heinemann, 2002.

Sarat, Austin. *When the State Kills: Capital Punishment and the American Condition*. Princeton, N.J.: Princeton University Press, 2001.

See also Capital punishment; Cruel and unusual punishment; Rape and sex offenses.

Cold cases

Definition: Unsolved cases, usually involving homicide, on which active police work has ceased

Criminal justice issues: Homicide; investigation; technology

Significance: Unsolved homicides provide no closure to relatives or friends of the victims. In some instances, a homicide's going unsolved may allow an at-large killer to com-

mit another homicide. Additionally, large numbers of open homicide cases can place a burden on detectives already struggling with high caseloads. These situations have led to the development of a specialized unit within the homicide division of certain police departments that deals specifically with "cold" cases.

Police departments are, at times, plagued with such high caseloads that their performance is adversely affected. For example, increased homicide rates leading to a backlog of cases could slow results from crime laboratories, autopsies, and medical examiners. Case overloads can be frustrating to detectives who may already be working in departments that are short-staffed. All of these factors can hurt police performance, while allowing homicide cases to remain unsolved.

Unsolved homicides are commonly referred to

Workers use ground-penetrating radar to search a farm field in South Dakota during the 2004 investigation of a thirty-three-year-old missing-persons case. Investigators sought the car that the two girls had been driving when they disappeared and thought it might be buried at the farm on which their chief suspect had lived at the time of the disappearance. Radar failed to find the car but did turn up two hubcaps, miscellaneous auto parts, and a 1968 license plate. *(AP/Wide World Photos)*

as cold cases. The phrase "cold case" can apply to any unsolved crime but mainly refers to homicides because there is no statute of limitations on murder, and these cases, despite the passing of months, remain open. Police department policies vary regarding the length of time that passes before a case is considered cold. Depending on the size of the department and its number of homicide detectives, a case could become cold after three months or after one year.

An increase in cold cases has resulted from a rising number of homicides, generally attributed to gang- and drug-related murders. Such cases are among the most difficult to solve. Traditionally, murder victims and their killers usually had some kind of relationship. However, deaths involving illegal immigrants, homeless people, transients, unsolved police shootings, and prostitutes are less likely to be rooted in long-standing personal relationships; thus the cases have a greater likelihood of becoming cold.

The Development of the Cold Case Squad

Cold case squadrons are a viable solution for police departments that have a high number of unsolved homicides. A high volume of new cases may prevent regular homicide detectives from looking into old cases. The cold case squad originated in Washington, D.C., where the homicide rate had skyrocketed to the point at which overwhelmed detectives solved very few cases, and murders kept increasing. This situation left many cases unsolved, with no detectives to work on them.

The Washington, D.C., Metropolitan Police Department (MPD) needed to address this issue. In a joint effort with the FBI, the Cold Case Homicide Squad or the Cold Case Squad (CCS) was formed. The squad, which would not respond to new homicide cases, worked exclusively on unsolved murders. Other law-enforcement agencies had formed similar squads in the past, but this was the first time the FBI contributed agents to assist in investigations.

Staffing

Personnel make up the most important element of a cold case squadron. Old cases are among the most frustrating to work on because evidence could have been lost and witnesses are

Cold Cases: A Hot Topic

Cold cases attracted wide public attention in 2004, when a new crime drama, *Cold Case*, began airing on network television. The show followed the exploits of Detective Lily Rush, played by Kathryn Morris, one of four detectives from the Philadelphia homicide division assigned to investigate cold cases. The show presented a fairly accurate portrayal of a true-life cold case squad. However, due to its time constraints and need to appeal to a mass audience, it fell short of depicting the meticulous detective work that goes into investigating real cold cases.

A more realistic representation of how true cold case detectives operate was broadcast on the A&E Channel's show *Cold Case Files*, which followed actual cold case investigations and portrayed the great detective work and ingenuity that goes into investigations of old cases. The A&E show depicted both the hard work and the innovative techniques required of real cold case detectives in order to solve these types of cases.

missing or are now deceased. These are cases that, after all, one or several competent detectives have failed to solve. Only experienced, innovative, and resilient detectives are recommended for cold case investigations. These agents should have knowledge in investigating and prosecuting various types of homicides. Experience with violent crimes is also helpful in these types of cases as well as experience in gang- and drug-related homicides.

Most full-time cold case squads employ two to four investigators. Usually they also have a lieutenant supervisor from the homicide division or a sergeant who manages the squad. Some departments that are too small to carry a full-time cold case squad instead have a part-time squad made up of detectives who split their time between cold cases and their regular caseloads.

Process

A case is usually referred to a cold case squad by a homicide division supervisor or another homicide detective. Sometimes a prosecutor will decide to reopen an unsolved case and will request assistance from local law enforcement. Cases are then prioritized, usually being ranked by their likelihood of being solved.

After reviewing the case file, cold case detectives assess previously collected evidence for usability. Investigators then attempt to fill in any information missing from the original investigation. This includes speaking with the original case investigators, obtaining missing notes from the case file, and reinterviewing old witnesses.

One of the main challenges in a cold case investigation is locating and interviewing unknown or reluctant witnesses. These witnesses may be difficult to find or reluctant to speak, but the hope is that enough time has passed so that they are now willing to cooperate with the police. In this instance, the passage of time could aid, rather than hinder, detectives.

Once the process is completed, if no arrest is made or no viable suspect is identified, the detectives write a summary of their new investigation and recommend either further investigation or to close the case. A cold case can either be closed through an arrest or administratively. A case can also be considered closed if the suspect believed to be guilty is deceased or is serving a life sentence for another crime. Ultimately, the effectiveness of a cold case squad is measured by the number of cases it clears.

Technology

A significant advantage possessed by modern cold case investigators is the benefit of improved technology. Advancements in forensic analysis and investigative techniques have improved investigators' capabilities; these resources were not available to previous examiners.

New technology can shed new light on previously unsolved cases. DNA analysis and new methods in fingerprint technology have been great tools in clearing cases. Cold case investigators have also been known to utilize external resources, such as assistance from the FBI and U.S. Marshals Service, medical officers, and coroners.

Mark Anthony Cubillos

Further Reading

Ramsland, Katherine. *The Science of Cold Case Files*. New York: Berkley, 2004. Extracts from real-life cases, collected by a forensic psychologist, that inspired television shows.

Reavvy, Pat. "Deputy's Diligence Pays Off." *Deseret Morning News*, September 27, 2004, p. B4. Describes detective work that solved the murder of a fourteen-year-old boy eleven years after the event, and the advances in DNA technology that led to the killer's conviction.

U.S. Department of Justice, Office of Justice Programs. *Using DNA to Solve Cold Cases*. Washington, D.C.: National Institute of Justice, 2002. This special report, which is also available online, covers DNA fingerprinting among other modern technologies whose use can be applied to cold cases.

See also Autopsies; Bloodstains; Computer forensics; Coroners; Crime labs; Crime scene investigation; Criminal history record information; DNA testing; Fingerprint identification; Forensic accounting; Forensics; Medical examiners; Murder and homicide; Murders, mass and serial.

Color of law

Definition: Action that has the appearance of authority and legality but is actually unauthorized and illegal

Criminal justice issues: Constitutional protections; government misconduct; legal terms and principles; police powers

Significance: The color of law provision in the U.S. Code has been important in civil rights cases, particularly in enforcement of the rights guaranteed by the Fourteenth Amendment.

Government employees and especially law-enforcement officers are said to act "under color of law" when they presume to act in official capacities in the course of depriving others of their civil rights. The phrase therefore suggests an abuse of the powers entrusted to law-enforcement agents and other officials, constituting misconduct. The deprivation of rights "under color of law" can amount to criminal offenses or lead to civil lawsuits. At the federal level, allegations of color of law violations constitute the majority of federal civil rights cases initiated by the Federal Bureau of Investigation (FBI).

Color-of-law complaints, frequently leveled at law-enforcement personnel, include charges of excessive force, sexual assaults, false arrest or fabrication of evidence, wrongful deprivation of property, and failure to keep persons from harm. The Department of Justice can pursue remedies under civil law when entire police departments engage in patterns or practices of rights violations, and similar civil actions can be initiated against institutions that violate the rights of institutionalized persons, including inmates in jails, prisons, and mental hospitals. All citizens and residents enjoy rights that may be threatened by official misconduct under color of law, but the deprivation of the civil rights of aliens and members of minorities, or differential treatment of aliens and minorities, is a problem of special interest and importance, in both criminal and civil law contexts.

The phrase "color of law" is also used in the context of immigration to refer to aliens permanently residing in the United States under color of law, suggesting that the Immigration and Naturalization Service (INS) is permitting their residence in the United States indefinitely. The color of law has also been used to suggest that racial privileges and racial discriminations are institutionalized or embedded in the legal system.

T. J. Berard

Further Reading

Howard, John R. *The Shifting Wind: The Supreme Court and Civil Rights from Recon-*

struction to Brown. Albany: State University of New York Press, 1999.

O'Brien, David M. *Constitutional Law and Politics.* 6th ed. New York: W. W. Norton, 2005.

See also Deadly force; Fines; Perjury; Police civil liability; Police powers.

Commercialized vice

Definition: Business enterprises catering to various human desires that lead to statutory crimes

Criminal justice issues: Deviancy; morality and public order; victimless crime

Significance: Commercialized vice constitutes an ambivalent area in American justice as it involves mostly voluntary and consensual activities that are widely regarded as not harming anyone and thus frequently designated as victimless crimes.

When not merely viewed as a social deviance, commercialized vice is often described as crime against public morality. These so-called victimless crimes include prostitution and related offenses, obscenity and pornography, gambling, certain drug-related crimes, and alcoholism.

Prostitution and Related Crimes

In addition to actual or attempted prostitution, commercialized vice includes keeping bawdy houses, procuring, and transporting women for immoral purposes (less frequently, men or minors). At first, prostitution was not an offense per se under English or American law. It was only in 1914 that an Indiana statute defined the trade and only in 1917 that Massachusetts made prostitution directly punishable instead of charging solicitation, vagrancy, disorderly conduct, loitering, and the like.

By 1920 most states, using their police powers to protect

Examples of Color of Law Violations

Two notable civil rights cases that involved the color of law provision were *Monroe v. Pape* (1961) and *United States v. Price* (1966). In *Monroe*, thirteen police officers were accused of misusing their authority by entering a home without warning, ransacking it, and using their authority in a manner inconsistent with state law. Supreme Court justice William O. Douglas held that because the police action occurred under color of law, the victim had recourse to the courts. Color of law was held to apply to all rights guaranteed by the Fourteenth Amendment. In *Price*, eighteen people were implicated in the Mississippi murder of three civil rights workers. Justice Abe Fortas's opinion in the case stated that even private citizens—in contrast to state officials—can be said to be acting under color of law when they are working in concert with state officials.

Prostitutes in one of Nevada's legal brothels line up before customers in early 2003. Nevada has considered taxing prostitution to raise revenue for the state, but some opponents of legalized prostitution oppose taxing brothels for the reason that doing so would tend to legitimize a business that they regard as vice. *(AP/Wide World Photos)*

the health, safety, welfare, and morale of the citizens, criminalized prostitution, with the exception of Nevada, where the matter is still decided at the county level. Despite variations, state and local criminal statutes may apply to the prostitute, panderer, pimp, customer (the "john" or the "jill"), the economic beneficiary of the prostitute's activity (if other than the pimp), and the trafficker in prostitutes.

The federal government, using the commerce clause of the U.S. Constitution as its authority, has taken part in regulating these offenses beginning with the Mann (White Slave Traffic) Act of 1910, which bars the interstate transportation, persuasion, or coercion of women or girls into prostitution. Under its war powers, the U.S. Congress subsequently banned prostitution around military bases beginning in World War I.

Streetwalkers, who make up an estimated 10 percent to 20 percent of all prostitutes, account for some 85 percent or more of all arrests because they are the most visible prostitutes. In this regard, they differ from prostitutes in other categories such as call girls, in-house sex workers, and workers in massage parlors, photo studios, strip clubs, and elsewhere. There is little empirical evidence about the effectiveness of such arrests in curbing prostitution, as pimps often pay fines or hire lawyers to get their employees released from jail. Police often consider that more serious priorities than prostitution need attending to, and the general public and even the courts are ambivalent about this area of the law. Still, there are some notable examples of city mayors publishing lists of "johns" or of police vice squads, a few headed by women, strictly enforcing the laws relating to public morality or decency.

Male prostitutes also ply their trade, primarily in the gay sex market. Many of these cater to pedophiles, often older men for whom children are the preferred sex objects. A few males are hired by older women, especially at tourist resorts where the customers, seeking adventure and fun, can also retain their anonymity. As with their female counterparts, male prostitutes fall into various categories, such as street hustlers, bar hustlers, call boys, kept boys, and escorts. Even in the twenty-first century, which has seen an unprecedented acceptance of homosexual activity, there are still antisodomy laws at the state and federal levels, and in 2004 the U.S. Supreme Court had yet to set aside its *Bowers v. Hardwick* decision of 1986, thus refusing to overturn antisodomy laws, even those involving consensual adults.

Obscenity and Pornography

The crime of obscenity or pornography ("porn" is the nonlegal term for obscenity) involves the selling, delivering, airing, or supplying in any form any sex-related materials that are considered offensive according to certain standards. Generally, these materials or acts have to go beyond the customary lines of candor in description or representation. Just what the benchmarks of acceptability should be has been hard for the U.S. Supreme Court to define. As Justice Potter Stewart stated in *Jacobellis v. Ohio* (1964), he could not describe pornography, "but I know it when I see it." Justice John Marshall Harlan opined in *Cohen v. California* (1971) that "one man's vulgarity is another man's lyric."

Beginning with the case of *Roth v. United States* (1957), the Supreme Court has held that once it is ascertained, obscenity falls outside the protection of the First Amendment of the U.S. Constitution guaranteeing freedom of speech, actual or symbolic. For all that, the justices made it clear that nudity and sex are not by definition obscene but only if they are "hard-core pornography." To be obscene, according to the landmark ruling of *Miller v. California* (1973), a work, taken as a whole, must be deemed by "the average person applying contemporary community standards" to appeal to the "prurient interest" or to depict "in a patently offensive way, sexual conduct specifically defined by applicable state law" and lacking "serious literary, artistic, political, or scientific value."

For all that, the courts will always have difficulty negotiating the fine line between the right of citizens (even children) to read, see, and hear what they wish and the right of others to protect minors and the community in general from moral "degradation." Accordingly, recognizing that in a pluralistic society differing values will be in evidence, by the twenty-first century the Supreme Court, referring to artistic, literary, scientific, or political merit or deferring to community standards, had shown wide fluctuations of opinion in the decisions handed down in this area of commercialized vice.

Drug-Related Crimes

Of relatively recent origin, the so-called drug crisis in the United States relating to the abuse of narcotics is not a single problem but, in fact, a broad range of them. It is part of a global situation involving a vast network of growers, smugglers, wholesale dealers, and street retailers—even criminal justice officers who cannot resist the money involved in payoffs, in extorting money from the dealers themselves, or in selling the confiscated goods.

Historically, the substance most widely used in the United States has been marijuana, at one time often employed, just as cocaine, in popular elixirs. By the 1970's cocaine had again become the preferred "hard" narcotic. The invention of newer and more powerful or customized drugs, such as crack cocaine, has reportedly popularized addiction even more, despite fluctuations in the use of all drugs.

Beginning in 1906 with the Pure Food and Drug Act and in 1914 with the Harrison Narcotic Drug Act, the federal government has imposed gradual control over drug use involved in interstate and foreign commerce. In 1919, two U.S. Supreme Court decisions (*United States v. Doremus* and *Webb v. United States*) declared almost all forms of drug addiction illegal. Federal control was tightened in the 1930's, as heroin use spread and as organized crime became more involved in the distribution and sale of illegal drugs. State control was not far behind.

In 1970, the Comprehensive Drug Abuse Prevention and Control Act consolidated all existing measures in the federal code. Stricter penalties for drug abuse and trafficking went into force in the wake of the Vietnam War-era drug epidemic. Most states began to follow the U.S. Department of Justice-recommended uniform code, updated by the Uniform Controlled Dangerous Substances Act of 1974.

Since then, some states have relaxed the rules, including decriminalization of a few of the drugs, such as marijuana, which have been shown to have therapeutic value. In its 2004-2005 term, the U.S. Supreme Court was scheduled to decide whether Congress has the authority to prohibit the medical use of marijuana in states where the voters or the legislature have approved the drug's use under a doctor's care. Even in states like New York that have harsh drug laws, it was likely that this would happen in short order. Most observers agree that drug abuse and convictions are an important reason behind prison overcrowding and public budgets squeezed by law-enforcement outlays.

Gambling

Gambling is the staking of money or something else of value on an uncertain future event. The element of luck is the controlling factor in gambling, so wagers are made on the outcome of a game of chance or skill. The range of games, devices used, and places where bets are made is very wide.

Since 1948, after a half century of regulation by states, the federal government expanded its role in regulating gambling. By the 1970's, federal statutes had been enacted to control, among other things, interstate and foreign transporta-

tion of gambling paraphernalia, the transmission of wagering information through wire facilities, state-conducted lotteries, and taxes on betting. Accordingly, by the twenty-first century, the federal government was extensively involved in regulating the promotion of illegal gambling and in sanctioning violators. At the state level, wagering on dog races or cock fights—especially as these activities often violate animal rights legislation—are widely outlawed.

At the same time, however, a number of gambling activities are being legalized—for example, church raffles and bingo games, state lotteries, and gambling casinos run by American Indians. As in the case of other so-called victimless crimes such as drug use, arguments are being made that legalizing games of chance will reduce the profits of running illegal ones, especially by organized crime, and that this, in turn, will curtail the corruption of officials and law-enforcement agents who apply gambling laws in a discriminating manner. There is disagreement on most of these points, and the fear, also voiced in connection with decriminalizing other so-called victimless crimes, is that ancillary criminality—such as prostitution—may increase at gambling casinos and other gaming locations.

Alcoholism

This form of commercialized vice involves drunkenness and intoxication with alcoholic beverages. In the United States the consumption of

So-Called Victimless Crimes

Crime	Total number of arrests in 2002
Prostitution and commercialized vice	58,758
Other sex offenses (except forcible rape and prostitution)	67,833
Drug abuse violations	1,103,017
Gambling	7,525
Liquor law violations	463,849
Drunkenness	413,808
Disorderly conduct	482,827
Vagrancy	19,678
All other offenses (except traffic)	2,606,294

Notes: Police departments reporting these figures are often inconsistent in their classifications. Also, as the conduct involved is consensual, many victimless crimes are unreported.

Source: Federal Bureau of Investigation's *Crime in the United States 2002: Uniform Crime Reports*

such beverages—beer, wine, and hard liquor—is relatively high. As in the case of drug abuse, alcoholism—defined as excessive use of these beverages—is closely linked to violent crime, driving while intoxicated with the resulting automobile crashes, problems in the workplace such as absenteeism, disorderly and violent conduct of various kinds, family abuse and breakup, and other social ills.

Criminal law has attempted to check the consequences of some alcohol abuse by raising the minimum drinking age in states (often to as high as twenty-one years) in public places, limiting bar hours, and checking secondary criminality flowing from middlemen profiting from the national addiction by operating after-hour bars and the like. However, the dismal experience of the Prohibition era (1919-1933), when the Eighteenth Amendment of the U.S. Constitution, implemented by the Volstead Act of 1919, unsuccessfully barred the manufacture, sale, transportation, import, or export of intoxicating liquors taught an object lesson. Thus, the "demon rum," seemingly as American as apple pie, is no longer perceived as a major public menace.

Vice Control

Law, including in the field of criminal justice, is always the product of the forces of time and place, and undoubtedly the American mosaic has evolved. Thus, when it comes to commercialized vice, what was considered widely reprehensible in an earlier, more puritanical age—as socially or legally deviant—may not be so today. Paralleling a supposedly better-educated and more sophisticated public and the socializing influence of the media, there has been a corresponding change in mores and in the laws and court decisions that reflect them over time.

Peter B. Heller

Further Reading

Aggleton, Peter, ed. *Men Who Sell Sex: International Perspectives on Male Prostitution and HIV/AIDS*. Philadelphia: Temple University Press, 1999. A series of essays about the numerous, complex dimensions of male sex work in several different locations across the world and its regulation by legislation and police. Includes index.

Chapkis, Wendy. *Live Sex Acts: Women Performing Erotic Labor*. New York: Routledge, 1997. Profile of the trade of prostitution and those engaged in it, with a chapter on "Legalization, Regulation, and Licensing." Includes photographs, bibliography, and index.

Lane, Frederick S., III. *Obscene Profits: The Entrepreneurs of Pornography in the Cyber Age*. New York: Routledge, 2000. How various social and technological developments have reduced or eliminated the stigma previously attached to pornography. Includes index.

Liska, Ken. *Drugs and the Human Body, with Implications for Society*. 7th ed. Saddle River, N.J.: Prentice-Hall, 2004. The social, medical, and psychotropic aspects of narcotic drugs. Includes bibliography, illustrations, and index.

Mason-Grant, Joan. *Pornography Embodied: From Speech to Sexual Practice*. Lanham, Md.: Rowman & Littlefield, 2004. The debate about pornography in the women's movement. Includes appendix, bibliography, and index.

O'Brien, Timothy L. *Bad Bet: The Inside Story of the Glamour, Glitz, and Danger of America's Gambling Industry*. New York: Random House/Times Business, 1998. The nature of compulsive gambling and its regulation. Includes bibliography and index.

See also *Bowers v. Hardwick*; Decriminalization; Disorderly conduct; Drug legalization debate; Gambling; Mafia; Mann Act; Opium Exclusion Act; Pandering; Pornography; Pornography, child; Prohibition; Public-order offenses; Victimless crimes.

Common law

Definition: Body of law arising from judicial decisions, rather than from written statutes, that reflect customs, tradition, and precedent

Criminal justice issues: Law codes; legal terms and principles

Significance: With roots that go back to the eleventh century, English common law served as the foundation for the American legal system, and both civil and criminal law in the United States reflect the English common-law tradition.

The American criminal justice system, especially the substantive criminal law that defines criminal offenses, defenses, and specifies criminal punishments, is derived from English common law. Common law is the body of law that first emerged in England during the eleventh century. It grew out of the manner in which judges settled disputes. Before the eleventh century, English courts were often informal assemblies in which judges based their decisions on local traditions and customs. As a consequence, England lacked uniformity in how judges defined the law and decided cases.

After the Norman Conquest in 1066, the new Norman kings appointed royal judges to settle disputes. These royal, or common-law, judges recorded their decisions and the kings ordered the distribution of the decisions throughout the country to serve as precedents to guide judges in similar future cases. These precedents served as a basis for developing a common body of law in both civil and criminal cases. The doctrine of deciding cases based on precedent initiated by the common law became known as *stare decisis*. Legal scholars often refer to common law as judge-made law because its development was dependent on judicial interpretation. By 1200, England had established a unified system of common law by incorporating decisions based on local custom and tradition to the national level.

As the English common law evolved, judges created criminal offenses to protect individuals from conduct that society judged wrongful. These common-law crimes became known as *mala in se* offenses; they were the types of offenses that societies have almost universally condemned since ancient times. For example, judges defined what constituted the crimes against persons such as the homicidal crimes of murder, manslaughter, and suicide. They also defined the crimes against property such as robbery, burglary, and larceny. Moreover, the judges articulated what constituted defenses to each of the defined crimes. For example, at common law a homicide could be excusable if it were committed for necessary self-protection.

Finally, the common law judges also developed a consistency in determining punishments for crimes. In addition to defining the substantive criminal law, the English courts also instituted trial by jury and an adversarial system of justice in which trial lawyers (known as barristers in England) argued cases in front of judges whose roles were to remain neutral. The eighteenth century English jurist Sir William Blackstone described the principles of English common law in *Commentaries on the Laws of England*, which he published in 1769.

Common Law in North America

As England colonized North America, government officials transferred English common-law legal traditions and common-law crimes to the colonies. After the United States proclaimed its independence from England during the late eighteenth century, its individual states adopted English common law to the extent to which it did not conflict with provisions of the U.S. Constitution and their own state constitutions.

Eventually, states developed a preference for defining crimes, defenses, and punishments by statute. By the twentieth century, most of the principles of common law were codified into statutes, as state legislatures enacted each state's principles and definitions of criminal law and criminal procedure. Most states now have comprehensive codes of criminal law and criminal procedure that set forth general principles of criminal responsibility, criminal offenses, defenses to crimes, and the rules of law governing how crimes are investigated, prosecuted, adjudicated, and punished. However, most states also ground and interpret these statutes in the tradition of English common law.

Important examples of common law are the definitions of murder as the unlawful killing of one person by another with malice aforethought and manslaughter as the unlawful killing of a human being without malice. Common law also defined two categories of manslaughter: voluntary manslaughter, or intentional unlawful killing that occurs in the heat of passion, and involuntary manslaughter—the unintentional killing due to gross negligence. American statutory criminal laws pertaining to homicide reflect these common-law ideas concerning homicide, although states typically classify homicide differently than the common-law classification. Most states classify murder as either first- or second-degree murder. First-degree murder requires malice aforethought or premeditation while second-degree murder usually requires outrageous conduct that results in the death of another person. Similarly, most states have changed their classifications of manslaughter and no longer make the formal distinction between voluntary and involuntary manslaughter but rather classify the crime in terms of degrees. However, the degrees of manslaughter specified in state statutes still reflect the common-law distinction between intentional and unintentional killing.

Although the modern American criminal justice system reflects the English common-law tradition, it also contains many modifications and additions that reflect social and economic changes in society. For example, common law defined rape as unlawful sexual intercourse with a female without her consent. Common law held that a husband could not be guilty of raping his wife. In addition, English common law held that it was an offense for a man to have sexual intercourse with a child less than ten years of age, with or without the child's consent. Common law defined this type of offense as statutory rape. Legislation in many states now modifies the crime of rape in several ways. First, the common law rule that a husband cannot be guilty of raping his own wife is no longer the law. Second, statutes specify that other sexual situations besides sexual intercourse constitute criminal behavior when performed without the victim's consent or with a minor whether or not the minor consents. Third, many states define sex offenses as gender-neutral offenses. This means that states can charge both men and women as the perpetrators of these crimes. Finally, statutory rape laws also protect young teenagers. These laws vary from state to state but typically specify an age range of from two to five years between victims and perpetrators in order to impose criminal penalties.

While many additions and modifications to the American criminal justice system have occurred since the introduction of English common law, the American criminal justice system remains steeped in the features of English common law. These include the principle of *stare decisis*, the definitions of criminal offenses, criminal defenses, the adversarial system, and trial by jury. Therefore, while each state has its own criminal justice system, most state legislatures have left unchanged many principles developed under English common law.

Patricia E. Erickson

Further Reading

Holmes, Oliver W. *The Common Law*. Boston: Little, Brown, 1881.

Scheb, John M., and John M. Scheb II. *Introduction to the American Legal System*. Albany, N.Y.: Delmar Learning, 2001.

Schweber, Howard. *The Creation of American Common Law, 1850-1880: Technology, Politics, and the Construction of Citizenship*. New York: Cambridge University Press, 2004.

See also Arson; Burglary; Case law; Crime; Criminal justice in U.S. history; Criminal law; Criminal procedure; Defenses to crime; Excuses and justifications; Felonies; *Mala in se* and *mala prohibita*; Misdemeanors; Model Penal Code; Precedent; Principals (criminal); *Stare decisis*; Statutes; United States Code.

Community-based corrections

Definition: Sentence, or post-sentence arrangement, in which offenders are allowed to remain in their own communities, with supervision and sometimes assistance with rehabilitation and reintegration into their communities

Criminal justice issues: Probation and pretrial release; punishment; rehabilitation

Significance: Community-based corrections are alternatives to incarceration and are increasingly and innovatively being used by judges and corrections administrators to alleviate prison and jail overcrowding.

An array of community-based correctional strategies is in use, but this was not always the case. Around the time of the American Revolution, offenders were routinely punished in their local communities, with public humiliation as the goal. Criminals, for example, were placed in stocks and forced to endure thrown garbage and insults while they were, literally, on display in the town square. Such punishments aimed to deter would-be offenders and provided obvious retribution for wrongdoing. These early humiliating punishments, however, did not aim to reintegrate the offender.

Over time, penal reformers argued that rehabilitation should also be an objective of punishment and that offenders could be corrected within their communities. By the mid-nineteenth century, some offenders were placed on probation and parole, the earliest attempts at their correction outside an institution. Until the late 1950's, these were the only widely employed community-corrections strategies. During the 1960's and 1970's, increased interest and support for the idea of correction in the community led to the proliferation of work-release programs, halfway houses, substance-abuse centers, and other community-based corrections. By the 1980's, support for rehabilitation and community-based corrections had decreased; the number of offenders removed from society via incarceration grew. Prison and jail populations skyrocketed. Consequently, alternatives to incarceration are now sought, if only to alleviate institutional overcrowding.

Probation and Parole

Probation and parole began to be used in the United States during the nineteenth century. Probation originated in Boston in 1841, through the work of John Augustus, an influential business owner. As a sentence, probation allows convicted offenders to remain in their communities, under supervision and with specified conditions. Liberty is, therefore, conditional. The conditions of probation quite often focus on an offender's rehabilitative needs. For example, an offender with substance-abuse problems will likely be required to attend Narcotics Anonymous or other appropriate meetings.

Unlike probation, parole is not a sentence. A parole board, rather than a judge, decides whether an offender may soon rejoin society. If the decision is favorable, an inmate is granted early release from prison. Therefore, all parolees have recently been incarcerated. New York, through its adoption of an indeterminate sentencing law in 1876, was the first state to allow prisoners to be released on parole.

The aim of parole, like that of all community-based corrections, is to assist with an offender's reintegration. Like a probationer, a parolee is supervised while in the outside community and must abide by conditions of release. For both probationers and parolees, failure to abide by the conditions specified for release may result in reimprisonment.

The Mid-Twentieth Century

From the late-1950's to the late-1970's, the scope of community-based corrections expanded beyond probation and parole. Penal reformers argued that released inmates faced many problems as they made the transition from imprisonment to life back in the community. To combat the challenges former inmates faced, organizations such as the International Halfway House Association (now known as the International Association of Residential and Community Alternatives) and the American Correctional Association were instrumental in increasing the resources available for community-based corrections, and some were secured through legislation. For example, the Federal Prisoner Rehabilitation Act of 1965 authorized the establishment of halfway houses for both juveniles and adults. Largely because of these efforts, from 1966 to 1982 the number of halfway houses operating in the United States and Canada increased from fewer than fifty to more than fifteen hundred. The aim of halfway houses, both then and now, is to assist with an offender's successful reintegration back into society. Some halfway houses also provide in-house rehabilitation, which may include job skills training, substance-abuse treatment, or mental health counseling.

The number of inmates granted temporary release from prisons and jails also grew notably. In 1957, for example, North Carolina became the first state to permit selected convicted felons to leave prisons during the day to work in the local community. Other states followed suit. The U.S. Congress, in 1965, allowed work release for prisoners in federal institutions. Authorization for other temporary-release programs, such as furlough release and study release, also became more widespread. The aim of all temporary-release programs is to promote offenders' positive ties to society by allowing them to maintain regular societal interaction.

The 1980's and Beyond

Belief in the value of rehabilitation waned in the 1980's. Critics argued that high recidivism rates were indicative of a correctional system that was not working, suggesting that "correction" was not possible. Consequently, deterrence, retribution, and incapacitation became the primary justifications for punishment. With this came an increased likelihood of incarceration for an offender.

By 2004, the rate of incarceration was at an all-time high. Prisons and jails in many jurisdictions across the United States remained severely overcrowded. One method of reducing overcrowding is to sentence offenders to something other than incarceration. Intermediate sanctions, which are simply punishments that are more severe than probation but less severe than incarceration, provide an alternative.

Use of most intermediate sanctions originated in the 1980's or 1990's. For example, Georgia became the first state to implement intensive supervised probation (ISP), in 1982, and widely to use correctional boot camps, in 1983. Both were done, in part, to avoid a federal takeover of its overcrowded prison system. New Jersey and Massachusetts also began utilizing ISP during the early 1980's.

The use of house arrest, with or without electronic monitoring, has also spread rapidly. In 1984, Florida was the first state extensively to use the sanction of home confinement. For many offenders, this punishment is the last chance to avoid incarceration in jail or prison. As technology has advanced, more and more jurisdictions have added electronic monitoring into their repertoire of punishment options.

Day-reporting centers are among the newest of intermediate sanctions. In 1990 only thirteen day-reporting centers existed in the United States. By 2004, most major jurisdictions had at least one center to which offenders are sentenced to report on a daily basis. At the center, where offenders may spend up to eight hours of their days, focus is placed on an offender's rehabilitation needs. Over time, expectations are that intermediate sanctions will increasingly be used.

Pauline K. Brennan

Further Reading

Abadinsky, Howard. *Probation and Parole*. 7th ed. Upper Saddle River, N.J.: Prentice-Hall, 2000. Detailed description of probation and parole in the United States.

Allen, Harry E., Clifford E. Simonsen, and Edward J. Latessa. *Corrections in America: An Introduction*. 10th ed. Upper Saddle River, N.J.: Pearson Education, 2004. An introductory discussion of the history of corrections, sentencing, incarceration, alternatives to confinement, types of offenders under correctional supervision, and reintegration.

Clear, Todd R., and Harry R. Dammer. *The Offender in the Community*. 2d ed. Belmont, Calif.: Wadsworth/Thomson Learning, 2003. Systematic review of a number of community-based corrections.

Haas, Kenneth C., and Geoffrey P. Alpert. *The Dilemmas of Corrections*. 4th ed. Prospect Heights, Ill.: Waveland Press, 1999. Provides readings on rehabilitation, community-based corrections, and critical problems and issues faced by corrections institutions.

Stohr, Mary K., and Craig Hemmens. *The Inmate Prison Experience*. Upper Saddle River, N.J.: Pearson Education, 2004. Describes life behind bars and the challenges of reintegration for former inmates.

See also Community service; Criminology; Deterrence; Drug courts; Electronic surveillance; Forestry camps; Halfway houses; House arrest; Incapacitation; "Not-in-my-backyard" attitudes; Parole; Prison overcrowding; Probation, adult; Recidivism; Rehabilitation; Restorative justice; Sentencing; Work camps; Work-release programs.

Community-oriented policing

Definition: Philosophy of law enforcement that encompasses aspects of social service as police officers work with members of the communities they serve to solve local problems

Criminal justice issues: Crime prevention; law-enforcement organization

Significance: Community policing practices have been adopted in one form or another by a vast majority of police departments throughout the United States.

Formal policing is less than two centuries old, and a community-oriented approach is being advanced as the new philosophy of policing for the twenty-first century. Although the variety of roles police have played during the history of the United States is not well documented, an understanding of what is known will aid in understanding the concept of community-oriented policing.

Historical Background

At the turn of the twentieth century, American police officers performed duties that amounted to social services. Such activities included assisting the unemployed to find jobs, operating soup kitchens, and making police stations available as night shelters for the indigent. During the first decade of the twentieth century, the New York City police commissioner initiated a number of policies that facilitated community-oriented policing. The commissioner believed that the rank-and-file police officers held positions of social importance of great public value. The community-oriented policies should not only be considered for their benefits to the police but also as beneficial to the public. The New York City Police Department held that every police officer was accountable for the social condition on the beat that he patrolled.

Many disciplines in the social sciences now hold that employment is a deterrent to crime. The 1990's saw a verification of this theory: The United States had both a low unemployment rate and a low crime rate. Likewise, in the early twentieth century, the New York City police commissioner considered unemployment to be a major cause of crime, and beat officers were expected to distribute employment information and assist the unemployed in locating employment. One of the overall responsibilities of beat officers was to improve the safety of their beats and make them safe.

Initiatives by the New York City Police Department in its early, community-oriented approach to policing included creating so-called play streets. Play streets were designated for youngsters in neighborhoods that had no playgrounds, parks, or safe open places. For several hours during the day, the police would close streets in specific neighborhoods by placing barricades to vehicle traffic.

The police also referred teenage boys who were involved in delinquent acts to social services agencies, such as the Young Men's Christian Association and Big Brothers. One more creative approach to community-oriented policing was the police department's communication with ethnic newspapers of that era. Greek-, Italian-, and Yiddish-language papers were encouraged to publish city ordinances, so that immigrants could read about the laws in their native languages.

Eras of Policing

Historians recognize that policing in the nineteenth century was primarily decentralized and neighborhood-oriented. The major problems of this policing model were inefficiency, corruption, incompetence, and undue political influence on police officers. That era has been called the "political era," during which the police and politicians had close relationships. Meanwhile, as towns and cities were developing, policing was in its initial stages, under the control of local governments. In the cities, the politicians oversaw all police operations. Although the police were usually organized in centralized, semimilitary, and hierarchical structures, they generally did not function along those lines. Rather, they made up decentralized units, with each ward politician running the police department in his ward.

Around the turn of the twentieth century, the Progressive movement emerged as a voice that sought to improve city government. The Progressive movement reflected upper-middle-class values that emphasized honesty in government officials, and it ushered in uniform, well-defined police procedures and policies. This period of policing has been called the "reform era." It saw attempts to free the police from control by politicians. Civil service reforms in police departments led to decreased influence by politicians, who lost their power in the hiring and firing of police officers. The reforms in policing emphasized the law-enforcement functions of policing over their social service functions. Although some law-enforcement scholars have suggested different policing eras and models, the terms "political era" and "reform era" have become generally accepted as the names of the eras preceding the modern era of community-oriented policing.

Problem-Oriented Policing

The road to modern change may have been laid down in 1979, when Herman Goldstein published an article on problem-oriented policing that would greatly influence modern-day practices. Goldstein claimed that the reform approach to policing was not working. Police responded to citizens' calls to handle specific incidents then returned to their patrol cars. According to Goldstein, beat officers were responding to events that kept occurring over and over again. Goldstein recommended that the police address the cycles themselves by developing a problem-oriented approach in order to solve the underlying issues that lead to problems. The emphasis of problem-oriented policing, he said, should be on the police working proactively to resolve situations that generate the reactive calls for help from beat officers.

In community-oriented policing, as in problem-oriented policing, the police take an active role in problem solving, but the goal of community-oriented policing is for officers to develop partnerships with members of the communities they serve. Problem-oriented policing has been incorporated into community-oriented policing as an important tool. Police departments that have adopted the community policing

philosophy refer to problem-oriented policing (POP) projects, in which beat officers are expected to be involved.

The literature of various police departments reveals that the philosophy of community-oriented policing has a variety of meanings. Some police administrators believe that community-oriented policing has always taken place in small towns, where police officers typically know everyone on a first-name basis. Some administrators equate problem-oriented policing with community-oriented policing. Still others equate community-oriented policing with specialized units that work in high-crime areas. Also, there are police administrators who tout community-oriented policing because they consider it the latest fad and have instituted it for public relations purposes. Community policing has become so fashionable that a vast majority of police departments are claiming they are doing it.

The Nature of Communities

Basically, community-oriented policing involves police working with people in the communities they serve as equal partners to solve local problems. The term "community" may refer to a

In an effort to gain greater control over prostitution and drug dealing in Indianapolis's rough eastside, police officers began returning to foot patrols in place of squad cars during the late 1990's. (AP/Wide World Photos)

specific geographical area, such as a neighborhood, precinct area, or a patrol beat. Different areas of the city or community typically have different problems, the solutions to which should be determined by the police officers assigned to these areas in partnership with the local residents. A major premise of community-oriented policing advocates that strategies to solve problems are developed in concert with the citizens, whether the community refers to neighborhood or beat.

What is the value of community-oriented policing? Will it produce safer communities? Will citizens be more willing to cooperate with and support the police? Will the police be willing to share decision-making when it comes to controlling and preventing crime within the community? At present, no definitive answers can be provided. Because of a lack of scientific evidence that community-oriented policing has been successful, supporters are stressing other benefits to the community that are easier to demonstrate, based on surveys of residents taken both before and after implementation of community-oriented policing strategies in their neighborhoods. These successes involve citizens' attitudes, specifically regarding their fear of crime, their evaluation of the police, and their satisfaction with their neighborhoods.

In addition, the distribution of police newsletters informing residents about crime prevention and police programs; community projects, such as cleanup campaigns, property identification, and "safe" houses for children are considered to be successful attributes of community policing. Other benefits that community-oriented policing offers include public scrutiny—the public has a close view of police practices—and accountability—community-oriented policing provides the public with greater control over the police and law enforcement. Obviously, because community policing is implemented by individual police departments throughout the United States, it should be expected that some communities will be further advanced than others in community-oriented policing.

The community-oriented policing philosophy is not completely new, but it represents a major break with the reform or crime control model of policing that dominated the United States for most of the twentieth century. Many of the strategies of community-oriented policing are based on concepts that have been used by police departments in the past. Community-oriented policing has adapted from police-community relations ideas that have been proposed since the 1960's. The team-policing concept adopted in the 1970's could be considered a forerunner to the philosophy of community-oriented policing. The strategy of directed patrol, or patrolling guided by analysis of crime patterns and directed toward the solution of specific neighborhood problems was used in the 1970's and is being used in community policing today.

In large part, community-oriented policing has been advocated because of the failures of previous crime control methods to prevent, solve, or reduce crimes substantially. The concept of community policing has a variety of definitions and meanings, but generally it includes a problem-solving, results-oriented, public-oriented approach which emphasizes collaboration and partnership with the members of the community. The police-community collaboration focuses on solving problems of crime, fear of crime, public disorder, and neighborhood decay. Although its effectiveness in preventing crime has not clearly been proven, community-oriented policing can have a positive effect on citizen attitudes, decreasing the fear of crime and increasing satisfaction with neighborhoods of residence. Community-oriented policing can also have a positive effect on the police, who gain a more positive image of the public, enjoy increased grassroots support, and see improved police morale.

Possible Problems

Potential problems with community-oriented policing might include actions by police to uphold local norms of order and respectability that go beyond the legal bounds, such as harassment of the homeless. Also, police strategies may selectively favor the affluent and powerful in the community at the expense of the less privileged. Officers could use their close ties with the community members for political ends or for corrupt personal gain; the police could also become too intrusive into the private lives of residents.

In addition, implementation of community-oriented policing may face several obstacles.

Many aspects of the reform or traditional policing organization and culture should be expected to resist change. Even in departments that have had community policing for several years, there are officers who resist the community-oriented philosophy and want a return to traditional policing. Also, community support and involvement can be difficult to obtain. Reasons behind lack of support could range from lack of residents' time to commit to community-oriented programs to residents' mistrust of the police, fear of neighborhood criminals, or lack of infrastructure in high-crime neighborhoods. Community support has to be obtained by the police and should never be assumed by them.

Michael J. Palmiotto

Further Reading

Bennet, W., and Karen Hess. *Management and Supervision in Law Enforcement*. 4th ed. Belmont, Calif.: Wadsworth, 2004. Comprehensive textbook on all aspects of local police work, including community-oriented policing.

Miller, L., and Karen Hess. *Police in the Community: Strategies for the Twenty-first Century*. 3d ed. Belmont, Calif.: Wadsworth, 2002. Evaluation of the direction in which community-oriented policing was headed at the beginning of the twenty-first century.

Palmiotto, Michael J. *Community Policing: A Policing Strategy for the Twenty-first Century*. 2d ed. Boston: Jones and Bartlett, 2005. Comprehensive and up-to-date survey of all aspects of community-oriented policing.

_____. "The Influence of 'Community' in Community Policing." In *Visions for Change: Crime and Justice in the Twenty-first Century*, edited by Roslyn Muraskin and Albert Robert. 4th ed. Upper Saddle River, N.J.: Prentice-Hall, 2004. Chapter on the nature of communities involved in community-oriented policing.

Palmiotto, Michael J., M. Birzer, and N. Unninthan. "A Suggested Curriculum for Police Recruit Training in Community Policing." *Policing: An International Journal of Police Strategies and Management* 23, no. 1 (2000). Practical suggestions for the special training required for officers involved in community-oriented policing.

See also Criminology; McGruff the Crime Dog; Neighborhood watch programs; Peace Officers Standards and Training; Police; Police academies; Police civil liability; Police ethics; Police powers; September 11, 2001, attacks; Strategic policing.

Community service

Definition: Form of punishment that as an alternative to incarceration requires offenders to do work that improves the community or restores the damage their actions have caused

Criminal justice issues: Punishment; restorative justice

Significance: Community service has proven to be a cost-effective alternative to incarceration and offers other benefits to communities. At the same time, it requires a measure of accountability and responsibility on the part of the offenders.

Offenders who are sentenced to perform community service are typically required to do set amounts of unpaid labor for some project or operation that benefits the community in which they have been convicted. The logic behind this practice follows a principle of restorative justice holding that reparations to victims or communities as a whole create a better end than simply punishing offenders through incarceration. While part of restoration may include imposition of fines, the amounts of the fines may be influenced by the offenders' ability to pay and thus have unequal impact on the communities. Restitution to the community as a whole through tangible service can be a more even-handed way of achieving restorative justice, as the sentences imposed on the rich and the poor are more likely to be the same.

Community service offers many benefits. While still holding offenders accountable for their actions, the communities can receive tangible forms of compensation. Moreover, monitoring completion of community service is nearly always less expensive than incarceration, allowing the limited incarceration resources to be directed to offenders who pose greater risks to the community. Another benefit is the offering of positive, structured activities for the offenders' free-time. However, although offenders themselves may benefit from performing their service, being forced to give up leisure time or opportunities to earn money clearly has a punitive aspect.

The quality of community service is often dependent on the relationships between the court officers overseeing the work and the organizations for which the offenders perform services. An important aspect of community service is that the work performed serves genuine needs in the community, and that it is actually done. Assignments may be client-specific, to take advantage of individual offenders' special skills, or offense specific, such as assigning someone charged with animal cruelty to work in an animal shelter.

Most offenders reside in their homes while completing their service, but some states have created centers in which the offenders are required to reside while performing their service. Residents of such centers are supervised twenty-four hours a day, but the centers create opportunities for the residents to work in programs that help the community. Upon release, the residents are generally better prepared to be reintegrated into their communities, and they may have developed new marketable job skills, along with positive feelings of involvement in the community.

While research findings on the effectiveness of community-service programs have been mixed, most studies find that offenders sentenced to community service are, at the least, no more likely to become repeat offenders afterward than offenders who are incarcerated. On the other hand, if community service is overused for repeat offenders and jail is not an alternative, incentives for offenders to provide quality service may be diminished. One thing is clear, however: The cost savings and general benefit of the offenders' work to the community makes the programs attractive alternatives to traditional sentences of incarceration for many offender populations.

John C. Kilburn, Jr.

Further Reading

Clear, Todd R., and Harry R. Dammer. *The Offender in the Community*. 2d ed. Belmont, Calif.: Wadsworth/Thomson Learning, 2003.

Karp, David R., and Todd R. Clear. *What Is Community Justice? Case Studies of Restorative Justice and Community Supervision*. Thousand Oaks, Calif.: Sage Publications, 2002.

McDonald, Douglas. *Punishment Without Walls: Community Service Sentences in New York City*. New Brunswick, N.J.: Rutgers University Press, 1986.

See also Animal abuse; Chain gangs; Community-based corrections; Punishment; Restitution; Restorative justice; Sentencing; Sentencing guidelines, U.S.

Competency to stand trial

Definition: Determination of whether defendants are mentally able to understand the charges against them and to understand trial proceedings

Criminal justice issues: Defendants; mental disorders; trial procedures

Significance: A long-standing American and English legal tradition holds that mentally incompetent persons should not be subjected to criminal trials.

The idea that a person judged to be incompetent should not be forced to stand trial on criminal charges has its basis in English common law. In the United States it has been considered a constitutional principle as well since the Supreme Court case *Drope v. Missouri* (1975). Part of the rationale is that if an accused party does not have the capacity to participate in the trial, then the American adversarial system of justice cannot be fairly applied, and the accused will therefore not receive due process of law.

Dusky v. United States (1960) established that the standard of incompetency for federal trials was to be whether the accused has "sufficient present ability to consult with his lawyer with a reasonable degree of rational understanding" and could have a rational and factual understanding of court proceedings. To be "competent," a person must be able to confer with a lawyer, testify coherently, and follow evidence that is presented. State courts generally follow this standard as well, although the wording of state statutes varies. Although the federal incompe-

Brian David Mitchell (center) singing a hymn at a competency hearing in Salt Lake City in early 2005. A self-proclaimed prophet who claimed to have been sent by God to reform the Church of Jesus Christ of Latter-day Saints, Mitchell was arrested in 2002 for the highly publicized nine-month abduction of teenager Elizabeth Smart, whom he planned to make one of his plural wives. However, through early 2005, his case still had not come to trial because of his disruptive behavior during his many competency hearings. *(AP/Wide World Photos)*

tency statute refers to mental incapacitation, some cases of severe physical incapacitation have been held to constitute incompetency.

Determining competency involves three stages: initiating an inquiry, making a preliminary determination as to competency, and, if there is sufficient evidence, holding a competency hearing. An inquiry is usually initiated by counsel, either prosecution or defense. Generally a psychiatric examination is then mandatory. If the examination indicates that the defendant may be incompetent, a competency hearing is mandatory. The hearing is adversarial in nature; the main witness is usually the psychiatrist who gave the psychiatric examination, but other witnesses may also be called. The trial judge usually rules on the defendant's competency, and the judge may consider the defendant's appearance and demeanor

as well as the witness's testimony. A finding of incompetency does not mean that the person has been judged not guilty. Traditionally, a person found incompetent would be committed to a psychiatric institution, and there were no restrictions on how long such confinement could be. In 1972, however, in *Jackson v. Indiana* the Supreme Court held that commitment could not exceed a "reasonable period of time" for determining whether the person could be expected to regain competency.

Elizabeth Algren Shaw

Further Reading

Bardwell, Mark C. *Criminal Competency on Trial: The Case of Colin Ferguson*. Durham, N.C.: Caroline Academic Press, 2002.
Conley, Ronald W., Ruth Luckasson, and George

N. Bouthilet. *The Criminal Justice System and Mental Retardation: Defendants and Victims.* Baltimore: Brookes, 1992.

Reed, E. F. *The Penry Penalty: Capital Punishment and Offenders with Mental Retardation.* Lanham, Md.: University Press of America, 1993.

See also Arraignment; Common law; Criminal intent; *Ford v. Wainwright*; Forensic psychology; Insanity defense; Malice; Mental illness; Psychological evaluation.

Comprehensive Crime Control Act

The Law: Federal legislation that selectively overhauled the federal criminal code
Date: Became law on October 19, 1984
Criminal justice issues: Federal law; law codes
Significance: This act expanded the government's law-enforcement power and emphasized the rights of the public over those of the criminal or accused criminal.

Work on this legislation began in the 1970's in a Democratic-controlled Senate. Passage of the bill (by a vote of 94 to 1) reflected close cooperation between Democrat Edward Kennedy and Republican Strom Thurmond. Democrats in the House of Representatives were less cooperative because they wanted a more piecemeal approach to the revision of the federal criminal code than the major recodification supported in the Senate. Thus a collection of procedural and substantive crime proposals were made instead of a systematic overhaul.

Fearing that the Democratic House leadership would block passage of the proposals, Republican Dan Lungren moved to add the crime proposals to an unrelated resolution on continuing appropriations, which would require urgent consideration on the House floor in order to keep the government in operation. Facing reelection in November, 1984, congressional Democrats voted in favor of law and order rather than explain a recorded "no" vote to their constituents. When the joint appropriations resolution emerged from the House, it had tacked to it a Title XI: the Comprehensive Crime Control Act of 1984.

For the first time, federal judges could detain repeat offenders in preventive detention, without bail, before trial. They could also detain individuals accused of certain major crimes if they were deemed dangerous to the community. In the past, bail was granted unless there was reason to believe the defendant would flee. Moreover, if the detained defendant were later acquitted or the charges dismissed, no recompense would be given for the time spent in jail awaiting trial.

Under the act, federal judges follow a system of guidelines in imposing sentences. The guidelines, established by a presidentially appointed sentencing commission, eliminate disparities in sentences for the same crimes and dismantle the early-release parole system. Under the guidelines, federal prosecutors are able to select charges that carry the likelihood of the longest sentence. Judges are required to explain in writing any departure from the guidelines, while both prosecutors and defendants are entitled to appeal sentences that depart from the standard.

The act also restricts the use of insanity as a defense to individuals who are unable to understand the nature and wrongfulness of their acts. The law prevents expert testimony on the ultimate issue of whether the defendant has a particular mental state or condition. It shifts the burden of proof from prosecutors, who formerly had to prove that defendants were not insane, to the defendants, who must prove that they are. This change in the insanity defense was a direct response to the John Hinckley, Jr., case. Hinckley's lawyer proved that Hinckley was psychotic and depressed. The jury found him not guilty because of insanity in the attempted assassination of President Ronald Reagan on March 30, 1981.

Finally, the legislation allows the government to seize profits and assets, including real estate, that are used in organized crime enterprises such as drug trafficking.

Bill Manikas

Further Reading
Calder, James D. *The Origins and Development of Federal Crime Control Policy.* Westport, Conn.: Praeger, 1993.

Federal Criminal Code and Rules. St. Paul, Minn.: West Group Publishing, 2003.

Marion, Nancy E. *A History of Federal Crime Control Initiatives, 1960-1993*. Westport, Conn.: Praeger, 1994.

See also Bail system; Crime; Insanity defense; Mandatory sentencing; National Narcotics Act; Omnibus Crime Control and Safe Streets Act of 1968; Organized Crime Control Act; *Schall v. Martin*; United States Sentencing Commission; Wiretaps.

Comprehensive Drug Abuse Prevention and Control Act

The Law: Federal legislation encompassing a major reformulation of drug law and policy

Date: Signed into law on October 27, 1970

Criminal justice issues: Federal law; medical and health issues; substance abuse

Significance: This legislation provides the legal foundation of the federal government's fight against the abuse of drugs and other substances.

The Comprehensive Drug Abuse Prevention and Control Act was enacted at a time when the federal government was grappling with the escalating drug abuse of the 1960's. The legislation addressed two aspects of the drug abuse problem: treatment and law enforcement. Title I of the act provided funding for substance abuse treatment, research, and prevention initiatives. The act's impact on the criminal justice system came through Title II, more commonly known as the Controlled Substances Act (CSA). The CSA provides a framework for categorizing drugs into one of five categories, or "schedules," reflecting a drug's degree of medical usefulness and potential for abuse and dependence. Drugs categorized into Schedule I were deemed by the federal government to have no medical usefulness and a high potential for abuse and dependence. Consequently, they cannot be prescribed by a medical professional and are illegal to possess, manufacture, or distribute.

Drugs in Schedules II through V are deemed to have medical purposes and progressively fewer risks for abuse and dependence. Penalties for drug law violations are linked with a drug's scheduling. Thus, violations involving Schedule I and Schedule II drugs carry more severe penalties than do violations involving drugs in the other schedules. Among other initiatives, the CSA established a drug enforcement agency called the Bureau of Narcotics and Dangerous Drugs, which later became the Drug Enforcement Administration.

Damon Mitchell

Further Reading

Gray, James. *Why Our Drug Laws Have Failed and What We Can Do About It: A Judicial Indictment of the War on Drugs*. Philadelphia: Temple University Press, 2001.

Maccoun, Robert J. *Drug War Heresies: Learning from Other Vices, Times, and Places*. New York: Cambridge University Press, 2001.

Musto, David F. *The American Disease: Origins of Narcotic Control*. New York: Oxford University Press, 1999.

See also Commercialized vice; DARE programs; Decriminalization; "Drug czar"; Drug Enforcement Administration; Drug legalization debate; Drugs and law enforcement; Mandatory sentencing; National Narcotics Act; Opium Exclusion Act; Organized crime.

Computer crime

Definition: Illegal intrusions into computers and the use of computers for the perpetration of other crimes

Criminal justice issues: Business and financial crime; computer crime; fraud; technology

Significance: Computer crimes cause immense harm and present a national problem that is difficult to control because of constantly changing technology and the inconsistent and often unenforceable national and international laws enacted to counter the crimes.

Computer crime comprises a broad range of illegal acts in which computers, other types of electronic information-processing devices, and information systems are the objects, targets, or instruments of crimes. They may also be the sites from which "attacks" are launched or the cyber environments harmed in the course of attacks on information systems.

The term "computer crime" has historically conveyed different meanings to criminal justice officials, policymakers, researchers, the media, and the general public. For example, computer crime was once regarded as any illegal act requiring knowledge of computer technology for its perpetration, investigation, or prosecution. Computers have also been conceptualized as symbols for intimidation, particularly in situations in which intended crime victims do not understand or become fearful about the functional capabilities of computers.

The absence of a widely accepted definition of computer crime has much to do with the technical and special nature of computer abuses, such as computer "hacking," the releasing into computer systems of viruses, and interruptions of service. Also important are the technologically evolving nature of computers and the crimes in which they are used, the pace of computerization, and increasing adoption of computers for illicit purposes throughout the United States and other nations. As a consequence of these complexities, several different terms and labels have come into use to describe crimes in which computers—often networked and used in combination with other electronic devices—are used for criminal purposes. Terms generally considered to be synonymous with computer crime include computer-related crime, high-tech crime, information technology-related crime, information/new age crime, Internet crime, and cybercrime. In addition, computer crimes are also frequently given sensational labels in the media, such as "data rape" and "cyber stalking." These terms, too, further complicate wide acceptance of any specific term or label.

History

Computer crimes emerged in the United States with the computerizing of banking services. The first recorded instance of computer crime occurred in 1958. It involved "salami slicing," in which a bank employee in Minneapolis, Minnesota, used a computer to divert and deposit rounding errors of financial transactions into a special account. Over the years, as evolving computer technology made possible new banking services, such as personal credit cards, automatic teller machines (ATMs), and online banking, new forms of computer-enabled financial crimes arose.

Computer hacking—the unauthorized accessing of computerized information systems—also began during the late 1950's. At that time, the nation's first computer science students, at the Massachusetts Institute of Technology, were intent on discovering new uses for computers and called themselves "computer hackers."

Throughout the 1960's and 1970's the number, variety, and impact of computer abuses and crimes increased significantly. However, official estimates of such trends are not available. Nonetheless, growing concern about computer crime during the 1980's, coupled with the beginning of widespread Internet operations in 1984, resulted in several state governments and the federal government enacting special computer crime laws. In 1984, the federal government enacted the Computer Fraud and Abuse Act, which made it illegal to access computer systems without prior authorization. During that same period, several new types of computer crimes arose and several famous computer crime cases occurred. For example, in 1984 Fred Cohen, a famous computer-security instructor and consultant, introduced the term "computer virus" to describe self-replicating programs capable of infecting networked computers. On November 2, 1988, Robert Morris released an infamous computer "worm"—a program that shut down significant portions of the Internet.

After 1994, the World Wide Web made online computing more accessible, versatile, and interesting to millions of computer users. The development invariably gave rise to more and increasingly imaginative forms of computer abuse. During the first decade of the twenty-first century, computer crimes included disruptions of computer services by writing and distributing malicious computer programs (viruses, worms, and trojans), and trespassing into information systems without authorization in order to explore, steal, modify, or destroy data.

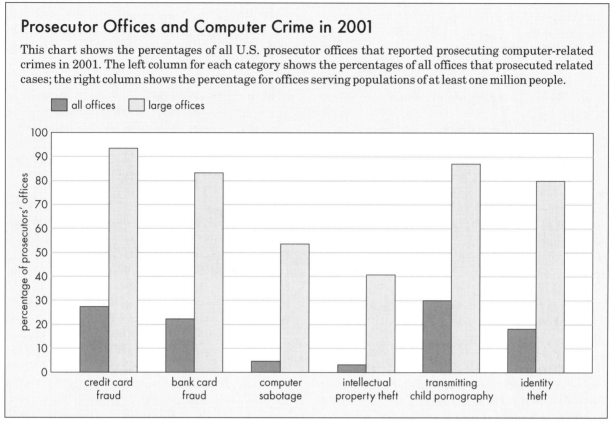

Prosecutor Offices and Computer Crime in 2001

This chart shows the percentages of all U.S. prosecutor offices that reported prosecuting computer-related crimes in 2001. The left column for each category shows the percentages of all offices that prosecuted related cases; the right column shows the percentage for offices serving populations of at least one million people.

■ all offices   □ large offices

Source: U.S. Bureau of Justice Statistics.

Computer crimes now also include such financial crimes as embezzlement, securities fraud, unlawful use of credit card account numbers, identity theft, and fraud in online auction and retail-purchasing Web sites. Other forms of computer crime include piracy of digitized music, film, and application files; sending of unwanted spam; online harassment and stalking; and accessing, distributing, and possessing computer media containing child pornography.

Prevalence

Computer crime now reportedly occurs throughout the United States at record rates, in more complex variations and combinations, and with increasing social and economic impacts. Computer crime is also raising fears of lost, damaged, or stolen data among computer users everywhere, and is generally raising concerns about information security throughout society, including at the highest levels of government. Never-

theless, reliable estimates of the numbers and impact of computer crimes remain largely undetermined, as few studies of the problem have been undertaken. Moreover, even when such studies are conducted, they seldom employ random sampling and other research methods capable of producing results that are scientifically valid and applicable to society as a whole. This condition is the consequence of unclear or imprecise definitions of computer crime and categorizations of offenses and offenders, the unwillingness on the part of many computer crime victims to reveal successful attacks on their information systems, the lack of criminologists specializing in computer crime issues, and a general lack of federal government funding for computer crime research.

Three basic ways of estimating the prevalence of computer crime are victimization surveys, self-report (offender) surveys, and crime reporting systems such as the Uniform Crime Report

(UCR) system, which is operated by the Federal Bureau of Investigation (FBI) with voluntary participation of state and local law-enforcement agencies. None of these methods is systematically and consistently used within the United States for reporting computer crime occurrences or trends.

In 2001, the federal government began considering how best to measure the prevalence and costs of computer crime to businesses in the United States. A pilot Computer Security Survey administered in 2001 and responded to by 198 businesses revealed that 74 percent of the businesses had been victims of computer crimes, and 68 percent of the companies experiencing incidents had losses totaling $61 million. These findings are not nationally representative but may illustrate the feasibility and utility of a data collection program that in 2004 the federal government was planning to initiate among some 36,000 U.S. businesses.

Other research efforts to establish the prevalence of computer crime indicate that most large corporations and government agencies surveyed have detected computer security breaches that resulted in financial losses within the previous twelve months. For example, 223 organizations surveyed in 2002 reported $455,848,000 in total financial losses from thefts of proprietary information and financial fraud. The organizations surveyed also reported that their Internet connections and internal systems were the most frequent points of attack.

Internet auction fraud is a frequent form of computer crime, along with credit- and debit-card fraud, computer intrusions, unsolicited e-mail (spam), and child pornography. Of 75,063 complaints received by the Internet Fraud Complaint Center of the National White Collar Crime Center in 2002 and subsequently referred to law-enforcement and regulatory agencies for investigation, Internet auction fraud constituted 46 percent. Auction fraud problems included nondelivery of merchandise and account payment matters.

It also appears that the levels of automation in attack tools are increasing as attack-tool developers use more advanced techniques. The number of newly discovered vulnerabilities continues to rise at a rate more than double each year, making it difficult for systems administrators to keep up with information security patches. Attack technologies are being designed to bypass typical computer firewall configurations. The security of the Internet and other systems is interdependent, as it can only be as strong as its weakest point. Attacks against critical information infrastructures are increasing concern because of the number of organizations and users on the Internet and their increasing dependency on the Internet to perform their daily functions.

Investigation

The investigation, prosecution, and punishment of computer abuse and crime began during the late 1950's as financial transactions and other types record-keeping by banks were computerized. The first federally prosecuted case of computer crime occurred in 1966; it involved a perpetrator using a computer to manipulate computerized banking records. During the early years of computer crime, many investigators and prosecutors considered the problem to arise mainly in isolated instances in which computers were merely tools being used in innovative ways to commit already well-understood forms of white-collar and financial crimes, such as fraud and embezzlement.

The onset of computer abuse and crime also arose from establishment of the computer hacker subculture, whose participants believed in the "hacker ethic" of unconstrained discovery, exploration, and sharing of information. Although such motives may have been noble in their original intent, they underscored a considerable portion of unauthorized hacking into computer systems and remain today a justification for many acts of computer trespassing, software piracy, and illegal sharing of digitized music and film files.

Prosecution

During the 1970's and throughout the 1980's computers were increasingly used to commit other new forms of computer abuse and crime, including the creation and distribution of digitized child pornography. Fraud and exploitation of children and the elderly by means of computer bulletin boards and online information services were also commonplace during this period, as were traditional types of crimes committed with the aid of computers, such as counterfeiting, robbery, illegal gambling, kidnapping, prostitution, racketeering, drug trafficking, and homicide. Hate crimes and acts of terrorism were also facilitated by the use of computers. As a result, the U.S. Department of Justice published the first *Computer Crime Criminal Justice Resource Manual* in 1979.

In 1987, the federal government passed the nation's first Computer Fraud and Abuse Act. The following year, Robert Morris became the first offender prosecuted under this law for releasing an Internet worm program that infected thousands of connected computers in November, 1988, and essentially shut down significant portions of the Internet throughout the eastern United States.

In 1989, the Department of Justice published a second edition of its computer crime resource book for criminal justice officials and also explained how state and local law-enforcement officials could go about creating special computer crime investigation and prosecution units. Afterward—and especially after the creation of the World Wide Web and the explosion of new forms of computer crime that ensued—numerous state and local law-enforcement agencies, as well as the federal government, established computer investigation and prosecution units. In 1994, the Computer Crime Prosecution Unit of the Department of Justice published its first set of federal guidelines for searching and seizing computers.

Several professional associations and organizations, such as the international and regional chapters of the High Technology Crime Investiga-

FBI agent Rubin Garcia (left) and U.S. attorney general Janet Reno address a May 8, 2000, press conference at which they announced creation of the Internet Fraud Complaint Center, which was created to combat the rapidly growing problem of commercial fraud on the Internet. (AP/Wide World Photos)

tion Association, the Computer Security Institute, and SANS are now instrumental in developing training programs that teach and promote best practices for investigating and prosecuting computer crime, as well as enhancing information-systems security. In 2000, agencies of the federal government, including the Department of Homeland Security, the National Security Agency (NSA), and the National Institute for Standards and Technology, began establishing technical standards and recommending best practices to meet the goals of improved security. These and other government agencies and private associations and organizations now routinely provide updated resource materials at no charge for law-enforcement investigators, prosecutors, and information security professionals.

Despite such capacity-building to prevent and control computer crimes, the international and transnational aspects of investigating and prosecuting computer crimes are immensely complex and problematic for criminal justice officials. In 2004, there was no universally accepted body of international law or treaty governing search, seizure, and the admissibility of computer evidence. There were also no universally recognized methods for effecting arrests of offenders beyond U.S. borders or extraditing them back to the United States to stand trial for alleged crimes.

The general requirements for successful investigations and prosecutions of computer crimes do not substantially differ from those for other types of crime. However, greater understanding, curiosity, and technical knowledge about computers and other types of electronic information processing systems is required in some instances. Computer crimes range from offenses that involve little computer usage to those that involve significant usage. Evidence of computer crimes may be testimonial and either tangible or cyber, as well as circumstantial. Human factors surrounding motives, means, and opportunities to commit computer crimes, as well as the skills, knowledge, resources, and access to information systems possessed by perpetrators also matter from the standpoints of investigating and prosecuting computer crimes.

Investigations of computer crimes are subject to the same rules that govern the search, seizure, and analysis of evidence in other crimes. For example, search warrants are required to search computers for digital evidence of crimes unless exceptional circumstances exist. Ultimately, judges and juries decide on the acceptability and relative value of evidence in cases that go to trial.

Punishment

Depending on the types of computer crimes involved, suspected perpetrators may be charged with either misdemeanor or felony crimes. Adults convicted of misdemeanors are normally subject to punishment of up to one year in jail, fines of up to one thousand dollars, or both. Adults convicted of felony computer crimes may be sentenced to spend more than one year in prison, pay fines greater than one thousand dollars, or both. However, amounts of fines vary among state and federal courts. Other sanctions, such as performing community service and paying victims of crimes financial restitution may also be imposed.

Early computer criminals typically received light punishments. However as the number and seriousness of computer crimes increased, courts began imposing more severe sanctions. In an incomplete but regularly updated list of punishments imposed on convicted computer crime offenders, the Department of Justice reported that penalties ranged from five to sixty months incarceration, often combined with fines of thousands or even hundreds of thousands of dollars, depending on the circumstances of the cases.

Samuel C. McQuade III

Further Reading

Baase, Sara. *A Gift of Fire: Social, Legal, and Ethical Issues for Computers and the Internet.* 2d ed. Upper Saddle River, N.J.: Prentice-Hall, 2003. Broad examination of criminal and other issues relating to computer use.

Clifford, Ralph D., ed. *Cybercrime: The Investigation, Prosecution, and Defense of a Computer-Related Crime.* Durham, N.C.: Carolina Academic Press, 2001. Collection of articles on all aspects of investigating and prosecuting cybercrime; includes discussions of selected court cases.

Grance, T., K. Kent, and B. Kim. *Computer Security Incident Handling Guide: Recommendations of the National Institute of Standards and Technology.* Washington, D.C.: U.S. Department of Commerce, 2004. Government report on the latest methods of enhancing computer security.

Himanen, P. *The Hacker Ethic and the Spirit of the Information Age*. New York: Random House, 2001. Examination of the philosophy of computer hackers and their impact on the computer world's growing interconnectedness.

Rantala, R. R. *Cybercrime Against Businesses*. Washington, D.C.: Bureau of Justice Statistics, 2004. Report of a U.S. Department of Justice study of the impact of computer crime on American businesses.

Stephenson, Peter. *Investigating Computer-Related Crime*. Boca Raton, Fla.: CRC Press, 2000. Moderately technical discussion covering types of computer crime, their impacts, investigations, and different forensic technologies available for investigating them.

See also Blackmail and extortion; Computer forensics; Computer information systems; Corporate scandals; Cryptology; Electronic surveillance; Embezzlement; Fraud; National Stolen Property Act; Privacy rights; Spam; Trespass; White-collar crime.

Computer forensics

Definition: Search of computers, networks, and communication devices for existing or deleted electronic-evidence

Criminal justice issues: Computer crime; evidence and forensics; technology

Significance: Used to detect, trace, or prove a diverse range of crimes or cause of action, including fraud, negligence, malpractice, child pornography, violent crime, money laundering, and terrorist activity.

Computer forensics is the search for electronic data or documents for use as evidence. When electronic data or documents are used as evidence, they are referred to as electronic evidence, or e-evidence. Broadly defined, e-evidence is any electronically stored information on any type of computer device that can be used as evidence in a legal action.

During computer forensics investigations, there is a search for e-evidence by analyzing electronic devices (for example, computers, personal digital assistants (PDAs), cell phones, voice mail, servers, computer discs, Zip drives, or backup tapes) and communication media (such as instant messaging or chat rooms.) Computer forensics has played a critical role in crime investigations because criminals use computers, electronic mail, and the Internet to help them plan or carry out their crimes. For example, Ramzi Yousef, the mastermind of the 1993 World Trade Center bombing, stored detailed plans to destroy U.S. airliners in encrypted files on his laptop computer. Those files were discovered and recovered using advanced computer forensics tools.

Evidence Search

Unlike physical evidence, e-evidence exists only in digital format, requiring specialized computer forensics tools and techniques for its recovery. Typically, computer forensics involves a two-stage process: the discovery, recovery, preservation, and control of electronic data or documents; and the analysis, verification, and presentation of those documents as e-evidence in court or investigations. Like all evidence collection methods, computer forensics specialists must follow legal protocols to ensure that the e-evidence is admissible. That means that the operations used to collect, analyze, control, and present e-evidence cannot modify the original item in any manner.

Any alteration to the primary source of e-evidence could contaminate it and render it inadmissible in court. Therefore, as with other types of evidence, the handling of e-evidence must follow the three "Cs" of evidence: care, control, and chain of custody. Everyone who touches the e-evidence can contaminate it, so care and control of the computer files and digital audit trails must be kept safe and secured. Chain of custody is necessary to ensure that the e-evidence presented at court is the same as that which was seized. Maintaining the chain of custody for e-evidence is more difficult than for physical evidence because it is more easily altered.

Federal Rules

In 1970, Rule 34 of the Federal Rules of Civil Procedure was amended to address changing technology and communication methods. The amended Rule 34 made electronically stored information subject to subpoena and discovery. Therefore, any communication or file storage device is subject to computer forensic searches to identify, examine, and preserve potential e-evidence—the electronic equivalent of a "smoking gun."

Clearly, this rule has far-reaching implications for electronic records and communications—gateways to evidence of a person's or organization's activities and conduct. Every computer-based activity—whether it is using the Internet for money laundering or identity theft or sending electronic mail with an incriminating or threatening message—leaves an electronic trace that computer forensics may recover. Thus, deleted or not, there is a good probability that electronic mail, Web site visits, drafts and revisions of documents, spreadsheets, or messages can be retrieved. Computer forensics is playing a growing and major role in legal cases, as new legislation is passed to combat cybercrimes, traditional crimes, and terrorism.

Types of Computer Forensics

Computer forensic investigators perform several types of e-evidence searches. There are forensics techniques based on what is searched for, such as computer disc (data) forensics, network forensics, electronic-mail forensics, Internet forensics, and portable device forensics. In data forensics, the situation under investigation is seldom live, so the data being searched for is already stored. In contrast, network forensics cases involve "live" situations, so the data capture must be done on online data feeds. Electronic mail, Internet, and portable device forensics involve the search of both live and stored data. The portable devices subject to forensics searches are flash cards, PDAs, Blackberries, electronic mail pagers, cell phones, video cameras, and instant messaging devices. Also, investigations involve forensics tools and techniques that are specific to the operating system being searched, such as Windows, Macintosh, Unix, and Linux.

Law Enforcement and Forensics Labs

The Federal Bureau of Investigation (FBI) has made computer crimes a top priority, just behind terrorism-related work, because computers are used in such a wide variety of crimes. In July, 2004, the FBI opened a new computer forensics lab in New Haven, Connecticut, for detecting computer-related crimes and training federal, state, and local police to catch Internet pedophiles, frauds, and thieves. It is the second such lab the FBI has opened in the United States, and it will serve one of fifty computer crime task forces that have been set up around the country to increase cooperation among law-enforcement agencies.

The caseload of the U.S. Department of Defense Computer Forensics Lab (DCFL) grows each year. In 2000, the DCFL investigated 148 crime and intrusion cases. In 2003, that number was 425.

Linda Volonino

Further Reading

Casey, Eoghan. *Digital Evidence and Computer Crime*. 2d ed. San Diego, Calif.: Elsevier Academic Press, 2004. Explains how computers and networks function, how they can be involved in crimes, and how they can be used as a source of evidence.

Littlejohn Shinder, Debra, and Ed Tittel. *Scene of the Cybercrime: Computer Forensics Handbook*. Rockland, Mass.: Syngress, 2002. Covers law and technology issues, including rules of evidence, control of crime scenes, and technology for fighting crime.

Prosise, Chris, Kevin Mandia, and Matt Pepe. *Incident Response and Computer Forensics*. 2d ed. New York: McGraw-Hill Osborne Media, 2003. Written by FBI insiders, this book describes the legal, procedural, and technical steps of incident response and computer forensics.

Vacca, John R. *Computer Forensics: Computer Crime Scene Investigation*. Hingham, Mass.: Charles River Media, 2002. Overview of computer forensics, including how to gather evidence, data recovery techniques, auditing methods, and terrorist cyber-attack tactics.

Volonino, Linda, and S. R. Robinson. *Principles and Practice of Information Security*. Upper Saddle River, N.J.: Prentice-Hall, 2004. Explains the legal and technical issues of computer forensics and electronic evidence.

See also Chain of custody; Cold cases; Computer crime; Computer information systems; Crime scene investigation; Criminal procedure; Cryptology; Cybercrime; Evidence, rules of; Search and seizure.

Computer information systems

Definition: Systems designed to bring together people, computers, and departmental rules and procedures to gather, store, retrieve, analyze, and apply information to meet organizational goals

Criminal justice issues: Computer crime; crime statistics; law-enforcement organization; technology

Significance: Modern computer technology is helping to revolutionize law-enforcement by helping police departments to deploy officers more rapidly and efficiently and enabling both departments and officers in the field to gather and assess information rapidly.

Police use of computers is a relatively recent development. The first commercially available computer was not released until 1951. Four years later, the New Orleans police adopted the first arrest and warrant computer system. The St. Louis, Missouri, police department installed the first computer-aided dispatch system in 1960. During the 1970's, law enforcement began embracing computer-based information systems even more quickly than the courts and corrections departments. However, during those early years, computer applications were generally limited to basic record keeping, crime reporting, and traffic violations.

Large police departments developed computerized data-searching capabilities during the 1980's; however, they were often disappointed that the much-anticipated benefits in productivity and efficiency were not materializing. This was due, in part, to the problem of integration: Different agencies used different types of equipment that were either incompatible with one another or could not easily be integrated into larger systems. To a lesser extent, the same problem still exists today.

By the 1990's, most police departments with one hundred or more full-time sworn officers had expanded their uses of computers to include staff allocation, dispatching, budgeting, and criminal investigations. In 1994, the U.S. Congress established the National Law Enforcement and Corrections Technology Center (NLECTC) to promote the development and production of promising technologies with law enforcement and corrections applications. In 1995, the NLECTC, in turn, created the Justice Information Network (JUSTNET) to serve as a clearinghouse for the dissemination of information about new and proven technology specifically geared for policing and corrections.

During the early stages of the information technology revolution, law-enforcement agencies relied upon computers primarily to speed up their processing of such traditional functions as crime reporting, dispatch, payroll, and traffic tickets. However, with advances in hardware and software, new ways of thinking gradually emerged. The old uses of computers were still in heavy demand. In fact, they had become indispensable. However, computers were soon expected to do more than simply gather, organize, and retrieve information. They were expected to generate new knowledge as well. Information technology is now heavily used in law enforcement in computer-aided dispatch, mobile data computing and automated field reporting, records management systems, and geographic information systems and crime mapping.

Specialized Applications

Computer-aided dispatch (CAD) is designed to handle all information relating to both mundane and emergency calls for service. Based on a "geofile," or geographic database, using map-based x and y coordinates, CAD can accurately establish the locations of callers and incidents, whether the information is provided in the form of addresses, business names, street intersections, or other fragments of information. CAD fully automates the receiving of calls and the dispatching of police vehicles. When it is used with automated vehicle location (AVL) systems that contain information on the status and location of every vehicle in a police department, CAD can help prioritize calls for service and make suggestions about which vehicles should be sent out, based upon which officers are currently occupied and which are closest to the locations where help is needed. More advanced CAD systems can also provide officers with useful information, such as the numbers and types of prior calls made from the locations in question, whether there are any outstanding warrants on the residents who live there, and so on.

Mobile data computing allows police vehicles to become "offices" on wheels. In typical cases, officers receive dispatch information about incidents through mobile laptop computers in their squad cars. When they arrive at the scenes of incidents, they can quickly retrieve useful information electronically from remote local, state, and national databases. Officers equipped with mobile data computing can, in fact, perform a wide variety of functions using laptop and wireless hand-held units. They can, for example, access information about departmental policies and procedures, look up pertinent law in the penal code, and call up digital photographic images.

Mobile computing can significantly assist officers in on-the-spot decision making by providing them with immediate access to much-needed information. When the incidents are concluded, the officers can then prepare reports through their laptop or hand-held units. The officers then electronically submit their reports to supervisors. When the supervisors approve the reports, they can forward them electronically to their departments' records management systems. If a report requires revisions, a supervisor can send it back to the officer for corrections. Mobile data computing is enhanced by automated field reporting (AFR) software. AFR software offers time-saving features such as drop-down menus, spell-checking, error correction, pre-filled fields on the report forms, and other features.

Records management systems are designed to allow law-enforcement agencies to enter, store, manipulate, and retrieve data about virtually every aspect of police work, not merely crime reports, arrest reports, and crime analysis data. Before the 1960's, almost all law-enforcement agencies kept information of this sort in hard-copy files. Mainframe computers improved data retrieval during the 1970's but were not owned by many law-enforcement agencies themselves. Instead, police departments had to share time on the mainframes with other municipal agencies, and control of the mainframes was located outside the law-enforcement agencies. Now, advanced records management systems can be interfaced with other city, county, state, and federal law-enforcement systems, including their databases such as the National Crime Information Center (NCIC), the Interstate Identification Index (III), the Integrated Automated Fingerprinting Identification System (IAFIS), and the National Incident Based Reporting System (NIBRS). The last, which

A criminal records specialist in Vermont uses a computer database to study fingerprint records in 2002. *(AP/Wide World Photos)*

was only partly operational in 2004, is the planned successor to the Federal Bureau of Investigation's Uniform Crime Reports.

State-of-the art records management systems can be integrated with other intradepartmental systems, such as computer-aided dispatch and mobile data terminals. Records management systems are not without problems, however. They are expensive to purchase and maintain and require skilled staff with extensive—and ongoing—training.

Geographic information systems (GIS) are computer-based systems that store both spatial and nonspatial information in "layers" that can be called up simultaneously and depicted in the nuanced forms of maps. Replacements for the old-fashioned, color-coded pin maps traditionally used by police departments, geographic information systems can generate sophisticated maps showing, for example, relationships among illegal drug sale locations and the locations of schools, housing projects, and public telephones. GIS maps can also accurately identify "hot spots" and "hot times," enabling reallocation of police resources.

A good example of GIS usage is New York City's CompStat program. Begun in 1994, CompStat is a unit designed to analyze the statistics of daily crime reports from the city's police precincts. The data and maps generated by CompStat are used by the chief of police to evaluate the performances of precinct commanders, who, in turn, evaluate the performances of the officers on their beats.

In addition to pinpointing the locations of armed robberies over designated periods of time, a geographic information system can include information such as liquor store locations and unemployment rates in specific neighborhoods and the addresses of all probationers and parolees in the area. When combined with the satellite technology of a global positioning system, law-enforcement and correctional officials can then accurately monitor the whereabouts of known offenders in any given community.

Robert Rogers

Further Reading

Dunworth, T. "Criminal Justice and the IT Revolution." *Federal Probation* 65, no. 2 (2001): 52-

65. Discussion of the impact of information technology on criminal justice generally.

Harris, K. J., and W. H. Romesburg. *Law Enforcement Tech Guide*. Washington, D.C.: U.S. Department of Justice, Office of Community Oriented Policing Services, 2002. Federal government manual on technology available to law-enforcement agencies.

Lin, C., P. J-H. Hu, and H. Chen. "Technology Implementation Management in Law Enforcement." *Social Science Computer Review* 22, no. 1 (2004): 24-36. Brief survey of the practical application of modern computer information systems in law enforcement.

Reaves, B. A., and M. J. Hickman. *Law Enforcement Management and Administrative Statistics, 2000: Data for Individual State and Local Agencies with One Hundred or More Officers*. U.S. Department of Justice, Office of Justice Programs, 2004. U.S. Department of Justice study of the employment of computer information systems in large police departments.

Vann, Irvin B., and G. David Garson. *Crime Mapping: New Tools for Law Enforcement*. New York: P. Lang, 2003. Broad study of geographic information systems.

See also Booking; Coast Guard, U.S.; Computer crime; Computer forensics; Criminal history record information; Criminal records; Fingerprint identification; Geographic information systems; Homeland Security Department; Interpol; Violent Criminal Apprehension Program.

Comstock law

The Law: Federal law that amended postal regulations to enforce a prohibition against using the mail to send sexually suggestive material, including birth-control information

Date: Became law on March 3, 1873

Criminal justice issues: Federal law; morality and public order; women's issues

Significance: The most restrictive obscenity statute ever passed by Congress, the Comstock law limited the availability of even mild forms of pornography until the courts

Anthony Comstock. *(Library of Congress)*

law made it a federal offense to use the mails to sell or otherwise distribute any obscene printed or pictorial material, as well as all drugs and articles designed to prevent human contraception or to cause abortions. First offenders faced jail terms ranging from six months to five years and fines ranging from one hundred to two thousand dollars. Repeat offenders could be fined up to ten thousand dollars and jailed for as long as ten years. Fines collected by the federal government were shared with Comstock's Society for the Suppression of Vice.

At the end of his first year on the job, Comstock reported that he had seized and destroyed nearly 200,000 obscene pictures, seventy tons of books, and tens of thousands of condoms, along with more than thirty thousand boxes of substances alleged to be aphrodisiacs. Over the years, he used his special powers to prosecute thousands of people who used the mail to distribute what he defined as obscene materials.

Women's rights reformers ran afoul of the Comstock law when they attempted to mail information on sexuality, birth control, and abortion. Meanwhile, authors grew afraid to write on sensitive subjects, and book publishers grew more cautious about what they published. Modern postal authorities still have the power to prevent the distribution of obscene materials through the mail, but they tend to focus their censorship efforts on child and violent pornography.

Thomas C. Mackey

expanded First Amendment protections during the 1950's.

The late nineteenth century moral reformer Anthony Comstock was a New York postal official who came to national prominence for his antiobscenity crusade. In 1873, he helped to form what became the New York Society for the Suppression of Vice. Together with the Young Men's Christian Association (YMCA), he lobbied the U.S. Congress to enact more effective laws to prohibit the distribution of what he regarded as immoral materials through the U.S. mail. Congress responded by passing the Act for the Suppression of Trade in, and Circulation of, Obscene Literature and Articles for Immoral Use. The law was afterward popularly dubbed the Comstock law.

President Ulysses S. Grant signed the bill on March 3, 1873, and appointed Comstock as a voluntary "special agent" of the U.S. Postal Service with special enforcement powers. The Comstock

Further Reading

Beisel, Nicola Kay. *Imperiled Innocents: Anthony Comstock and Family Reproduction in Victorian America.* Princeton, N.J.: Princeton University Press, 1997.

Boyer, Paul S. *Purity in Print: The Vice-Society Movement and Book Censorship in America.* New York: Charles Scribner's Sons, 1968.

Mackey, Thomas C. *Pornography on Trial: A Handbook with Cases, Laws, and Documents.* Santa Barbara, Calif.: ABC-Clio, 2002.

See also Criminal law; Mann Act; Pornography; Pornography, child; Sex discrimination.

Concurrent sentences

Definition: Sentences for separate convictions that an offender serves at the same time

Criminal justice issues: Judges; legal terms and principles; punishment; sentencing

Significance: Judges determine whether defendants serve their sentences concurrently or consecutively based on factors related to the specific crimes and the offenders.

When defendants are convicted of more than one crime at the same time, the judges in their cases have the option of deciding whether the sentences for the individual crimes should run consecutively (one after the other) or concurrently (at the same time). When judges choose to order defendants to serve their sentences concurrently, the total time that the offenders serve—barring other complications—is equivalent to the lengths of their longest sentences.

Concurrent sentences sometimes arise out of plea-bargain agreements. Additionally, judges may decide to be more lenient on particular offenders or may view the crimes of which defendants are convicted as being so closely related to one another as to amount to a single crime. However, state laws may set the conditions under which judges can decide to have sentences run concurrently. Typically, state laws require judges to impose consecutive sentences, instead of concurrent sentences, when the crimes, or purposes behind the individual crimes, are distinct.

A major criticism of the principle of concurrent sentences is that offenders who serve their sentences concurrently spend only as much time in prison as they would if they were convicted of only the most serious charges brought against them. They thus go unpunished for their additional crimes, while other defendants who commit the same combinations of crimes may serve longer sentences.

Sheryl L. Van Horne

Further Reading

Demleitner, Nora V., Douglas A. Berman, Marc L. Miller, and Ronald F. Wright. *Sentencing Law*

Malcolm X's "Concurrent" Sentences

In 1946, the future black nationalist leader Malcolm X and a friend were convicted on fourteen counts of burglary in Massachusetts. The *Autobiography of Malcolm X* (1965) offers a vivid description of the moment that a county judge passed down the men's sentences:

> "Count one, eight to ten years—
> "Count two, eight to ten years—
> "Count three . . . "
> And, finally, "The sentences to run concurrently."

As Malcolm's partner Shorty heard the judge reading off the fourteen counts, he nearly collapsed: "not understanding the word 'concurrently,' [Shorty] had counted in his head to probably over a hundred years; he cried out, he began slumping. The bailiffs had to catch and support him."

Malcolm's and Shorty's net sentences were ten years. Two white women with whom they had collaborated in their crimes received sentences of only one to five years each. Malcolm's and Shorty's sentences were doubtless harsher because the men were black, but they were not nearly as harsh as they would have been, if they were not to be served concurrently.

Malcolm X. *(Library of Congress)*

and Policy: Cases, Statutes, and Guidelines. New York: Aspen Publishers, 2003.

Tonry, Michael. *Sentencing and Sanctions in Western Countries.* New York: Oxford University Press, 2001.

United States Sentencing Commission. *Federal Sentencing Guidelines Manual 2003.* St. Paul, Minn.: West Publishing, 2004.

See also Convictions; Defendants; Judges; Mandatory sentencing; Plea bargaining; Prison and jail systems; Sentencing.

Confessions

Definition: Criminal suspects' oral or written acknowledgments of guilt

Criminal justice issues: Confessions; interrogation

Significance: Because confessions are of high evidentiary value at criminal trials, law-enforcement officers must secure the admissibility of the confession by utilizing proper interrogation methods in custodial settings.

Traditionally, any statement made by a criminal suspect, regardless of how the statement was obtained, was admissible at trial. This rule had the effect of producing unreliable statements, especially when the interrogators had used extreme force or brutality. Beginning during the late nineteenth century, American courts began to recognize that a confession was of little evidentiary value if it was not made voluntarily. To that end, the U.S. Supreme Court determined that the Fifth Amendment right against self-incrimination made involuntary confessions inadmissible.

A confession may be deemed involuntary in one of two ways. First, if the confession is obtained by the use of coercion, such as physical or mental torture, that confession is considered involuntary because it was not made of the suspect's free will. Second, if the confession is obtained while the suspect is in a custodial setting and is not free to leave, that confession is presumed to be compelled and will be inadmissible at trial, even if police have not used coercive tac-

tics. The U.S. Supreme Court has set forth numerous procedural guidelines designed to assist police officers during the interrogation process in order to obtain admissible confessions while safeguarding suspects' constitutional rights.

Voluntariness

Aware that the pressures one faces when subjected to police interrogation might stimulate false confessions and therefore undermine the integrity of the criminal justice system, the Supreme Court mandated in *Miranda v. Arizona* (1966) that police officers advise suspects in custody, prior to interrogation, that they have the right to remain silent, that anything they say can be used against them in court, and that they have a right to an attorney present during questioning. If a police officer fails to read these rights before questioning a suspect, the suspect's statements will not be admissible at trial. In addition, any evidence obtained as a result of the illegal interrogation can be considered tainted and excluded from trial as "fruit of the poisonous tree." It is important to note that the *Miranda* doctrine only applies to a suspect who is in custody.

The *Miranda* decision has come under attack. Some prosecutors and law-enforcement officers view the rigid guidelines as the primary reason for losing valuable evidence that could have been used at trial. Instead, they have argued that *Miranda* should be overturned and that the admissibility of confessions should be determined by the totality of the circumstances surrounding the interrogation. In 2000, however, the Supreme Court reaffirmed *Miranda*'s constitutional underpinnings in *Dickerson v. United States* when it held that Miranda rules are "concrete constitutional guidelines" which may not be overturned by legislation enacted by Congress in favor of the pre-*Miranda* case-by-case voluntariness standard.

While *Miranda* may appear to place significant restrictions on police interrogation procedures, it does not bar police officers from lying, using tricks, or cajoling a suspect into speaking. Although threatening a suspect would be considered coercive, and evidence gained in that way would be inadmissible, police may, for example, tell a suspect that evidence exists, even when it does not, in order to coax the suspect into confessing. Similarly, while physical mistreatment will render a confession invalid, an officer pretending to be angry to induce a confession or playing on a suspect's sympathies may not be. In short, there is a fine line between what is considered coercive and what is not, and it takes a skilled practitioner to extract a confession in a manner that is constitutionally acceptable.

The Sixth Amendment Right to Counsel

Laws regulating admissibility of confessions do not only apply to police interrogation before trial. After a suspect is arrested and charges are filed by a district attorney, the suspect becomes a criminal defendant and is entitled to legal representation. In *Massiah v. United States* (1966), the Supreme Court held that a criminal defendant may not be questioned by any police or officers of the court outside the presence of counsel. If any illegal interrogation occurs, or if any tricks are used, such as informants or wiretaps, to deliberately elicit a statement from the accused, that statement will be inadmissible at trial.

There is a major difference between the Fifth Amendment right to avoid self-incrimination and the Sixth Amendment right to counsel. The *Massiah* doctrine is offense-specific and only applies to those charges for which adversarial criminal proceedings have been initiated. It does not bar police from questioning criminal defendants about other cases. Additionally, if defendants are released from custody, they are no longer considered to be under arrest, and *Miranda* does not apply. In such cases, the suspects need not be advised of their rights prior to interrogation.

Kimberly J. Belvedere

Further Reading

Dressler, Joshua. *Understanding Criminal Procedure*. 3d ed. New York: LexisNexis, 2002. Comprehensive text regarding constitutional criminal procedure, with several chapters on confession law and relevant defenses.

Inbau, Fred, John Reid, Joseph Buckley, and Brian Jayne. *Criminal Interrogations and Confessions*. 4th ed. Boston: Jones and Bartlett, 2001. Explanation of the popular nine-step process used by many police departments that shows police officers how to distinguish between truth and falsity.

A Dubious Movie Confession

One of the most famous films about capital punishment ever made is director Robert Wise's *I Want to Live!* Loosely based on the true-life story of Barbara Graham, who was executed in California in 1955, this 1958 film stars Susan Hayward as Graham, a woman who is convicted of participating in a robbery and murder. Although Graham insists on her innocence to the end, she is executed in a gas chamber after a series of appeals.

A key element behind Graham's conviction is the confession that she apparently made to a fellow prison inmate, who promised to provide her with an alibi if she would confess. This bit of trickery, made at a time when the defendant was represented by an attorney, probably made her confession inadmissible, and the film is now unrealistic for failure to note this fact.

Timothy L. Hall

Orth, John V. *Due Process of Law: A Brief History*. Lawrence: University Press of Kansas, 2003. Traces the development of the concept of due process as well as the logic underlying the issue from as early as the Magna Carta to Supreme Court decisions that may shed light on how and why certain tactics used during interrogations might be considered unconstitutional.

Stephen, John, and Earl Sweeney. *Officer's Interrogation Handbook*. New York: LexisNexis, 2004. Primarily designed for police officers, this handbook explains the constitutional constraints applicable to statements, admissions, and confessions as they apply to the Fifth and Sixth Amendments.

Zalman, Marvin. *Criminal Procedure: Constitution and Society*. 3d ed. Upper Saddle River, N.J.: Prentice-Hall, 2002. Highlights how legal doctrines, including those dealing with the Bill of Rights, interact with the criminal justice system through a comprehensive account of the issues from both a legal and social perspective.

See also Due process of law; False convictions; Fifth Amendment; Forensic accounting; *Massiah v. United States*; *Minnick v. Mississippi*; Miranda rights; *Miranda v. Arizona*; Police ethics.

Consent searches

Definition: Searches based on permission, usually given by the parties who are the objects of the search

Criminal justice issue: Search and seizure

Significance: Under most circumstances, a search warrant, or at least probable cause, must be present to allow law-enforcement agents to undertake a legal search. However, if consent to a search is freely and voluntarily given, a warrant need not be present. A large number of searches are based on consent.

The issue of what constitutes a "consent search" has been a recurring one for the U.S. Supreme Court. One principle consistently upheld by the Court is that for such a search to be valid, consent must be freely given. Law-enforcement officers, however, have no blanket obligation to inform individuals of their right to refuse to consent to a request to search.

The Court has also held that consent may be freely given when an individual is engaged in a consensual encounter with the police, that is, when the individual is not in the position of having been "seized." Consequently, the Court has had to deal with a number of cases defining "seizure." In general, if a person feels "free to leave" an encounter with the police, that person is considered to be in a position to freely grant consent. The Court has held that the determination of being free to leave—indeed, of being able to freely consent to a search—is based on the "totality of the circumstances" doctrine, which is used in a number of other instances. For example, under this doctrine it is acceptable for police to enter a bus at a station and seek consent to search luggage stored in the racks above the seats, as the Court held in *Florida v. Bostick* (1991).

It is also permissible for police to search after gaining the consent of a third party, if that party shares "common authority" or "apparent authority" over the item to be searched. Moreover, once consent is given, the scope of the search is limited only by the nature of the item for which the search is being conducted.

The use of consent searches is controversial, in part because of the Supreme Court's holding that the police need not inform citizens of their right to refuse. Critics feel that under the circumstances of a police-citizen encounter, most people do not feel able to refuse.

David M. Jones

Further Reading

Bloom, Robert M. *Searches, Seizures, and Warrants*. Westport, Conn.: Praeger, 2003.

Yarborough, Tinsley E. *The Rehnquist Court and the Constitution*. New York: Oxford University Press, 2000.

See also Automobile searches; Bill of Rights, U.S.; Due process of law; Exclusionary rule; Forensic accounting; Fourth Amendment; *Knowles v. Iowa*; Probable cause; Reasonable suspicion; Search and seizure; Search warrants; Vehicle checkpoints; *Whren v. United States*.

Conspiracy

Definition: Planning of an illegal act by any two or more persons

Criminal justice issues: Business and financial crime; fraud; legal terms and principles; white-collar crime

Significance: The criminal charge of conspiracy is used to fight terrorism, prevent overt commissions of crimes, and bring to justice accessories and accomplices who aid and abet in the planning or commission of crimes ranging from violent crimes against persons to business crimes against consumers or stockholders.

Conspiracy is one of several inchoate crimes that involve talking about the commission of crimes that are to take place in the future. An increasing number of white-collar criminal prosecutions include charges of conspiracy. In the past, it was assumed that businesses and other organized groups were artificial constructs, without minds of their own, and therefore incapable of forming the intention necessary to commit crimes. This view has been changing, however, so that businesses, as well as individuals, are now held liable for conspiracy and fined accordingly.

Conspiracy involves two or more actors who come together or communicate with one another to plan to engage in criminal activity. These actors may be individual persons, businesses, families, gangs, or groups. They must mutually agree either to engage in criminal conduct themselves, to solicit other persons to engage in criminal conduct, or to aid other persons in planning, committing, or attempting to solicit someone to engage in criminal conduct.

Agreement among actors is essential to the charge of conspiracy. Agreements need not be written, oral, or even explicit. Agreements among actors may simply be inferred when actors meet together or are in communication, and there exists a general understanding that those involved are working toward a common purpose. The agreements may be to commit unlawful acts, such as robberies, or to do lawful acts by unlawful means, such as businesses setting lawful prices by unlawful collusion among competing storeowners. Some participants in conspiracies may limit their own involvement to legal activities; however, if the end result of a conspiracy's combined activities is illegal, then all its actors may be held accountable for conspiracy.

Prosecution of Conspiracies

Prosecutors can gain several advantages by filing conspiracy charges against defendants. First, because law-enforcement officials often learn about conspiracies while they are still being planned, they can bring charges against conspirators before their intended crimes actually take place, thereby preventing the intended crimes. Second, defendants who are only marginally involved in conspiracies can be charged and brought to trial together with those who are more actively involved. Juries tend to find defendants guilty simply because of their proven association with other defendants who are more deeply involved in crimes. This is especially true with chain conspiracies.

Chain conspiracy involves multiple participants in a single long criminal chain. An example is a series of illegal drug deals that begins with the manufacture of a drug and extends to the dealers on the street. Conspiracy defendants are held responsible for the actions of all participants in the chain, even if they never meet or communicate with the other participants and even if some of the actors in the chain engage in entirely lawful activities. Members of a chain can also be charged with vicarious criminal liability and be punished as though they themselves have committed the end crime, if the end crime can be proven to have been reasonably foreseeable by the actors.

Hub-and-spoke conspiracies involve multiple individuals conspiring with a single central individual, or "hub," but not with any of the other spokes. It is a more difficult form of conspiracy to prosecute, as defendants can claim that their own communications with the hub person are separate and disconnected from the hub's communications with the other spokes and thus not part of true conspiracies.

Many popular conspiracy theories are hub-and-spoke conspiracies in which one central actor, or group of actors, plans an objective—such as controlling world oil prices or maintaining secrecy about the crash of an alien spacecraft—and use their connections with, or their control over, multiple spokes to further their objectives. Each of the spokes may or may not know the objectives of the hub and usually do not know the roles that the other spokes play in the conspiracy.

Defense Against Conspiracy Charges

To prevent prosecutorial abuses, such as law-enforcement entrapment schemes and violations of the freedoms of speech, assembly, or association, many states require that at least one of the actors involved in an alleged conspiracy commit some overt act in furtherance of the objectives of the conspiracy. For example, if antiwar activists were to meet to discuss assassinating political leaders to help bring an end to the war that they oppose, they could not be charged with conspiracy if none of them takes active steps toward implementing the assassinations. Such persons would merely be involved in free speech. However, if one of the participants in such a meeting were subsequently to purchase a sniper rifle, hire an assassin, or begin hoarding cash, charges against the entire assemblage might be possible.

Conspiracy is a continuing course of conduct. A conspiracy is considered to be abandoned if none of its actors takes overt action within a reasonable time to pursue the conspiracy's objective. An individual actor can also abandon or renounce the actor's role in the conspiracy either by telling the fellow conspirators or by reporting the conspiracy to law-enforcement authorities.

Gordon Neal Diem

Further Reading

Formisano, Ronald. *The Great Lobster War*. Amherst: University of Massachusetts Press, 1997. Fascinating account of multiple conspiracies and a conspiracy trial in the lobster industry.

Knight, Peter, ed. *Conspiracy Nation: The Politics of Paranoia in Postwar America*. New York: New York University Press, 2002. Collection of scholarly articles on conspiracy theories in popular culture.

McSorley, Joseph F. *A Portable Guide to Federal Conspiracy Law: Tactics and Strategies for Criminal and Civil Cases*. Chicago: American Bar Association, 2003. Advanced-level discussion, with cases, of the complete definition of conspiracy, indictment for conspiracy, and the relationship between conspiracy and aiding and abetting.

Marcus, Paul. *Prosecution and Defense of Criminal Conspiracy Cases*. New York: Matthew Bender, 1978. Two loose-leaf volumes that are constantly updated and revised, this publication covers evidentiary matters, constitutional issues, practical prosecutorial and defense matters, and the text of relevant federal statutes and important conspiracy cases.

Parish, Jane, and Martin Parker, eds. *The Age of Anxiety: Conspiracy Theory and the Human Sciences*. Oxford, England: Blackwell/Sociological Review, 2001. Collection of scholarly articles on conspiracy theories in popular culture.

Podgor, Ellen S., and Jerold Israel. *White Collar Crime in a Nutshell*. St. Paul, Minn.: West, 2004. Chapters on each inchoate and white-collar crime, including conspiracy.

See also Accomplices and accessories; Attempt to commit a crime; Chicago Seven trial; Criminal law; Entrapment; Forensic accounting; Freedom of assembly and association; Hobbs Act; Immunity from prosecution; Inchoate crimes; Multiple jurisdiction offenses; Organized crime; Principals (criminal); Ruby Ridge raid; Solicitation to commit a crime; Teapot Dome scandal; Vicarious liability; Voting fraud.

Constitution, U.S.

The Law: Foundation document representing the supreme law of the United States of America, as applied to the body of law dealing with offenses against the state, which may be penalized by fine or imprisonment

Date: Ratified in 1789

Criminal justice issue: Constitutional protections

Significance: Most criminal justice activity is conducted under the auspices of state and local governments empowered by and limited by the U.S. Constitution.

The foundation of American criminal justice is the U.S. Constitution, including the first ten amendments, which form the Bill of Rights. The Constitution guarantees all legal residents of the United States fundamental rights, freedoms, and liberties and strongly emphasizes the protection of the rights of defendants in the criminal process. One of the most important functions of the U.S. Supreme Court in interpreting the Constitution is the maintenance of constitutional standards for criminal prosecutions conducted in both federal and state courts.

The main body of the Constitution contains seven provisions specifically addressing aspects of criminal justice that protect all people, including criminal defendants, from tyrannical excesses of the majority. Article I, section 9 restricts suspension of the privilege of *habeas corpus* (a writ requiring government officials who have custody of a person to explain why they have the authority to detain or imprison that person) unless the public safety requires it. Section 9 also prohibits bills of attainder (legislative acts declaring a person guilty of a crime and passing sentence without benefit of trial) and ex post facto laws (laws that make something illegal that was not illegal when it was done or which increase the penalty for the act after it has occurred).

Article II, section 2 empowers the president to grant reprieves (temporary suspension of the execution of a sentence) and pardons. Article III, section 2 provides for trial by jury for all crimes, except in cases of impeachment, and requires that the trial be held in the state where the crime had been committed. Article III, section 3 defines treason against the United States, and Article IV, section 2 sets forth the procedure for the extradition of criminal defendants from one state to another.

Fair trial procedures were considered of such importance as to be included in five of the first eight amendments to the Constitution. Twenty-three separate rights are enumerated in the Bill of Rights, and thirteen specifically concern the treatment of criminal defendants. These Bill of Rights provisions include the broad guarantee of due process of law as well as a number of procedural protections that were thought to be fundamental and beyond invasion by the national government.

The Fourth Amendment contains an unqualified prohibition against violation of the rights of the people to be secure in their persons, houses, papers, and effects against unreasonable searches and seizures. This amendment reflected untoward colonial experience with the British crown's writs of assistance, searches and seizures at the discretion of government officials. Such unrestrained government searches have characterized totalitarian police states. The Fourth Amendment, more directly than any other constitutional provision, governs police investigations. That

One of the most controversial trials in U.S. history occurred during the 1920's, when Italian immigrants Nicola Sacco (second from right) and Bartolomeo Vanzetti (second from left) were convicted in Massachusetts for murdering two men during a 1920 payroll robbery. Because of fervent public dislike of Italian immigrants and the anarchist views the men held, Sacco and Vanzetti had no chance of receiving a fair trial. Despite worldwide protests, both were executed in 1927. Since that time, American courts have worked to ensure that the protections guaranteed by the U.S. Constitution and its amendments are observed so that all defendants receive fair trials. *(AP/Wide World Photos)*

Supreme Court Decisions on Selective Incorporation in Criminal Justice Cases

Date	Case	Constitutional provision	Amendment
1948	*Cole v. Arkansas*	Notice clause	Sixth
1948	*In re Oliver*	Public trial	Sixth
1949	*Wolf v. Colorado*	Search and seizure	Fourth
1961	*Mapp v. Ohio*	Exclusionary rule	Fourth
1962	*Robinson v. California*	Cruel and unusual punishment	Eighth
1963	*Gideon v. Wainwright*	Right to counsel in felony cases	Sixth
1964	*Malloy v. Hogan*	Self-incrimination	Fifth
1965	*Pointer v. Texas*	Confrontation clause	Sixth
1966	*Parker v. Gladden*	Impartial jury	Sixth
1967	*Klopfer v. North Carolina*	Speedy trial	Sixth
1967	*Washington v. Texas*	Compulsory process clause	Sixth
1968	*Duncan v. Louisiana*	Jury trial	Sixth
1969	*Benton v. Maryland*	Double jeopardy	Fifth
1971	*Schilb v. Kuebel*	Excessive bail	Eighth
1972	*Argersinger v. Hamlin*	Right to counsel in misdemeanor cases with possible jail terms	Sixth

amendment requires a standard of probable cause and particularity of description of persons and premises in procuring a search warrant from a judge.

The Fifth Amendment requires indictment by grand jury before an accused can be prosecuted in "capital, or otherwise infamous" crimes (except in certain military cases) and protects defendants against double jeopardy (being tried more than once for the same offense by the same authority) and against being required to testify against themselves in criminal cases (self-incrimination). Most significant, the Fifth Amendment also protects the right to "due process of the law," interpreted by the courts to confer on defendants a broad array of protections and rights.

The Sixth Amendment guarantees defendants in all criminal prosecutions a speedy and public trial by an impartial jury of the state and district wherein the crime shall have been committed. It also entitles defendants to be confronted by (and to cross-examine) the witnesses against them, to have compulsory processes for obtaining witnesses in their favor, and to have the "assistance of counsel" for their defense. This last protection has been expanded by court interpretation over the years to guarantee defendants adequate counsel in most criminal trials.

The Eighth Amendment prohibits excessive bails and fines and the infliction of cruel and unusual punishments. The "cruel and unusual" prohibition has been interpreted by the courts to limit the kinds of punishments that can be inflicted.

Supreme Court Interpretation of Criminal Justice Provisions

The criminal justice provisions in the original Constitution and the Bill of Rights were at first understood to apply only to the federal government. Traditionally, the states had possessed nearly complete autonomy in the areas of criminal law and procedure. This standard was upheld in the landmark Supreme Court decision *Barron v. Baltimore* (1833), which held that the Bill of Rights applied to the federal government only, not to the states. The adoption of the Fourteenth Amendment with its due process and equal protection clauses in 1868, however, imposed upon the Court some responsibility over the caliber of criminal justice dispensed in the states.

Over the years the Supreme Court interpreted its responsibility more narrowly for standards of criminal justice in state courts than for those in the federal courts. Until the 1960's there had been great controversy as to whether the provisions of the Fourth through the Eighth Amendments were applicable to the states. The due process clause of the Fourteenth Amendment had been accepted as imposing certain limitations on state judicial procedure which would guarantee a fair hearing before an unbiased tribunal. In a series of decisions between 1884 and 1937 the Court had held that indictment by grand jury, trial by jury, and protections against self-incrimination and double jeopardy were not such fundamental attributes of a fair trial as to be protected against state action by the due process clause. The result was that practices that would be unconstitutional in federal prosecutions were not necessarily considered as grounds for reversing state convictions.

In considering the idea that the Fourteenth Amendment imposed upon the criminal law of the states all the restrictions contained in the Bill of Rights, the Court chose to follow the rule expressed by justice Benjamin Cardozo in *Palko v. Connecticut* (1937). Cardozo's fundamental fairness doctrine held that only those provisions of the first eight amendments are applicable to the states which were "implicit in the concept of ordered liberty" as declared by the Supreme Court. The Court then was to adjudge the constitution-

ality of state fair trial procedures by determining in each case whether the principle of justice involved was "so rooted in the traditions and conscience of our people as to be ranked as fundamental.

Critics of the *Palko* rule contended that this left the interpretation of due process up to some "natural law" theory of the justices, who would decide on what they thought were fundamental rights on the basis of nothing more than their own preferences. To counter the uncertainty of such a doctrine, in the 1940's, four justices of the Court—Hugo L. Black, William O. Douglas, Frank Murphy, and Wiley B. Rutledge— advocated the total incorporation theory, the idea that the Fourteenth Amendment imposed upon the states all the restrictions contained in the Bill of Rights. Advocates of total incorporation never constituted a majority on the Court, however.

Selective Incorporation

During the 1960's, the Earl Warren court was to formulate a third view of the appropriate relationship between the Fourteenth Amendment and the Bill of Rights, combining aspects of both

"Dirty Harry" and Constitutional Rights

The 1971 film *Dirty Harry* (directed by Don Siegel) was produced only five years after the U.S. Supreme Court's famous decision in *Miranda v. Arizona* (1966), which required police to advise criminal defendants of their rights upon arrest. *Dirty Harry* represents a strong antipathy toward constitutional doctrines that allow defendants to escape conviction on "technicalities." The film's title character, Harry Callahan, a San Francisco street cop played by Clint Eastwood, captures a kidnapper and tortures him to reveal the location of his kidnapping victim, only to find the victim dead. Afterward, the fact that Callahan has disdained the suspect's constitutional rights by torturing him results in the suspect's being released from custody. Callahan is naturally furious.

Clint Eastwood, as film detective "Dirty Harry" Callahan, in a scene from *Sudden Impact* (1983). *(AP/Wide World Photos)*

Later, when the suspect hijacks a school bus filled with children, Callahan again tracks him down and finds an excuse to kill him. In that climactic scene, Callahan corners the suspect and issues the now-famous taunt, "Go ahead, make my day!" That line became so famous that President Ronald Reagan— himself a former film actor—used it in 1985 to taunt members of Congress.

Timothy L. Hall

the fundamental rights and the total incorporation interpretations. This approach, called "selective incorporation," recognizes that the Fourteenth Amendment encompasses all rights that are "of the very essences of a scheme of ordered liberty" but focuses less on the particulars of the case and instead determines whether the guarantee as a whole should apply to the states. By determining that an enumerated right within the first eight amendments is fundamental, the Court incorporates that guarantee into the Fourteenth Amendment due process clause "whole and intact" and enforces it against the states according to the same standards applied to the federal government. The Warren court used selective incorporation as the basis of a "due process revolution" in the 1960's to incorporate almost all provisions of the Bill of Rights to apply to the states. The Court also has used the equal protection clause of the Fourteenth Amendment to guarantee fair trials.

By 1972, only two Bill of Rights guarantees related to criminal justice had not been held to apply to the states: the Fifth Amendment requirement of prosecution by grand jury indictment and the Eighth Amendment prohibition against excessive fines. The Court, on a case-by-case determination, has achieved almost the same result as if it had endorsed the total incorporation interpretation.

The incorporation doctrine dramatically transformed American criminal justice and fundamentally altered the nature of the federal system. Interpretation of the Constitution, however, sets a minimum standard, not a ceiling, on the rights of citizens against police, prosecutors, courts, and prison officials. The states may grant more rights to criminal defendants. For example, the state of New York frequently is cited as providing more protection of the rights of criminal suspects and criminal defendants than does the U.S. Supreme Court.

The changing nature of criminal justice under the U.S. Constitution demonstrates the flexibility, and ultimately the supremacy, of that document. With the U.S. Supreme Court as a watchdog over civil liberties, neither Congress nor the states can pass criminal laws that violate the Constitution.

Theodore M. Vestal

Further Reading

Banner, Stuart. *The Death Penalty: An American History*. Cambridge, Mass.: Harvard University Press, 2003. A richly detailed overview of American attitudes toward and implementation of capital punishment throughout its history.

Berger, Raoul. *The Fourteenth Amendment and the Bill of Rights*. Norman: University of Oklahoma Press, 1990. Argues that expansive interpretation of the Fourteenth Amendment to apply the Bill of Rights to the states is contrary to the original intent of the Fourteenth Amendment, which should be understood in the light of the Tenth Amendment.

Bodenhamer, David J. *Fair Trial: Rights of the Accused in American History*. New York: Oxford University Press, 1997. A succinct history of fair trials in the United States.

Levy, Leonard. *Origins of the Bill of Rights*. New Haven, Conn.: Yale University Press, 1999. A classic history of the Bill of Rights by a noted constitutional historian.

Lewis, Anthony. *Gideon's Trumpet*. New York: Vintage, 1989. A journalist's account of the landmark case of James Earl Gideon's fight for the right to legal counsel; includes explanations of other criminal justice rights and the work of the U.S. Supreme Court.

Lewis, Thomas T., ed. *The Bill of Rights*. 2 vols. Pasadena, Calif.: Salem Press, 2002. Comprehensive coverage of the Bill of Rights, with articles on each of the amendments, the Constitution, the incorporation doctrine, and many other topics, as well as 280 individual court cases.

Sunstein, Cass R. *Designing Democracy: What Constitutions Do*. New York: Oxford University Press, 2002. Analysis of how the U.S. divisions of conviction and belief can be used to safeguard democracy.

See also Bill of attainder; Bill of Rights, U.S.; Counsel, right to; Double jeopardy; Due process of law; *Ex post facto* laws; Freedom of assembly and association; Gun laws; Incorporation doctrine; Judicial review; Magna Carta; Precedent; Privacy rights; Right to bear arms; Search and seizure; Self-incrimination, privilege against; Supreme Court, U.S.; Treason.

Consumer fraud

Definition: Intentional deception of consumers with untruthful or misleading information about goods, services, and other aspects of business transactions, such as financial terms

Criminal justice issues: Business and financial crime; fraud; white-collar crime

Significance: There are many ways that consumers can fall victim to fraud by corporations and individuals. The financial cost of such crimes to the United States as a whole is immeasurable.

Consumer fraud takes many forms. Consumers fall victim to fraudulent acts such as false advertising, telemarketing and Internet scams, price gouging, chiseling, investment fraud, and many others. Such crimes are so prolific it is impossible accurately to estimate the total number of victims and costs to consumers. "Let the buyer beware" is a fundamental principle within a capitalistic economy. This assumption lends itself to consumer fraud by shifting responsibility from sellers, producers, and providers of goods and services to the consumers. Consumers should naturally be leery of products or services that seem too good to be true. Failing to distrust corporations and businesspersons, believing their claims to be true, is too often viewed as irresponsibility on the part of the consumer rather than victimization.

False Advertising and Bait and Switch Techniques

Goods and services are advertised almost everywhere. Television, magazines, billboards, sides of buses, and even park benches are sites of advertisements used to entice consumers to try new products, services, and companies. Consumers are bombarded with information intended to entice them into spending money. Using deceitful means or misrepresentations of facts to get people to buy particular products and services is the essence of fraud.

Consumers cannot make informed decisions about how to spend their money when the information they are given is untrue or misleading.

For example, actors dressed in white laboratory coats are often used in television commercials. The professional-looking attire of the actors gives them the appearance of medical professionals making claims about the quality of products. Audiences may be more inclined to believe the claims made in the commercials because they assume that the persons presenting them are experts.

Similarly, celebrity endorsements can sway consumers' purchasing decisions because people are often willing to trust the word of well-known individuals. It has only been since the 1990's that the Federal Trade Commission has required celebrity endorsers to base their remarks in commercials on their own personal findings or experiences with products. Before this requirement was instituted, celebrities were free to endorse products and services without any firsthand knowledge of their quality. Sellers occasionally included disclaimers within the fine print of their products' packaging. Such disclaimers were both easy to overlook and often difficult to understand, but their mere existence left victimized consumers with little or no legal recourse if they found that their purchases did not match up to the claims made in endorsements.

Another fraudulent technique used by sellers is known as "bait and switch." The "bait" is typically an exceptionally low-priced product or service designed to lure customers. The appeal of the bait is short-lived, however. Once customers are in the place of business, they are encouraged to purchase different and more expensive or more profitable goods or services—hence the "switch." Sellers lure consumers in with little intention of actually selling the advertized bait to them. The products are advertised only to draw in customers who might buy different goods or services. Sellers generally do carry limited quantities of the advertised bait, but it usually sells out quickly or may be of such poor quality that customers are easily talked into buying something else.

Chiseling and Price Gouging

A second sales technique used to defraud consumers is chiseling, a systematic means of taking money from consumers, typically without their knowledge. Chiseling takes a variety of forms, such as scales calibrated to overweigh products such as meat and produce sold by retailers, gas pumps calibrated to over-measure the quantities of fuel dispensed, and phone calls that are charged to the nearest whole minute. Consumers are often unaware they are being overcharged because the overcharge amounts are too small to be detected without special tools. However, the cumulative profits that can be generated from chiseling techniques can be substantial. Regardless of how small the overcharges are, consumers are ultimately defrauded by paying for goods or services they do not receive.

An equally sinister means of defrauding consumers is through the practice of price gouging. Price gouging occurs when sellers take advantage of emergency situations, such as gas shortages, to inflate prices for their goods and services. The threat of a shortage of a product or the increased need of a product might result in inflated prices and is in essence "gouging" the consumer. In times of natural disasters, for example, opportunistic sellers may inflate prices for emergency items. A bag of ice that normally sells for one dollar might instead go for three to five times as much.

Rumors of shortages of "must have" products, such as popular children's toys, often drive up prices for consumers. The examples are endless but the outcomes are the same. Consumers are forced to pay higher prices for goods or services often in times of crisis, fear, or disadvantage. The poor are often especially vulnerable to price gouging because of their lack of purchasing options. As a result, the poor often pay much higher prices for the same goods and services that the rich buy for less.

Another aspect of price gouging is the practice of selling "knockoff" products—inferior goods designed to look like high-quality products, such as designer clothes. Consumers are often aware when they are purchasing knockoff products because of where they buy them. For example, an open-air flea market is an unlikely place to buy a genuine designer product. However, when consumers are unaware that the items they are purchasing are not genuine, they are victims of fraud.

Investment Frauds

Named after its most notorious perpetrator, Charles Ponzi, Ponzi schemes are fraudulent investment schemes that promise to return high profits to investors but are actually only methods of funding lavish lifestyles for their originators. The promise of high returns on an investment is appealing to consumers. Initial investors in Ponzi schemes often receive returns, which make the offers more appealing to later investors. However, the returns the initial investors receive are simply the money paid into the schemes by new investors. The schemes work as long as investors receive returns, but they never pay at the levels promised.

Pyramid schemes are closely related to Ponzi schemes. Consumers are promised large returns by purchasing or selling goods or services and bringing additional investors into the businesses. The schemes are pyramid-shaped, with the initial investors at the top. As in a real pyramid, each lower level of investors must be larger. Each level makes its profits from the investments of the lower levels; the more levels below, the more return an investor receives. Eventually, however, the scheme collapses when no new investors come in, and the most recent participants receive no return at all on their investments.

Consumers are defrauded out of billions of dollars each year through investment fraud. Low-priced penny stocks are offered to investors with misrepresentations about their money-making potentials. Investment insiders inflate the prices of the stocks only long enough to sell their own shares when the market prices reach their peak. These investors make large amounts of money while outsiders lose money.

Fraudulent investment firms, often called "boiler rooms," make phone calls to unsuspecting investors telling them about "hot" stocks that will make them rich if they invest immediately. Brokers often make false claims about the stocks, their ability to make money for investors, and the inside information they have about the stocks. The investment firms profit from both the sales of the worthless stock and from the commissions they receive on the sales.

Telemarketing Scams

Smooth-talking telemarketers bilk billions of dollars from the unsuspecting public. Their offers are often too good to pass up. Good telemarketers quickly develop such trust with their customers that they can persuade them to pay for goods and services before they are received, even though the goods may never materialize or be of inferior quality.

Telemarketers often use travel scams and time-share vacation packages as their hooks. A typical travel scam works by informing consumers of "prizes" they have won. The prizes are typically expensive vacations to wonderful locations. However, in order to claim their prizes, the consumers must first purchase memberships in travel clubs or pay service fees. After the consumers pay the required fees, the vacation packages they receive often have so many restrictions placed that they are virtually impossible to use. The consumers are then left with little legal recourse because the vacation packages have been provided. Even when consumers do use the vacation vouchers, they often find that the quality of their vacations has been grossly misrepresented.

Similarly, time-share vacations are a lucrative and common type of scam. Consumers are again informed about the "no further obligation" prize(s) they have won and can claim if they attend an information session. The consumer is met with high-pressure sales people trying to sell them membership in the time-share. The prize they won rarely comes to fruition.

Amie R. Scheidegger

Further Reading

Rosoff, Stephen, Henry Pontell, and Robert Tillman. *Looting America: Greed, Corruption, Villains, and Victims*. Upper Saddle River, N.J.: Prentice Hall, 2003. Includes discussions and examples of a wide variety of fraudulent crimes and their impact on victims.

_____. *Profit Without Honor: White-Collar Crime and the Looting of America*. Upper Saddle River, N.J.: Prentice Hall, 2002. Critical evaluation of corporate criminals as well as government wrongdoing and the public's perceptions of such crimes.

Simon, David. *Elite Deviance*. Boston: Allyn & Bacon, 2002. Examination of various deviant and criminal acts performed by corporations and the impact such behaviors have individually and collectively.

Swierczynski, Duane. *Complete Idiots Guide to Frauds, Scams, and Cons*. Indianapolis, Ind.: Alpha Books, 2003. Popular guide to the ele-ments of confidence games that includes a typology of con men and illustrations of the most common scams and frauds.

Wells, Joseph. *Corporate Fraud Handbook: Prevention and Detection*. Hoboken, N.J.: John Wiley & Sons, 2004. Examines an array of fraudulent schemes and provides insight on prevention and detection.

See also Antitrust law; Background checks; Cable and satellite television signal theft; Corporate scandals; Cybercrime; Fraud; Insider trading; Insurance fraud; Sherman Antitrust Act; Tax evasion; Telephone fraud; Theft; White-collar crime.

Contempt of court

Definition: Conduct that obstructs a court's administration of justice or undermines its dignity

Criminal justice issues: Courts; punishment; trial procedures

Significance: Citing persons who disrupt court procedures or disobey court orders with contempt of court can be a powerful tool for maintaining order and decorum within courtrooms, and judges can use contempt of court to send offenders to jail without the help of police or trials.

Just as law-enforcement officers use discretion in deciding whom to arrest, judges use discretion when deciding to hold persons in contempt of court. However, just as police officers do not issue tickets to all motorists who exceed posted speed limits, judges do not cite all those who disrupt court proceedings with contempt. Judges typically reserve contempt citations for those who they believe are creating the most serious disorders and for situations in which they wish to set examples for other persons present in their courtrooms.

Contempt of court can also be used as a prosecutorial tool for imprisoning wrongdoers without trials. For example, prosecutors might call certain witnesses to testify, knowing that they are likely not to cooperate and then be jailed for con-

During the early nineteenth century the abolitionist Passmore Williamson was jailed for contempt of court for giving evasive testimony about his own part in freeing three slaves. Later Supreme Court rulings have limited the courts' contempt power to prevent abuses. *(Library of Congress)*

tempt of court. In fact, everyone who fails to comply with subpoenas or other court orders can be punished with contempt. In addition, those who disobey gag orders can also be held in contempt of court. Those who are found in contempt of court can be subjected to fines, jail time, or both, depending on the decisions of the judges holding the offenders in contempt. Those held in jail can be kept there without trial until they comply with the original court orders.

A justification for the courts' power to punish those guilty of contempt of court is deterrence. The sanctioning of individuals with contempt of court may deter others from being disruptive in court or from disobeying court orders. It can be especially useful in persuading news reporters to obey gag orders.

Jenephyr James

Further Reading

Neubauer, D. W. *America's Courts and the Criminal Justice System*. 7th ed. Belmont, Calif.: Wadsworth, 2002.

Rabe, Gary A., and Dean John Champion. *Criminal Courts: Structure, Process and Issues*. Upper Saddle River, N.J.: Prentice-Hall, 2002.

See also Chicago Seven trial; Deterrence; Discretion; Fines; Gag orders; Judges; Obstruction of justice.

Contributing to delinquency of minors

Definition: Any acts or omissions perpetrated by adults that encourage juveniles to engage in behaviors that may lead to delinquency

Criminal justice issues: Crime prevention; juvenile justice

Significance: American laws are designed to protect naïve juveniles from the depredations of adults.

Contributing to the delinquency of a minor is, like the term "juvenile delinquency," relatively recent in origin. For centuries, childhood was the most precarious period in an individual's life. Scant knowledge existed concerning illnesses and bacteria, and, as a result, it was common for people to die in infancy or childhood—the central reason that married couples had big families. If children were strong enough to survive, around age seven they entered the workforce alongside their parents and older siblings, becoming "little adults."

Views regarding childhood began changing in the nineteenth century because of the paradigm shift caused by the Industrial Revolution. Instead of families working together at the farm, people began migrating into the cities. Children competed with their elders for the new jobs created by the industrial boom. Up to this point, most children could not read or write, because education was not a particularly important issue for individuals tilling the soil.

With the growth of urban populations, education became increasingly important. Most parents were happy for their children to gain educations because it meant they might not have to work twelve to fifteen hours a day in factories. In addition to providing an academic education, many reformers attempted to teach the children that certain activities or vices were unhealthy and that it would be advantageous to leave certain things alone. For example, many children enjoyed the same unhealthy habits as their parents, such as smoking, using snuff or chewing tobacco, and drinking alcohol. Once society started seeing childhood as separate from adulthood, the social and moral mores changed, and what had once been done in the open (such as smoking cigarettes) now became surreptitious. Likewise, behaviors considered normal for adults began to be seen as taboo for juveniles.

Over time, statutes and law codes were written describing the punishments, usually mild, that adults would receive if they engaged in any activities that might lead juveniles toward delinquency. Furthermore, if adults allowed juveniles to engage in behavior considered "out-of-bounds," they could face charges based on not restricting the child. For example, adults who catch children smoking cigarettes but do nothing could conceivably be brought before a judge, as tobacco use is a proscribed activity for individuals who have not reached the age of majority. Furthermore, if a parent indulges in an illegal activity, such as smoking marijuana, the state has the right to arrest the parent for setting an example that could conceivably cause the juvenile to seek out opportunities for further drug exploration.

Cary Stacy Smith

Further Reading

Champion, Dean John. *The Juvenile Justice System: Delinquency, Processing, and the Law.* 4th ed. Upper Saddle River, N.J.: Prentice-Hall, 2003. Broad overview of delinquency and the treatment of juveniles in the justice system. Examines juvenile legal rights and the courts' decisions regarding adjudication, disposition, and sanctions.

Cox, Steven M., John J. Conrad, and Jennifer M. Allen. *Juvenile Justice: A Guide to Theory and Practice.* 5th ed. New York: McGraw Hill, 2003. Comprehensive examination of the juvenile justice system that connects theory and practice.

Malmgren, K. W., and S. M. Meisel. "Examining the Link Between Child Maltreatment and Delinquency for Youth with Emotional and Behavioral Disorders." *Child Welfare* 83, no. 2 (2004): 175-189. Examination of one cause contributing to juvenile delinquency.

Paternoster, R., S. Bushway, R. Brame, and R. Apel. "The Effects of Teenage Employment on Delinquency and Problem Behaviors." *Social Force* 82, no. 1 (2003): 297-336. Sociological treatment of one contributing factor in juvenile delinquency.

Shoemaker, D. J. *Theories of Delinquency: An Examination of Explanations of Delinquent Behavior.* 4th ed. New York: Oxford University Press, 2000. Survey of theoretical approaches to explaining delinquent behavior. Clearly written evaluations of the various individualistic and sociological theories.

Siegel, Larry J., Brandon C. Welsh, and Joseph J. Senna. *Juvenile Delinquency: Theory, Practice, and Law.* 8th ed. Belmont, Calif.: Wadsworth/Thomson Learning, 2002. Comprehensive examination of juvenile justice along with policies, theories, landmark court decisions, and contemporary issues. The eighth edition of this perennial textbook pays special attention to multimedia and Web resources.

Vander Ven, Thomas. *Working Mothers and Juvenile Delinquency.* New York: LFB Scholarly, 2003. Sociological study of the special problems of children with working mothers.

See also Antismoking laws; Indecent exposure; Juvenile courts; Juvenile delinquency; Juvenile Justice and Delinquency Prevention, Office of; Juvenile Justice and Delinquency Prevention Act; Juvenile justice system.

Convictions

Definition: Legal process through which judges and juries establish the guilt of criminal defendants

Criminal justice issues: Convictions; defendants; prosecution; verdicts

Significance: The focus of all criminal trial proceedings is the prosecution's efforts to obtain convictions by proving defendants guilty and the defendants' efforts to avoid convictions.

Convictions may be established in several ways: Defendants may enter pleas of guilt, they may enter pleas of *nolo contendere*, or they may be found guilty at trial. In each instance, the courts enter final judgments, in which the factual and legal allegations are sustained, and orders of conviction. Upon entry of the orders, the courts may then proceed to the sentencing phase. The combined process of entering judgments, convictions, and penalties are known as the judgment and sentence phase.

A conviction may only be entered when the legal and factual allegations reach the appropriate level of proof. In all criminal matters, the level of proof required is beyond a reasonable doubt. This is the level of factual certainty in which no mere skeptical condition of the mind exists but in which the evidence may fall short of absolute proof beyond all doubt. It means simply that the proof must be so conclusive and complete that all realistic doubts of the facts are removed from the minds of ordinary persons.

After Convictions

The legal status of defendants changes substantially once they are convicted. Convictions bring with them restrictions and losses of certain due process and other rights. The most significant loss is that of the defendants' freedom, which may be ordered as part of the sentences. In addition, convictions confer the status of having been found guilty of crimes. In some instances a conviction may also terminate or limit personal rights, such as the ability to own firearms, vote, be bonded, serve in the U.S. military, or obtain professional licenses, such as those of attorneys, medical doctors, or accountants.

Convictions are generally considered permanent parts of the defendants' criminal records. A person who has multiple convictions—especially for the same or similar crimes—may receive an enhanced punishment for the later offenses. For example, in most states conviction of the felony crime of burglary carries penalties of from one to seven years in the states' penal systems. Second and subsequent convictions generally increase punishments up to life in prison. Similar crimes carry similar punishments, which may be enhanced based on the type or number of prior convictions.

In instances in which more than one crime is charged against a defendant, each conviction may affect the penalties for any other convictions. In such instances, the courts tend to treat the companion cases either as separate crimes requiring individual punishments or as parts of a larger group of crimes.

The courts may run sentences concurrently or consecutively, depending on how they wish the individual convictions to be treated. Concurrent sentences are served and completed at the same time. For example, a person convicted both of driving under the influence of alcohol (DUI) and of manslaughter (both arising from the

The moment that defendants are pronounced guilty, their legal status changes. While they have the right to appeal their convictions, they nevertheless fall under the jurisdiction of the courts in which they are convicted and begin to lose their personal rights and freedoms. *(Brand-X Pictures)*

same set of facts), may be punished for both convictions at the same time. Thus, if a court were to order the defendant to serve a one-year sentence for the DUI conviction and a two-year sentence for the manslaughter conviction, the defendant would serve both sentences at the same time and spend a total of only two years in prison. By contrast, if a defendant were convicted of the exact same pair of crimes and instead received one- and two-year sentences to be served consecutively, the defendant would spend a total of three years in prison.

Convictions may also be used to prove conduct in civil cases as well. The burden of proof in criminal cases is higher than that required in civil actions. This means that once the burden is met for a criminal case, as proven through existence of the conviction, the burden will also be met for the civil action. The key is that the facts leading to the conviction must be the same as those used in the civil case. Thus, defendants who are convicted of driving under the influence of alcohol may find themselves civilly liable for car crashes arising from the same set of facts.

One must be careful when associating convictions with a jury trial. The duty of the jury is to determine the facts in a case. It is always the duty of the judge to determine the given law. A conviction can only be entered when both facts and law combine to prove the elements of the particular crime. While a jury may reach a verdict as to the facts, it is only the judge that may enter a conviction as part of the final judgment.

Carl J. Franklin

Further Reading

Christianson, Scott. *Innocent: Inside Wrongful Conviction Cases*. New York: New York University Press, 2004. Investigative reporter's account of forty-two wrongful conviction cases.

Connors, E., T. Lundregan, N. Miller, and T. McEwen. *Convicted by Juries, Exonerated by Science: Case Studies in the Use of DNA Evidence to Establish Innocence After Trial*. Alexandria, Va.: National Institute of Justice, 1996. Close examination of some of the first cases of false convictions that were overturned by DNA evidence.

Hanson, Roger A. *Federal Habeas Corpus Review: Challenging State Court Criminal Convictions*. Washington, D.C.: U.S. Department of Justice, Bureau of Justice Statistics, 1995. Statistical study of *habeas corpus* petitions in eighteen federal district courts in nine states.

LaFave, Wayne. *Criminal Law Hornbook*. 4th ed. Belmont, Calif.: West Publishing, 2003. Detailed treatise of criminal law with lengthy explanations and references to cases.

LaFave, Wayne R., Jerold H. Israel, and Nancy J. King. *Criminal Procedure*. 4th ed. St. Paul, Minn.: Thomson/West, 2004.

See also Acquittal; Aggravating circumstances; Burden of proof; Concurrent sentences; Criminal records; Double jeopardy; Execution of judgment; False convictions; Mitigating circumstances; Plea bargaining; Pleas; Presentence investigations; Recidivism; Sentencing; Verdicts.

Coroners

Definition: Public officials who investigate deaths when there are reasons to suspect those deaths did not occur naturally

Criminal justice issues: Evidence and forensics; investigation; medical and health issues

Significance: A coroner is the officer responsible for finding out how a person died if that death appears to have been violent. The coroner may hold an inquest and order an autopsy to be performed if the manner of death is not obvious.

When a person dies and the manner of death is deemed either uncertain or violent, it is the coroner's job to investigate the death. A coroner is called to the scene of a crime to determine whether a death occurred by accidental, suicidal, homicidal, natural, or uncertain means. Even if law-enforcement officials feel that there already exists enough evidence to proceed with a criminal investigation, they still must wait for the coroner's decision before they act. The coroner may order an autopsy and wait until its completion before making a final decision on the manner of death.

Coroners can be elected officials who do not necessarily possess any medical or law-enforcement

Thomas Noguchi, shortly before his retirement from the Los Angeles County Coroners Office in 1999. Although famous as the "coroner to the stars," Noguchi was actually a medical examiner. *(AP/Wide World Photos)*

mission from the deceased's next of kin in order for an autopsy to be performed. The coroner will usually order a full autopsy, so as much information can be gathered as possible. The results of the autopsy will determine whether law-enforcement agencies should continue with their own investigations.

Everybody is under the jurisdiction of the coroner, from the pathologists or medical examiners who perform the autopsy to the laboratory technicians who run further tests on dissected organs (such as toxicology). The coroner can issue arrest warrants and subpoenas as needed if investigations warrant it; in some counties the coroner is legally more powerful than the sheriff. The coroner also identifies remains, testifies regarding insurance and estate claims, and warns the community about dangerous new illegal drugs as they are discovered.

knowledge. Usually, though, the coroner is a mortician, doctor, or other local law-enforcement official. In big metropolitan areas such as Los Angeles, a coroner's position is a full-time job and is assisted by deputies who do the fieldwork.

Responsibilities

A coroner's responsibilities are many, including the primary one of determining whether or not enough evidence accompanies a death to justify a criminal investigation. A coroner may investigate against the will of the deceased's relatives or hospital employees; conversely, a coroner may declare the matter closed, stating there should not be an investigation at all. Coroners are also responsible for notifying the proper authorities regarding deaths and signing death certificates. A human body must be certified as legally dead before any funeral arrangements are made. If the body is eventually going to be cremated, an autopsy may be mandatory according to regional laws.

If the cause of death is not obvious at the crime scene, the coroner will usually hold an inquest and order an autopsy. For medicolegal or forensic investigations, a coroner does not have to get per-

History

Throughout history, there have been coroners or people like them whose job it was to say whether someone's death was intentional or not. The English were the first to establish a coroner's office: In 1194, as a way to raise ransom funds for King Richard I, knights in each county were given the task of selling the goods of hanged felons. These knights were known as "crowners," a word that eventually became "coroner" (taken from *corona*, a Latin word for "crown").

Eventually the coroner's job became that of ensuring all taxes were collected honestly by the sheriff. This meant that all deaths of a sudden or violent nature were investigated. Matters became complicated when suicide was concerned. The laws of medieval England stated that all possessions belonging to someone who committed suicide become the property of the Crown. The Church of England added that the suicide victim's soul was condemned to hell unless the victim had suffered from demoniac possession or insanity. This the coroner had to determine, and the first inquests were held.

The first written work about forensic medicine was Sung Tz'u's *Hsi Yuan Chi Lu* (washing away

of unjust imputations or wrongs), written in 1247. The first university department of legal medicine opened at the University of Edinburgh, Scotland, in 1807, and in England, coroners became officials who dealt with deaths that were suspicious. The United States adopted the British coroner system but eventually began to change how it worked by using professionally trained physicians who had studied forensic pathology.

The Coroner in the United States

In the United States, a coroner was either elected or appointed to the job until 1877. In that year, a physician in Massachusetts was chosen instead to be the coroner. The job's description changed, also, so that coroners were only supposed to investigate violent deaths. In 1915, New York became the first city to give a coroner the authority to order an autopsy, and Maryland began a statewide medical examiner system in 1939.

Modern coroners are not only invaluable assets to medicolegal investigations, but they can also become celebrities in their own rights. Thomas Noguchi, Los Angeles County's chief coroner from 1967 to 1982, became known as the "coroner to the stars" because he supervised the investigations of Hollywood celebrity deaths such as those of Natalie Wood and John Belushi. Noguchi also invented a method of trace metal identification that is now used throughout the United States.

Kelly Rothenberg

Further Reading

Blanche, Tony, and Brad Schreiber. *Death in Paradise: An Illustrated History of the Los Angeles County Department of Coroner*. New York: Four Walls Eight Windows, 2001. Details what a forensic coroner does and gives examples from famous Hollywood murders.

Burton, Julian L., and Guy N. Rutty. *The Hospital Autopsy*. New York: Oxford University Press, 2001. Contains a chapter about coroners and autopsies.

Kadish, Sanford H. *Encyclopedia of Crime and Justice*. Vol. 1. New York: Free Press, 1983. Detailed history of coroners and what their job entails.

Noguchi, Thomas T. *Coroner*. New York: Simon & Schuster, 1983. Autobiography of Los Angeles County coroner Thomas Noguchi.

See also Autopsies; Cold cases; Forensics; Inquests; Medical examiners; Toxicology; Trace evidence.

Corporal punishment

Definition: Infliction of physical pain or discomfort as the means to punish behavior that violates established rules, including criminal laws

Criminal justice issues: Confessions; interrogation; medical and health issues; punishment

Significance: Although corporal punishments were once commonly applied, they were eliminated from the American justice system as the United States moved toward exclusive reliance on fines and restrictions on freedom, such as probation and incarceration, as methods of criminal punishment.

In seventeenth and eighteenth century Europe and colonial America, people routinely received physical punishments for violating society's rules. These corporal punishments included branding, whipping, cutting off ears, fingers, hands, or tongues, and placing people in stocks—wooden structures in a town square into which a person's head, arms, or legs could be locked. These corporal punishments were legacies of religious beliefs that had also encouraged torture, burning people at the stake, and public executions for a variety of offenses, both serious and minor. A basic belief that underlay these physical punishments of people's bodies was an assumption that people who misbehaved were possessed by the devil and therefore unable to conform their behavior to God's rules for society.

During the Enlightenment period of the late eighteenth century, the emphasis on corporal punishment in Europe began to be displaced by reforms intended to rehabilitate offenders. Instead of branding or whipping them, various localities began to incarcerate them with a Bible or make them work in prison shops in the hope that they would discover God and self-discipline and thereby become good people.

Punishment in the United States

During the colonial and postrevolutionary periods, the United States employed many of the corporal punishments that had been brought from Europe, including whipping, branding, and placing in stocks. The movement away from corporal punishments in favor of incarceration occurred during the nineteenth century.

In the southern United States, corporal punishments of the most vicious kinds, particularly whipping, branding, and dismemberment, were applied against African American slaves as punishment for escapes or any other infractions as defined by slave owners. Local law-enforcement officials and courts reinforced the institution of slavery by actively supporting these forms of punishment.

After the Civil War, corporal punishments began disappearing as formal punishments for crimes, but their use still flourished on an informal basis. Police in many localities throughout the country utilized beatings and even torture as a means to punish people informally and to obtain confessions. While corporal punishment was used successfully to obtain many confessions, these confessions often came from innocent people who had simply been selected for victimization by unethical police officers. Such abusive behavior by police officers became less common in the twentieth century as policing began to become a profession with training, and as judges scrutinized the activities of police.

Corporal punishment was used in prisons and jails until the 1960's. Prisoners in some states were beaten, locked in small compartments, and otherwise physically coerced into obeying orders. Officials sometimes permitted inmates to abuse other inmates in order to force prisoners to perform labor under harsh conditions. These practices were outlawed by federal judges as a result of lawsuits in the 1960's and 1970's.

Whippings and other forms of corporal punishment that did not interfere with slaves' productivity were frequently inflicted on American slaves before the Civil War. *(Library of Congress)*

Corporal Punishment and the Law

By 1969, all but two states had abolished whipping as a punishment for prison inmates. The final two states were effectively barred from further use of corporal punishment when a U.S. court of appeals decision said that Arkansas's continuing use on prisoners of the "strap"—a leather whip attached to a wooden handle—violated the prohibition on cruel and unusual punishments (*Jackson v. Bishop*, 1969).

Beginning in the 1970's, prison officials, like police officers, could not use corporal punishments. They could, however, use physical force for self-defense and for gaining control over people who were fighting, threatening, or disruptive. Despite the prohibition on corporal punishments, occasional lawsuits are still filed against police officers and corrections officials who have beaten criminal defendants and inmates.

The formal abolition of corporal punishment in the criminal justice system did not mean that corporal punishment no longer existed in the United States. Parents are permitted to apply corporal punishment to their children as long as that punishment does not cause injuries or break laws against child abuse. In addition, corporal punishment is permitted in schools in many states. In 1978, the Supreme Court decided that the Eighth Amendment's prohibition of cruel and unusual punishments did not apply to disciplinary corporal punishments in schools (*Ingraham v. Wright*, 1978). Thus many schools continued to use corporal punishments, most frequently paddling with a wooden paddle, as a means to punish misbehaving students. By 1992, twenty states and the District of Columbia had banned the use of corporal punishment in schools, and many individual school districts in the remaining states had done the same.

In 1994, public debates resumed concerning the desirability of corporal punishment when Singapore sentenced Michael Fay, an American teenager, to six lashes with a bamboo cane for committing acts of vandalism. Although the U.S. government protested on Fay's behalf that the punishment ("caning") was barbaric, leaders in many American local communities seized on the issue to advocate the reintroduction of corporal punishment as a cheaper and more effective punishment for juvenile offenders. Corporal punishment was not reinitiated, but the debate demonstrated that many Americans still consider corporal punishment to be an effective deterrent to misbehavior by young people.

Christopher E. Smith

Further Reading

Berkson, Larry. *The Concept of Cruel and Unusual Punishment*. Lexington, Mass.: Lexington Books, 1975. Examination of the legal aspects of corporal and other forms of punishment.

Foucault, Michel. *Discipline and Punish: The Birth of the Prison*. Translated by Alan Sheridan. New York: Vintage Press, 1995. Traces the history of punishment from brutal public events to subtle exertions of power over individuals in everyday life.

Garland, David. *Punishment and Modern Society*. Chicago: University of Chicago Press, 1990. General overview of punishment.

Genovese, Eugene D. *Roll, Jordan, Roll: The World the Slaves Made*. New York: Pantheon Books, 1974. Discusses the use of whipping and other corporal punishments of slaves in the antebellum South.

Hyman, Irwin A., and James H. Wise, eds. *Corporal Punishment in American Education: Readings in History, Practice, and Alternatives*. Philadelphia: Temple University Press, 1979. Examination of the debates over corporal punishment in schools.

Rothman, David J. *The Discovery of the Asylum: Social Order and Disorder in the New Republic*. Boston: Little, Brown, 1971. Broad history of punishment in the U.S.

See also Auburn system; Bill of Rights, U.S.; Cruel and unusual punishment; Police brutality; Punishment; Rehabilitation.

Corporate scandals

Definition: Crimes in which investors in corporations, including both stockholders and creditors, lose money due to falsehoods perpetrated by corporate management

Criminal justice issues: Business and financial crime; fraud; white-collar crime

Significance: Corporate scandals have seemingly increased in the early twenty-first century, but such crimes have occurred throughout the history of the corporate form of business.

Frauds perpetrated by corporate insiders and the scandals that result are not new phenomena; they have occurred since the beginnings of the corporate form of business during the mid- to late nineteenth century. As early as the mid-nineteenth century, corporate fraud in railroads occurred with regularity. For example, during the early 1850's, the Mobile & Ohio Railroad found that a corporate engineer learned the route on which a new railroad was going to be built. He went out and bought land along that route from farmers and plantation owners and then sold the land to the railroad at inflated prices. It was his insider information that allowed him to defraud his employer. By the 1870's, one-half of the railroads in the United States were in receivership, many because of the immoral acts of corporate leaders. Many aspects of law involving corporate bankruptcy and reorganization emanated from the railroad receiverships.

Corporate scandal is known as the "agency problem." As agents, corporate officers utilize corporation assets on behalf of the stockholders (owners). At the same time, they have a vested interest in maximizing their own well being. The result is that stockholders need some form of governance over the officers of corporations. This is theoretically accomplished through boards of directors, audit committees, and internal auditors, who oversee the activities of management.

Kreuger and the Securities and Exchange Acts

Modern government oversight of corporate dealings has grown out of one of the most notorious scandals of the twentieth century—the failure of Kreuger & Toll, a Swedish match conglomerate that had been founded and headed by Ivar Kreuger, who was supposedly the richest man in the world. During the 1920's, the most widely held securities in America—and the world—were the stocks and bonds of Kreuger's company.

The bankruptcy of Ivar Kreuger's empire in 1932, following his suicide, led to a national outcry that resulted in the passage by the U.S. Congress of the Securities and Exchange Act the following year. Prior to 1933, companies that depended on stockholder financing were not required to have audits. Even companies listed on the New York Stock Exchange often did not issue audited financial statements. That situation changed because of Kreuger—one of the greatest swindlers the world has ever seen.

Kreuger's securities had been popular because they sold in small denominations and paid dividends and interest that often reached as high as 20 percent annually. Financial reporting as it is now known was in its infancy; stockholders based their investment decisions almost solely on companies' dividend payments. However, Kreuger's dividends were paid out of capital, not profits. Kreuger was essentially operating a giant pyramid scheme that was hidden from the investing public by his insistence that financial statements not be audited. He argued that financial secrecy was paramount to corporate success. In his defense, some secrecy was truly needed because he was often dealing with foreign powers about government monopolies and taxes on wooden matches. Subsequently, it was discovered that many of his companies' assets were in the form of intangible monopolies.

The stock market crash in 1929 made it more difficult for Kreuger to sell new securities to fuel his pyramid scheme. Finally, he committed suicide in March, 1932. Within three weeks, his companies were in bankruptcy, as it became apparent that there were few assets to support the financial statements they had issued over the years. The Kreuger bankruptcy was the largest on record up to that time and resulted in numerous changes in financial reporting. Newspaper articles kept Americans aware of the extent of Kreuger's fraud at the same time that Congress was considering the passage of the federal securities laws. The timing of the Kreuger bankruptcy and the corresponding media coverage made it politically expedient to pass laws that would make similar schemes difficult in the future. A single event, the corruption of Ivar Kreuger, had shaken investors' confidence and provided the media event of the decade. As a result, both the passage of the Securities and Exchange Act of 1933 and the issuance by the New York Stock Exchange of rules mandating audits of listed companies can be attributed to the Kreuger case. In fact, it might be argued that Kreuger ultimately did more good than harm to the financial community.

The federal Securities and Exchange Acts of 1933 and 1934 provided both civil and criminal penalties for perpetrators of corporate frauds. The acts also provided for civil penalties, under specific circumstances, for accountants and lawyers who were involved in the preparation, registration, or audits of financial statements hiding corporate frauds. Section 11(a) of the Securities and Exchange Act of 1933 covers the failures of experts, including accountants, who certify financial statements that contain material misstatements of facts or omission of such facts in registration statements of new securities.

Under federal law, accountants may be held liable on either fraud or negligence charges. Plaintiffs do not even have to prove that they have relied on erroneous statements; they merely have to prove that the errors existed. Also, privacy of contract is not required under the securities laws. Accountants, brokers, and lawyers may assert the due diligence defense in cases involving Section 11(a) violations. The landmark U.S. Supreme Court case involving the due diligence defense is *Escott v. BarChris Construction Corporation* of 1968.

Whereas the 1933 Securities and Exchange Act applies only to issues of new securities, the 1934 act applies to subsequent issues of stocks and bonds. Rule 10b-5 of the Securities and Exchange Act of 1934 is the most formidable weapon available to federal prosecutors attempting to fight corporate fraud. Rule 10b-5 outlaws fraudulent financial statements, misstatements, or omissions of material facts in the sale of securities. Unlike the provisions of the 1933 act, negligence by itself is not a crime because injured parties must prove that defendants have acted with intent. This rule was tested in the 1976 Supreme Court case of *Ernst and Ernst v. Hochfelder*.

McKesson & Robbins and Later Cases

In 1938, the McKesson & Robbins drug company was the victim of insider fraud in the person of Philip Musica (also known as Donald Coster). The senior management of McKesson & Robbins had used a facade of false documents to conceal the fact that $19 million in inventory and receivables did not exist. A federal Securities and Exchange Commission (SEC) investigation concluded that Price Waterhouse & Company had adhered to generally accepted auditing procedures. The auditors had obtained management assurances as to the value of the inventories and had checked the inventories to purchase orders, which had been fabricated to conceal the fraud. The SEC concluded that although generally accepted procedures had been followed, the procedures themselves were inadequate. As a result, the American Institute of Accountants in 1939 issued a statement that required auditors to observe inventories and confirm receivables. Other cases followed during the twentieth century that influenced auditors and regulators, but probably none to the extent of the Kreuger and McKesson & Robbins cases.

Corporate frauds appeared to be slightly less newsworthy during the 1940's and 1950's. During the 1960's, the news media focused on the salad oil swindle at the Allied Crude Vegetable Oil Refining Corporation and the crooked schemes of Billie Sol Estes in the fertilizer and grain industries. The salad oil swindle was perpetrated by Anthony De Angelis, the corporate president who moved a small amount of soybean oil around in hundreds of large tanks. He then got the American Express Field Warehousing Company to certify that all the tanks were full of oil, when in reality the tanks were full of water, with small amounts of oil on top. Based on the phony warehouse receipts he accumulated, De Angelis persuaded New York bankers to lend him hundreds of millions of dollars.

The fraudulent scheme used by Estes was to use the same collateral for multiple loans. When he sold fertilizer tanks to farmers, the farmers signed notes to pay for the tanks in installments. Estes then took their notes to financial institutions and used them as security for loans. However, he used each note several times to secure many more loans than there were notes from farmers. By the time his scheme was uncovered, Estes had obtained approximately 30,000 loans on only 1,800 tanks of fertilizer. Both auditors and lenders had been misled by a shell game of switching identification plates on fertilizer tanks.

The Estes case also tended to give big business

a bad name as many people believed that all business deals were at least somewhat shady. Politicians, particularly then Vice President Lyndon Johnson, also suffered from public relations problems since Estes claimed that he made payoffs to many prominent individuals. In 1963, Estes received a fifteen-year sentence following his conviction for fraud.

Late Twentieth Century Scandals

The 1970's witnessed the dawn of computer frauds, with extensive news coverage of the use of computers to defraud shareholders in the huge insurance company Equity Funding Corporation of America. The company's top management created imaginary policyholders on its computers. At that time, auditors were not widely familiar with computers, so they failed to uncover the fraud. After the imaginary policyholders were created, their policies were resold to other insurance companies. As a result of the fraud, both stockholders and other insurance companies lost money. Most of the corporate executives were eventually convicted of fraud and violations of insurance laws.

The decade of the 1970's saw the passage of two federal laws that subsequently played important roles in the fight against corporate fraud. The 1970 Racketeer Influenced and Corrupt Organizations Act (RICO) was designed to curtail the role of organized crime in corporate frauds. However, the use of RICO in civil cases not involving organized crime has been more extensive because of the all-encompassing wording of the act.

RICO allows the awarding of treble damages in civil cases. In 1977 the corporate environment changed when Congress passed the Foreign Corrupt Practices Act (FCPA). Although the media emphasized that the purpose of the new law was to eliminate payments by U.S. corporations to foreign officials, a secondary purpose of enhanced internal controls was more important to corporate management.

Congress included in the new law a provision that companies should have controls to ensure that illegal payments are uncovered by the accounting system. Thus, if a corporation is guilty of making an illegal payment, management could not escape conviction by claiming lack of knowl-

edge of the payments. If management did lack knowledge, then they were guilty of having a system that could not uncover illegal payments. As a result of this law, corporate management began placing more emphasis on internal controls. The result was the hiring of more internal auditors by corporations with internal audit departments and the establishment of new audit departments by organizations that did not have them. This increase in internal controls resulted in a reduction in corporate fraud. Although the intent of the law was to target a single type of fraud, the fact that companies now have more internal auditors and better systems of control means that all types of fraud can be uncovered.

During the 1980's, hundreds of financial institutions, primarily savings and loan associations, failed due to insider fraud, leading to a congressional investigation headed by Michigan congressman John Dingell. The conclusions of the Dingell Committee included recommendations that large corporations should all have internal auditors and audit committees of the boards of directors. The oddity about the cases of the 1980's was that so many companies were involved, and most of them were all in the same industry. Technically, the savings and loan fraud of the 1980's was the worst fraud in history—totaling well over $200 billion in losses. However, these losses were the result of hundreds of similar frauds at financial institutions throughout the country.

Twenty-first Century Cases

During the first years of the twenty-first century, scandals at HealthSouth, Global Crossing, Tyco, Enron, and WorldCom were in the news; however, these scandals are simply modern extensions of the nineteenth century railroad schemes and the Kreuger debacle of the early 1930's. In every case, corporate governance systems broke down or simply did not exist, and greedy individuals took corporate assets for their own personal use and manipulated stock prices to defraud stockholders.

In most of these cases, external auditors were blamed for either agreeing to questionable accounting practices or failing to uncover the transactions recorded by management. Enron Corporation was a highly publicized failure uncovered in late 2001. When Andersen & Company (for-

Bernard Ebbers, the former chief executive officer of WorldCom leaving the Manhattan federal courthouse on March 15, 2005, after being convicted on all counts of financial fraud with which he had been charged. *(AP/Wide World Photos)*

merly Arthur Andersen & Company), an external auditor that had approved some questionable transactions, was discovered to have shredded thousands of documents related to its audit of Enron, the once revered firm was destroyed. By the spring of 2002, Andersen essentially ceased to exist—not because it had failed in conducting an audit, but because it attempted to hide its audit coverage by shredding key documents. One Andersen audit partner eventually pleaded guilty to obstruction of justice for ordering the documents to be shredded.

As media coverage of Enron receded, a new fraud was uncovered at WorldCom, a major telecommunications firm in Clinton, Mississippi, that was also audited by Andersen & Company. The internal auditors at WorldCom discovered that its chief financial officer, controller, and other accounting employees had recorded expenses as assets, which resulted in higher income and generated huge bonuses for top employees. WorldCom

was essentially the straw that broke the camel's back; the investing public insisted that Congress do something about the amoral acts of corporate executives.

The result was the passage on July 31, 2002, of the Sarbanes-Oxley Act, which set limits on the types of nonaudit work that external auditors are allowed to perform for their clients and required corporate executives to certify the accuracy of their companies' financial statements. Several WorldCom accountants, including chief financial officer Scott Sullivan and controller David Myers, pleaded guilty to accounting fraud under the Securities and Exchange Acts of 1933 and 1934. The company's chief executive officer, Bernard Ebbers, was also indicted.

A similar story unfolded at HealthSouth Corporation in Birmingham, Alabama, where the government quickly worked out plea deals with corporate financial officers. However, prosecution of the company's chief executive officer was less of a certainty. Thus, at WorldCom, Enron, and HealthSouth the chief executive officers all claimed their own innocence by trying to place blame on lower-level workers, whom they claimed were trying to inflate corporate earnings in attempts to profit from stock options and bonus agreements.

The seemingly endless string of financial frauds in public corporations has cast public doubt on the credibility of even untarnished corporations. Such trust, once lost, is slow to return. The results have been slowdowns in the financial markets during the 1930's, 1960's, 1980's, and the early years of the twenty-first century. However, there are now more tools available for prosecutors to use against corporate fraud perpetrators. In addition to common law, there are the Securities and Exchange Acts of the 1930's, the Racketeer Influenced Corrupt Organizations Act of 1970, the Foreign Corrupt Practices Act of 1977, and the Sarbanes-Oxley Act of 2002.

Dale L. Flesher

Further Reading

Akst, Daniel. *Wonder Boy: Barry Minkow—the Kid Who Swindled Wall Street*. New York: Charles Scribner's Sons, 1990. Describes the details behind the $200-million ZZZZ Best fraud of the 1980's. An international accounting firm, a top law firm, New York investment bankers, and a multitude of investors all succumbed to a fraud perpetrated by a teenager.

Cruver, Brian. *Anatomy of Greed: The Unshredded Truth from an Enron Insider*. New York: Carroll & Graf, 2002. An Enron insider, Cruver was a lower-level employee who tells his story of the events at Enron, including how he continued to receive paychecks for several months after he was fired.

Fox, Loren. *Enron: The Rise and Fall*. Hoboken, N.J.: Wiley, 2003. This volume examines Enron's culture, its rise, and its fall. Also discussed are the impacts on financial markets, American energy policy, and the U.S. economy.

Jeter, Lynne. *Disconnected: Deceit and Betrayal at WorldCom*. Hoboken, N.J.: John Wiley & Sons, 2003. This is the first book to look into the downfall of the telecom industry giant WorldCom. Includes a discussion of the possible role of former chief executive officer Bernie Ebbers in the largest bankruptcy in U.S. history.

Keats, Charles. *Magnificent Masquerade: The Strange Case of Dr. Coster and Mr. Musica*. New York: Funk & Wagnalls, 1964. The complete story of Philip Musica, the man who perpetrated the McKesson & Robbins fiasco of 1938. Surprisingly, Musica had been previously convicted of earlier corporate frauds, but his sentence had been commuted by the president of the United States. The result was major changes in the ways accountants conducted their audits.

Miller, Norman C. *The Great Salad Oil Swindle*. New York: Coward McCann, 1965. This volume tells the story of how one man manipulated millions of gallons of nonexistent salad oil, resulting in the bankruptcy of two Wall Street brokerage houses, the demise of a subsidiary of American Express Company, and destruction of the stability of stock markets throughout the world.

Minkow, Barry. *Clean Sweep*. Nashville, Tenn.: Thomas Nelson Publishers, 1995. Memoir describing the author's leadership of one of the largest corporate frauds of the 1980's.

Pilzer, Paul Zane, and Robert Deitz. *Other People's Money: The Inside Story of the S&L Mess*. New York: Simon & Schuster, 1989. The story

behind the largest federal bailout in U.S. history—the frauds of the savings and loan associations of the 1980's. The federal government ultimately allowed a series of scandalous deals with corporate raiders who were able to acquire the portfolios of savings and loan investments for pennies on the dollar.

Shaplen, Robert. *Kreuger: Genius and Swindler*. New York: Alfred A. Knopf, 1960. Explains the role of Ivar Kreuger in what was in 1932 the largest corporate bankruptcy in history. Kreuger's securities were the most widely held in the world, and this volume unravels some of the intricacies of the fraud.

Swartz, Mimi, and Sherron Watkins. *Power Failure: The Inside Story of the Collapse of Enron*. New York: Doubleday, 2003. An Enron accountant and former auditor, Watkins tells how the company went from trading in tangible goods to abstractions, complete with questionable accounting practices and huge compensation packages. She also includes stories about how she warned corporation executives about cooked books and phony reports.

See also Antitrust law; Bribery; Commercialized vice; Computer crime; Consumer fraud; Embezzlement; Forensic accounting; Fraud; Insider trading; Insurance fraud; Money laundering; Obstruction of justice; Racketeer Influenced and Corrupt Organizations Act; Regulatory crime; Tax evasion; Watergate scandal; White-collar crime.

Counsel, right to

Definition: Entitlement provided for criminal defendants by the U.S. Constitution to receive representation by an attorney during criminal proceedings

Criminal justice issues: Attorneys; constitutional protections; defendants

Significance: An essential aspect of the American adversary system of justice employed is the principle that criminal defendants receive professional representation in order to protect their constitutional rights and prevent the conviction of innocent people.

American legal proceedings employ an adversary system of justice which assumes that the truth will emerge through the clash of professional advocates who oppose each other in the courtroom. In criminal cases, the permanent advocate for the government is the prosecutor. If individuals accused of crimes did not have professional advocates to represent them, there would be grave risks that the prosecution would automatically overwhelm the average citizen-defendant in the courtroom and thereby obtain convictions, whether justified or not. Defendants who have sufficient funds can hire their own attorneys, but poor people who are accused of crimes cannot afford to secure their own professional representation. In order to increase the fairness of legal proceedings and provide protection for criminal defendants' rights, the U.S. Supreme Court gradually interpreted the words of the U.S. Constitution to provide a broad right to counsel for people who otherwise could not afford to hire an attorney on their own.

One of the fundamental principles of the American criminal justice system is the right of all defendants to professional legal counsel—whether they can afford it or not. *(Brand-X Pictures)*

Constitutional Law

The Sixth Amendment to the U.S Constitution includes various rights intended to ensure that criminal defendants receive fair trials. One of those rights is the right "to have the Assistance of Counsel for his defense." For most of American history, the application of this right to counsel was limited for two reasons. First, until the middle of the twentieth century, the Bill of Rights was regarded as protecting people only against the federal government. Thus the Sixth Amendment applied only to federal criminal cases, which are a tiny proportion of the total criminal cases processed each year. Second, the right to counsel was interpreted to mean that people could not be prevented from having an attorney if they could afford to hire one. It did not mean that an attorney would be provided for people who could not afford to hire their own.

The Supreme Court began to alter its interpretations of the Sixth Amendment in the 1930's. In a case concerning several unrepresented African American youths convicted of rape and sentenced to death in a lynch-mob atmosphere in Alabama (*Powell v. Alabama*, 1932), the Supreme Court declared that poor defendants facing the death penalty must be provided with attorneys. In *Johnson v. Zerbst* (1938), the Supreme Court said that all defendants facing felony charges in federal court must be provided with attorneys if they are too poor to hire their own. During the 1940's, the right to appointed counsel was expanded to cover poor state felony defendants who needed professional representation because of "special circumstances" such as illiteracy or mental retardation.

During the 1950's and early 1960's, state legislatures, state supreme courts, and local state judges began to require that poor defendants be supplied with attorneys in criminal cases. By 1963, seven states still did not ensure that defense attorneys were provided for all felony defendants. The Supreme Court brought the entire country into line in 1963 with its decision in *Gideon v. Wainwright* (1963), which applied the Sixth Amendment to all state courts by requiring that poor defendants be given attorneys in felony cases. In subsequent decisions, the Supreme Court expanded the right to counsel to cover initial appeals after conviction (*Douglas v. California*, 1963) and misdemeanor cases in which the defendant faces the possibility of incarceration for less than one year in jail (*Argersinger v. Hamlin*, 1972). The Supreme Court also applied the right to counsel to pretrial processes by declaring that the Sixth Amendment required that defense attorneys be made available during police questioning of suspects, during preliminary hearings, and at identification line-ups after a defendant has been charged with a crime.

Limitations on the Right to Counsel

Under the Supreme Court's interpretations of the Sixth Amendment, the right to counsel applies only when a criminal defendant faces a charge that might result in incarceration. If a defendant faces only a small fine, then the county or state government is not required to supply a defense attorney unless mandated by that state's laws.

The right to counsel does not apply at all to civil cases. Poor people who want to file lawsuits usually must obtain their own attorneys, unless they qualify for free representation through the Legal Services Corporation, a federal government agency.

The right to counsel for criminal defendants does not guarantee that the defense attorney supplied by the state will take the case all the way to trial or will do an outstanding job in representing the defendant. Whether the state chooses to supply defense attorneys for poor people through state-salaried public defenders or through assignments to private attorneys who receive a small sum for each case, most attorneys work to obtain plea bargains for their clients. If the defendants are unhappy with their court-appointed attorney or public defender, there is little that they can do about it. It is difficult to prove that an attorney's performance was so bad that it violated the Sixth Amendment by providing "ineffective assistance of counsel." Thus there is often distrust and dissatisfaction evident in the relationships between poor defendants and the attorneys provided for them by the state.

Christopher E. Smith

Further Reading

Lewis, Anthony. *Gideon's Trumpet*. 1964. Reprint. New York: Vintage, 1989. History of the right to counsel in American jurisprudence built around the story of the *Gideon v. Wainwright* case, which expanded the right to counsel to all state courts.

Smith, Christopher E. *Courts and the Poor*. Chicago: Nelson-Hall, 1991. Examination of the special problems of poor defendants in the criminal justice system, with special attention to the issue of the right to counsel.

Taylor, John B. *Right to Counsel and Privilege Against Self-Incrimination: Rights and Liberties Under the Law*. Santa Barbara, Calif.: ABC-Clio, 2004.

Tomkovicz, James J. *The Right to the Assistance of Counsel: A Reference Guide to the United States Constitution*. Westport, Conn.: Greenwood Press, 2002.

Wishman, Seymour. *Confessions of a Criminal Lawyer*. New York: Penguin, 1982. First-person account of the work of a criminal defense attorney.

See also *Argersinger v. Hamlin*; Arraignment; Arrest; Attorney ethics; Bill of Rights, U.S.; Constitution, U.S.; Death-row attorneys; Defendant self-representation; Defense attorneys; *Gideon v. Wainwright*; *Massiah v. United States*; *Minnick v. Mississippi*; *Miranda v. Arizona*; *Powell v. Alabama*; Public defenders.

Counterfeiting

Definition: Illegal copying of currency for the purpose of committing fraud or creating political and economic instability

Criminal justice issues: Business and financial crime; federal law; fraud; technology

Significance: The counterfeiting of currency has been a problem in the United States since the founding of the nation in the late eighteenth century, but modern technology has made it so much easier for criminals and foreign enemies to duplicate currency that the U.S. government has been forced to redesign its currency and find new methods of countering the problem.

The counterfeiting of a national currency is a process used by governments and individuals for different goals. Governments sometimes attempt to undermine the financial and political stability of other countries by debauching their currency and weakening their political and financial stability. On the other hand, individual counterfeiters usually engage in the crime to take advantage of existing instability to make profits. For these reasons, incidents of counterfeiting tend to rise during periods of economic or political instability.

History

During the American Revolution, the Continental Congress attempted to create a single currency for the new republic. The British government responded by printing large amounts of counterfeit continental dollars and dumping them into the American market. This made the American government's valid currency worthless and had a devastating impact on the colonial economy during and after the war. Counterfeiting continued even after the Revolution ended as states struggled to fix their own economies and were unable to protect their individual currencies from local counterfeiters.

During the first seventy years of its history, the United States suffered through chaotic and tumultuous financial conditions. The new federal government was given the exclusive power to issue a currency and punish counterfeiters, but no single currency was recognized throughout the country until the Civil War. Meanwhile, individual states issued bills of credit that could be used to pay off debts. These documents were easily copied by counterfeiters, and the counterfeit versions were used to defraud both individuals and the government in purchases of land and other commodities.

Enforcement of counterfeiting laws was left to the states and localities as the federal government itself had no law-enforcement agency to investigate or prosecute counterfeiters. Catching counterfeiters was made more difficult by the ease with which the paper money could be copied and the variety of bills of credit offered by states and their banks.

The counterfeiting of currency became a national problem during the Civil War, when more thousands of different legal currencies were in circulation. The high cost of the war ended the country's dependence on coins and the gold standard for currency and forced both the Union and Confederate governments to issue paper money to pay their bills. As paper became the main currency, criminals seeking to make quick profits began to print counterfeit federal currency and distribute it in order to undermine the war effort.

Federal Counterfeiting Laws

In response to the growing problem of counterfeiting, the federal government created the Secret Service on July 5, 1865. The agency was given the task of tracking down and prosecuting counterfeiters. At the same time, one of the first federal laws punishing counterfeiters was passed as Title 18 of the United States Code. Title 18 remains in force in the twenty-first century and is used by the Secret Service as counterfeiting has again become a more frequent practice.

One of the earliest cases prosecuted by the new Secret Service involved an instance of insider involvement in a counterfeiting scheme. The Bureau of Engraving and Printing is part of the Treasury Department, the same department that originally oversaw the Secret Service. A clerk in that bureau stole the metal plates used by the bureau to print currency. He then gave the plates to two professional counterfeiters, Tom Hale and Charlie Adams, who printed large quantities of unauthorized currency and distributed it into the economy.

Hale and Adams were eventually caught in the first instance of the Secret Service's protection of U.S. currency. The service spent much of the rest of the nineteenth century tracking more amateurish counterfeiters, who did not have access to government plates. However, it was not until creation of the Federal Reserve Bank in 1913 that the mass production of U.S. currency made counterfeiting a truly lucrative crime and one that could be used by other countries to undermine the U.S. economy and political system.

During World War II, counterfeit currency was used by both the Allied and Axis Powers as a tool for weakening the economies and war-fighting abilities of their enemies. The U.S. government itself printed and distributed counterfeit German currency, while the German government sought to flood the American economy with millions of fake U.S. bills. Neither effort succeeded, however. Germany's fake American dollars were destroyed at the end of the war before they could be distributed in the United States.

While counterfeiting is usually undertaken for profit, there have also been instances in which counterfeiting laws have been used to prosecute people who publish photographs of currency to promote stories or products. For example, a 1981 issue of *Sports Illustrated* magazine used a cover picture showing currency to dramatize the rise of money in professional sports. The Treasury Department responded by charging the magazine's publisher, Time Inc., with violating Title 18, which prohibited the copying of currency. However, in its *Regan v. Time Inc.* (1984) ruling, the U.S. Supreme Court struck down that portion of Title 18 as a violation of free speech. Nine years later, Title 18 was revived in a ruling prohibiting the copying of currency under certain specific conditions.

New Counterfeiters

Through the nineteenth and most of the twentieth centuries, professional counterfeiters were generally experts at printing and engraving. Some counterfeiters created metal printing plates that were nearly identical to the plates used by the government to print currency. High levels of expertise in engraving and printing were usually required for successful large-scale counterfeiting operations. However, as advanced computer technology and digital printing reached consumer markets during the late twentieth century, the levels of knowledge required to counterfeit currency declined. By the twenty-first century, any person with a computer and a good color printer could make counterfeit U.S. currency that many people—especially in other countries—would accept.

During the 1990's, the Secret Service handled counterfeiting charges against high school and college students who used public copy machines to print and distribute fake U.S. currency. Meanwhile, as small-scale counterfeiting became more prevalent at the individual level, it grew to nearly epidemic proportions at the international level,

as foreign states and organized groups began counterfeiting American currency to fund their political schemes. The federal government responded by redesigning currency notes to make them more difficult to duplicate.

At the end of the twentieth century, the Secret Service reported that the twenty-dollar bill was the most counterfeited piece of U.S. currency, followed by the one-dollar bill. Larger denominations were less frequently counterfeited because changes in their designs were making it more difficult to duplicate them. By contrast, the twenty- and one-dollar bills had yet to be redesigned. However, as the lower denominations were redesigned, it was expected that counterfeiting of those bills would also decline.

International Dimensions

As U.S. currency has been adopted as the currency of some other nations, it has increasingly become the target of foreign counterfeiters, particularly in Central and South America. At the turn of the twenty-first century, the largest producers of counterfeit American currency were in Colombia. With narcotic drug production and distribution a central part of the Colombian economy, the drug cartels and Marxist rebels in the country have attempted to use counterfeit American currency to advance their own ends. South America is also a convenient part of the world for counterfeiting of U.S. currency, as several South American nations, such as Bolivia, use American dollars as their own currency. Another South American state, Chile, was the second-largest producer of counterfeit American currency at the turn of the century. Bulgaria, in Central Europe, is another major source of counterfeit currency, with Great Britain just behind it.

Although billions of dollars in counterfeit U.S. currency is produced abroad, only a small portion of it enters the U.S. economy. It has been estimated that $600 billion in counterfeit money circulates around the world; however, the Secret Service has been able to find less than $49 million of the bills in circulation. In 2001, the largest amount passed was in Hong Kong; the second-largest amount circulated in Mexico. Most of the counterfeit dollars that were discovered were found inside the United States. In 2001, the Secret Service charged some five thousand people with counterfeiting and closed more than six hundred counterfeiting "plants," in which the phoney bills were produced.

Counterfeiting is expected to remain a problem so long as paper currency is a medium of exchange in modern economies. Making counterfeiting more expensive and time consuming to undertake reduces the profits to be made in counterfeiting. However, as counterfeiting technology continues to advance, governments must also develop new methods of combating the crime.

Investigation

One of the first American attempts at stifling counterfeiting was made by the North American colonies' most famous printer, Benjamin Franklin. A prolific inventor, Franklin was assigned the task of printing notes by the colonial government and created a system of raised leaves on the documents that made copying them nearly impossible. However, the expenses associated with such printing also made it nearly impossible for the governments to afford printing the notes on a large scale. During the American Revolution, the continental government was unable to prevent the mass counterfeiting of its currency by criminals in the colonies and by the British government. Counterfeiting again became a major problem during the Civil War. To combat the fake currency being distributed, the federal government created the Secret Service to investigate and prosecute counterfeiters.

The Secret Service is required to find counterfeiters, but another government agency, the Bureau of Engraving and Printing, is responsible for creating currencies that are difficult to counterfeit. Created in the 1870's, the bureau long used highly skilled engravers to design bills with ornate decorations, making them difficult to copy. Through much of the nineteenth and twentieth centuries, American currency was dif-

ficult to counterfeit because there were few craftsmen who could duplicate the finely designed details in government currency. Moreover, the special currency paper used by the federal government also made it all but impossible for undetectable counterfeit bills to be created. Finally, the printing technology available to counterfeiters was so primitive that only a small number of people could mass-produce counterfeit bills of any quality.

The development of computer technology, digital printing, and color copying made counterfeiting much easier for ordinary people. The ornate decorations and engraving quality on bills could be easily reproduced on photocopiers and by computers. By the 1990's, both individuals and countries were engaged in counterfeiting for profit. The Treasury Department and Bureau of Engraving and Printing responded by issuing redesigned currency notes developed specifically to prevent counterfeiting.

A Secret Service officer points out the nuances of counterfeit currency. *(AP/Wide World Photos)*

In 1996, new one-hundred-dollar bills were issued; lower denominations followed. The faces on the fronts of the bills were enlarged and given finer details that could not be copied by machines. Watermarks were added, providing another feature that machines could not copy. These changes impeded counterfeiting by amateurs and foreign governments and organized crime groups.

While the new bills were created to make counterfeiting more difficult, detecting counterfeit bills fell mainly on the efforts of the private sector. When counterfeit bills are passed to merchants, it is their responsibility to make quick determinations of the bills' authenticity. Modern bills have several special features that allow quick and easy determination of their genuineness. People can hold them up to a light source or use special pens to mark them to see if color changes occur. In addition, many commercial establishments now utilize computer systems to read the bills by looking for such features as strips of printing down the sides of the bills.

When fake bills are suspected, local police should be contacted. Although the Secret Service is given the task of investigating and prosecuting counterfeiters, most counterfeiting cases begin at the local level. Local police usually conduct the preliminary investigations of counterfeit bills then pass their findings along to the Secret Service, which collects the evidence and makes arrests.

Punishment

The basic punishments for counterfeiting are outlined in Title 18 of the United States Code. Under this section of the law, counterfeiters can be imprisoned for up to fifteen years and fined up to fifteen thousand dollars for creating or knowingly distributing counterfeit currency.

While local law enforcement is willing to work with the Secret Service within the United States and federal law can be used to punish domestic counterfeiters, a considerable amount of counterfeiting occurs outside U.S. borders, where the Secret Service lacks authority to enforce American laws. Halting overseas counterfeiting requires cooperation from the countries in which fake bills are being created and distributed. The main foreign sources of counterfeit American currency have been Colombia, Mexico, Great Britain, and China. Most of these countries have been willing to work with the U.S. Secret Service, allowing the agency to establish offices in their territory and to help train local police to detect counterfeit bills. Some countries, such as China, that have closed political and economic systems have been less cooperative. However, as all the world's nations become more closely tied to the world economy, it is becoming more difficult for any nation to allow fake American currency to be used within its own economy.

While counterfeiting remains a problem both domestically and in foreign countries, the creation of new types of currency which is harder to counterfeit and greater international cooperation has made counterfeiting easier to detect and counterfeiters easier to catch.

Douglas Clouatre

Further Reading

Green, Edward J., and Warren Weber. "Will the New $100 Bill Decrease Counterfeiting?" *Federal Reserve Bank of Minneapolis Quarterly Review* (1996): 3-10. Early analysis of the first completely redesigned unit of currency to be placed in circulation.

Johnson, David. *Illegal Tender*. Washington, D.C.: Smithsonian Institution Press, 1995. Fascinating history of the early years of counterfeiting and the rise of the U.S. Secret Service.

Motto, Carmine J. *In Crime's Way: A Generation of Secret Service Adventures*. Boca Baton, Fla.: CRC Press, 1999. Firsthand stories by a retired Secret Service agent who specialized in counterfeiting investigations.

The Use and Counterfeiting of U.S. Currency Abroad. Washington, D.C.: U.S. Department of the Treasury, 2003. One of a series of annual Treasury Department reports to Congress on the department's ongoing fight against counterfeiting.

See also Annotated codes; Federal Crimes Act; Forgery; Money laundering; Secret Service, U.S.; Treasury Department, U.S.; United States Code; United States Statutes at Large.

Court reporters

Definition: Courtroom employees who are responsible for recording all testimony and utterances that take place during legal proceedings

Criminal justice issue: Courts

Significance: Court reporters are an integral component of the court system as their main function is preservation of spoken testimony.

The inception of this career began more than two thousand years ago, when a scribe recorded speeches during the Roman Senate. In 2004 there were approximately fifty thousand court reporters across the United States. It is expected that this number will continue to soar throughout the next several decades. Court reporters play a fundamental role in the criminal justice system by ensuring the preservation of the spoken word as a legible written transcript. Their main function is to record testimony, speeches, judges' rulings, judges' instructions to juries, attorneys' objections, and comments by attorneys, verbatim, during all court proceedings.

Court reporters assist judges and attorneys in the retrieval of information for official records, including reading back all or any portion of the court record, as requested. Court reporters edit the translation to correct grammar, identify proper names and places, and prepare written transcripts to file with the clerk of the court. In addition, court reporters are also expected to have knowledge of real-time technology, to enable them to provide closed-caption services and translating for the deaf where required.

The most common method by which court reporting is administered is stenotyping. This employs the use of computer-aided transcriptions (CAT) to translate combinations of letters that represent words and phrases into complete and legible transcripts. Because maintaining a high degree of accuracy is essential, coordination, concentration, and strong grammatical skills are required.

Lisa Landis Murphy

Further Reading

Knapp, M. H., and R. W. McCormick. *The Complete Court Reporters Handbook*. 3d ed. Englewood Cliffs, N.J.: Prentice-Hall, 1998.

Schmalleger, Frank. *Criminal Justice Today: An Introductory Text for the Twenty-first Century*. 8th ed. Upper Saddle River, N.J.: Pearson/Prentice-Hall, 2005.

See also Court types; Criminal justice system; Testimony; Trial transcripts; Trials.

Court types

Definition: Courts of narrow and broad functions

Criminal justice issues: Appeals; courts; jurisdictions; military justice

Significance: The judicial system in the United States is complex. Each state has courts of specialized, limited, and general jurisdiction. A separate hierarchy of federal courts parallels the fifty state judiciaries. In many states efforts have been made to reduce the number of court types.

In contrast to Japan and many European countries, the United States has a highly complex network of courts. In nations with unitary political systems, such as France, there is a single judicial hierarchy. Because of federalism, however, there are two sets of trial and appellate courts in the United States, one state and the other federal. At the state level many courts of original jurisdiction can hear only a single type of case, such as that dealing with wills (probate courts) or claims for small amounts of money. Courts differ also in whether jury trials are possible, in what types of procedures are used and in what types of remedy judges can provide complaining parties. Selecting the correct court in which to file a complaint is so complicated that most law schools offer students a course called "Conflict of Laws" to help them make the right choice.

Types of Jurisdiction

There are a number of fundamental characteristics that distinguish one court from another.

Jurisdiction is the power, or authority, of a particular court to hear a case. Courts of original jurisdiction, or trial courts, hear cases for the first time. Courts of appeal review the decisions of trial judges to determine if they made any reversible errors. Courts of common law can provide monetary compensation to injured plaintiffs in civil suits. Equity courts, or chancery courts, issue injunctions, which are orders to act or to refrain from acting in a particular way, such as polluting a river. The right to trial by jury can be exercised in common law and criminal courts but not in equity courts. Courts of specialized jurisdiction can hear only one type of case. Courts of limited jurisdiction hear several kinds of cases but not all.

The most important state trial courts are the civil and criminal courts of general jurisdiction, which can hear and determine any case. State courts hear cases involving state law, while federal courts determine legal disputes arising under the U.S. Constitution or federal laws. There are circumstances, however, in which a state court can hear a case that requires the interpretation of federal law and in which a federal court can determine controversies arising under state legislation. In the former type of case, the losing party may appeal to the U.S. Supreme Court after the state supreme court has rendered its decision. Criminal courts try cases in which the government seeks punishment of a defendant for violating the law. Civil courts resolve disputes between private parties in which a complainant alleges harm as a result of a defendant's failure to fulfill a legal duty. A court of record is a trial court whose determinations of fact are final.

Criminal Courts

States have established a variety of judicial tribunals to handle criminal cases. Municipal courts are trial courts of limited jurisdiction with the authority to determine misdemeanor cases. Other names for criminal courts of limited jurisdiction are justice or general sessions courts. Night court, or police court, is available in many large urban areas to process cases in which defendants are charged with petty offenses, such as public drunkenness. Police forces in populous cities issue citations ordering drivers caught breaking the law to appear in traffic court. In rural areas, justices of the peace often hear cases involving minor criminal charges. Municipal courts preside over preliminary hearings to determine if evidence is sufficient to hold over felony defendants for trial in superior court. Felonies are prosecuted in criminal courts of general jurisdiction, often called superior or county courts. It is in these courts that most jury trials occur. Other names for such bodies are circuit, district, or criminal courts.

Civil Courts

Trial courts of limited and general criminal jurisdiction in most states have the power to determine civil controversies. Municipal courts may hear legal disputes in which the amount of compensation requested is relatively low, usually under $30,000. County and superior courts hear civil cases in which the monetary amount in dispute exceeds that. Most states have established a court of specialized jurisdiction, or small claims court, to make the civil courts more accessible to ordinary citizens. In these courts parties typically are not represented by lawyers, the filing fees are low, and the waiting period before trial is relatively short. The jurisdiction of small claims courts is typically confined to cases not exceeding $5,000.

Probate courts exercise jurisdiction over wills, estates, and guardianship questions. Probate judges determine how the assets of deceased persons are to be allocated and who is legally responsible for frail elderly or mentally incompetent persons. Family law courts, or domestic relations courts, process divorce cases and resolve often contentious issues of child custody, visitation, child support, alimony, and the division of property. Family law court judges have broad equitable powers. Youths charged with delinquency or youths in need of protection appear in family law or juvenile courts. Juvenile courts are civil courts; they do not mete out punishment, but rather provide treatment. In mediation court, or conciliation court, judges help parties negotiate mutually acceptable compromises rather than impose solutions to conflicts. In states with unified judicial systems, such as California, the trial court of general jurisdiction, the superior court, may sit as a probate court, juvenile court, family law court, and conciliation court.

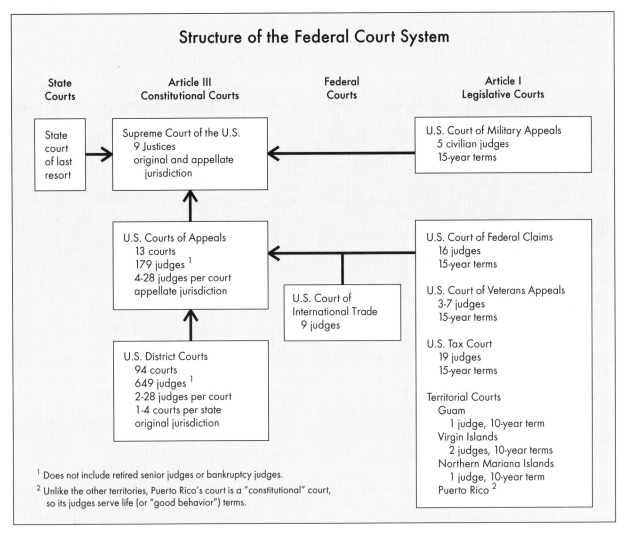

Structure of the Federal Court System

State Courts	Article III Constitutional Courts	Federal Courts	Article I Legislative Courts

State court of last resort

Supreme Court of the U.S.
9 Justices
original and appellate
jurisdiction

U.S. Court of Military Appeals
5 civilian judges
15-year terms

U.S. Courts of Appeals
13 courts
179 judges [1]
4-28 judges per court
appellate jurisdiction

U.S. Court of International Trade
9 judges

U.S. Court of Federal Claims
16 judges
15-year terms

U.S. Court of Veterans Appeals
3-7 judges
15-year terms

U.S. Tax Court
19 judges
15-year terms

U.S. District Courts
94 courts
649 judges [1]
2-28 judges per court
1-4 courts per state
original jurisdiction

Territorial Courts
Guam
1 judge, 10-year term
Virgin Islands
2 judges, 10-year terms
Northern Mariana Islands
1 judge, 10-year term
Puerto Rico [2]

[1] Does not include retired senior judges or bankruptcy judges.

[2] Unlike the other territories, Puerto Rico's court is a "constitutional" court, so its judges serve life (or "good behavior") terms.

Appellate Courts

While trial courts consist of a single judge, appellate courts are collegial bodies with three or more judges. They review trial courts' decisions at the request of losing parties. A reversible error is one that is so egregious that a trial judge's decision must be overturned. In general, appellate courts can reverse only a trial judge's interpretation of the law and not the trial court's determinations of fact. This rule exists to prevent appellate judges from undermining the jury system. In the United States, each loser in a trial has the right to one appeal. A consequence of this tradition is that some appellate courts have no control over their dockets. They must hear and decide every appeal that is filed.

The final court of appeal is the state supreme court (known in New York as the Court of Appeals). If a case involves matters of state law only, the decision of a state supreme court cannot be further appealed. In many states, the state supreme court is the only appellate court. In twenty-five states, however, there are intermediate courts of appeal. In these states the state supreme court enjoys discretion over the cases it wishes to review. Some states have separate intermediate courts of appeal for criminal and civil cases.

Several states, including New Jersey, Virginia, and California, have taken steps to simplify their judicial hierarchy. Their goal is to establish an integrated judicial pyramid embracing only a few kinds of trial courts and a single type of intermediate appellate court.

Federal Courts

Article III of the U.S. Constitution authorizes Congress to establish trial and appellate courts to determine cases arising under federal law, cases involving foreign ambassadors, and suits between citizens of different states. The federal courts of general trial jurisdiction are the ninety-four U.S. district courts. Federal jury trials occur in the district courts. They have both civil and criminal jurisdiction. Federal law requires that judges give preference to criminal over civil cases when scheduling trials.

There are a number of federal trial courts of specialized jurisdiction. Each district court has a bankruptcy unit. Bankruptcy courts determine whether petitioners can be relieved of the obligation to repay debts. Magistrate judges handle misdemeanor trials and many of the procedural disputes that must be resolved before a trial in the district court can begin.

Appeals of district court decisions are made to one of the thirteen U.S. courts of appeals. The judges sit in panels of three. They also hear appeals from the decisions of federal administrative agencies, such as the National Labor Relations Board (NLRB) and the Federal Communications Commission (FCC). The courts of appeal must accept for review all appeals. A specialized federal court is the U.S. Court of International Trade. It reviews the rulings by federal customs inspectors governing tariffs on imported goods.

When a federal question is at issue, appeals of decisions of the U.S. courts of appeals and the state supreme courts may be filed with the U.S. Supreme Court. The U.S. Supreme Court has complete discretion and only grants review to approximately 1 percent of the cases that are filed before it. All nine justices of the U.S. Supreme Court participate in the decision of every case accepted for review.

From time to time the U.S. Congress has established tribunals to assist administrative agencies in the performance of their adjudicative functions. U.S. Tax Court, for example, was set up to hear taxpayers' appeals of decisions of the Internal Revenue Service (IRS). Such so-called Article I courts differ from their Article III coun-

terparts in the judges' tenure. Article I judges serve for a limited number of years while Article III judges are appointed for life. There are four other federal legislative courts: the U.S. Court of Federal Claims, the U.S. Court of Military Appeals, the U.S. Court of Veterans Appeals, and territorial courts.

The Court of Federal Claims adjudicates plaintiffs' claims for compensation from the federal government. The Court of Military Appeals is a body of civilian judges who hear appeals from military courts-martial. The Court of Veterans Appeals reviews decisions of the Board of Veterans Appeals denying benefits to former military personnel. Appeals from the Court of Federal Claims, the Court of International Trade, and the Court of Veterans Appeals must be filed with the U.S. Court of Appeals for the Federal Circuit. The federal territories Guam, the Virgin Islands, and the Northern Mariana Islands have territorial courts, which can hear matters involving both local and federal law. Because Puerto Rico has its own set of local courts, the territorial court in Puerto Rico has the same jurisdiction as a U.S. district court.

Kenneth M. Holland

Further Reading

Abraham, Henry. *The Judicial Process: An Introductory Analysis of the Courts of the United States, England, and France.* 7th ed. New York: Oxford University Press, 1998. Offers a clear description of differences among courts.

Banks, Lenore. *The Judicial Maze: The Court System in New York State.* Albany, N.Y.: League of Women Voters, 1988. Practical advice, from a citizen's viewpoint, on the daunting task of selecting the correct court in the state of New York.

BNA's Directory of State and Federal Courts, Judges, and Clerks. Washington, D.C.: BNA Books, 1997. Detailed listings of the various types of courts are available. Includes state court structure charts, which show the routes of appeal for all courts of record. Also includes listings of Internet sites for federal and state courts.

State Justice Institute. *Improving the Quality of American Justice, 1987-1997.* Alexandria, Va.: State Justice Institute, 1997. Exploration of ways in which the courts might be improved through unification.

Want's Federal-State Court Directory 1998: All Fifty States and Canada. New York: Want Publishing, 1997. Another catalog of courts.

See also Change of venue; Citations; Clerks of the court; Court reporters; Criminal justice in U.S. history; Criminal justice system; Judicial system, U.S.; Jurisdiction of courts; Juvenile delinquency; Night courts; Supreme Court, U.S.; Trials.

Courts-martial

Definition: Military equivalents of civilian criminal trials

Criminal justice issues: Courts; military justice

Significance: Courts-martial judge major infractions of military law by members of the armed forces.

To preserve discipline and ensure order, military commanders have three ways to punish violations of the rules, regulations, and laws governing the Army, Navy, Air Force, Marine Corps, Coast Guard, and National Guard: administrative action, nonjudicial punishment, and courts-martial. In administrative action the commander punishes by withdrawing common privileges with the offender's acquiescence. In nonjudicial punishment a small-unit commander tries minor infractions and assesses limited penalties. Courts-martial can consider any accusation of misconduct as defined in the Uniform Code of Military Justice (UCMJ) of 1950, published and elaborated on in the *Manual for Courts-Martial* (1995). The sentences of some courts-martial include long-term imprisonment and the death penalty. Punishments under administrative action or nonjudicial punishment are internal military affairs; conviction by court-martial becomes part of a person's permanent criminal record.

All officers, enlisted personnel, and reservists on active duty are subject to the UCMJ, and each branch of the armed forces has jurisdiction over members of all the other branches. The Supreme Court has ruled that military courts cannot try civilians (*Ex parte Milligan*, 1866) or civilian employees of the services, even when functioning under martial law (*Duncan v. Kahanamoku*, 1946). Courts-martial have exclusive jurisdiction over all purely military offenses, such as disobedience of orders or desertion. An action violating both military and civilian law can be tried either by court-martial or by a civilian court, although local civilian authorities usually have precedence over military courts.

Generally similar to civilian criminal courts, courts-martial nevertheless differ in their pretrial procedures, their questioning of witnesses, their method of reaching verdicts, and the variety of punishments they may impose. Three types of courts-martial exist: general, special, and summary. They differ in the crimes they judge and in the severity of punishment they may impose. All three are ad hoc courts convened by a commanding officer to judge a specific case or a small number of related cases. In general and special courts-martial, the "accused" (not "defendant," as in civilian courts) has the right to counsel; in summary courts-martial, counsel may be excluded if military circumstances require it.

Pretrial Procedure

The responsible officer, such as a company commander in an infantry regiment, acts as the accuser of subordinates suspected of having violated a provision of the UCMJ, who must be warned that any statements they make can be used against them during judicial action. The responsible officer can prefer charges and recommend the type of court-martial to the next higher-level commander, such as a battalion commander. This higher-level commander may convene either a summary court-martial or a special court-martial to hear the charges. This procedure, known as an "Article 32 investigation," performs the same function as a grand jury in civilian law. However, the accused has several rights not granted to civilian defendants, including the power to cross-examine witnesses and to submit and examine evidence. The investigating officer reports the findings to an officer who has the authority to convene a general court-martial. That commander may convene the court, refer the charges back to a lower court, or drop the charges. If a general or special court-martial is initiated, the convening authority also appoints the trial counsel, a commissioned officer certified as a competent military lawyer by the service's judge advocate general, and the defense counsel, who must likewise be a certified military lawyer. In some cases the accused may also hire a civilian lawyer.

During the discovery phase of a court-martial proceeding attorneys take depositions from witnesses, gather documentary evidence, and arrange for the appearance of witnesses. The equivalent of the prosecuting attorney in a civilian court, the trial counsel must provide the defense with copies of documents and papers relating to the charge, reports of physical or psychological examinations performed on the accused, and a list of witnesses to be called. The defense must also disclose the names of its witnesses to the trial counsel. The accused may agree at this time to a plea bargain, as in civilian courts. A military judge may grant the accused or witnesses transactional immunity, which protects them from trial for one or more offenses under the UCMJ, or testimonial immunity, which excludes later trial action based on statements made in depositions or in court.

Conduct of Courts-martial

The president of the United States, service secretaries, or high-ranking commanders, usually generals or admirals, convene general courts-martial. Those who convene courts-martial select members of their command to act as members of the court. The court consists of five to seven officers; one must be a qualified military judge, who is the presiding officer, and the rest fulfill much the same function as a civilian jury. Enlisted accused may request that one-third of the court be enlisted personnel. Except in capital cases, the accused can choose to be tried before a military judge alone.

The presiding officer instructs the members of the court on points of law, controls the proceedings, rules on questions of law and procedure, issues judgments on questions of fact, rules against trial participants who are in contempt of court, and may summon witnesses in addition to those called by the court and defense counsel. The court takes testimony, assesses the evidence, and may directly question witnesses, unlike the jury of a civilian court. The panel then retires to discuss the verdict, which must be based strictly on the evidence presented in court. Finally, after instruction from the presiding officer on the consequences of different verdicts, the panel votes.

A Few Good Men

Director Rob Reiner's 1992 film *A Few Good Men* explores several aspects of courts martial. The fictional story centers on the legal case of two Marines who are charged with undertaking a disciplinary action known as a "code red" that inadvertently led to another Marine's death. The defendants claim that their base commander (Jack Nicholson) ordered the code red. A brash young military lawyer (Tom Cruise), who is skilled at settling cases but not at trying them, is assigned as lead defense counsel in the case. His cocounsel (Demi Moore) shames him into looking beneath the surface of the case and believing his clients' story. The lawyer eventually calls the formidable base commander to testify as a witness and taunts him into revealing that he did indeed order the code red.

Tom Cruise. *(Castle Rock Entertainment)*

The film portrays the defense lawyer as putting his career on the line and risking a court-martial for himself by accusing a superior officer of wrongdoing without having an adequate basis for making such an accusation. In real life, military lawyers cannot be court-martialed for such conduct. However, challenging an influential superior officer might well subject a lawyer to a variety of less formal and equally career-ruining consequences.

Timothy L. Hall

A two-thirds majority is required for conviction, which means that there is never a deadlocked jury, as in civilian courts. Court is reconvened and the verdict announced. If the accused is acquitted, the proceedings end and the accused is released.

If the accused is convicted, the sentencing phase begins. The court again hears arguments from the trial counsel and defense counsel in favor of a specific punishment and reviews pertinent evidence, such as records of previous convictions. The panel deliberates once more and votes by secret written ballot on the sentence. General courts-martial may impose any punishment authorized under the UCMJ. While a simple majority vote is sufficient for most sentences, such as dismissal from the service and dishonorable discharge, three-fourths of the panel must approve a sentence of imprisonment for ten years or more and a unanimous vote is required to impose the death penalty.

Special courts-martial convene under the authority of commanders of small units, such as regiments, or small installations, and consist of three members, unless the accused chooses to be tried by a military judge alone. Enlisted accused may also demand that one member of the panel be enlisted. A special court-martial verdict may include a bad conduct discharge if the court includes a military judge. Otherwise, the court may convict the accused to as many as six months of confinement, forfeiture of two-thirds pay for six months, hard labor for three months, or reduction in rank.

Unlike general and special courts-martial, which can try officers, summary courts-martial have power over only enlisted personnel. An Army or Marine officer of the rank at least of captain (equivalent to a lieutenant in the Navy and Coast Guard) is the convening authority and appoints the single member of the court. When no other commissioned officer is available, convening authorities in courts-martial may appoint themselves. The purpose of the court is to hear charges of minor offenses promptly. For accused noncommissioned officers, the presiding officer may impose sentences not to exceed forfeiture of two-thirds of one month's pay, restriction for two months, or reduction of one rank. Accused who are in the fourth enlisted pay grade or below may receive one month's confinement or hard labor for forty-five days as well.

After adjourning a court-martial, the trial counsel must notify the accused's commander or the convening authority of the verdict and sentence, and this officer executes the court's decision by ordering confinement, the withholding of pay, or imposing other punishments. The military judge or convening authority may call for post-trial sessions to correct errors or rectify improper procedures by reopening the proceedings. A complete record of a court-martial's proceedings is assembled and forwarded to an appropriate reviewing authority.

Reviews and Appeals

The provisions for review and appeal of decisions by courts-martial are as varied as those for civilian courts, but they invest considerable review authority in individuals as well as in appellate panels. Lawyers in the office of the staff advocate general, a unit under the authority of the local commanding general or admiral, review the conduct and decisions of courts-martial to ensure that proper procedures were followed. The convening authority also reviews the verdict of a court-martial and may vacate or reduce a sentence.

The accused has two years in which to appeal a conviction to the service's judge advocate general. After examining court-martial records, the judge advocate general may modify or set aside the findings or refer the case to the court of criminal appeals for the appropriate branch of the service. This court may modify a sentence but may not vacate it or alter the changes made by the convening authority. The judge advocate general may then refer the case to the Court of Appeals for the Armed Forces, whose three judges are appointed for fifteen-year terms by the president of the United States and confirmed by the U.S. Senate. The accused may also petition this appeals court. Furthermore, the Court of Appeals for the Armed Forces must review all verdicts that affect general or flag officers and death sentences, which, if approved, may be carried out only upon orders from the president.

Federal courts may review courts-martial when their jurisdiction is questioned or when the accused petition for writs of *habeas corpus* (applications to a court to consider whether a person in custody is being held lawfully). The U.S. Supreme Court may review decisions of the Court of Appeals for the Armed Forces and return cases to the lower court for further hearings or direct the president or service secretary to act upon its directives.

Roger Smith

Further Reading

Bishop, Joseph W., Jr. *Justice Under Fire*. New York: Charterhouse, 1974. Argues that military law affords as many guarantees of due process, and sometimes more, than civil law.

Finn, James, ed. *Conscience and Command: Justice and Discipline in the Military*. New York: Random House, 1971. Contains essays critical of military justice, claiming it is outmoded and detrimental to discipline.

Frost, Lawrence A. *The Court Martial of General George Armstrong Custer*. Norman: University of Oklahoma Press, 1968. Entertaining account of one of the most celebrated military trials in U.S. history. ·

Joint Service Committee on Military Justice. *Manual of Courts-Martial*. Washington, D.C.: Government Printing Office, 1995. Practical handbook on how courts-martial should be conducted, with details on questions relating to jurisdiction and sentencing.

Military Justice Trial Procedure. Washington, D.C.: Headquarters, Department of the Army, 1973. How-to manual for lawyers participating in courts-martial.

Schug, Willis E., ed. *United States Law and the Armed Forces: Cases and Materials on Constitutional Law, Courts-Martial, and the Rights of Servicemen*. New York: Praeger, 1972. Outlines of court procedures and celebrated cases that illustrate them.

Sherrill, Robert. *Military Justice Is to Justice as Military Music Is to Music*. New York: Harper & Row, 1969. Bitter indictment of the influence of local commanders on courts-martial proceedings; inspired by cases from the Vietnam War.

Ulmer, S. Sidney. *Military Justice and the Right to Counsel*. Lexington: University Press of Kentucky, 1970. Concise and lucidly written inquiry into individual rights under military law.

West, Luther. *They Call It Justice*. New York: Viking Press, 1977. Critical examination of the military justice system by a veteran military lawyer, who pays particular attention to cases arising during the Vietnam War.

See also International tribunals; Martial law; Military justice.

Crime

Definition: In narrow legal terms, violations of criminal laws that ban or command acts whose commission or omission are subject to penalties.

Criminal justice issues: Criminology; legal terms and principles; robbery, theft, and burglary

Significance: Crimes are seen as offenses against the state rather than against the individual, the latter being civil violations subject to restitution, rather than punishment. Historically scholars have challenged the strict legal definition and developed several different views about the criteria that should be used to define crime. These criteria emphasize moral, cultural, social, political and integrational dimensions of intended or avoidable harm.

Crime is the category of behavior to which criminal justice is a response. It has several defining features that make it "unwanted" behavior, including the extent of harm to its victims, the intent and culpability of the offenders, degree of public consensus over its moral significance, the severity of society's response, and the visibility of its effects.

Although different crimes share some common features—such as the use of instruments of power to gain advantages over others—crime is not a single kind of behavior but a category that comprises multiple types of behavior, each with its own range of causes. Criminologists study crime, its causes, and society's criminal justice responses. What is defined as crime determines how big a problem society confronts, which areas of society are affected, what resources are put into policing to control the crime, and what systems of justice should be deployed to deal with it.

What behaviors are considered criminal has varied through history and among different cultures and in different situations. This is because behaviors that are defined as crimes essentially reflect values, or express what the legal scholar Jerome Hall termed "disvalues." Anthropologists and sociologists have observed that values, and therefore behaviors that are sufficiently unwanted to be designated "crimes" by societies, change over time, depending upon the cultures, and are subject to the interpretation of meaning of local contexts and social situations.

The seriousness of offensive behavior depends upon the interpretation of the meanings of acts, and these are affected by society's concept of who the acts allow to be victims. Moreover, since crime is defined by laws, and laws are made by legislators and politicians with particular interests, what comes to be defined as criminal need not reflect a universal set of harmful behaviors, but those that lawmakers consider significant. Socio-political factors as well as economic and political interests affect what legislators judge to be sufficiently offensive to be criminalized.

Some behaviors that are considered harmful to American society and its members fall within American definitions of crime. These behaviors include such acts as murder (homicide), rape, robbery, theft, physical violence, and arson. At the same time, other behavior that can be equally or even more harmful, are excluded from the definition. Examples include industrial pollution, creating dangerous working conditions for employees, faulty product manufacture, and violations of food and safety standards. Such acts are typically designated as "white-collar" crimes and are usually subject to administrative regulation, rather than criminal law, and are thus often technically not considered "crimes." Since the 1980's, the United States has seen an accelerating movement to criminalize many white-collar and corporate harms and to subject their perpetrators to criminal sanctions.

Views of Crime

In their 1933 book *Crime, Law and Social Science*, social philosophers Jerome Michael and Mortimer Adler clarified the legal view of crime in the United States. They stated that criminal law itself gave behavior its quality of criminality. By this they meant that any behavior that has not been designated—by case or statutory law—as a felony or a misdemeanor offense is not a crime.

The law crudely distinguishes crimes by their seriousness, and this is indicated by the severity of the punishment associated with individual offenses. A crime is called a felony if it is punishable by a prison sentence, usually of more than a year, or by the death penalty; it is a misdemeanor if punishable by a fine or a prison sentence of less than a year (typically served in a jail). Felonies and misdemeanors are typically categorized as crimes against persons such as murder, rape, and assault; crimes against property, such as theft, burglary, arson, and fraud; and crimes against morality and public order, such as substance abuse and rioting. The law also distinguishes between two kinds of acts: those seen as bad in and of themselves (*mala in se*) and those legislated as crimes (*mala prohibita*).

Criminals are, by definition, persons who commit crimes. They may include collectivities, such as criminal corporations, as well as criminal individuals. Sociologist Paul Tappan argued in 1949 that to be a criminal one had to be convicted by a court of law. To be found guilty of a crime a person or collectivity has to have both criminal intent (*mens rea*, or a guilty mind) and have acted voluntarily (*actus reus*) meaning that a perpetrator must act willingly rather than being coerced. In the case of a corporation or organization, the "criminality" that produces criminal harm is seen to be in the collective mind, such as that of a board of directors, or an agency policy. Since the mid-twentieth century the strict legalistic view has been increasingly challenged.

There are several deficiencies with the narrow legal view. First, what is included is historically and culturally relative, meaning that at different periods in history and in different cultures and places, the behaviors that are defined as criminal change, not least because values change or are different. For example, it was once not considered criminal to use cocaine, for a man to rape his wife, or for symbols of racial hate to be directed at members of minorities. In the twentieth century, smoking in public places and in government buildings is being increasingly banned and defined as a crime.

In 1939, sociologist Edwin Sutherland pointed out that the criminal law is biased; it includes some harms but excludes others, particularly those produced by corporations, which are handled as violations of administrative regulations rather than as violations of criminal laws. Increasingly in the second half of the twentieth century this regulatory approach changed as "white-collar crime" was seen as a significant omission from criminal law. However, critics have pointed out that "socially injurious acts" by the powerful—whether corporations, organizations, or state agencies—still manage to largely escape being classified in law as crimes.

This relates to a third problem with the narrow legal view that highlights its selectivity because of the influence of power on the legislative process as a result of judges' affinity for business ideology and because of legislators' ties to business, and being subject to industry lobbyists and political action committees financed by interested parties.

Moral Consensus and Cultural Conflict Views

A fundamental assumption embodied in the legalistic view is that criminal laws reflect a moral sentiment of the public. What is defined as a crime is behavior that arouses moral indignation, or as nineteenth century French sociologist Émile Durkheim stated, behavior that "shocks the common conscience." The difficulty with this view is that such indignation is filtered through interested legislators and moral entrepreneurs rather than being tied specifically to the state of public opinion. For this reason, the early conflict sociologist Thorsten Sellin argued in 1938 that value-neutral social scientists, rather than politicians, should map which behaviors the public is concerned about enough to ban by identifying naturally occurring "conduct norms" and use these as the basis to construct laws. Indeed, there have been some studies that index public views about crime, which have revealed that previously ignored harms by corporations and professionals such as doctors are rated as more serious than many more conventional crimes of violence, yet the latter are typically "reacted to" more severely.

The argument that crime is a variable rather than a fixed body of behaviors reflecting social values that are subject to change led some to the view that cultures and even subcultures within a society should be allowed to develop their own laws, depending upon their norms of conduct, rather than having these imposed by the dominant group of a mainstream culture. Indeed, in this view what Sellin called "culture conflict" comes into play, wherein different subcultural groups have conflicting allegiance to their own cultural norms and societal laws, which may clash. This tendency can be seen in immigrants to the United States, who may have norms different from those of mainstream Americans.

Immigrants from Mediterranean and Middle Eastern honor cultures believe that private family vengeance should be taken on those who dishonor a family, such as by having sexual relations outside marriage. Acts of private vengeance are illegal by American criminal law. In a clash between laws and norms, which should prevail? Are there generalized social values that transcend the specific interests of mainstream culture and its subcultures and serve a functional value to society as a whole, as implied by Hall's view of crime as an expression of "disvalues"? Alternatively, do the values of a society, and thereby the behavior banned by criminal law, depend upon which interest groups and which major political forces mobilize most effectively to criminalize the behavior of those most threatening to themselves?

The Social Conflict View

Those who see conflicts of interest, whether based on wealth, status, political power, honor, religion, etc., as the driving forces of society, believe that the behavior most criminalized is that which offends those in positions of power. These critics are also concerned with the broader question of values tied to banned behavior. They say that the idea of "appropriate" or "wanted" behavior, versus "unwanted" behavior, as used by some analysts, such as the Law Commission of Canada in its deliberations on *What Is a Crime?* (2004), begs several critical questions. Not least of these is who decides what counts as unwanted. The key issue is how far behavior interpreted as "unwanted" is the result of powerful audiences finding the behavior problematic/unacceptable or harmful to them, rather than to the society as a whole.

As sociologist Howard Becker pointed out in his studies of social deviance, it is important to consider the role of those interest groups (moral entrepreneurs) who can whip up moral support and advocacy, through the media, for turning some "problem behaviors" into "deviance" or "crimes." According to this view, the questions can be reframed: To whom is a particular behavior problematic? On what basis is it problematic, implying a need to distinguish between harmful and morally unacceptable? Who decides that this behavior should be acted upon?

This view is ultimately concerned with the politics of defining behavior as "unacceptable"? Which levels of society are involved and which are excluded? Whose views prevail in "opinion" or popular culture, and whose views are translated into formal law? How do those who prevail draw on the resources of government, agencies, and media to defeat others who may have different views? Clearly there are political struggles between interested groups over what is defined as crime. In part this involves the fight to control the symbolic meaning of laws, but it also involves the issues of whose behavior is criminalized and what behavior counts as punishable and in what ways.

Social Interactionist and Situational Constructionist Views

Social constructionism, the idea that people construct their social worlds through symbolic meanings and shared discourse, sees a significant role played by the media in defining crime. It is not just that the media influence the content of definitions of crime by shaping what actions people take as serious and offensive, but also that the media are used as resources in the struggle over some groups asserting their interests over others. As British criminologist Stanley Cohen first noted, one way of doing this is to create a "moral panic" about some kinds of behavior, although the actual behavior need not have actually occurred, and the demonized offenders need not actually engage in the practices that have been claimed. Of central concern of constructionists and critical theorists is how groups with different

resources gain equal access to the media in asserting their position; how they make truth claims that lead to the banning of behavior and how the production of mass mediated images of "crime" is shaped by those in positions of power?

Rather than taking consensus or conflict as significant factors in defining crime, some social constructionists see the situational context and the interaction between local actors as important. For example, criminologists Leroy Gould, Gary Kleck, and Marc Gertz see crime defined as a social event, involving many players, actors, and agencies. Beyond the offenders and victims, a "crime event" includes bystanders and witnesses, police officers, and members of political society. A crime event is a particular set of interactions among offenders, crime targets, police, community, and society's institutional agencies. This social situational view of crime emphasizes the complexities associated with defining crime by recognizing its socially constructed nature. The local situation involves the claim making and legitimating process by local community agencies, and that necessarily involves issues of power.

Critical Conflict View

Critical theorists also question how the interests of the powerful influence the selection of societal responses, or penalties, such that the most punitive seem to disproportionately affect the powerless (resulting in their predominance in the criminal justice system), yet the most harmful offenses are committed by those who receive the least punitive sanctions (resulting in their relative absence from the criminal justice system. For example, multimillion-dollar corporate fraud receives considerably less punitive sentencing than conventional street crimes of burglary or robbery.

Critics ask how the powerful avoid having their "unwanted" yet harmful behavior criminalized and how they seem to attract the most constructive societal responses, such as rewards for conforming to regulation? There appears to be one law for the rich and another for the poor. The example of the punishment for using "crack cocaine," a drug used mostly by African Americans, is compared to the punishment for using "powder cocaine" used primarily by white substance abus-

ers. Here sentences can be 10 percent of the level
of those convicted of crack use.

If people want to use less punitive criminal law
in responses to "unwanted" behavior, argue these
theorists, equity should prevail between responses to the crimes of the powerful compared
with crimes of the powerless. To deal with these
concerns it would be necessary to criminalize and
punish some crimes of the powerful, while decriminalizing and regulating the behaviors of the
powerless.

Critical criminologists Herman and Julia
Schweindinger and Richard Quinney built on the
early work of Sutherland to suggest that definitions of crime need to be more expansive and include behavior that violates the human rights of
others and the socially injurious acts by the struc-
turally powerful toward the powerless in society.
For example critical theorist Raymond Micha-
lowski used the term "analogous social injury" to
describe a range of currently legal behaviors by
corporations, organizations, and state agencies
that produce social, environmental, and health
problems. Examples are promoting cigarette and
alcohol production and distribution and setting
work production targets that force employees to
cut health and safety protective practices.

Postmodernist and Power-as-Crime Views

Postmodernist-influenced constitutive criminologists such as Dragan Milovanovic, Bruce
Arrigo, and Stuart Henry have developed definitions of crime that take account of the total
context of powerful relations and the situational
context. Postmodernism rejects claims that
knowledge is true or can be true. Instead, like social constructionists, its advocates believe that
"claims to know" are simply power plays used to
dominate others. For example, Henry and Milovanovic define crime as an agency's (individual, corporation, or organization) ability to make a negative difference to others. They define crimes as

> nothing less than moments in the expression of
> power such that those who are subjected to these
> expressions are denied their own contribution to
> the encounter and often to future encounters.
> Crime then is the power to deny others . . . in
> which those subject to the power of another, suf-
> fer the pain of being denied their own humanity,
> the power to make a difference.

From a similar perspective, anarchist criminologists Larry Tifft and Dennis Sullivan argue
that the power in social organizations, institutions and processes operate through hierarchical structure and social arrangements to produce harm that evades the legal definition. They,
like the critical Marxist theorists, argue for a
greatly expanded definition of crime that will
include as crimes the activities of many contemporary legal industries and commerce. Paradoxi-
cally, this approach would also question many
of the criminal justice system's responses to
crime, because these too produce harm, not
merely by definition, but by exerting power over
others.

Integrative View

It is clear that defining crime is far more complex than the simplistic idea that crime is behavior defined by law. In an attempt to take account
of several of these themes Canadian criminologist John Hagan developed a concept of crime as a
continuous variable expressed through his pyramid of crime; each slope represents one dimension of the crime phenomenon. Regardless of who
defines behavior as "unwanted," a related issue is
the degree of "unwantedness," which Hagan argued ranges from apathy through mild to severe.
The question of unwantedness is different from
how much consensus exists about unwantedness
and also different from the degree of severity of
any reaction or societal response. At a minimum,
says Hagan, the issue of unwantedness exists
along three dimensions: first, the degree of harm
caused; second, the degree of consensus about the
harm caused; and third, the severity of society's
response.

In expanding Hagan's pyramid into the concept of a "crime prism," Stuart Henry and Mark
Lanier added further dimensions. A fourth dimension is the degree of consensus about the severity of society's response: Does everyone agree
with the sentence or is there wide disagreement
that it is either too severe or too lenient? A fifth
dimension is the degree of visibility of unwanted
behavior—and the role of mass mediated culture
in sensitizing populations to fear of some unwanted behavior/crime rather than others. A
sixth dimension is the extent of harm caused
(which is different from how harmful the act is in

itself), for example, a terrorist act that kills one hundred people is seen as more harmful than an act of terrorism that kills one person, even though the act itself may be the same. Seventh is the selectivity of society's responses to such behavior, which relates to the equality of responses across the different levels of society and the degree to which power and resources of those in different levels are drawn on to resist.

By integrating these different dimensions it is possible to develop a more balanced and comprehensive definition of the crime phenomenon. This necessarily takes account of crime's complexity, recognizes its multiple victims, and acknowledges the critical role of power in various aspects of the crime creation process.

Stuart Henry

Further Reading

Barak, Gregg. *Media, Process and the Social Construction of Crime: Studies in Newsmaking Criminology*. New York: Garland, 1994. Useful examination of the media's role in defining crime.

Hagan, John. *The Disreputable Pleasures*. Toronto: McGraw-Hill Ryerson, 1977. Explanation of the integrated view of defining crime.

Hall, Jerome. *General Principles of Criminal Law*. Indianapolis: Bobbs-Merrill, 1960. Old but still useful foundational statement of the legal perspectives on defining crime.

Henry, Stuart. "What Is School Violence? An Integrated Definition." *The ANNALS of the American Academy of Political and Social Science* 567 (January, 2000): 16-29. An application of the integrative view of crime.

Henry, Stuart, and Mark Lanier, eds. *What Is Crime? Controversies Over the Nature of Crime and What to Do About It*. Boulder, Colo.: Roman & Littlefield, 2001. In-depth coverage of a wide variety of views on what constitutes crime.

Law Commission of Canada, ed. *What Is a Crime? Defining Criminal Conduct in Contemporary Society*. Vancouver: University of British Columbia Press 2004. Penetrating study that tries to grapple with concrete problems of defining crime.

Surette, Raymond. *Media, Crime and Criminal Justice*. 2d ed. Pacific Grove, Calif.: Brooks Cole, 1997. Another useful examination of the media's role in defining crime.

See also Accomplices and accessories; Common law; Comprehensive Crime Control Act; Crime Index; Criminal justice in U.S. history; Criminal law; Criminal liability; Criminals; Criminology; *Ex post facto* laws; Felonies; Lesser-included offenses; Malice; Misdemeanors; Psychopathy; Uniform Crime Reports.

Crime Index

Definition: Part of the Federal Bureau of Investigation's annual Uniform Crime Reports (*Crime in the United States*)

Criminal justice issues: Crime statistics; legal terms and principles

Significance: The Crime Index is the most complete compilation of national reported crime statistics for the eight most serious types of crime, as determined by the Federal Bureau of Investigation.

The Federal Bureau of Investigation (FBI) Crime Index is part of the FBI's annual Uniform Crime Reports (UCR), which is a compilation of crime statistics reported monthly to the FBI by more than sixteen thousand police agencies. These agencies, taken together, have jurisdiction over 98 percent of the United States, making the index the best single source of information concerning national crime levels. The Crime Index consists of arrests and reported crimes of the eight types ("index crimes") deemed most serious by the FBI: murder and nonnegligent homicide, forcible rape, robbery, aggravated assault, burglary, larceny, motor vehicle theft, and arson. This last category, a late addition to the index, has been included since 1981.

National estimates of the volume and rate of Crime Index incidents for every 100,000 people over the past two decades are included as well as the number of reported crimes cleared by arrest or other means. Information for the entire United States is broken down into various geographical divisions, including individual states, metropolitan areas, cities, towns, counties, and college and university campuses. Crimes are also classified according to types of weapons used and the value of property stolen or recovered, as well as by the sex, race, and age of victims and perpetrators. The Crime Index does not attempt to explain the reasons for an increase or decrease in crime. It is used by law-enforcement agencies and others to identify long-term trends and assess police effectiveness.

Several factors should be borne in mind by the reader when interpreting data from the Crime Index. First, although most major cities report crime statistics, not all police agencies do, so while the Crime Index is the most inclusive compilation of national crime statistics that is available, it is not 100 percent complete. Second, while the FBI issues definitions for the eight major crimes tabulated in the crime index, each of the reporting agencies independently interprets those definitions, causing considerable potential variation in the meaning of the reported statistics. Third, the number of crimes actually occurring is unknown and may or may not be proportional to the number of crimes reported to the various law-enforcement agencies who then report to the FBI.

When assessing the geographical distribution of crimes, readers are cautioned to consider the size of the region's population as well. Finally, the FBI warns that crime can vary dramatically from year to year and advises against drawing sweeping conclusions about long-term trends on the basis of a few years' data.

Jean Sinclair McKnight

Further Reading

Federal Bureau of Investigation. *Crime in the United States, 2002*. Washington, D.C.: Government Printing Office, 2003.

Reebel, Patrick A., ed. *Federal Bureau of Investigation: Current Issues and Background*. New York: Nova Science, 2002.

U.S. Bureau of Justice Statistics. *Sourcebook of Criminal Justice Statistics*. Annual. Washington, D.C.: Government Printing Office.

See also Cold cases; Crime; Federal Bureau of Investigation; Felonies; National Crime Victimization Survey; Robbery; Uniform Crime Reports.

Crime labs

Definition: Facilities—mostly government-run—designed to analyze physical evidence of crimes

Criminal justice issues: Evidence and forensics; investigation; technology

Significance: Crime labs process, analyze, and sometimes collect physical evidence from crimes and crime scenes. As the field of criminalistics has become increasingly important within the criminal justice system, crime labs have provided the expertise to use and understand scientific methods of analysis of evidence.

Most crime labs are funded and administered by governmental agencies, such as the Federal Bureau of Investigation (FBI), state departments of justice, and local law-enforcement agencies. There are also private, for-profit crime labs. The criminalists who work within crime labs typically have degrees in chemistry, biology, and other sciences, and often have masters and doctoral degrees.

Crime labs perform a wide variety of analyses. One of their most common tasks now is DNA analysis. Among other things, DNA analysis is done to identify criminal offenders and crime victims. DNA analysis can be performed on body tissues and on body fluids, such as blood, saliva, and semen. Other common crime labs tasks include fingerprint analysis; identification of trace evidence such as clothing fibers and paint particles; screening of body fluids for alcohol, drugs, and toxins; identification and matching of firearms and ammunition; identification and matching of marks made by hammers, screwdrivers, saws, and other tools; and analysis of written documents, such as matching handwriting samples to those of suspects. Depending on the types of analysis being performed, criminalists use a wide variety of scientific equipment and techniques.

Modern Challenges

As crime labs become increasingly important in the investigation of crime, they face a growing number of challenges. One of these is overwhelming caseloads and limited personnel and budgets. In 2002, for example, the fifty largest crime labs in the United States received more than 1.2 million requests for services. Although these labs had 4,300 full-time employees, they had a backlog of 270,000 requests by the end of that year. As a result of these backlogs and contrary to what is often depicted on television shows such as *CSI*, it often takes well over a month for a real-life law-enforcement agency to obtain results of scientific analysis. This contributes to slowing down the criminal justice system's response to crimes. The delays allow some guilty people to escape justice, while innocent suspects may be detained for longer periods of time.

Another challenge that crime labs face is the quality of their work. The first years of the twenty-first century have seen a number of high-profile incidents involving crime labs and crime lab employees that have provided false and misleading results. These problems have been caused by such factors as high caseloads and inadequate personnel training and supervision. Faulty crime lab analyses are particularly troubling because they can lead to mistaken convictions of innocent people. In fact, according to the Innocence Project, defective and fraudulent science was a major contributor to the false convictions of dozens of men for crimes as serious as murder and rape. Some of these innocent men even received death sentences, and many of them spent long years in prison.

In response to the problem of bad science, there has been a recent trend toward accrediting crime labs. Under a formal accreditation process, an external agency such as the American Society of Crime Laboratory Directors audits and inspects labs. The accrediting agency checks for such things as proper employee education and training, availability of appropriate equipment

Crime lab of the New Jersey State Police Forensic Science Center, in Hamilton, New Jersey, which employed about ninety scientists in such fields as entomology, chemistry, biology, and anthropology in 2004. *(AP/Wide World Photos)*

and space, and correct evidence handling and analysis techniques. In addition, the U.S. Department of Justice has published several reports providing guidelines on forensic science training and techniques.

Accreditation and guidelines are likely to do little to help alleviate the backlogs in lab work. However, they should improve the accuracy and quality of the labs' work, thus leading to more accurate crime investigations.

Phyllis B. Gerstenfeld

Further Reading

Bureau of Justice Statistics. *Fifty Largest Crime Labs, 2002.* Washington, D.C.: U.S. Department of Justice, 2004.

Evans, C. *The Casebook of Forensic Detection: How Science Solved One Hundred of the World's Most Baffling Crimes.* New York: John Wiley & Sons, 1998.

Genge, N. *The Forensic Casebook: The Science of Crime Scene Investigation.* Beverly Hills, Calif.: Ballantine Books, 2002.

Lee, H., T. O'Neil, and C. Gill. *Cracking Cases: The Science of Solving Crimes.* Amherst, N.Y.: Prometheus Books, 2002.

National Institute of Justice. *Education and Training in Forensic Science: A Guide for Forensic Science Laboratories, Educational Institutions, and Students.* Washington, D.C.: U.S. Department of Justice, 2004.

See also Bloodstains; Cold cases; Crime scene investigation; Criminology; Cryptology; DNA testing; Document analysis; Fingerprint identification; Forensic anthropology; Forensic entomology; Forensic odontology; Forensic palynology; Forensics; Police detectives; Shoe prints and tire-tracks; Toxicology; Trace evidence.

Crime scene investigation

Definition: Meticulous preservation of physical evidence at specific locations by use of photographs, sketches, and collection and preservation of crime-related evidence

Criminal justice issues: Evidence and forensics; investigation; technology

One of the first things that police do on their arrival at crime scenes is seal off the areas to prevent contamination of evidence. *(Brand-X Pictures)*

Significance: Securing the crime scene and meticulously protecting evidence contributes to successful prosecution. Crime scene procedures allow proper coordination among investigators, scientific laboratory personnel, and prosecutors; interagency cooperation is essential to exoneration of the innocent and conviction of the guilty.

The primary objectives of the first responding officers at a crime scene are to arrive safely and render aid to crime victims. The officers' next immediate task is to isolate, contain, and preserve the crime scene. Officers use barriers to create an exclusion zone and prevent unauthorized access. In most cases, the responding officers conducting the preliminary investigation release the crime scene to the follow-up investigators and the Crime Scene Investigation unit (CSI). The ultimate purpose of crime scene investigation is to maintain proper care, custody, and control of evidence. Well-delineated procedures result in competent, material, and reliable evidence for presentation in a criminal trial.

Crime Scene Coordination

Lead investigators coordinate logistical resources for crime scene investigation. Requests for technical CSI unit services—crime scene processing and a mobile crime laboratory—require approval of the senior investigator. CSI technicians process the crime scene; they do not conduct follow-up investigations or arrest suspects. The media, however, portray CSI roles inaccurately.

The CSI's primary role is to record the crime scene, including photographing it, and collect evidence. The CSI evidence team coordinates with forensic laboratory scientists and investigators. In smaller agencies with limited resources, state police or the State Bureau of Investigation (SBI) may assist local officers with the follow-up investigation.

The lead follow-up investigator establishes a systematic search plan at the crime scene. Officers estimate boundary determinations; inner and outer crime boundaries divide the scene. The investigator attempts to identify potential offender routes. For example, in a homicide, the inner crime scene might include the victim's home and immediate property. The outer crime scene may include several blocks or open fields. A wounded criminal may provide a travel pattern of blood trace evidence from the bedroom window, backyard, and to a specific vehicle. The vehicle, once traced to another location, may provide additional evidence. Additional locations to be investigated may include those of other crimes or dump sites. These areas may contain other evidence that will lead police to offenders.

Investigative service teams may assist in interviewing witnesses, recording statements, and canvassing neighborhoods or vehicles. Lead investigators conduct liaison activities with technical and investigative services personnel. Specialists in criminal investigative analysis and criminal profiling may assist in linking physical and psychological evidence. Criminal information is stored, collated, analyzed, and disseminated to appropriate agencies and personnel.

Crime Scene Inspection

The basic rule of criminal investigation requires that evidence never be touched, altered, or moved before being photographed. The CSI team records the crime scene according to specific photography and videography procedures. Specialists such as fingerprint examiners, blood evidence technicians, and footprint technicians may gather fragile trace evidence. A sketch team further documents and measures the location of the physical evidence. Standard search methods ensure the successful collection of all crime scene evidence. The collection team secures, marks, and tags the evidence and initiates the chain of custody forms.

In the after-action briefing review, the investigative team and the CSI team share findings. Investigative teams compare preliminary notes for potential follow-up procedures. Discussions focus on essential evidence and its connection to primary suspects. The process identifies potential suspects and the need for laboratory examination to develop associative trace evidence.

The final survey is the last official step before the crime scene is released according to agency reg-

Because the importance of individual items of evidence may not be apparent until well after the initial investigation of a crime scene, it is important to record every detail that may later prove relevant. One such detail in a homicide investigation is the exact position in which a body is found—a detail that is often recorded in a chalk outline. *(Brand-X Pictures)*

A Typical Crime Scene Application

Officers respond to a homicide call and discover the body of a young woman in the bedroom. After securing the scene, they set up the crime scene log, which controls all people having the right of access to the crime scene. The preliminary survey requires written notes, sketches, and identification of fragile evidence. Officers identify footprints outside the bedroom window. They alert investigators and CSI specialists to the location of fragile evidence.

Officers establish a pathway for medical personnel; this pathway prevents destruction of physical evidence. If emergency medical responders request assistance from the pathologist, the pathway allows such follow-up investigators opportunities to locate obvious physical evidence, for example, a weapon, blood, and footprints. The initial point-to-point search turns up additional evidence to be photographed.

Special attention to points of entry windows and exits will assist in identifying the offender's travel pattern. Officers locate broken glass near a damaged window and notice a bloody fingerprint below the putty line. This is a strong indicator that the offender pulled the broken glass from the window frame.

The corpse represents a secondary crime scene. The autopsy examination provides essential information on cause of death. There are three possible explanations for death crime scenes: accidental, suicide, or homicide. The case of death in this scenario is homicide. The autopsy report links trace evidence from the victim to the scene and offender.

Crime scene interpretation is the result of hypothesis formulation, experimentation, laboratory examination, and logical analysis.

Thomas E. Baker

Further Reading

Becker, Ronald F. *Criminal Investigation*. Gaithersburg, Md.: Aspen Publications, 2000. A handbook for use by crime laboratory personnel.

Gilbert, James N. *Criminal Investigation*. Upper Saddle River, N.J.: Prentice-Hall, 2001. Includes index and bibliography.

Ogle, Robert R. *Crime Scene Investigation Reconstruction*. Upper Saddle River, N.J.: Prentice-Hall, 2004.

See also Arson; Bloodstains; Bombs and explosives; Chain of custody; Cold cases; Computer forensics; Crime labs; Evidence, rules of; Fingerprint identification; Forensic anthropology; Forensic entomology; Forensic odontology; Forensic psychology; Forensics; Plain view doctrine; Police detectives; Psychological profiling; Shoe prints and tire-tracks.

ulations or other legal requirements. Standing procedures require final inspection by the lead investigator and CSI team leader. The purposes of the final survey are to check for and collect uncovered evidence, police equipment, and dangerous materials.

In summary, crime scene reconstruction requires critical thinking and problem-solving strategies. Investigators apply scientific analysis to determine an accurate sequence of events and reconstruct what happened at a crime scene. Physical evidence determines the suspects and the manner in which the crime was carried out.

Crimes of passion

Definition: Crimes that are regarded as having been committed impulsively, without premeditation or malice aforethought

Criminal justice issues: Defendants; homicide; women's issues

Significance: This concept is most frequently used in distinguishing the crime of murder, in which the killing is done with premeditation or malice aforethought, from the lesser crime of manslaughter.

One concept in determining the seriousness of a crime is the mental state of the perpetrator. A crime of passion, often known by the French term *crime passionnel*, is one committed under the influence of such strong feelings as rage, anger, hatred, furious resentment, wild desperation, or terror that occur so suddenly or extremely as to render the mind incapable of cool reflection. Such passion can be considered as a mitigating, although not an exonerating, factor.

The distinction between premedicated murder and manslaughter in American jurisprudence goes back to a Pennsylvania law enacted in 1794 to remove the death penalty from murders not considered willful, deliberate, and premeditated. If a killing follows from adequate provocation on the part of the victim and there is insufficient time for a reasonable person to have recovered self-control, the perpetrator is assumed to lack the *mens rea*, or evil intent, required for a murder charge.

To distinguish between a premeditated act and a crime of passion, all circumstances must be considered, including the length of time between the provocation and the crime, the manner in which the crime was committed, and the relationship between the parties. The application of this law has of course been influenced by contemporary mores. The traditional example of the homicidal crime of passion used to be the man who caught his wife *in flagrante delicto* (in the act) with another man. There was some disagreement as to whether this was an extenuating circumstance for killing the wife, the man, or both, but men who killed in that situation were often given minimal sentences on the grounds that they were impelled by their passions.

In modern America that approach is questioned. Feminists have argued that overly mild sentences in such cases all but license killing, and some would ask whether the supposedly masculine reaction of quick, angry violence should be privileged. Women, it is argued, are more likely to wait and build up courage before acting, and the "heat of passion" argument does not cover that. These issues came to the forefront in a Maryland case in 1994, when Kenneth Peacock was convicted for killing his wife. After catching his wife in an act of adultery, Peacock had argued with her for several hours, then shot her to death. He was allowed to use the crime-of-passion defense, pleading guilty to voluntary manslaughter. He was given a minimum three-year sentence with half of it suspended, a decision that brought widespread public criticism, especially when the judge publicly said that he might have done the same thing himself.

Arthur D. Hlavaty

Further Reading

Daly, Martin, and Margo Wilson. *Homicide*. New York: Aldine de Gruyter, 1988.

Geberth, Vernon J. *Practical Homicide Investigation*. 2d ed. New York: Elsevier, 1990.

Mandelsberg, Rose G., ed. *Crimes of Passion: From the Files of True Detective*. New York: Pinnacle Books, 1993.

See also Adultery; Criminal intent; Criminal law; Criminals; Manslaughter; Motives; Murder and homicide.

Criminal history record information

Definition: Record, or a system of records, that includes the identification of a person and describes that person's arrests and subsequent court dispositions—also known as a rap sheet

Criminal justice issues: Arrest and arraignment; investigation; technology

Significance: Criminal history records are widely used in investigations, sentencing, licensing, background checks, and other purposes.

Typical criminal history records begin with the names, dates of birth, sex, and other identifying characteristics of persons arrested by the police, followed by listings of subsequent instances in which the persons came in contact with the criminal justice system. For example, the first event on a person's record might be an arrest on June 1, 2004, for vehicle theft, showing which law-enforcement agency arrested the suspect; the next event might be a dismissal of the charge of vehicle theft against that person on June 11, 2004, showing which court dismissed the charge.

Normally, records do not include information about arrests and dispositions that occurred when subjects were juveniles. When juvenile cases have been waived to adult court, however, the adult court disposition does appear in criminal records. Criminal history records also do not contain intelligence information on their subjects or entries

The Federal Bureau of Investigation's high-tech computer center at its Washington, D.C., headquarters, can serve as a national control center during crisis situations by supplying information and coordinating responses of different agencies. *(AP/Wide World Photos)*

about parking violations, drug abuse treatment, mental health treatment, or similar matters.

As several people may have the same name and be born on the same date (or criminal offenders may lie about their names or dates of birth), criminal history records are accompanied by a positive identification of the person, normally fingerprints. Arrests that occurred in different cities, counties, or states are linked though a computerized interstate identification index operated by the Federal Bureau of Investigation (FBI). The information from different states may be combined into a single FBI criminal history record or stored in computers in the different states, ready to be combined electronically upon request. Linking records in different states for the same person is facilitated by automated fingerprint identification systems.

A person who was never arrested does not have a criminal history record, even if the FBI or a state agency has a copy of the person's fingerprints from an employment background check or for another reason.

Originally, criminal history records were considered highly confidential, and access was restricted to employees of criminal justice agencies for specified purposes, such as trying to find perpetrators of crimes or prosecuting and sentencing offenders in accordance with law. Beginning in the 1990's, state and federal legislation has facilitated access to criminal history records (or selected portions of those records) for a variety of purposes, including background checks of applicants for purchase of a firearm, employment related to public safety, or volunteer work involving care of children or the elderly. Sex offender registries, which are completely available to the public in some states, are separate from criminal history records.

Jan M. Chaiken

Further Reading

Bureau of Justice Statistics. *Improving Criminal History Records for Background Checks*. Washington, D.C.: U.S. Department of Justice, 2003.

SEARCH, The National Consortium for Justice Information and Statistics. *Public Attitudes Toward Uses of Criminal History Information*. Washington, D.C.: Bureau of Justice Statistics, 2001.

See also Arrest; Background checks; Bureau of Justice Statistics; Cold cases; Computer information systems; Criminal records; Criminals; Federal Bureau of Investigation; Fingerprint identification; Gun laws; Juvenile justice system; Juvenile waivers to adult courts; Sex offender registries; Uniform Crime Reports.

Criminal intent

Definition: Necessary state of mind needed to assign criminal responsibility to persons for their actions

Criminal justice issues: Defendants; prosecution

Significance: Criminal intent is one of the conditions that must be met in order to find a defendant criminally responsible.

In order to establish criminal responsibility, the easiest condition to recognize is the act, known as the *actus reus*. This is the outward behavior that makes up the crime. An equally important component is a person's state of mind when committing the act, known as *mens rea*. Justice Robert Houghwout Jackson in the U.S. Supreme Court case of *Morissette v. United States* (1952) defined crime as "a compound concept . . . constituted only from concurrence of an evil-meaning mind and an evil-doing hand." In common law the evil mind has also been referred to as a guilty mind, felonious intent, guilty knowledge, evil purpose, or mental culpability. All these terms signify that persons charged with crimes meant to cause the natural and probable results of their actions.

In 1962 the American Law Institute published the Model Penal Code, which suggested that confusion in this and other areas of law could be avoided if specific, uniform definitions were incorporated into statutes. It determined that four culpable mental states compose criminal intent. In order of severity, crimes may be committed purposely, knowingly, recklessly, and negligently. In most statutes the mental states required to categorize crimes are specifically stated.

Persons act purposely when they desire a result. For example, persons act purposely if they plan to kill other persons by lying in wait and ambushing them using techniques that ensure success. Acts are carried out knowingly when persons act in such a way that they are clearly aware that a certain result is likely. When persons point guns at others and pull the trigger, they are fully cognizant that this will most likely cause death. Persons act recklessly when they disregard an obvious and considerable risk. Driving under the influence of alcohol is an example of a crime based on the criterion of recklessness as a mental state. Negligence is present when persons deviate significantly from a standard of care that would constitute normal behavior in the situation. If a gun owner in a home with children leaves a weapon on a nightstand and a child shoots a playmate with it, the owner is negligent in creating the situation and is criminally liable.

One type of act may be judged differently depending solely on the criminal intent involved. If persons driving cars hit pedestrians, they do so purposely if they aim their cars at the pedestrians. They do so knowingly if they see the pedestrians crossing the street and refuse to slow down, expecting the pedestrians to move out of the way. They do so recklessly if they have been drinking heavily and are unable to react to the pedestrians in a crosswalk. They do so negligently if they drive significantly over the speed limit and are unable to stop quickly enough. However, they have committed no crime whatsoever if the pedestrians have darted from between two parked cars into the middle of the street.

Michael L. Barrett

See also Attempt to commit a crime; Crimes of passion; Criminal law; Criminal liability; Criminals; Defenses to crime; Duress; Ignorance of the law; Inchoate crimes; Insanity defense; *Mala in se* and *mala prohibita*; Malice; *Mens rea*; Motives; Principals (criminal); Solicitation to commit a crime; Strict liability offenses.

Criminal justice education

Definition: Methods of increasing the awareness of criminal justice students with careers in their field

Criminal justice issues: Criminology; professional standards

Significance: Many undergraduate students in criminal justice are not fully aware of the wide variety of career choices available in their field. They can broaden their educations by looking beyond their regular academic course work. The broader their experiences are, the better their chances of selecting and succeeding in their criminal justice careers.

A variety of methods and techniques can be helpful in assisting undergraduate students in becoming more aware of the variety of criminal justice positions. For example, internships are an excellent means of allowing students to find out at firsthand what various government agencies do and the services they provide. Internships usually require students to work within law-enforcement agencies, courts, corrections agencies, or forensics labs for a specific number of hours. Interns work under the supervision of staff officers and mentors in the agencies. Some internships are paid, but the main advantage offered by internships is experience. Students also usually receive college credit for their intern work.

Service learning is another means for students to gain insight, knowledge, and experience in areas that interest them. The students agree to perform certain services that agencies provide and work alongside regular staff members on projects related to the college courses in which they are registered. Such assignments may be fixed course requirements or be individual choices that the students make to complete course work. The students benefit by gaining valuable work knowl-

edge and experience. Service-learning assignments usually entail fewer hours than internships.

Volunteering work in criminal justice agencies is another good way in which to learn more about possible careers. Voluntary work usually earns neither college credits nor payment. However, such work can be easy to get, as most criminal justice agencies rarely turn down would-be volunteers.

Many educational institutions host guest speakers from a variety of criminal justice agencies and careers to address students interested in the discipline. Such occasions can provide excellent opportunities for students to hear from practitioners in the field about the particulars of their work. They can also provide students with opportunities to make contacts for future reference.

Many educational institutions host career fairs, which as many as fifteen to thirty representatives from criminal justice agencies may attend. The agencies typically set up booths or tables to distribute information about their work. Such fairs can provide excellent opportunities for students to meet and talk directly to working criminal justice professionals. They can also make contacts for possible internships and future employment.

Campus career centers and offices are usually separate departments at most colleges. They normally maintain listings and contacts encompassing the majority of criminal justice careers available. Depending on their staffing, they can assist students with interviewing techniques, résumé writing, application procedures, and other job-search tasks. In addition, they can help students secure internships.

Criminal justice clubs and associations invite new members at many colleges and universities. These groups are usually operated by students majoring in criminal justice, with the help of faculty advisers from the criminal justice departments. The main goal of such groups is to disseminate information by hosting guest speakers, taking field trips, and helping organize career fairs.

Criminal justice advisory boards are another means of enhancing students' awareness of various criminal justice agencies. For example, many jurisdictions maintain youth service commissions. These bodies encompass cross sections of individual citizens—including students—who would serve as advisory groups to judiciary and juvenile justice agencies. They recommend programs and other means of dealing with juvenile offenders. In addition, they may recommend preventive programs to agencies dealing with at-risk juveniles.

Other types of community advisory boards are youth and young-adult boards that advise criminal justice agencies. Their purpose is to communicates the ideas of young people to advise criminal justice agencies on how to deal with offenders of the same ages. A wide variety of juvenile and adult advisory groups exist that invite community participation.

John M. Paitakes

Further Reading

Bolles, Richard Nelson, and Mark Emery Bolles. *What Color Is Your Parachute? 2005: A Practical Manual for Job-Hunters and Career-Changers*. Berkeley, Calif.: Ten Speed Press, 2004. One of the most popular general guides ever published for job hunters filled with practical, no-nonsense advice.

Champion, Dean John. *Review of Seeking Employment in Law Enforcement, Private Security and Related Fields*. Upper Saddle River, N.J.: Prentice-Hall, 1994. Job-hunting manual focusing on criminal justice careers.

Harr, Scott J., and Karen M. Hess. *Seeking Employment in Criminal Justice and Related Fields*. Belmont, Calif.: Wadsworth, 2003. Compendium of information on criminal justice professions that provides tips on job-search strategies, including information on résumé writing and interviewing techniques.

Taylor, Dorothy L. *Jump Starting Your Career*. Upper Saddle River, N.J.: Pearson Education, 2004. Popular general guide to planning careers.

See also Bureau of Prisons; Community-based corrections; Criminal justice in U.S. history; Criminal justice system; Drug Enforcement Administration; Judges; Neighborhood watch programs; Omnibus Crime Control and Safe Streets Act of 1968; Parole; Parole officers; Prison and jail systems; Television news.

Criminal justice in U.S. history

Criminal justice issues: Courts; law-enforcement organization; punishment; trial procedures

Significance: The evolution of the American criminal justice system provides insights into understanding the system as it is presently constituted.

The development of the criminal justice system in the United States is closely tied to that of Great Britain, from which the United States drew the basis of its own government and legal system. The origins of the British criminal justice system date back to tenth century England, when the mutual pledge system arose. Under that system, families banded together in groups of ten called tithings. The tithings in turn banded together in groups of ten, each helping to keep order among the others. An officer called the shire rieve—which later gave rise to "sheriff"—oversaw groups of hundreds. That system began the development of criminal justice, but there was poor law enforcement because there was no supervision and some people did not want to participate in the mutual pledge system. Mutual pledge did not reduce or deal effectively with crime; this led to the creation of the *posse comitatus* system, in which members of communities were chosen to help victims of crime bring justice to offenders.

Colonial America

Early courts in England—both the courts of the king and the church courts—were highly unpredictable and corrupt. After England started founding colonies in North America, the settlers created many of their own rules for criminal justice, in part because of their dissatisfaction with the shortcomings of England's system. Early American law drew on English legal traditions, biblical law, and the colonists' own ideas.

Every British colony had its own criminal code, but all laws fell into four major crime categories: crimes against persons, crimes against property, crimes involving sexual acts, and misconduct considered socially harmful. Colonists used the English law-enforcement system, bringing with them the concepts of trial by juries of peers, taking of testimony under oath, and impartial courts. English legal tradition relied heavily on death as a form of punishment, but the North American colonists preferred to have a wider variety of punishments to choose from, including incarceration, whipping, and banishment.

The criminal justice system in the colonial era differed greatly from modern American criminal justice. Public police forces were not yet established, public prosecutors and public defense attorneys did not yet exist, there were no criminal appeals, a separate juvenile justice system had not been established, and there were no specialized courts, such as modern drug courts. Responsibility for law enforcement rested primarily on private individuals, through dueling to uphold codes of honor, church tribunals, and vigilante groups. Among peace officers, there was a great amount of corruption, including accepting bribes and assaulting citizens without cause. Grand juries of twelve to sixteen members acted as "sworn presenters," responsible for watching the other townspeople and bringing illegal activities to the attention of the courts. The powers of arrest of untrained peace officers, constables, and sheriffs were limited to only those crimes that they personally witnessed. Some colonies adopted England's hue-and-cry system for pursuing offenders. Under that system, constables and sheriffs called for all able-bodied men to pursue criminals.

When suspected offenders were arrested, they were brought before judges, who decided whether to issue bail. After the arrestees entered pleas of guilty or not guilty, their cases went to trial. Persons familiar with the law were occasionally called upon by the accused to clarify laws during trials; however, defense attorneys were not commonly involved in the courtroom until the 1730's. Around the time of the American Revolution, the role of defense attorneys became more important as greater emphasis was placed on individual rights.

Defendants who pleaded guilty or who were found guilty by juries were punished publicly. Punishments included admonitions to behave correctly in the future; fines, which were paid in money or tobacco; forced public displays of guilt, such as wearing a scarlet letter A in cases of adultery, B for burglary, and D for drunkenness; temporary confinement in stocks and pillories; indentured servitude; whipping; banishment; and hanging. Most crimes during the colonial period were minor violations such as trespassing. Major predatory crimes were virtually nonexistent. Jail terms were rarely used as punishments, and such jails as existed were primarily holding facilities, in which accused persons awaited trial.

The Nineteenth Century

The first modern police force in the world was created in London, England, in 1748, when Henry Fielding designed a full-time force from among men who wanted to be police officers. His untrained and nonuniformed force became known as the Bow Street Runners. Many of the men who wanted to be police were criminals or violent, and the Bow Street Runners became unpopular because of their corruption and violence. Following Fielding, Sir Robert Peel created the first trained, professional police force in 1829 under England's Metropolitan Police Act. Members of this force became popularly known as "Bobbies," after Peel's given name. Like the Bow Street Runners, the Bobbies were initially unpopular, as poor residents of London viewed them as protecting the rich. However, the Bobbies carried no weapons, and the public gradually began to accept them.

British ideas about police carried over to America. However, the first American police were mostly private forces made up of part-time police officers and had only loose ties to government bodies. In 1838, Boston created a police department that modified and consolidated the existing law-enforcement practices and began regular patrols of the city. Soon afterward, New York City formed a modern police force, with police officers who walked beats.

Social and economic changes brought by large-scale immigration and rapid urbanization and industrialization led to many riots and disorders that prompted changes in the criminal justice system. From the 1840's to the 1930's, private law-enforcement bodies and vigilante groups slowly lost popularity, as modern police forces were developed. There was a general trend in criminal justice toward professionalism, with uniformed police, professional public prosecutors, defense attorneys, and the development of plea bargaining to resolve cases in criminal courts. Meanwhile, the idea of separate juvenile courts and "schools" began to emerge. Chicago established the first juvenile court in 1899. Executions moved from public hangings to gas chambers and electric chairs.

Although the idea of prisons originated in England in the sixteenth century, they were used sparsely in America to rehabilitate inmates through hard labor and religion. Pennsylvania's Walnut Street Jail opened in 1790 with a similar purpose, but its conditions were harsh, and it provided only limited amounts of work for its inmates. Penitentiaries became common tools for incarcerating offenders in the United States dur-

Criminal Justice and *An American Tragedy*

Theodore Dreiser's classic novel *An American Tragedy* (1925) offers a generally realistic depiction of criminal justice during the early twentieth century. The novel's protagonist, Clyde Griffiths, the young son of a Kansas City preacher, moves to New York, where he has an affair with Roberta Alden. He subsequently falls in love with the wealthy, young Sondra Finchley. By this time, however, Roberta is pregnant. After she threatens to tell Clyde's family if he does not marry her, Clyde decides to kill her. While the two are boating, Clyde accidentally capsizes the boat, which strikes Roberta in the head. Clyde makes no effort to rescue her, and she drowns. After her body is discovered, Clyde is arrested, convicted, and executed for her murder.

Dreiser based his novel on the real-life murder trial of Chester Gillette, who was executed in 1908. His novel fairly replicates the actual course that a real criminal investigation and trial would take, although—as happens in real life—the participants in the criminal process do not always follow the law. For example, one of the prosecutor's assistants manufactures evidence to incriminate Clyde, and the prosecutor himself conceals this evidence when, by law, he is obligated to reveal its existence to the defense counsel. Clyde's attorney, for his part, fails to advance a defense of insanity that might save Clyde, because Clyde's family—which is paying the attorney's fees—will not permit that defense to be asserted. Although attorneys are often pressured to abide by the wishes of the clients paying their fees, their profession expects them steadfastly to resist such pressure and seek only to further the interests of their clients.

Dreiser's narrative only briefly summarizes the *voir dire* portion of the trial, when Clyde's jury is selected. This process, though undoubtedly tedious, is of crucial importance in a real criminal trial, for it is

Author Theodore Dreiser. *(Library of Congress)*

the point when the prosecution and the defense have the greatest influence on the choice of who will ultimately decide the fate of criminal defendants such as Clyde. Dreiser's account of the trial focuses on the "tragic" inability of the justice system to deal fairly with the underlying event, since all its participants are linked in the same quest for social and material advancement—the American Dream—as the accused.

Timothy L. Hall

ing the mid-1820's. Instead of punishing offenders publicly, the prisons isolated them from their communities.

In 1850, there were only 6,737 inmates of prison in the thirty-one states. That number rose to 30,659 inmates in 1880 and 57,070 inmates in 1904. Due to appalling conditions in the prisons, there were many calls for prison reform. Suggestions included moving inmates from prisons to reformatories and focusing the time the inmates spent in incarceration on productive work, education, and religion. By end of the nineteenth century, separate reformatories were being built for women prisoners.

The Early Twentieth Century

While trying to create professionalism in the criminal justice system, the new police forces were still characterized by their corrupt practices. The police officers themselves were often hired by corrupt government officials and politicians, whom they, in turn, tried to protect. Police officers collected bribes, kickbacks, and regular payoffs from criminals to overlook criminal activity.

During Prohibition, from 1920 to 1933, the public began to view police negatively for the first time because the police enforced the extremely unpopular laws banning alcohol. With this and the great corruption exposed by the Wickersham Commission Report in 1931, the public greatly resented the police and called for reform.

The Prohibition era also saw the emergence of gangsters, such as Al Capone, and rising government and public concern about organized crime. There appeared to be a great surge in crime, but the government had no empirical evidence to support that notion. Under the leadership of J. Edgar Hoover, the Federal Bureau of Investigation began compiling crime statistics in what is known as the Uniform Crime Reports (UCR). Modern police departments around the country now submit annual reports to the UCR, which maintains the database of crimes known to police.

From the 1930's to the 1970's, police departments began following a more legalistic style of policing, based on strict adherence to the law. With advancing technologies, the police were moving away from walking beats to responding to crime from departmental offices. Ideas about corrections changed as well, with the creation of probation and parole officers to monitor offenders in communities.

Civil Unrest and the Criminal Justice System

The 1960's saw new law-enforcement challenges in the Civil Rights movement, protests against the Vietnam War, urban unrest, and rising crime rates. These changes increased public distrust of both government and the criminal justice system. Increasingly, police were challenged about the ways in which they operated, and Supreme Court decisions such as *Miranda v. Arizona* (1966) and *Mapp v. Ohio* (1961) imposed new regulations on police practices.

Consistent with the social climate of the day, a renewed emphasis on individual rights within the criminal justice system developed. Advocates for individual rights support the due process model, which would rather allow some guilty people go free than convict innocent people. The 1960's thus saw a focus on individual rights throughout the criminal justice system, giving the convicted enhanced opportunities for appeals, improving prisoners' rights, and shifting sentencing more toward rehabilitation than incarceration. Also, for the first time, research was conducted on how to enforce laws effectively through scientific policing. In 1965, the President's Commission on Law Enforcement and Administration of Justice was formed, providing new funding to the police to do research.

Community Era of the Criminal Justice System

During the 1970's, the notion of community policing gained popularity. This was characterized by a service style of law enforcement, emphasizing the role of the police as public servants, while placing less stress on strict law enforcement. This development tended to move police back to the streets. In 1974, the Kansas City Preventive Patrol Experiment compared different methods of patrolling—traditional random patrols, traditional random patrols with more officers, and reactive policing in which officers waited at police stations for emergency calls—to determine which worked best. The Kansas City Experiment found no differences in crime rates and no differences in levels of public fear of crime among the different methods. The conclusion was that more police do not necessarily reduce crime rates. However, because of the experiment, police departments implemented more direct patrols in an effort to identify areas with the most crime and place the most police in those areas.

The death penalty temporarily was abolished in the United States during this time. In 1972, the U.S. Supreme Court ruled that the death penalty was unconstitutional in its *Furman v. Georgia* decision. Four years later, in *Gregg v. Georgia*, the Court ruled that the state of Georgia had correctly changed its legislation regarding capital punishment to uphold the Constitution. The Court's new ruling permitted the death penalty in other states, as well. Nevertheless, many scholars have argued that capital punishment still disproportionately affects certain races.

Increasing violent crime rates during the 1960's and early 1970's caused the public to become disillusioned with the recent emphasis on individual rights. This disillusionment was enhanced by the Martinson Report of 1975 on crime, which proclaimed that nothing works.

The 1980's brought about a new focus on preserving public order, and the criminal justice system placed a renewed emphasis on punishment. During the years of the Reagan administration, a new drug, crack cocaine, emerged, bringing with it a large drug problem. The Reagan administration waged a "war on drugs," emphasizing public order.

Public order advocates support the crime-control model, which favors giving police greater powers to arrest, making justice system processes faster and more efficient, making it easier to convict offenders, and allowing fewer appeals. Sentencing guidelines were created out of the federal Sentencing Reform Act of 1984 to ensure "truth in sentencing" and reduce judicial discretion with the object of eliminating reduced sentences.

Modern Structure of the System

In the twenty-first century, the criminal justice system operates like a funnel in which people leave the system at each stage. The first stage is the criminal investigation and arrest. The more serious the offenses, the more likely it is that arrests will take place. Arrests are also more likely in stranger crimes—those in which the victims do not know the offenders. However, most offenses are actually never investigated or processed.

After arrests are made, personal information of the alleged offenders and the crimes with which they are charged is recorded in the booking process. The third stage is the initial appearance. The alleged offenders—now called defendants—must appear before judges, who decide whether to jail them or release them on bail until trial. The next time the defendants appear in court is at preliminary hearings, at which judges determine whether there is enough evidence to continue with trials.

At the fifth stage, the indictment, the prosecution presents its cases to grand juries, who decide whether there is cause for reasonable persons to believe that the defendants have committed the crimes with which they are charged. At the sixth stage, arraignment, defendants are officially notified of the charges against them and are asked to enter pleas.

Although most cases are resolved through plea bargaining, some proceed to trial, the seventh stage. When trials result in convictions, judges decide what the sentences should be at the sentencing/adjudication stage. Finally, at the correctional phase, the convicted defendants serve their sentences—which may include probation, community service, or incarceration.

Law Enforcement

Modern law enforcement is organized at three different government levels: federal, state, and local. There are also unofficial, or private, law-enforcement bodies specially created to protect certain properties and individuals. At the federal level, the best-known law-enforcement bodies are the Federal Bureau of Investigation (FBI), the Drug Enforcement Administration (DEA), the U.S. Marshals Service, the Bureau of Immigration and Customs Enforcement (ICE), the Bureau of Alcohol, Tobacco, Firearms and Explosives (ATF), and the U.S. Secret Service. After the terrorist attacks of September 11, 2001, on the United States, the federal government created a new cabinet-level department called Homeland Security, which brought most of the federal law-enforcement agencies together under the same department.

Declining Violent Crime Rates, 1973-2003

Source: U.S. Bureau of Justice Statistics, 2005. Data represent aggregate violent victimization rates for murder, rape, robbery, and assault.

Different types of law-enforcement agencies can be found in the various states, but there are only two basic models. In the centralized model, state law-enforcement agencies are responsible for all law enforcement, including traffic laws. By contrast, in the decentralized model, there are separate, limited-purpose law-enforcement agencies. For example, one agency may enforce criminal law, while another enforces traffic law. Some states have crime-specific task forces. There tends to be less communication among different branches in the latter model.

Local law-enforcement agencies are more diverse and are more numerous than state and federal agencies combined. No general model exists, and local law-enforcement bodies have many different tasks. During the late 1980's and early 1990's, the philosophy of community policing began broadening police functions to incorporate citizen input and vary services among different neighborhoods to focus on specific needs of individual communities. Problem-oriented policing

diverges from the traditional reactive response to crime in that police actively look for the causes of crime to try to prevent crimes from occurring.

Courts and Sentencing

As with law-enforcement organizations, there are different levels of courts. At the state level, courts of general jurisdiction—names of the courts vary—deal with a variety of cases. Most cases do not involve juries but are resolved through plea bargaining. States also have intermediate appellate courts that handle appeals from lower courts, as well as supreme courts.

The federal court system has three levels. At the lowest level, U.S. district courts try cases dealing with violations of federal law. Courts at the next level—U.S. courts of appeal—do not have trials but review cases referred from the district courts. At the top is the U.S. Supreme Court, which is also the supreme court over the entire federal and state judicial system. The Supreme Court reviews cases raising important constitutional questions and issues rulings that must be followed throughout the country.

The United States incarcerates more offenders than any other country in the world. However, at the beginning of the twenty-first century, the nation was again exploring alternative sanctions, including day fines, house arrest, and shock incarceration. Restorative conferencing is also becoming increasingly popular, designed for victims and offenders to discuss the crimes, allowing the offenders to admit their guilt and express remorse to their victims to help return the victims to the state that they were in prior to the offenses.

Jennifer C. Gibbs

Further Reading

Chapin, Bradley. *Criminal Justice in Colonial America, 1606-1660.* Athens: University of Georgia Press, 1983. Detailed description and analysis of the origins of the early American criminal justice system, including criminal law, courts, and punishment.

Friedman, Lawrence M. *Crime and Punishment in America History.* New York: Basic Books, 1993. Study of changes in the criminal justice system—including criminal law, police, courts, sentencing, and punishment—from the colonial era through the early 1990's.

Hall, James P. *The History and Philosophy of Law Enforcement.* Dubuque, Iowa: Kendall/Hunt, 1975. Study of the changing philosophies in law enforcement from ancient times through early English history and the American colonial period to law enforcement in the United States in the 1970's.

Law Enforcement Assistance Administration. *Two Hundred Years of American Criminal Justice: An LEAA Bicentennial Study.* Washington, D.C.: U.S. Department of Justice, 1976. Official U.S. Justice Department history of criminal law in the United States from 1776 through 1976.

Miller, Wilbur R. *Cops and Bobbies: Police Authority in New York and London, 1830-1870.* 2d ed. Columbus: Ohio State University Press, 1999. Study of police forces in the United States and England from 1830 to 1870 that pays special attention to the question of how countries with similar legal histories developed markedly different models of policing.

Ruth, Henry S., and Kevin R. Reitz. *The Challenge of Crime: Rethinking Our Response.* Cambridge, Mass.: Harvard University Press, 2003. Examination of crime policy, including policing, sentencing, incarceration and the juvenile justice system from 1970 into the early twenty-first century.

Schmalleger, Frank. *Criminal Justice Today: An Introductory Text for the Twenty-first Century.* 7th ed. Upper Saddle River, N.J.: Prentice-Hall, 2003. Introduction to the criminal justice system that includes a discussion of the history of criminal justice in the United States.

Walker, Samuel. *Popular Justice: A History of American Criminal Justice.* 2d ed. New York: Oxford University Press, 1998. Review of the evolution of the criminal justice system in the United States, from the colonial era through the 1990's.

See also Canadian justice system; Common law; Court types; Crime; Criminal justice system; Criminal prosecution; Criminals; Judicial system, U.S.; Justice Department, U.S.; Juvenile justice system; Law enforcement; Outlaws of the Old West; Prison and jail systems; Slave patrols; Vigilantism; Violent Crime Control and Law Enforcement Act; Wickersham Commission.

Criminal justice system

Definition: Interrelationships among law enforcement, the courts, corrections, and juvenile justice

Criminal justice issues: Courts; juvenile justice; law-enforcement organization; punishment

Significance: The American criminal justice system is a multilayered complex that interconnects courts, law-enforcement agencies, and corrections of federal, state, and local governments in the common goal of reducing crime, punishing wrongdoers, and rehabilitating offenders.

Crime is found in all societies, and every culture develops its own mechanisms to control and prevent it. The ways in which the different peoples of the world confront crime vary considerably. Great dissimilarities can be found in the very definitions of what constitute illegal acts and in the variety of methods used to judge and punish criminals. The ways that a society employs to confront crime often reflect the society's political and cultural values.

The United States is a democracy, and the ways in which Americans control crime reflect the national political philosophy. The usual meaning of a democratic government is a representative one in which those in authority are periodically elected by the people. The basic philosophy of an elected government should thus reflect the will of the people. However, on many issues, the people may disagree with their government. Even when they agree, they may differ among themselves on how the majority opinions should be put into effect.

A key element in a democracy is consent of the people. Democratic governments operate on agreement and not on the basis of coercion. It is understood that a democracy's citizens concur as to its existence. If not, then its citizens are free to withdraw from the society or to work within the system for change. Another element of democracy is that of participation. Democratic governments allow and encourage their citizens to participate in making policies and, at times, executing them as well. In a democracy the dignity of the people will be assumed along with all citizens being treated with fairness and justice.

People, Personalities, and Politics in Criminal Justice

Although the depictions of the criminal justice system conveyed by Hollywood films are often distorted and inaccurate, many films nevertheless provide realistic insights into the ways in which criminal justice actually works. An example is director Alan J. Pakula's *Presumed Innocent* (1990), a thriller based on the best-selling 1987 novel of the same title by veteran attorney Scott Turow. This film demonstrates that the law is not simply a matter of books and treatises but one of people and the tangles of their lives. The film also reveals the criminal justice system as not merely a structure of rules but also a maze of personalities and personal agendas—from a sexy prosecutor willing to trade on her sensuality to a judge with a secret and a district attorney worried about getting reelected.

In fact, the law, as depicted in *Presumed Innocent*, is mostly incompetent or corrupt. District Attorney Rusty Sabich (Harrison Ford) is initially assigned to investigate the murder of his former mistress and fellow prosecutor (Greta Scacchi), only to be charged later with the murder himself. Sabich's wife, who has been cheated on, is the real murderer, and although she makes a valiant attempt to frame her husband for the murder, the incompetence and corruption of various actors within the criminal justice system frustrate her attempt to exact revenge for her husband's infidelities. A police officer friendly with Sabich holds onto evidence (a glass with the defendant's fingerprint planted in the victim's apartment) that would have incriminated him. The police decline to get a warrant to search the defendant's house, where they would have discovered the murder weapon, still caked with blood, in the defendant's toolbox, where his wife had left it. The defense attorney uses a dirty secret from the judge's past to pressure him into dismissing the case.

Harrison Ford as the government prosecutor who finds himself on trial for murder in *Presumed Innocent. (Warner Bros., Inc.)*

Timothy L. Hall

The foundation of American democracy traditionally holds the value in the confidence and consent of the people as the primary basis for justice.

The governmental system that deals with the nature of crime in society, as well as analyzing the social agencies and formal processes, has come to be known as the criminal justice system. The word "system" implies an integrated process that works to control crime. Some scholars consider criminal justice to be more of a process than a coordinated system working together to control and prevent crime and prefer the term "criminal justice process." However, the term "criminal justice system" has become accepted when discussing the process of handling crime through the legal channels to arrest, convict, and punish criminal offenders.

Framework of the Criminal Justice System

The basic framework of the American criminal justice system is found in the legislative, judicial, and executive branches of government. The legislative branch defines the laws determining criminal conduct and establishing criminal penalties. Appellate courts interpret laws and review their constitutionality. The executive branch has administrative responsibility for criminal justice agencies and program planning. Also, public agencies such as police departments and parole boards function as parts of the government and are established to implement specific legislation.

All three branches of government generally work together to direct the criminal justice system. The legislative branch is not completely independent of the executive branch, nor is the judiciary branch independent of the other two branches of government. For example, if a legislature passes a criminal statute making conviction for possession of a handgun a mandatory prison sentence, both the judiciary and executive branches are involved in the law's implementation and influence the criminal justice system. A gun law may be the product of the executive branch, requiring legislative approval and eventually judicial review.

The criminal justice system has three separately organized components: law enforcement, the courts, and corrections. Some scholars consider the juvenile justice system to be a fourth component of the criminal justice system. The primary reason for this is that juvenile offenders are handled in noncriminal procedures. Terms from civil law, and not from criminal law, are used when juveniles are accused of criminal offenses. The philosophy of the juvenile justice system is completely different from that of the adult system. Since the creation of the first juvenile system by the Illinois legislature in 1899, the philosophy of juvenile justice has been to "save the child." In contrast, the goals of the adult criminal justice system have been either to punish or to rehabilitate offenders.

Each of the three components of the criminal justice system—law enforcement, the courts, and corrections—has distinct tasks. However, these components are not independent of one another. What each one does and how it operates have direct bearings on the work of the other components. For example, courts can deal with only those whom the police arrest, and correctional institutions handle only those who are sentenced to incarceration by the courts. Moreover, the successful reform of prisoners by correctional institutions determines whether the offenders may again come into contact with law-enforcement officers and influence the sentences judges pass. In addition, law-enforcement activities are scrutinized by the courts, and court decisions establish law-enforcement procedures.

The concept that the agencies of justice form a system has become increasingly popular among academicians, practitioners, and other professionals involved in the criminal justice field. The term, theoretically, refers to interrelationships among all the agencies concerned with the prevention of crime in society. Generally, it has become acceptable to some students of the criminal justice system to assume that if a change occurs in one of the major criminal justice components, that change will affect the other components. This approach implies that coordinating of policies and procedures occurs among the various components composing the system.

The various elements of the criminal justice system—law enforcement, courts, and corrections—are all related, but only to the extent that they are influenced by each others' policies and procedures. They are not well coordinated. Adjectives such as "fragmented," "divided," and "splintered" are often used to describe the criminal justice system.

Criminal justice is a field of study, an interrelated system of agencies, and a system that involves moving offenders from the arrest stage to the release stage from a correctional institution. The goals of the system may be broken down to two basic categories: theoretical and practical. Theoretical goals include retribution, deterrence, incapacitation, and rehabilitation. Practical goals include crime prevention, diversion of offenders from the criminal justice system, fairness in handling offenders, and efficiency in criminal justice operations.

Law Enforcement

The functions and goals of the different components of criminal justice all differ from one another. The law-enforcement component consists of all police agencies at the federal, state, and local levels. Included at the local level are county and municipal agencies. Law-enforcement agencies are part of the executive branches of government and work toward deterring and preventing crime. Their mission is to reduce crime or to eliminate the opportunities for criminal acts.

The police have the function to apprehend and arrest criminal law violators. They are responsible for investigating crimes, collecting and preserving evidence, and preparing criminal cases for prosecution. The police play an important role from the investigative phases of criminal acts through the arrests and prosecution of cases against offenders. Without sufficient evidence collected by the police, prosecutors will not prosecute cases against suspects charged with crimes.

Another function of police is protection of life and property. The strategies of this have included crime prevention, crime repression, apprehension of criminals to protect society, and the performance of specialized services to maintain public safety.

Law enforcement functions at all three levels of government—local, state, and federal. In 2005, there were approximately 18,000 local police agencies in the United States. They vary in size from a single police officer to the approximately 40,000 officers of the New York City Police Department. Most police officers serve as patrol car

officers; in some instances, they walk beats. The largest departments contain many specialized sections. These may include investigation units, planning units, drug units, juvenile units, traffic units, and SWAT teams.

Several counties in the United States have established county police departments to police unincorporated areas of the county. County police departments are given law-enforcement duties when local sheriff's departments have limited jurisdiction. Among the best-known county police departments are those of Maryland's Baltimore County and New York's Nassau and Suffern Counties. All three are counties with urban populations of sufficient size and resources to provide full law-enforcement services.

State constitutions generally provide that sheriffs are the chief law-enforcement officers of counties. Services provided by sheriffs' offices vary from county to county and often from state to state. Some sheriffs may have virtually no fixed responsibilities at all, or they can be responsible for a full range of law-enforcement services.

The federal government's role in law enforcement evolved during the twentieth century. Until the 1960's, the federal government emphasized that federal law-enforcement agencies should concentrate on enforcing federal laws. In 1968, the U.S. Congress passed the Omnibus Crime Control and Safe Streets Act, which was designed to provide resources to local law enforcement for equipment, training, and personnel. Local law-enforcement officers are now often incorporated into federal task forces directed by the Drug Enforcement Agency and Federal Bureau of Investigation.

There are approximately fifty federal law-enforcement agencies. Most of these agencies have specific powers and their investigative powers are specified by federal legislation. In 2002, several federal investigative agencies were placed under the new Department of Homeland Security.

State Courts

The second criminal justice component, the court system, includes those judicial agencies at all levels of government. The courts ensure that the accused receive fair and impartial trials un-

Criminal Justice Process

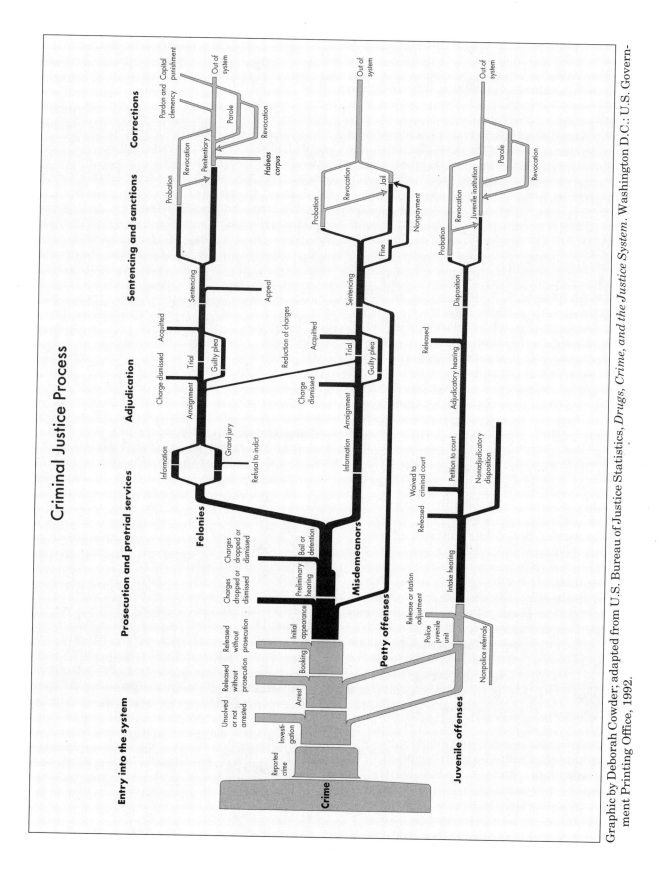

Graphic by Deborah Cowder; adapted from U.S. Bureau of Justice Statistics, *Drugs, Crime, and the Justice System.* Washington D.C.: U.S. Government Printing Office, 1992.

der the relevant laws of the jurisdictions in which they are charged with criminal offenses. There two basic types of courts: trial courts and appellate courts. All criminal crimes take place in trial courts.

The names of the state trial courts differ from state to state. In Kansas, for example, they are called district courts. In Pennsylvania, they are called courts of common pleas. The federal court system calls its trial courts district courts. In jurisdictions, trial courts have the responsibility of determining by the evidence presented whether defendants should be convicted of crimes. The trial courts review all evidence presented by prosecutors and consider its relevance and admissibility, while examining and reviewing the circumstances surrounding the crimes.

The trial courts have the responsibility of protecting the rights of accused offenders. They review the actions of the law-enforcement agencies to ensure that the police have not violated the constitutional rights of the accused. Upon conviction, the trial courts examine the backgrounds of the defendants and consider sentencing alternatives. Since the trial courts have a duty to protect their communities and repress criminal behavior, they have the task of imposing specific penalties. When imposing penalties, the trial courts usually take into consideration the circumstances of the crimes, the characters of the offenders, and the potential threats that the offenders may pose to public safety.

Federal Courts

Article III of the U.S. Constitution provides that "the judicial power of the United States shall be vested in one Supreme court and in such inferior courts as the Congress may from time to time ordain and establish." The United States has a "dual court system" meaning that there is one federal court and fifty state courts. The fifty-one court systems are independent of one another and are not hierarchically related, except for the fact that the constitutional decisions of the U.S. Supreme Court are binding on both state and federal courts at all levels.

The U.S. Supreme Court is the highest court in the country. Although it can conduct ordinary trials, it functions primarily as appeals court. The Court hears cases appealed from either the fed-

eral court of appeals or from the highest courts of appeal of the individual states. Below the Supreme Court are thirteen U.S. courts of appeals, each of which handles appeal from its own designated region of the country or its territories. These courts hear appeals from federal district courts, the trial courts of the federal government. The district courts conduct trials in ninety-four districts scattered throughout the United States and its territories.

Most states have appeals courts comparable to the U.S. Supreme Court. Their various names include Court of Appeals, Supreme Court of Appeals, and Supreme Judicial Court. Below the states' highest courts of appeals lie intermediate courts of appeals and trial courts.

Cases generally enter the federal and state judicial systems at the trial court level. In these courts, defendants are either convicted or held to be innocent. Losers in the cases may appeal the verdicts to the appeals court. Appeals courts do not re-evaluate the evidence presented in trial courts. Instead, they determine whether errors of law have been made and provide remedies for prejudicial errors. The federal and state court system merges at the Supreme Court of the United States. The Supreme Court reviews only claims and defenses found in the U.S. Constitution or laws enacted under its authority.

Corrections

Corrections, the third component of the criminal justice system, comprises the executive agencies of the federal, state, and local government that are responsible both directly and indirectly for housing and controlling persons convicted of crimes. The first duty of corrections is to maintain prisons, jails, and halfway houses. The purpose of corrections is to provide protection for law-abiding citizens by isolating criminal offenders in secure facilities. The confinement of offenders prevents them from committing further crimes.

At various periods in the history of American corrections, consideration has been given to reforming offenders. Reforming offenders consists of providing services that will assist them to be released and returned to society to lead law-abiding lives. The trial courts also encourage crime deterrence by incarcerating convicted of-

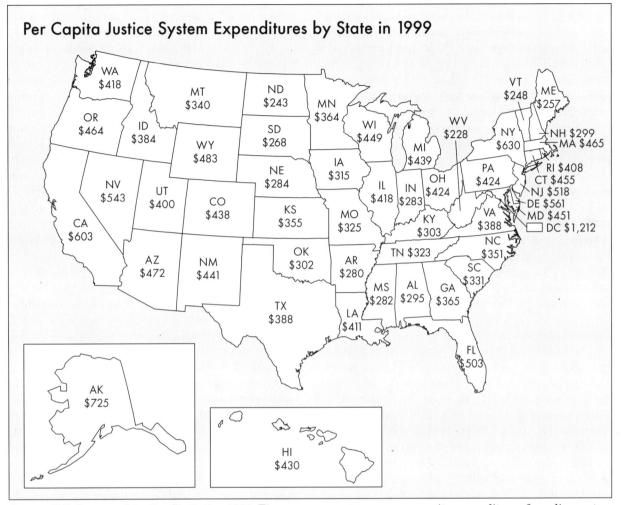

Per Capita Justice System Expenditures by State in 1999

WA $418
MT $340
ND $243
MN $364
VT $248
ME $257
OR $464
ID $384
WY $483
SD $268
WI $449
WV $228
NY $630
NH $299
MA $465
NV $543
UT $400
CO $438
NE $284
IA $315
MI $439
PA $424
RI $408
CT $455
CA $603
KS $355
IL $418
IN $283
OH $424
NJ $518
DE $561
MD $451
DC $1,212
AZ $472
NM $441
MO $325
KY $303
VA $388
NC $351
TN $323
SC $331
OK $302
AR $280
MS $282
AL $295
GA $365
TX $388
LA $411
FL $503

AK $725

HI $430

Source: U.S. Bureau of Justice Statistics, 2002. Figures represent average per capita expenditures for police protection, judicial and legal systems, and corrections. Figures are rounded off to the nearest dollar. Per capita expenditure for federal judicial system in 1999 was $442.10.

fenders. This act may deter potential criminal offenders from violating the law by the threat of the loss of their freedom of movement.

The federal government's Bureau of Prisons was established in 1930, under the Department of Justice. Facilities within the federal system consist of correctional institutions, detention centers, medical centers, prison camps, metropolitan corrections centers, and penitentiaries.

All fifty states maintain their own corrections systems. State departments of corrections generally divide their facilities according to their levels of security: minimum, medium, and maximum. Large states, such as New York, Texas, and California, operate a wide variety of units, encompassing all levels of security and beyond. Smaller states generally have fewer and less-specialized facilities.

Jails are another type of corrections facility that are used for temporary detentions at the local level. Depending upon the jurisdiction, jails may be called lockups, workhouses, detention centers, or stockades. Most jails are overcrowded. They usually employ minimal staff, who are usually poorly paid and poorly trained. These limitations can result in giving inadequate attention to inmate needs and the mistreatment of the inmates by the jailers.

An important part of the corrections component is community-based corrections, which involve activities and programs within local communities. Emphasis in community-based corrections programs is on rehabilitation rather than punishment. Rehabilitation may include education, employment, and social services. Community-based corrections sometimes include diversion programs that remove offenders from the direct application of the criminal law process. Criminal proceedings are stopped in favor of noncriminal dispositions.

Probation and parole are other forms of community-based corrections. Probation is a conditional release from a prison upon conviction of a crime provided the probationers follow the guidelines established by the court. Parole provides for prison inmates to be released early, then follow the guidelines established by their parole boards.

Juvenile Justice

The fourth component of criminal justice deals primarily with juveniles who have not reached the age of majority. Because of their age, juveniles are deemed to have a special status. The philosophy of the juvenile justice system holds that children should be treated in ways that protect them and correct their misbehavior.

The state of Illinois established the first juvenile court system in 1899. Under Illinois law, all children were placed under one jurisdiction. The juvenile court was given jurisdiction over dependent, neglected, and delinquent children. The first juvenile court was established in Cook County, which included the city of Chicago. All juveniles under the age of sixteen alleged to be delinquents came under the jurisdiction of the juvenile courts, which were created by the legislatures as courts of limited jurisdiction.

Illinois's juvenile courts were designed to protect and correct the inappropriate behavior of juvenile offenders. These courts were to provide protective services, which included placing youthful offenders with families that would function as surrogate parents. The intent of the Illinois legislature was for juvenile court settings to be informal and for proceedings to function in a civil manner rather than in a criminal-court manner. The hope was that humane judges would function as substitute parents who would prescribe and apply individual treatment based on the needs of the children and the communities.

Juvenile courts differ from adult criminal courts in several ways. First, their judges are assigned to handle juvenile cases. Also, records of juvenile courts are separated from those of adult criminal court; juvenile court records are confidential. Juvenile courts employ more informal court procedures than adult courts, and their courtrooms are physically separated from courtrooms used in adult cases. In theory, juvenile courts do not consider juveniles defendants or criminals and regard them as children in need of care, protection, and rehabilitation.

In contrast to procedures in adult criminal court, juvenile courts do not readily recognize due process for the juvenile defendants. Juvenile courts have the power to punish juveniles for specific offenses and the responsibility to determine if the juveniles are immoral, wayward, in need of supervision, incorrigible, or living in unfit homes.

The chief objective of juvenile courts is to promote the rehabilitation of juvenile offenders and to assist them to become useful citizens. To achieve this goal, judges are appointed specifically to deal with juvenile cases, and probation officers are hired to supervise the juveniles. Juvenile court facilities are separated from adult courthouses and usually offer physical environments that are less severe and threatening. Juvenile judges sit behind desks rather than benches, and terms such as "intake hearing," "petition," and "adjudication inquiry" are used in place of "hearing," "arrest," and "arraignment."

Michael J. Palmiotto

Further Reading

Champion, Dean John. *Criminal Justice in the United States.* 2d ed. Chicago: Nelson Hall, 1997. General survey of the modern legal system of the United States, with an extensive treatment of juvenile crime and alternatives to incarceration.

_____. *The Juvenile Justice System: Delinquency, Processing, and the Law.* 4th ed. Upper Saddle River, N.J.: Prentice-Hall, 2003. Broad overview of the treatment of juveniles in the justice system. Examines juvenile legal rights and court decisions regarding adjudication, disposition, and sanctions.

Cole, George F., and Christopher Smith. *American System of Criminal Justice*. 10th ed. Belmont, Calif: Thomson/Wadsworth, 2004. Standard textbook that covers all aspects of criminal justice in the United States.

Inciardi, James A. *Criminal Justice: 2004-2005 Update*. Boston: McGraw-Hill, 2005. Comprehensive overview of the criminal justice system: law enforcement, courts, and corrections, along with up-to-date statistics and major court decisions and important changes in the criminal justice system.

Travis, Lawrence F., III. *Introduction to Criminal Justice*. 4th ed. Cincinnati: Anderson Publishing, 2001. Another excellent textbook covering all aspects of the criminal justice system.

See also Appellate process; Arrest; Bail system; Counsel, right to; Court types; Criminal justice in U.S. history; Criminal procedure; Criminal prosecution; Criminology; Judges; Judicial system, U.S.; Justice; Justice Department, U.S.; Juvenile justice system; Law enforcement; Police; Prison and jail systems; Special weapons and tactics teams (SWAT); State police; Women in law enforcement and corrections.

Criminal law

Definition: Body of law that defines criminal offenses and sets out appropriate punishments for convicted offenders

Criminal justice issues: Law codes; law-enforcement organization; prosecution; punishment

Significance: Criminal law sets out formal codifications and definitions of crimes against which to measure actions.

Crimes are generally regarded as offenses against society, even though they are often committed against single persons or small groups. Nevertheless, the fundamental concept assumes that criminal acts injure society as a whole. Therefore, the state, acting as the injured party, begins the process of bringing offenders to justice in criminal proceedings. Violations of the criminal law can result in the imposition of punishments that express society's outrage or displeasure with the offensive behaviors.

Criminal law is said to have numerous goals: punishment of wrongdoers, deterrence of future criminal acts by making wrongdoers examples to others, retribution justifying punishment on the ground that it is correct to inflict pain on criminals in order to prevent future crimes, rehabilitation aiming to change criminals' behavior so that they will conform to the law, and incapacitation of criminals through confinement. Despite these goals, studies have indicated that many convicted criminals are recidivists, or repeat offenders.

Elements of a Crime

Every statutory crime has three elements: a wrongful act, or *actus reus*; an evil intent, or *mens rea*; and causation. At trial, prosecution must prove the presence of each element of a crime separately and beyond a reasonable doubt in order to convict a wrongdoer of a crime.

For an act to be wrongful, it must be willful and not an involuntary action, such as a physical spasm or an action undertaken while sleepwalking or under hypnosis. A failure to act in a situation in which one has a legal duty to act may also constitute a wrongful act. Examples might include parents who neglect the proper care of their children or a lifeguard who does not attempt to rescue a drowning swimmer. The duty to act may also be imposed by statute, such as a citizen's duty to file an income tax return or register with the selective service. Failure to perform moral duties does not constitute criminal omission.

Possession offenses constitute an exception to the requirement of a physical act. For example, a person found with a controlled substance, such as cocaine, in a pocket may not be engaging in any physical act; however, the law would treat the fact of possession of the illegal substance as the equivalent of a wrongful act.

The principle of *mens rea* recognizes the mental component to crime. It focuses on the intent of wrongdoers at the moments the crimes are committed, rather than the mental state of the wrongdoers at some earlier or later times. People rarely express intent overtly. Therefore, the law determines intent by indirect or circumstantial evidence. Intent is inferred from actions in the absence of direct observation. *Mens rea* is said to be present when people should know that the consequences of their actions are likely to result in serious bodily injury or death, even if such consequences are not part of their original intent. A legal presumption exists that people intend the natural and probable consequences of their actions. For example, if a person shoots a loaded gun into a crowd of people intending to frighten them and someone is killed, the law supplies the *mens rea* to convict the wrongdoer.

The third element of criminal activity is causation. Clear links must be established between wrongful acts and their resulting harm. Criminal liability attaches to conduct that is determined to be the proximate, or legal, cause of the resulting harm. A person who sets in motion a chain of events that eventually results in harm may be the indirect cause of the harm. There must also be concurrence of events in order for an action to constitute a crime. For example, a person who mistakenly takes another person's umbrella and leaves his own in its place commits a wrongful act; however, there is no wrongful intent, so no crime is committed. Some scholars regard concurrence as a fourth element of criminal activity.

Classifications of Crime

Crimes are classified as felonies and misdemeanors. Felonies are serious crimes punishable by imprisonment of more than one year. They generally include murder, rape, aggravated assault, robbery, burglary, and arson. Misdemeanors constitute crimes punishable by prison sentences of less than one year or incarceration in local jails. It should be noted that precise classifications vary among different jurisdictions.

The common law classified crimes as either *mala in se* or *mala prohibita*. The former are offenses that are intrinsically bad; the latter are acts that are considered criminal only because the law defines ("prohibits") them as such. An example of the latter would be a parking violation that is illegal but not evil. Petty offenses or violations are punishable by imposition of fines.

Parties to Crime

The doctrine of complicity, or being a party to a crime, establishes the conditions under which more than one person incurs liability before, dur-

ing, and after the commission of criminal activity. At common law there were four parties to crime. principals in the first degree actually commit the crime. Principals in the second degree are aiders and abettors who are present when the crimes are committed; they might include lookouts, getaway-car drivers, and co-conspirators. Accessories before the fact are aiders and abettors who are not present when the crimes are committed, such as persons who provide weapons used in the crimes. Accessories after the fact are persons who give aid and comfort to known criminals, such a person who harbors a fugitive from justice.

In common law, only after principals were convicted could the government try their accomplices. Modern statutes have removed those distinctions by defining accomplices (accessories before and during the crime) principals. However, most jurisdictions retain the common-law accessory-after-the-fact category for complicity following crimes. Courts have established that mere presence of a person at the scene of a crime is generally insufficient to establish guilt.

Based on the relationships between persons who commit crimes and others, the principle of vicarious liability applies primarily to business relationships, such as employer-employee or buyer-seller. Vicarious liability generally punishes the principals (employers) for the wrongful acts of their agents (employees) acting within the scope of their employment. States have occasionally imposed vicarious liability on parents for minor children and on owners of cars for those who drive them.

Inchoate Crimes

Certain acts are preliminary or incomplete crimes that may involve attempts, conspiracies, and solicitation. Each aspect of inchoate crimes is considered a separate offense, and each has its own elements. All share the *mens rea* of specific intent to commit a crime and the *actus reus* taken to fulfill the crime, but each falls short of completion of the crime. Attempt constitutes the intent to commit a crime and some overt act taken in pursuance of the intention that falls short of completion of the crime. The law must distinguish between mere preparation to commit a crime—which is not in itself a criminal attempt—and some steps taken toward completion of the crime that fall short of actually completing the crime.

If a crime ultimately is accomplished, the inchoate crime of attempt merges with the completed crime, so that the defendant is tried only for the greater offense. For example, one cannot be tried for attempted murder of a person and murder of the same person. The former, inchoate, offense merges with the latter crime.

Conspiracy is an agreement between two or more persons for the purpose of committing an unlawful act or doing a lawful act by an unlawful means. The agreement does not have to be formal, and the parties do not have to know one another. Conspiracies are of two kinds: wheel, or hub and spoke, and chain conspiracies. In the former, one or more defendants participate in every transaction. They constitute the "hub" of the wheel. Each other member of the conspiracy participates in only one transaction and constitutes a spoke of the wheel. Chain conspiracies usually involve the distribution of some commodity such as illegal drugs. Every participant handles the same commodity at different distribution points. Failure to convict one party in the chain does not prevent conviction of other parties.

Solicitation is a command, urging, or request to a third person inducing that person to commit a crime. Criminal solicitation does not have to result in a completed criminal act. The law considers those who urge others to commit crimes dangerous enough to warrant punishment, even if the crimes are not actually committed.

Defenses to Crime

Defendants can avoid criminal liability in certain instances. For example, they may have alibis and contend that others have committed the crimes for which they are charged. In defenses of justification, defendants admit their responsibility for the wrongful acts but argue that what they have done was right under the circumstances. In defenses of excuse, defendants admit what they have done was wrong but argue that they were not responsible for their actions under the circumstances.

Justifications include self-defense, which justifies the use of force only when defenders are resisting unlawful force used against them by aggressors or reasonably believe that they are in imminent danger of unlawful force. Moreover, defenders can use only the amount of force they reasonably believe necessary to repel the attacks; excessive force is not permitted. Defense of others includes third persons. Nearly all states authorize the use of force to protect one's own home and property. However, this authorization does not include the use of deadly force. Execution of public duties is another justification. It applies to persons such as government executioners, soldiers killing during wartime, and police officers using force to make arrests.

Excuses include duress and brainwashing situations, in which persons commit crimes because they are coerced to do so. Such coercion negates both *actus reus* and *mens rea*. Involuntary intoxication—which occurs when persons do not know they are taking intoxicants or do so under duress—is also an excuse to criminal liability. Voluntary intoxication is not.

Mistakes of fact can excuse criminal liability if the mistakes are honest and reasonable. A mistake of law does not excuse liability under the principle that ignorance of the law is not an excuse. Immaturity has also excused criminal liability. At common law a presumption existed that people under age seven lack the mental capacity to commit crime because they cannot form *mens rea*. Under common law, everyone over the age of fourteen was presumed to have mental capacity, and those between ages seven and fourteen were presumed incapable. About half the states in the United States adopted the common-law approach but altered specific ages. Other states have granted juvenile courts exclusive jurisdiction up to a certain age, generally between fifteen and sixteen.

Entrapment is another excuse for criminal liability but is often misunderstood. Entrapment excuses crime when law-enforcement officers lead citizens to commit crimes. If, however, a person would have committed the crime in any case, the defense of entrapment does not apply.

A final excuse to criminal liability is insanity. Four primary tests determine insanity: the right-wrong test or M'Naghten rule, stating that defendants did not appreciate the nature and quality of their acts, or, if they did, they did not know that their acts were wrong. The Durham rule, or product test, used only in New Hampshire, states that

Photograph that John W. Hinckley, Jr., took of himself some time before he tried to assassinate President Ronald Reagan in 1981. During his trial, Hinckley's defense argued that he was mentally ill and therefore not responsible for his actions. *(AP/Wide World Photos)*

acts that are products of mental disease or defect excuse crime. With the irresistible impulse test, defendants cannot controls their conduct, and under the Model Penal Code or substantial capacity test, defendants must lack substantial mental capacity, either to appreciate the criminality of their conduct or to conform their conduct to the law. Diminished capacity is used in a few jurisdictions, and guilty-but-mentally-ill pleas are allowed in others. The latter was the defense pleaded by John Hinckley, Jr., who attempted to assassinate President Ronald Reagan in 1981.

Crimes Against Persons

Homicide, or the taking of the life of another person, is divided into murder and voluntary and involuntary manslaughter. Premeditated, or first-degree, murder is the most serious form of homicide. Most jurisdictions include in second-degree murder all homicides that are neither first-degree murder nor manslaughter. Pennsylvania has an additional category: Killings that occur during the commission of felonies are classified as second-degree, or felony, murder. All other murders constitute third-degree murder.

Manslaughter is divided into voluntary and involuntary. Voluntary manslaughter is the intentional killing of another under circumstances constituting provocation, during the heat of passion without time to cool off. A commonly cited example of voluntary manslaughter is that of a husband who catches his wife in the act of adultery and kills her lover. Involuntary manslaughter is criminal homicide in which the killers do not intend to cause the deaths of their victims. The deaths result from reckless or negligent legal acts or the commission of illegal acts. Negligent homicide is an unintentional killing in which the actors should know that they are creating substantial risks of death by engaging in conduct that deviates grossly from the norm.

Another crime against persons, rape is sexual intercourse by force or threat and without consent. Statutory rape is carnal knowledge of a person under the age of consent—which age varies by jurisdiction. Battery is a harmful or offensive touching and covers a wide spectrum. Battery requires some injury, at least of an emotional nature in most jurisdictions. Assault is the fearful apprehension of an imminent battery. Words alone do not constitute assault; they must be accompanied by threatening gestures. False imprisonment is forcible detention or confinement that interferes substantially with the victims' liberty. Kidnapping requires a carrying away or transportation of victims. Modern statutes in some states have removed the transportation requirement, replacing it with the requirement that the kidnappers intend to confine or significantly restrain their victims in secret.

Crimes Against Habitation and Property

At common law, burglary was defined as the breaking into and entering of the dwelling place of another at nighttime with intent to commit a felony. Over time, the requirements have become modified, so that the element of "breaking" was satisfied simply by an unauthorized entry or surreptitious remaining. The concept of "dwelling place" was broadened to include the dwelling structures, as well as garages and yards. Vehicles are also included in many burglary statutes.

The "nighttime" requirement no longer exists, and the "felony" requirement has been replaced by an intent to commit a "crime." Arson is the burning or setting on fire of structures and includes the use of explosives and scorching. The structures do not have to be completely destroyed for the crime to be considered arson.

The common law crimes against property included larceny, embezzlement, false pretenses, receiving stolen property, robbery, and extortion. Many modern statutes have grouped the first three of these under the umbrella term "theft." Larceny included the wrongful taking and carrying away of the property of others with intent permanently to deprive the rightful owners of their possessions. Larceny was limited to movable objects and also excluded stocks, bonds, checks, and negotiable instruments. Modern statutes include virtually all property within their scope.

Embezzlement is the retention of the property of others by those already lawfully in possession of it, such as bank tellers handling customers' money, parking lot attendant handling other people's cars, and dry cleaners handling customers' clothes. False pretenses requires obtaining the property of another through false misrepresentation of a material past or present fact.

Receiving stolen property requires that property taken or acquired by deception comes into the receiver's control for at least a short time period and also an intent on the part of its receivers permanently to dispossess the rightful possessors. Robbery is the taking and carrying away of others' property from their persons, or in their presence, through force of threat or force with intent permanently to deprive them of their property. Actual force is not always required; threatened force is sufficient. Most states have divided robbery into degrees according to the injury committed or the force or threat used. The force must be imminent or immediate. Extortion, in contrast, involves threats of future harm. The consolidated theft statutes eliminate the need to decide the nature of the action in order to distinguish among larceny, embezzlement, and false pretenses. Instead, the offenses deal with the social problem of criminal property misappropriation and group the offenses together.

Marcia J. Weiss

Further Reading

LaFave, Wayne. *Criminal Law*. 4th ed. Belmont, Calif.: West Group, 2003. Detailed treatise on criminal law with lengthy explanations and reference to cases.

Loewy, Arnold H. *Criminal Law in a Nutshell*. 4th ed. Belmont, Calif.: West Group, 2003. Concise summary of modern American criminal law.

Reid, Sue Titus. *Criminal Law*. 6th ed. New York: McGraw-Hill, 2003. College text containing edited cases highlighting timely issues.

Samaha, Joel. *Criminal Law*. 8th ed. Belmont, Calif.: Wadsworth, 2004. Clearly written college text containing criminal law principles and edited legal cases illustrating the principles.

Schmalleger, Frank M. *Criminal Law Today: An Introduction with Capstone Cases*. 2d ed. Upper Saddle River, N.J.: Pearson Education, 2001. Basic college text containing an overview, opening stories, and illustrations of the law in practice.

See also Accomplices and accessories; Attempt to commit a crime; Common law; Constitution, U.S.; Crime; Criminal intent; Criminology; Defenses to crime; Due process of law; Felonies; Ignorance of the law; Inchoate crimes; *Mala in se* and *mala prohibita*; *Mens rea*; Misdemeanors; Proximate cause; Strict liability offenses; United States Code; Vicarious liability.

Criminal liability

Definition: Accountability under criminal law
Criminal justice issues: Defendants; prosecution
Significance: Criminal liability is the foundation upon which the criminal justice system is based.

The commission of crimes without legal justification or excuses, criminal liability is responsibility under criminal law. In contrast to civil law—which concerns the rights and responsibilities of private citizens—criminal law is designed to maintain the safety and order of the state and is that part of law that codifies offenses committed against society. Criminal law carries within it the possible sanction of loss of freedom, incarcerating those who are held responsible for violating it, in addition to fines and other penalties.

Crimes have main parts: mental and physical. For crimes to occur, criminal law defines such mental elements as intention, knowledge, recklessness, and gross criminal negligence. It also defines the physical elements of crimes as the actual actions offenders complete, or attempt to complete, while committing crimes. The mental elements together constitute criminal intent or culpability (*mens rea*), but are not considered criminal unless they are coupled with actual acts or omissions that are defined as crimes.

To be held criminally liable, one must either voluntarily perpetrate a crime or fail to perform an act that one is legally mandated to perform. For example, assault may be defined by the law as an intentional or reckless (mental element) injury (physical element) perpetrated on another person. The perpetrator can be prosecuted criminally—or held criminally liable—for the violation of the law.

An example of a criminal act omission might be a parent or guardian's failure to protect a child from physical, mental, or moral harm. Parents and guardians who refuse to provide needed medical care for the children in their care can be prosecuted criminally—or held criminally liable—for violating criminal law.

Criminal liability differs from vicarious liability. The latter holds one responsible for the actions of another and is primarily defined by civil law. Similarly, criminal liability differs from strict liability, a civil law concept that concerns itself with crimes without the intent or culpability (*mens rea*) that are required elements of criminal law. Criminal liability focuses on the actors who violate the law.

Jennifer C. Gibbs

Further Reading

Brody, David C., James R. Acker, and Wayne A. Logan. *Criminal Law*. Gaithersburg, Md.: Aspen Publishers, 2001.

Garner, Bryan A., ed. *Black's Law Dictionary*. 8th ed. St. Paul, Minn.: Thomson/West, 2004.

Ross, Darrell. *Civil Liability in Criminal Justice*. 3d ed. Cincinnati: Anderson, 2003.

See also Attempt to commit a crime; Crime; Criminal intent; Excuses and justifications; Ignorance of the law; Immunity from prosecution; Lesser-included offenses; *Mens rea*; Sports and crime; Strict liability offenses; Trespass; Vicarious liability.

Criminal procedure

Definition: Stages and points at which particular decisions are made in the criminal justice process that are mandated by statutes and constitutional judicial decisions

Criminal justice issues: Arrest and arraignment; probation and pretrial release; trial procedures

Significance: The procedural steps in the processing of criminal cases are designed to ensure that correct decisions are made about guilt and innocence and that authorities respect the rights of criminal defendants.

Every country has the authority to decide how it will determine which individuals will be punished for committing crimes. In some systems, the police or the army may have complete authority to identify and punish wrongdoers. The individual suspect may have no ability to question the law-enforcement officers' decisions or swift imposition of punishment. In the United States, however, criminal procedure has been established to ensure that only guilty defendants receive punishment and to protect the public from abusive practices that police and prosecutors might employ in investigating, convicting, and punishing suspected criminals.

Historical Background

American criminal procedure, like other aspects of law, traces its roots to legal practices in England. The practice of using trials as a procedural mechanism to determine guilt and innocence began in England. Originally, England used physical trials to identify guilty offenders. Suspects were forced to place their hands in boiling oil, for example, or fight in a public duel with the assumption that God would protect the innocent but injure the guilty during such events. Eventually, the church discontinued its sponsorship of such events, and England gradually shifted to the use of trials involving the presentation of testimony and the use of witnesses and jurors. Juries assumed an important role by protecting the public against abusive decisions by prosecutors. If there was insufficient evidence of guilt presented by the prosecutor, then the jury could acquit the defendant and the defendant would go free. The American jury trial, a key component of criminal procedure, developed from these English origins.

The U.S. Constitution

The first ten amendments to the Constitution, commonly known as the Bill of Rights, contain several provisions that mandate procedures to be followed in the investigation, prosecution, and punishment of criminal offenders. The Fourth Amendment protects people against "unreasonable searches and seizures." It also requires that search warrants and arrest warrants be supported by probable cause and that they specifically describe places to be searched and persons or things to be seized.

The Fifth Amendment requires indictment by a grand jury before serious charges are prosecuted. The amendment also provides protection against compelled self-incrimination and the possibility of being tried twice for the same offense. The Sixth Amendment provides rights to speedy and public trials by impartial juries, as well as the right to be informed of charges, to obtain relevant documents and witnesses, to be confronted by adverse witnesses, and to have the assistance of a defense attorney. The Eighth Amendment prohibits excessive bail and fines and bans cruel and unusual punishments. The Fourteenth Amendment, which was added to the Constitution in 1868, provides additional rights to due process and equal protection of the laws. All of these provisions help shape the procedures used in crimi-

The U.S. Constitution and its amendments guarantee defendants a number of important rights in criminal trials, including the right to have the assistance of defense attorneys. *(Brand-X Pictures)*

nal cases by defining suspects' rights, limiting the authority of police, prosecutors, and judges, and mandating elements that must be incorporated into the legal process.

The provisions of the Bill of Rights originally applied only in federal court cases concerning defendants accused of violating criminal laws enacted by Congress. From the 1920's through the 1960's, the U.S. Supreme Court made many decisions that incorporated individual provisions of the Bill of Rights into the due process clause of the Fourteenth Amendment and made them applicable in state criminal cases. The only federal constitutional right concerning criminal procedure that has not been incorporated is the Fifth Amendment right to be indicted by a grand jury. State courts are not required by the Supreme Court to use grand juries, but many use such proceedings on their own. States are required to abide by all the other provisions of the Bill of Rights concerning criminal procedure.

State and Federal Criminal Justice System

The legislatures for each state have the authority to design procedures that will be used within their state courts to process the cases of criminal defendants. Congress possesses this authority with respect to the federal courts. In addition, all court systems must obey the U.S. Supreme Court's decisions that apply to them and mandate the use of certain procedures or respect for specific rights. State court systems must also obey the decisions of their own state supreme courts. The highest court in each state has the authority to interpret its state constitution and apply those decisions to the procedures used in processing criminal cases within that state. If legislatures want to change the kinds of procedures used within their own state's courts, they can enact reforms as long as those reforms respect the relevant provisions of the state and federal constitutions as interpreted by the state supreme court and the U.S. Supreme Court.

Because each state legislature and Congress possess the power to design procedures for the courts under their authority, there are differences in the criminal procedures used in different court systems. Although certain requirements of the U.S. Constitution that apply to all court systems, such as the use of defense attorneys and the availability of jury trials, provide common elements to all systems, other aspects of states' criminal procedure are quite different, especially with respect to preliminary proceedings.

Pretrial Proceedings

Immediately after an arrest is made by police officers, the individual arrested by the police is processed through the various steps of the state or federal court's criminal procedure. Two issues are decided shortly after arrest: first, whether the defendant will be released from custody on bail while the case is being processed; second, whether there is enough evidence to justify pursuing charges against the person arrested.

The process for setting bail varies from state to state and from county to county within states. If suspects are arrested for minor charges, the police may have the authority to release them after fingerprinting them, photographing them, and obtaining relevant personal information. Suspects may be released on their "own recognizance," which means that they do not have to post any amount of money with the police or court in order to gain release. The suspects merely sign promises to appear at scheduled court dates. They may also be required to post set amounts of money, which will be forfeited if they fail to appear in court. It is more common for bail to be set by judges in initial court hearings, and judges always handle bail decisions when suspects are charged with very serious crimes.

In some state constitutions, there is a right granted for each defendant to have bail set. Judges, however, will set a very high bail, perhaps even in the millions of dollars, if they do not want the person released while the case is being processed. In the federal courts and some states, the judge can deny bail by finding that the person would endanger the community if released or by deciding that no amount of money would guarantee that the person would return to court. In other states, suspects arrested for the most serious crimes, such as first-degree murder, may not be eligible for bail at all.

If a suspect is arrested through a decision by a police officer rather than through an arrest warrant issued by a judge upon the presentation of evidence, then the suspect is entitled to an initial hearing to make sure that evidence exists to support the arrest. The U.S. Supreme Court has interpreted the Fourth Amendment's prohibition on unreasonable seizures to require that initial hearings be held within forty-eight hours after a warrantless arrest (*County of Riverside v. McLaughlin*, 1991).

People who are arrested have a right to have an attorney represent them in court. The police must inform them of this right before any questioning takes place (*Miranda v. Arizona*, 1966), and defendants who are too poor to hire an attorney have a right to have an attorney provided for them by the government (*Gideon v. Wainwright*, 1963; *Argersinger v. Hamlin*, 1972). Attorneys need not be provided immediately after arrest if the police do not intend to question the suspect or if the suspect agrees to answer questions without an attorney present. Attorneys must be made available, however, to represent defendants at arraignments in which an initial plea is entered and at preliminary hearings in which a judge determines whether there is enough evidence to proceed with the case. Attorneys can also seek to have bail set or the amount of bail reduced by presenting arguments at a bail hearing.

At arraignments, the courts officially inform the suspects of the charges against them and give the suspects the opportunity to plead "guilty" or "not guilty." Few suspects plead guilty at felony arraignments because their attorneys have just begun to work for them, and even if they will plead guilty eventually, as most defendants do, their attorneys need time to develop plea-bargain proposals. It is more common for guilty pleas to be entered immediately in traffic courts or in misdemeanor cases, because defendants usually face only fines or probation and are anxious to get the cases resolved quickly. At preliminary hearings, prosecutors must present enough evidence to persuade a judge that sufficient grounds exist to proceed in a case against the defendant.

In some states, arraignments and preliminary hearings take place in lower level courts, often called municipal courts or district courts. After these initial proceedings, felony cases will be transferred to upper-level courts, often called superior courts, circuit courts, or courts of common pleas. Defendants frequently waive formal proceedings for arraignments and preliminary hearings because they are aware of the charges and they already know that enough evidence exists to move the cases forward.

Some states and the federal government use grand jury proceedings to make the final determination about whether sufficient evidence exists to prosecute a defendant on serious charges. Grand juries are composed of citizens drawn from the community who meet in secret proceedings to hear witness testimony and examine the prosecutor's other evidence to determine whether charges should be pursued. The suspect has no right to be present in the grand jury proceedings. Defense attorneys are barred from the courtroom when grand juries meet. If the grand jury believes that charges are justified, it issues an indictment against the defendant.

Defense Attorneys and Criminal Procedure

Beginning with the preliminary hearing, defense attorneys file motions in an effort to have evidence excluded or to learn more about the evidence possessed by the prosecutor. Motions provide the basis to protect the defendant's rights against unreasonable searches and seizures. The defense attorney often argues during the preliminary hearing and subsequent pretrial motion hearings that specific evidence should be excluded from trial because it was obtained in violation of the defendant's rights.

The defense attorney also often initiates plea negotiations with the prosecutor. More than 90 percent of defendants whose cases are carried forward past grand jury indictments or preliminary hearings eventually enter guilty pleas in exchange for agreements about what punishment will be imposed. Although felony defendants have a right to have their cases decided at trial under constitutional rules for criminal procedure, most defendants prefer to make a plea agreement. Such agreements frequently produce lighter punishments than those that might have been imposed after a trial. Defendants' guilty pleas may be entered at any point in the process, from the arraignment through the middle of a jury trial.

The Trial Process

Defendants who face felony charges are entitled to a jury trial. Many defendants choose to have a bench trial before a judge alone rather than a jury if their case is controversial or if they believe that a judge will be fairer or more understanding. Misdemeanor defendants are entitled to jury trials under some states' laws, but they may have only bench trials under the laws of other states. The U.S. Supreme Court has said that the Sixth Amendment's right to trial by jury applies only to serious charges (*Blanton v. North Las Vegas*, 1989).

Under the Supreme Court's interpretations of the Sixth Amendment right to an impartial jury and the Fourteenth Amendment right to equal protection, jurors must be drawn from a fair cross-section of the community, and jurors cannot be excluded because of their race or gender. Through a process called *voir dire*, the prosecutor and defense attorney question potential witnesses and ask the judge to exclude those who might be biased because of their attitudes or personal experiences.

Although the federal government and most states use twelve-member juries in criminal cases, many states use six- to eight-member juries for misdemeanor cases. Six states use six- or eight-member juries for felony cases. The Supreme Court has declared that six-member juries must reach unanimous verdicts (*Burch v. Louisiana*, 1979), but nonunanimous verdicts are permissible for convicting defendants before twelve-member juries if permitted under a state's laws (*Apodaca v. Oregon*, 1972).

At the trial stage of criminal procedure, the prosecutor and defense attorney present evidence, question witnesses, and raise objections to each other's evidence and arguments. Each attorney attempts to persuade the jury or judge (in a bench trial) about the defendant's guilt or innocence. A conviction requires a finding of guilt beyond a reasonable doubt. In considering whether the evidence presented by the prosecutor achieves that standard, jurors must follow the judge's instructions about how to interpret the relevant law and evidence. Throughout the trial, the judge must follow the relevant laws of procedure and evidence that govern the state or federal court in which the trial is being conducted. The relevant laws are created by the state legislature for state courts and by Congress for the federal courts, and then they are refined and clarified by decisions of appellate courts, such as the state supreme court and U.S. Supreme Court. Decisions by the U.S. Supreme Court guide trial judges with respect to constitutional rights, such as those concerning double jeopardy, compelled self-incrimination, and confrontation of adverse witnesses, that can arise in the context of a trial.

Post-trial Procedures

After the jury or judge reaches a verdict, a defendant who is found guilty will be sentenced by the trial judge. In some states, juries determine the sentence in death-penalty cases. Death-penalty cases have special hearings in which the judge or jury must consider aggravating and mitigating circumstances, which are any circumstances making the crime or criminal especially deserving or not deserving of execution. Every sentence imposed for a crime must follow the punishments established by the legislature for that crime. The sentence must not violate the Eighth Amendment's prohibitions against excessive fines and cruel and unusual punishments.

Convicted defendants have a right to appeal their convictions by filing legal actions in appellate courts. These legal actions allege that the trial judge made specific errors that violated relevant laws or the defendant's constitutional rights. In most states, such appeals go first to an intermediate appellate court, usually called the state court of appeals, and then may be pursued in the state supreme court. In twelve states, however, there is no intermediate appellate court, so appeals go directly to the state supreme court. A few states have special appellate courts that hear only criminal appeals. There is a right to counsel only for the first appeal (*Douglas v. California*, 1963).

Subsequent appeals may have to be prepared and presented by the convicted offenders unless they can hire attorneys, or unless the relevant state law provides assigned counsel for convicts beyond the first appeal. Unsuccessful appeals to state supreme courts can subsequently be filed in the U.S. Supreme Court, but the nation's highest court accepts very few cases for hearing.

Convicted offenders can also file writs of *habeas corpus*, a traditional legal action from English history that permits a person to seek release or a new trial through a claim of wrongful detention. In the American system, prisoners must be able to show that their federal constitutional rights were violated in the course of the case and conviction. Very few prisoners prevail in such actions, but several thousand *habeas corpus* petitions are filed in the federal courts each year.

Christopher E. Smith

Further Reading

Abraham, Henry. *Freedom and the Court*. 5th ed. New York: Oxford University Press, 1988. Broad history of criminal procedure in the United States.

Bodenhamer, David. *Fair Trial*. New York: Oxford University Press, 1992. Brief and readable perspective on the development of criminal procedure.

Decker, John. *Revolution to the Right: Criminal Procedure Jurisprudence During the Burger-Rehnquist Court Era*. New York: Garland, 1992. Collection of reviews of Supreme Court criminal procedure decisions during the 1970's and 1980's.

Del Carmen, Rolando V. *Criminal Procedure: Law and Practice*. 6th ed. Belmont, Calif.: Thomson/Wadsworth, 2004. Comprehensive and readable review of criminal procedure, including constitutional rights, that covers each stage of criminal procedure, with special attention given to Supreme Court cases.

Garcia, Alfredo. *The Sixth Amendment in Modern American Jurisprudence.* Westport, Conn.: Greenwood Press, 1992. Examination of the previous three decades of U.S. Supreme Court rulings in the Sixth Amendment—a period during which rights of defendants were eroded, according to Garcia.

Kamisar, Yale, Wayne R. LaFave, and Jerold H. Israel. *Modern Criminal Procedure: Cases, Comments, and Questions.* 6th ed. St. Paul, Minn.: West, 1986. Textbook providing deeper coverage of legal cases.

See also Appellate process; Arraignment; Bail system; Booking; Chain of custody; Common law; Criminal justice system; Defendants; Due process of law; Grand juries; Judicial system, U.S.; Jurisdiction of courts; Jury system; Miranda rights; Preliminary hearings; Preventive detention; Public defenders; Standards of proof.

Criminal prosecution

Definition: Area of legal practice that involves the charging and trying of persons for criminal offenses

Criminal justice issues: Courts; prosecution; trial procedures

Significance: Criminal prosecution, or the work of criminal prosecutors, is an integral part of the criminal justice system.

The U.S. criminal justice system is an adversarial system based on the model of two opposing sides presenting their best cases to an impartial fact finder—either a jury or a judge. The side presented by the government in an effort to prove beyond a reasonable doubt that defendants committed the offenses for which they have been charged is presented in criminal cases by the prosecution.

The work of criminal prosecution in the United States is wider than simply presenting a case to a fact finder. Criminal prosecutors sometimes assist law-enforcement authorities in the investigation of suspected crimes, assess the strength of evidence, and make critical decisions about whom—if anyone—to charge with criminal offenses and what charges to bring. They often present these charges to a grand jury in order to have the grand jury weigh the evidence of a suspected crime and—if it is sufficient—return an indictment, or a statement of charges. Prosecutors handle hearings and arguments in court following the formal institution of charges and deal with questions such as bail or the suppression of evidence under the exclusionary rule. The vast majority of criminal charges in the United States that result in convictions never go to trial but are resolved through plea bargaining.

The prosecutor, as the representative of the government's position in legal cases, is the principal player in this process. If a case goes to trial, the prosecutor tries it and attempts to convince the fact finder that the defendant is guilty as charged. Finally, whether a case is resolved through negotiation or trial, if a conviction is handed down, the prosecutor presents the government's recommendation for sentencing. In many jurisdictions, the prosecutor's sentencing recommendation is weighed heavily by the judge. In jurisdictions in which sentencing is constrained by guidelines, such as in federal court and an increasing number of states, the prosecutor's charging decision before the case ever reaches court can have a dramatic impact on sentencing. Throughout this wide range of responsibilities, the prosecutor's discretion in these matters is virtually unconstrained.

Systems of Prosecutors

There are three distinct levels of prosection in the United States, each of which focuses on different offenses. Local prosecutors, often called district attorneys, handle prosecution of criminal offenses in state court for a particular county or judicial district, which may span several counties. Local prosecutors are usually elected, although some are appointed, and they may be employees of the county or state. They primarily prosecute crimes against persons or property or drug offenses. They may prosecute very serious offenses such as murder, but most of the important events and facts surrounding the offenses they prosecute generally occur within their local jurisdictions. The national organization of local district attorneys is the National District Attorneys Association.

State prosecutors, usually under the supervision of a state attorney general, represent the state in state and federal courts. The state attorney general is often elected, although sometimes this is an appointed position. State prosecutors handle criminal appeals (defending the validity of convictions on appeal) and the prosecution at the trial level of certain types of more complex criminal offenses, which are often committed in several counties or districts or even several states. These types of more complex offenses involve environmental crimes, consumer fraud, civil rights violations, and securities offenses. The organization of state attorney generals is the National Association of Attorneys General.

Finally, federal prosecutors are located in each federal judicial district, which is either a state or in more populous regions a portion of a state. Federal prosecutors, called U.S. attorneys, operate under the control of the U.S. attorney general, an officer in the cabinet of the president of the United States. The attorney general runs the U.S. Justice Department, which has hundreds of prosecutors handling the prosecution of different types of federal crimes in its "criminal division." The attorney general also supervises U.S. attorneys, who are responsible for the local prosecution of offenses in the federal court in their judicial districts. U.S. attorneys are appointed by the U.S. president. Besides these systems of prosecutors, there are also military prosecutors, who handle cases arising under military law.

State and Local Prosecutors

State and local prosecutors in the United States are spread over more than two thousand offices. According to the 1994 statistics from the U.S. Justice Department's Bureau of Justice, there were 2,343 offices of state prosecutors employing about 65,000 lawyers, investigators, and support personnel. Slightly more than 10 percent of these offices, or 127, were concentrated in major metropolitan centers with populations over 500,000 people. These large offices employed an average of 179 persons. A few large offices in the nation's most populous counties employed several times this number of persons. About 65 percent of the prosecutors' offices in the United States served smaller cities and towns and employed an average of ten persons. About 30 percent of the country's prosecutor's operated only part-time offices.

State and local prosecutors' offices and procedures vary widely from jurisdiction to jurisdiction. Some have particular units to prosecute particular types of offenses, such as drug crimes, sex offenses, or homicides. Others organize their staffs according to the particular courts in which they practice. In most jurisdictions prosecutors review criminal charges before they are filed. One of the most important functions of the prosecutor is to screen prospective cases and identify those that present the most significant violations, for which the public benefit from prosecution will be greatest.

Federal Prosecutors

The U.S. Justice Department is responsible for the prosecution of federal crimes in federal court. In each federal judicial district, the local U.S. attorney's office handles federal prosecutions. From its main office in Washington, D.C., the Justice Department also centrally investigates and prosecutes violations of criminal laws and laws that may carry criminal penalties, such as civil rights violations, antitrust offenses, and consumer fraud offenses. These investigations often span more than a single federal district. The agency responsible for investigating and assisting in the prosecution of federal offenses is the Federal Bureau of Investigation (FBI).

The U.S. attorney is the lawyer who represents the federal government in each judicial district. A U.S. attorney is appointed by the president of the United States with the advice and consent of the U.S. Senate in each of the ninety-four federal judicial districts in the country and in U.S. territories. U.S. attorneys serve four-year terms. The U.S. attorney is the chief federal law-enforcement officer in a federal judicial district and is assisted by assistant U.S. attorneys. U.S. attorneys have extensive discretion over their staffs, resources, and prosecutorial efforts. Different districts characteristically have different focuses of investigation and prosecution. Major financial and securities cases, for example, are characteristically brought in large urban areas—particularly the southern district of New York—which includes the financial area of Wall Street in Manhattan. Drug prosecutions are brought in virtually every district and are the most common cases heard in federal court. Prosecutions for drug offenses are particularly common in the border areas of the southern districts of Florida and Texas.

The Role of the Prosecutor

The job of prosecutors is to seek justice. This is different from the role of lawyers representing accused persons. Although prosecutors represent the government, they are also charged with representing the public interest and seeing that justice is done. The prosecutor, for example, has the authority to bring and to dismiss charges. This responsibility, a public trust, has been formalized in standards of practice for prosecutors prepared by the American Bar Association (ABA), the largest bar association in the United States. First published in 1968, these Standards for Criminal Justice set forth guidelines for effective and ethical conduct by both prosecutors and defense lawyers.

The ABA standards explain that "the duty of the prosecutor is to seek justice, not merely to convict." This means that prosecutors not only must pursue the most compelling cases for conviction but also must pursue them properly, within the applicable legal and ethical rules. They must disclose to defendants' lawyers any evidence suggesting that defendants are innocent.

Prosecutorial Discretion

Prosecutors in the United State wield extraordinary power. Their discretionary decisions concerning the investigation, charging, prosecution, and disposition of cases are largely unreviewable. This is a uniquely American phenomenon, for which several explanations have been offered. Criminal codes are the products of political processes; many offenses appear in criminal codes not necessarily because they are common problems but because legislatures seek to declare their public abhorrence of them. Sufficient evidence is not present in every potential case, and prosecutors must make hard judgments not only

about the public importance of particular cases but also the likelihood of conviction. As prosecutorial resources are limited, they must be put to the most efficient use possible. Finally, justice must be done in every case for every offense, and some defendants are better candidates for informal types of sanctions or penalties (often called "diversion") than for formal criminal prosecution.

David M. Siegel

Further Reading

American Bar Association. *Standards for Criminal Justice: The Prosecution Function*. 3d ed. Washington, D.C.: Author, 1992. Guidelines for ethical conduct by prosecutors.

Barnes, Patricia G. *CQ'S Desk Reference on American Criminal Justice: Over 500 Answers to Frequently Asked Questions from Law Enforcement to Corrections*. Chicago: University of Chicago Press, 2000. Answers to questions often asked about the U.S. legal system. Reference materials include significant laws and court decisions, and a glossary of common legal terms.

Jacoby, Joan E. *The American Prosecutor: A Search for Identity*. Lexington, Mass.: Lexington Books, 1980. Thorough social science analysis of several prosecutors' offices and the problems they face.

Schmalleger, Frank. *Criminal Justice Today: An Introductory Text for the Twenty-first Century*. 8th ed. Upper Saddle River, N.J.: Pearson/Prentice-Hall, 2005.

Senna, Joseph J., and Larry J. Siegel. *Introduction to Criminal Justice*. 7th ed. Minneapolis, Minn.: West Publishing, 1996. Textbook on criminal justice with a sociological emphasis.

Stewart, James B. *The Prosecutors*. New York: Simon & Schuster, 1987. Interesting account of major federal prosecutions.

See also Antitrust law; Attorney general of the United States; Bail system; Criminal justice system; Dismissals; District attorneys; Exclusionary rule; Eyewitness testimony; Grand juries; Harmless error; Jurisdiction of courts; Plea bargaining; Pleas; Presumption of innocence; Sentencing; Speedy trial right; Statutes of limitations; Trials.

Criminal records

Definition: Official documents that list individuals' past convictions for misdemeanors and felonies and that sometimes include arrests that do not result in convictions

Criminal justice issues: Convictions; defendants; sentencing

Significance: Criminal records allow police agencies and courts to know the histories of criminal suspects' and defendants' violations of laws and are often used as sentencing tools in evaluating convicted persons' eligibility for probation and parole.

Local, state, and federal law-enforcement agencies and courts all compile criminal records. Effective national coordination of criminal records is now a clear goal of the Federal Bureau of Investigation (FBI) and other law-enforcement agencies, but there are still holes in the system of record keeping that make it difficult to track mobile offenders, particularly low-level misdemeanants.

Data Collection

The FBI has national responsibility for the compilation of criminal records. These records are stored at the FBI's Criminal Justice Information Services (CJIS) division, which is headquartered in Clarksburg, West Virginia. The CJIS is now the world's largest fingerprint repository; it cooperates with both national and international law information agencies. As of May, 1997, CJIS had more than 219 million fingerprint cards. Of these more than 132 million were criminal record cards and more than 187 million were civil record cards.

Although submission of records to the CJIS is voluntary for state and local law-enforcement agencies, data submission increased during the

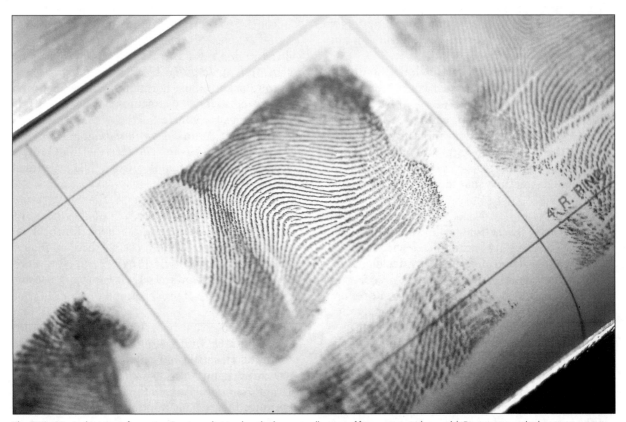

The FBI's Criminal Justice Information Services division has the largest collection of fingerprints in the world. Fingerprints, which are unique to every person, provide one of the most valuable tools in making positive identifications. *(Brand-X Pictures)*

late twentieth century. The CJIS also receives the fingerprints of aliens who seek permanent residence, naturalization, and asylum in the United States, as well as the fingerprints of Americans seeking to adopt children abroad. Alien residents who are convicted of felonies are automatically deported if found, and aliens with serious criminal records cannot be admitted to the United States legally.

In some states, state law requires those arrested for felonies and class A and B misdemeanors to be fingerprinted, and two sets of fingerprint records are made so that both local authorities and the state bureau of investigation can maintain appropriate records. Juveniles charged with offenses that would be felonies or class A and B misdemeanors for adults also must submit fingerprints. Minor misdemeanors slip through the cracks of states' recording systems.

Private and Public Use of Criminal Records

In addition to law-enforcement, court, and corrections use of criminal records, private citizens increasingly seek access to criminal records. Employers must know whether they are hiring individuals with criminal histories that raise serious concern about their fitness to deal with vulnerable populations in day-care centers, schools, summer camps, and nursing homes.

If an employer fails to do a background check and hires an employee whose record would have indicated that he or she posed a potential threat, the employer can be sued for negligent hire. Judgments now average more than $1 million per case. Specialized search firms have proliferated to meet employer needs to learn of potential employees' criminal histories and other potentially damaging background information. Potential employees must often sign a consent form agreeing to a criminal record check or forfeit further consideration for employment even in low-level jobs.

Law-enforcement agencies use criminal records to track offenders over time. While juvenile records were once sealed when juvenile offenders became adults, many states now make them available to courts sentencing former juvenile felons for adult crimes.

Prosecutors and courts use criminal records in determining how serious punishment should be for particular crimes. In some states, first-time offenders may be granted a diversion that keeps them out of the criminal justice system if they accept responsibility for their offenses and honor restitution and other conditions imposed on them. The successful completion of diversion leaves persons with no formal criminal record, although prosecutors have access to records that indicate who has been granted diversions. Judges in many states use mandated sentencing guidelines that impose sentences for specific offenses based on the severity of the offense and individuals' prior criminal records. Judges must justify departures from a recommended sentencing range.

Coping with a Criminal Record

Former offenders find themselves severely handicapped by their criminal records. In addition to losing voting rights and the right to bear arms, those with felony convictions are barred from obtaining many occupational and professional licenses in most states. Sometimes criminal background checks are required for health care workers who deal directly with patients, and some states have passed laws that revoke the teaching certificates of public school teachers with felony records. Some states have a formal process called "expungement," through which persons who can demonstrate that they have been rehabilitated can have convictions for most crimes removed from their records. Expunged records are not totally destroyed, however. In addition, expunged records can be reopened if further offenses are committed.

Susan A. Stussy

Further Reading

Bureau of Justice Statistics. *Improving Criminal History Records for Background Checks*. Washington, D.C.: U.S. Department of Justice, 2003.

Niam, Edward, Jr. "Do You Know Who You Are Hiring?" *USA Today Magazine* 125 (July, 1997). Describes the legal problems that can confront employers who hire employees without thoroughly researching their pasts. If someone with a serious criminal record is hired and then commits a felony, the employer may be liable in tort for negligent hiring practices.

Sontag, Deborah. "U.S. Deports Felons but Can't Keep Them Out." *New York Times*, August 11, 1997. Reports on the efforts of the INS to exclude deported criminal aliens from the United States.

Vail, Kathleen. "Privacy Rights Versus Safety." *American School Board Journal* 184 (April, 1997). Reports on trends to open juvenile records of serious offenders to school superintendents and other educators.

See also Background checks; Booking; Computer information systems; Convictions; Criminal history record information; Criminals; Immigration and Naturalization Service; Misdemeanors; Sentencing; Three-strikes laws; Traffic schools.

Criminals

Definition: Perpetrators of criminal offenses

Criminal justice issues: Defendants; deviancy; legal terms and principles

Significance: Although the concept of "criminals" may seem obvious, identifying and understanding criminals is actually fraught with ambiguity, disagreement, and misunderstanding.

Definitions of "criminals" are inexorably intertwined with definition of "crime." All societies have laws. Therefore, all societies have crimes as well as criminals. The maintenance of order in any social group, whether small or large, primitive or advanced, requires that laws governing the interactions among its members be established and enforced. However, definitions of "crime" and "criminals" vary widely across societies. Conduct that makes a person a criminal in one society might be regarded as neutral or even heroic in another society. Nevertheless, despite ambiguities in definitions of crime and criminals, it is useful to categorize different types of criminals. At least five basic types can be identified.

Classifying Criminal Types

Perhaps the most frightening criminals are those who commit crimes of violence. Robbers, murderers, and rapists all qualify as violent criminals. It is also important to recognize that, under Western law, violence can occur even when no clear bodily harm results. For example, a rapist who psychologically coerces or manipulates an underage victim is considered a violent offender.

What is not commonly understood is that many violent criminals are not repeat offenders. Many violent crimes of passion, such as aggravated assault and murder, are unique events that occur under extraordinary circumstances involving highly charged emotional conflicts that are often fueled by drugs or alcohol. Nevertheless, in the United States, fear of violent crime and concern about so-called "repeat violent offenders" has spurred interest in stiff mandatory sentencing laws.

Far more common than violent criminals are property criminals, who include shoplifters, purse and wallet snatchers, and vandals who deface or destroy public or private property. Many property criminals are drug addicts who steal to finance their addictions. Others, such as cat burglars and professional car thieves, are experienced professional criminals who can make steady livings from their crimes.

A third category of criminals includes members of organized crime syndicates. These include the Mafia, drug and prostitution rings, and stolen car "chop shops." Criminal organizations often profit from so-called consensual crimes, such as illegal narcotics and prostitution.

A fourth category, white-collar criminals, includes professionals such as stock traders who use improperly acquired information to make stock transactions, industrialists who violate occupational safety and environmental laws, and embezzlers. The proliferation of electronic commerce in the late twentieth century generated new types of white-collar criminals, such as identity thieves, who steal personal information to tap their unaware victims' bank and credit card accounts.

The category of political criminals may be the most controversial of all. Figures such as the American civil rights leader Martin Luther King, Jr., and Indian nationalist leader Mohandás K. Gandhi are now celebrated as heroes who opposed injustice. However, both men were once

Now honored as a national hero because of his leadership of the Civil Rights movement, Martin Luther King, Jr., was regarded as a criminal law-breaker in many states and spent a considerable amount of time in jails. *(Library of Congress)*

considered criminals by their governments' law-enforcement officials and spent considerable time in jails. Gandhi became a criminal under British colonial law when he opposed imperialism in South Africa and India.

In the United States, many white southerners regarded King as a criminal because of his open defiance of segregation laws. J. Edgar Hoover, the head of the Federal Bureau of Investigation (FBI) regarded King as a dangerous subversive and kept special files on him. Both Gandhi and King were political criminals because their political positions made them the targets of the institutions of law. However, their opponents never opened called them "political criminals." The descriptions most often applied to them include "anarchists," "seditionists," and "traitors."

Terrorists are also political criminals. However, definitional issues beset even this example.

To Americans, the September 11, 2001, attacks against the United States were barbarous acts of murder, and their perpetrators were international "criminals." However, in many parts of the Arab and Muslim worlds, the attacks were praised as justified retaliation for perceived mistreatment of Muslims in American foreign policy, and the hijackers are regarded as holy warriors and martyrs.

In any attempt to identify general crime types, it is important to remember that criminals—like the crimes they commit—are not easily boxed within mutually exclusive categories. For example, the September 11 hijackers can be considered violent criminals for their murders of thousands of people; they can be considered property criminals because of their destruction of billions of dollars worth of private and public property; and they can also be classified simply as "terrorists" and might even be considered members of an organized crime syndicate, al-Qaeda.

Biological and Psychological Theories

A subfield of sociology, criminology is the social science of observing and explaining the behavior of criminals. Criminologists and political scientists have long debated the causes of criminality. There have historically been many competing views of crime causation. Basic theories of crime can be divided into four very broad categories.

One category falls under the heading of biological/psychological theories. The idea that innate human tendencies explain the existence of criminals has a long history in criminology. Primitive and early religious societies generally attributed antisocial behavior to individual moral defects or the temptations introduced by demons or devils. Even throughout most of Western history, there was no meaningful distinction between ecclesiastical and secular law. "Illegal" was synonymous with "un-Christian."

The Age of Enlightenment saw the introduction of more scientific explanations of crime. In 1876, Italian physician Cesare Lombroso wrote *The Criminal Man*, in which he argued that autopsies showed that criminals were more likely than other people to exhibit so-called atavistic traits, such as asymmetrical faces, exceptionally large or small brains, and unusually long arms.

Lombroso's notions are now generally dismissed as pseudoscience, but the idea that innate individual attributes can explain criminal behavior persists.

Studies of twins separated at birth indicate that antisocial tendencies are at least partially inheritable, suggesting a biological component to crime—often oversimplified as the idea of a "crime gene." There is also evidence that life experiences, especially early childhood events, can powerfully shape individual psychology for better or worse. Inmates of modern prisons are disproportionately likely to have had traumatic pasts—such as abuse or neglect—that can solidify psychological trajectories toward criminal behavior.

Environmental Theories

Many sociologists deny or downplay the importance of psychological or biological attributes in explanations of why some people become criminals. They argue that even if there are variations in criminal tendencies among different individuals, the most powerful causes of criminal behavior are immediate environmental factors, such as family and peer influences, work and education opportunities, and socioeconomic conditions.

These sociological views of crime are numerous and well researched. For example, various social-learning theories contend that some individuals become criminals by imitating the behaviors and adopting the values of criminal peers. "Strain" theorists contend that poor and marginalized individuals are blocked from traditional means of survival and success in a competitive society such as the United States. These individuals turn to crime in reaction to the "strain" resulting from the incongruity between their aspirations and their legitimate prospects.

Social-Control and Critical/Conflict Theories

Rather than attempting to explain why some people become criminals, social-control theories approach the question of crime by explaining why most people do not become criminals. For example, the general theory of crime holds that individuals with propensities for analogous high-risk behaviors are also more likely to become criminals. Early childhood experiences can condition this propensity for high-risk behaviors. Children not properly disciplined and socialized can later become adults without the ability to empathize with others or appreciate the consequences of their actions, and they are thus more likely to become criminals.

"Critical," or "conflict," criminologists argue that criminals are neither made nor born. Instead, criminals are defined into existence by law. These theorists argue that the institutions of law favor the interests of the privileged and powerful who make the laws. Members of racial and ethnic minorities are economically, socially, and politically marginalized, making it easy for the dominant interests to frame them as "dangerous criminals" whose crimes should be aggressively targeted by the institutions of law. At the same time, these theories downplay or ignore crimes committed by the social elite, such as securities fraud, occupational safety violations, and environmental crimes.

A potential limitation of the critical/conflict perspective is accommodating "absolute" moral imperatives. Some legal/ethical restrictions are nearly universal, suggesting that some moral understanding beyond the hegemony of arbitrary law explains them. For example, almost everyone would agree that murder, rape, and incest should be forbidden, even if there are substantive differences on the exact definitions of these crimes. However, in other cases, the conflict interpretation is more compelling.

One oft-cited instance is the schedule of penalties for drug offenses under federal law. For example, the penalties for crack cocaine are much harsher than those for powder cocaine, even though no proven medical differences between the two exist. Since crack cocaine is disproportionately used by poor members of minorities, the latter are more aggressively prosecuted and overrepresented for drug crimes in federal prison, even though the proportions of white and minority drug use are roughly equal. Conflict criminologists argue that this focus on the drug crimes of marginalized classes is a classic example of how law itself creates criminals.

The explanations of crime summarized here focus on individual-level crime and are only a basic typology of the vast literature of criminological theory. There are other individual theories of crime, as well as a host of sociological theories explaining why some geographic areas and social groups, as opposed to individuals, are especially prone to pervasive crime.

The Social Construction of Criminals

The word "criminal" can conjure any number of images. However, in a mass media-dominated society such as the United States, the public's understanding of "criminals" is generally confined to television, film, and newspaper presentations. These media images of criminals can be both powerful and constricting, because most people have limited firsthand knowledge of criminals. Commonly held beliefs about criminals are thus socially constructed, not formulated from direct observations.

Television crime dramas emphasize plots about lurid and bizarre crimes and the heroic law-enforcement professionals who solve or prevent such crimes. Television and print news sources generally emphasize sensational car chases, shoot-outs, and murders in an effort to attract viewers and maximize advertising revenue. In the print media, many editors openly admit that "If it bleeds, it leads." White-collar and corporate crimes, by contrast, tend to be less sensational and less amenable to "sound byte" news coverage, and thus often receive less attention.

Additionally, some argue, there are institutional barriers that prevent the crimes of powerful individuals and corporate entities from coming to light in the mainstream media. These media images, and omissions, can create or reinforce dubious assumptions in an unaware public. Citizens can easily come to believe that the typical "criminal" is a young, disheveled, thuggish, male member of a dark-skinned minority group who commits his crime out of naked greed or barbarous impulse, or that serial killers pose a frequent and pervasive threat. There are, in fact, some criminals who fit these caricatures.

More common, however, are the drug-addicted prostitutes, burglars, and thieves, minor juvenile offenders, and tormented individuals who commit tragic, atypical crimes of passion. However, little media attention is paid to them or to the underlying economic and social conditions that are arguably responsible for much crime. These incomplete media images could in turn distract both the public and elected policymakers from the best solutions to crime. If the socially constructed image of "criminal" is limited to include only physically menacing, impenitent brutes or serial killers, the public might be less sympathetic toward social policies that can alleviate the underlying social and psychological conditions that create most criminals, and less inclined to invest public resources in potentially effective rehabilitation and drug treatment programs to help them.

Timothy Griffin

Further Reading

Akers, Ronald L. *Criminological Theories: Introduction and Evaluation*. 2d ed. Los Angeles: Roxbury Publishing, 2000. Summary of competing theories of what makes individual criminals.

Andrews, Donald A., and James Bonta. *The Psychology of Criminal Conduct*. Cincinnati: Anderson Publishing, 1998. Overview of different psychological and biosocial bases of criminal conduct.

Geldenhuys, Deon. *Deviant Conduct in World Politics*. New York: Palgrave MacMillan, 2004. Examination of international criminal behavior by individuals, organizations, and states.

Wilson, James Q., and Richard J. Herrnstein. *Crime and Human Nature*. New York: Simon & Schuster, 1985. Detailed analyses of the various attempts to account for individual differences in propensity for crime, with an outline for a general theory to explain how criminals are made.

See also Crime; Crimes of passion; Criminal history record information; Criminal intent; Criminal justice in U.S. history; Criminal records; Criminology; Defendants; Gangsters of the Prohibition era; *Mens rea*; Organized crime; Outlaws of the Old West; Print media; Psychopathy; Terrorism.

Criminology

Definition: Interdisciplinary field that relies heavily on scientific methods to study crime phenomena, including patterns and rates of crime and victimization, etiology of crime, social responses to crime, and crime control

Criminal justice issues: Criminology; legal terms and principles

Significance: Criminological knowledge of all sorts has saturated American society, making it increasingly difficult to know what information is valid and reliable. One must pay close attention to how information is created, what its purpose is, and how it is used. Criminology usually refers to a body of knowledge that is developed by professional experts associated with academic and research institutions, whose main goal is to further knowledge and understanding.

The term "criminology" was first employed by the French anthropologist Paul Topinard in 1897 to refer to a separate area of study of crime and criminal behavior. Since then, there has been controversy over the term's common definition. The controversy stems from the fact that criminology represents many scientific disciplines, such as biology, psychology, and sociology, as well as such professional fields as law and criminal justice. Each of these fields emphasizes its own definitions and employs different units of analysis, such as offenders, victims, specific offenses, or crime rates.

While it is difficult to argue that one field or another is superior in terms of explaining crime phenomena, it may be claimed that the various fields together offer a fuller understanding of crime. Recent developments in criminology confirm the trend toward integrating theories and methods so that information gathered from the perspectives of several disciplines can be combined for more explanatory power and comprehensiveness. This trend reinforces the fact that crime is not caused by a single factor but is more likely to be the result of complex interactions of individuals and structural and cultural phenomena.

The Scope of Criminology

Criminologists have disagreed over whether criminology should limit its study to strict legal definitions of crime and those persons who have been convicted, or extend its study to include all conduct that violates group norms. The latter view, which serves to broaden the definition, was not widely accepted when it was first introduced in 1938 by Thorsten Sellin, yet it takes on new significance today. Rapid technological changes and expanding global relationships provide opportunities for the rise of new types of crime such as computer identity theft, unauthorized electronic fund transfers, toxic-waste dumping, selling harmful products to underdeveloped nations, and global terrorism. These developments give criminologists new issues to study even before laws are enacted to cover them.

Although criminology is a multidisciplinary and multiparadigm field drawing on the many competing theoretical and research approaches used in the study of crimes and criminals and the debate over the fundamental nature of the subject matter, criminology has evolved into a separate discipline with a body of knowledge meriting its own status. Criminologists Marvin Wolfgang and Franco Ferracuti have argued that criminology might be considered a separate, autonomous discipline because it has its own scientifically oriented knowledge base that includes its own set of systematically organized data, research questions, and theoretical propositions. The field of criminology also has its own scholarly learned societies and professional associations, conferences, and a wide range of pure and applied research journals representing the field as a whole as well as its many sub-areas on state, regional, national and international levels.

Within the discipline of criminology one can delineate several sub-areas that, taken together, make up what has been called the "criminological enterprise." These areas include law, measurement, victimology, etiology, criminal typologies, and the criminal justice system, as well as cross-cultural studies, ethics, and critical criminology.

Law

The study of law, legal prescriptions, and legal definitions of offenses such as crimes of violence and public-order crimes is an indispensable part of criminology. Scholars, however, have varying interpretations of the role of criminal law. Legal thinkers, such as Roscoe Pound, who espouse a consensus perspective, assume that the law arises from social agreement over commonly held interests and values. According to this view, the criminal law functions to uphold society and the social order.

Proponents of the conflict perspective, such as William Dahrendorf and William Chambliss, maintain that any social order may be traced to the dominance of one group temporarily coercing another group. According to this position, the criminal law functions to protect the interests of the rich and powerful in society. It has been held that if crime represents conduct that is forbidden by law, law itself is a formal cause of crime.

Measurement

Determining the actual volume or prevalence of crimes committed in society is among one of the most difficult questions to answer by criminologists, who simply do not know how much real crime occurs in society at any given time. The many criminal acts that go undiscovered or unreported constitute the "dark figures of crime." Traditionally, criminologists have relied on official crime statistics such as the Federal Bureau of Investigation's Uniform Crime Reports (UCR). Statistics provided by the Bureau of Justice Statistics (BJS) and federal statistics have also provided valuable information.

It is important to keep in mind that these statistics sources are not without limitations. For example, problems related to underreporting or selective reporting have plagued the UCR ever since the implementation of crime reporting systems in the United States during the early 1930's. In fact, most crime statistics must be considered cautiously because they are subject to the organizational politics of the various types and levels of agencies that collect them. For example, certain types of crimes such as white-collar or corporate crimes are less likely to come to the attention of local police and more likely to attract the attention of federal authorities. It has been observed that criminal statistics based on crimes known to the police tend to reflect more how citizens and officials respond to crime and their per-

ceptions of crime, rather than how prevalent the problem itself is.

During the 1960's, interviews with representative samples of crime victims in major American cities began to be conducted periodically to augment official police crime statistics. Known as the National Crime Victimization Survey, the results have revealed that the volume of crime reported to police substantially underestimates the true incidence of crime in the United States.

Data about crime can also be obtained using other research strategies such as self-report studies, in which members of the general public—usually high school students—are surveyed through questionnaires and interviews about their delinquent or criminal involvement. These studies, which are aimed at overcoming the bias and selectivity associated with official police crime statistics, have also provided criminologists with insights into the dark figures of crime or unknown crimes, suggesting that official sources grossly underestimate crimes in society.

The accurate measurement of crime is of vital importance in society. It not only determines the numbers of personnel needed to handle law violators and the amounts of money spent on crime, but also relates to the public's fears and peace of mind.

Victimology

Until recently, most of the emphasis in the field of criminology was on offenders. Criminologists have studied the motives, treatment, and rehabilitation of offenders almost exclusively, while paying little attention to their victims. Although some researchers studied victims as early as 1948, it was not until the 1970's that victimology became a special area of criminology study.

Broadly defined, victimology is the study of victim-offender relationships. Much of the interest of victimologists has been centered on determining the vulnerability or susceptibility of crime victims to victimization, as well as victim precipitation—how they contribute to their own victimization. Victimologists warn, however, that victim precipitation should not be used to blame victims, as has long been the case for rape victims, who have been notoriously discriminated against by the criminal justice system.

The notion that victims should have a role in criminal justice has only recently been recognized. Now, victims are occasionally allowed to have a say in the sentencing decisions of offenders. Moreover, victimization research has led to the establishment of local, state, and federal victim compensation programs that offer financial and psychological support for victims of crimes.

Etiology

Although controversy surrounds crime measurement, the numbers of crimes can be predicted with uncanny precision. What cannot be predicted with any reasonable degree of accuracy is who the criminals and their victims will be. Research has suggested that fluctuations in crime rates may be explained more by social variables than by psychological or biological characteristics. For this reason, most modern analyses of crime rates are sociological in nature.

Psychology, biology, and sociology have all contributed to criminologists' understanding of the nature of offenders, motivations underlying different offenses, patterns of offending, and the circumstances surrounding various offenses. Usually presented in a logical framework, theories address questions of why and how criminal behaviors or events occur. The question of what causes crime, however, is difficult to answer. The history of criminology suggests that no one theory can explain the phenomenon of crime. For this reason criminology comprises many rival etiological perspectives.

Most of the research on the causes of crime is scientific. The relative strengths and weaknesses of the different explanatory models are determined by scientific merit, with positions supported or dismissed on the basis of reliability and validity of evidence. Since no theory has sole hold on truth, it is critical to take into account the contributions of all perspectives to enhance understanding of crime. Theories are important. They underlie the way society and individuals respond to crime and criminals and fundamentally what members of society think of one another.

Criminal Typologies

No universally accepted typology exists in the field of criminology. A number of typologies are used. Most typologies are based on legal or semilegal definitions of offenders, in addition to information related to the seriousness of offenses, the psychological and sociological characteristics of offenders, and the career patterns of offenders.

The development of typologies is no simple matter, especially considering the changing nature of crimes and laws. Early criminologists focused on street violence, theft, and public order crimes, such as drug use, gambling, and sex crimes. Modern criminologists have expanded their attention to include organized crime, white-collar crime, and corporate and political crimes, as well as human rights violations, terrorism, and other types of global offenses and perpetrators.

The Criminal Justice System

Another integral component of criminology is the study of the criminal justice system itself—law enforcement, courts, and corrections. The criminal justice system comprises several layers: local, state, and federal. During the early years of the twenty-first century, total expenditures on justice in the United States exceeded $167 billion annually for civil and criminal justice, and the criminal justice system alone employed approximately 2.3 million persons.

Law enforcement represents the largest element of the criminal justice system. Law-enforcement practices of crime prevention and control have changed a great deal since the first establishment of metropolitan police departments in major cities across the United States during the mid-nineteenth century. Technological advancements, formalization of police procedures, and urban development are among the main influences of transformation of law enforcement in America. Among the topics of current interest to criminologists are police and community relations, professionalization of the police, police use of deadly force, community policing in action, police discretion, and the proper role of the police in modern society.

Courts represent the second component of the criminal justice system. There are now approximately 17,000 municipal, county, state, and federal courts across the United States. Criminologists study many issues connected with the adjudicatory process, including adequacy of representation, plea-bargaining, pretrial detention, sentencing disparities, jury selection, trial process, and court reform.

The third component of the criminal justice system is corrections. According to BJS data, more than two million inmates were incarcerated in the nation's prisons, jails, and juvenile facilities in 2004. The number of inmates had grown significantly over the previous decade.

Because funding for prisons is balanced against funding for other domestic priorities, such as new schools, criminologists and legislators have debated correctional ideologies. Corrections officials face many problems in prisons, such as racial conflicts, overcrowding, understaffing, AIDS among inmates, violent gang activity, high recidivism rates, rising costs, and a trend toward privatizing prisons. All these problems are inspiring serious consideration of alternatives to incarceration, such as community corrections.

Cross-Cultural Studies

Research on crime in only one society cannot explain all aspects of crime. Increases in global terrorism and sociopolitical crimes, international drug trading, illegal arms trading, money laundering, and violations of human rights of all kinds suggest the necessity of studying crime throughout the world. Although criminologists have studied topics such as international terrorism as a form of political violence, the terrorist attacks on the United States of September 11, 2001, have stimulated renewed interest in the complex intricacies associated with the causes and control of terrorist violence and other types of international crimes.

The challenges presented by crime are no longer the concern of any one nation; crime is a global phenomenon. Comparative criminology may be defined as the cross-cultural study of all aspects of crime and criminal justice in two or more societies. Researchers conducting cross-cultural studies may analyze crime in a particular country by focusing on any one of several units of study such as the national crime trends, individual offender, the specific offense, the criminal law, the criminal justice system, scholarly contributions, and public opinions.

Comparative criminology is generally based on the premise that crime is relative and is inherent in the social structure of a society and that changes in crime patterns can be attributed to changes in the social structure. Variations in crime patterns and in types of crime control systems are, therefore, studied as reflections of different social, political, and economic conditions.

Ethics

Ethics concerns the principles of moral conduct that govern individuals and groups. As experts in the area of crime and justice, criminologists must recognize their own ethical responsibilities with respect to their research methods as well as their findings and recommendations, which may form the basis for establishing or dismantling social programs and policies. For example, criminological research results often directly or indirectly impact local, state, and federal criminal justice policies regarding such things as crime prevention and control of juvenile and adult law violators and the operation of the various components of the criminal justice system.

Concrete policies regarding issues such as the use of capital punishment, mandatory sentences, three-strike laws, and treatment and rehabilitation modalities have been influenced by criminological research and theories. Professional organizations in the field such as the American Society of Criminology and the Academy of Criminal Justice Sciences offer professional codes of ethics to give guidance to criminologists; however, ultimate responsibility for ethical conduct and the appropriate use of knowledge rests with individual researchers and practitioners. Since the late twentieth century, growing concern over the ethics of research and associated applications and practices has led to the development of a body of knowledge and research as well as specialty courses and concentrations related to these topics.

Critical Criminology

Most people, including many experts, take an uncritical stance toward their society and often take the social order for granted. Mainstream criminology has been built on the consensual view of the law, suggesting that there is agreement in society over what is right and what is wrong. The social order is not questioned. Crime in this context is perceived as a major problem and a threat to society. The preservation of order and eradication of crime (at any cost) are considered to be desirable goals and in the public interest. Flaws within the criminal justice system, while recognized, are usually approached with an attitude that while no system is perfect, the present system is an improvement over some dim past, and that progress will continue in the future. The political state is assumed to be neutral and to serve the public good and, therefore, the criminal justice system is fundamentally fair and necessary.

Critical criminologists question this worldview and set of assumptions. They argue that crime is ultimately a product of unequal power relations and clashing interests in society. Critical criminologists claim that the groups with the most power are able to determine existing definitions of crime and enforce adherence to such definitions. Scholars working within this framework question everything. They look for hidden agendas and latent consequences and they look for evidence of discrimination of any kind such as that based on age, sex, race, ethnicity, nationality, religion, class, education, residence, physical appearance, and individuals' beliefs or lifestyles. The object of the work of critical criminologists is to demystify the taken-for-granted world and to uncover injustices.

Over the course of its two centuries or so of development, the field of criminology itself has become enormous and diversified. Modern criminologists are now focusing on bridging various theoretical models and different areas of investigation, emphasizing "relativity" over predictability and "complementarity" over rivalry. Today there is greater appreciation of the complexities of crime; it cannot simply be understood within a cultural or historic vacuum. Moreover, there is recognition that not all contradictory evidence suggests that one is right or wrong; it may be that different results represent different aspects of the same reality. While in the past century criminology may have required contributions from various areas of specialization for its development, the present time may warrant a more integrated, synthetic criminology to meet the challenges of the twenty-first century.

Lydia Voigt

Further Reading

Braswell, Michel C., Belinda R. McCarthy, and Bernard J. McCarthy, eds. *Justice, Crime and Ethics*. 3d ed. Cincinnati: Anderson Publishing, 1998. Collection of short essays and articles that consider personal and social values, offer philosophical perspectives, and develop a foundation for making more informed decisions about criminal justice issues and practices.

Carrington, Kerry, and Russell Hogg, eds. *Critical Criminology: Issues, Debates, and Challenges*. Portland, Oreg.: Willan Publishing, 2002. Bringing together leading scholars from the United Kingdom, Australasia, and the United States, this collection of essays explores the key issues and debates as well as the future direction of critical criminology.

Clinard, Marshall B., Richard Quinney, and John Wildeman. *Criminal Behavior Systems: A Typology*. 3d ed. Cincinnati: Anderson Publishing, 1994. Classic work that discusses the construction of different types of crimes and introduces a typology of criminal behavior systems.

Coleman, James William. *The Criminal: Understanding White-Collar Crime*. 5th ed. New York: Worth Publishers, 2002. Discusses illegal acts committed by middle- and upper-class persons in conjunction with their ordinary occupational pursuits, examining these criminal acts, which have become prevalent in the modern high-tech world, and bringing light to the common forms and causes of white-collar crime.

Derber, Charles. *The Wilding of America: Money, Mayhem and the American Dream*. 3d ed. New York: Worth Publishers, 2004. Offers an analysis of societal fears related to violent crime and terrorism, arguing that there is a disconnect between America's goals of success and the prospects of success, and considers illustrations of recent social scandals and horrific events ranging from major cases of corporate corruption and Roman Catholic Church sex abuse to the terrorist attack on the World Trade Center and the war in Iraq and, finally, provides recommendations and community-based solutions to the wilding trends in contemporary society.

Geis, Gilbert, and Mary Dodge. *Lessons of Criminology*. Cincinnati: Anderson Publishing, 2002. Presents stories as well as lifestyle conclusions and advice of famous criminologists regarding their research and careers.

Inciardi, James A. *Criminal Justice, 2004-2005 Update*. Boston: McGraw-Hill, 2005. Provides a comprehensive overview of the criminal justice system: law enforcement, courts, and corrections, along with up-to-date statistics and major court decisions and important changes in the criminal justice system.

Miethe, Terance D., and Richard C. McCorkle. *Crime Profiles: The Anatomy of Dangerous Persons, Places, and Situations*. 2d ed. Los Angeles, Calif.: Roxbury Publishing, 2001. Examines offender, victim, and situational elements surrounding seven major forms of crime.

Muraskin, Roslyn. *It's a Crime: Women and Justice*. 2d ed. Upper Saddle River, N.J.: Prentice-Hall, 2000. A comprehensive text with topical readings on subjects related to the involvement of women in crime and the treatment of women offenders by the criminal justice system.

Siegel, Larry J. *Criminology*. 8th ed. Belmont, Calif.: Wadsworth/Thomson Learning, 2004. Gives a thorough overview of the discipline of criminology and the entire criminal justice process, legal concepts, and justice perspectives, featuring high-profile cases, events, and relevant materials in a comprehensive, balanced, and objective fashion.

Williams, Frank P., III, and Marilyn D. McShane. *Criminological Theory*. 4th ed. Upper Saddle River, N.J.: Pearson Prentice-Hall, 2004. Provides an overview and critique of the major sociological theories of crime including classical and current theories.

See also Community-based corrections; Community-oriented policing; Crime labs; Criminal justice system; Criminal law; Criminals; Document analysis; Graffiti; Incapacitation; International law; Punishment; Victimology; Youth gangs.

Cross-examination

Definition: Procedure in which witnesses testifying in trials and depositions are questioned by attorneys representing opposing sides

Criminal justice issues: Attorneys; interrogation; trial procedures; witnesses

Significance: The fact that unexpected revelations from witnesses can upset the development of cases makes cross-examinations one of the most dramatic—and sometimes perilous—parts of the judicial process.

In trial testimony, attorneys try to establish the credibility of their own witnesses through direct examinations. When they complete their questioning, the opposing attorneys then cross-examine the same witnesses and try to undo their credibility. In the popular mind and media, cross-examination offers the appealing prospect of a

Cross-examination is a central feature of the American adversarial system of justice, as it is a primary way in which attorneys challenge the evidence presented by the opposing sides. *(Brand-X Pictures)*

Cousin Vinny as a Cross-examiner

Among the comic highlights of the 1992 film *My Cousin Vinny* are scenes in which an inexperienced New York lawyer played by Joe Pesci cross-examines eyewitnesses in his first trial—the murder trial in Alabama of his young cousin and the latter's friend. Vinny discredits one witness after another, until almost nothing remains of the prosection's case. One witness he discredits by demonstrating in the courtroom that her eyesight is not strong enough for her to identify the escaping criminals as confidently as she initially claims. Another witness he discredits by making him admit that his estimate of the time that passed between two crucial events is grossly inaccurate. A third witness he discredits by producing photographs of the dirty windows through which the witness saw the criminals escape, getting him to admit that he could not have seen clearly enough to provide a positive identification. Finally, he completes his case by discrediting the prosecution's expert witness on the subject of tire-track evidence. After his own expert witness, his fiancé (Marisa Tomei), convincingly debunks the prosecution's interpretation of the evidence, the prosecution's expert recants his testimony.

Many of the legal matters treated in *My Cousin Vinny* are unrealistic—most notably the willingness of the trial judge (Fred Gwynne) to allow Vinny to appear in court without verifying his legal background. Nevertheless, the film's courtroom scenes accurately depict the frequent unreliability of eyewitness testimony and the crucial importance of effective cross-examination.

clever interrogator—such as Erle Stanley Gardner's fictional Perry Mason, or one of his innumerable imitators—uncovering deception and establishing guilt.

For legal experts as well, cross-examination is at the heart of judicial proceedings. John Henry Wigmore, a famous early twentieth century theorist of the law of evidence, said of the matter:

> If we omit political considerations of broader range, then cross-examination, not trial by jury, is the great and permanent contribution of the Anglo-American system of law to improved methods of trial procedure.

The Sixth Amendment to the U.S. Constitution guarantees the right of defendants to confront witnesses brought against them. Cross-examination gives defendants—through counsel—the opportunity to put their opponents' evidence to the test. However, within the adversarial format of the American judicial system, emphasis in cross-examination is often less on testing the truth of claims than on discrediting inconvenient witnesses.

Many standard cross-examination techniques involve rhetorical maneuvers designed to capitalize on favorable concessions and to minimize the impact of unfavorable testimony on juries. The first question that trial counsel face is whether to cross-examine at all. Legal lore is replete with stories of attorneys who asked one question too many and elicited unanticipated answers that damaged, instead of helped, their cases.

The primary aim of cross-examination is to impugn the veracity of witnesses and thereby lessen the weight of the evidence supporting the opposing side. In practice, achieving that goal involves suggesting—if not actually proving—that a witness's testimony is incorrect or incomplete. Witnesses seem less believable to juries if they are shown to be biased, to have interests in the outcomes of cases, to be generally careless with the truth, or to lack the ability or opportunity to secure the knowledge they claim to possess.

For reasons well known to psychologists, judges, attorneys, and witnesses, even eyewitnesses, are often mistaken in their claims about who did what to whom. Members of juries, however, are less likely to be sophisticated about such matters, so one purpose of cross-examination is to alert them to the natural and inevitable limitations of testimony.

Witnesses in special categories, such as court-recognized experts, or children, require special treatment. In general, however, the basic object of cross-examination is to attack witnesses' credibility, without alienating judges or—especially—juries.

Edward Johnson

Further Reading
Mauet, Thomas A. *Trial Techniques*. 6th ed. New York: Aspen Publishers, 2002.

Wellman, Francis L. *The Art of Cross-Examination*. New York: Macmillan, 1936. Reprint. New York: Simon and Schuster, 1997.

Wigmore, John Henry. *Evidence in Trials at Common Law*. 2d ed. Boston: Little, Brown, 1961.

See also Attorney ethics; Depositions; Due process of law; Effective counsel; Expert witnesses; Eyewitness testimony; Hearsay; *Maryland v. Craig*; Perjury; Testimony; Witnesses.

Cruel and unusual punishment

Definition: Treating convicted offenders in unnecessarily abusive ways

Criminal justice issues: Convictions; government misconduct; medical and health issues; punishment

Significance: The U.S. Constitution prohibits cruel and unusual punishment, and the courts are responsible for interpreting the meaning of that provision.

The Eighth Amendment to the U.S. Constitution forbids the use of cruel and unusual punishments. The words are not complex, but exactly what they prohibit is not obvious. In 2004, much debate surrounded arguments about whether the death penalty violates the Eighth Amendment. Some legal scholars argue that the Eighth Amendment should be read to mean exactly what it meant to the founders and that they did not intend to restrict the use of death itself as a punishment.

Critics claim that capital punishment, because it treats a human life as disposable, is inherently cruel and therefore unconstitutional. Others look to the framers of the Constitution and assert that they had no qualms about capital punishment. They cite the Fifth Amendment's guarantee that no one should be deprived of *life*, liberty, or property without due process of law. It is possible to read that guarantee as meaning that deprivation of life is permissible if due process has been followed. Likewise, the Fifth Amendment's restriction on double jeopardy, providing that no one should twice be forced to risk *life* or limb, could imply that life is an acceptable stake if one only has to risk it once.

When the Constitution was written during the late eighteenth century, "cruel and unusual punishment" was a familiar phrase taken from the English bill of rights. Many states included similar wording in their constitutions. The terminology involved the ideas that punishments should be proportionate to crimes and that punishments not authorized by law were prohibited. The founding generation had vivid memories of gruesome punishments devised by kings for retribution against their enemies. The founders wished to avoid such creative use of unusual sanctions by placing the authority to codify crimes and punishments in the hands of the people's representatives, the legislatures. In deciding how and when to apply the legislated punishments, the courts and the executive branch enjoyed wide latitude.

The Eighth Amendment could be read to forbid punitive measures that were unnecessarily painful or too oppressive. Exactly how those characteristics were to be defined was based on the notion that the sensibilities of a republic placed a high value on human dignity. In a society where all free citizens were believed to share inalienable rights, punishments should not purposely degrade but should be severe enough only to accomplish a social purpose.

Ultimately, the responsibility for defining "cruel and unusual" rests with the courts, especially the U.S. Supreme Court. For more than a century after the Constitution was written, the justices considered only a few cases that addressed the issue. The idea that the death penalty itself might be unconstitutional because it violated the Eighth Amendment was not brought before the Court until the middle of the twentieth century. The Court, for the most part, assumed that the forbidden cruel and unusual punishments were the obvious tortures and barbaric cruelties that offended modern, civilized communities. They did not need to rule that boiling in oil or drawing and quartering would not be permitted under the U.S. Constitution. They did, however, rule that two less dramatic but still violent means of execution did not violate the Eighth Amendment.

Although hanging remained the most widely used form of capital punishment in the United States throughout the nineteenth century, the leaders of the Utah Territory preferred death by firing squad. As the territory was settled, largely by Mormons who believed in blood atonement for the crime of murder, being shot by riflemen was considered more theologically correct than being swung from the gallows. Use of the firing squad was challenged as cruel and unusual punishment in *Wilkerson v. Utah* (1878). In that case, the Court ruled that shooting was a traditional method of execution, long favored by the military. Utah and Idaho still offered condemned prisoners the choice of a firing squad or lethal injection in the twenty-first century. Another innovation in capital punishment techniques came in 1890, when the Supreme Court decided that death by electrocution was not a violation of the Eighth Amendment. Its ruling *in re Kemmler* held that, even though no human being had yet been put to death in the electric chair, the method would produce "instantaneous, and therefore, painless death."

Aside from recognizing that there were outer limits to the humane treatment of offenders, in the nineteenth century the Court avoided most discussion of capital punishment, believing its methods and application were matters for the individual states to decide.

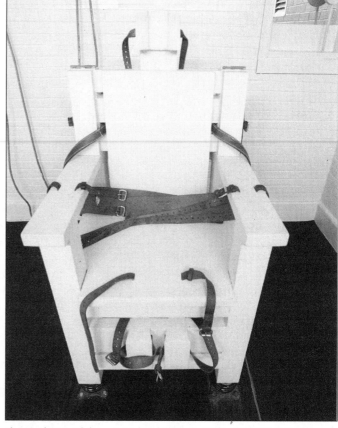

Electric chair in Alabama's Holman Prison in 1996. An 1890 U.S. Supreme Court decision ruled that execution by electrocution did not constitute cruel and unusual punishment because it was assumed—in the absence of empirical evidence—that electric chairs would kill painlessly and instantaneously. By the end of the twentieth century, however, most states were abandoning electric chairs and gas chambers in favor of lethal injections to avoid constitutional challenges to capital punishment based on the Eighth Amendment. *(AP/Wide World Photos)*

Eighth Amendment Cases

In 1910, the Supreme Court made a significant Eighth Amendment ruling in a case that did not concern the death penalty. *Weems v. United States* involved an American official in the Philippines who was sentenced to fifteen years of hard labor for forging a minor document. Weems challenged his punishment as cruel and unusual, and the Court agreed, holding that the sentence was so disproportionate to the crime as to be a violation of Weems's constitutional rights.

Almost a half century later, in *Trop v. Dulles* (1954), the justices revisited the Eighth Amendment and added the concept that cruel and unusual should be measured against contemporary public beliefs and attitudes. The case involved Army private Trop, who had left his unit for one day in 1944 during World War II. Trop thought better of going absent without leave and was voluntarily returning to his base when he was stopped by the military police. He was convicted of desertion, sentenced to three years at hard labor, and given a dishonorable discharge. Eight years later, when Trop applied for a passport, he learned that a dishonorable discharge for wartime desertion had resulted in the loss of his American citizenship. The Court examined the law that deprived a person of citizenship for desertion and found it unconstitutional. It spelled out one of the major premises of modern Eighth Amendment jurisprudence: It held that the words "cruel and unusual" must draw their meaning from "the evolving standards of decency that mark the progress of a maturing society."

Thus, the Court provided a new test for determining whether a punishment violated the Constitution. The criteria were dynamic. As ideas about human dignity evolved and changed, the attitudes about what constituted acceptable treatment of offenders would presumably become more refined.

Virtually every Eighth Amendment and capital punishment case that followed *Trop v. Dulles* invoked the concept of "evolving standards of decency" and wrestled with how to measure and apply those standards. The National Association for the Advancement of Colored People (NAACP) was one group who brought cases during the 1950's and 1960's challenging the application of the death penalty on Eighth Amendment grounds. They raised the claim that racial bias in capital sentencing violated the evolving standards and was therefore unconstitutional. They developed and presented social science research on racial bias and the arbitrariness with which the death penalty was applied. In 1972, the Supreme Court heard *Furman v. Georgia*, an attempt by the NAACP to win from the Court a statement that capital punishment violated the Eighth Amendment.

Furman v. Georgia

In 1972, the Court heard three death-penalty cases grouped under the title *Furman v. Georgia*. Furman was a black man who had shot a white homeowner, apparently by accident, during a robbery. The other two cases, from Georgia and Texas, involved rapes in which the offenders were black and the victims were white. No injury, aside from the rape, had occurred in either case. All three defendants were sentenced to death. Each justice wrote a separate opinion, and although a majority of five members of the Court found that the death penalty, as administered, was unconstitutional, the explanations for the justices' holdings varied widely. The four dissenting justices found no constitutional flaws with

the system of capital punishment. All nine justices argued that evolving standards of decency were the measure of cruel and unusual punishments. They differed over what those standards were.

Those who voted to uphold the death sentences believed that the only objective ways to assess contemporary standards were through the actions of legislatures and the decisions of juries. Neither had found capital punishment per se to be cruel and unusual—and therefore unconstitutional. Without that endorsement from lawmakers and jurors, the four dissenting justices held that the Court could not move on the issue. On the other side, Justice William Brennan argued that the death penalty was, by definition, unconstitutional. In this view, degrading punishments were not only those that caused pain, but also included those that dehumanized people and treated them as disposable objects. He maintained that even vile criminals retained their humanity and dignity.

Brennan's fellow opponents believed that capital punishment failed every constitutional test. It was unusually severe. There was a strong possibility of its arbitrary and biased use. It was substantially rejected by every modern democratic society, and it accomplished no greater purpose than less severe punishments. From this perspective, standards of decency had already evolved to the point where the death penalty was unacceptable. It remained only for the Court to formalize that position by declaring it unconstitutional on Eighth Amendment grounds. Thurgood Marshall, the first African American justice on the Supreme Court, reiterated that the "cruel and unusual" clause must be reexamined continually in the light of changing human knowledge. He asserted that if citizens were fully informed about the injustices inherent in the death penalty, they would find it unacceptable and reject it.

Justices taking a middle position in *Furman* identified the problem that the death penalty was being applied in an "arbitrary and capricious" manner, that death sentences were cruel and unusual "in the same way that being struck by lightning is cruel and unusual." In other words, it was the randomness in the application of capital punishment that made it cruel and unusual. *Furman* thus suspended executions until state legislatures could devise new laws that met the constitutional objections. The new legislation would be measured by its conformity with evolving standards of decency.

Gregg v. Georgia

The Court had found the laws at issue in *Furman* arbitrary and capricious, allowing too much discretion to juries and permitting the consideration of unacceptable factors such as race. North Carolina was one state that tried to meet those concerns by making the death penalty mandatory for certain offenses. To the majority of the Supreme Court in *Woodson v. North Carolina* (1976), this approach violated contemporary standards of decency and was therefore considered cruel and unusual under the Eighth Amendment.

On the same day as *Woodson*, however, the Court upheld the new Georgia capital statute again invoking contemporary standards of decency in their analyses of the death penalty. The majority in *Gregg v. Georgia* (1976) read the eagerness of thirty-five states to create new death-penalty laws as significant evidence that the punishment itself did not violate public sensibilities. They determined that a death sentence could serve to express a community's belief that because certain crimes were so reprehensible, only death was an adequate response. They also deferred to the theory of federalism, holding that each legislature can best evaluate the moral consensus in its state, determining what its constituents find cruel and unusual.

Gregg was a 7-2 decision. Since then, the Court has operated on the assumption that the death penalty itself is not cruel and unusual punishment and does not violate the evolving standards of decency. The justices have constructed an elaborate structure of law around the death penalty, providing for a process of guided discretion to choose who will die. Many of those decisions have employed the notion of evolving standards of decency to define the meaning of cruel and unusual punishment as it applies to specific crimes or to categories of defendants.

Evolving Standards

Just one year after *Gregg*, the Court ruled that the punishment of death for the rape of an adult woman violated the Eighth Amendment. In *Coker v. Georgia* (1977), they reasoned that execution was disproportionate for a crime in which the victim did not lose her life. On several occasions, the Court considered whether an accomplice to a crime, who did not actually commit murder, could be put to death without violating the ban on cruel and unusual punishments. In *Enmund v. Florida* (1982), the justices found the death penalty too severe for someone who participated in a crime but did not kill nor intend to kill. Five years later, however, in *Tison v. Arizona* (1987), the Court seemed to reverse itself and allowed for the execution of defendants whose recklessness allowed a murder to occur. *Coker*, *Enmund*, and *Tison* all attempt to measure whether punishment by death for those who did not take a life violates evolving standards and is therefore cruel and unusual punishment. Rather than drawing a bright line, the Court seems to have linked its judgment with the degree of the defendant's responsibility.

In other cases, the Supreme Court has ruled on whether the Eighth Amendment is violated if certain categories of defendants—the mentally ill, the developmentally disabled, juveniles, or the factually innocent—are executed. In *Ford v. Wainwright* (1986), they found it would offend basic standards of humanity to put a mentally ill person to death. The Court has not decided, however, whether a state may medicate inmates to make them "sane" enough for the death penalty to be carried out. In 2002, the justices ruled that there was a national consensus that executing the developmentally disabled violated standards of decency and was cruel and unusual punishment in *Atkins v. Virginia*. The ruling left it up to the states to determine who met the criteria as mentally retarded. In a 1989 case, *Stanford v. Kentucky*, the Court held that executing a juvenile who was sixteen years old at the time of his crime did not violate the Eighth Amendment. Since that ruling, the majority of states have raised the age of eligibility for the death penalty, and virtually every country in the world has outlawed the execution of juveniles. On March 1, 2005, the Supreme Court overturned its 1989 decision by ruling that executions of juveniles constituted cruel and unusual punishment.

The Supreme Court has not been clear with respect to whether it violates the Eighth Amendment when an innocent person is punished with death. In *Herrera v. Collins* (1993), the majority of the justices held that the Herrera had a fair trial, that he was not denied due process, and that if he were truly innocent, he should ask the governor for clemency. Therefore, he was not permitted to introduce new evidence of innocence in court. Five justices wrote separately that executing an innocent person would be constitutionally intolerable, but the Court has not ruled officially on the subject.

More Noncapital Issues

Citing the doctrine against cruel and unusual punishment, the Court required prisons to end the policy of whipping inmates in the 1960's. However, the justices have also ruled that prison officials cannot be sued for excessive use of force unless it is proved that they used force maliciously and sadistically and that they intended to cause harm. Thus, although inmates are theoretically protected from violent punishments, the remedies for such violations are difficult for those inside prison walls. Likewise, if corrections facilities fail to meet humane standards in food, housing, or health care, prisoners must prove the conditions were caused by the officials' deliberate indifference. The Supreme Court has also ruled that the Eighth Amendment applies only to convicted offenders. Therefore, people held in jail awaiting trial are not covered by the ban on cruel and unusual punishment. Nor do the provisions apply to children in public schools. The Court has been unwilling to view school officials who beat or paddle students as violating the students' constitutional rights.

Mary Welek Atwell

Further Reading

Banner, Stuart. *The Death Penalty: An American History*. Cambridge, Mass.: Harvard University Press, 2002. An examination of capital punishment in the United States since the colonial era. Puts the application of the death penalty into the social milieu of each period.

Bedau, Hugo Adam, ed. *The Death Penalty in America: Current Controversies*. New York: Oxford University Press, 1997. A collection of articles, statistics, and court opinions that summarize the major issues in the death penalty debate, including substantial attention to Eighth Amendment jurisprudence.

Irons, Peter. *A People's History of the Supreme Court: The Men and Women Whose Cases Have Shaped Our Constitution*. New York: Penguin, 1999. A readable history of important cases and judicial behavior beginning with the writing of the Constitution.

Kaufman-Osborn, Timothy V. *From Noose to Needle: Capital Punishment and the Late Liberal State*. Ann Arbor: University of Michigan Press, 2002. Considers the way capital punishment is inflicted as it relates to the overall functioning of modern capitalist society in the United States.

Latzer, Barry, ed. *Death Penalty Cases: Leading Supreme Court Cases on Capital Punishment*. 2d ed. Burlington, Mass.: Butterworth Heinemann, 2002. A comprehensive, edited collection of major death penalty rulings by the Supreme Court from *Furman v. Georgia* to *Atkins v. Virginia*.

Lifton, Robert Jay, and Greg Mitchell. *Who Owns Death? Capital Punishment, the American Conscience, and the End of Executions*. New York: Perennial, 2002. An analysis of the workings of the modern death penalty, including its randomness and its impact on those who work within the criminal justice system.

Sarat, Austin. *When the State Kills: Capital Punishment and the American Condition*. Princeton, N.J.: Princeton University Press, 2001. A critical examination of the politics and purpose served by capital punishment in the modern state.

Smith, Christopher E. *Constitutional Rights: Myths and Realities*. Belmont, Calif.: Thomson Wadsworth, 2004. A thorough discussion of the rights included in the Bill of Rights that challenges conventional wisdom about the application of constitutional rights.

See also Bill of Rights, U.S.; Capital punishment; *Coker v. Georgia*; Corporal punishment; Execution, forms of; *Ford v. Wainwright*; *Furman v. Georgia*; *Gregg v. Georgia*; *Harmelin v. Michigan*; Miscarriage of justice; *Robinson v. California*; *Rummel v. Estelle*; *Solem v. Helm*; Solitary confinement; *Stanford v. Kentucky*; Supermax prisons; Three-strikes laws; *Tison v. Arizona*.

Cryptology

Definition: Science of enciphering and deciphering codes, ciphers, and cryptograms

Criminal justice issues: Computer crime; evidence and forensics; technology

Significance: With the rise of electronic commerce and numerous hackers on the Internet in the twenty-first century, cryptology has become essential in people's everyday affairs.

Cryptology's Ancient Roots

Although the science of cryptology is a comparatively recent development and one that has been accelerated by the rapid growth of computer and Internet technology, the word itself has ancient roots. The word comes from Greek's *kryptos*, which means "hidden" and *logos*, which means "word." "Cryptology" literally means "hidden words," and cryptology is thus the branch of science that deals with secret communications.

One effective way to keep communications secret is to transmit them in codes, ciphers, or both.

Julius Caesar is generally recognized as the earliest military leader to utilize ciphers to encrypt and decode messages. His ciphering system became the basis for many of the more advanced ciphers in later centuries. Eventually, mechanical devices were invented to make encryption and decryption faster and easier. Thomas Jefferson described a drumlike device that was used to encode and decode messages. During World War II, the Enigma machine, a brilliant conception of the German military, was used to add complexity to codes. Enigma's scheme was eventually broken, first by Polish mathematicians suspicious of the intentions of Germany's Nazi rulers. It was then passed along to the French and British. None of these early pioneers in cryptology could envision the impact computers would have on the necessity of having covert communications, not just to be used in wars and by spies, but in daily life.

The computer industry has revolutionized cryptology. People who send messages over the Internet want to hide information from prying eyes, but at the same time, messages must be deciphered on the receiving ends. Public-key encryption uses not one key, but two. One key is used to encrypt a message, the other to decrypt it. The most important feature is that knowing the encryption key does not help outside parties to figure out how to decrypt the messages. For this type of encrypting to be effective, it must be easy for cryptographers to calculate a pair of keys (private and public) but virtually impossible for other cryptanalysts to recover either key. The encryption and decryption operations should be easy for legitimate users to carry out. Currently no cryptosystem ever devised has satisfied all these conditions, which is why hackers remain in the news for breaking into systems deemed secure by their designers.

Heidi V. Schumacher

A Cryptology Lexicon

Cipher	Structure in which units of plain text, usually letters, are transposed or substituted according to a predetermined code.
Code	System of symbols representing letters, numbers or words.
Cryptanalysis	Science of recovering information from ciphers without prior knowledge of their keys.
Cryptography	Study of techniques and applications that depend on the existence of difficult problems.
Cryptology	Field of cryptography and cryptanalysis combined.

Further Reading

Barr, Thomas. *Invitation to Cryptology*. Upper Saddle River, N.J.: Prentice-Hall, 2002.

Garrett, Paul. *Making, Breaking Codes: Introduction to Cryptology*. Upper Saddle River, N.J.: Prentice-Hall, 2000.

Spillman, Richard J. *Classical and Contemporary Cryptology*. Upper Saddle River, N.J.: Prentice-Hall, 2004.

See also Computer crime; Computer forensics; Crime labs; Cybercrime; Document analysis.

Cultural defense

Definition: Legal defense designed to diminish or eliminate criminal responsibility by establishing that the cultural traditions of the defendants have led them reasonably to believe in the propriety of their otherwise criminal acts

Criminal justice issues: Defendants; civil rights and liberties; domestic violence

Significance: The principle of cultural defense creates conflicts between the American commitment to justice for the individual and the establishment of common values among all members of society.

As the cultural diversity of the United States has grown, courtrooms have encountered increasingly frequent problems in addressing the rights of immigrants and members of minorities. American courts have historically been reluctant to allow defendants to use their different cultural backgrounds as independent and substantive defenses in criminal trials. On the other hand, cultural factors are often considered during the charging and sentencing phases in criminal processing, when prosecutors and judges are permitted to exercise more discretion than they are during the trial proceedings. Although courts are permitted to consider cultural factors in criminal cases, the legal framework of American courts during the early twenty-first century does not include a formal cultural defense.

The theory behind the cultural defense is that defendants—who are typically recent immigrants—have acted appropriately according to the dictates of their native cultures and thus deserve to be found not guilty of the crimes with which they are charged or to be treated with greater leniency. A common example of a case in which a cultural defense is evoked is the charging of Asian immigrants with cruelty to animals for cooking and eating pet dogs or cats—practices that are both legal and socially acceptable in the immigrants' home countries.

The cultural defense is considered an excuse defense. Although the behavior at issue may be deemed criminal, some peculiarity of the offender or the situation reduces the offender's moral blameworthiness. By explaining the criminal conduct on cultural grounds, the defendant seeks to receive some benefit from the court or prosecutor, including lessened punishment, reduced charges, or a dismissal of the charges.

The prospect of formalizing cultural defense generates criticism. Some opponents of the cultural defense maintain that the protection of victims, principally women and children, might be compromised. Others suggest that the deterrent effect of the law might be undermined by a defense of this kind, thus jeopardizing the preservation of social order.

Advocates of the cultural defense insist that its acceptance recognizes and respects the American commitment to cultural pluralism. Additionally, such a defense vindicates the principles of fairness and equality that underlie the American system of individualized justice. Further, treating those raised in foreign cultures differently is not deemed favoritism. The cultural defense is considered necessary because recently arrived immigrants have not had the same opportunities to absorb, through exposure to important socializing institutions, the norms upon which American society's laws are based.

If formalized, the cultural defense would join a growing group of new criminal defenses including the battered spouse defense and the Vietnam veterans' defense. Such defenses have been created to address those situations in which conviction would be unfair, but traditional defenses of self-defense and insanity would prove inappropriate.

Christine Ivie Edge

Further Reading

Kahn, Paul. *The Cultural Study of Law: Reconstructing Legal Scholarship*. Chicago: University of Chicago Press, 1999.

Renteln, Alison D. *The Cultural Defense*. New York: Oxford University Press, 2004.

See also Animal abuse; Crime; Defenses to crime; Excuses and justifications; Ignorance of the law; Mitigating circumstances.

Cybercrime

Definition: Crimes that involve use of the Internet and computers

Criminal justice issues: Business and financial crime; computer crime; technology; vandalism

Significance: One of the major areas of computer crime, cybercrime is expanding rapidly, costing Americans hundreds of millions of dollars per year. Victims seldom see or know the perpetrators, and the criminal justice system is only beginning to address the problem directly.

The first useful electronic computer was built in 1946. By the mid-1960's, the term "computer crime" was in the general lexicon and in legal jargon by the 1970's. The term "cybercrime" entered general use with the development and expansion of the Internet. The two terms, cybercrime and computer crime, are often used interchangeably. This, however, is not precisely correct. A cybercrime is one that is committed using the Internet and, by definition, computers. Most observers would agree that a computer must be the tool of the attack, the object of the attack, or both. Computer crime, on the other hand, does not need the Internet to be committed.

Many crimes that have been around since before the development of computers can be committed today via computer. Computers, most of the time, add an increased shroud of anonymity to criminal acts. Crimes perpetrated over the Internet can be committed from almost any place on the planet.

Types of Cybercrime

When thinking of cybercrime, most people think of releasing so-called viruses, trojans, worms, and denial-of-service attacks. Other cybercrime includes snooping, hacking and cracking, spoofing, and various forms of theft and fraud. Stalking takes place on the Internet, and

Internet pornography is abundant. Finally, organized crime and terrorists are using the Internet. The following discussion briefly covers prominent types of criminal activity on the Internet.

Computer viruses of many kinds have been developed, Each is able to replicate itself and to become part of another file; this is how viruses spread. Not every virus does damage, but every virus is potentially dangerous. Trojans differ from viruses in two important ways: They do not replicate themselves, and they can stand alone as files. Trojans are disguised as files that users want, such as music files, video files, games, or other software. Once inside victims' computer systems, trojans are free to release the hidden programs for which they are designed. These can be anything from harmless pranks to outright destruction of computer hard drives.

Worms spread copies or segments of themselves to other computers, usually via electronic mail. Worms differ from viruses because they do not need to attach to other files. Worms occupy increasing amounts of system resources, eventually bringing down the system. The first worm program was released in 1988. Its spread across the United States shut down a significant part of the Internet.

A denial-of-service attack makes the computer service unavailable to authorized users. The attack hogs resources or damages resources to the extent that they cannot be used.

Web-jacking occurs when someone takes control of a site and either changes it or otherwise manipulates it. Cases have occurred in which sites have been vandalized, instructions have been altered, and other types of changes have been made.

Logic bombs are dormant until triggered by some specific logical event. This event might be a specific date and time, the removal of a person's name from the system, or some other specific event. Then the bomb delivers its payload, which can be very destructive within the computer system.

Spoofing occurs when an Internet user is redirected from a legitimate Web site to a fake site set up to look like the original. This is done to get the victim to give personal information to the "company" when transacting business.

Snooping, hacking, and cracking are all forms

of unauthorized intrusion into computer systems. Snoopers are usually just curious people who enter a system to browse around. Hackers are persons with varying degrees of expertise who break into computer systems for many reasons. The challenge may merely be to see if they can do it, or it may be for more sinister reasons, such as stealing information or vandalizing the computer or Web site. Hackers also work for hire. Some consider themselves to be advanced and elegant programmers, and they consider the term "hacker" a badge of honor. These people think that hackers who ply their trade for nefarious purposes should be called "crackers," the type of hacker who should be viewed with contempt. Crackers communicate with one another online, on Web-based bulletin boards or private electronic mail lists. Sometimes crackers form groups with strange names like the Legion of Doom or the Chaos Computer Club and seek out more and more challenging exploits for their computer expertise. In 1995, the Department of Defense was subjected to more than 250,000 attacks by hackers and crackers.

Personal Crimes

A variety of thefts and fraud can take place online. The most damaging type of theft is identity theft. Hackers and crackers look for Social Security numbers and other types of personal information. Corporate and government databases are the largest sources of this kind of data. Illegal use of the victim's Social Security number, for example, can enable a criminal to borrow money, even qualify for mortgage loans, under the victim's name. Purchases of all kinds can be made, with victims unaware of it until they apply for a loan or credit card, or until they check their credit reports. It can take months, or even years, to get credit issues arising from identity theft resolved.

Fraud can take many forms, old and new. The Nigerian letter scam, formerly perpetuated by postal mail, is an example. In it, electronic mail appears in the victims' in-boxes offering to transfer large sums of money to the victims' banks if they will provide their account numbers so that the transfer can take place. Victims are offered a percentage for their cooperation. More recent examples include investment schemes and lottery or inheritance scams.

It is possible to gamble online. Players buy "chips" using a credit card, can play any game in the "house," and bet as much money as they want. Where gambling is illegal, such online gambling is illegal, too. The games may be rigged against the players. Also, some online gambling is used for money laundering.

Cyberstalking involves sending harassing or threatening electronic mail to a specific individual repeatedly and over time. It may also include visiting chat rooms frequented by victims and harassing them there. Usually, women are the victims of stalking crimes. Children may also fall victim to cyberstalkers, especially if the perpetrators are pedophiles. As many as 200,000 people stalk someone each year.

Internet pornography is another new version of an old problem. Thousands of pornographic Web sites offer pictures and videos of all kinds to anyone who can find them. All Internet sites that offer pornographic material, whether on a subscription basis or for free, are supposed to have a warning about the contents that instructs minors to exit the site. The most serious problems associated with pornography are in the area of child pornography. Child pornography can be encrypted (hidden) on computers and exchanged. In 2003, authorities in Europe and the United States uncovered an international child pornography ring leading to the arrest of hundreds of defendants.

Organized crime and terrorists also use the Internet, mainly for money laundering and transfers. The written text is encrypted to hide its meaning before it is sent over the Internet. A process called steganography hides graphic images and sends them undetected over the Internet. Gangsters operate gambling sites online as well as other illegal enterprises. Terrorists operate Web sites that incorporate elaborate symbols to deliver hidden messages. They also use the sites as recruitment tools and propaganda dissemination vehicles.

Prevalence

In 2004, a survey by the Gartner research group indicated that 1.98 million people in the United States had been victimized for $2.4 billion in checking account fraud. The same report estimates that more than fifty-seven million Amer-

Milestones in Cybercrime History

1971 John Draper discovers that a whistle from a cereal box makes a 2,600-hertz tone, which lets him trick telephone company computers and allows him to make free phone calls. "Phone phreaking" is born.

1981 First virus "in the wild" is spread on Apple II operating-system discs. Called Elk Cloner, the relatively harmless virus appears in computers after their fiftieth boot-ups; it presents a two-verse poem, then reappears after every fifth boot-up.

1982 During a nine-day period, hackers break into more than sixty computer systems before being caught; victims include computers of the Sloan-Kettering Cancer Center and Los Alamos Laboratories.

1982 First documented virus is demonstrated by Fred Cohen at a security seminar.

1984 Magazine *2600* is launched to provide information and tips to hackers and phone phreaks. The Legion of Doom and the Masters of Deception computer clubs form to provide hackers and phreaks other venues for exchanging information.

1984 Federal Comprehensive Crime Control Act gives the Secret Service jurisdiction over computer fraud.

1986 First PC-based trojan is released in PC-Write, a shareware program.

1987 Donald Burleson of USPA Insurance is the first person convicted of "harmful access to a computer" for setting off a logic bomb in his former employer's computer system after being fired. His bomb wiped out 168,000 company records.

1988 Morris worm is released on the ARPANet (which will later become the Internet) and spreads to more than six thousand networked computers, causing havoc in university and government systems.

1988 Kevin Mitnick is convicted of violating network security at Digital Equipment Corporation and is sentenced to one year in prison.

1988 First National Bank of Chicago is victimized in a $70 million electronic robbery.

1990 Secret Service launches Operation Sundevil sting operation, and computer hackers in fourteen U.S. cities are arrested for credit card theft and telephone and wire fraud.

1990 Woman calling herself Natasha Grigori founds antichildporn.com, a group of hackers who hunt for child pornography on the Internet and report sites or addresses they find to law-enforcement authorities.

1992 Virus Creation Laboratory distributes first virus-creation kits, with pull-down menus and selectable payloads.

1995 Kevin Mitnick is arrested and charged with wire fraud and possession of stolen computer files; he is held without trial for four years.

1995 Department of Defense computers are attacked online more than 250,000 times, and hackers vandalize several federal Web sites.

1999 First combination virus and worm, known as Melissa, uses Microsoft Outlook and Outlook Express address books to send itself around the world.

2000 Love Letter worm becomes first major denial-of-service attack, shutting down Web sites as large as Yahoo and Amazon.com.

2003 "Phishing" appears as a new crime fad, as hackers send out millions of e-mail messages disguised as legitimate inquiries from well-known sources that seek personal information.

2004 Two America Online (AOL) employees are arrested for stealing 92 million names from AOL records over the previous year.

2005 In plea-bargain agreement, federal government convicts self-styled "Robin Hoods of cyberspace" of copyright violation for putting millions of dollars worth of films, software, and computer games on the Internet for free distribution.

ican Internet users received electronic mail phishing for personal information, and nearly two million people had been tricked into sending their personal data to scammers.

Criminal justice professor Marjie Britz estimated that "the vast majority of Fortune 500 companies have been electronically compromised to the tune of at least $10 billion/year." If less than 20 percent of corporate crime is reported, the number of companies and their losses could be far higher.

Internet "baby-sitter" software has been developed for use by parents to safeguard their children from deleterious Internet material and chat rooms, but it is no substitute for careful monitoring of children's online activity.

Internet crime continues to expand, and criminals find new ways to victimize people. Major companies have been founded on virus-scanning technology. Many other private companies have been formed to investigate cybercrime.

Investigation

At issue in investigating cybercrime effectively are training enough officers to conduct investigations, developing sufficient case law and knowledge among prosecutors to prosecute criminals, and establishing effective punishments to deter cybercriminals and effectively protect the private and public sectors of American society.

Since the mid-1960's, the Federal Bureau of Investigation (FBI) has effectively promoted crimefighting through the use of task forces. These have been used to fight organized crime, distribution of drugs and guns, and many other crime problems. In 1996, the FBI formed the Computer Investigations and Infrastructure Threat Assessment Center (CITAC) to coordinate computer crime initiatives. When it comes to cybercrime, the FBI continues to coordinate task forces but also offers investigative help and support, training, grants and other assistance to state and local agencies as they try to handle the growing problem.

Even though computer crime and cybercrime have been in the public consciousness since the late 1980's, the majority of police departments, and perhaps the majority of states' law-enforcement agencies, do not have well-trained, well-equipped computer crime investigation units. A few large cities, such as New York, Washington, D.C., and San Francisco, have had computer crime units since the late 1980's. These units were formed with the help of the FBI. In 2004, however, only large and well-funded departments had effective cybercrime investigative capabilities. Mid-sized and small cities had no capability for such investigations. Larger cities like the ones mentioned above and regional cooperative ventures, like the Sacramento Valley High-Tech Crimes Task Force, emerged as leaders in the field.

The Institute for Security Technology Studies at Dartmouth College convened a meeting of leading national and state agencies in 2003 to draft a coordinated research and development agenda for fighting cybercrime. Training and research were slowly being implemented to equip investigators with the necessary expertise to investigate cybercrime. The FBI and some of the larger, better-funded law-enforcement agencies offered training opportunities in the field of cybercrime. A few colleges and universities offered classes in the subject. A growing literature on cybercrime and investigations was emerging. Nevertheless, most investigation was still carried out by private sector employees of computer firms and by companies created to conduct cyberinvestigations.

Most police agencies do not have the necessary resources to provide adequate training for their officers and investigators. The ability to conduct investigations of cybercrime includes not only all the training to investigate normal street crime but also a thorough knowledge of computer systems, electronic evidence collection, preservation and analysis techniques, both logical and physical analysis, and forensic analysis techniques. Most departments that do any cyber-investigation are fortunate enough to have staff members who had learned about computers before they arrived. Others have learned on the job. Organized training is still emerging and is still expensive.

Prosecution

When criminal activity on the Internet was first being recognized, it was not taken very seriously by law-enforcement agencies. Women who complained of being harassed or stalked were told to avoid particular chat rooms or to delete electronic mail messages from the harassers. Victims of fraud were told that nothing could be done to recover their money. Hackers were considered to be harmless curiosities. As the phenomenon of cybercrime gradually came to be understood, law-enforcement personnel realized the criminal justice field would be changed forever.

One of the problems with successfully prosecuting cybercrime is that of establishing jurisdiction. At issue is who should have jurisdiction when an offense occurs. Considering that the victim and the offender may be thousands of miles apart, the answer to this question has been difficult. Some have expressed the idea that cyberspace should be designated a separate and unique jurisdiction. A consensus has yet to emerge. However, the number of cases that have been tried has rapidly expanded, so the issue of jurisdiction is expected to become clearer.

Perhaps the most important computer crime statute, the Computer Fraud and Abuse Act of 1984, was the first major piece of legislation to govern cyberspace. Since its passage, a number of other laws have been enacted to address computer crime. Because there are a large number of types of such crimes, many laws are necessary.

Important on the list are the Electronic Communications Privacy Act of 1986, the Computer Abuse Amendments Act of 1994, the Electronic Espionage Act of 1996, the Electronic Theft Act of 1997, and the Digital Theft Deterrence and Copyright Damages Improvement Act of 1999.

On January 1, 2004, Congress passed a new federal antispam law in response to dramatically increasing levels of spam arriving in citizens' electronic mail in-boxes. The FBI, in cooperation with the Direct Marketing Association, launched an antispam initiative called Operation Slam-Spam. As of May, 2004, this operation had turned fifty cases over to state and federal prosecutors. In a similar case from 2003, New York State prosecutors sent Howard Carmack to prison for three-and-a-half years for sending 825 million junk electronic messages from his home. Big Internet providers have been involved in suing spammers for several years. Now federal and state agencies are also getting involved.

Along with an expanding amount of federal law to curtail cybercrime, states also have an expanding collection of statutes to deal with the issue. Among the topics covered under these laws are: computer tampering, which includes modification to programs or to the way a network or networked computer operates; computer trespassing, or unauthorized access to computer systems; disruption of computer services statutes, which seek to protect the integrity of Internet service providers; computer fraud statutes, which include all forms of fraudulent activity but specifically cover cases in which a computer is used to conduct the activity; spam-related statutes, which generally focus on using a network to falsify the header information on mass electronic mail; unlawful use of encryption statutes, which are aimed at using this technology to hide information passed between cybercriminals and increasingly among terrorists and drug traffickers.

Cyber-stalking laws make it illegal to use the Internet to harass or threaten individuals, especially for purposes of extorting money. Other

After earning notoriety as a convicted computer hacker, Kevin Mitnick, seen here in 2002, was barred by the terms of his probation from working on computers but received permission to use a computer to write books and emerged as the author of several best-selling works on cybercrime. *(AP/Wide World Photos)*

broad categories of crime that have had to be covered in the cybercrime rubric include money laundering and monetary transactions, racketeering, economic espionage, theft of trade secrets, swindles, embezzlement, gambling, pornography, stalking, and terrorism.

Punishment

Early computer criminals were not punished very severely. There was little specific case law under which to punish their crimes, and most cases were novelties. When Robert Morris was convicted for releasing the first worm in 1988, the Cornell University graduate student was dismissed from school, fined $10,000 and placed on three years' probation. This was despite the fact that the worm had spread to six thousand computers and clogged both government and university systems at an estimated $100 million in damages. In 1992, Kevin Poulsen, who was wanted for other Internet crimes, rigged the phone system of a radio station in order to win a contest fraudulently. He spent five years in prison for computer and wire fraud. In 1994, Vladimir Levin was sentenced to three years in prison for stealing $10 million from Citibank.

The courts are beginning to realize that cybercrimes are at least as bad as any white-collar crimes and that they deserve to be punished accordingly. In early 2005, a federal court found nineteen-year-old Minnesota resident Jeffrey Lee Parsons guilty of "intentionally causing or attempting to cause damage to a computer." In August, 2003, Parsons had released onto the Internet a worm that affected more than seven thousand computers. Conviction for this crime can carry sentences of up to ten years in prison and $250,000 in fines, but a federal judge sentenced Parsons to the minimum term of eighteen months in prison.

According to estimates, cyber-thieves take an estimated $100 billion annually, with 97 percent of the crimes going undetected. Brown, Esbensen, and Geis (2001) say hackers' offenses cost an average $104,000 per incident in damage and labor and productivity costs. The criminal justice system is just beginning to address the issue effectively but is constantly having to catch up to the challenges posed by cybercriminals.

Donald R. Dixon

Further Reading

Baase, Sara. *A Gift of Fire: Social, Legal, and Ethical Issues for Computers and the Internet.* 2d ed. Upper Saddle River, N.J.: Prentice-Hall, 2003. Broad discussion of issues related to computers, cybercrime, and related issues.

Clifford, Ralph D, ed. *Cybercrime: The Investigation, Prosecution, and Defense of a Computer-Related Crime.* Durham, N.C.: Carolina Academic Press, 2001. Collection of chapters by different authors detailing cybercrime and investigation, including selected court cases.

Shinder, D. L., and Ed Tittle. *Scene of the Cybercrime: Computer Forensics Handbook.* Rockland, Mass.: Syngress, 2002. Chapter 2 contains a brief history of cybercrime.

Stephenson, Peter. *Investigating Computer-Related Crime.* Boca Raton, Fla.: CRC Press, 2000. Moderately technical discussion covering types of computer crimes, their impacts, investigations, and different forensic technologies available.

See also Bank robbery; Cable and satellite television signal theft; Computer forensics; Consumer fraud; Cryptology; Fraud; Identity theft; Pornography; Private detectives; Spam; Stalking; Telephone fraud; Terrorism; Theft; Trespass; White-collar crime.

D

DARE programs

Identification: Drug abuse prevention programs targeted at schoolchildren
Date: Founded in 1983
Criminal justice issues: Crime prevention; juvenile justice; substance abuse
Significance: The DARE programs, designed to help youths make life-affecting decisions, represent a cooperative effort between police departments and the local school systems.

Escalating drug abuse in the 1980's prompted the development of the Drug Abuse Resistance Education (DARE) program by the Los Angeles Police Department in 1983. The program's original goal was to focus on fifth- and sixth-grade elementary school children, helping them to build self-esteem and providing them with information about the detrimental effects of drug abuse, ideas for resisting peer pressure, and strategies for avoiding participation in gang and violent activities. Instruction was provided in seventeen lessons by trained law-enforcement officers as part of the curriculum in public schools. The program was later extended and included in middle- and high school curricula.

By the late-1990's, the DARE program had been implemented in almost 80 percent of the school districts in the United States, as well as in more than fifty-four countries throughout the world. Although it was a very popular program, results of numerous studies showed that DARE was not greatly effective in reducing drug abuse. In many cases, the program heightened the curiosity of its student participants about drug use, leading some to experimentation. The program also tended to alienate socially deviant youth. Further analysis of DARE revealed questionable objectives and content.

By 2004, a new DARE program was being implemented by many school districts in the United States. The number of lessons was reduced to ten, which focused on interactive, real-life, problem-based activities that emphasize decision-making skills. Lessons and related activities were being developed for elementary, middle-school, and high school curricula.

Alvin K. Benson

Further Reading

Maran, Meredith. *Dirty: A Search for Answers Inside America's Teenage Drug Epidemic.* San Francisco: Harper, 2003.

U.S. National Institute of Justice. *The D.A.R.E. Program: A Review of Prevalence, User Satisfaction, and Effectiveness.* Washington, D.C.: U.S. Department of Justice, 1994.

See also Comprehensive Drug Abuse Prevention and Control Act; Drug courts; Drug Enforcement Administration; Drug testing; Drugs and law enforcement; Office of Juvenile Justice and Delinquency Prevention; Juvenile justice system; Peace Officers Standards and Training.

Date rape

Definition: Rape committed by persons with whom the victims are voluntarily engaging in social outings
Criminal justice issues: Domestic violence; sex offenses; women's issues
Significance: Date rape is the most common form of rape committed against women between the ages of fifteen and twenty-five.

Rape, as defined by the U.S. Justice Department's National Violence Against Women Survey in 2000, is forced vaginal, anal, or oral sex. Acquaintance rape is a form of rape perpetrated by persons whom the victims already know. Approximately 85 percent of all rapes are committed by persons whom the victims know. Date rape is a specific form of acquaintance rape that most commonly occurs when a man (less than 2 percent of rapists are women) forces sex on a woman by means of threats or physical strength.

Men who rape women on dates may believe that the women owe them sex because they are spending money on them. Those who are likely to rape their dates often exhibit warning signs. For example, they tend to be physically or emotionally abusive to their dates or others, they talk negatively about women in general, they try to get their dates intoxicated, and they become hostile or aggressive when their dates reject their sexual advances.

It is estimated that more than 50 percent of all rapes occur during dates. However, while 55 percent of rapes committed by strangers are reported, only 19 percent of acquaintance rapes and only 2 percent of date rapes are reported to the police. One of the most common reasons for nonreporting is the fear of reprisal from the assailants.

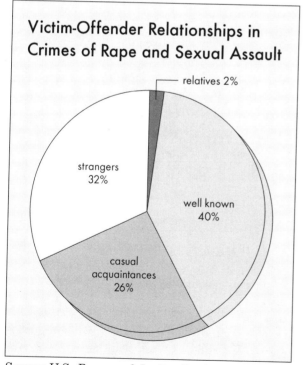

Victim-Offender Relationships in Crimes of Rape and Sexual Assault

relatives 2%

strangers 32%

well known 40%

casual acquaintances 26%

Source: U.S. Bureau of Justice Statistics, *Criminal Victimization.* Figures are based on all reported rapes and sexual assaults in the United States in 2002.

At colleges and universities, an estimated 20 to 25 percent of female students are victims of date rapes during the years they spend on campus. College fraternity members are more than twice as likely as other male students to commit date rape. Date rapes are also disproportionately committed by college athletes.

When date-rape cases go to trial, they differ from stranger-rape cases, in which defenses may argue that the accused rapists have been misidentified, or that no sexual acts occurred. Defenses in criminal date-rape cases often argue that the alleged sexual acts were consensual. Therefore, the prosecution must look for evidence demonstrating the use of physical force, such as photographs of genital and other physical injuries, damaged clothing, the existence of alcohol or other drugs in the victims' blood or urine, interviews with people to whom the victims have disclosed information about their assaults, and evidence from the rape scenes. In an estimated 90 percent of rape cases, physical evidence is available. However, only 3 to 10 percent of that evidence is actually collected.

From the perspective of the victims, date rape is often more traumatic than stranger rape because the victims are more likely to blame themselves for being raped. Moreover, the experience of being raped by trusted friends causes the victims to lose their ability to trust others.

Elizabeth M. McGhee Nelson

Further Reading

Sanday, Peggy Reeves. *A Woman Scorned: Acquaintance Rape on Trial.* Berkeley: University of California Press, 1997.

Smith, Merril D., ed. *Sex Without Consent: Rape and Sexual Coercion in America.* New York: New York University Press, 2001.

Warshaw, Robin. *I Never Called It Rape: The MS Report on Recognizing, Fighting and Surviving Date and Acquaintance Rape.* New York: HarperPerennial, 1994.

See also Campus police; Domestic violence; Pornography; Rape and sex offenses; Sexual harassment; Stalking; Statutory rape; Victimology.

Deadly force

Definition: Killing of people by police officers through the use of choke holds, firearms, or other methods of physical control

Criminal justice issues: Government misconduct; homicide; police powers

Significance: Because of controversies about excessive, inappropriate, and discriminatory applications of force to citizens by police officers, fatalities caused by the police have been reduced through training programs, regulations, and court decisions.

To control crime and maintain order in society, law-enforcement officers have traditionally been granted the authority to use physical force to capture or gain control of people who violate the law. American police officers, unlike those in some other countries, carry firearms, and police throughout the country have used their guns to kill people in the course of seeking to enforce the law and maintain order. Police officers have also caused people's deaths through the use of choke holds around people's necks and blows to the head administered with nightsticks, flashlights, or pistols.

The Context of Police Deadly Force

Deaths caused by the police were not randomly distributed throughout the broad spectrum of society, but instead occurred most frequently among poor people and members of racial minority groups who lacked the political power to complain effectively about improper police behavior. Because criminal offenders have easy access to firearms in the United States, American police officers know that they risk being shot; therefore they sometimes overreact to persons whom they suspect of being armed and dangerous. The problem has been compounded throughout American history because of negative attitudes toward poor people and members of minority groups. Officers have used guns, nightsticks, and choke holds more frequently in seeking to capture or gain control over people in inner-city neighborhoods. Lethal

physical force was applied not only to people suspected of committing felonies but also sometimes to people who argued with officers about parking tickets or failed to cooperate with the police about other relatively minor matters.

During the 1960's and 1970's, as African Americans became more assertive about gaining equal rights and American society became less tolerant of discrimination, many police departments came under sharp criticism for their harsh behavior toward members of minority groups. In the urban riots of the late 1960's, for example, most of the fatalities were caused by police officers' shooting of suspected looters and rioters. The actual nature and extent of police deadly force varied by city, depending on the training provided to officers and the guidelines developed by police departments for the use of firearms and other physical interventions. Deadly force was more likely to be applied by officers whose police chiefs saw their job as attacking criminal segments of society as opposed to serving the entire public in a professional manner.

Police work is one of the few professions in the United States whose practitioners are authorized to carry firearms and use deadly force; however, not all the world's police forces authorize their officers to carry firearms. *(Brand-X Pictures)*

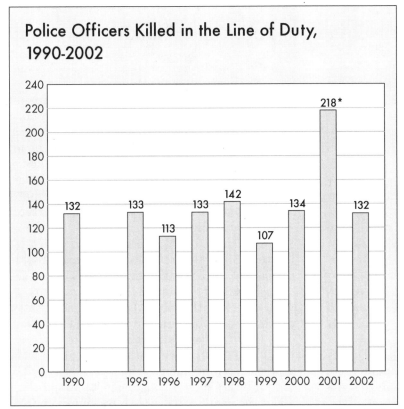

Police Officers Killed in the Line of Duty, 1990-2002

Source: Federal Bureau of Investigation, *Law Enforcement Officers Killed and Assaulted*. Figures include all state and federal officers killed feloniously and accidentally while in the line of duty. *Note that the figure for 2001 includes 72 officers killed in the September 11 terrorist attacks.

Control of Police Deadly Force

Controversies over highly publicized killings by the police led many police departments to develop stricter rules about the use of force. Greater attention was given to the precise situations in which officers would be justified in firing their guns or hitting someone with a nightstick. Officers also received more training in crowd-control techniques and immobilizing holds that would not threaten the lives of resisting civilians. Most important, courts and juries increasingly found police officers and their departments liable for needlessly causing the deaths of citizens. The threat that a city might have to pay millions of dollars in damages to the family of a person killed by police created even greater incentives for police chiefs to address the deadly force issue through stricter guidelines, better supervision, and increased training. Such guidelines still permit officers to use their weapons against armed offenders who pose an immediate threat, but they significantly narrow the circumstances in which it is reasonable for potentially lethal force to be applied.

As a result of these changes, the number of people killed annually by police officers in major U.S. cities dropped from approximately 350 in 1971 to 170 in 1984. Yet the guidelines for officers had developed unevenly, and some states still permitted officers to shoot unarmed suspects if they were suspected of fleeing from the scene of a felony. In 1985, in *Tennessee v. Garner*, the U.S. Supreme Court provided a common national rule regarding the use of deadly force on fleeing felons. The Court declared that it was an unconstitutional violation of a person's rights to shoot at an unarmed suspect who is fleeing from the scene of a crime. Under Fourth Amendment rules, such actions constituted an unreasonable use of force to seize people.

This ruling helped to clarify and standardize the application of deadly firearms force, but it could not solve the problem completely. Some police departments, including that of Los Angeles, faced further controversy and lawsuits over deaths that resulted from the use of choke holds—especially given that the holds appeared to be applied most frequently to members of minority groups.

Although police use of deadly force will inevitably remain an issue, particularly because of the need for American police to confront armed criminals, developments since the 1970's have reduced the scope of this problem.

Christopher E. Smith

Further Reading

Alpert, Geoffrey, and Lorie A. Fridell. *Police Vehicle and Firearms: Instruments of Deadly Force*. Prospect Heights, Ill.: Waveland Press, 1992. A broad overview of negligence and liability issues concerning vehicular pursuits and police shootings.

Del Carmen, Rolando V. *Civil Liabilities in American Policing*. Englewood Cliffs, N.J.: Prentice-Hall, 1991. Examination of problems of civil liability faced by individual police officers, departments, and municipal governments.

Fyfe, James J., ed. *Readings on Police Use of Deadly Force*. Washington, D.C.: Police Foundation, 1982. Collected essays on aspects of police use of deadly force.

Kappeler, Victor E. *Critical Issues in Police Civil Liability*. Prospect Heights, Ill.: Waveland Press, 1993. Examination of legal rules and consequences affecting police use of deadly force.

Milton, Catherine H., et al. *Police Use of Deadly Force*. Washington, D.C.: Police Foundation, 1977. Another collection of essays on the subject.

Skolnick, Jerome H., and James J. Fyfe. *Above the Law: Police and the Excessive Use of Force*. New York: Free Press, 1993. Examination of police use of deadly force in the larger context of police brutality.

Stroud, Carsten. *Deadly Force: In the Streets with the U.S. Marshals*. New York: Bantam Books, 1996. Exploits of modern federal fugitive hunters.

Thrasher, Ronald. "Internal Affairs: The Police Agencies' Approach to the Investigation of Police Misconduct." In *Police Misconduct*, edited by Michael J. Palmiotto. Upper Saddle River, N.J.: Prentice-Hall 2001. This college-level course reader covers many aspects of police misconduct, including brutality and corruption.

See also Arrest; Branch Davidian raid; Civilian review boards; Color of law; High-speed chases; Miami riots; MOVE bombing; Nonlethal weapons; Police brutality; Reasonable force; Ruby Ridge raid; Special weapons and tactics teams (SWAT); *Tennessee v. Garner*.

Death qualification

Definition: Procedure used in selecting jury members to try death-penalty cases

Criminal justice issues: Capital punishment; convictions; juries

Significance: The screening process in which prospective jurors are questioned about their views on capital punishment tends to exclude anti-death-penalty candidates. Critics argue that the juries, when finally chosen, are more likely to convict as a result of the screening.

Death qualification refers to a process that some prospective jurors undergo. In a capital case, potential members of the jury must be able to convince the court that they will be able to consider death as a possible punishment should the defendant be convicted of the capital crime.

Though this sounds like a simple exercise, the process is complicated by the fact that many potential jurors have strong, long-standing beliefs about the death penalty that prevent them from being able to ever consider death as an appropriate punishment for any crime. Because both the defendant and the prosecution have a right to expect that jurors on a case will consider the appropriate law, anti-death-penalty jurors pose a potential problem for the system.

The law, as developed by the U.S. Supreme Court in the cases of *Adams v. Texas* and *Wainwright v. Witt*, states that jurors' personal beliefs or biases must not "prevent or substantially impair" their ability to follow the law. The importance of this standard is that prospective anti-death jurors, in order to serve, must convince courts that they can put aside their personal beliefs and consider death as a possible punishment after hearing the evidence.

There is a strongly held belief by some in the criminal justice system that, simply by being exposed to this death qualification process, the entire jury becomes "conviction-prone." In other words, because jurors have been probed at length by the judge and the attorneys about their death-penalty views, jurors have been given the clear impression that this case is more serious than most and that this defendant is very dangerous.

Some research supports the notion that jurors going through this process go into the guilt phase of the case with a bias against the defendant before any evidence has been heard.

William L. Shulman

Further Reading

Bohm, Robert M. *Deathquest II*. Cincinnati: Anderson, 2003.

Rivkind, Nina, and Steven Shatz. *Cases and Materials on the Death Penalty*. St. Paul, Minn.: West Publishing, 2001.

See also Bifurcated trials; Capital punishment; Jury system; *Voir dire*; *Witherspoon v. Illinois*.

One State's Requirements for Death-row Attorneys

Colorado is an example of a state in which trial courts appoint the attorneys to represent capital defendants. Each death-row attorney in Colorado must

✓ be licensed to practice law in the state of Colorado

✓ have at least five years of criminal litigation experience, including trials and post-conviction appeals

✓ have a minimum of three years of experience trying felony cases

✓ have at least three years of experience handling felony appeals

---

Death-row attorneys

Definition: Attorneys who specialize in representing defendants charged with capital crimes

Criminal justice issues: Attorneys; capital punishment; defendants

Significance: Outcomes of capital trials depend at least in part on the skills and resources of the defense attorneys who present defendants' cases to the judges and juries who decide whether the defendants are to live or die.

The right of defendants to effective representation in capital cases was established in the U.S. Supreme Court's 1932 *Powell v. Alabama* decision, in which the Court held that a capital defendant "must not be stripped of his right to have sufficient time to advise with counsel and prepare his defense." Attorneys who represent capital defendants are now required to meet certain special qualifications. In addition to being licensed to practice law in the jurisdictions in which their cases are heard, these attorneys must demonstrate their commitment to providing high-quality and zealous defenses. They must also satisfy certain training requirements in relevant state, federal, and international laws; pleading and motion practice;

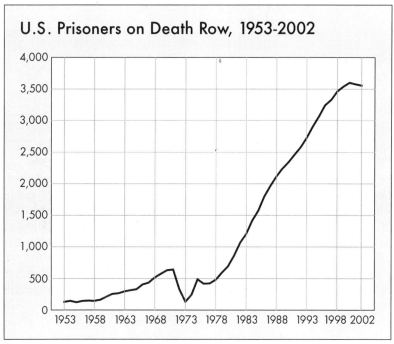

U.S. Prisoners on Death Row, 1953-2002

Source: U.S. Bureau of Justice Statistics, 2004.

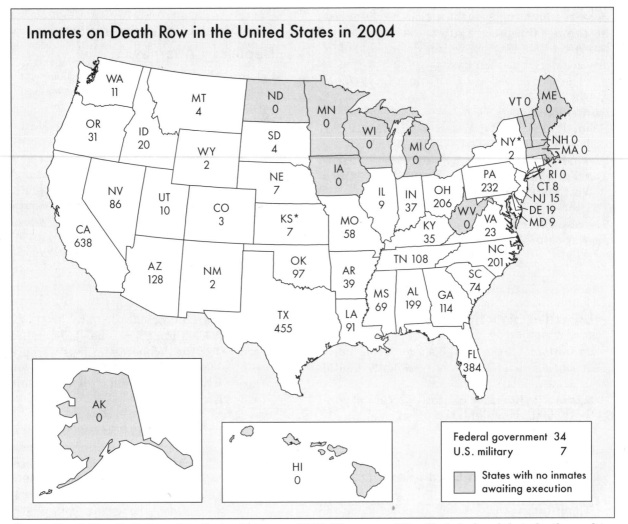

Inmates on Death Row in the United States in 2004

WA 11
MT 4
ND 0
MN 0
VT 0
ME 0
OR 31
ID 20
WY 2
SD 4
WI 0
NY* 2
NH 0
MA 0
NV 86
UT 10
CO 3
NE 7
IA 0
MI 0
PA 232
RI 0
CT 8
NJ 15
DE 19
MD 9
CA 638
KS* 7
MO 58
IL 9
IN 37
OH 206
KY 35
WV 0
VA 23
AZ 128
NM 2
OK 97
AR 39
TN 108
NC 201
SC 74
TX 455
LA 91
MS 69
AL 199
GA 114
FL 384
AK 0
HI 0

Federal government 34
U.S. military 7

☐ States with no inmates awaiting execution

Source: Death Penalty Information Center, February, 2005. *Kansas and New York declared their death penalties unconstitutional in 2004. Inmates on death row in 2004 totaled 3,479.

pretrial investigation; jury selection; trial preparation; and ethics.

In 1984, the American Bar Association (ABA) began publishing guidelines for the appointment and performance of defense counsel in death-penalty cases to create a national standard that would ensure high-quality legal representation for all defendants facing possible death sentences. The ABA guidelines apply to every legal stage of every case.

Issues concerning death-row attorneys include the right to competent counsel and the right to mitigation investigation. Legal representation of indigent defendants has become an in-

creasingly controversial topic of debate. Most concern is not over the question of whether death-row defendants have representation, as in the past, but rather how well they are represented. The Supreme Court's 1984 *Strickland v. Washington* decision created a standard for measuring the effectiveness of counsel. That ruling established a standard for death-row defendants to demonstrate that their representation has been ineffective and requires them to prove not only that they received substandard representation but also that such representation directly affected the outcomes of their cases. In *Wiggins v. Smith* (2002), a federal appeals court held that an effective defense must include the investigation of mitigating factors—evidence that may lessen the severity of the crime.

Allison M. Cotton

Further Reading

Lane, Nelson, and Burk Foster. *Death Watch: A Death Penalty Anthology*. Upper Saddle River, N.J.: Prentice-Hall, 2001.

Monk, Richard C. *Taking Sides: Clashing Views on Controversial Issues in Crime and Criminology*. 6th ed. Connecticut: Dushkin/McGraw-Hill, 2001.

U.S. Bureau of Justice Statistics. *Capital Punishment 2000*. Washington, D.C.: U.S. Government Printing Office, 2000.

See also Capital punishment; Counsel, right to; Defendants; Defense attorneys; Effective counsel; Execution, forms of; *Gideon v. Wainwright*; *Powell v. Alabama*.

Decriminalization

Definition: Process of lessening penalties for violations of specified laws

Criminal justice issues: Law codes; substance abuse

Significance: Decriminalization is a hotly debated alternative to the severe penalties and enforcement costs associated with legislation pertaining to social issues such as drug laws.

Decriminalization is a legal concept with applications in many areas of criminal law, ranging from assisted suicide to so-called victimless crime. However, the term is associated most frequently with illegal drug use, which until recent decades was an offense subject to severe penalties in virtually all states. During the last decades of the twentieth century, however, several states began enacting statutes that redefined possession of small amounts of marijuana as offenses to be punished with citations similar in severity to speeding tickets. Under these laws, penalties for possession of the illegal drug are light, usually no more than small fines, which are often suspended. Moreover, those found guilty of possession are not saddled with felony or even misdemeanor convictions and face no additional criminal or civil prosecutions.

The process of drastically reducing penalties for drug possession, or other offenses formerly treated as felonies, is called decriminalization. Decriminalization is an intermediate step between severe penalties and no substantial ramifications at all. Decriminalization is often wrongly equated with legalization, which is the complete removal of all penalties. As a concept, decriminalization of drug-possession offenses started gaining attention and support during the 1980's. By the end of the 1990's, eleven states had passed laws that decriminalized the possession of small amounts of marijuana—amounts meant only for personal use—while leaving in place, or even strengthening, criminal penalties for possession of large amounts.

There has been considerable opposition to the concept of decriminalization. Many Americans believe that the liberalization of drug laws will lead to a massive increases in usage of presently illegal drugs and that these increases will be associated with more crime, health, and unemployment problems. Additionally, some social commentators regard marijuana as a so-called gateway drug that leads directly to use of more dangerous and addictive drugs such as heroin.

Thomas W. Buchanan

Further Reading

Gray, Mike. *Drug Crazy: How We Got into This Mess and How We Can Get Out*. New York: Random House, 1998.

Husak, Douglas N., and Peter de Marneffe. *The Legalization of Drugs*. New York: Cambridge University Press, 2005.

Zimmerman, Bill, with Rick Bayer and Nancy Crumpacker. *Is Marijuana the Right Medicine for You? A Factual Guide to Medical Uses of Marijuana*. New Canaan, Conn.: Keats, 1998.

See also Commercialized vice; Comprehensive Drug Abuse Prevention and Control Act; Criminals; Drug courts; Drug Enforcement Administration; Drug legalization debate; Drugs and law enforcement.

Defendant self-representation

Definition: Situations in which criminal defendants reject professional legal counsel and represent themselves

Criminal justice issues: Attorneys; defendants; trial procedures

Significance: Defendant self-representation is a right of criminal defendants that has been recognized by the U.S. Supreme Court. However, that right sometimes comes into conflict with the right of defendants to counsel and their right to have fair trials.

First recognized by the U.S. Supreme Court in *Gideon v. Wainwright* (1963), the right of criminal defendants to counsel is now a cornerstone of the criminal justice system. The recognition of that right has generated questions about what rights, if any, criminal defendants have to waive counsel. The Supreme Court also found there was a right to self-representation in *Faretta v. California* (1975). The basis of this decision rests on the notion that personal autonomy means that counsel cannot be foisted on unwilling defendants. However, the right to self-representation raises a number of difficult practical and legal issues.

Limitations on the Right to Self-Representation

As a practical matter, virtually no judge wants criminal defendants to represent themselves. Even otherwise well-educated defendants who lack legal training almost inevitably inhibit the smooth functioning of courts because they lack knowledge of criminal procedures, the norms and rules governing pretrial proceedings, and the trial proceedings themselves. Defendant self-representation almost always makes for lengthier and more laborious proceedings. Moreover, criminal defendants who represent themselves raise difficult questions about the degree to which judges should intercede on their behalf when they neglect to make motions or raise objections that competent lawyers would.

Despite these questions, courts must acknowledge the right to self-representation recognized in the Supreme Court's *Faretta* ruling. They do so, first, by advising defendants of their right to counsel, and then, by trying to ensure that the defendants' decisions are unequivocal, voluntary, and intelligently made. This second step almost always includes a recitation of the dangers and disadvantages of not having lawyers. In addition, most courts inquire as to whether requests for defendant self-representation are made to delay the proceedings, in which cases judges will not grant the requests.

The Issue of Competence

The most difficult and controversial issues surrounding exercise of the right to self-representation involve whether such an exercise is "voluntary and intelligent." In a typical situation, a criminal defendant suffering from a mental disorder seeks to exercise the right to self-representation. Such circumstances raise profound and troubling questions. When do defendants' autonomy and personal choice become so tainted by their mental disorders that the state should not permit them to pursue paths that are almost certainly more likely to result in their convictions and harsher sentences? Is it possible that the right of self-representation in such circumstances might conflict with the defendants' right to receive fair trials? How should these rights be balanced?

The so-called "insanity defense" is sometimes the most powerful defense available to a criminal defendant. However, a characteristic of some mental disorders is the inability of afflicted persons to recognize that they have the disorders. Defendants with mental disorders may not want their counsel to present evidence concerning their mental status and run into conflicts with their attorneys who believe that such evidence might be the most effective evidence available. In such situations, defendants may demand to represent themselves. How to handle these questions becomes all the more difficult in light of how challenging it is to draw definitive conclusions about the nature or even existence of mental illness.

Two cases illustrate the difficult of these issues. The first involves the "Unabomber" Theodore Kaczynski, who was tried during the late 1990's for a series of bombings. Kaczynski vigorously tried to prevent his attorneys from presenting evidence about his mental status but failed. The court then denied his request to represent himself. Faced with a choice between an inquiry into his mental status and a guilty plea, he chose the latter, and later unsuccessfully appealed his conviction on the grounds that his plea was "involuntary." What makes Kaczynski's case especially difficult is continuing debate about what mental illness afflicted him, or even whether he suffered from mental illness at all.

The second case involved Colin Ferguson, a man accused of shooting nineteen people on a commuter train and killing six. He successfully requested that he represent himself at trial. While virtually all commentators agreed that an insanity defense would be Ferguson's best hope at trial, he chose to argue that another assailant committed the murders after stealing his gun, thus contradicting the testimony of numerous witnesses. Ferguson's defense itself might well have been an example of psychosis. The bizarre trial that ensued ended in Ferguson's conviction.

The Kaczynski and Ferguson cases—both controversial and both representing different decisions as to whether criminal defendants should represent themselves—demonstrate the extraordinary challenges faced by the criminal justice system in reaching principled approaches in such cases.

Robert Rubinson

Further Reading

Bardwell, Mark C. *Criminal Competency on Trial: The Case of Colin Ferguson*. Durham, N.C.: Carolina Academic Press, 2002. Full description of the Ferguson case.

Mello, Michael. *The United States of America Versus Theodore John Kaczynski: Ethics, Power, and the Invention of the Unabomber*. New York: Context Books, 1999. Description of the Kaczynski case by an attorney who assisted Kaczynski's appeal.

Rhode, Deborah L., and David Luban. *Legal Ethics*. 4th ed. New York: Foundation Press, 2004. Casebook that excerpts portions of judicial opinions in the Kaczynski case, asks pointed questions about the conduct of the case, and provides additional citations to other commentators and sources.

Sabelli, Martin, and Stacey Leyton. "Train Wrecks and Freeway Crashes: An Argument for Fairness and Against Self-Representation in the Criminal Justice System." *Journal of Criminal Law and Criminology* 19 (2000): 161-235. Examination of the importance of mental illness evidence and the right of self-representation.

See also Attorney ethics; Counsel, right to; Effective counsel; *Faretta v. California*; *Gideon v. Wainwright*; *Habeas corpus*; Insanity defense; Mental illness; Psychological evaluation; Psychopathy; Unabomber.

Defendants

Definition: Persons or organizations who are formally accused of crimes; litigants in lawsuits

Criminal justice issues: Constitutional protections; defendants; trial procedures

Significance: The American criminal justice system is designed to pit litigants against one another in virtual fights for justice. Criminal justice procedures attempt to balance defendants' rights and government's interests in speedy and efficient trials with the desire for justice. The rules of criminal procedure are therefore designed to ensure that defendants' rights are protected.

The Sixth Amendment to the U.S. Constitution grants to all defendants the right to speedy and public trials decided by impartial juries in the states and districts in which the crimes are alleged to have been committed. The Sixth Amendment also grants accused persons the right to be informed of the nature and cause of the accusations against them, to be confronted by witnesses against them, to present witnesses of their own to testify on their behalf, and to consult with attorneys.

The Fifth Amendment to the Constitution grants defendants the right not to be tried more than once for the same crimes (the double jeopardy clause), the right not to testify against themselves (self-incrimination clause), and the right to established courses of judicial proceedings designed to protect the legal rights of citizens (due process clause). These are all federal constitutional protections that states can supplement but cannot take away.

Defendants are subject to criminal or civil procedures depending on whether they are accused of violating criminal or civil statutes. The rules of criminal procedure differ from those of civil procedure because criminal and civil proceedings have different objectives and results. Criminal cases involve violations of criminal law, while civil cases involve violations of tort law, such as negligence and wrongfulness. In criminal cases, the states bring the suit against defendants and must prove guilt beyond a reasonable doubt. By contrast, in civil cases, private citizens and organizations bring the suits against defendants, and they are required only to show that the defendants are liable by a preponderance of the evidence.

Allison M. Cotton

Further Reading

Abramson, Leslie, with Richard Flaste. *The Defense Is Ready: Life in the Trenches of Criminal Law*. New York: Simon and Schuster, 1997.

Acker, J. R., and D. C. Brody. *Criminal Procedure: A Contemporary Perspective*. 2d ed. Sudbury, Mass.: Jones and Bartlett, 2004.

Ingram, Jefferson L. *Criminal Procedure: Theory and Practice*. Upper Saddle River, N.J.: Prentice-Hall, 2005.

See also Change of venue; Criminal procedure; Criminals; Double jeopardy; Due process of law; Equal protection under the law; Indictment; Mitigating circumstances; Plea bargaining; Pleas; Presumption of innocence; Public defenders; Self-incrimination, privilege against; Suspects; Verdicts; *Voir dire*.

Realistic Fiction

In Joyce Carol Oates's 1989 novel *American Appetites*, Ian and Glynnis McCullough are a long-married couple who get into a drunken quarrel over the wife's suspicions that her husband has been unfaithful. As the quarrel turns into a brawl, Glynnis accidentally falls through a plate-glass window and is fatally injured. Afterward, Ian is tried for second-degree murder. During the trial, the prosecution's evidence eventually appears so weak that the prosecutor reduces the charges against Ian to manslaughter. However, the jury acquits Ian of even that charge.

The novel is a generally realistic depiction of how the criminal process might affect a middle-class citizen who becomes a defendant. It is a suburban variant of a similar setting in Tom Wolfe's *The Bonfire of the Vanities* (1987). One of the more interesting dynamics in Oates's book involves the continued insistence of Ian's lawyer to him that nothing will come of the police investigation, the grand jury consideration of his wife's death, and so forth. In reality, attorneys must walk a careful line between encouraging their clients and seeming to be in control of matters, on one hand, and accurately conveying to their clients the possibilities of an adverse conclusion, on the other hand.

Timothy L. Hall

Defense attorneys

Definition: Attorneys who are engaged to represent criminal defendants and are paid by the clients

Criminal justice issues: Attorneys; defendants; pleas

Significance: Private attorneys are essential to fair defenses in criminal cases.

Private defense attorneys engage in the representation of persons charged with crimes in local, state, federal, or tribal courts. Unlike public defenders, private defense attorneys are engaged and paid by their clients, rather than by the state.

Criminal defense lawyers must be members of the bar in good standing in the jurisdiction in which they practice. A law student wishing to become a criminal defense lawyer will usually take (in addition to the courses in criminal law generally required in law school) specialized courses preparing them for criminal trial work, including

A Movie Lawyer's Mixed Motives

Director Gregory Hoblit's 1996 film *Primal Fear* reveals one of the less attractive sides of attorneys. Actor Richard Gere plays prominent Chicago defense attorney Martin Vail, who represents a shy, stuttering, altar boy (Edward Norton) who is accused of murdering an archbishop after being caught near the scene of the crime covered in the archbishop's blood. Attorney Vail is less concerned with whether his client is innocent than with the publicity that the sensational murder case will attract to him. On this point at least, the film tracks reality. For successful lawyers, a prominent criminal case can generate an even more prominent—and more remunerative—case. In fact, the potential for publicity that the murder case in *Primal Fear* has makes the film realistic by having Vail represent his client for free. Lawyers refer to such arrangements as *pro bono* representation, short for *pro bono publicum*, meaning "for the good of the public." However, in the case of the lawyer in *Primal Fear*, it might be more accurate to say that he takes the case "*pro bono Vail*"—for the good of himself.

Timothy L. Hall

advanced criminal law, trial practice, criminal procedure, and negotiation. Many defense lawyers begin their career as prosecutors in local district attorney offices and go into private practice after receiving some criminal trial experience.

The defense lawyer's task is to represent the client zealously, regardless of any personal feelings about the defendant or the crime. If the client has not yet been charged, the defense attorney's job is to advise the client on communicating with the grand jury, to accompany the client to meetings with police and prosecutors, and to advise the client as to evidence. Once the client is arrested, the defense attorney will represent the client at bail hearings and arraignment. The defense attorney will often try to "build a Chinese wall" around the client, denying the police and prosecution access to the client and regulating the prosecution's access to evidence to the extent possible. The defense attorney is entitled to any information the prosecution has on the crime and defendant prior to trial, and the defense attorney will often use a private investigator to evaluate this information and discover new information. At trial, the criminal defense lawyer will seek to exclude damaging evidence, or at least minimize its impact, and will present evidence to introduce a "reasonable doubt" in the jury's mind as to guilt.

If a defendant is convicted, a criminal defense attorney may participate in filing an appeal, but a different attorney will usually represent the defendant on appeal.

While criminal defense lawyers often take cases to trial, they also spend considerable time negotiating plea bargains for their clients. A plea bargain is an agreement between the prosecutor's office and the defendant for the latter to plead guilty to a particular charge in exchange for a predetermined sentence. A defense lawyer must be prepared to offer a plea bargain to a prosecutor, evaluate any offer of a plea bargain by the prosecuting attorney, make sure that the client understands any offer, and help the client decide either to take the offer or to go to trial. It is, however, ultimately the client's responsibility (not the lawyer's) to decide whether to make or accept a plea-bargain offer.

Gwendolyn Griffith

Further Reading

Clehane, Dianem, and Nancy Grace. *Objection! How High-Priced Defense Attorneys, Celebrity Defendants, and a 24/7 Media Have Hijacked Our Criminal Justice System*. New York: Hyperion, 2005.

Neubauer, David W. *America's Courts and the Criminal Justice System*. 8th ed. Belmont, Calif.: Thomson/Wadsworth, 2005.

Wishman, Seymour. *Confessions of a Criminal Lawyer*. New York: Penguin, 1982.

Wolfram, Charles. *Modern Legal Ethics*. St. Paul, Minn.: West Publishing, 1986.

See also Attorney ethics; Celebrity trial attorneys; Counsel, right to; Criminal justice system; Death-row attorneys; Defendant self-representation; District attorneys; Effective counsel; Paralegals; Public defenders; Public prosecutors; *Voir dire*.

Defenses to crime

Definition: Justifications and excuses offered by criminal defenses in attempts to win cases or have charges dropped or reduced

Criminal justice issues: Defendants; medical and health issues; pleas

Significance: Many potential justifications and excuses are offered by criminal defendants for their illegal acts, and it is up to the courts to determine their validity.

To protect themselves from prosecution, persons accused of committing criminal acts can use a variety of defenses, which fall into two broad categories: denying all involvement in the acts and acknowledging involvement while denying responsibility. *Actus reus* is the actual commission of a criminal act. Defendants who deny *actus reus* are denying having committed the acts with which they are charged. In effect, they are simply asserting that their prosecutors are accusing the wrong people. *Mens rea* pertains to the mental elements behind commissions of crimes—what is known as criminal intent. Defendants who deny *mens rea* are acknowledging their commission of the acts in question but are also claiming either that their acts were justified or that their actions must be excused because of the circumstances surrounding them.

Justifications

Justifications involve situations in which accused persons admit to committing criminal acts but claim their acts were legally justified for any of various reasons. The accused persons are admitting to committing the acts. They understand fully that the acts are wrong and illegal but are submitting that they were legally justified in committing those acts because of circumstances.

Otherwise criminally punishable acts can be justified under numerous circumstances. The best known justification is self-defense. For defendants to make that claim successfully, they must prove that they had a reasonable belief that they were in imminent danger and used reasonable force to quell the danger. Justifiable self-defense can also include defending family members, friends, and the helpless. It does not apply to preemptive strikes against possible threats or acts of vengeance.

Most states adhere to a retreat doctrine that requires defendants claiming self-defense to show that they took all means to avoid or escape the dangerous situations before using force. However, this doctrine usually does not apply in situations in which persons are attacked within their own homes, from which they are not expected to retreat.

A second justification for criminal acts is performance of a public duty—committing criminal acts in order to acknowledge a higher loyalty, such as upholding the law. This concept supports issues of military justice and diplomatic immunity and covers police behavior, including shooting looters after natural disasters cause a breakdown in public order. The main idea regarding this defense is that upholding the law is a higher authority that may permit otherwise criminal behavior.

The justification of necessity involves committing one criminal act in order to avoid having to commit, or avoid, a greater wrong. Examples of situations in which the necessity of justification might apply include violating a speed limit to get a gravely ill person to a hospital, dispensing drugs without a prescription in a medical emergency, breaking and entering an empty structure to avoid freezing to death, and destroying property to prevent the spread of a fire. In most jurisdictions, economic necessity is not acceptable as a justification for stealing; however, the government's power to pardon may be invoked in special cases.

The consent of victims is sometimes recognized as a justification by courts in cases in which it can be shown that the victims of criminal acts voluntarily consented to the offenders' acts in advance. For such a defense to be acceptable, it must be proved that the victims were capable of giving informed consent, that offenses themselves were "consentable" (murder and statutory rape are examples of crimes that are not considered consentable); consent was not obtained by fraud; and the persons giving consent had authority to do so.

Excuses

Legal excuses for criminal behavior may be acceptable for defenses in situations in which the accused admit to committing the acts but provide satisfactory reasons why they should not be held responsible for those acts. Such defenses typically argue that the accused did not act from their own volition or free-will and thus did not have the true criminal intent necessary for criminal liability.

A common excuse is duress: being forced by others to do something wrong. The principle behind the idea of duress as a defense is that people who are forced to commit illegal acts should not be held responsible for those acts. An often-cited example of duress is cases involving persons who are forced to rob banks or commit other criminal acts while under gunpoint. The laws of different states vary on the specific circumstances in which duress defenses apply. However, the general rule is that if the lives of the accused—or others—are immediately threatened, the accused are judged to be under duress and excused from their behavior.

Involuntary intoxication is another legal excuse for criminal behavior. Involuntary intoxication may occur when people are forced, against their will, to consume alcohol or intoxicating drugs and when people consume intoxicants unknowingly, as when drugs are slipped into their drinks or food. Defendants who have been intoxicated under those conditions may be said to have lost their volition or free will. The validity of that type of defense may rest on the strength and dosage of the intoxicants that are involved.

Honest mistakes are sometimes accepted as legitimate excuses for criminal acts. A classic example of an honest mistake is a man leaving a restaurant with someone else's umbrella, thinking it is his own. In such a case, no criminal act occurs because there is no criminal intent *mens rea*. Such situations are referred to as mistakes of fact. On the other hand, ignorance of the law itself is not an acceptable excuse, unless the accused has made a reasonable effort to learn the law.

The youthfulness of defendants may also be an acceptable excuse for criminal acts. The general assumption is that individuals cannot have true criminal intent until their brains have fully developed to make rational adult decisions. In the common-law tradition, persons under the age of seven are presumed to be psychologically incapable of committing criminal acts. In modern American law, the states vary on what constitutes the age of accountability. In most, the dividing line is fourteen years, but the modern trend has been to lower that age.

Another excuse is entrapment—being induced by government to commit crimes that the perpetrators would not otherwise commit. This defense to criminal responsibility arises from the idea that it is wrong for state authorities, usually undercover police officers, to encourage criminal behavior. When police officers play upon the weaknesses of individuals to lure them into committing criminal acts, such actions may be ruled entrapment, and evidence against the defendants would be barred according to the exclusionary rule.

The Insanity Defense

The principle behind the so-called insanity defense holds that persons who lack the mental capacity to form the intent to commit crimes cannot be held legally responsible for their criminal acts. For that defense to be acceptable, the defendants must be judged legally insane. States vary in the legal standards they use to determine the sanity of defendants.

One of the standards for measuring sanity is the so-called M'Naghten rule, or right-wrong test. This rule holds that persons who do not have the mental capacity to differentiate right from wrong do not have the intellectual awareness necessary to form criminal intent. To be held criminally responsible for their actions, defendants must be able to grasp the significance of their acts. A modified version of the M'Naghten rule is the irresistible impulse test. This latter tests focuses more on the idea of volition to consider whether the accused have the ability to exercise free will to inhibit their criminal behavior. Persons who are judged to suffer from diseases of the mind so strong that they have lost the power to avoid committing criminal acts cannot be held criminally responsible according to this standard.

Under the substantial capacity test, "substantial capacity"—as defined by the American Legal Institute—is lost when persons lack the capacity to appreciate the wrongfulness of their criminal acts at the time they commit them.

Emerging Mental-Related Defenses

✓ Adopted child syndrome
✓ Accommodation syndrome
✓ American Dream syndrome
✓ Antisocial personality disorder
✓ Arbitrary abuse of power
  syndrome
✓ Attention deficit disorder
✓ Battered child syndrome
✓ Battered woman syndrome
✓ Black rage syndrome
✓ Cherambault-Kandinsky
  syndrome
✓ Chronic fatigue syndrome
✓ Computer addiction
✓ Cultural norms defense
✓ Distant father syndrome
✓ Drug-abuse defense
✓ Elderly abuse syndrome
✓ Failure-to-file syndrome
✓ Fan obsession syndrome
✓ Fetal alcohol syndrome
✓ Football widow syndrome
✓ Gangster syndrome
✓ Genetics defense

✓ Gone with the Wind syndrome
✓ Gulf War syndrome
✓ Holocaust survivor syndrome
✓ Legal abuse syndrome
✓ Meek-mate syndrome
✓ The minister-made-me-do-it
  defense
✓ Mob mentality defense
✓ Mother lion defense
✓ Multiple-personality disorder
✓ Munchausen-by-proxy
  syndrome
✓ Nice-lady syndrome
✓ Nicotine withdrawal
  syndrome
✓ Not-in-my-backyard syndrome
✓ Parental abuse syndrome
✓ Parental alienation syndrome
✓ Patient-therapist sex
  syndrome
✓ Pornography syndrome
✓ Posttraumatic stress disorder
✓ Premenstrual stress syndrome
✓ Prozac defense

✓ Rape trauma syndrome
✓ Repressed (or recovered)
  memory syndrome
✓ Ritual abuse syndrome
✓ Road rage
✓ Rock-and-roll defense
✓ Self-victimization syndrome
✓ Sexual abuse syndrome
✓ Sexually transmitted disease
  syndrome
✓ Sitting duck syndrome
✓ Situational stress syndrome
✓ Stockholm syndrome
✓ Super Bowl Sunday syndrome
✓ Super-jock syndrome
✓ Sybil (multiple-personality)
  syndrome
✓ Television defense
✓ Tobacco deprivation syndrome
✓ Twinkie defense
✓ UFO survivor syndrome
✓ Unhappy gay sailor syndrome
✓ Urban survival syndrome
✓ Vietnam syndrome

The insanity defense is often viewed by the media and public as a way for offenders to evade punishment for their criminal actions. However, the principle actually gives government the authority to incarcerate without conviction offenders who are judged to be mentally abnormal. The insanity defense is thus usually reserved for very serious cases. Defendants who are found to be legally insane in serious cases are often incarcerated in mental and psychiatric institutions for periods longer than the prison sentences that they would receive if they were convicted of the criminal charges against them.

A related defense is diminished capacity, a concept that stems from the idea that certain mental disorders may reduce offenders' culpability for their criminal acts while falling short of rendering them legally insane. Successful diminished capacity defenses usually result in reductions of charges or less severe punishments of convicted defendants. The automatism defense comes into play when it can be claimed that the accused acted unconsciously or semiconsciously because of some physical problem or mental problem aside from insanity. Reasons for such behavior may include epilepsy, concussions, blackouts, childhood traumas, and brainwashing.

As medical and psychiatric professionals continue to decipher the mysteries and development of the human brain, it is likely that new mental-related defenses will emerge. Numerous syndromes have already been advanced as criminal defenses as they have been diagnosed by medical professionals. Many of these syndromes are creations of industrious defense attorneys, but others are fully acknowledged by medical and legal professionals. All, however, have been presented as defense at one time or another. Because defending the criminally accused is an ever-evolving endeavor—much as criminal law itself is—new defenses may always be expected to emerge.

Theodore Shields

Further Reading

Conley, R, R. Luckasson, and G. N. Bouthilet. *The Criminal Justice System and Mental Retardation: Defendants and Victims*. Baltimore: Brookes, 1992. Broad study of the special legal problems of both defendants and victims who have mental disabilities.

Dershowitz, Alan M. *The Abuse Excuse*. Boston: Little, Brown, 1994. Thoughtful consideration of one of the most frequently cited excuses by criminal offenders by a prominent law professor and attorney.

Nicholson, R. "A Comparison of Instruments for Assessing Competency to Stand Trial." *Law and Human Behavior* 12, 313-322. Provides examples of the techniques used to screen for mental disorders.

Szegedy-Maszak, M. "The Brainwashing Defense." *U.S. News and World Report* (December 22, 2003): 135. Case study showing why a person who has experienced brainwashing may not be competent to stand trial.

Whitlock, Francis Antony. *Criminal Responsibility and Mental Illness*. London: Butterworths, 1963. Now classic study of the general issue of mental disability and criminal responsibility.

See also Aggravating circumstances; Battered child and battered wife syndromes; Common law; Criminal intent; Cultural defense; Diminished capacity; Duress; Excuses and justifications; Ignorance of the law; Insanity defense; *Mens rea*; Mental illness; Mitigating circumstances; Motives; Self-defense.

Deportation

Definition: Forcible expulsion of foreign visitors from a host nation, usually back to their home nations

Criminal justice issues: Espionage and sedition; international law; terrorism

Significance: Traditionally a tool for ridding countries of ordinary criminals and other foreign undesirables, deportation can also be used to remove political radicals or suspect terrorists.

The nations of the world have long used deportation as a criminal sanction. In U.S. history, however, deportation has tended to be regarded not so much as a judicial process involving punishment but as an administrative process to aid in shaping the composition of the national population. Indeed, in one of the Chinese exclusion cases, *Fong Yue Ting v. United States* (1893), the U.S. Supreme Court formally declared that deportation was an administrative process for removing undesirable and unwelcome resident aliens from the United States in the interest of "public welfare." With that ruling, due process provisions for deporting aliens persons were severely curtailed since deportation was not considered to pose a risk of "punishment."

Nevertheless, deportation was still deemed a serious matter that could significantly affect a person's future and required administrative hearings in order to be handled fairly. To that end, government interpreters have long been made available to aliens facing possible deportation. However, the services that such interpreters rendered to aliens during the early twentieth century were questionable, as the interpreters often took liberties in translating. In some deportation cases, the interpreters were provided by government prosecutors and occasionally even testified against the people for whom they were interpreting.

Aliens facing deportation also had a right to counsel. However, the significance of that right was often not made clear to them, and many chose not to utilize it. Moreover, even in cases in which aliens chose to use counsel, their attorneys sometimes had serious conflicts of interest, such as being employees of the Department of Justice or acting on primarily mercenary interests.

Federal Laws

One of the earliest deportation laws enacted in the United States was the Alien Act of 1798, which empowered the president of the United States to deport persons considered dangerous. The Immigration Act of 1903 permitted deportations in response to the social and economic changes accompanying late nineteenth century industrialization. After these laws came the Deportation Acts of 1917 and 1918, which made it easier for the federal government to deport anar-

The black nationalist movement of Marcus Garvey was dealt an irreparable blow during the 1920's, when the federal government deported Garvey back to his homeland, Jamaica. In 1923, Garvey was convicted on a trumped-up mail-fraud charge and sent to a federal prison. Four years later, President Calvin Coolidge commuted Garvey's sentence, only to have him deported immediately. Garvey was never allowed to return to the United States. *(Library of Congress)*

Stopping Deportations

Deportation proceedings can be stopped under the terms of the Immigration and Nationality Act of 1952, the first comprehensive federal immigration law that consolidated previous immigration laws into one coordinated statute. That law, and its many amendments, remains the basic federal immigration and nationality statute. The law empowers the U.S. attorney general to issue cancellations of departure, working through immigration judges or successful appeals of immigration court decisions to the Board of Immigration Appeals.

Cancellations of deportations can take several forms. One is a waiver of deportability in which an alien demonstrates that deportation would lead to unusual hardships for a parent, spouse or child who is a U.S. citizen or a permanent resident of the United States. Another form is a cancellation of removal for aliens who have been classified as permanent residents for at least five years and have resided in the United States continuously for at least seven years without any convictions for aggravated felonies.

Aliens can also get deportation orders cancelled when they can show that they have been in the United States continuously for ten years, while exhibiting good moral character and not engaging in document falsification, security violations, criminal activities, or marriage fraud. They must also show that their deportation would result in exceptional hardships to parents, spouses, or children who are U.S. citizens or permanent residents. Aliens resident in the United States for only seven years who otherwise meet the same qualifications can have their deportation orders suspended.

Political factors are also considered in suspending deportation orders, as when aliens can demonstrate that returning to their countries of origin would result in their persecution because of their race, religion, political opinions, nationality, or membership in certain groups.

Camille Gibson

chists. Sweeping immigration reforms in 1996 facilitated the deportation of resident aliens with criminal convictions, including those serving sentences for offenses as serious as first-degree murder.

In the twenty-first century, deportation remains an administrative tool for the removal of undesirable aliens from the United States. Reasons for deportation include entering the country improperly; violating the terms of admission or conditional residency; certain criminal convictions—in either the United States or abroad—including most serious felonies and "moral turpitude"; membership in a forbidden organization, such as a known terrorist group; certain cases in which immigrants become government dependents within five years of arriving in the country as the result of conditions that preceded their entry into the United States.

Further Reading

Cassese, Antonio. *International Criminal Law*. New York: Oxford University Press, 2003. A readable introduction to international criminal law examining the substantive aspects of the law and the procedural dimensions of state practice.

Panunzio, Constantine M. *The Deportation Cases of 1919-1920*. New York: Da Capo Press, 1970.

Preston, William. *Aliens and Dissenters: Federal Suppression of Radicals, 1903-1933*. Cambridge, Mass.: Harvard University Press, 1963.

Rush, George E. *The Dictionary of Criminal Justice*. 5th ed. New York: Dushkin/McGraw-Hill, 2000.

See also Attorney general of the United States; Diplomatic immunity; Extradition; Homeland Security Department; Illegal aliens; Immigration and Naturalization Service; Moral turpitude.

Depositions

Definition: Out-of-court statements from persons involved in cases

Criminal justice issues: Courts; legal terms and principles; witnesses

Significance: Depositions can provide attorneys with valuable information prior to trials and be useful during the trial process.

The formal and informal exchange of information between prosecutors and defense attorneys is called "discovery." One of the most common methods of discovery involves depositions, which are out-of-court statements given under oath by people involved in cases. They usually consist of oral examinations, followed by opposing attorneys' cross-examinations. Most states permit both prosecutors and defense attorneys to take depositions, and both sides have the right to be present during oral depositions.

Information collected through depositions can be used at trial or during the preparations for trials. The chief benefit of depositions is that they allow both prosecution and defense to know in advance what witnesses will say at the trials.

Depositions can take the form of written transcripts, videotapes, or both. There are instances in which information can be gathered prior to trial by either side by submitting sets of questions to the opposing side. This procedure requires that the questions be answered in writing and under oath.

In addition to depositions being taken so that attorneys are aware of what witnesses will say at trial, they also serve the purpose of questioning the credibility of witnesses' testimony. At the conclusion of a deposition, both sets of attorneys are provided with transcripts of the statements. This is a particularly useful function of the deposition when a witness's testimony at trial differs from what is offered in the deposition.

Depositions can also be taken to obtain testimony from important witnesses who cannot appear during trials, due to death or other reasons. When this is the case, testimony from depositions is read into evidence.

In contrast to testimony during trials, in which there are strict standards regarding what types of questions can be asked, questions asked during depositions are not held to such restrictions. Attorneys from either side have much wider latitude in the questions they may ask witnesses about different facets of the issues at hand.

Another obvious benefit of depositions is that they help preserve witnesses' recollections while the information is still fresh in their minds. This is especially important when long periods of time separate events and trials. Moreover, it sometimes happens that in the process of collecting depositions and reviewing all information collected, opposing attorneys find compromises that allow them to avoid the expense and time of trials.

Jenifer A. Lee

Further Reading

Meyer, Jon'a F., and Diana R. Grant. *The Courts in Our Criminal Justice System*. Upper Saddle River, N.J.: Prentice-Hall, 2003.

Rabe, Gary A., and Dean John Champion. *Criminal Courts: Structure, Process, and Issues*. Upper Saddle River, N.J.: Prentice-Hall, 2002.

See also Cross-examination; Discovery; Privileged communications; Subpoena power; Testimony; Witnesses.

Deterrence

Definition: Notion that harsh punishments discourage individuals from future involvement in criminal conduct

Criminal justice issues: Crime prevention; legal terms and principles; punishment

Significance: Prevention of crime is a major public issue; if punishments could indeed be shown to deter crime, the finding would be of considerable importance to numerous public policy questions.

There are two categories of deterrence, specific (or simple) and general. Both involve the idea that the threat of punishment will influence individuals not to commit crimes. Specific deterrence focuses on the individual and rests on the assumption that if the punishment imposed on a specific offender is severe enough for a crime, the offender will not commit crimes in the future. General deterrence focuses on society and is based on the idea that potential offenders will be deterred by the fear of being punished. Both categories of deterrence are based on the assumptions that potential offenders are rational and will perceive the possible punishment for crime as painful.

Does punishment, in fact, deter? Although many people would intuitively argue that it does, scholarly studies have not proven with certainty that punishment, or the fear of it, deters. There are several problems with the notion that punishment or fear of punishment will prevent crimes in the future.

A major assumption of deterrence theory is that people are rational and will consider the costs of committing a crime before committing the act. While this may be true in some cases, many crimes are unplanned events resulting from chance and opportunity.

Another assumption of deterrence theory is that swift punishment proportional to the seriousness of an offense will deter. In the American crim-

inal justice system, however, many offenders are provided with the opportunity for numerous delays prior to trial. Moreover, many cases end in plea bargains that call for punishment for less than the actual offense.

Both specific and general deterrence theories rest on the notion that most offenders fear being caught. Critics of deterrence policies, however, note that many potential offenders do not believe that they will be caught and prosecuted. Victimization surveys reveal that fewer than half the crimes committed in the United States are known to law-enforcement authorities. Violent crimes are the crimes most frequently reported to the police, yet studies reveal that fewer than 47 percent of all violent crimes are reported. Fear of punishment is further mitigated by the fact that fewer than 5 percent of all crimes reported to police are ultimately prosecuted.

A final argument used to bolster deterrence theory is the assertion that potential offenders

A primary justification of incarcerating offenders in prisons is that loss of freedom should be a powerful deterrent to committing crime. However, studies have found that many prisoners do not regard incarceration as especially painful, and a high proportion of former prisoners repeat their crimes and find themselves in prison again. *(Brand-X Pictures)*

Public Opinion on Effectiveness of the Death Penalty as a Deterrent to Violent Crime

Numbers in parentheses are responses of supporters of capital punishment versus opponents of capital punishment.

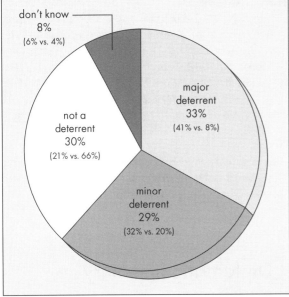

don't know
8%
(6% vs. 4%)

major
deterrent
33%
(41% vs. 8%)

not a
deterrent
30%
(21% vs. 66%)

minor
deterrent
29%
(32% vs. 20%)

Source: ABCNEWS.com Poll, June 2000. Percentages reflect responses of 1,004 adults from throughout the United States.

will avoid criminal activity because they fear the pain associated with punishment. Yet some studies have shown that although substantial portions of the offender population in prisons acknowledge that prison is recognized as a cost of criminal activity, many offenders do not consider it an especially painful experience. Even with regard to crimes that carry the potential for the death penalty, most studies reveal, few criminals fear the pain of punishment prior to the crime because they do not believe that they will ever receive such a punishment. Although politicians and the public often clamor for stiffer penalties as a solution to rising crime rates, few scholars would argue that such remedies are likely to prove very effective.

Robert R. Wiggins

Further Reading

Colvin, M. *Penitentiaries, Reformatories, and Chain Gangs: Social Theory and the History of Punishment in the Nineteenth Century*. New York: St. Martin's Press, 1997.

Foucault, Michel. *Discipline and Punish: The Birth of the Prison*. Translated by Alan Sheridan. New York: Vintage Press, 1995.

Friedman, Lawrence M. *Crime and Punishment in America History*. New York: Basic Books, 1993.

Tonry, Michael, and Richard Fraser. *Sentencing and Sanctions in Western Countries*. New York: Oxford University Press, 2001.

See also Capital punishment; Community-based corrections; Contempt of court; Crime; Fines; Incapacitation; Just deserts; Prison and jail systems; Punishment; Punitive damages; Rehabilitation.

Diminished capacity

Definition: Defense tactic used to reduce the culpability of a criminal defendant

Criminal justice issues: Defendants; legal terms and principles; mental disorders; pleas

Significance: Diminished capacity is a significant legal defense in crimes involving developmentally disabled persons.

Diminished capacity is a defense tactic wherein defendants argue that although they did break the law, they should not be held criminally accountable for doing so because of their impaired, or diminished, mental functions. This defense is invoked in attempt to reduce a defendant's culpability.

The diminished capacity defense is somewhat similar to that of insanity, but in diminished capacity cases defendants have not been diagnosed with mental illnesses that restrict their abilities to know right from wrong. The insanity defense was first recognized in 1843 in Great Britain when the delusional Daniel McNaghten killed the secretary to Prime Minister Robert Peel because McNaghten believed that the government was plotting against him. He was acquitted on the grounds of insanity.

In 2001, the Michigan Supreme Court ruled, in *People v. Carpenter*, that "evidence of mental incapacity less than insanity cannot avoid or reduce criminal responsibility by negating specific intent. Rather, only mental illness constituting insanity can negate intent, and mental illness or mental retardation not rising to insanity can result in entitlement to psychiatric treatment during incarceration."

The best-known examples of diminished mental capacity include the developmentally delayed condition sometimes called mental retardation. Pleading diminished capacity is not likely to result in a finding of not guilty but rather would be considered as a mitigating circumstance, resulting in the defendant being charged with a lesser offense. In some cases the diminished capacity is taken into consideration at sentencing.

In 1989, the American Bar Association promulgated a policy position recommending that the practice of execution of developmentally delayed persons be abolished. On June 20, 2002, the U.S. Supreme Court, in *Atkins v. Virginia*, held that "it is a violation of the Eighth Amendment ban on cruel and unusual punishment to execute death-row inmates with mental retardation." This landmark decision resulted in a moratorium on the execution of mentally disabled inmates.

The issue of chronological age as diminished capacity is controversial. In response to increasing violent criminal behavior by adolescents, most states have increased the number of juvenile offenders waived to adult court for prosecution. States have reduced the age for waiver of jurisdiction and established policies pertaining to mandatory waiver for specific crimes.

Developmental psychologists agree that preadolescent children lack the cognitive ability of abstract thinking and, consequently, cannot truly appreciate the seriousness of their conduct. The situation is exacerbated with adolescents who have lower than average intelligence. Chronologically, their age may qualify them for waiver; however, their mental age is below their chronological age due to limited intelligence.

Defense attorneys have attempted to extend the legal concept of diminished capacity to include the influence of alcohol and drugs as mitigating circumstances. These defenses are not successful and are commonly restricted by law. Some states have passed legislation that abolishes both the insanity defense and the defense of diminished capacity.

Duane L. Dobbert

Further Reading

Conley, R, R. Luckasson, and G. N. Bouthilet. *The Criminal Justice System and Mental Retardation: Defendants and Victims*. Baltimore: Brookes, 1992.

Reed, E. F. *The Penry Penalty: Capital Punishment and Offenders with Mental Retardation*. Lanham, Md.: University Press of America, 1993.

See also Bifurcated trials; Capital punishment; Defenses to crime; Jury duty; *Mens rea*; Mental illness; Mitigating circumstances.

Diplomatic immunity

Definition: Legal immunity that exempts foreign diplomats and their families from the laws of the host countries in which they work

Criminal justice issues: Espionage and sedition; immunity; international law

Significance: Diplomatic immunity is a commonly recognized practice in countries in which diplomatic personnel are legally exempt from laws within their host countries.

The purpose behind diplomatic immunity is the protection of diplomats from harassment or arrest while they are engaged in important international diplomacy while visiting other countries. The Vienna Convention on Diplomatic Relations (1961) first promoted the idea behind diplomatic immunity. During that convention, many nations signed a document that outlined how diplomacy should be carried out around the world. With few exceptions, this unifying agreement granted exemption from both criminal and civil laws for all international diplomats, representatives, and ambassadors. This exemption became commonly known as diplomatic immunity.

From that time, diplomatic agents became immune to arrest, trial and other related jurisdictions while abroad. They cannot be held for any form of arrest or detention. All diplomatic personnel are granted freedom of communication. Therefore, in any legal case, international diplomats are also excused from giving testimony, serving as witnesses, or providing evidence.

Diplomatic immunity also extends to the families of diplomatic representatives. Their homes and personal belongings are also exempt from legal searches. Diplomats are also excused from paying local dues and taxes. Ultimately, diplomatic immunity allows diplomatic agents and personnel authorization to function under their own laws while abroad. These are merely some of the comforts that all international diplomats enjoy.

Although it may seem that international diplomats benefit from the principle of diplomatic immunity, their home governments expect them always to regard all local laws and regulations while working for, or visiting, their host countries. They may not interfere in domestic matters and may be recalled to their home countries if they do so. If a foreign representative, diplomat, or ambassador breaks a local law; law-enforcement officials can pursue them legally. Individuals who fall into this category are usually deported back to their home countries for prosecution. However, diplomatic agents sometimes go unpunished for such crimes, claiming that they have diplomatic immunity and are therefore exempt. When this occurs, the host countries may ask the home governments to recall the offending representatives. It is then up to the diplomats' own governments to deal with their offenses.

It is possible for the diplomats' home countries to waive diplomatic immunity. This extreme case usually occurs when a diplomat commits a serious crime including, but not limited to, espionage, smuggling, violating child custody laws, or murder. In such rare cases, the diplomats would be expelled from their host countries. No longer welcomed, they would be deemed undesirable. In a familiar Latin phrase, such a person would be *persona non grata*.

Emily I. Troshynski

Further Reading

Denza, Eileen. *Diplomatic Law: A Commentary on the Vienna Convention on Diplomatic Relations*. 2d ed. Oxford, England: Clarendon Press, 1998.

McClanahan, Grant V. *Diplomatic Immunity: Principles, Practices, Problems*. Washington, D.C.: Institute for the Study of Diplomacy, 1989.

Von Glahn, Gerhardt. *Law Among Nations: An Introduction to Public International Law*. 7th ed. New York: Longman, 1996.

See also Deportation; Extradition; International law; International tribunals; Privileged communications; Testimony; Witnesses; World Court.

Discovery

Definition: Court process that requires prosecution and defense attorneys to share the information they gather

Criminal justice issues: Attorneys; legal terms and principles; prosecution; trial procedures

Significance: An overriding goal of the criminal justice system is fairness and impartiality in all phases of trial processes, and the principle of discovery helps achieve that goal.

American courts operate under an adversarial system in which opposing legal teams attempt to further their versions of the truth while being overseen by neutral judges. This system is based on the premise that adversarial proceedings provide the best way to uncover the truth and determine the facts in a case. Another premise of the system is that the accused must be considered innocent until proven guilty. It is thus the task of prosecutors to prove that defendants have committed the crimes of which they are accused beyond a reasonable doubt. To do that, prosecutors submit evidence and testimony. In contrast, the role of defense attorneys in the adversary system is to contest the criminal allegations made against the defendants and dissuade the courts or juries from concluding that the defendants are guilty.

Purpose of Discovery

When preparing for trial, both prosecutors and defense attorneys need to examine all available evidence that has been collected by police investigators, the results of any tests that have been conducted, and information about who is to be called to testify at the trials. American courts insist that both sides have equal opportunities to present complete cases, so that one side does not have an unfair advantage over the other. Discovery ensures that both sides to have equal access to the same information.

Discovery involves both the formal and informal exchange of information between prosecutors and defense attorneys. The types of information considered "discoverable" vary from state to state. Items that are particularly likely to be considered discoverable include laboratory reports, fingerprint results, ballistic tests, witness statements, defendants' confessions, psychiatric reports, and police reports.

The implementation of discovery tends to focus on the actions of prosecutors more than on defense attorneys because prosecutors have greater access to investigators (usually police officers), laboratory technicians, and advanced equipment for the analysis of evidence. If prosecutors were to restrict access to such information, it would jeopardize the right of defendants to fair trials. Defense attorneys therefore depend on strong discovery rules to secure their defendants' rights. Allowing defense attorneys to learn what the prosecutors know, or possess in the form of evidence, may spare defense attorneys from the difficult task of attempting to force their clients voluntarily to disclose information that they are reluctant to admit.

In addition to the formal process of discovery, there is an informal process. Informal prosecutorial disclosure operates under the long-held theory that providing defense attorneys with advance viewings of the prosecutors' cases encourages guilty pleas. Because prosecutors believe that defendants tell their attorneys only part of the story, informal disclosure allows the defense attorneys to be armed with the same information possessed by the prosecutors. The defense attorneys can use the evidence to confront their clients with more complete pictures of the events. This process often convinces both defendants and their attorneys to conclude they would be better served by entering guilty pleas.

Informal and Reciprocal Disclosure

The process of discovery does not require that only prosecutors turn over their evidence to defense attorneys. Defense attorneys must reciprocate by disclosing all relevant materials in their possession. This step seems only fair considering the goal of the adversary system to achieve fairness. If trials are to be conducted fairly, both sides must start on a level playing field and be prevented from presenting surprise evidence.

As with many issues in state courts, reciprocal-disclosure requirements

---

Vinny's Discovery

In the popular 1992 film *My Cousin Vinny*, Joe Pesci plays a cocky self-taught Brooklyn attorney whose first trial experience comes when he defends his cousin and a friend in a murder case in Alabama. Much of the film's humor emerges from Vinny's bumbling attempts to comply with formal courtroom procedures. Although he has passed the New York bar exam, he is a complete novice in a southern courtroom. There are many holes in Vinny's legal education, and one of the most glaring is exposed midway through the trial.

While Vinny takes smug satisfaction in persuading the prosecutor (Lane Smith) to give him copies of his files in the murder case, his girlfriend (Marisa Tomei) learns—from browsing through a legal textbook—that the prosecution is *required* to do just that. The girlfriend's revelation of that fact to Vinny generates powerful comic tension, but it also touches on a central feature of modern criminal practice: Prosecutors are required to reveal any evidence to the defendants that might possibly exonerate them.

In *My Cousin Vinny*, the prosecutor agrees to give Vinny copies of his files while the two men are out hunting during a break in the trial. Such fraternization between opposing attorneys is unusual during trials, but the film reflects another reality about attorneys: They may be fierce opponents inside a courtroom but cordial professional acquaintances outside.

Timothy L. Hall

vary from state to state. Some jurisdictions require defense attorneys to file notices of alibi defense—claims that their clients were elsewhere when the crimes with which they are charged were committed—along with lists of witnesses to be called to support the alibis. Such pretrial notices allow prosecutors to investigate witnesses before they testify in court so they can counter the claims of the defendants. Some jurisdictions require defense attorneys to disclose to prosecutors, prior to trial, that insanity pleas will be entered or that expert witnesses will be called. Some states require defense attorneys to turn over to prosecutors the names, addresses, and statements of the witnesses they plan to call at trial.

The process of discovery is meant to ensure that trial processes result in verdicts based on all available evidence. The process achieves that goal when no side in a case is permitted to ambush the other with surprise evidence or witnesses because both sides have exchanged all relevant information.

Jenifer A. Lee

Further Reading

Hancock, Barry W., and Paul M. Sharp. *Criminal Justice in America: Theory, Practice, and Policy.* 3d ed. Upper Saddle River, N.J.: Prentice-Hall, 2003. General text on criminal law.

Neubauer, David W. *America's Courts and the Criminal Justice System.* 8th ed. Belmont, Calif.: Thomson/Wadsworth, 2005. Comprehensive analysis of the dynamics of criminal justice in action as seen in the relationship of judge, prosecutor, and defense attorney.

Rabe, Gary A., and Dean J. Champion. *Criminal Courts: Structure, Process, and Issues.* Upper Saddle River, N.J.: Prentice-Hall, 2002. Comprehensive textbook on the workings of criminal courts that includes a thorough discussion of discovery

Stolzenberg, Lisa, and Stewart J. D'Alessio. *Criminal Courts for the Twenty-first Century.* 2d ed. Upper Saddle River, N.J.: Prentice-Hall, 2001. Another fine textbook that examines all aspects of the criminal court processes.

See also Bill of particulars; Criminal procedure; Depositions; Due process of law; Subpoena power; Testimony; Trials; Witnesses.

Discretion

Definition: Flexibility allowed to the police and the courts to make decisions such as whether to arrest and prosecute individuals and the severity of sentences to be imposed

Criminal justice issues: Courts; legal terms and principles; police powers

Significance: Public officials may employ conscience and good sense, not only the letter of the law, in the reasonable exercise of power; however, discretion, particularly judicial discretion, has many critics.

Discretion is the ability of a public official to decide whether and how a law will be enforced. It allows a range of judgments to be made to fit particular circumstances while still maintaining the spirit of the law. Discretion exists in many areas

How Lawyers Can Learn from Fiction

Billy Budd, Foretopman (1924), a posthumously published novella by Herman Melville, the author of *Moby Dick* (1851), poses a question about the law that is so fundamental that the book is studied by lawyers. Set on a British Royal Navy vessel during the early nineteenth century, *Billy Budd* tells the story of an innocent seaman—Budd—who is falsely accused of mutiny by a sadistic officer. When confronted with the officer's outrageous accusations, the seaman is too dumbfounded to speak; he strikes the officer without thinking and kills him. Afterward, the ship's captain assembles a court to try Budd, who is convicted of mutiny and executed.

The crucial issue in Budd's shipboard trial is whether military law permits the consideration of any mitigating issues in determining Budd's guilt and punishment. The short novel remains a frequently studied text among lawyers and law students interested in pondering whether the law is a black-and-white affair, or whether judges and other legal decision makers inevitably have discretion to reach a result they believe to be morally right.

Timothy L. Hall

of the criminal justice system, from the actions of the police to the sentencing of a criminal by a judge. Discretion is therefore a very important aspect of the system, and it is one reason that the law as written often differs from the law in practice. Regarding police actions, for example, a law may prohibit all incidents of public drunkenness, but police officers may arrest only certain violators of the law who are particularly disorderly or appear disheveled. Officers always have the power to decide whether or not to arrest a person at the scene of a disturbance or suspected crime. In addition, administrative discretion exists within the police department: The administration decides where and how to deploy what numbers of officers, and particularly in the case of large-scale disturbances, how much force officers should be instructed to use.

Various aspects of discretion in the courts apply to the prosecution, defense, and judge. Prosecutorial discretion comprises deciding whether to prosecute, what charges to bring, the method of conducting the trial, and the type of sentence requested. In defense of a matter, discretion permits counsel to choose to present a case under one of several equal provisions of the law. The discretion of the judge at the time of sentencing has been the most criticized aspect of discretion in the system. The judge typically weighs a number of factors, such as the convicted person's criminal history and character, in deciding how severe a sentence to pass within the guidelines of the law. A first-time offender may receive a suspended sentence or probation, while a person with many past convictions may receive the maximum sentence allowable. Reforms such as strict sentencing guidelines and mandatory sentencing laws (including "three-strikes" laws) have attempted to reduce the allowable amount of judicial discretion. Discretion exists even after sentencing, in the corrections system. For example, corrections officers have discretion in determining who will be eligible for parole and when.

Elizabeth Algren Shaw

Further Reading

Neubauer, David W. *America's Courts and the Criminal Justice System*. 8th ed. Belmont, Calif.: Thomson/Wadsworth, 2005.
Tonry, Michael, and Richard Fraser. *Sentencing and Sanctions in Western Countries*. New York: Oxford University Press, 2001.
Walker, Samuel. *Taming the System: The Control of Discretion in Criminal Justice, 1950-1990*. New York: Oxford University Press, 1993. Broad review of bail reform.

See also Aggravating circumstances; Arrest; Deadly force; Diversion; Lesser-included offenses; Mandatory sentencing; Mitigating circumstances; Model Penal Code; Parole; Plea bargaining; Presentence investigations; Preventive detention; Sentencing; Sentencing guidelines, U.S.

Dismissals

Definition: Formal terminations of legal proceedings
Criminal justice issues: Legal terms and principles; prosecution; trial procedures; verdicts
Significance: Dismissals end judicial proceedings in legal matters without the completion of trials and generally without conclusive findings of law or facts.

In the broadest sense of the term, a dismissal is simply the termination of a legal proceeding. In criminal law it is the cancellation of an indictment, information, complaint, or charge. A dismissal may be done with or without prejudice to the refiling of a subsequent complaint. A dismissal without prejudice means the prosecution may seek new charges either through indictment, information, or complaint. However, a dismissal with prejudice does not allow the prosecution to file the same charge against a defendant again at a later time.

Dismissals may be voluntary, as in cases when the prosecution chooses to stop pursuing a matter, or involuntary. In cases of voluntary dismissals, the prosecution usually has tactical or legal reasons for its actions. Tactical reasons for dismissal may include the absence of key witnesses or the need to take more time to process important evidence. So long as the relevant statute of limitations on filing a charge does not expire, a

Vinny Wins a Dismissal

In the 1992 film *My Cousin Vinny*, Joe Pesci plays the title character, an inexperienced New York lawyer who defends his young cousin and a friend in an Alabama murder trial. Although Vinny has trouble coping with unfamiliar trial procedures, he eventually casts so much doubt on the prosecution's eyewitnesses and so thoroughly discredits the prosecution's expert witness on a key point of evidence that the prosecutor finally agrees that his case has no merit and dismisses all charges against the defendants. This is the appropriate action for a prosecutor to take in the circumstances, but it is unlikely that a real-life prosecutor would dismiss a case on the spot, as the film's prosecutor does. A prosecutor would probably use an evening recess to consider the new developments in the case before taking a step that is, by its nature, irrevocable. If he later discovers that he has made a wrong decision, he can not recall the defendants and try them again.

Timothy L. Hall

prosecutor may choose to dismiss the original complaint and refile at a later time when the case is better prepared.

Strict due process rights are common reasons that for dismissing cases for legal reasons. Once a criminal charge is brought against someone, due process rights attach and place a heavy burden on the prosecution to move forward. Any failure to proceed with a case in a timely fashion may subject the matter to either voluntary or involuntary dismissal. One example would be the use of evidence obtained without probable cause or a search warrant. Prosecutors who recognize that their cases rest on such evidence may voluntarily dismiss the cases in the hope of finding supported evidence later. If they do not dismiss at that time, they run the risk that courts will dismiss their cases later, possibly with prejudice, when defenses make motions or raise the troublesome issues at trial.

In circumstances in which dismissals are involuntary, courts generally make decisions as to the prejudice or harm caused to the parties. An involuntary dismissal does not always mean that it is with prejudice to the refiling. Involuntary dismissals are generally used when the interests of justice mandate the judicial action. One exam-

ple is found in cases in which the defendants' affirmative defenses are sustained by the court. For example, when defendants can prove their alibis, then the prosecutors or the judges, upon proper motions, may enter dismissals based on the perfected defenses.

It is important to recognize that dismissals do not include rulings or judgments on the issues at trial. In most instances, dismissals occur prior to trial, and in almost all instances before verdicts or judgments are rendered. Thus, the dismissals are not legal determinations in the truest sense. Nevertheless, they may have impact similar to those of judgments. For example, dismissals with prejudice have the same weight in preventing subsequent charges for the same offense that findings of "not guilty" have at trial.

Another important point in criminal cases is that dismissals prior to the start of jury trials do not necessarily violate the concept of double jeopardy. This means that a dismissal at any time up to the point of picking a jury or beginning the trial does not restrict the later prosecution of the same case, unless prejudice has been ordered by the court.

Carl J. Franklin

Further Reading

Acker, J. R., and D. C. Brody. *Criminal Procedure: A Contemporary Perspective.* 2d ed. Sudbury, Mass.: Jones and Bartlett, 2004.

Del Carmen, Rolando V. *Criminal Procedure: Law and Practice.* 6th ed. Belmont, Calif.: Wadsworth, 2004.

LaFave, Wayne R., Jerold H. Israel, and Nancy J. King. *Criminal Procedure.* 4th ed. St. Paul, Minn.: Thomson/West, 2004.

See also Acquittal; Criminal prosecution; Hung juries; Mistrials; Trials; Verdicts.

Disorderly conduct

Definition: Any public behavior that disturbs or shocks the senses of the public or community, including disturbing the peace, which is considered as basically destroying the tranquillity or settled state of the public arena

Criminal justice issues: Morality and public order; victimless crime

Significance: Violation of disorderly conduct statutes in most states are prosecuted as misdemeanors, and the extent of punishment is usually based on the specific nature of the disorderly conduct.

The term disorderly conduct is used in statutes to identify various acts against the public peace. It has been held to include the use of obscene language in public, the blocking of public thoroughfares, and the making of threats. It may also include conduct that is perceived as threatening morals or public decency or that constitutes a disturbance of a controversial or disorderly matter. Almost every state has a disorderly conduct law that makes it a crime to be drunk in public, to disturb the peace, or to loiter in certain areas. A statute for disorderly conduct, however, must identify acts that constitute the prohibited conduct with sufficient clarity in order to avoid being held unconstitutional because of vagueness of exactly what is prohibited by the statute.

Disorderly conduct is usually charged as a misdemeanor. Minors and the drunken adults are the most common offenders of this statute. Disorderly conduct violations are common during celebrations, such as Mardi Gras or sporting events. Although offenders are sometimes jailed in order to calm them down while they are intoxicated,

New Jersey police officer arresting a woman for disorderly conduct during a protest demonstration against an appearance by President George W. Bush in March, 2005. (AP/Wide World Photos)

Disorderly Conduct Under California Law

The Riverside County Sheriff's Department specifies what acts are considered "disorderly conduct" under a California statute. Six of the acts are classified as offenses against a "moral lifestyle." They include dissolute or lewd behavior in public, engaging in prostitution, begging or solicitation, loitering to engage in lascivious conduct, public intoxication, and occupation of buildings or private places without consent of the owners.

Two acts under the California statute can be linked to Federal Bureau of Investigation profiler Roy Hazelwood's study of the dangers of voyeurism: peering into the windows of inhabited dwellings and prowling at night on private property without consent of the owner. Hazelwood found that 68 percent of the violent sexual offenders he studied engaged in voyeurism as a precursor to violent sexual behavior. While most acts under California's statute involve minor infractions against the "moral code," several have been linked by research to more serious offenses and are becoming law-enforcement priorities.

the most common forms of punishment range from fines, to probation and community service. Disorderly conduct is usually not regarded as a serious blot on a person's criminal record, unless it is accompanied by more serious offenses.

Bernadette Jones Palombo

Further Reading

Michaud, Stephen G., with Roy Hazelwood. *The Evil That Men Do: FBI Profiler Roy Hazelwood's Journey into the Minds of Sexual Predators*. New York: St. Martin's Press, 1999.

Sanders, Pete, and Steve Myers. *Getting into Trouble or Crime*. Brookfield, Conn.: Copper Beech Books, 1999.

Scott, Michael. *Disorderly Youth in Public Places*. Washington, D.C.: U.S. Department of Justice, Office of Community Oriented Policing Services, 2001.

See also Breach of the peace; Commercialized vice; Loitering; Pandering; Public-order offenses; Resisting arrest; Vagrancy laws.

District attorneys

Definition: Prosecuting attorneys for local government
Criminal justice issues: Attorneys; prosecution
Significance: District attorneys are responsible for pursuing charges against persons accused of violating state criminal laws.

In many cities the chief prosecutor responsible for enforcing state criminal laws is called the district attorney and is often referred to as the DA. In some places these officials are called county prosecutors or state's attorneys. They make decisions about which people will be charged with crimes, which charges will be filed, and which plea agreements will be accepted for presentation to a judge.

Duties of District Attorneys

District attorneys work closely with local police officials to identify suspects and crimes that should be investigated. They often must approve police officers' requests for search warrants and arrest warrants before those requests are presented to judges in order to obtain the actual warrants. After a suspect is arrested, DAs and their assistants often make arguments to the court about setting bail or other conditions for the pretrial release of individual defendants. They must also represent the government in preliminary hearings, in which judges may consider whether there is sufficient evidence to move a case forward. District attorneys determine which charges will be filed against each defendant based on an evaluation of the evidence gathered by the police. They have the authority to drop charges and have suspects released if they believe there is insufficient evidence to pursue a case. District attorneys are not obligated to prosecute every suspect arrested by the police. Even if the prosecutor believes that the suspect might be guilty of a crime, the district attorney has a professional obligation to pursue only those cases in which there is sufficient evidence to justify initiating criminal charges.

Many cases conclude after either a plea agreement or a trial. In the plea-bargaining process the district attorney determines whether any concessions will be made, such as dropping or reducing charges, in order to gain a guilty plea from the defendant. If a defendant agrees to plead guilty, the district attorney often agrees to recommend that the judge impose a sentence less than the maximum possible punishment for the crime. If no plea agreement is arrived at after discussions between the district attorney and defense attorneys representing the defendant, then the case will go to trial. The district attorney is responsible for organizing the available evidence and then preparing and presenting evidence and arguments in court before a judge or jury. After a defendant is convicted, the district attorney may represent the government in opposing any appeals filed by the convicted offender.

Selection of District Attorneys

District attorneys must be law school graduates who have passed their state's bar exam and have become licensed to practice law. In most places lawyers must run for election in order to become district attorneys. Successful efforts to gain election to local office usually require that attorneys be active in a political party and have the support of local political party leaders. Successful election campaigns also require that candidates raise money and gain public visibility.

The electoral process may pose problems for district attorneys. There are risks that reelection campaigns may take up so much time that they interfere with the effective fulfillment of the district attorney's prosecutorial responsibilities. In addition, some observers fear that the process of raising money from supporters and gaining favor with politicians make district attorneys unable to make fair and equitable decisions if financial supporters or political colleagues become suspected of wrongdoing. A few states attempt to avoid such problems by having the state attorney general or chief state prosecutor appoint and supervise local prosecutors.

After a lawyer is elected district attorney, the lawyer must hire and train assistant DAs. In small cities there may be only one assistant, but in major metropolitan areas there may be hundreds of assistants under the supervision and direction of the district attorney. The district attorney must also attempt to establish policies for determining which cases will be prosecuted and which kinds of plea agreements will be accept-

---

"District" vs. "State's Attorneys"

The terms "state's attorney" and "district attorney" are often used interchangeably; however, they are not synonymous. A district attorney may be an officer of a municipality, a district, or a state, while a state's attorney represents only a state. Both types of government attorneys are called prosecuting attorneys. A district attorney for a particular federal district is known as a United States attorney. Special prosecutors, or United States attorneys, may be appointed to investigate possible criminal activities of the executive branch of the federal government.

---

able. Assistant district attorneys often have substantial freedom to make decisions about what will happen in their own cases, but they must generally follow guidelines developed by the district attorney so that there is an element of consistency in the processing of criminal cases within a particular city.

Key Relationships

As the central figure in the criminal justice process, the district attorney must develop and maintain relationships with various court actors and constituents. The district attorney must cooperate with the police in order to prosecute cases effectively. The DA relies on the police to gather evidence properly and to serve as witnesses for many criminal cases. The district attorney must also work well with victims and witnesses from among members of the public. These people must be questioned with sensitivity and care, and they must be informed about the court processes and questions they will encounter in preliminary hearings and trials.

The district attorney must develop good relationships with defense attorneys and judges. The plea-bargaining process can operate smoothly if the prosecutor and defense attorney do not permit personal animosity to develop. Instead, both lawyers must recognize that they are likely to meet together repeatedly over the years as they discuss the possibility of concluding criminal cases without undertaking the time and expense of a trial.

Plea bargaining is not always adversarial, because both the prosecution and defense may gain benefits from a quick plea bargain that saves court time and seals a conviction while permitting the offender to avoid the strongest possible sentence. Similarly, district attorneys are likely to appear before the same judges year after year. Thus, there is a strong incentive to become well-acquainted with the judge and the judge's preferences for sentencing. The district attorney does not want to waste the court's time by, for example, recommending sentences in plea agreements that are known to be unacceptable to the presiding judge. Instead, the district attorney must often talk regularly with judges to gain an understanding of their values and philosophies about punishment and the criminal justice system.

District attorneys also seek to maintain good relationships with the news media and political parties. Such relationships are essential in efforts to gain reelection to office at the end of a term in office. These contacts also help if DAs seek higher office, because many DAs subsequently seek election to judgeships and legislatures. Thus, district attorneys often hold press conferences and submit to interviews with reporters. Typically, they attempt to portray themselves as being very tough on criminals in order to impress the voters with their effectiveness in combating crime. Relationships with political party officials are important for most district attorneys, because DAs need the parties to mobilize campaign workers and voters at each election.

Christopher E. Smith

Further Reading

Carter, Lief. *The Limits of Order*. Lexington, Mass.: Lexington Books, 1974. Examinations of the work of local prosecutors.

Heilbroner, David. *Rough Justice: Days and Nights of a Young D.A.* New York: Pantheon Books, 1990. Presents perspectives of actual district attorneys on their jobs.

McDonald, William. *The Prosecutor*. Beverly Hills, Calif.: Sage, 1979. Broad presentation of topics concerning prosecutors in the United States and other countries.

Neubauer, David. *Criminal Justice in Middle America*. Morristown, N.J.: General Learning Press, 1974.

Parrish, Michael. *For the People: Inside the Los Angeles District Attorney's Office, 1850-2000*. Santa Monica, Calif.: Angel City Press, 2001.

Rowland, Judith. *The Ultimate Violation*. New York: Doubleday, 1985.

See also Attorney ethics; Attorneys, U.S.; Attorneys general, state; Criminal prosecution; Defense attorneys; Inquests; National District Attorneys Association; Plea bargaining; Preliminary hearings; Public prosecutors; Trials; *Voir dire*.

Diversion

Definition: Decision that may be made at several stages of the juvenile justice process to avoid formal court processing

Criminal justice issues: Juvenile justice; legal terms and principles

Significance: Commonly employed in juvenile justice, diversion helps youthful offenders avoid formal court processing and reduces court caseloads; it can also be an effective response to some delinquent behaviors.

Diversion is based on the reality that formal responses to youths such as arrest and referral to court are not always in the best interests of young offenders or the communities in which they live. Consequently, efforts designed to spare youths from the potentially negative consequences of formal court processing have existed since colonial times. Efforts designed to divert some youths from formal juvenile court processing are now common throughout the United States.

Diversion consists of true diversion (radical nonintervention) or referral to a diversion program. True diversion occurs when police officers or other authorities decide to warn, counsel, or release juvenile offenders to parents or guardians without making arrests or formal court referrals. Referrals to diversion programs occur when youths, and perhaps their families, are referred to community programs in lieu of making court referrals or taking formal court actions.

Diversion is based on labeling theory, which maintains that the repeated processing of youths by juvenile justice agencies may lead to additional deviance by those labeled as delinquents. This typically happens when youths began to see themselves as deviants or delinquents, and the opportunities of youths to engage in law-abiding behaviors are limited because they have been labeled as delinquents. Diversion is typically reserved for behaviors that do not seriously threaten public safety, and diversion decisions are typically limited by police department and juvenile court policies.

Preston Elrod

Further Reading

Champion, Dean John. *The Juvenile Justice System: Delinquency, Processing, and the Law.* 4th ed. Upper Saddle River, N.J.: Prentice-Hall, 2003.

Elrod, Preston, and R. Scott Ryder. *Juvenile Justice: A Social Historical and Legal Perspective.* Gaithersburg, Md.: Aspen, 1999.

Lundman, Richard J. *Prevention and Control of Juvenile Delinquency.* 3d ed. New York: Oxford University Press, 2001.

See also Criminal records; Discretion; Juvenile delinquency; Juvenile Justice and Delinquency Prevention Act; Juvenile justice system.

DNA testing

Definition: Comparison of DNA samples from body tissues and fluids to identify people

Criminal justice issues: Evidence and forensics; investigation; privacy; technology

Significance: A new and highly accurate way to identify people and match evidence with victims and suspects, DNA testing is revolutionizing investigative techniques in law enforcement and forcing major reconsiderations of the possibilities of convicting the innocent, particularly in capital cases.

DNA stands for deoxyribonucleic acid, the basic building blocks of biological genes. Because every human being has a unique pattern of genetic material, every human being has a pattern of DNA molecules that is like that of no other human being. For this reason, DNA taken from samples of human body tissues and fluids can be used to determine very accurately from what individual person those tissues and fluids come.

Criminal justice agencies have long sought better methods of linking suspects with particular crime scenes, especially when eyewitnesses to crimes are not available. Early methods of establishing such links included fingerprint analysis, blood-typing, and analyses of such trace evidence as cloth fibers and hair. Fingerprint evidence has the potential of establishing positive identifications; however, good fingerprint evidence is often difficult to obtain at crime scenes. Materials such as cloth fibers, human hairs, and blood samples can be helpful but can rarely be used to establish definitive links to any one suspect. In contrast, good DNA evidence not only is generally more readily obtainable, it is more reliable because no two human beings have exactly the same DNA patterns.

Since the mid-1980's, DNA testing has been used as a valuable tool for solving crimes. Criminalists can, for example, tell whether a single human hair or tiny blood spatter found on a victim comes from the victim or from someone else. Moreover, if the police have a suspect in the case, criminalists can determine whether the hair or blood comes from that suspect. The certainty with which tiny quantities of human tissue and fluids can be matched to criminal suspects makes it easier for prosecutors to secure convictions and lessens the chances of wrongful convictions.

History of DNA Testing

DNA was first discovered in 1868, but it was not until 1953 that scientists discovered its physical structure. For this discovery, the American scientist James Watson and the British scientists Francis Crick and Maurice Hugh Frederick Wilkins shared a Nobel Prize in 1962.

Most DNA is identical in all humans, and much of it even matches the DNA of other animals. However, in 1983, British biochemist Alec Jeffreys discovered that certain portions of the DNA sequence vary from individual to individual. These sequences were soon dubbed "DNA fingerprints," because they—like the patterns of ridges on human fingertips—were thought to be unique to individual human beings. Jeffreys and

Henry C. Lee, the head of Connecticut's state forensic laboratory examines a DNA profile retrieved from a computer database, whose information has proven useful in solving murder cases. *(AP/Wide World Photos)*

his colleagues created methods of probing DNA samples to examine the DNA fingerprints, a process that became known as DNA profiling.

Criminal justice agencies quickly realized the potential of DNA profiling as a tool for solving crimes. In 1985, Jeffreys used his techniques to help British government authorities determine whether a Ghanaian boy who wanted to come to England from West Africa to be reunited with his mother was indeed the woman's son. Jeffreys's DNA analysis proved that he was. One year later, Jeffreys helped police in Leicestershire, England, solve cases involving the rape and murder of two fifteen-year-old girls. Using traces of semen found on the victims, Jeffreys determined that both girls had been attacked by the same man. Moreover, those samples established that a suspect whom police were holding in custody could not have been the girls' assailant. After DNA samples were collected from many local men,

Jeffreys was eventually able to connect a local resident to the murders.

DNA Testing Techniques

DNA is present in every part of the human body that contains nucleic cells. These include body tissues and such fluids as blood, sweat, semen, and urine. DNA cannot be collected from strands of hair that are cut, but it can be extracted from the roots and follicles of hairs that are pulled from a body or shed naturally. Material in the follicles contains DNA, as do flakes of dandruff and other minute fragments of skin that are naturally shed.

DNA typing was originally done through a process known as RFLP—which is short for "restriction fragment length polymorphisms." The process used enzymes in a fashion much like chemical scissors to cut out portions of a DNA sample. Those portions were then subjected to various electrical and chemical processes that allowed their structures to be seen. Scientists then compared the patterns observed in those portions with patterns in samples taken from materials found at crime scenes.

During criminal investigations, portions from several different sites on a DNA strand are compared. If one particular person is the source of all the samples, the patterns will match on all sites. The chance of samples from two different persons matching on all sites is minuscule.

During the mid-1990's, a new testing technique was invented: PCR, or polymerase chain reaction. Using the new PCR technique, extremely minute amounts of DNA are chemically replicated until there is a quantity large enough to analyze. Because less than one-billionth part of one gram of DNA material is sufficient for PCR analysis, it can be used to analyze DNA taken from samples as minute as the dried saliva found on cigarette butts and envelope flaps.

In 2005, the latest form of DNA testing technology in use was called short tandem repeat (STR) analysis. Because of the types of DNA strands that STR examines, STR can be used on samples that have reached advanced states of decomposition. PCR and STR techniques are now used in combination: PCR is used to replicate DNA to enlarge the samples, which STR is then used to analyze. As few as nine human cells may be all that is needed to obtain sufficient DNA for STR analysis.

In the criminal justice system, thirteen different sites along the DNA strand are used for analysis. The chance of the DNA of any two individuals being identical in all thirteen sites is less than one in 575 trillion. Since the latter figure is roughly 40 million times greater than the number of all the human beings who have lived, it is clear that DNA testing offers an exceptionally powerful method of identifying and exonerating criminal suspects.

A final type of DNA testing that is sometimes used is mito-chondrial DNA analysis, or mtDNA. Mitochondrial DNA is found outside cell nuclei, and exists in greater quantities than nuclear DNA. MtDNA testing can be done on samples in which nuclear DNA is too degraded to analyze, or on samples in which nuclear DNA is absent altogether, such as hair shafts. However, mtDNA analysis is costly and more difficult to do, and few labs are able to perform it. Moreover, all human beings have mtDNA that is identical to that of their mothers. Thus, because mtDNA patterns are not unique to each individual, mtDNA analysis is limited in its usefulness as a tool for identifying suspects.

CODIS

The Federal Bureau of Investigation (FBI) has created a computer database program called CODIS, an acronym for "Combined DNA Index System." Data from DNA evidence from unsolved crimes and from certain convicted offenders are entered into CODIS by local, state, and federal law-enforcement agencies. DNA patterns from different unsolved crimes and from known offenders can now be easily compared. In this regard, CODIS is similar to AFIS, the FBI's Automated Fingerprint Identification System. By early 2005, CODIS had produced nearly 20,000

DNA Testing and Privacy Rights

In early 2005, police in Truro, Massachusetts, tried to solve the January, 2002, murder case of fashion writer Christa Worthington by asking men in the town voluntarily to submit to DNA testing. Investigators hoped to find the murderer by matching a DNA sample with DNA samples found in semen collected from the body of Worthington, who had had sexual intercourse before she was killed. Hundreds of Truro residents complied with the request by allowing swabs to be taken from inside their mouths; however, the investigation's attempt to test the entire town alarmed civil libertarians concerned with unwarranted intrusion into privacy rights. Particularly troubling was the fact that the police were recording the names of men who refused to comply with the request for DNA samples. The American Civil Liberties Union of Massachusetts sent letters to the Cape Cod County prosecutor and Truro's chief of police asking them to stop the DNA collection.

In 2003, police in Baton Rouge, Louisiana, collected DNA samples from about 1,200 men in an effort to catch a serial killer. The authorities eventually arrested a suspect but did not reveal whether DNA evidence figured into the arrest.

DNA matches, or "hits," that helped solve many cold cases.

The CODIS system is not without critics. Some people have argued that mandated collection of DNA samples invades citizens' privacy. A major part of this objection is the fact that DNA, unlike fingerprints, contains information about its owners' physical, behavioral, and health characteristics. Critics are concerned about the ways such personal information might ultimately be used by the government. Some people also are concerned that in some states, such as California, DNA information is collected not only from convicted felons but also from some adults and juveniles who are simply charged with certain crimes.

The Challenges of DNA Testing

In addition to legal and ethical disputes, DNA testing also faces practical challenges. The first of these is the great care that must be used in collecting, storing, and analyzing of DNA evidence. With improper handling, DNA evidence can be contaminated easily. There are methods of detecting contamination during analysis; however, contamination makes analyses more difficult and less certain. There have also been cases in which lab employees have engaged in sloppy and improper techniques of handling and analyzing DNA that have resulted in incorrect data.

A second major challenge of DNA analysis is the time and expertise that it requires. Steadily improving technology has simplified and speeded up testing processes. Nonetheless, the demand for DNA analyses far outstrips the equipment and trained personnel of the crime labs that perform the analyses. Most crime labs have long backlogs in their work, and law-enforcement agencies may have to wait several months before they receive the results of the analyses they request. To complicate matters, the DNA evidence awaiting testing is often stored, not at crime labs, but rather at the law-enforcement agencies, which typically lack the facilities for proper storage. This fact increases the chance of evidence becoming contaminated or degraded.

Other Uses for DNA Testing

In addition to matching suspects to crime scenes, DNA testing has found other important uses in the legal system. As often as it is used to identify offenders, it is used at least equally often to prove that suspects have not committed crimes. In 1992, the Innocence Project was created at Yeshiva University's Benjamin N. Cardozo Law School in New York City. By early 2005, the Innocence Project had combined with DNA testing to prove the innocence of 157 people who had been convicted of serious crimes. Under new laws, states must now allow certain convicted prisoners access to DNA testing if there is any chance that it might help prove their innocence.

DNA testing is also widely used to establish paternity; that is, to determine whether two particular people are blood relatives. An instance of this type of testing that captured world headlines occurred after Asia's devastating tsunami in late 2004. In Sri Lanka, it was reported that nine different families claimed the same four-month-old infant who was found in the debris of the tsunami. DNA testing was used to identify his actual parents, with whom he was reunited. During large-scale disasters such as the Asian tsunami and the September 11, 2001, destruction of New York City's World Trade Center, DNA testing has been used to identify human remains. DNA evidence can also be used to identify human remains in missing persons cases or whenever human remains are discovered.

Phyllis B. Gerstenfeld

Further Reading

"DNA Evidence: What Law Enforcement Officers Should Know." *National Institute of Justice Journal* 249 (2003): 10-15. Manual for police officers describing techniques for collecting and storing materials for DNA evidence.

Fridell, R. *DNA Fingerprinting: The Ultimate Identity*. London: Franklin Watts, 2001. Written for high school students, this book describes the process and uses of DNA testing.

National Institute of Justice. *Using DNA to Solve Cold Cases*. Washington, D.C.: U.S. Department of Justice, 2002. Federal government pamphlet describing how DNA testing can be used to solve old cases.

Scheck, B., P. Neufeld, and J. Dwyer. *Actual Innocence: Five Days to Execution, and Other Dispatches from the Wrongly Convicted*. New York: Doubleday, 2000. Book about Cardozo

Law School's Innocence Project, with details on many of the cases that were solved with DNA evidence.

Wambaugh, J. *The Blooding*. New York: Bantam Books, 1989. Fascinating account of how Alec Jeffreys's DNA testing methods were used to solve the murders of two teenage girls in England.

See also Bloodstains; Cold cases; Crime labs; Eyewitness testimony; False convictions; Forensic anthropology; Forensic entomology; Forensics; Latent evidence; Simpson trials; Toxicology; Trace evidence.

Document analysis

Definition: Forensic techniques used to ascertain the authenticity of documents

Criminal justice issues: Business and financial crime; evidence and forensics; fraud; investigation

Significance: Determining the authenticity of documents is important in the fields of both criminal and civil law. Modern document analysis now encompasses computer documents, but even in the twenty-first century's increasingly paperless world, people and institutions continue to rely heavily on handwritten and printed documents, and the need for trained document analysts is continuing to grow.

Document analysis is a diversified area of forensics that encompasses a wide spectrum of methods of investigation. In trying to determine whether documents are legitimate, examiners employ such techniques as handwriting and signature identification; typewriter, computer, fax, and copier identification; pencil lead and ink examinations; and paper analysis. The field was pioneered by Albert S. Osborn, whose 1910 book, *Questioned Documents*, was the first major work in the field; it is still considered an important and useful work.

Handwriting and signature identification is used in the examination of such documents as letters, checks, wills, ransom notes, and suicide

notes. During the Lindbergh baby kidnapping and murder trial of 1935, Osborn testified that the writing on the ransom notes was consistent with the handwriting of the defendant Bruno Hauptmann, who was convicted and later executed.

Handwriting and Signature Identification

Generally, the genuineness of any writing is established by comparing the writing on suspect documents with handwriting samples known to have been written by the purported signers of the suspect documents. Examiners prefer to have a variety of authentic writing samples to use for comparisons. Since the handwriting of individual writers tends to vary with the circumstances in which they are writing, document examiners need authentic samples that have been written under a variety of circumstances.

A skilled forger may succeed in faithfully copying a number of aspects of another person's handwriting; however, there are always noticeable differences between authentic and forged writing specimens. For example, forgeries often differ from authentic specimens in the speed with which they are written and the pressure that the forgers apply to their writing instruments. Even when there is a successful mimicry of speed and pressure, it is almost impossible for forgers to remove all traces of the peculiarities of their own writing from their forgeries.

Typed, Printed, Faxed, and Copied Documents

Document examiners must sometimes question whether suspect documents originated from particular machines. Unlike human handwriting, which has numerous individual characteristics, brand-new printing devices are generally very much alike and possess only the class characteristics that make new machines of the same models produce nearly identical documents. However, after machines are used repeatedly, they begin to develop individual characteristics, the same way that shoes develop individual characteristics with increased wear. Examiners focus on these individual differences.

Manually powered typewriters were prone to having some letter keys strike their ribbons and paper with less pressure than others, and individual typists using the same machine would not all use the same force on the same keys. Photocopying machines often have imperfections in their glass plates or distribute their toner powder in ways that make them unique. All fax transmissions received by a single machine have unique identifying lines. Computer printers also develop their own individual characteristics over time.

Professional handwriting expert Samuel Small comparing the handwriting of Bruno Hauptmann with that in the ransom notes written by the Lindbergh baby's abductor. Small made his analysis after Hauptmann was convicted in a trial in which the prosecution produced an expert witness who testified that Hauptmann's handwriting matched that of the ransom notes. *(AP/Wide World Photos)*

To improve their ability to make correct identifications of typed, printed, and duplicated documents, examiners like to work with at least ten documents from each machine they examine. It is also helpful to obtain the examples as soon as possible after the suspect documents are crated, as the individual characteristics of the machines continue to change over time.

Pencil Lead, Ink, and Paper Analysis

Paper documents can be altered in many ways. They may be erased or obliterated. They may also be overwritten. Attempts may be made to completely destroy documents by burning. Document examiners are often faced the challenge of enhancing or reconstructing writing on documents. Using different light sources is often helpful in this type of work. Unless the inks used to alter documents are the same as the inks originally used on them, they will reveal different chemical and light-reflecting properties to examiners. Document reconstruction and enhancement can be done using infrared photography or digital-image processing.

Inks are especially important to identify when the ages of documents and signatures are in question. Inks are also examined when it appears that something on a document has been altered by simply writing over the document's original text. For example, forgers may simply add zeros to the dollar amounts written on checks. Ink analysis can also help determine the age of a document or the writing on it. Very old inks are easy to spot because of their chemical compositions, as the manufacture of ink products changed dramatically after 1950. Examiners must also be familiar with computer inks. The chemical compositions of inks can be revealed through the use of thin-layer chromatography.

Papers are analyzed in a variety of ways by examiners, who pay particular attention to the physical characteristics of paper. Watermarks, which are regularly used in currency, can be examined, and analyses can be conducted on the fibers, chemicals, and trace elements that make up individual papers. Examiners must also be familiar with the types of papers used by computer printers, fax machines, and copiers, as well as standard writing and typing papers.

Ayn Embar-Seddon
Allan D. Pass

Further Reading

Dines, Jess E. *Document Examiner Textbook*. Irvine, Calif.: Pantex International, 1998. Detailed textbook that covers almost every aspect of document forging, from written contracts, deeds, and wills through computer files and graffiti. Discusses the history of document analysis and offers practical instructions.

Ellen, David. *The Scientific Examination of Documents: Methods and Techniques*. 2d ed. Boca Raton, Fla.: CRC Press, 1997. Guide to methods of examining handwritten, printed, typed, and photocopied documents. Written for lawyers, law-enforcement professionals, and others who investigate the authenticity of documents but accessible to general readers.

Herbertson, Gary. *Document Examination on the Computer: A Guide for Forensic Document Examiners*. Berkeley, Calif.: Wideline Publishing, 2002. Practical handbook on computer document analysis by a professional document examiner who learned his craft during his career in the FBI, for which he created and taught the first course on document examination.

Slyter, Steven A. *Forensic Signature Examination*. Springfield, Ill.: C. C. Thomas, 1996. Detailed guide to detecting forgeries by a certified document examiner. Covers handwriting analysis, paper types, inks, copying equipment, and other subjects.

See also Circumstantial evidence; Crime labs; Criminology; Cryptology; Fingerprint identification; Forensics; Forgery; Latent evidence; Trace evidence.

Domestic violence

Definition: Emotional, sexual, or other physical abuse committed by a spouse, intimate partner, or other relatives living in the same household as the victim

Criminal justice issues: Domestic violence; medical and health issues; sex offenses; women's issues

Significance: Domestic violence involves acts of abuse formerly considered to be private family matters and now considered crimes.

Domestic violence is characterized by a recurring and often escalating pattern of emotional and physical control and coercion of a vulnerable victim who is dependent, physically, emotionally, or financially, on the abuser. Definitions of domestic violence differ from state to state and among practitioners who deal with domestic violence victims and offenders.

The broadest definitions of domestic violence include various kinds of maltreatment, from yelling, shoving, slapping, or "inappropriate" touching to rape or murder. Specific legally included acts may include battering (injurious physical assaults) and stalking (repeated unwanted following, phone calls, or other unwanted communications). States differ in whether they limit domestic violence to acts involving bodily injury or the threat of bodily injury and whether they include psychological abuse such as harassment.

Some categories of domestic violence depend on the relationship between the victim and abuser. Family violence covers a range of victims, from infants and children to elderly parents. Abuse of an aging parent by an adult child or other adult in the household is called elder abuse. Abuse committed by one's husband or wife is termed spousal or marital abuse. Women who are repeatedly assaulted by their husbands are called battered wives, and their husbands are called batterers. Abuse committed by a current or former intimate partner or spouse is called partner abuse or intimate partner abuse. Partner abuse can involve partners of either sex.

While assault or abuse of women can occur outside a domestic relationship, the term "violence against women" is often used to mean abuse committed by husbands, boyfriends, or former husbands or boyfriends. Child abuse, too, can occur outside of a domestic situation but is considered a form of domestic violence when committed by a parent or other adult living in the same home as the victim. In some states, children who witness abuse of their parents are considered to be victims of those same acts. In the remaining sections of this article, the focus is on domestic violence involving adults. Readers who want to know more about child abuse are referred to the separate sections.

History of the Crimes

Throughout much of recorded history, domestic violence short of murder was not believed to be a crime. Women were considered the property of first their fathers and then their husbands. Men were formally or informally given the right to use physical force against their wives. Forcible sex between a husband and wife was considered a private matter and, as late as the twentieth century, treated in novels and motion pictures as romance, not rape. While several religions formally prohibited use of excessive physical force or defined some marital rights of wives, the common perception was that a man's home was inviolate and that authorities should not interfere with spousal relationships.

Historically, women who willingly participated in intimate relationships with men other than their husbands were considered to be immoral and had even fewer rights than wives. Same-sex partners were also viewed as engaging in illegal relationships and were allowed no rights to protection from abusive partners.

Early in the twentieth century, a few efforts were made in progressive cities to prevent abuse

Hispanic women in wedding dresses demonstrating in New York City on September 26, 2003, in the city's third annual march in remembrance of women killed by their domestic partners. *(AP/Wide World Photos)*

and assist battered women, but domestic violence was rarely publicly recognized until the 1960's, after the emergence of the women's movement.

During the 1960's, women began to organize to provide emergency shelter for battered wives, often in private homes, and to call for designation of domestic violence as a crime. Highly educated women, many of whom had previously been active in the Civil Rights movement, campaigned at local, state, and national levels to end discrimination against women in general and to call attention to women who were battered at home. It was not until the 1970's, when more women had entered legislatures and professions dealing daily with domestic violence victims, that shelters for battered wives were created by community organizations and criminal justice agencies began to recognize domestic violence as a crime.

In 1976, the first national directory of shelters and victim services for battered women was published. In 1978, the National Coalition Against Domestic Violence (NCADV) was founded. At this time, women affiliated with the NCADV, together with state and local domestic violence coalitions, began pressuring legislators and police departments to recognize and respond to battered women as victims and not as participants in private feuds. For example, in 1977 the state of Oregon passed the Family Abuse Prevention Act, which included statutes for mandatory arrests of batterers. A few months later, Massachusetts enacted the Abuse Prevention Law, which criminalized wife battering and enabled victims to obtain civil protection orders free of charge.

During the late 1970's, the phrase "battered woman's syndrome" was coined and first used in expert legal testimony in cases in which battered women were tried for killing husbands who had repeatedly abused them. During the 1980's, an increasing number of states officially recognized domestic violence as a crime and enacted legislation favoring the arrests of perpetrators, streamlining the process for victims to obtain restraining orders, and providing public funds for emergency shelters and other services for children. A growing number of police began to institute mandatory or pro-arrest policies for domestic violence offenders, in part based on highly publicized research that found that mandatory arrest led to fewer subsequent incidents of abuse. (The findings was challenged by other research findings but was later validated using more advanced statistical techniques.)

Also during the 1980's, a strong national victims' rights movement, initiated in part by families of homicide victims, succeeded in passing federal legislation that provided resources for domestic violence victims and agencies that served them. The 1982 Victim and Witness Protection Act addressed issues of victims' rights, services, and safety within justice agencies. The 1984 Victims of Crime Act (VOCA) provided federal funds to supplement state allocations for victim services and shelters.

Five major developments in 1994 led to increased public awareness of domestic violence and greater commitment among criminal justice agencies to deal with the crime. The murder of Nicole Brown Simpson and the subsequent trial of her former husband, O. J. Simpson, raised public interest in the plight of battered women. NCADV and state coalitions implemented an annual concerted national campaign to publicize and remember the names of all victims of domestic violence homicide. The Violence Against Women Act (VAWA) was enacted, providing federal funds for state and local criminal justice agencies to combat domestic violence. VAWA also provided new federal legislation to strengthen convictions and sentences of domestic violence offenders who used guns. It also defined more responsibilities for U.S. Attorneys in domestic violence cases involving interstate jurisdictions.

Prevalence

Given the hidden nature of domestic violence and the varying definitions of it, most statistics on the prevalence of domestic violence must be considered estimates. Primary data on prevalence come from the National Crime Victimization Survey (NCVS) and state and local police reports collected by the Federal Bureau of Investigation (FBI).

Homicides are more likely to be reported and recorded by police than any other form of domestic violence and therefore are relatively accurate. Based on Supplementary Homicide Reports police departments provide to the FBI, in the year 2000 women were far more likely to be murdered by an intimate partner, including spouses or former

National Domestic Violence Hotline

Funded by the federal Violence Against Women Act of 1994 (VAWA), which Congress reauthorized in 2000, the National Domestic Violence Hotline opened its telephones to victims of domestic violence in February, 1996. The organization takes calls twenty-four hours a day and fields questions in many languages. By 2005, the hotline was receiving more than thirteen thousand calls per month. More than 75 percent of the calls are from victims of domestic violence or concerned relatives and friends, and about 70 percent of the callers who are victims of domestic violence are women.

The hotline now offers referrals to more than four thousand shelters and service providers throughout the United States, Puerto Rico, and the U.S. Virgin Islands. Information on the hotline can be found at its Web site, at www.ndvh.org

Information for those who need help immediately can be found by calling the hotline directly: 800-799-7233 or 800-787-3224. Hearing-impaired persons can find help by calling the teletypewriter (TTY) line: 800/787-3224.

than men to be victims of all types of intimate partner violence.

The NCVS also shows that elderly people, those sixty-five years or over, are far less likely to be victims of any form of crime, especially violent crime, than younger people. Elderly victims of nonlethal assault are also less likely to have been attacked by a relative or intimate partner than younger victims of nonlethal violence. However, elderly murder victims are much more likely to be killed by a relative or intimate partner than younger murder victims. While many researchers believe that same-sex partners are just as likely to be victims of domestic violence as heterosexual partners, scientific evidence is currently lacking.

Investigation

Initial investigation of domestic violence incidents is usually carried out by police officers or sheriffs' deputies who respond to calls from the victim or another party who hears or sees the abuse in progress.

When domestic violence was still considered a private family matter, police commonly believed that family fights posed a relatively high danger of injury to the responding officers. Policy and training for responding police focused on reducing danger to both police and the involved couple by providing a "cooling off" period. Unless one party required immediate medical care, the couple was separated into different rooms, or the police strongly suggested that the husband or boyfriend leave the home for a while.

Police departments later adopted mandatory-arrest or pro-arrest policies, but these were difficult to enforce because offenders often told police that the victim attacked them first, while the victim remained silent. Under these circumstances the police might have been compelled to arrest both attacker and victim.

Now community-based victim advocates help improve the effectiveness of investigations in

spouses (1,247), than were men (440). Among all men murdered in 2000, only 3.7 percent were murdered by an intimate partner; 33.5 percent of murdered women were killed by an intimate partner. Although there had been a precipitous decline in the number of men murdered by an intimate after 1976, the number of women murdered by an intimate has been only slightly reduced.

Far more victims of intimate partner abuse suffer nonfatal assaults. In 2001, based on the NCVS, close to 700,000 adults, or 3 out of every 1,000 persons, were victims of nonlethal intimate partner violence. The majority of these victims—about 85 percent—were women. Another national survey indicated that 25 percent of women in the United States are victims of intimate partner violence at some point in their lives. Most acts of intimate partner violence, more than 68 percent, involved simple assault, including punching resulting in black eyes or bruises, while 17 percent involved aggravated assault, including attacks with a weapon or attacks that result in serious injury or more than one day of hospitalization.

Other, less frequent, acts of intimate partner violence include robbery and rape or other sexual assault. Although there is a common perception that men are just as likely to be victims of some forms of domestic violence as women, research shows that women are significantly more likely many jurisdictions. They provide training to police officers and educate them about the many reasons victims refuse to cooperate with police. In some cities, police and advocates form response teams; police officers call advocates to the crime scene once the safety of the advocate can be ensured, or they transport victims to a safe place where advocates meet the victims and help them receive needed services, such as shelter or assistance in obtaining a restraining order against the abuser.

Rather than depending on victim cooperation, police also are being trained to gather more evidence when they respond to domestic violence incidents. Methods include noting evidence that helps them to distinguish between the so-called primary aggressor and the victim, recording "excited utterances" of the victim about the attack, interviewing witnesses, including children, and checking to see if a court previously issued a re-

straining order that should have prevented the abuser from contacting the victim.

A growing number of law-enforcement departments have special domestic violence units staffed by officers who receive special training for initial and follow-up investigations. One function of officers in these units is to interview victims a day or two after the incident, when the victims are calmer and in a safe place. Because bruises are more visible a day or two after an attack, the officers also take photographs of the victim at that time to use as evidence in court. Many officers are able to provide victims with cell phones so they can call for immediate response if they are being threatened again.

Prosecution

Prosecutors' offices were the first among criminal justice system agencies to provide victim assistance programs and to institute specific programs for victims of domestic violence. Victims are contacted by the prosecutor's office, informed about the court process and the dates when they will be needed to appear in court, provided information about changes in schedules, and, if needed, provided assistance with transportation to and from court.

Prosecutors have also taken a leading role in coordinating their offices with those of police and other agencies addressing domestic violence. In addition to forming interagency teams with police, prosecutors have taken several other steps.

Vertical prosecution, in which one prosecutor is assigned to handle a domestic violence case from intake to disposition, has been instituted in a number of counties. Vertical prosecution helps ensure that the prosecuting attorney who appears in court is familiar with the victim and with all aspects of the case.

Some prosecutors have also formed specialized domestic vio-

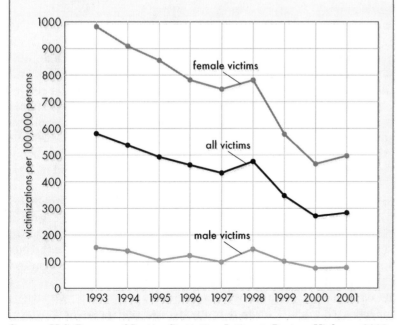

Violent-Incident Rates Among Intimate Partners, 1993-2001

Violent acts include murder, rape, sexual assault, robbery, and assault. Intimate partners include current and former spouses, and current and former girlfriends and boyfriends.

Source: U.S. Bureau of Justice Statistics, *Intimate Partner Violence*, 2003.

lence units. Attorneys assigned to these units receive special instruction about changes in state domestic violence laws as well as training in interviewing domestic violence victims and advising them about services available to help them as they go through the justice system. Still, most prosecutors still deal with uncooperative victims by issuing subpoenas to compel them to testify, a procedure that may revictimize already vulnerable persons.

To deal with domestic violence defendants, some prosecutors have instituted diversion programs. If a first-time defendant meets certain conditions such as attending treatment, not reoffending, and obeying restraining orders, the case is dropped.

A number of prosecutors' offices have instituted a "no drop" domestic violence case policy, in which attorneys have less discretion to drop a case because of a lack of victim cooperation or weak evidence. "No drop" policies are very controversial and are opposed by many victim advocates.

Punishment

Most domestic violence offenders who are found guilty are sentenced to probation and released, rather than being sentenced to jail or prison. Many prosecutors and victims advocates feel that these sentences are too lenient. To prevent these convicted offenders from continuing to batter, some probation departments have formed special domestic violence probation teams or units. Officers assigned to these teams or units regularly check up on the convicted offenders and contact the victims to make sure they are not being further intimidated or harmed.

Some cities have formed special domestic violence courts in which judges not only adjudicate cases but also continue to review records collected by probation officers and deal with offenders who are rearrested for domestic violence.

Marcia R. Chaiken

Further Reading

Ammerman, Robert T., and Michel Hersen, eds. *Case Studies in Family Violence*. New York: Plenum Press, 2000. Scholarly essays on legal, medical, social, and psychological issues involved in domestic violence.

Bureau of Justice Statistics. *Intimate Partner Violence, 1993-2001*. Washington, D.C.: U.S. Department of Justice, 2003. This brief report presents data in simple tabular form on the prevalence of domestic violence and changes over time.

Jasinski, Jana L., and Linda M. Williams, eds. *Partner Violence: A Comprehensive Review of Twenty Years of Research*. Thousand Oaks, Calif.: Sage, 1998. Chapters by different social scientists summarize what is known about partner violence, based on twenty years of research.

National Research Council. *Understanding Violence Against Women*. Washington, D.C.: Author, 1996. A panel of experts presents information on the nature and scope of crimes against women, causes, consequences, prevention, and treatment.

Office for Victims of Crime. *Enforcement of Protective Orders*. Washington, D.C.: U.S. Department of Justice, 2002. Information is provided for victims and victims' advocates about laws and legal issues in each state relevant for obtaining restraining orders.

Violence Against Women Office. *Toolkit to End Violence Against Women*. Washington, D.C.: U.S. Department of Justice, 2001. Practical advice for community organizations and individuals.

See also Adultery; Animal abuse; Battered child and battered wife syndromes; Child abuse and molestation; Date rape; National Crime Victimization Survey; Rape and sex offenses; Restraining orders; Sexual harassment; Simpson trials; Stalking; Victim assistance programs; Victimology; Violent Crime Control and Law Enforcement Act.

Double jeopardy

Definition: Criminal due process right that protects a defendant from being prosecuted twice for the same crime

Criminal justice issues: Appeals; constitutional protections; legal terms and principles; prosecution

Significance: The rule against double jeopardy is a civil liberty specified in the Fifth Amendment to the U.S. Constitution, which applies this right to persons prosecuted for federal crimes. The Fourteenth Amendment's due process clause applies double jeopardy to the states, thereby protecting people charged with state crimes. In particular, a person acquitted of a crime cannot be prosecuted and tried again for that same crime, even if the prosecution finds more evidence implying guilt.

Double jeopardy applies only to crimes and not to civil cases, such as private lawsuits. For example, in a famous murder case, O. J. Simpson was acquitted of murdering two people. In a wrongful-death civil suit, however, a court ruled that Simpson was responsible for the wrongful deaths of the two persons. Therefore, despite Simpson's previous acquittal in a criminal case, he could still be sued and found liable in a civil case based on the same facts.

There are other exceptions to double jeopardy. If a person is convicted of a crime and appeals the case to a higher court, the appellate court may overturn the conviction. In such a case, a person may be tried again for the same crime. Also, a person may perform a criminal act that violates the laws of more than one jurisdiction. For example, if a person violates the laws of two or more states or federal law, that person may be prosecuted by more than one state or the federal government. A person who steals a car in Indiana and then drives it to Michigan can be prosecuted by Indiana, Michigan, and the federal government. This is covered by the doctrine of dual sovereignty.

A more complex legal doctrine that may affect a defendant's use of and a court's interpretation of double jeopardy is collateral estoppel. Rarely used in criminal law, collateral estoppel prohibits a factual or legal issue from being used against a criminal defendant if that issue was resolved in his favor in a previous trial within the same jurisdiction. For example, a state prosecutes a person for robbing three people at the same time, choosing to prosecute the person in three separate cases for the robbery of each victim. A defendant acquitted for the robbery of the first victim may claim that acquittal in the first case means that it is impermissible to be prosecuted for the other two robberies because the facts and issues are the same. By using collateral estoppel, the defendant uses a type of double jeopardy defense. Defendants do, however, have the burden of proving which facts or issues were decided in their favor at earlier trials and how relevant they are to their new cases.

Sean J. Savage

Further Reading

Garcia, Alfredo. *The Fifth Amendment: A Comprehensive Approach*. Westport, Conn.: Greenwood Press, 2002.

Holmes, Burnham. *The Fifth Amendment*. Englewood Cliffs, N.J.: Silver Burdett Press, 1991.

Levy, Leonard W. *Origins of the Fifth Amendment*. 1968. Reprint. New York: Macmillan, 1986.

See also Acquittal; Constitution, U.S.; Convictions; Defendants; Dismissals; Due process of law; Fifth Amendment; Jurisdiction of courts; King beating case; Lesser-included offenses; Mistrials; *Palko v. Connecticut*; Simpson trials; Verdicts.

Drive-by shootings

Definition: Use of firearms to shoot at people from moving vehicles that enable rapid getaways

Criminal justice issues: Homicide; juvenile justice; violent crime

Significance: Because they provide the offenders with quick escapes from the scenes of their crimes, drive-by shootings are popular amongst criminals with violent intentions, particularly youths who are members of violent gangs.

Commonly associated with gang activity, drive-by shootings are used not only to kill rival gang members but also to terrorize rivals. Drive-by shootings have also been associated with systemic drug violence, as drug dealers use them to eliminate rival drug dealers or buyers who fail to pay for their drug purchases.

Funeral procession in Brooklyn, New York, of the "gangsta" rapper Notorious B.I.G. (Christopher Wallace), who was killed in a drive-by shooting in Los Angeles, in March, 1997. (*AP/Wide World Photos*)

Although they first gained national notoriety during the 1980's, drive-by shootings are not a modern development. Indeed, the Prohibition era of the 1920's is well known for the large numbers of drive-by shootings associated with gangsters. Moreover, even before the invention of the automobile, outlaws simply rode horses when they staged similar hit-and-run attacks on their rivals.

Just as prohibition of alcohol was associated with drive-by shootings, drug-related policies are a primary factor in the twenty-first century. Because drive-by shootings allow perpetrators to flee the scene with less chance of identification or immediate retaliation, many drug dealers employ them as low-risk forms of attack on rivals who may themselves be armed. Automobiles provide convenient cover for concealing weapons and surprising victims. Because drug dealing is most commonly done outdoors, on the streets of low-income neighborhoods, drive-by attacks are often effective in achieving their purpose.

Drive-by shootings have also provided a popular way for members of street gangs to strike rivals. The public nature of the attacks is an effective way of sending public messages to rival gangs. Indeed, drive-by shootings are predicated on a rationale similar to that used by international terrorists who prefer to make their violent strikes as public as possible. For this reason, drive-by shootings are listed under antiterrorism statutes in a number of states.

One ramification of drive-by shootings has been their impact on gun-control legislation. The use of automatic weapons in drive-by attacks, particularly those in which innocent bystanders are injured or killed, has increased pressure on politicians to eliminate such weapons.

Brion Sever

Further Reading

Curry, David, and Scott Decker. *Confronting Gangs: Crime and Community*. Los Angeles: Roxbury, 2002.

Hutson, Range, Dierdre Anglin, and Marc Eckstain. "Drive-by Shootings by Violent Street Gangs in Los Angeles: A Five-year Review from 1989 to 1993." *Academic Emergency Medicine* 3 (1996): 300-303.

Leet, Duane, George Rush, and Anthony Smith. *Gangs, Graffiti, and Violence: A Realistic Guide to the Scope and Nature of Gangs in America*. 2d ed. Belmont, Calif.: Wadsworth, 2000.

Sanders, William. "Drive-bys." In *The Modern Gang Reader*, edited by Jody Miller, Cheryl Maxson, and Malcolm Klein. 2d ed. Los Angeles: Roxbury, 2001.

_____. *Gangbangs and Drive-bys*. New York: Aldine de Gruyter, 1994.

See also Drugs and law enforcement; Gun laws; Juvenile delinquency; Murder and homicide; School violence; Youth gangs.

Drug courts

Definition: Recently developed alternative to traditional prosecution of drug-related offenses that focuses on ending offenders' drug habits while integrating them into their communities

Criminal justice issues: Courts; crime prevention; medical and health issues; substance abuse

Significance: Drug courts are a new component of the criminal justice system that try to remove, at least temporarily, cases of drug offenders from traditional criminal processing and to place them in less formal hearings in which judges, prosecutors, public defenders, case workers, and the defendants themselves work together as teams to correct the offenders' drug and alcohol problems.

Drug and alcohol abuse tend to make people more likely to commit crimes for many reasons. Placing drug addicts and alcoholics on probation or incarcerating them in prisons typically does nothing to address the fundamental problems of their substance abuse. Drug courts combine accountability to the criminal justice system and protection of the public with treatment for alcoholism, addiction, and related mental health problems. The first drug court was established in Miami, Florida, in 1989. By 2005, more than one thousand drug court programs were in operation throughout the United States, and several hundred more were being planned.

Drug Court Processes and Characteristics

The drug court process begins when defendants are arrested for drug possession or offenses related to drug or alcohol use, such as committing thefts to buy drugs. After suspects are arrested, prosecutors screen their cases to determine if they are eligible for adjudication in drug courts. In some cases, defendants are not screened until after they are convicted of crimes or they violate the terms of their probation. Drug court participants are usually long-term users of more than one drug.

After defendants are classified as being eligible for drug courts, the requirements of the drug court program are explained to them. Depending on how far the judicial processing of their cases has developed, defendants can benefit by having the prosecution, adjudication, or sentencing of their cases postponed until after their successful completion of the drug court program. Defendants who "graduate" from drug court are typically rewarded by having the charges against them dropped, having their cases dismissed, or having their probation ended.

Drug courts differ from traditional criminal justice in many ways. For example, they incorporate drug testing into case processing. Participants in the programs may be subjected to random urine testing as often as three times a week. Those who test positive or miss tests may be subject to such penalties as weekend jail stays, increased testing, or restrictions on their freedom to leave their homes. On the other hand, participants who do well may receive such rewards as advancement to the next phase in their treatment, gifts, or tokens. Most often, however, successful participants are rewarded merely by praise from the judges at their court hearings and applause from fellow participants in the programs.

Relationships between participants and the courts are nonadversarial. The courts sees their mission as assisting participants to recover from alcohol or drug addiction. The courts try to identify defendants in need of treatment and refer them to treatment as soon as possible after their arrests, rather than having them wait several months for trials and sentencing.

Participants in drug courts programs are provided with extensive mental and physical health services, job skills training, education, and housing services to help them stay clean, sober, and out of trouble. Participants are usually required to attend meetings of Alcoholics Anonymous or Narcotics Anonymous.

The Team Approach

Judges, prosecutors, public defenders, probation officers, and treatment case managers (usually social workers or counselors) work as teams to monitor and assist participants. They try to reach consensus on how to reward participants who comply with their programs and penalize those who do not.

Drug court judges see individual participants as often as every week at court sessions attended by all participants. Every participant is called to the bench by the judges; together, they review their fellow participants' progress. Judges commend those who are doing well and may warn or penalize those who are not doing well. These proceedings all take place in open courts, before other participants and all members of the drug court teams.

Drug court teams seek to continually evaluate their programs' progress against their goals. They also work to incorporate innovations in substance abuse treatment, the technology of monitoring participants, and lessons learned from the experiences of other drug courts. Drug courts work in partnership with local government, community agencies, businesses, churches, and health professionals.

Effectiveness of Drug Courts

Several studies have suggested that drug courts are effective in reducing drug use, retaining participants, reducing repeat offending, and costing taxpayers less money than such alternative programs as incarceration. However, these findings must be treated with caution. Many of these studies are not scientifically rigorous, and even the studies that use sound methods shed little light on *how* drug courts achieve their positive results. Until more research is done, it will not be clear which components of the drug court model—such as drug testing and weekly court appearances—are essential to the court's success.

The successes indicated by early research may have led to unrealistic expectations for drug courts. Most studies of drug court effectiveness have been short term. If drug courts function in ways that are similar to those of other programs that show similar short-term successes, it is probable that as more time passes after participant graduate from the programs, they will become increasingly likely to relapse and commit new crimes. As with vaccinations for diseases, treatments for criminal behavior and addiction tend to weaken over time

Issues and Concerns

During the first years of the twenty-first century, jurisdictions were launching new drug courts at an amazing rate. However, it was expected that some of these new programs either would not or could not implement the drug court model fully, as the model requires local jurisdictions to abandon their "business as usual" practices and become open to innovation. As jurisdictions move to adapt the drug court model to use with juvenile delinquents and the parents of children who have been abused and neglected, these issues will intensify.

Despite their apparent success, drug courts still reach only a small percentage of offenders who might benefit from their programs. Many early drug courts began their operations with the help of generous federal and state grants. However, some local jurisdictions may lack either the will or the means to continue operating their drug courts after their grant money is exhausted.

Although drug courts face numerous challenges, they show great promise as alternatives to "revolving door" justice in which the same offenders are repeatedly processed. In some criminal justice circles, the growth of drug courts is referred to as a "movement," and one that reflects the enthusiasm about this new way of dealing with crime and addiction.

Jerome McKean

Further Reading

Cole, David. "Doing Time—In Rehab." *The Nation* 269, no. 8, September 20, 1999.

Drug Court Programs Office, Office of Justice Programs. *Defining Drug Courts: The Key Components*. Washington, D.C.: U.S. Department of Justice, 1997. Federal government guide to the organization and administration of drug courts.

Gaines, Larry K., and Peter B. Kraska, eds. *Drugs, Crime, and Justice*. Prospect Heights, Ill.: Waveland Press, 2003. Broad collection of articles addressing drug control, the industry of drug distribution, and law-enforcement strategies.

Goode, Erich. *Drugs in American Society*. Boston: McGraw-Hill, 2005. Complete and up-to-date review of drug use in America, the drug crime connection, and law-enforcement efforts to control drug abuse and drug related crimes.

Gray, James P. *Why Our Drug Laws Have Failed and What We Can Do About It*. Philadelphia: Temple University Press, 2001. A critical critique of the war on drugs from the personal perspective of a California trial judge.

See also Alcohol use and abuse; Community-based corrections; DARE programs; Decriminalization; Drug Enforcement Administration; Drug legalization debate; Drug testing; Drugs and law enforcement; Mandatory sentencing; Recidivism; Victimless crime; Violent Crime Control and Law Enforcement Act.

"Drug czar"

Definition: Nickname for the federal government official in charge of the Office of National Drug Control Policy

Criminal justice issues: Federal law; law-enforcement organization; substance abuse

Significance: The so-called drug czar is the leading federal government official responsible for efforts to curtail the use of illicit drugs.

Government efforts to curtail the consumption of illicit drugs in the United States date from World War I. With the spread of crack cocaine use in the 1980's, however, Republican administrations under presidents Ronald Reagan and George Bush launched a renewed effort in the form of a "war on drugs." A key development occurred in the latter presidential administration with the creation in 1988 under the Anti-Drug Abuse Act of the Office of National Drug Control Policy. Its head, officially known as the director of the White House Office of National Drug Control Policy, quickly was nicknamed the drug czar by the American media.

The drug czar was given the power to direct strategy and to speak officially on the issue. The first person to hold the job was William J. Bennett, a longtime Republican and former secretary of education in the Reagan administration. Under Bennett's tenure, which set the tone for subsequent drug czars, the emphasis on curtailing drug use was on law enforcement—including stiff prison sentences for those convicted—and not on treating the matter as a medical problem requiring education and treatment. In response to the failure of the government's approach to lessening the drug problem, others would advocate new policies, including decriminalization.

Steve Hewitt

Further Reading

Maccoun, Robert J. *Drug War Heresies: Learning from Other Vices, Times, and Places*. New York: Cambridge University Press, 2001. Part of the RAND Studies in Policy Analysis series, this work contains a bibliography and index.

Schlosser, Eric. *Reefer Madness: Sex, Drugs, and*

Cheap Labor in the American Black Market. New York: Mariner Books, 2004. This exposé highlights the prevalence of illegal drugs within U.S. borders.

See also Comprehensive Drug Abuse Prevention and Control Act; Crime; Drug Enforcement Administration; Drug legalization debate; Drugs and law enforcement; Mandatory sentencing; National Narcotics Act; President, U.S.; Sentencing.

Drug Enforcement Administration

Identification: Federal agency responsible for enforcing federal laws and regulations concerning controlled substances

Date: Established as a branch of the Bureau of Internal Revenue in 1915; became the Drug Enforcement Administration in 1973

Criminal justice issues: Federal law; law-enforcement organization; medical and health issues; substance abuse

Significance: In carrying out its mission, the Drug Enforcement Administration brings to justice organizations involved in producing or distributing controlled substances destined for illicit traffic in the United States.

The Drug Enforcement Administration (DEA) proactively investigates and prosecutes major growers, manufacturers, and distributors of controlled substances. It also conducts drug awareness and abuse prevention programs targeted toward demand reduction in the domestic and international illicit drug markets.

The DEA, compared to other federal criminal

An agent of the Drug Enforcement Administration with six hundred pounds of marijuana seized in Oklahoma City in June, 1999. The contraband drugs had an estimated street value of $1,200,000. *(AP/Wide World Photos)*

justice agencies, has a brief history. Its origins are traceable to the Harrison Narcotic Drug Act of 1914; it was originally classified as a "miscellaneous division" of the Bureau of Internal Revenue in 1915. In its first year, the agency seized 44 pounds of heroin and produced 106 convictions. Major expansion and reorganization over the following decades resulted from the Narcotics Drugs Import and Export Act of 1922, legislation establishing the Federal Narcotics Control Board; the Marijuana Tax Act of 1937, which levied a fine of $100 per ounce on untaxed marijuana; and the Boggs Act of 1956, which made heroin illegal.

The Bureau of Narcotics and Dangerous Drugs (BNDD) was created in 1968 through a congressionally approved merger of the older Bureau of Narcotics and the Bureau of Drug Abuse Control. Congress then passed the Controlled Substances Act, known as Title II of the Comprehensive Drug Abuse Prevention and Control Act of 1970, legislation that established consolidated oversight of both narcotics and psychotropic drugs. Rapid growth in the BNDD's domestic and foreign operations and the rise of recreational drug use in the popular culture prompted the creation of the Drug Enforcement Administration in 1973.

The DEA engages casework and prepares for the prosecution of major violators of controlled substance laws. Its operations focus on disrupting and dissolving violent drug trafficking organizations. The agency also is responsible for maintaining a national drug intelligence program that collects, analyzes, and disseminates drug intelligence information. Additionally, the DEA serves as the U.S. liaison to the United Nations and Interpol and is responsible for the seizure and forfeiture of assets that are associated with criminal drug enterprises.

According to the DEA, in 2004 it had an annual budget of $1,897 million and 9,629 employees (4,680 special agents plus support staff) and operated 237 domestic field offices throughout the United States plus foreign field offices in 58 countries. From 1986 to 2004, the DEA made approximately 443,600 domestic drug arrests and seized nearly 61,594 kilograms of cocaine, 705 kilograms of heroin, 195,644 kilograms of marijuana, and more than 118,049,279 dosage units of methamphetamines.

During its brief history, the DEA has established a significant worldwide presence. The agency's primary mission of drug law enforcement involves coordination and cooperation with federal, state, and regional authorities on mutual drug law-enforcement efforts as well as nonenforcement methods such as crop eradication or substitution, drug resistance education, and awareness efforts.

Theodore M. Vestal

Further Reading

Drug Enforcement Administration. *Tradition of Excellence: The History of the DEA from 1973-1998*. Washington, D.C.: U.S. Department of Justice, 1999.

Machette, R. B. *Guide to Federal Records in the National Archives of the United States*. Washington, D.C.: National Archive and Records Administration, 1995.

See also Attorney general of the United States; Comprehensive Drug Abuse Prevention and Control Act; DARE programs; Decriminalization; Drug courts; "Drug czar"; Drug legalization debate; Drug testing; Drugs and law enforcement; Homeland Security Department; Justice Department, U.S.; National Narcotics Act; Opium Exclusion Act.

Drug legalization debate

Definition: Ongoing public and criminal justice debate over whether use of currently illicit drugs should be legalized

Criminal justice issues: Crime prevention; morality and public order; substance abuse

Significance: The ongoing "war against drugs" in the United States is a massive social commitment that is rarely debated publicly. Fuller understanding of the debate over issues of legalization should help both those who support and those who oppose current drug policy to clarify their perspectives.

Since the early twentieth century, American society has sought to control the problem of drug abuse largely through its criminal justice system.

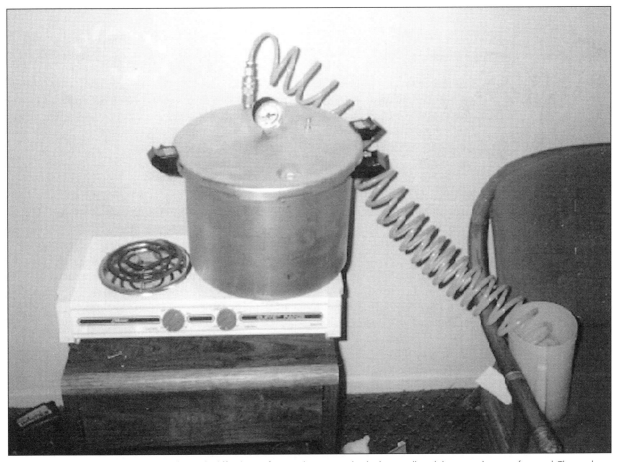

Among the reasons that drug laws are inherently difficult to enforce is the ease with which some illegal drugs can be manufactured. This methamphetamine lab seized by the Drug Enforcement Administration in 1997 is made from common household items and uses such readily available ingredients as starter fluids, lithium batteries, Styrofoam cups, and Sudafed capsules. *(AP/Wide World Photos)*

During the 1970's and 1980's, sharp increases in drug use and the emergence of such dangerous new drug menaces as crack cocaine fueled what has been dubbed a "war on drugs." This led to massive increases in state and federal narcotics enforcement efforts and stiffer criminal penalties for drug offenders that in turn led to sharp increases in prison populations. These increases have especially affected the federal Bureau of Prisons, more than 50 percent of whose 140,000 inmates in 2004 were drug offenders—up from 16 percent of 21,000 prisoners in 1970.

Arguments Pro and Con

Proponents of the war on drugs defend it as necessary to prevent the spread of drug abuse and its associated problems. However, its critics argue that the programs are expensive, ineffective, counterproductive, and immoral. Critics also argue that most, if not all, drugs should be made legal and regulated by methods similar to those in place for alcohol and tobacco products.

Opponents of legalization, or "prohibitionists," often note the social ills associated with illegal drugs in defending the war on drugs. They point out that most prison and jail inmates are involved with illegal drugs, that even so-called "minor" drugs, such as marijuana, have been shown to have serious negative health effects, and that illicit drugs devastate the most disadvantaged communities. To address these problems, they argue, harsh penalties for drug crimes should be enacted to deter prospective drug users and traffickers.

Critics reject the prohibitionist logic. First, they question whether the criminal justice system itself is the appropriate place in which to respond to what is essentially a medical and personal problem. They cite the example of alcohol and tobacco products containing nicotine. Like illegal drugs, those substances pose serious health challenges to their users and generate enormous costs to society, but society addresses those problems through means other than arrest and punishment.

Drug war critics also note that, despite massive efforts by drug enforcement agencies to combat drug use, research surveys have suggested that drug-use patterns have remained remarkably stable since the war on drugs programs began during the 1970's. Meanwhile, the drug war has endangered the lives of valuable law-enforcement personnel and wasted precious financial resources. Prohibitionists respond by pointing to marginal decreases in the use of some drugs during the 1990's as possible evidence of the drug war's success. However, their critics counter that those decreases may be attributable either to improvements in the national economy that alleviated the social conditions that tend to drive drug use or to mere changes in drug fashions.

Critics also contend that the war on drugs contributes to the problems that prohibitionists use to justify current policy. The crucial problem with attempting to control drugs through law enforcement is the demand for illegal drugs, which inevitably entices people into the lucrative illicit drug trade. Drug addicts commit crimes to support their habits and must enter the dangerous criminal underworld to purchase their drugs, whose prices are made artificially high by the fact of their being illegal. Drug traffickers engage in extortion, kidnapping, and murder to establish and defend their illegal trade.

Among the other arguments advanced in favor legalizing drugs is the need to protect the health and safety of addicts. Because illicit drugs are unregulated, there can be no guarantees of their purity and their safety to the people who use them. Another line of argument concerns the impact of drug law enforcement on the innocent. For example, the use of incarceration to punish drug crimes disrupts the families of incarcerated drug offenders, worsening the conditions of poverty and instability that breed youth criminality, including drug offenses, thereby tending to perpetuate the cycle of drug use that the drug war is intended to end. Critics of current drug policies argue that if drugs were legalized and regulated, the current black market, and most of the crime, health risk, and social cost associated with drug use, would vanish.

Prohibitionists counter with a number of effective criticisms at those who support legalization. First, even if it is true that prohibition has failed to eradicate all drug use, legalization could easily result in increased levels of use as the legal consequences of drug crimes are removed. Second, government's legalization of drugs might send a message, especially to young people, that drug use is acceptable, thereby encouraging the spread of drug abuse.

Weighing the Positions

Drug war critics can produce no compelling response to the prohibitionists' first criticism, since legalization is not the current policy and its effects are thus unknown. However, some legalization proponents suggest that the decision to use drugs is a function of complex personal and social factors, of which prospective legal penalties are only a small part. By this reasoning, decriminalization might not result in the dramatic increase in consumption that prohibitionists fear.

Critics also challenge the idea that legalization "sends the wrong message." First, by the logic of this prohibitionist argument, the use of *all* dangerous substances, including nicotine and alcohol, should be subject to the criminal law. However, American society does not rely on the justice system to impress on the public the undesirability of the use of those substances. Furthermore, it is argued that there are more constructive ways to "send the *right* message," including public awareness campaigns about the social consequences of drug abuse—much like those already used to discourage cigarette smoking and alcohol abuse.

Regardless of how these issues are settled, some proponents of legalization argue that mere drug use should be legal in any event, because drug use, by itself, carries no personal culpability in the same sense as robbery or murder. However, prohibitionists dispute that "mere" use is a morally neutral act, since a society in which drugs are commonly available would be less able to prevent drug use among the young and misinformed. Even mere consensual use is part of, and certainly no solution to, the problem of drug abuse.

Deciding which side of the debate—prohibition or legalization—is most compelling may hinge on the answers to three difficult questions: What are the likely social costs of decriminalization? How do those costs compare with the costs of the current war on drugs? And, to what extent are drug "crimes," such as mere possession or trafficking, punishable under an ethical system of law? The fact that the answers to these questions are currently in such sharp dispute demonstrates that the drug legalization debate is far from resolved.

Timothy Griffin

Further Reading

Gray, James. *Why Our Drug Laws Have Failed and What We Can Do About It: A Judicial Indictment of the War on Drugs*. Philadelphia: Temple University Press, 2001. Historical analysis of the failures of drug interdiction.

Husak, Douglas. *Legalize This! The Case for Decriminalizing Drugs*. New York: Verso, 2002. Not actually a comprehensive case for decriminalization, but a philosophical argument that punishing personal drug use is unjustified.

"Should Drugs Be Legalized?" In *Drugs: Should We Legalize, Decriminalize, or Regulate?*, edited by Jeffrey A. Schaler. New York: Prometheus, 1998. Argument for penalties against even minor drug offenders to curb the spread of drugs.

Trebach, Arnold S., and James A. Inciardi. *Legalize It? Debating American Drug Policy*. Washington, D.C.: American University Press, 1993. Trebach argues for legalization while Inciardi argues against it in this "opposing viewpoints" format.

Wilson, James Q. "Drugs and Crime." In *Drugs and Crime*, edited by Michael Tonry and James Q. Wilson. Chicago: University of Chicago Press, 1990. Drawing distinctions between currently legal and regulated drugs and illicit drugs to justify policies of interdiction.

See also Antismoking laws; Commercialized vice; Comprehensive Drug Abuse Prevention and Control Act; Decriminalization; "Drug czar"; Drug Enforcement Administration; Drugs and law enforcement; National Narcotics Act; Opium Exclusion Act; Prohibition; Victimless crimes.

Drug testing

Definition: Procedures involving standard sets of guidelines and technologies that are used to examine physical specimens—such as urine, blood, hair, perspiration, and saliva—to detect the presence of illegal psychoactive drugs—such as cocaine, heroin, and marijuana

Criminal justice issues: Courts; probation and pretrial release; substance abuse; technology

Significance: Drug testing is a tool that can be used at every stage of the criminal justice process; it is an especially useful aid to making decisions about the sentencing, supervision, placement, treatment, and release of offenders.

Illegal drug use is common within offender populations, which include arrestees, detainees, probationers, prison inmates, and parolees. During sustained periods of drug use, offenders commit more crimes and commit them at higher rates and severity levels. This fact and the continued national emphasis on the enforcement of drug laws have increased the importance and role of drug testing in criminal justice practices.

Drug-Testing Procedures and Accuracy

Urinalysis is the oldest and most common type of drug-testing procedure. The two primary methods for detecting drugs in the urine are immunoassay and chromatography. Immunoassay tests use human antibodies to reveal the presence of certain substances in urine. Relatively inexpensive, these tests can be conducted in criminal justice agencies and do not require highly specialized laboratories. Drug-testing experts, known as toxicologists, recommend that positive immunoassay tests be followed by chromatography. The latter is a more costly procedure but is also more reliable and legally defensible test that separates drugs from the biological components of urine specimens.

Urinalysis must be performed shortly after suspected use because such tests lose their effectiveness with delays between drug ingestion and drug testing. For example, amphetamines, cocaine, and heroin can be detected by urinalysis for only two or three days following their use. In addition, drug testing has greater deterrent effect on potential offenders when it is conducted frequently and randomly.

Urine specimens can be analyzed by instruments in machines or manually, in noninstrument tests. The former methods uses machines to sample, measure, and produce quantitative results on a numeric scale that specifies the detectable levels of ingested drugs. The latter methods use manual techniques in which specimens are collected by hand. Point-of-contact strips are dipped into the specimens and produce dichotomous results that are either positive or negative.

The two possible types of drug-testing errors are false positives and false negatives. False positives occur when tests indicate the use of illegal drugs when none have been ingested. False negatives occur when tests fail to detect drugs that have been ingested. Ingestion of legal drugs, such as ibuprofen and other anti-inflammatory medicines, can lead to false positive findings. False negative results can occur when quantities of ingested drugs are too small to be detected by the tests, or when the tests are not sensitive enough to detect the amounts of drugs typically ingested. Confirmation, or follow-up, tests can help avoid drug-testing errors.

Newer drug-testing technologies are expected eventually to replace urinalysis as the predominant mode of drug testing for offenders. Among

A chemist in the crime laboratory of the Massachusetts State Police holds a test tube showing positive results of a marijuana test. The test indicates traces of marijuana in human urine by separating the fluid into different color bands. (*AP/Wide World Photos*)

the new technologies are hair analysis, saliva testing, and sweat patches. Compared with urinalysis, newer drug-testing technologies are less invasive, easier to administer, and capable of detecting drug use for much longer periods of time after ingestion.

Uses of Drug Testing

Drug testing can improve assessment and case-management strategies for drug-using offenders, and can be used at the pretrial and posttrial levels, that is, both before and after sentencing. At the pretrial stage, drug testing can be done while arrestees and detainees are awaiting bail, arraignment, or disposition of their cases. Defendants on pretrial release who use illegal drugs are more likely to continue committing crimes and miss their court dates. Hence, drug testing is often used to monitor defendants who participate in pretrial release programs that allow them to remain in their communities under court-ordered conditions of release. Participation in day reporting centers is an example of such a program, in which defendants receive services during the day and return to their residences in the evenings under a curfew restriction.

Detection of illicit drug use can help courts determine defendants' suitability for community supervision. The results can also be used to develop specific service plan for defendants in pretrial programs. Positive test results can hold defendants accountable to the courts when judges have imposed abstinence on them as a condition of their pretrial release. In these situations, the detection of illicit drugs often leads to such sanctions as pretrial confinement or the imposition of more restrictive conditions of release.

After offenders are sentenced to probation or prison or are released on parole, drug testing can be used to achieve different goals, depending on the offenders' progress in the recovery process. As at the pretrial level, positive drug test results can yield confirmatory evidence that is part of a more comprehensive assessment of drug use. Moreover. the threat of continued testing can increase the honesty and candor of offenders' self-reports of their illicit drug use. During their early stages of recovery, when offenders' acceptance of their drug use problems is paramount, drug testing can produce objective evidence of illicit drug

use and be another mechanism to confront the offenders' resistance to treatment. During treatment and relapse prevention, testing can be a barometer of abstinence, encouraging offenders to remain drug free for increasing lengths of time.

Drug testing often has been ordered as a condition of release for offenders in intensive probation supervision programs, a popular sentencing option for managing drug-using offenders in the community. Officers who administer intensive probation programs have smaller caseloads than those who manage offenders on standard probation supervision. They use drug testing to evaluate drug problems, monitor offender behavior, and deter continued drug use.

The results of drug tests performed at the pretrial and probation stages can be used to make decisions about the placement of incoming prison inmates. For example; offenders who violate their probation and are sent to prison because of positive drug-test results might be housed in special drug treatment units or facilities. In these situations, drug-test results are used to develop drug-treatment plans.

As with all criminal justice clients, both drug testing and treatment must be mandated to be most effective. Numerous studies have shown that offenders in mandatory treatment programs remain in treatment longer—an essential component of successful recovery. Mandatory testing can exert more leverage over offenders by being a deterrent to continued drug use, but only if positive test results lead to swift, consistent, and meaningful sanctions.

Limitations of Drug Testing

The current technology of drug testing is limited in several respects. For example, it provides no specific information about the quantity of drugs ingested, the precise times of drug ingestion, the modes of ingestion, the degree of functional impairment experienced by drug users, or the severity of the users' problems. Some offenders who test positive are only occasional or "recreational" drug users who experience few problems from use. Others who test positive may be addicted to drugs and experience intense cravings and an inability to function without the substances. As a general rule, offenders who test positive on multiple occasions are more likely to abuse or be dependent on drugs and should be further assessed.

Little evidence suggests that drug testing by itself significantly reduces pretrial arrests or failure-to-appear rates. In addition, drug testing during pretrial release has questionable utility in predicting rearrests before sentencing. The use of drug testing as part of pretrial or post-trial supervision programs might actually increase the sizes of jail populations by giving defendants and offenders additional ways to violate the conditions of their release and to be returned to detention as a consequence.

Drug testing is also a costly and sometimes unreliable method of detecting illicit drug use. Moreover, results can infringe on constitutional or due process rights when, for example, persons who test falsely positive for illicit drug use lose their freedom.

Because of its limitations, drug testing should be used judiciously. Positive tests should lead to further assessments, increased contacts with case managers, and plans for treatment and other interventions that are designed to reduce drug use. For defendants on pretrial supervision, the lengths of time they spend on release may be too brief to produce lasting benefits from treatment. Therefore, participation in treatment readiness sessions may be a more appropriate option for drug-involved defendants.

For probationers, positive test results must be linked to drug treatment services and interventions to reengage them in the recovery process. These same principles apply to parolees with drug-use problems. In short, drug testing and treatment together are more effective than drug testing alone in changing offenders' drug-using and criminal behaviors.

At all stages of the criminal justice system, professionals must recognize that addiction is a chronic brain disease, and relapses are to be expected in the recovery process. For this reason, one or two positive test results should rarely, if ever, be considered sufficiently serious violations of supervised release to justify termination of treatment or other services. Instead, positive drug-test results should be seen as valuable opportunities to identify and challenge the factors in individual offenders' lives that precipitate relapses, and case workers should refocus the of-

fenders on the elements of their treatment and other community resources that promote sobriety.

Drug testing is a useful tool for managing drug-involved offenders at the pre- and post-sentencing stages. At the pretrial stage, drug-test results provide objective indicators of the need for further evaluation and placement in treatment readiness programs. At the post-sentencing stage, drug-test results confirm the findings of more comprehensive assessments, help motivate offenders to continue their recovery, and identify episodes of relapse that can be exploited as opportunities to facilitate treatment.

Arthur J. Lurigio

Further Reading

Belenko, S., I. Mara-Drita, and J. E. McElroy. "Drug Tests and the Prediction of Pretrial Misconduct: Findings and Policy Issues." *Crime and Delinquency* 38 (1992): 557-582. Professional study of correlations between drug-test results and criminal behavior by defendants during pretrial release.

Drug Treatment in the Criminal Justice System. Washington, D.C.: Office of National Drug Control Policy, 2001. Federal government report on drug-treatment programs through the criminal justice system.

Goldkamp, J. S., M. R. Gottfredson, and D. Weiland. "Pretrial Drug Testing and Defendant Risk." *Journal of Criminal Law and Criminology* 81 (1990): 585-652. Similar study on the connections between drug-test results and pretrial release behavior.

Mieczkowski, T., and K. Lersch. "Drug Testing in Criminal Justice." *National Institute of Justice Journal* 3 (1997): 9-15. Brief but broad overview of the uses of drug testing in the criminal justice system.

Wish, E. D., M. Toborg, and J. Bellassai. *Identifying Drug Users and Monitoring Them During Conditional Release.* Washington, D.C.: National Institute of Justice, 1988. Federal government report on the use of drug testing to monitor defendants in pretrial release.

See also DARE programs; Drug courts; Drug Enforcement Administration; Drugs and law enforcement; Parole; Privacy rights; Probation, adult; Sobriety testing; Toxicology.

Drugs and law enforcement

Criminal justice issues: Federal law; law-enforcement organization; substance abuse

Significance: Drug abuse and drug enforcement are major concerns for law-enforcement agencies and the criminal justice system as a whole. Drug enforcement activities account for a large portion of federal and state law-enforcement budgets, and drug offenders are a growing population in both state and federal prisons.

At the turn of the twentieth century there was a growing concern on the part of many Americans regarding the use of so-called patent medicines, many of which contained opium. One of the most common of the numerous "cures" for various ailments was Laudanum, which was a mixture of opium and alcohol. At that time, drugs were considered a medical issue subject to control at the individual state level, and it was usually left to the determination of the medical community as to what constituted appropriate and inappropriate use. Drugs officially became a national law-enforcement issue in 1914 with the U.S. Congress's passage of the Harrison Narcotic Drug Act.

The Harrison Act made drugs and drug abuse federal law-enforcement concerns with the creation of the Narcotics Division within the U.S. Treasury Department. In 1930, Congress's passage of the Porter Act created the federal Bureau of Narcotics under the direction of the Treasury Department; it became the predecessor to the modern Drug Enforcement Administration (DEA).

Throughout the twentieth century, drug enforcement efforts changed the focus from one drug of choice to another, and increased authority was granted to law enforcement in attempts to control the illicit importation and distribution of controlled substances. Some of the most significant legislative enforcement efforts include the Comprehensive Drug Abuse Prevention and Control Act of 1970 (also known as the Controlled Substances Act), the Omnibus Crime Control Act of 1984, the Violent Crime Control and Law Enforcement Acts of 1990 and 1994, and the Home-

land Security Act of 2002. Each of these federal laws provided additional tools and authority for law enforcement to identify, apprehend, penalize, and incapacitate those involved in the trafficking and use of controlled substances.

Types of Drugs

In general, law-enforcement efforts in the United States focus primarily on five major categories of what are collectively known as "controlled substances": stimulants, depressants, narcotics, hallucinogens, and cannabis. Cocaine and methamphetamines are the two primary controlled stimulants that require law-enforcement action. Depressants include barbiturates, rohypnol ("roofies"), methaqualone, and gamma hydroxy butyrate (GHB).

Law-enforcement agencies are concerned with both natural and synthetic narcotics. Natural narcotics derive from the opium poppy and include heroin, morphine, and codeine. Synthetic narcotics, which are manufactured from chemicals in laboratories, include such substances as methadone, demerol, and oxyContin. Hallucinogens cover a wide range of naturally occurring substances such as peyote and psilocybin and synthetically produced substances such as lysergic acid diethylamide (LSD), phencyclidine (PCP), methylenedioxymethamphetamine (MDMA or Ecstasy), and ketamine. Finally, the cannabis category of drugs includes marijuana, hashish, and any other substance containing tetrahydrocannabinol (THC).

Drug Schedules

The federal Drug Enforcement Administration is charged with the responsibility of regulating the manufacture, distribution, and scheduling of controlled substances in the United States. Controlled substances are scheduled according to their potentials for abuse, propensities for user dependency, and levels of accepted medical use within the United States. Drugs are classified in five schedules.

Schedule I controlled substances have no currently accepted medical uses within the United States. They also have high potentials for abuse and lack accepted safety for use even under medical supervision. Examples include heroin, LSD, GHB, marijuana, and MDMA.

Schedule II substances also have a high potential for abuse, but they differ from Schedule I substances in that they have accepted medical uses in the United States. Despite the latter fact, abuse of these substances can lead to severe physiological or psychological dependence. Schedule II substances include cocaine, methamphetamines, methadone, PCP, and oxyContin.

Schedule III substances have less potential for abuse than those on Schedules I and II and also have well-documented and accepted medical uses in the United States. They present low or moderate potentials for physical dependence but high potentials for psychological dependence. Drugs in this schedule include ketamine, codeine, many diet pills, and steroids.

Schedules IV and V controlled substances have a low potentials for abuse. They are well known as useful in medical treatments in the United States and present limited potential for either physical or psychological dependence.

Federal Drug Law Enforcement

The Treasury Department was originally tasked with enforcement of the Harrison Narcotic Drug Act because this act was a taxation measure and fell under the same jurisdiction as other taxation matters. The Federal Bureau of Narcotics was established within the Treasury Department in 1930 to focus specifically on controlled substances and narcotics violations. In 1968 jurisdiction was transferred from the Department of Treasury to the Bureau of Narcotics and Dangerous Drugs within the U.S. Department of Justice. In 1973 the Drug Enforcement Administration was created and charged with primary responsibility for drug and narcotics enforcement within the United States. In 2004, the DEA employed approximately 3,300 agents and 400 intelligence specialists deployed throughout the United States and in fifty foreign countries.

Federal Drug Seizures, 1990-2003

(pounds)

total seizures by agents of the DEA, FBI, U.S. Customs, and U.S. Border Patrol

Source: U.S. Drug Enforcement Administration.

In 1982, the Federal Bureau of Investigation (FBI) was given concurrent jurisdiction with the DEA on drug enforcement-related investigations. Since then, the FBI has focused mainly on organized crime's role in drug trafficking and has employed specific legislative enforcement tools in this effort. Continuing criminal enterprise (CCE) statutes and the Racketeer Influenced and Corrupt Organizations Act of 1970 (RICO) laws are two of the primary law-enforcement tools used by the FBI to combat organized crime's role in drug trafficking. The FBI established the Organized Crime Drug Enforcement Task Force (OCDETF) in 1983 to detect and prosecute large criminal organizations that traffic in drugs. The OCDEFT is a multiagency endeavor, with both state and federal participation, that boasts a highly successful record of apprehending and prosecuting large drug trafficking organizations and their associates.

Along with law-enforcement efforts to identify, apprehend, and prosecute drug users and distributors at the federal and state levels, federal agencies also focus on the interdiction of drugs prior to their entry into the United States and during their transportation from point of entry to distribution locations. Interdiction efforts attempt to prevent the entry of drugs into the United States by concentrating efforts on the supply routes on land, air, and sea.

The United States Coast Guard plays an active role in the identification and interception of drug smugglers on the oceans and in the coastal waters that surround the United States. The Coast Guard employs advanced intelligence systems and utilizes interdiction patrols on known smuggling routes to profile "mother ships" that may be loaded with drugs being shipped from one of the many source countries. The Bureau of Immigration and Customs Enforcement (ICE) is responsible for securing the nation's borders and transportation systems and is charged with the prevention of smuggling drugs, weapons, and instruments of terrorism across U.S. nation's borders or through the numerous ports of entry either by air or from the sea.

State and Local Drug Law Enforcement

State and local drug law enforcement is similar to the federal system in organization. However, most state and local law-enforcement agencies are heavily dependent on federal funding to support their enforcement activities. Drug investigations can be both personnel and time intensive and are often beyond the capability of small local agencies; they can even place severe strains on some state law-enforcement budgets. Federally sponsored multijurisdictional task forces and the involvement of the federal agencies in major cases are frequently utilized techniques at the state and local levels of drug enforcement.

A common method of effective drug investigations at both state and federal levels is drug interdiction. In drug interdiction, law-enforcement agencies attempt to intercept and seize illegal drugs during their transportation from their source locations to their intended distribution sites. Federal efforts focus on intercepting drugs before they enter the United States, while state

A member of one of the California Highway Patrol's specially trained drug interdiction teams dismantles the dashboard of a car believed to be used for smuggling drugs. (*AP/Wide World Photos*)

and local efforts focus on intercepting drugs before, or while, they enter the individual states and before they reach their points of distribution.

Interdiction efforts at the state and local levels include highly visible efforts by uniformed officers on major interstates and major routes of travel between source cities and areas of distribution. Another effective interdiction strategy involves the interception of drugs that are being moved from source to distribution locations by means of public transportation, such as buses, railways, and public airlines.

Special Operations

A highly visible drug investigative effort that is viewed by the general population as an effective strategy is known as the fish net operation. This type operation is a planned and coordinated labor-intensive effort targeting both buyers and sellers of drugs at the street level. This strategy is used most frequently in open-air drug markets that are commonly located in inner cities. Known drug-selling locations are subjected to intense surveillance in this type of operation. Individuals observed selling or purchasing drugs are contacted away from the sites of the sales and are arrested for possession or distribution of controlled substances. This technique is often enhanced by the use of undercover police officers making buys from targeted individuals.

As may be expected, these operations receive strong support from local communities and serve as effective public relations strategies for law-enforcement agencies. Fish net operations are effective in disrupting the flow of illegal drugs for short periods of time but have limited impact on long-term drug control or drug reduction strategies.

The most highly publicized drug enforcement investigative technique involves the use of undercover operatives to make purchases or to infiltrate drug trafficking organizations. There are two primary types of undercover operations employed at the state and local level. The first type involves the use of police officers in undercover roles; the second involves the use of informants to make undercover purchases or gather other evidence.

Each type of undercover operation has specific benefits and limitations. When utilizing police of-ficers in undercover roles, the primary concern throughout the operations is focused on the safety of the officers. These operations must be well planned and coordinated with adequate surveillance and "cover" units in place to ensure the safety of the undercover officers. The value of using undercover police officers, instead of informants, is the level of confidence that is obtained in the details of the drug purchases and in the evidence obtained. Basically, judges and juries trust police officers more readily than informants.

The use of informants to make undercover purchases or obtain evidence for use in drug prosecution requires detailed efforts to "validate" the information obtained. Since many informants have less-than-credible pasts (some may even be currently involved in illegal activities), it is imperative that interviews and searches of the informants be conducted immediately before and after they make their drug purchases or collect their evidence. Consequently, a primary focus of undercover operations utilizing informants is on the credibility of the evidence the informants obtain. Informants must be kept under constant surveillance during and after their drug purchases to ensure that all collected evidence is recovered and that no evidence is "planted" or stolen by the informants. The primary benefit of using informants is in that they can often infiltrate organizations or gain the trust of individuals to which undercover law-enforcement officers would not have access.

Another form of undercover operation used by larger agencies and at the federal and state level is the so-called "reverse sting." In a reverse sting, the police are the individuals "selling" drugs. These operations are usually large in scale and target mid- and upper-level dealers who show a predisposition to drug trafficking activities. Reverse sting operations require detailed planning and coordination and can pose serious dangers to the officers involved.

There have been reported instances of individual law-enforcement agencies setting up reverse sting operations whose intended drug buyers were from other law-enforcement agencies. Such situations can hold dramatic and unfortunate outcomes when each agency involved believes the other side to be the "bad guy." Another issue of concern in the reverse sting is the defense of entrapment that is frequently presented at trial. It is important in this type investigation to establish the predisposition of the targeted individual prior to the actual conduct of the operation.

Summary

In 2005, law enforcement had been officially fighting the "war on drugs" for three decades, and the battle was still raging on. Strategies have changed over the years, as has the focus on the different types of drugs being smuggled into, or produced within, the United States. Although drug trafficking efforts continually evolve to meet the changing demand for the drugs of choice, law enforcement has rallied to meet this evolution with newer and more effective enforcement strategies. Although many critics of the war on drugs believe that the war has already been lost, law-enforcement agencies at the federal, state, and local levels have neither surrendered nor retreated.

Michael L. Arter

Further Reading

Gaines, Larry K., and Peter B. Kraska, eds. *Drugs, Crime, and Justice*. Prospect Heights, Ill.: Waveland Press, 2003. Broad collection of articles addressing drug control, the industry of drug distribution, and law-enforcement strategies.

Goode, Erich. *Drugs in American Society*. Boston: McGraw Hill, 2005. Very thorough review of drug use in America, the drug crime connection, and law-enforcement efforts to control drug abuse and drug related crimes.

Gray, James P. *Why Our Drug Laws Have Failed and What We Can Do About It*. Philadelphia: Temple University Press, 2001. Critique of the war on drugs from the personal perspective of a California trial judge.

Lee, Gregory D. *Global Drug Enforcement: Practical Investigative Techniques*. Boca Raton, Fla.: CRC Press, 2004. Comprehensive presentation of investigative techniques used in drug investigations.

Lyman, Michael D. *Criminal Investigation: The Art and the Science*. Upper Saddle River, N.J.: Prentice-Hall, 2002. Thorough description of drug abuse and the investigative techniques utilized by law enforcement.

Manning, Peter K. *The Narcs' Game: Organizational and Informational Limits on Drug Law Enforcement*. Prospect Heights, Ill.: Waveland Press, 2004. Wide-ranging review of drug control policies and the police role in drug enforcement.

See also Alcohol use and abuse; Coast Guard, U.S.; Comprehensive Drug Abuse Prevention and Control Act; Decriminalization; Drug courts; "Drug czar"; Drug Enforcement Administration; Drug legalization debate; Drug testing; Entrapment; Federal Bureau of Investigation; Homeland Security Department; Opium Exclusion Act; Organized crime; Racketeer Influenced and Corrupt Organizations Act; Victimless crimes.

Drunk driving

Definition: Operating or controlling motor vehicles while under the influence of intoxicants

Criminal justice issues: Substance abuse; traffic law

Significance: Drunk drivers are involved in accidents that result in more than 600,000 injuries and 17,000 fatalities annually in the United States. The fact that nearly 1.4 million drivers are arrested for drunk driving every year indicates that the criminal justice system is committed to reducing the devastation caused by drunk driving.

The term "drunk driver" is loosely applied to all persons who operate motor vehicles on public or private roads while under the influence of alcohol or any other drugs. Motor vehicles are defined by state vehicle codes as vehicles that are propelled by means other than human power. In the broadest sense, therefore, a person could be considered a drunk driver for riding a horse while under the influence of alcohol or other drug. Some jurisdictions go further by defining drunk drivers to include bicycle and scooter riders and skateboarders. Additionally, operators of road-building equipment have been charged and convicted of drunk driving. It is more generally accepted, however, that the term "drunk driver" applies to persons who drive motor vehicles upon highways while intoxicated.

Every U.S. state has a legally defined presumptive limit for determining levels of driver intoxication. Forty-eight states have set 0.08 grams of alcohol per deciliter of blood as the maximum acceptable blood alcohol levels (BAL) for drivers. Delaware and Colorado have set the figure at 0.10. These standards mean that drivers whose blood alcohol levels exceed the acceptable state levels are presumed by the laws of those states to be "driving under the influence" (DUI) of alcohol. California holds drivers of trucks to a more stringent BAL standard of 0.04.

Persons of average height and weight generally reach blood alcohol levels of 0.10 after consuming the equivalent of five ounces of alcohol during a one-hour period. Absorption rates vary with body mass and food consumption, but blood alcohol levels tend to drop at the rate of 0.02 per hour after consumption of alcohol stops.

History of Drunk Driving

Sanctions against drunk driving may be said to have originated during the mid-nineteenth century, when railroads began disciplining employees who operated their locomotives while intoxicated. However, similar sanctions would not be placed on operators of motor vehicles operated on highways until nearly fifty years later. East Coast states such as New York, Pennsylvania, and Massachusetts were the first to adopt drunk driving laws shortly after the turn of the twentieth century. As motor vehicles became more common on the roadways, other states began following suit. However, most states still lacked basic vehicle codes for drivers.

In a trend that moved gradually from the East Coast to the West Coast, states began developing motor vehicle codes. New York was the first, outlawing drunk driving in 1910. At that time, the offence was defined simply as operating a motor vehicle while intoxicated, and there was no set standard by which officers could gauge levels of intoxication. Drunk driving arrests were thus made strictly at the discretion of the arresting officers. By the mid-1930's, all forty-eight states in the Union had laws on the books prohibiting drunk driving. Many of these laws were adopted in response to the new post-Prohibition drinking

and driving culture. In 1939, Pennsylvania became the first state to implement laws that connected blood alcohol content of drives to drunk driving offenses.

During those early years, driving while intoxicated was not considered to be a major social concern. Even after V-12 and other high-performance engines began taking to the highways in the 1930's, law-enforcement officials did not regard drunk driving as a major problem. That attitude changed after American servicemen and women returned following World War II.

America's love affair with the automobile and the wide-open spaces offered by a rapidly expanded network of interstate highways drew more traffic than ever before to the roadways. During the 1940's and 1950's, deaths from motor vehicle accidents increased significantly, and the automobile industry worked to improve vehicle safety. Drivers, for the most part, were ignored in assessments of motor vehicle safety. Public awareness of the hazards of driving while intoxicated finally began to develop as the findings of traffic safety studies were published. Federal traffic safety guidelines began to surface in the mid-1960's as a result of these studies. Law enforcement responded to the problem, but generally only passively.

During the 1940's and 1950's, when police officers cited drunk drivers, they typically parked the drivers' cars and either took the drivers home or called taxis for them. That practice was socially accepted as good enforcement policy. During the 1960's, the numbers of arrests for drunk driving increased as federal highway funding became contingent upon state enforcement of DUI laws.

Public attitudes toward drunk driving underwent a dramatic change after a young pedestrian was struck and killed by a drunk driver in a Sacramento, California, suburb in 1980. Thirteen-year-old Cari Lightner was hit by a car driven by a drunk driver who was a repeat offender. Cari's mother, Candace (Candy) Lightner, started a grassroots campaign to increase public awareness of the social harm caused by drunk driving. The organization she founded, Mothers Against Drunk Driving (MADD), developed into a major national force for tougher drunk driving laws and enforcement.

Meanwhile, as public concern over drunk driving increased, so too did law-enforcement response. A new emphasis on arresting suspected drunk drivers replaced the old informal sanction of parking the drivers' cars and assisting them to get home. The result of tougher enforcement of DUI laws was a notable reduction in alcohol-related traffic fatalities. In 1982, there were 26,173 alcohol-related traffic deaths in the United States. That number would decline over the next two decades.

Prevalence of Drunk Driving

It is difficult to estimate how many drivers operate motor vehicles while under the influence of alcohol or other drugs. One measure of the prevalence of drunk driving can be found in data on alcohol-related traffic fatalities. According to the National Highway Traffic Safety Administration (NHTSA), 17,419 alcohol-related traffic fatalities occurred in the United States in 2002. That number represents nearly 41 percent of all traffic fatalities nationwide during that year. Between 1982 and 2002, every state in the Union saw a decrease in alcohol-related traffic fatalities. The only increase noted occurred in Washington, D.C. However, alcohol-related traffic fatalities are only one measure of the prevalence of drunk driving. In addition to fatalities, nearly 600,000 injuries occur as a result of alcohol-related accidents each year.

Another measure of the prevalence of drunk driving can be found in arrest records. According to the National Hardcore Drunk Driver Project, there were approximately 186.6 million motor vehicle drivers in the United States in 2001. During that same year, approximately 1.4 million persons were arrested for drunk driving. (Those figures do not include Wyoming, Ohio, Colorado and Montana, whose arrest records are maintained at local jurisdictions and are not shared in a centralized database.) According to the Bureau of Justice Statistics, approximately 513,000 people were in jails or on probation in 1997 for drunk driving offenses. That figure compares with nearly 270,000 people in jails or on probation for such offenses in 1986.

According to Bureau of Justice Statistics (BJS), typical DUI offenders are white, male, and older and better educated than other classes of criminal offenders. In 1983, female drivers repre-

Billboard warning motorists they are approaching a sobriety checkpoint near Indianapolis, Indiana. In 2003, Indiana posted similar billboards throughout the state to deter motorists from drinking and driving although many of the vehicle checkpoints never actually existed. *(AP/Wide World Photos)*

sented only about 5 percent of all DUI arrests. That figure rose to nearly 7 percent of all DUI arrests in 1996. The increase may indicate that more women are driving while drunk, or that law-enforcement officers (an increasing number of whom are themselves women) are becoming more willing to arrest female offenders than in the past.

Even arrest figures do not complete the picture of the prevalence of drunk driving. Those numbers reflect only those offenders who are actually observed and apprehended. It is impossible to know the actual numbers of drunk driving offenders because many—perhaps most—are not detected.

Investigation

Almost all drunk drivers enter the criminal justice system through arrests by law-enforcement officers. Some arrests result from police investigations of motor vehicle accidents, but most offenders are arrested in the course of their driving. Patrol officers from sheriffs' departments, highway patrol agencies, and city police departments are now trained in detecting drunk drivers.

There is no one thing that officers look for to detect drunk drivers. Although most offenders are arrested between the hours of 10:00 P.M. and 2:00 A.M., arrests are made at all hours of the day and night. Some law-enforcement agencies have special drunk driver task forces that work during peak detection periods. Officers watch for cars that are traveling too slowly or too fast, aggressive driving behavior, and other traffic offenses. Many drunk drivers are detected simply because they allow their vehicles to drift from side to side in their traffic lanes.

When officers suspect drivers to be under the influence of alcohol or drugs, traffic stops are initiated. If, after stopping the suspect drivers, the officers observe objective symptoms of alcohol or drug consumption, such as slurred speech or bloodshot and watery eyes, they ask the drivers to perform field sobriety tests (FSTs). Every department has policies on the administration of such tests, which may include balance tests, such as standing on one foot or walking in a straight line, and tests involving mental dexterity, such as counting on fingers or reciting the alphabet backward. When drivers fail to perform the test

satisfactorily or refuse to take them, arrests are made.

Prosecution

After they are arrested, suspected drunk drivers are transported to facilities where chemical tests of their alcohol levels are made. When blood tests are made, they are administered at hospitals. Breath and urine tests are usually administered at local jail facilities. When breath tests are taken, the results can be assessed immediately. When test results indicate blood alcohol levels below the acceptable limits, the drivers may be released without undergoing prosecution. However, such decisions are at the sole discretion of the arresting officers and are made when the officers consider all relevant facts in the cases. For example, an officer who suspects that a driver has ingested drugs as well as alcohol may elect to pursue prosecution. The ultimate decisions of whether to prosecute are made by local prosecutors' offices.

Drunk driving is categorized as a misdemeanor in all fifty states, but under some special circumstances it is treated as a felony. Although what constitutes special circumstances varies from jurisdiction to jurisdiction, drunk driving is always a felony when persons other than the drivers are injured as a result of accidents caused by drunk drivers. Felony charges are also pursued against repeat offenders.

Punishment

Specific laws vary among the states, but most states follow similar general guidelines in the punishments that administer to convicted drunk drivers. In the case of first offenses, offenders are generally required to remain in jail a minimum of four hours—the approximate length of time they need to sober up. First-offense fines usually range from $200 to $1,000. Many jurisdictions allow first-time offenders to go to traffic school to have their arrests expunged from their driving records.

Subsequent drunk driving arrests result in stiffer sanctions. Fines for second and third offenses generally result in fines of more than $1,000 and jail sentences of thirty to ninety days. Offenders who violate DUI laws more than three times are considered habitual and are given six-to-nine-month jail sentences and are assessed fines of around $2,500. In many jurisdictions, felony charges are brought against offenders with more than four drunk driving arrests.

Average jail sentences for DUI offenders are eleven months, with half of all offenders serving at least six months. Those figures suggest that most DUI offenders who serve jail time are repeat offenders. In fact, the BJS also reports that one-third of DUI offenders on probation and nearly one-half of all incarcerated drunk driving offenders admitted to prior arrests.

In addition to fines and jail time, DUI offenders face scrutiny by state departments of motor vehicles. In all fifty states, driving is considered a privilege, and motor vehicle departments reserve the right to suspend the driving privileges of drivers who are stopped for DUI and refuse to complete field sobriety tests. Such suspensions follow administrative hearings at which the drivers may have attorneys present. Driving privileges of drivers who accumulate excessive numbers of DUI arrests are also suspended. A new form of punishment that is gaining favor in America is the forced installation of ignition-locking devices that allow law-enforcement officials to shut down drivers' vehicles under certain conditions set forth by the courts.

Charles L. Johnson

Further Reading

Jacobs, J. B. *Drunk Driving: An American Dilemma.* Chicago: University of Chicago Press, 1992. Broad synthesis by a law professor on all aspects of drunk driving in the United States, from myths about the nature of the problem to the trend toward tougher enforcement of drunk driving laws.

Jasper, Margaret, et al. *DWI, DUI and the Law.* New York: Oceana, 2004. Layperson's guide to drunk driving laws in the United States. Covers criminal justice procedures, drunk driving statistics, and other related subjects.

Laurence, Michael D., John R. Snortum, and Franklin E. Zimring, eds. *Social Control of the Drinking Driver.* Chicago: University of Chicago Press, 1988. Sociological study of the causes and effects of drunk driving.

Light, Roy. *Criminalizing the Drunk Driver.* Brookfield, Vt.: Ashgate, 1994. Study of changing laws regarding drunk driving.

Robin, Gerald D. *Waging the Battle Against Drunk Driving: Issues, Countermeasures and Effectiveness.* Westport, Conn.: Greenwood Press, 1991. Fascinating study of the modern movement against drunk driving, with special attention to such grassroots movements as MADD.

Taylor, Lawrence E., and Steven Oberman. *Drunk Driving Defense.* New York: Aspen, 2003. How-to guidebook written by a lawyer to help people beat drunk-driving charges. While the ethics of publishing such a book may be questionable, the book provides revealing insights into the problems of prosecuting drunk driving offenses.

Watson, Ronald R., ed. *Alcohol, Cocaine, and Accidents.* Clifton, N.J.: Humana Press, 1995. Collection of ten research papers on the roles of alcohol and cocaine in motor vehicle, aviation, and aquatic accidents that are addressed to policymakers and people in law enforcement. Particular attention is given to the behavior of young people.

Wilson, R. Jean, and Robert E. Mann, eds. *Drinking and Driving: Advances in Research and Prevention.* New York: Guilford Press, 1990. Interdisciplinary collection of articles on a wide variety of aspects of drunk driving. The first section covers efforts to understand impaired drivers; the second section examines efforts to deter drunk driving; and the third section examines other preventive measures.

See also Blue laws; Fines; Hit-and-run accidents; Mothers Against Drunk Driving; Sobriety testing; Traffic courts; Traffic fines; Traffic law; Traffic schools; Vehicle checkpoints.

Due process of law

Definition: Fundamental principle of fairness in all legal matters, both civil and criminal, especially in the courts. All legal procedures set by statute and court practice, including notice of rights, must be followed for each individual so that no prejudicial or unequal treatment will result.

Criminal justice issues: Constitutional protections; legal terms and principles; professional standards

Significance: Due process of law is a safeguard of both private and public rights against unfairness.

The concept of due process originated in the Magna Carta (1215), by which English nobles limited the authority of the king. The document required the king and his agents to respect the "legal judgment of his peers" and "the law of the land." Over time, the ideas of that charter of liberties protecting the public against the government's arbitrary and random acts came to be represented in the phrase "due process of the law."

Essentially, the Anglo-American tradition of due process requires a fair hearing for persons charged with an offense and a decent opportunity to defend themselves. This is one of the major foundations of the American tradition of personal liberty. It is most highly developed in the oldest form of public action, the criminal prosecution.

Today, due process in the United States partially depends on written guarantees of the Constitution. The Fifth Amendment to the U.S. Constitution applies to the federal government and provides that "No person shall . . . be deprived of life, liberty, or property, without due process of law." The Fourteenth Amendment, with similar language, constrains the states. Many legal decisions determining both procedural and substantive rights—especially in criminal justice cases—arise from these two amendments. In criminal law, interests of "liberty" would include freedom from incarceration and a parolee's interest in staying on parole. Other constitutional amendments, from the Fourth through the Eighth, provide additional substance to due process.

Due process also depends on American values of fairness. The Constitution does not specify certain standards in criminal justice, such as the requirement that guilt be proved beyond a reasonable doubt, that the accused be presumed innocent until proved guilty, or that the burden of proof rests on the prosecution. Nevertheless, such standards are part of American custom dating back to the early years of the republic and are integral to the concept of due process. As Justice Louis Brandeis described it, procedural "funda-

One of the most distinguished American jurists who never sat on the U.S. Supreme Court, Learned Hand served more than thirty years on federal appeals courts and wrote more than three thousand opinions. *(Library of Congress)*

mentals do not change; centuries of thought have established standards."

Obviously, due process cannot be fully defined in a neat catchall rule. Perhaps Judge Learned Hand expressed it best when he stated that it embodies the English sporting sense of fair play. In the language of Justice Oliver Wendell Holmes, state administration of criminal law offends due process "if it makes you vomit."

Historically, the U.S. Supreme Court has interpreted due process in two distinct categories: substantive and procedural. Substantive due process is concerned with limitations on the power or authority of government to abridge any person's life, liberty, or property interests. The body of the Constitution and the Bill of Rights contain numerous limitations on the power of government to interfere with individual rights. Substantive due process is used to invalidate government actions interfering with individual freedoms in such areas as abortion, marriage, procreation, and interstate travel when no more specific constitutional ground can be found.

Procedural Due Process

Procedural due process is concerned with fair procedure when the government is a party in a case where an individual has been deprived of a recognized liberty or property interest. The Supreme Court, as guardian of the criminal justice systems, has provided general guidelines rather than precise delineations of due process. In each case the Court asks whether the challenged practice or policy violates "a fundamental principle of liberty and justice which inheres in the very idea of a free government and is the inalienable right of a citizen of such government." The Court has held that, at a minimum, due process means that an accused must be given notice of a charge and adequate opportunity to appear and be heard in his or her own defense. Criminal defendants have a right to a fair and public trial conducted in a competent manner and a right to an impartial jury. Laws must be written so that a reasonable person can understand what constitutes criminal behavior.

The Bill of Rights requires the federal government to observe explicit criminal procedure standards. The Fourth Amendment protects people from unreasonable searches and seizures and describes the requirements for a search warrant. In addition to protecting the right to "due process of the law," the Fifth Amendment requires indictment by grand jury and protects defendants from double jeopardy and from being required to testify against themselves. The Sixth Amendment provides the accused with the right to a speedy and fair trial by an impartial jury; the right to be confronted by the witnesses against them and the right to cross-examine such witnesses; the right of compulsory processes for obtaining witnesses in their favor; and the right to counsel. The Eighth Amendment prohibits excessive bails and fines and protects the guilty from cruel and unusual punishments.

Although Bill of Rights protections were enforced against the federal government, state criminal law and procedures were traditionally afforded greater autonomy under the American system of federalism. With respect to the state courts, the Supreme Court's authority had his-

torically been less extensive, as it had held in *Barron v. Baltimore* (1833) that the specific provisions of the Bill of Rights dealing with judicial procedure did not apply to the states. The adoption of the Fourteenth Amendment in 1868, however, required the Court to reconsider its position in *Barron*. In *Hurtado v. California* (1884), the Court rejected the claim that the due process clause incorporated the Fifth Amendment requirement of indictment by grand jury to apply to the states. What the Court did concede was that the due process clause was a general guarantee of fairness, prohibiting the states from interfering with fundamental principles of liberty and justice.

The Incorporation Doctrine

By the 1930's the Court had found that some provisions of the Bill of Rights had been made applicable to the states by the Fourteenth Amendment due process clause. In *Palko v. Connecticut* (1937), the Court held that the due process clause incorporated those parts of the Bill of Rights "so rooted in the traditions and conscience of our people as to be ranked fundamental" or which are "the very essence of a scheme of ordered liberty." For the Court, justice Benjamin Cardozo announced this "fundamental fairness doctrine" and found that double jeopardy protections did not meet its requirements. To require more than that would be to put a "straitjacket" on the states and their administration of criminal law according to proponents of the fundamental fairness theory.

During the 1940's, four justices of the Court— Hugo L. Black, William O. Douglas, Frank Murphy, and Wiley B. Rutledge—argued that the due process clause made every provision of the Bill of Rights applicable to the states. These proponents of "total incorporation" were never able to persuade a fifth justice to their view, so the Court continued to use the fundamental fairness approach in interpreting due process. As explained by justice Felix Frankfurter, the question of whether a state criminal procedure was consistent with the requirements of due process imposed upon the Court "an exercise of judgment" upon the whole course of the proceedings in order to ascertain whether they "offend those canons of decency and fairness which express the notions of justice of English-speaking peoples even toward those charged with the most heinous offenses."

During the 1960's, the Earl Warren court provided a third view of the appropriate relationship between the Fourteenth Amendment and the Bill of Rights—"selective incorporation." In cases dealing with state criminal prosecutions, the Court used selective incorporation that combined aspects of both the fundamental rights and the total incorporation interpretations. The Court agreed with proponents of the fundamental fairness approach that the due process clause of the Fourteenth Amendment protects only those rights that are "fundamental to ordered liberty." Whereas justices following the fundamental fairness concept would incorporate only the particular part of a constitutional guarantee involved in the specific case at hand, proponents of selective incorporation look less to the particulars of the case and instead determine whether the guarantee as a whole should apply to the states—a view similar to that of the total incorporation theory.

Applying this selective incorporation analysis, the Court in the twenty-first century has held that practically all the criminal procedural guarantees of the Bill of Rights include limitations that are fundamental to state criminal justice systems and that the absence of a particular guarantee denies a defendant due process of law (only the Fifth Amendment requirement of indictment by grand jury and the Eighth Amendment prohibition of excessive fines have not been incorporated to apply to the states). In making these determinations, the Court struggled with the problems of accommodating competing interests—the most important of which was the concept of a minimum national standard of due process competing with the position and authority of the states in maintaining their systems of justice within the structure of federalism. However, the due process clause of the Fourteenth Amendment is not limited to the specific guarantees of the Bill of Rights but also contains protection against practices that may violate values of fundamental fairness without abrogating a specific provision of the Constitution.

Other Elements of Due Process

Among elements of due process enunciated by the Court are: the void-for-vagueness doctrine

that requires detailed legislation providing ascertainable standards of guilt; statutory notice providing for definiteness in criminal statutes so that a person may know that something must not be done or, alternatively, that unless something is done criminal liability will result; the "entrapment" defense that protects people from punishment for illegal conduct induced or encouraged by police agents; the criminal identification process that regulates the conduct of police seeking to identify perpetrators of crimes by lineups or photographic displays; and indictment, which in the states may be by grand jury or information (a document issued by the prosecutor officially charging an individual with criminal violations) but must include adequate notice to defendants of the offenses charged against them and for which they are to be tried.

"Due process" also is used as a title of a social science model of the criminal justice system. The due process, or adversarial, model of criminal court operations emphasizes regularity of procedures, the elimination of mistakes, and prevention of official misconduct while maintaining that an individual accused of criminal conduct must be assumed innocent until proven guilty—even when doing so hinders the efficiency with which the criminal justice system operates. In contrast, the administrative, or crime control, model assumes that the accused is guilty and values efficient and cost-effective disposition of cases.

The large number of criminal due process cases that come before federal and state courts each year indicate the changing nature of the concept and its central position in American criminal justice.

Theodore M. Vestal

Further Reading

Alderman, Ellen, and Caroline Kennedy. *In Our Defense: The Bill of Rights in Action.* New York: Avon Books, 1992. Examines the freedoms expressed in the Bill of Rights, their legal and historical significance, and illustrates with stories of how lives have been affected by criminal justice issues.

Amar, Akhil. *The Constitution and Criminal Procedure: First Principles.* New Haven, Conn.: Yale University Press, 1998. A reconceptualization of the basic foundations of criminal justice to limit procedures that often reward the guilty while hurting the innocent.

Curtis, Michael Kent. *No State Shall Abridge: The Fourteenth Amendment and the Bill of Rights*. Durham, N.C.: Duke University Press, 1990. Argues that the Fourteenth Amendment was intended by the framers to incorporate the Bill of Rights and therefore to inhibit state action.

Nelson, William E. *The Fourteenth Amendment: From Political Principle to Judicial Doctrine*. Reprint. Cambridge, Mass.: Harvard University Press, 1995. Presents evidence that the framers of the Fourteenth Amendment intended to affirm the general public's long-standing rhetorical commitment to the principle of individual rights on one hand and to the principle of local self-rule on the other.

Neubauer, David W. *America's Courts and the Criminal Justice System*. 8th ed. Belmont, Calif.: Wadsworth/Thomson Learning, 2005. Comprehensive analysis of the dynamics of criminal justice in action as seen in the relationship of judge, prosecutor, and defense attorney.

Orth, John V. *Due Process of Law: A Brief History*. Lawrence: University Press of Kansas, 2003. A succinct and readable narrative tracing the history of due process from its origins in medieval England to its applications in the latest cases.

See also Arraignment; Bill of Rights, U.S.; Confessions; Consent searches; Constitution, U.S.; Criminal procedure; Equal protection under the law; Fifth Amendment; *Gault, In re*; Incorporation doctrine; Judicial review; Preliminary hearings; Preventive detention; Reasonable doubt; Self-incrimination, privilege against; Supreme Court, U.S.

Duress

Definition: Defense to a crime or contract based on the argument that one's will was overcome or overpowered by the threat of bodily harm or compulsion

Criminal justice issues: Defendants; legal terms and principles

Significance: Statutorily defined in most states, the defense of duress may be used in both criminal and civil cases.

The defense of duress is available in limited circumstances if a defendant's free will has been overcome by a threat of the imminent danger of death or great bodily harm from another. The defense of duress is also available in contract actions. The essence of duress in a contract action is that a person signing a contract or promissory note has done so under the threat of imminent bodily harm from another.

The defense of duress for crimes is statutorily defined in most states. In Oklahoma, for example, defendants are entitled to the defense of duress if they commit criminal acts or omissions that constitute the crimes because of a reasonable belief that they are in imminent danger of death or great bodily harm from another. In Oklahoma and other states, duress may be predicated on threats to one's spouse or children.

Courts refuse to instruct juries on the defense of duress when there is no evidence of actual force or fear to compel the defendant to commit crimes. The threatened harm must be continuous throughout the time the criminal act is being committed in order for there to be a duress defense.

The urgency of avoiding the harm is assessed according to ordinary standards of reasonableness. Serious bodily injury is bodily injury involving a substantial risk of death, extreme physical pain, disfigurement or the substantial impairment of a bodily member, organ, or mental facility. Jury instructions provide that if a defendant acted as a result of duress or there is a reasonable doubt as to whether the defendant acted as a result of duress, the defendant must be found not guilty. Duress is a defense even if defendants intentionally, knowingly, or recklessly placed themselves in a situation in which it was probable that they would be subject to compulsion.

Duress is also a defense to an ordinary contract action. Contracts signed under duress may be canceled or rescinded. Economic duress is not a defense to a contract. The type of duress that warrants excuse of contractual performance is a matter of local law. A holder in due course is a person who takes a negotiable instrument in good faith, for value, and without notice of defenses or claims. However, even a holder in due course takes an instrument subject to the defense of duress. The duress must render the obligation of the party a nullity. Duress rendering instruments void must be of such a nature that the signers believe themselves to have been under the threat of death or serious bodily injury at the time they signed the instruments.

Michael L. Rustad

Further Reading

Del Carmen, Rolando V. *Criminal Procedure: Law and Practice.* 6th ed. Belmont, Calif.: Thomson/Wadsworth, 2004.

Dressler, Joshua. *Understanding Criminal Procedure.* 3d ed. New York: LexisNexis, 2002.

Emanuel, S. L. *Criminal Procedure.* Aspen, Colo.: Aspen Publishing, 2003.

See also Blackmail and extortion; Criminal intent; Criminal law; Defenses to crime; Excuses and justifications.

Effective counsel

Definition: Legal representation of clients by fully qualified attorneys who are committed to providing their clients with the best possible defense

Criminal justice issues: Attorneys; constitutional protections; professional standards

Significance: All persons charged with the commission of crimes have a constitutional right to have lawyers who are qualified and competent to represent them.

Everyone charged with a crime in the United States is entitled under the U.S. Constitution to have a lawyer represent them, because having a lawyer has been held essential to ensuring a fair trial. The presence of lawyers on both sides of a case improves the fairness of a trial, enabling the adversary system to function as well as possible so that guilty persons can be identified and innocent persons set free. But because the presence of a lawyer only improves the fairness of a trial if the lawyer is qualified and competent, the U.S. Constitution has been held to guarantee not just the assistance of a lawyer but also the assistance of a competent lawyer, whose loyalty to the client is undivided and whose efforts on the client's behalf are not unduly restricted. This representation is termed "effective" assistance of counsel, and representation that does not meet this standard is described as "ineffective." If persons are convicted of a crime and their lawyers were constitutionally ineffective, these persons may have their convictions set aside and be eligible to receive new trials.

The Constitutional Right to Effective Counsel

The American model of criminal justice is based on the adversary system. This system requires attorneys on opposing sides who vigorously present their views of the law and the evidence. When one side is represented by lawyers who fail to present their parties' arguments, the adversary system may not function properly in reaching the truth. Such lawyers are said to be "ineffective," and the persons they represented are deprived of their constitutional right to effective assistance of counsel.

The guarantee of effective assistance of counsel applies only in criminal cases, because it is only in criminal, as opposed to civil, cases that persons have a right to be represented by lawyers. Regardless of whether criminal defendants can afford to hire (or "retain") their own lawyers or whether they cannot afford to do so and must have lawyers appointed for them by the court, the right to be represented has been held to be a guarantee of competent counsel.

How Counsel Can Be Ineffective

Lawyers can fail to provide effective assistance in any of three general ways. First, they can be ineffective because of a conflict of interest—something that prevents them from fully and zealously representing the interests of their clients. Second, lawyers can be ineffective if a judge restricts their ability to be effective—by preventing them from fully and zealously advocating on behalf of their clients. Third, lawyers can be ineffective through lack of competence to handle particular cases or types of cases.

Lawyers are ethically obligated to fully and zealously advocate first and foremost for the interests of their clients. Sometimes lawyers can have conflicting interests—for example, by representing more than one client in a case. If lawyers must choose between advancing the interests of one client or another, the client whose interests were not made the first priority may have received ineffective assistance of counsel. Besides making lawyers ineffective, conflicts of interest may also violate ethical rules and can be a basis for sanctions or penalties against such lawyers. Conflicts may result in lawyers' negligent performance of professional responsibilities and can be a basis for a civil action by clients against their lawyers for malpractice. Courts also have made lawyers ineffective—for example, by preventing them from making closing arguments

A Truly Ineffective Movie Lawyer

In director Sidney Lumet's 1993 film *Guilty as Sin*, an attorney played by Rebecca De Mornay agrees to represent a client (Don Johnson) accused of murdering his wife. The attorney eventually becomes convinced of her client's guilt. Concerned that he might not be convicted otherwise, she plants evidence designed to incriminate him. However, the client himself produces a surprise witness who lies to provide the client with an alibi that prevents the jury from convicting him. Afterward, the client attempts to kill the attorney.

The defense attorney in this film is unrealistically bad on several levels; she is a bad attorney when she initially believes her client is innocent and becomes even worse as she comes to believe that he is guilty. For example, the prosecution's key evidence against her client consists of statements written and made by the murdered wife that appear to implicate the

Don Johnson (left), Rebecca DeMornay and Jack Warden in *Guilty as Sin*. (Kerry Hayes, Hollywood Pictures Company. All Rights Reserved)

client. In real life, a competent attorney would categorically object to the introduction of this evidence because it violates the rule against hearsay evidence. This rule of evidence provides that testimony intended to prove the truth of some matter normally cannot be offered by a witness who is not present in court to be cross-examined. Thus, evidence from the dead wife tending to prove that her husband has killed her should not be admitted because the woman herself cannot appear in court.

Later in the film, when the attorney comes to believe that her client is, in fact, a murderer, she violates an even more fundamental rule. Attorneys are obligated to represent their clients diligently, whether they are innocent or guilty.

Timothy L. Hall

in bench trials (nonjury trials decided by judges alone) or by appointing lawyers shortly before trial and forcing them to proceed with their defense despite inadequate preparation. These practices have been found to render lawyers' assistance in such circumstances ineffective.

Effective Counsel and Successful Counsel

While conflicts of interest and court restrictions on lawyers' work can make lawyers' assistance ineffective, the most controversial area of ineffective assistance has dealt with incompetent or unqualified counsel. Incompetence can lead to mistakes, such as inadequate investigation of a case, failure to call certain witnesses, or inadequate presentation of evidence. Not all mistakes, however, render lawyers ineffective.

The U.S. Supreme Court has held that the Constitution guarantees defendants the right to have a lawyer who is competent but not necessarily successful. The Constitution guarantees only a fair trial, and if lawyers make trials fair—despite losing—they are considered constitutionally effective. For the purpose of establishing effectiveness, the Court has ruled that lawyers make trials fair by meeting the general level of professional performance of other lawyers. Lawyers need not do what the best lawyers or those with the most resources would do if they were handling the same case.

In the 1984 case of *Strickland v. Washington*, the U.S. Supreme Court created the standard by which lawyers' effectiveness was to be measured. The Court made it harder to bring successful claims against lawyers by requiring proof of "prejudice." Prejudice is the legal term for harm resulting from lawyers' mistakes or inaction. To find a lawyer ineffective, the Court required more than proof that the lawyer's performance was worse than that of most lawyers. It further required that this poor performance "prejudiced" or harmed the defendant, specifically by making it more likely that the defendant would be convicted.

Ensuring Effective Assistance of Counsel

A challenge to lawyers' effectiveness usually comes only after cases have been concluded and only when they result in convictions. Determining whether a lawyer was competent requires another proceeding, such as another trial, at which testimony and evidence are presented about the lawyer's work on the case. In such proceedings, lawyers often become principal witnesses. These proceeding are civil rather than criminal cases, even though they concern what happened in criminal trials. They can be held in either federal or state courts if the conviction originally occurred in state court (as most convictions do) and can result in the issuance of a writ of *habeas corpus* (a writ permitting prisoners to challenge wrongful convictions) if the reviewing court finds that lawyers' assistance was ineffective. A 1995 U.S. Department of Justice study of approximately half of all petitions for writs of *habeas corpus* in federal courts found that the largest percentage of such petitions, 25 percent, involved claims for ineffective assistance of counsel. Very few claims of ineffective assistance, however, are successful.

David M. Siegel

Further Reading

American Bar Association. *Model Rules of Professional Conduct and Code of Judicial Conduct*. Chicago: American Bar Association, 1992. Compilation of the codes establishing rules of ethics for lawyers. See also the ABA's *Code of Professional Responsibility and Judicial Conduct* (Chicago: American Bar Association, 1977).

Freedman, Monroe H., and Abbe Smith. *Understanding Lawyers' Ethics*. 3d ed. Newark, N.J.: LexisNexis, 2004. A compact treatment of lawyer's ethics, including chapters on prosecutors' ethics and the client perjury problem.

Taylor, John B. *Right to Counsel and Privilege Against Self-Incrimination: Rights and Liberties Under the Law*. Santa Barbara, Calif: ABC-Clio, 2004.

Tomkovicz, James J. *The Right to the Assistance of Counsel: A Reference Guide to the United States Constitution*. Westport, Conn.: Greenwood Press, 2002.

Wolfram, Charles. *Modern Legal Ethics*. St. Paul, Minn.: West, 1986. A treatise on legal ethics that addresses ethical obligations of prosecutors and defense attorneys in some detail.

See also Attorney ethics; Cross-examination; Death-row attorneys; Defendant self-representation; Equal protection under the law; *Habeas corpus*; Paralegals; Public defenders.

Elderly prisoners

Definition: Prison inmates who require special attention because of their advanced ages

Criminal justice issues: Medical and health issues; prisons; rehabilitation

Significance: Aging prison inmates present challenges to corrections administrators that go beyond the normal issues of custody and control in confinement settings.

With the advent of public policy encouraging longer sentences and the aging of the "boomer" population born shortly after World War II, the number and percentage of elderly inmates confined in American prisons and local jails has increased dramatically. The special challenges presented by elderly inmates reflect similar experience in the mainstream of American life. Those who are confined at older ages or those who grow old in confinement require different health care systems, different recreational and rehabilitation programs, special housing, different hygiene care, and different diets. They even have different preferences for the items sold in prison commissaries. Although free society is attuned to the interests of senior citizens outside prisons, most correctional institutions are struggling to meet the needs of elderly incarcerated persons.

One of the greatest challenges to corrections officials is providing adequate health care to aging inmates. Deteriorating health is a natural function of aging and elderly inmates face the same debilitating illnesses as those on the outside. Moreover, inmate health is typically worsened by prisoners' use of drugs, alcohol, tobacco, and other manifestations of unhealthy lifestyles. Correctional administrators are required by law to provide the same standards of health care to inmates that free members of society expect, but they often lack sufficient resources to deal with serious and lingering diseases, such as heart conditions, AIDS, cancer, and dementia.

Debilitating long-term medical conditions frequently require concerted and expensive medical care to preserve life or provide an acceptable quality of life. Some prison systems have developed hospice care inside their facilities to care for terminally ill inmates. Their goal is to keep such patients comfortable and allow them to come to terms with their coming deaths. In some prison systems, administrators seek compassionate releases from incarceration for terminally ill inmates.

Inmate-classification systems, which assign housing, programs, and privileges to inmates, make the safety of inmates a priority. Such systems face unique challenges in classifying aging inmates. On one hand, most elderly inmates are physically weaker than younger inmates; however, some possess criminal sophistication that allows them to continue to present serious dangers to other inmates, staff, and prison security. Older and more sophisticated inmates are often respected and renowned prison gang members who control the activities of fellow inmates. Because of the danger such inmates can present, they may be confined in the most secure settings that the prisons have. On the other hand, elderly inmates who are serving time for their first offenses may need to be protected from younger inmates who prey on the weak. Thus, no single formula exists for classifying aging inmates.

Older inmates often have special dietary and recreational needs. They may not be capable of playing common recreational games and need alternative exercise programs to maintain health and fitness. Human metabolism slows down as people age, so elderly inmates may require smaller meals with different food values. Even the range of items sold at inmate commissaries may need to be expanded to offer snacks and hygiene items preferred by aging inmates.

Michael Hackett

Further Reading

Allen, H. E., C. E. Simonsen, and E. J. Latessa. *Corrections in America*. 10th ed. Upper Saddle River, N.J.: Pearson/Prentice-Hall, 2004.

California Department of Corrections. *Older Inmates: The Impact of an Aging Inmate Population on the Correctional System: An Internal Planning Document for the California Department of Corrections*. Sacramento: California Department of Corrections, 1999.

Hackett, Michael. *The Impact of an Aging Inmate Population in Local Detention Facilities by the Year 2003*. Sacramento: California Commission on Peace Officer's Standards and Training Library, 1999.

Johnson, R. *Hard Time: Understanding and Reforming the Prison*. 3d ed. Belmont, Calif.: Wadsworth, 2002.

See also Prison and jail systems; Prison health care; Prison industries; Prison overcrowding; Prison violence; Work camps.

Electronic surveillance

Definition: Investigative technique used to monitor telephone conversations, electronic mail, pagers, wireless phones, computers, and other electronic devices

Criminal justice issues: Investigation; privacy; technology

Significance: Electronic surveillance significantly increases the ability of law-enforcement officers to conduct investigations of nontraditional or difficult-to-observe criminal targets.

Electronic surveillance is a tool utilized by law-enforcement agencies in the course of ongoing criminal investigations. Federal agencies have traditionally had broad legal powers to monitor telephone conversations, electronic mail, pagers, wireless phones, computers, and all other electronic devices. These powers were increased significantly after passage of the USA Patriot Act in 2001.

Popularly referred to as "tapping" in general discourse, electronic surveillance is governed by two statutes: the Federal Wiretap Act and the Foreign Intelligence Surveillance Act (FISA). The former, sometimes referred to as Title III, was initially passed in 1968 and expanded in 1986. It set procedures for court authorization of real-time surveillance in criminal investigations of all electronic communications, including voice, electronic mail, fax, and Internet.

Typically, before wiretaps can commence, court orders issued by judges must be obtained by the agencies requesting the surveillance. The government is responsible for providing the judges with affidavits detailing probable cause that crimes have been, are being, or are about to be committed. Wiretaps may be ordered for several activities, including but not limited to drug trafficking, child pornography, and terrorist activities. The Patriot Act expanded the list of criminal statutes for which wiretaps can be ordered. Wiretaps are used to prevent, as well as punish crimes, as the government can set up wiretaps in advance of crimes being executed. In such instances, the wiretaps are used to identify planning and conspiratorial activities related to criminal acts. Government requests for wiretaps are rarely denied.

The Foreign Intelligence Surveillance Act of 1978 allows wiretapping of aliens and citizens in the United States. Again, probable cause must be provided suggesting that the targets of surveillance are members of foreign terrorist groups or are agents of foreign powers. For American citizens and aliens who are permanent residents of the United States, there must also be probable cause to believe that the persons targeted are engaged in activities that may involve criminal violations. Suspicion of possible illegal activity is not required, however, in cases involving aliens who are not permanent residents of the United States. For such persons, membership in terrorist organizations is enough to justify surveillance, even if the activities in which they engage on behalf of their organizations are legal.

The Patriot Act and Electronic Surveillance

A major change introduced by the Patriot Act was to allow prosecutors to use FISA for the purposes of gathering evidence in criminal investigations of national security crimes. There are also no legislative limits on electronic observation conducted overseas, as neither Title III nor FISA has any application to intelligence collection activities outside the United States.

The most common form of electronic surveillance used in the United States is the pen register and trap-and-trace technology. Pen registers record and decode all numbers dialed by electronic devices such as telephones, while trap-and-traces capture the originating sources of incoming calls. Together, these are commonly referred to in law-enforcement jargon as dialed number recorders, or DNR. Standards governing the use of these devices are derived from the 1986 Electronic Communications Privacy Act. The Patriot Act has also expanded permissible uses of traditional pen register and trap-and-trace devices so that they may be used to monitor not only telephonic communications, but also Internet communications.

Another form of electronic surveillance is the "roving tap." Court orders permitting roving taps do not require specific telephone lines or electronic mail accounts to be named; they allow the tapping of any phone line, cell phone, or Internet account that the targeted suspects use. Unlike the traditional trap-and-trace and pen register, which numbers thousands of uses each year, roving taps are relatively rare with only six such taps approved during all of 2003.

Holly E. Ventura

Further Reading

Adams, James A., and Daniel D. Blinka. *Electronic Surveillance: Commentaries and Statutes*. Notre Dame, Ind.: National Institute for Trial Advocacy, 2003.

McGrath, J. E. *Loving Big Brother: Performance, Privacy and Surveillance Space*. New York: Routledge, 2004.

Monmonier, M. S. *Spying with Maps: Surveillance Technologies and the Future of Privacy*. Chicago: University of Chicago Press, 2002.

Stevens, Gina Marie, and Charles Doyle. *Privacy: Wiretapping and Electronic Eavesdropping.* Huntington, N.Y.: Nova Science, 2002.

See also Community-based corrections; Computer crime; Espionage; Fourth Amendment; House arrest; *Katz v. United States*; Mafia; Organized crime; Patriot Act; Privacy rights; Search and seizure; Stakeouts; Surveillance cameras; Telephone fraud.

Embezzlement

Definition: Theft or larceny of another's assets by a person who holds a position of trust

Criminal justice issues: Business and financial crime; fraud; robbery, theft, and burglary; white-collar crime

Significance: Embezzlement is a widespread crime that involves significant financial loss.

Embezzlement was first recognized as a distinct crime to include misdeeds by servants and clerks in England in 1799. Common law had failed to cover instances in which property or financial assets were entrusted to the care of another person or employee by the owner and then stolen or misappropriated. Earlier larceny laws required that the property be removed from another's possession, which necessitated that the offender take direct possession and walk off with the purloined article. Statutes also were passed in the United States that defined embezzlement as a felony delineated from theft based on the violation of trust that accompanies the conversion of the property. An office worker, for example, stealing supplies to keep and use at home is committing larceny, whereas a bookkeeper in the same office who siphons money from accounts receivable is committing embezzlement.

Embezzlement as a traditional white-collar crime is less clearly defined because in many cases the offender may lack a prestigious position and actually holds a lower-level job. The key element in embezzlement that categorizes the act as a white-collar crime is the violation of trust. Collective embezzlement, unlike other schemes, clearly represents a type of white-collar crime that emerged in the savings and loan scandal of the 1980's and refers to the embezzlement of funds, often with management involvement, from a financial institution for personal gain.

Motivations and Offender Characteristics

Early attributes and stereotypes for why men committed the crime of embezzlement included the three "W's": wine, women, and wagering or the three "R's": rum, redheads, and racehorses. The motivations of embezzlers, however, have come under intense scrutiny, as scholars, legal professionals, and victims attempt to understand why long-term, trusted, often well-paid employees risk their positions for financial gain. Research shows that gambling, extravagant lifestyles, drug addictions, and personal problems often provide the impetus for embezzlement.

Donald Cressey's 1953 study stands out as one of the most respected and cited research efforts on the actions and motives of embezzlers. Cressey interviewed 502 prison inmates who were identified as violators of trust; Cressey identified a specific process that occurs among embezzlers. First, employees are faced with financial problems that they cannot share with family or friends. Second, opportunities present themselves for solving the problems undetected. Third, the embezzlers rationalize their acts as "borrowing" to avoid internalizing a criminal identity.

Embezzlement schemes may be seen initially by the employees as borrowing money that they have every intention of repaying. Some embezzlers rationalize their behavior by claiming that their employers owe them money, or they may be disgruntled and seeking revenge against perceived unfairness in the workplace. Lifestyle improvements for most embezzlers create a downward spiral as they continue to steal, and any type of financial recovery or repayment becomes impossible. No business is immune from embezzlement, including small private organizations, major corporations, banks, and charity and nonprofit enterprises. Schemes for carrying out the crime vary tremendously, including, for example, pocketing cash, padding expense accounts, juggling billing, falsifying inventory, or manipulating payroll.

The involvement of women in the crime is significant. Statistics show a dramatic increase in the number of women convicted of felonies involving fraud. In 1996, Bureau of Justice Statistics found that women represented 41 percent of all felons convicted of forgery, fraud, and embezzlement. Major studies of women embezzlers suggest that women steal less money and have unique motives compared with men. The justifications used by women embezzlers tend to emphasize less greed, and the crime is more likely committed to meet the needs of family members. In one unusual case, a woman who had embezzled thirty thousand dollars used the ill-gotten gains to give fellow employees raises. The involvement of a high number of women may be related to the shift of family and career responsibilities as more women become sole providers for their children and acquire higher-level positions in the corporate world. In 2004, however, the majority of women embezzlers were likely to hold clerical positions.

Prevalence

Embezzlement is the fastest-growing crime in the United States and, according to Federal Bureau of Investigation (FBI) reports, showed an increase of 38 percent from 1984 to 1993. Embezzlement is listed as a Type II nonindex offense in the FBI's Uniform Crime Reports. Consequently, only arrests reported by state and local police departments are counted, and the incident rate includes a variety of trust violators. Losses from embezzlement range from conservative estimates of $4 billion to extreme projections of $400 billion. Less arguable particulars of the crime are that profits are large and risks of apprehension are low. Commentators have compared the average take of a bank robbery of about $3,000, whereas an embezzler averages around $40,000. The National White Collar Crime Center estimates that employee thefts range from $20 billion to $90 billion annually and may account for 30 percent to 50 percent of all business failures. New technologies offer easier manipulation and have contributed to an increase in embezzlement. The noted 56 percent increase in arrests from 1983 to 1992 is attributed mainly to the use of computers. The average embezzlement is estimated at $25,000, compared to computer-assisted acts at $430,000.

Investigation

Embezzlement is difficult to detect, and when successfully prosecuted, the punishment is generally more lenient than that for street-level offenses. Detecting and investigating embezzlement presents a difficult task for employers and law-enforcement agencies. Generally, the suspected employee is trusted and has a long, impeccable history with the company. Additionally, initial suspicions usually are based on circumstantial evidence that may or may not point directly to any one employee. The crime is more likely to be discovered during the later stages, as small amounts of stolen money accumulate into sizable sums. Company executives and business owners, who are often embarrassed by the loss of funds, are reluctant to report the theft to the authorities, and the situation is handled internally. Undetected and unreported incidents contribute to estimates that less than 50 percent of the employees who embezzle are arrested and prosecuted.

Initially, companies turn to an internal investigation and may employ legal counsel, forensic accountants, computer data specialists, and auditors. Publicly held companies are under greater scrutiny because executive officers must comply with securities law and fiduciary obligations. The expertise needed to gather evidence varies according to the size and complexity of the crime. Bank embezzlement schemes, which are difficult to unravel, for example, may be committed by nearly two hundred different methods.

Investigators rarely are able to find a clear paper trail because records are incomplete, missing, altered, or destroyed. The first step in any investigation is to identify the person with means and opportunity. Employers may use polygraph tests and credit checks, though internal investigators are limited by the Employee Polygraph Protection Act and the Fair Credit Reporting Act. Unwarranted or unproven accusations of embezzlement can result in defamation claims by the targeted employee.

Prosecution and Punishment

Civil actions against embezzlers represent an alternative to criminal prosecution and allow businesses to recoup losses. The expensive costs of litigation and limited assets of the wrongdoers, however, are prohibitive. Criminal proceedings are being pursued in a rising number of cases as attitudes toward financial crime become more punitive. Prosecution is a challenge, and many elements of the cases (motive, means, and opportunity) are difficult to prove. Motives are varied and include nonfinancial reasons. Prosecutors must prove that the defendants fraudulently appropriated money or property that was entrusted to their care for their own benefit.

Convicted embezzlers generally face short prison sentences. Often, restitution is part of the sentencing, but the amounts pale in comparison to what was stolen. After submitting phony expense reports and bills from an imaginary contractor, General Telephone and Electronics (GTE) managers were convicted of embezzling $1.3 million. The executives involved were sentenced to forty-one months in a federal prison and ordered to pay restitution of $355,685. An Ohio executive for the American Cancer Society was found guilty of stealing more than $7 million and was sentenced to thirteen-and-a-half years and $593,000 in restitution.

Mary Dodge

Further Reading

Cressey, Donald. *Other People's Money*. Glencoe, Ill.: The Free Press, 1953. Seminal research study examining the means, motives, and stories of male embezzlers.

Rosoff, Stephen M., Henry Pontell, and Robert H. Tillman. *Profit Without Honor: White-Collar Crime and the Looting of America*. Upper Saddle River, N.J.: Prentice-Hall, 2004. Comprehensive study of white-collar crimes that includes extensive case study examples.

Shichor, David, Larry Gaines, and Richard Ball, eds. *Readings in White-Collar Crime*. Prospect Heights, Ill.: Waveland Press, 2002. Collected articles that examine a wide range of white-collar crimes, including embezzlement.

Sifakis, Carl. *Frauds, Deceptions, and Swindles*. New York: Checkmark Books, 2001. Recounts a variety of scams, swindlers, and tales of deception.

Zietz, Dorothy. *Women Who Embezzle or Defraud*. New York: Praeger, 1981. Dovetails the work of Cressey with an in-depth examination of female perpetrators.

See also Circumstantial evidence; Computer crime; Corporate scandals; Criminal law; Forensic accounting; Forgery; Fraud; Money laundering; Polygraph testing; Private detectives; Theft; White-collar crime.

Entrapment

Definition: Legal concept that may be used as a criminal defense by defendants who believe that the government not only has created opportunities for them to commit crimes but also has gone so far as actually to encourage them to do so

Criminal justice issues: Defendants; police powers

Significance: The defense of entrapment has been created and upheld by court decisions. Although entrapment is not specifically named in the U.S. Constitution, there are constitutional principles that underlie it.

Due process implies fairness and notification. Entrapment is viewed as setting up a defendant to become a criminal. To ensure that the government does not abuse its power to arrest and charge citizens with crimes, it is forbidden from implanting or manufacturing crime in innocent minds. If the police do not have evidence of illegal activity, they may not get it by setting up an outrageous set of circumstances that would encourage law-abiding citizens to break the law.

An example of a successful use of the entrapment defense can be found in the U.S. Supreme Court case of *Sherman v. United States* (1956). In this case, the defendant was suspected of dealing in heroin. However, the police had no evidence to support their suspicions. To obtain the evidence to make an arrest, they used an informant, who asked Sherman to help him find some narcotics. Both Sherman and the informant were being treated for narcotics addiction. After being ignored on several occasions and persisting in his requests, the informant finally convinced Sherman to obtain narcotics for him. Sherman was arrested. The Supreme Court found that the tactics of the police constituted entrapment and that the police had gone too far in their efforts to enforce the law. In its decision, the Court stated that "the function of law enforcement is the prevention of crime and apprehension of criminals. Manifestly, that function does not include the manufacturing of crime."

Another notable case, *Jacobson v. United States* (1992), dealt with the purchasing of child pornography through the mail (a federal offense). While it was still legal to do so, Jacobson ordered magazines showing nude teenage boys. The law changed, making it illegal to receive such materials. When Jacobson's name was found on a mailing list from his previous order, law-enforcement agents encouraged him to purchase child pornography by repeatedly sending ads and solicitations to him. After more than two years of refusing the offers, he finally agreed to order a magazine and was arrested. In this case, the Court found that the defendant was not predisposed to committing the crime but had been lured by agents of the government to do something he would not ordinarily have done.

Victims of sting operations, including government officials who feel they have been set up by the police, often raise the defense of entrapment. Since the line between creating an opportunity for a crime to occur and actually inducing an innocent party to commit a crime is often blurry, the use of video cameras in enforcement has helped the courts decide if entrapment has occurred.

C. Randall Eastep

Further Reading

Holmes, Bill. *Entrapment: The BATF in Action.* El Dorado, Ark.: Desert Publications, 1998.

Lassiter, G. Daniel, ed. *Interrogations, Confessions, and Entrapment.* New York: Kluwer Academic/Plenum, 2004.

Marcus, Paul. *The Entrapment Defense.* Newark, N.J.: LexisNexis, 2002.

Mirfield, Timothy. *Silence, Confessions, and Improperly Obtained Evidence.* Oxford, England: Clarendon Press, 1997.

See also Bureau of Alcohol, Tobacco, Firearms and Explosives; Conspiracy; Defenses to crime; Drugs and law enforcement; Inchoate crimes; Police; Solicitation to commit a crime; Sting operations.

Environmental crimes

Definition: Violations of environmental laws, such as the dumping and discharging of pollutants into the atmosphere and water and the illegal production, handling, use, and disposal of toxic substances and hazardous wastes

Criminal justice issues: Business and financial crime; federal law; technology

Significance: Modern industrialization, technological advances, overdevelopment, and illegal business activities have contributed to environmental degradation, making enforcement of environmental laws increasingly important to the protection of public health and the preservation of natural resources.

In response to modern threats to the natural environment and public health, the U.S. Congress has enacted numerous environmental laws to protect the public health and natural resources. The federal Environmental Protection Agency (EPA), the Federal Bureau of Investigation, the U.S. Department of Justice Environmental Crimes Section, and state governments enforce these laws. Since 2003, the amounts of fines that are levied and lengths of prison sentences awarded under the U.S. Sentencing Guidelines for environmental crimes have increased.

Air and Water Quality

The federal Clean Air Act (CAA) of 1970 and its amendments have two major components: the establishment and enforcement of air quality standards and the regulation of mobile source emissions. The EPA is responsible for determining which adverse pollutants should be controlled and establishing national ambient air-quality standards to be attained within the hundreds of air-quality regions in the United States. Each state has responsibility for adopting a state implementation plan, establishing regulations, and enforcing its plan. The CAA requires operating permits for sources of air pollution and places limits on their emissions. The mobile source emissions portion of the CAA requires motor vehicle manufacturers to comply with EPA emission standards. In addition, the EPA requires the fuel industry to reformulate fuel products to reduce air-polluting emissions.

Criminal violations under the CAA include failure to obtain or comply with operating permits. Both acts are considered felonies that may subject violators to fines or imprisonment. Civil penalties, injunctive relief, and remedies for criminal negligence are also available under the CAA. Citizens may file actions against violators and are encouraged to report violations to appropriate officials.

The most significant water-quality laws include the Clean Water Act (CWA) of 1977 and its amendments, which protect surface waters from pollution, and the Safe Drinking Water Act (SDWA) of 1974, which is designed to ensure safe domestic drinking water through the protection of ground water. The CWA regulates discharges into surface waters through a permitting process that protects chemical, biological, and physical water quality; fisheries and habitats; and recreational uses of water.

Most violations of water-quality laws are failures to obtain discharge permits or violations of such permits. Violators may be subject to civil and criminal penalties including fines, injunctive relief, and imprisonment for criminal negligence and willful violations. An enforcement order may also include recovery of any economic benefit gained through noncompliance.

Toxic Substances

The EPA has authority to prohibit or permit development, distribution, and use of substances that may be harmful to humans and wildlife. The Toxic Substances Control Act (TSCA) of 1976 requires companies to provide scientific data and file premanufacturing notices with the EPA before producing toxic substances, while the federal Insecticide, Fungicide, and Rodenticide Act (FIFRA) of 1948 and its amendments require companies to register with the EPA and properly label pesticide products that are used in the United States.

Most violations of these laws are falsified records or failures to report to the EPA. In addition to the original registrant, violators might include wholesalers, distributors, retailers, and users of illegal substances. The laws provide for civil pen-

alties and criminal fines and imprisonment for knowing violations. The EPA may also stop sales of illegal substances and seize them.

Resource Protection

The Resource Conservation and Recovery Act (RCRA) of 1976 regulates disposal, transportation, storage, and treatment of wastes, including trash and hazardous wastes such as paint products. Regulation of hazardous wastes continues through generation to final disposal—a cradle-to-grave manifest tracking and management system in which any person coming in contact with the waste can be held liable for illegal handling, even without knowledge of a violation. Any treatment, disposal, or storage facility must also obtain a license to operate.

Most RCRA violations involve illegal dumping or operating without, or in violation of, permits. Civil and criminal penalties such as enforcement orders might provide for injunctive relief to stop improper activity. Criminal penalties for knowingly violating RCRA include daily fines, imprisonment, or both, and fines and prison terms are increased when there is the potential for immediate death or serious bodily injury to people.

Cleanup

The purpose of the Comprehensive Environmental Response, Compensation, and Liability Act (CERCLA) of 1980 is prevention and remediation of hazardous waste sites that might threaten serious harm to human health and the environment. Also known as the "Superfund Law," the act requires the EPA to establish a national priority list (NPL) of the most dangerous sites. The EPA then develops plans for remediation and assigns liability to potentially responsible parties (PRPs). The PRPs may include present and past owners of contaminated sites, even if they are not responsible for, and have no knowledge of, the disposal of illegal hazardous wastes.

All PRPs are subject to monetary penalties under CERCLA in order to replenish the Superfund and are likely to enter into consent decrees with the government to apportion damages and limit liability. Employees who commit environmental crimes subject their companies to liability, and many lawsuits brought under CERCLA encompass multiple PRPs and environmental crimes. Citizens also have the right to file suits under CERCLA and may sue the government and PRPs for environmental violations.

The EPA has declared the second full week in April of each year as the National Crime Prevention Week. All citizens, and especially students, are encouraged to take active roles in discovering and reporting environmental crimes to appropriate agencies during that week.

Carol A. Rolf

Further Reading

Burns, Ronald G., and Michael J. Lynch. *Environmental Crime: A Sourcebook*. New York: LFB Scholarly Pub., 2004. General reference work on environmental crime investigation techniques.

Grosz, Terry. *Defending Our Wildlife Heritage: The Life and Times of a Special Agent*. Boulder, Colo.: Johnson Books, 2001. Memoir of a person of who spent his career as a special agent responsible for enforcing federal wildlife protection laws.

Hersh, Heather B. *Environmental Crimes and Corporate Responsibility: A Legal Research Guide*. Buffalo, N.Y.: William Hein, 2001. Manual for legal professionals on environmental crime research methodologies.

Nolan, Andrea J. *Understanding Garbage and Our Environment*. New York: Terrific Science Press, 2004. Reader-friendly exploration of issues surrounding hazardous waste disposal.

Situ, Yingyi, and David Emmons. *Environmental Crime: The Criminal Justice System's Role in Protecting the Environment*. Thousand Oaks, Calif.: Sage Publications, 2001. Guide to the enforcement and prosecution of environmental crimes.

See also Federal Bureau of Investigation; Felonies; Fines; "Not-in-my-backyard" attitudes; Reckless endangerment; Regulatory crime; United States Code; Vicarious liability.

Equal protection under the law

Definition: Constitutional protection that forbids government from denying to any individual or group the rights and privileges accorded to others

Criminal justice issue: Civil rights and liberties; constitutional protections; trial procedures

Significance: The idea of equal treatment under the law is an expectation that most citizens have of the American justice system. However, the justice system has not always achieved that ideal.

The idea of equality under the law is symbolized in courthouses throughout the United States in various artistic depictions of the Roman goddess Justitia depicting the blindfolded deity weighing the considerations of justice on her scales without prejudice or favoritism. However, despite significant progress toward equality, the United States has often fallen short of this ideal, both in the quality of protection provided to citizens and in the treatment of those who stand accused.

The equal protection clause of the Fourteenth Amendment to the U.S. Constitution forbids state governments from denying their citizens equal protection under the law or imposing unequal punishments against them. Ratified in 1868, shortly after the Civil War, the Fourteenth Amendment was designed in large part to protect recently freed slaves. In actual practice, however, African American citizens were frequently denied equal protection under the law and many were victims of brutal lynch mobs, whose white citizens were rarely brought to justice by state or federal courts. At the same time, African Americans accused of crimes—especially rape—against white people were swiftly convicted in the courts by all-white juries and given severe punishments, including the death penalty. Members of other minority groups have also frequently found the courts to be particularly harsh in their treatment of nonwhite defendants and unconcerned with the crimes committed against them.

Women, too, have not always enjoyed equality

The principle of equal protection under the law means that justice must be dispensed with neither prejudice nor favoritism. Even a daughter of the president of the United States is subject to the law. In May, 2001, nineteen-year-old Jenna Bush (pictured) was punished by an Austin, Texas, court for a status offense violation: being a minor in possession of alcohol. After pleading no contest to the charge, a judge ordered her to pay court costs, perform community service, and attend alcohol abuse classes. (*AP/Wide World Photos*)

many officials in the justice system long regarded as personal issues outside the scope of the law.

Since the last decades of the twentieth century, excellent progress has been made toward achieving something like true equal protection under the law. Federal enforcement of civil rights legislation for minorities, increased participation of women and members of minority groups on juries, improvements in such due process rights as the right to counsel, and the inclusion of women and minorities in the various components of the justice system have all been important strides toward greater equality under the law.

Nevertheless, there remains much room for improvement before the American justice system can be said to have achieved its ideal of equality under the law. Evidence of continued disadvantages to minorities in the application of the death penalty, controversial law-enforcement practices such as racial profiling of narcotics suspects, inadequate representation for poor defendants, and the persistent inability of the justice system to control crimes against women and in disadvantaged neighborhoods continue to vex a justice system premised on the principle of equality.

Timothy Griffin

Further Reading

Belknap, Joanne. *The Invisible Woman: Gender, Crime, and Justice*. 2d ed. Belmont, Calif.: Wadsworth, 2000.

Cole, David. *No Equal Justice: Race and Class in the American Criminal Justice System*. New York: New Press, 1999.

Gertsmann, Evan. *The Constitutional Underclass: Gays, Lesbians, and the Failure of Class-Based Equal Protection*. Chicago: University of Chicago Press, 1999.

O'Brien, David M. *Constitutional Law and Politics*. 6th ed. New York: W. W. Norton, 2005.

Wilbanks, William. *The Myth of a Racist Criminal Justice System*. Monterey, Calif.: Brooks/Cole, 1987.

See also *Batson v. Kentucky*; Bill of Rights, U.S.; Defendants; Due process of law; Effective counsel; Freedom of assembly and association; *Gideon v. Wainwright*; Jim Crow laws; Lynching; *McCleskey v. Kemp*; Public defenders; Scottsboro cases; Sex discrimination.

under the law. Historically, women sometimes received lenient treatments from "chivalrous" police or judges. However, research has also shown that many women perceived as "unfeminine" or as living "wanton" lifestyles were severely punished by sexist court officials who sought to use the justice system to enforce what they regarded as appropriate gender roles. Furthermore, women victims have not always been adequately protected from rape and domestic violence, which

Escobedo v. Illinois

The Case: U.S. Supreme Court ruling on confessions

Date: Decided on June 22, 1964

Criminal justice issues: Arrest and arraignment; confessions; constitutional protections; interrogation

Significance: In this case, the Supreme Court overturned a murder conviction because the accused was never warned of his right to remain silent. This decision helped transform police behavior toward those accused of committing crimes.

Viewed historically, *Escobedo v. Illinois* was a transition case, bridging the right-to-counsel rulings in *Gideon v. Wainwright* (1963) and the capstone case of *Miranda v. Arizona* (1966). In *Gideon*, the Supreme Court ruled that criminal defendants are entitled to attorneys in their trials. *Gideon* thus definitely answered the question of the applicability of the Sixth Amendment's right-to-counsel guarantee to state action, which had been pending since the 1932 case of *Powell v. Alabama*, in which a coincidence of factors had prompted the Supreme Court to set aside a guilty verdict on the grounds that the defendants had not enjoyed adequate counsel. In *Miranda*, decided two years after *Escobedo*, the Supreme Court wove together several threads of developing judicial thought to rule that a person also has a right to counsel during pretrial questioning once the process moves to the (accusatory) stage of eliciting evidence to be used to convict the suspect being questioned. In between, *Escobedo v. Illinois* suggested the need to move the right to counsel from the courtroom to the precinct house because of the constitutionally objectionable nature of the questioning techniques used to elicit Escobedo's confession.

In a nutshell, Danny Escobedo was tricked into confession (he was falsely informed that his co-accused had fingered him for the crime) after requesting an attorney. Indeed, accounts of Escobedo's interrogation indicated that his lawyer was, at the time of Escobedo's confession, in an adjacent room being physically restrained by the police from seeing his client. This image was too much for the Supreme Court majority. In a 5-4 opinion, the Court ruled that the state's unwillingness to grant Escobedo's request for counsel rendered his confession inadmissible.

Escobedo v. Illinois is thus analogous to such cases as *Rochin v. California* (1952) in the Fourth Amendment area involving the admissibility of illegally seized evidence. In *Wolf v. Colorado* (1949), the Supreme Court absorbed the Fourth Amendment's protection against illegal searches and seizures into the due process clause of the Fourteenth Amendment, but it did not go so far as to exclude illegally seized evidence from being admitted in court. In a number of cases that followed, the zeal of the police to obtain conviction with minimal attention to a suspect's rights (as in *Rochin*, where the accused's stomach was illegally and involuntarily pumped to obtain damning evidence) prompted the Supreme Court to apply to state actors the exclusionary rule that already precluded federal law-enforcement agencies from introducing illegally obtained evidence (*Mapp v. Ohio*, 1961).

So it was with the *Escobedo* case. The case achieved instant notoriety; Danny Escobedo's face even graced the cover of one week's edition of *Time* magazine. In constitutional law, however, *Miranda v. Arizona* remains the major case involving both the pretrial right to an attorney and the admissibility of evidence and confessions obtained in pretrial interrogations.

Joseph R. Rudolph, Jr.

Further Reading

Fireside, Harvey. *The Fifth Amendment: The Right to Remain Silent*. Springfield, N.J.: Enslow, 1998.

Garcia, Alfredo. *The Fifth Amendment: A Comprehensive Approach*. Westport, Conn.: Greenwood Press, 2002.

Inbau, Fred, John Reid, Joseph Buckley, and Brian Jayne. *Criminal Interrogations and Confessions*. 4th ed. Boston: Jones and Bartlett, 2001.

Lassiter, G. Daniel, ed. *Interrogations, Confessions, and Entrapment*. New York: Kluwer Academic/Plenum, 2004.

Mirfield, Timothy. *Silence, Confessions, and Improperly Obtained Evidence*. Oxford, England: Clarendon Press, 1997.

Espionage

Definition: Attempting to secure secret information from a country or a company, using illegal or covert means

Criminal justice issues: Computer crime; espionage and sedition; technology

Significance: Protecting data about the military and technological capabilities of the United States, and discovering the intentions and capabilities of enemies, are vital to defending the national security of the country.

Espionage, counterespionage, and secret political intervention overseas are distinct operations. One actively seeks to procure secret information, the second guards against procurement of secrets by enemies, and the third, comprising clandestine operations such as assassinations and sabotage, is actually a political-military intrusion. The three are often confused with one another, a tendency encouraged by the fact that organizations such as the Central Intelligence Agency (CIA) may be concerned with all three, seeking data in foreign countries, carrying out paramilitary operations overseas, and trying to prevent attacks on the United States.

Espionage conducted by the CIA and other American government agencies against foreign powers is not a crime in the United States. Spying, sabotage, and terrorist attacks directed against the United States or its citizens are punishable crimes that the Federal Bureau of Investigation (FBI) seeks to discover and prevent as part of its national policing activity.

History of the Crime

Espionage has a lengthy genealogy. The Bible (Numbers 13) records that Moses sent agents to spy on the land of Canaan. The ancient Greeks and Romans devised ciphers to protect their communications from hostile eyes. George Washington, as commander of the American army during the Revolutionary War, employed numerous spies to keep him informed of British actions. The capture of British major John André, by alert American militiamen, with the plan of West Point in his boot and the subsequent flight of General Benedict Arnold have passed into legend, with Arnold's name becoming a synonym for traitor.

Modern American espionage and counterespionage techniques and institutions came of age during and shortly after World War II. President Franklin D. Roosevelt used a variety of secret organizations, some of which reported directly to him. William J. Donovan, a personal representative of Roosevelt, went to England in 1940 to study British antisabotage techniques and evaluate the probabilities of that country's surviving German air attacks. Donovan went on to head the Office of Strategic Services (OSS), which carried out espionage and sabotage missions inside occupied Europe and Germany. The OSS served as model when the CIA was created in 1947.

The FBI identified several German spy networks in 1941, aided by an American citizen born in Germany who had been recruited by German military intelligence against his will. The FBI arrested and convicted thirty-three operatives, effectively shutting down most German covert activity in the United States. Two separate attempts to land German saboteurs from submarines in 1942 and 1945 ended with the swift capture of ten agents, the conviction of all, and the execution of eight. The FBI was less successful in detecting atomic espionage for the Soviet Union carried out by members and sympathizers of the American Communist Party, even though the FBI was convinced the party was controlled by Moscow and had planted informants within it.

The greatest intelligence successes of the World War II were those of U.S. cryptanalysts who deciphered Japanese diplomatic and naval codes; their example would inspire the creation of the even more technologically adept National Security Agency in 1952.

Espionage in Fiction

The spy story has become a recognized literary genre, popular with readers and attractive to

Hollywood, which regularly creates films based on successful novels. The characters rarely resemble real-life spies. The protagonist of one of the earliest spy novels, John Buchan's *The Thirty-nine Steps* (1915, adapted to the screen by Alfred Hitchcock in 1935), is an amateur who stumbles upon a scheme to provoke a European war, which he successfully prevents.

Other extremely popular spy stories are often unrealistic, catering to readers' fantasies. Jack Ryan singlehandedly foils a terrorist attack on a member of the British royal family and ends up as a guest in Buckingham Palace in Tom Clancy's *Patriot Games* (1987). Interestingly, Clancy's *Debt of Honor* (1994) eerily prefigured the September 11, 2001, terrorist attacks on the World Trade Center, with its climactic description of a jumbo jet crashing into the United States Capitol. In films based on Ian Fleming's James Bond novels, the spectacular special effects became more and more fantastic as the series progressed. In contrast, novelist John le Carré effectively employed verisimilitude to express his disdain and disgust with Cold War espionage practices.

Espionage in the Twentieth Century

During World War II, Soviet spies within the United States were motivated by ideology, many being Communist Party members. Disillusionment with communism as an economic system and revelations of the excesses of Stalinism ended the ideological inspiration. Spies caught during the Cold War working for the Soviet Union were primarily motivated by cash, not idealism.

The Walker family spy ring operated for sixteen years, receiving money from the Soviet Union without showing any interest in ideology. John Walker, Jr., a U.S. Navy officer, began selling the Soviet Union cipher keys used by the Navy in 1968, as well as descriptions of cryptographic machines, enabling the Russians to decipher American messages using their own versions of the machines. When he retired from the Navy in 1976, Walker recruited his son, his older brother, and Walker's best friend to steal data on secret American electronic systems, which they did until the spy ring's members were arrested in 1985.

From 1985 to 1994, Aldrich Ames, a senior CIA officer, received more than $4 million from the Soviets for his services. He told the Russians of every active United States espionage and counterespionage operation involving the Soviet Union; the disclosures allowed the Russians to execute at least ten spies working for the United States. He revealed the names of American intelligence officers studying the Soviet Union and described techniques used by the CIA and FBI. By telling the Russians which areas the United States particularly wanted data regarding, Ames enabled them to offer false information that the CIA welcomed and presented to the president as fact.

Robert Hanssen, an FBI agent who sold the Russians six thousand pages of secret FBI documents, claimed that he acted as a spy because of the psychological pleasure he felt in fooling his coworkers. However, he did not reject the $1.4 million dollars he was offered for his services from 1985 until he was finally apprehended in 2001.

Twenty-first Century Cases

The continued employment of Hanssen by the Russian successor organization to the Soviet spy agency testified to the reality that espionage against the American government did not cease with the demise of the Soviet Union and the end of the Cold War. Interest in acquiring military secrets and in penetrating the FBI and CIA continues. However, technological and economic espionage was of increasing importance in the last decades of the twentieth century and the beginning of the twenty-first.

Different countries used varying techniques in acquiring information. China focused on ethnic Chinese working for American companies and research institutes, appealing to pride in the resurgence of China to motivate the delivery of documents and data. Japan did not appear to have a government organization coordinating its economic espionage, but each company worked on its own to secure valuable information and patents from its competitors. France preferred using Cold War techniques, including bribery, wiretapping, thefts, and combing through trash. In May, 1991, employees of the French consul in Houston, Texas, were caught stealing garbage bags from behind the house of a technology industry executive. Russia still seemed most interested in military technology, but France, Israel, and Germany spread their efforts much wider. The International Business Machines company and Texas Instruments complained of attempts by foreign governments to steal their technology for the benefit of competitors. Corning found its fiber optics proprietary information under attack by France.

Foreign governments were not the only culprits. Domestic corporations employed espionage techniques against one another in the search for competitive advantage. A major scandal rocked the aerospace industry in July, 2003, when the U.S. Air Force discovered that Boeing Corporation had stolen thousands of documents from Lockheed Martin when the two companies competed for a rocket launch contract.

Corporate espionage cases rarely involve criminal proceedings. Many instances never become public knowledge; companies involved often prefer to suffer losses rather than admit to security failures that might adversely affect their reputations and stock prices. If diplomats are implicated, the normal procedure is simply to declare the offenders *personae non gratae* and expel them. The Boeing-Lockheed affair was unique in that two accused employees were actually indicted under the 1996 Economic Espionage Act and faced trial for theft of trade secrets. The Air Force punished Boeing by withdrawing contracts worth $1 billion and awarding them to Lockheed. However, Boeing's disgrace did not keep it from winning an even more valuable bid to build air tankers.

Counterespionage within the United States is formally part of the internal police work of the FBI, with the CIA responsible for overseas activity. Detection of espionage is difficult. Investigations can run for years without uncovering definitive answers, and success can hinge on accidental discovery of long-running penetrations of American security. Prosecution of spies sometimes becomes impossible, as the display of convincing evidence in open court conflicts with the need to avoid revealing sensitive information. Electronic counterespionage has become increasingly useful in the struggle against terrorism.

Investigation

The successful Soviet penetration of American atomic bomb research was not discovered until after the war. Information about Soviet spies came from the defection in 1945 of Igor Gouzenko, a Soviet consular official in Canada, from the testimony of Elizabeth Bentley and Whittaker Chambers in 1946 and from the partial decipherment of intercepted Soviet diplomatic messages. American code breakers had begun working on Soviet communications during World War II, but it was not until the late 1940's that they had any success. Called the Venona archive, the dispatches revealed the existence of at least two Los Alamos security breaches—one involving the Rosenberg spy ring, the other the physicist Theodore Hall. Judith Coplon, identified as a Soviet spy in the Venona transcripts, was arrested with secret documents in her possession.

The activities of the U.S. naval officers who made up the Walker family spy ring were not discovered by counterespionage detective work but were disclosed by John Walker's estranged wife. Word of Hanssen's betrayal came from a source within the Russian intelligence community. The openly flamboyant lifestyle of Ames provided the decisive clues to his treachery; however, critics wondered why it took the CIA nine years to question how one of its employees making less than $70,000 a year got the money to charge more than $20,000 a month on his credit cards and to buy a $450,000 suburban Washington house with cash.

Prosecution and Punishment

Use of illegal wiretaps, break-ins, and mail openings by the FBI under its director J. Edgar Hoover created difficulties in securing espionage convictions. Such evidence was inadmissible in court. Of more than one hundred people named by Bentley and Chambers, only two (William Remington and Alger Hiss) were indicted and convicted—of perjury, not espionage. The Rosenbergs were prosecuted when members of their ring agreed to testify against them. Hall was never indicted because he refused to confess, and there were no witnesses to his activity; both the FBI and military intelligence objected to use of the Venona decipherment, which was not publicly disclosed until 1995. Successful prosecution of the Walkers and Hanssen involved plea bargains.

Julius and Ethel Rosenberg were convicted of espionage and executed by electrocution on June 19, 1953. David Greenglass and Harry Gold testified against the Rosenbergs; Greenglass was sentenced to fifteen years in jail, Gold to thirty. Judith Coplon escaped any jail time. Her conviction in June, 1949, was overturned on appeal because of use of illegal wiretap evidence. The FBI opposed a retrial, which would reveal that its agents had not detected Coplon's treason, instead learning of her spying through the Venona decodes.

John Walker agreed to plead guilty in exchange for lighter punishment for his son, Michael. Michael Walker received a sentence of twenty-five years and was paroled in February, 2000, after fifteen years in prison. John Walker, his brother, and Walker's friend Jerry Whitworth all received life sentences. Ames was convicted and sentenced to life in prison; his wife was jailed for five years for her share in his activity and deported in 1999. Hanssen hired a celebrity attorney who negotiated a plea bargain with the Department of Justice. In return for his wife's receiving a widow's pension of $38,000 a year, Hanssen agreed to accept a sentence of life without parole and take polygraph tests while describing all his transactions with the Soviets.

Counterespionage activity designed to combat terrorism is even more difficult than traditional spy catching. The FBI successfully pursued and convicted those responsible for the first World Trade Center attack in 1993. Detecting and preventing planned attacks is a much more challenging assignment, however, as the *9/11 Commission Report* (2004) demonstrated. Solving that problem will be a major concern of American security and intelligence agencies in the twenty-first century.

Milton Berman

Further Reading

Fialka, John. *War by Other Means: Economic Espionage in America*. New York: W. W. Norton, 1997. Detailed descriptions of how foreign countries and businesses spy on the American government and companies.

Gannon, James. *Stealing Secrets, Telling Lies: How Spies and Codebreakers Helped Shape the Twentieth Century*. Washington, D.C.: Brassey's, 2001. Credits cryptanalysis with playing a major role in military and counterespionage successes. Includes an excellent chapter on Venona transcripts.

Hitz, Frederick P. *The Great Game: The Myth and Reality of Espionage*. New York: Alfred A. Knopf, 2004. Compares espionage in fiction with real-life examples and concludes that the actual behavior of spies is stranger than that of their fictional counterparts.

Jeffreys-Jones, Rhodri. *Cloak and Dollar: A History of American Secret Intelligence*. New Haven, Conn.: Yale University Press, 2002. Critical examination of American espionage from the time of George Washington to 2001. Very skeptical of self-promotion and exaggerated claims by the CIA and FBI.

Owen, David. *Hidden Secrets: A Complete History of Espionage and the Technology Used to Support It*. New York: Firefly Books, 2002. Lavishly illustrated history of spying from ancient Greece to the modern-day challenge of gathering intelligence on terrorists.

Persico, Joseph E. *Roosevelt's Secret War: FDR and World War II Espionage*. New York: Random House, 2001. How Franklin D. Roosevelt used information from spies and code breakers to shape the American war effort during World War II.

Theoharis, Athan. *Chasing Spies: How the FBI Failed in Counterintelligence but Promoted the Politics of McCarthyism in the Cold War Years*. Chicago: Ivan R. Dee, 2002. A skeptical account of FBI activities reveals the difficulty of securing convictions in espionage cases.

See also Antiterrorism and Effective Death Penalty Act; Clear and present danger test; Electronic surveillance; Federal Bureau of Investigation; Forensic anthropology; Hoover, J. Edgar; National Stolen Property Act; Patriot Act; Rosenberg espionage case; Terrorism; Treason.

Evidence, rules of

Definition: Rules governing the admissibility of all forms of evidence at trial

Criminal justice issues: Evidence and forensics; testimony; trial procedures; witnesses

Significance: Proper application of the rules of evidence ensures that trials proceed in an orderly and predictable manner that best serves the goal of achieving just verdicts.

The rules of evidence evolved along with the jury trial system, which itself developed through history from a system in which jurors made their own findings of fact or based their decisions on their own knowledge, to the present system in which jurors are sworn to make decisions based solely on evidence presented at trial. To achieve that goal, it has been necessary to develop rules so that untrained jurors are not misled. Rules regulating various forms of evidence began to develop during the seventeenth and eighteenth centuries and continued developing thereafter.

The rules of evidence long existed independently in the form of judicial decisions, mandates, and separate statutes until 1975, when they were codified or brought together as statutes under the Federal Rules of Evidence. These rules govern procedures in the federal courts but are inapplicable in state court proceedings. The states have their own rules of evidence but frequently use the federal rules as models for their rules.

Types of Evidence

The two basic types of evidence are direct and circumstantial. Direct evidence tends to show the existence of facts in question without additional proof. Establishment of a fact is based on the credibility or value of the evidence. Circumstantial evidence requires that fact-finders make inferences or draw conclusions. An example of circumstantial evidence is snow on the ground that one sees after waking on a morning after a clear and dry day. Although the observer did not actually see the snow fall, it would be reasonable for the observer to infer a snow fall occurred during the night.

Testimonial evidence is based on the testimony of witnesses; nontestimonial evidence is based on physical objects presented as exhibits. Nontestimonial evidence may be real—actual physical objects from crime scenes—or demonstrative—objects used to assist fact-finders understand other testimony, such as maps or diagrams of crime scenes.

Admissibility of Evidence

The admissibility of evidence at trial depends on the rules. Fact-finders are permitted to evaluate only admissible evidence. Moreover, relevant evidence is admissible only if it is deemed competent. Relevant evidence must tend to prove or disprove disputed issues of consequence. Irrelevant evidence wastes time, confuses juries, and is often prejudicial.

Instances sometimes occur when relevant evidence is ruled inadmissible because its probative value is outweighed by the danger of unfair prejudice or confusion. Probative evidence tends to prove something of importance to the case. Relevant evidence that has little probative value is immaterial and should be excluded.

Materiality is part of the concept of relevancy under the federal rules but is defined as evidence tending to make the existence of facts more probable or less probable than it would be without the evidence. Evidence must also be competent (legally adequate) to be admissible. For example, for the evidence of witnesses to be considered competent, the witnesses must swear oaths affirming that they will testify truthfully. Nonexpert witnesses are limited to testimony about what they have personally seen or heard. Any opinions or conclusions they may express are considered incompetent. Witnesses who are experts through special training, knowledge, or experience may offer opinions or conclusions based on their expert knowledge. It is for juries to determine what value, if any, to place upon the testimony of competent witnesses, lay or expert.

Character Evidence

Human character is a collection of traits and features that make up individual person's disposition or nature, evidenced by consistent patterns of behavior. Character traits include such positive things as honesty, courage, and integrity and such negative traits as dishonesty, violence, and recklessness. In criminal cases, character evidence is generally not admissible to prove conduct to show that a person has acted in conformity on a particular occasion.

The prosecution cannot introduce evidence of a defendant's bad character, such as violent tendencies. By contrast, the defense has the option to introduce evidence of good character, such as a history of honest behavior. However, once the defense elects to introduce a character witness to testify about a defendant's good character, such an actin is said to "open the door" for the prosecution to provide rebuttal evidence. On the other hand, when the defense does not elect to introduce character witnesses, the prosecution may not comment on that fact to the jury.

Since their adoption in 1995, rules 413 and 414 of the Federal Rules of Evidence contradict the basic principles of character evidence. These new rules assert that evidence of similar crimes in sexual assault cases is admissible on any matter to which it is relevant. The same holds true in child molestation cases. However, such evidence must be examined privately, at "in camera" (in chambers) hearings, so that determinations about its admissibility can be made prior to its introduction at trial.

Evidence about particular character traits of victims may be admissible to prove conformity of the victims' actions. For example, defendants claiming self-defense in murder trials may introduce evidence of their victims' violent tendencies to support their claims that their victims were the aggressors during the incidents in question.

In sex offense cases, the federal rules prevent use of evidence about the reputations and past sexual behavior of the victims. Evidence of specific instances of sexual behavior is also inadmissible, except in three special circumstances. The first is cases in which it is constitutionally required, as in the right to confront adverse witnesses. The second circumstance may arise when the accused need to submit evidence on their alleged victims' earlier

past sexual relationships with others to show that they, the accused, were not the sources of the semen or injuries to the victims. A third circumstance permitting the accused to submit evidence about their victims' past sexual behavior occurs when such evidence is offered to show the victims' consent.

Despite the existence of one of these circumstances, the evidence will be reviewed privately to determine whether the probative value outweighs the danger of any unfair prejudice to the victims. In 1978, rule 412 was added to the Federal Rules of Evidence to limit the use of evidence of prior sexual experiences of victims of sexual assault. Up until that time, victims of sexual assault had traditionally been harshly cross-examined and had their morality called into question. In 1994, the rules were further amended to enhance the protections given to victims of sexual assault and were applied to all criminal cases, not merely sex offenses cases, and to civil cases.

The rules of evidence apply to all forms of evidence presented at trial, including oral testimony from witnesses. *(Brand-X Pictures)*

Rule 412 generally excludes evidence of both the past sexual behavior and sexual predispositions of victims.

Evidence of "other crimes, wrongs, or acts" is not admissible to prove character in order to show conformity, but may be admissible to establish "motive, opportunity, intent, preparation, plan, knowledge, identity, or absence of mistake or accident." For example, proof of a defendant's past crimes may be used to establish a pattern or manner of committing offenses (modus operandi). When the prosecution introduces evidence of a defendant's past crimes, the defense is permitted to introduce rebuttal evidence.

Hearsay Evidence

Hearsay evidence is defined in rule 801(c) of the federal rules as a "statement, other than one made by the declarant while testifying at the trial or hearing, offered in evidence to prove the truth of the matter asserted." Hearsay is excluded because the witnesses are not testifying from personal knowledge, but from repetition of what was said or written outside court by other persons who are not present to be cross-examined. Even if the witnesses report what they have heard accurately, it is possible that the out-of-court declarants may have been lying, joking, or speaking carelessly. The latters' statements have not been made under oath and thus have been expressed without fear of perjury. There is no opportunity to cross-examine the declarants in order to impeach their credibility. Additionally, since the hearsay statement are made out of court, the demeanor of the declarants cannot be observed by the fact-finders.

Additional problems of hearsay evidence are the possibilities that the testifying witnesses may have faulty memories, poor hearings, or other infirmities that may impeded their ability to report what they have heard accurately. For all these reasons, hearsay tends to lack reliability. Exclusion of hearsay testimony from trials prevents unreliable evidence from being considered. It should be noted that statements that would otherwise qualify as hearsay are admissible if they are introduced *not* to prove the truth of a matter asserted but merely to show that a statement was made.

Numerous exceptions to the hearsay rule make otherwise inadmissible hearsay evidence reliable and admissible. One of the most common exceptions is the so-called "present sense impression"—a statement describing or explaining an event or condition made while a declarant is perceiving an event or condition or immediately thereafter. Such statements are admissible because they are believed to have been made instinctively.

The "excited utterance" exception is considered trustworthy because a statement made under stress of a startling event allows no time for fabrication. A statement dealing with a person's "then existing mental, emotional, or physical condition" can be reported by anyone who heard the statement. Likewise, "statements for purposes of medical diagnosis or treatment" describing pain, symptoms, sensations, and the like are admissible because it is assumed that patients have strong motives to tell the truth.

Statements made by declarants who believe that their deaths are imminent are also admissible. Admissibility of so-called "dying declarations," or "death-bed" statements, is based on the presumption that people do not lie when confronted with imminent death. This exception applies in homicide cases and civil actions.

Hearsay within hearsay, also called "multiple hearsay" or "totem pole hearsay," occurs in situations in which hearsay statements contain other hearsay statements and a chain of hearsay exists. In such situations, every link must be examined separately to determine whether each part conforms with an exception to the hearsay rule. This is common in the area of business records and reports.

Marcia J. Weiss

Further Reading

Dix, George E., et al. *McCormick on Evidence*. 5th ed. St. Paul, Minn.: West Publishing, 1999. Part of a law school hornbook series, this treatise is considered to be the bible of the law of evidence and contains detailed explanations and case references.

Pelliocciotti, Joseph M. *Handbook of Basic Trial Evidence: A College Introduction*. Bristol, Ind.: Wyndham Hall Press, 1992. Concise but nevertheless comprehensive text outlining the rules of evidence with examples.

Schubert, Frank A. *Introduction to Law and the Legal System*. 8th ed. Boston: Houghton Mifflin, 2004. General college textbook with cases and explanations of evidentiary issues.

Stopp, Margaret T. *Evidence Law in the Trial Process*. Albany, N.Y.: West/Delmar, 1999. Comprehensive text outlining the rules of evidence with examples, explanations, and case excerpts.

See also Chain of custody; Circumstantial evidence; Computer forensics; Crime scene investigation; Expert witnesses; Eyewitness testimony; Forensic anthropology; Hearsay; Jury system; Latent evidence; Polygraph testing; Standards of proof; Testimony; Trace evidence; Trial transcripts.

The author of a lucid survey of the principles of common law as derived from important decisions in British case history, William Blackstone regarded *ex post facto* laws as "cruel and unjust." *(Courtesy of Art & Visual Materials, Special Collections Department, Harvard Law School Library)*

Ex post facto laws

Definition: Laws enacted "after the fact" of actions or occurrences that retrospectively alter the legal consequences of those original actions or occurrences

Criminal justice issues: Constitutional protections; law codes; legal terms and principles

Significance: The U.S. Constitution prohibits both federal and state governments from enacting *ex post facto* laws and thus protects individuals from suffering punishment for actions that were legal at the time they occurred.

Ex post facto laws rewrite legal history to change retroactively the legal significance of a past event. The most obvious example of an *ex post facto* law would be one that subjected an individual to criminal punishment for an act performed before the law's enactment that was innocent at the time of performance. *Ex post facto* laws violate elementary notions of fairness and justice. According to William Blackstone, the great eighteenth century legal commentator, individuals have no cause to abstain from engaging in actions that are innocent at the time performed and only later classified as criminal. To punish individuals on the basis of such retroactive determinations is, he insisted, "cruel and unjust."

Article I of the U.S. Constitution prohibits *ex post facto* laws, both those enacted by the federal government and those adopted by state governments. Many state constitutions also contain prohibitions against such laws. The Supreme Court, however, early interpreted the Constitution's prohibition against *ex post facto* laws as applying only to criminal or penal laws. The Court adopted this construction of the clause in 1798 in *Calder v. Bull* and has continued to maintain this view. Accordingly, civil statutes may be given retroactive effect without violating the prohibition against *ex post facto* law. Federal or state governments, for example, may generally pass statutes taxing income earned or limiting rights acquired before the statutes' enactment.

The Constitution's *ex post facto* clause embraces three kinds of prohibitions. First, it bars government from punishing as a crime an act that was innocent at the time it was committed. Second, it prohibits government from retroactively increasing the seriousness of the punishment for an act already defined as a crime. Finally, it restrains federal and state governments from eliminating criminal defenses that existed at the time the allegedly criminal act was performed. The *ex post facto* clause does not, however, completely foreclose retroactive legislation relating to criminal law or procedure. Government may, for example, retroactively vary the type of punishment imposed for a crime. It may substitute the electric chair for the hangman's noose without violating the prohibition against *ex post facto* laws. Government may also reduce the degree of punishment meted out for a particular crime. Finally, state and federal governments are free to punish individuals for continuing to engage in conduct that was once not subject to the criminal sanction but was subsequently made illegal. Thus, a person could not be punished for violating Prohibition laws for purchasing liquor before such laws went into effect but could be punished for continuing to possess liquor after possession had been outlawed.

Timothy L. Hall

Further Reading

Amar, Akhil Reed. *The Constitution and Criminal Procedure: First Principles*. New Haven: Yale University Press, 1997.

Barker, Lucius J., et al. *Civil Liberties and the Constitution*. 8th ed. Upper Saddle River, N.J.: Prentice-Hall, 1999.

Tomkovicz, James J. *The Right to the Assistance of Counsel: A Reference Guide to the United States Constitution*. Westport, Conn.: Greenwood Press, 2002.

Vile, John R. *A Companion to the United States Constitution and Its Amendments*. 3d ed. Westport, Conn.: Praeger, 2001.

See also Constitution, U.S.; Crime; Criminal law; International law; International tribunals; Lindbergh law; Prohibition.

Exclusionary rule

Definition: Legal principle requiring the exclusion of evidence obtained by means of unlawful police conduct

Criminal justice issues: Evidence and forensics; government misconduct; legal terms and principles

Significance: The exclusionary rule provides incentive for law-enforcement officers to honor citizens' civil liberties and helps deter police misconduct.

In a 1914 case titled *Weeks v. United States*, the U.S. Supreme Court created a rule of evidence, designed to deter overzealous federal police officers from violating citizens' rights. The Court refused to permit prosecutors to use unlawfully obtained evidence at trial, even if that evidence was relevant to the matter at hand. This became known as the "exclusionary rule."

The rule generally applies only in criminal trials, not in most civil trials. Although the rule requires the exclusion of evidence obtained by police misconduct, evidence obtained as the result of the independent actions of private citizens is generally admissible, even if the citizen has acted in violation of the law.

Changing Court Interpretations

At the time of its creation, this judicial construction was lauded by civil liberties advocates as an important step to deter police misconduct. Law-enforcement supporters warned that the exclusion of important but unlawfully obtained evidence would permit otherwise guilty defendants to go free. The rule was of limited effect, however, because it applied only to criminal cases tried in federal courts. It did not apply to criminal cases tried in state courts.

After 1914, various state supreme courts considered employing the exclusionary rule in their own jurisdictions. Some rejected the rule outright; they agreed with Supreme Court justice Benjamin Cardozo, who complained that "the criminal goes free because the constable has blundered." Other state supreme courts embraced the rule and mandated its application in their states.

By 1949, sixteen states had adopted the exclusionary rule; thirty-one states had rejected it. In that year, the U.S. Supreme Court was asked to consider a case titled *Wolf v. Colorado* and the issue of whether the exclusionary rule should be mandated in all state courts. The defendant in that case argued that all states were bound to provide criminal defendants with due process, or "fundamental fairness," under the Fourteenth Amendment. He reasoned that the admission of unlawfully obtained evidence in state criminal trials was fundamentally unfair. Justice Felix Frankfurter, writing for the majority, declared that the exclusionary rule was not essential to the notion of due process and refused to mandate it in state prosecutions. The Court reasoned that states should be free to determine for themselves the best way to address police misconduct and should not be forced by the U.S. Supreme Court to adopt a rule they found repugnant.

Mapp v. Ohio

In 1961, the Court was again asked to consider whether the exclusionary rule represented a right so essential to fundamental fairness that it should be mandated in all state courts. The case was *Mapp v. Ohio*. By this time, the Court had become concerned about the disparities among criminal trial outcomes caused by the uneven application of the exclusionary rule. In similar cases with similar evidence, criminal defendants in areas where the exclusionary rule was applied were more likely to be acquitted, while defendants in jurisdictions without the rule were more likely to be found guilty. In a 5-4 decision, the Supreme Court reversed its earlier decision in *Wolf* and concluded that exclusion of unlawfully obtained evidence was a right that all defendants should possess, whether they were tried in a federal or state court. Thus, the exclusionary rule became mandatory in all state courts. This decision significantly expanded the application and reach of the rule and served to increase the controversy surrounding its implementation.

In the years following the *Mapp* case, legal scholars posed persuasive arguments defending and criticizing the effects of the exclusionary rule. The purpose of the rule, as stated by the Court, was to deter police misconduct. The operative effect of the rule, however, was to permit some guilty defendants to go free. Those support-

ing the rule argued that the rule does what it was intended to do: deter police misconduct. This was substantiated by the fact that prior to the *Mapp* case, in states without an exclusionary rule, police officers rarely obtained a search warrant before conducting a search. In those cases, even if the court ruled that the evidence had been obtained illegally, there were simply no consequences for this behavior, and the evidence was admitted against the defendant. After *Mapp*, however, it became routine police procedure in all states to obtain search warrants whenever possible before conducting a search. Failure to do so could easily result in the exclusion at trial of the unlawfully obtained evidence and the subsequent acquittal of the defendant.

Proponents further argued that the exclusionary rule gave vitality to the protections promised to all citizens in the Bill of Rights. With the rule, there are protections for an aggrieved citizen and consequences for the misbehaving officer. The rule thereby not only deters police misconduct but also serves to protect civil liberties.

Opponents argued forcefully that the exclusionary rule results in the withdrawing of valuable evidence. If judges and juries are charged with the task of determining the truth, the exclusion of evidence that is both relevant and reliable is likely to result in a miscarriage of justice: An otherwise guilty defendant would go free because of a technicality. Others argue that the rule does not effectively deter police misconduct and may actually encourage it. These critics point to instances where officers may fabricate reasons for a stop or a search, simply to avoid the sometimes egregious effects of an unbendable exclusionary rule. Otherwise respectable officers may even lie on the witness stand if they feel that dangerous defendants would otherwise go free. An additional criticism of the rule is that U.S. laws and their interpretations have become so complex that even police officers trying their very best cannot possibly be expected to know and follow them all the time. The exclusionary rule, under those circumstances, is applied even when there is really no police misconduct to deter.

Later Supreme Court Rulings

These criticisms resulted in three 1984 U.S. Supreme Court decisions that modified the rule.

In *Segura & Colon v. United States*, the Court adopted the "independent source" exception to the exclusionary rule. This exception states that if the police come by the same evidence in two ways, one legal and the other illegal, the evidence will be admissible even though there has been some police misconduct. That is, as long as the police come by the evidence in at least one legal way, the fact that there has been some police misconduct will not cause the evidence to be excluded.

In the case of *Nix v. Williams*, the "inevitable discovery" exception to the exclusionary rule was delineated. The U.S. Supreme Court held that evidence that would have inevitably been found by the police would be admitted in court. The Court reasoned that the purpose of the exclusionary rule was to put the police in the same position they would have been in had they not engaged in any misconduct—not to withhold from them evidence they would have found lawfully in a matter of time.

The most widely applied exception to the exclusionary rule, the "good faith doctrine," was created in two U.S. Supreme Court cases handed down on the same day. Those cases are *United States v. Leon* and *Massachusetts v. Sheppard*. In both of those cases, the Court found that when police have first obtained a judicially approved search warrant, and executed the warrant in accordance with the law, the evidence seized will be admitted, even if there were infirmities in the warrant. This exception recognized the fact that police are entitled to rely on determinations made by a judge as to the sufficiency and lawfulness of a search warrant. If the judge who approved the warrant was in error, the police should not be punished by excluding the evidence seized pursuant to the warrant. Essentially, the fault lies with the judge, and there is no police misconduct to deter.

By the year 2000, the exclusionary rule was widely accepted among law-enforcement officers and constitutional scholars. While the rule occasionally permits a criminal to go free, there is general agreement that the benefits of the rule greatly outweigh its weaknesses. Police have become more professional in their investigations and prosecutions, and individual rights have been given much stronger protections.

Jana Nestlerode

Further Reading

Barnett, Randy. "Resolving the Dilemma of the Exclusionary Rule: An Application of Restitutive Principles of Justice." *Emory Law Journal* 32 (1983). For students seeking an advanced analysis of the rule and its implications.

Kennedy, Caroline, and Ellen Alderman. *The Right to Privacy*. New York: Vintage, 1997. A layperson's guide to the Bill of Rights.

Lynch, Timothy. "In Defense of the Exclusionary Rule." *Harvard Journal of Law and Public Policy* 23 (2000). Advanced study of the rule that should be understandable to undergraduate college students.

McWhirter, Darien A. *Search, Seizure, and Privacy*. Phoenix, Ariz.: Oryx Press, 1994. Written to make subjects such as search and seizure and the exclusionary rule interesting for high school and undergraduate college students.

Mason, Alpheus T., and Donald Grier Stephenson. *American Constitutional Law: Introductory Essays and Selected Cases*. Englewood Cliffs, N.J.: Prentice-Hall, 2001. A readable primer for undergraduate college students.

Mirfield, Timothy. *Silence, Confessions, and Improperly Obtained Evidence*. Oxford, England: Clarendon Press, 1997. An engaging discussion of the admissibility of evidence at criminal trials.

Osborne, Evan. "Is the Exclusionary Rule Worthwhile?" *Contemporary Economic Policy* 17 (1999). A readable article presenting multiple views of the subject.

See also Bill of Rights, U.S.; Consent searches; Criminal prosecution; Defenses to crime; Fourth Amendment; Harmless error; *Knowles v. Iowa*; *Leon, United States v.*; *Mapp v. Ohio*; *Massachusetts v. Sheppard*; *Massiah v. United States*; Plain view doctrine; Search and seizure; *Weeks v. United States*; *Whren v. United States*.

Excuses and justifications

Definition: Distinction between two ways of denying responsibility for misconduct

Criminal justice issues: Defendants; pleas

Significance: American criminal justice systems allow for various defenses against charges of wrongdoing; successfully used, these defenses exonerate or mitigate liability.

Excuses and justifications are two distinct defenses recognized in American criminal law. In justification, defendants deny that what they had done was wrong and claim that, given the circumstances, their actions were right and justified. By contrast, when people offer excuses for misconduct, they concede their actions to be wrong but state that they are not fully to blame. With excuses, culpability is denied, and so is responsibility—or, at least, full responsibility—for the misconduct. This differs from justifications, whereby the individuals take responsibility for their conduct but insist that it was the proper way to act in that situation.

A paradigm of a justification is killing in self-defense. The killing of an aggressor in defense of one's own life is not considered a violation of the law against murder but rather a "justifiable homicide." In this situation, a defendant admits to killing another person, often along with a concession that the taking of life is typically wrong. Modern American law recognizes that in certain circumstances, the killing of another person to protect one's own life is permissible. The law also covers other forms of justifiable killing.

Another type of justification is necessity, or the lesser of evils defense. An example would be a ship's crew tossing cargo overboard in a storm in order to prevent the ship from sinking.

Excuses commonly recognized in American law include duress, ignorance, mistake, and insanity. These are subject to careful definition and limitation. In the Model Penal Code, "duress" is said to be a defense when the actor "was coerced . . . by the use of, or a threat to use, unlawful force against his person or the person of another." The threat has to be sufficiently strong that a reasonable person would not be able to resist it. In *Peo-*

ple v. Court, for example, a man's conviction for perjury during a murder trial was overturned; he had not been able during the trial to present evidence of duress—namely, that numerous threats against his life had been made to prevent him from testifying against the murderer.

Allowance for excuses and justifications shows that a legal system is concerned with linking criminal liability and punishment to individual culpability. Distinguishing between justification and excuse is important because when seemingly wrongful conduct is deemed justified, the law is, in effect, condoning that action. Although this is not true for excused conduct, it may be troubling to exempt individuals from full or partial responsibility for wrongdoing even when they have some excuse, especially when the excuse seems contrived.

The distinction is quite clear, but the categorizing of defenses may be difficult and controversial. Two examples that may arguably be counted as excuses or as justifications are the defense of superior authority's orders and the battered woman's defense.

Mario F. Morelli

Further Reading

Fletcher, George. *Basic Concepts of Criminal Law.* New York: Oxford University Press, 1998.

Singer, Richard, and J. Q. La Ford. *Criminal Law: Examples and Explanations.* 3d ed. New York: Aspen, 2004.

See also Common law; Criminal law; Criminal liability; Cultural defense; Defenses to crime; Duress; Ignorance of the law; Insanity defense; Mental illness; Mitigating circumstances; Model Penal Code; Motives; Self-defense.

Execution, forms of

Definition: State-sanctioned ending of a condemned prisoner's life

Criminal justice issues: Capital punishment; medical and health issues; punishment; technology

Significance: As the legality of capital punishment in the United States drew increasing criticism during the twentieth century, technological innovations were sought in order to carry out executions in more humane and dignified manners.

Executions were once conducted in public and in ways intended to be both brutal and disrespectful of the accused. Burnings, crucifixions, and dismemberments sought not only death but also the total annihilation of the condemned through the destruction of the body. Societies of the past two centuries have shown increasing concern for the dignity of the individual, extending this concern even to those convicted of heinous crimes.

Where capital punishment remains a part of the legal regime, the state has faced the issue of how to take a convict's life in a way that is different from—and morally superior to—the crime for which the prisoner stands condemned. Resolution of this question has involved searching for a method of execution that inflicts a minimum of physical pain upon the condemned and that respects human dignity by avoiding spectacle and disfigurement of the body. This concern also extends to execution team members who perform the act of terminating a life and to the community at large, in whose name the execution will be carried out. Critics charge that this has been a futile pursuit and that the only way human dignity can be honored is by eliminating capital punishment altogether.

Hanging and Firing Squads

Death by the hangman's noose was the dominant form of execution in colonial America, and it remained the most common method used until the turn of the twentieth century. Hangings could be conducted at the local level of government. At first, they were elaborately staged public events. The execution process included a ritualized procession from the jail to the nearby gallows, speeches by local officials, and a sermon on the depravity of human nature and the wages of sin from the local clergy. The condemned was offered a chance to make a public statement, with the expectation of a demonstration of contrition, although not all prisoners performed according to script.

Finally, the condemned would be hooded and the noose affixed to the neck. A trap door was sprung from beneath the prisoner, causing him to drop until his fall was arrested by the rope. Death came through the severance of the spinal cord and was thought to be fast and painless. However, all executions involve some risk of error. Calculating the proper drop of the prisoner turned out to be an imperfect science, and botched executions were common. Too short a drop produced a slow death by strangulation, with its accompanying struggle, while too long a drop resulted in decapitation of the prisoner. Largely for this reason, states began to remove hangings from public view, and by the late nineteenth

Gas chamber of the Mississippi State Penitentiary in Parchman in 1983. Mississippi used the gas chamber for only one execution before switching to the use of lethal injections. (AP/Wide World Photos)

Methods of Execution by Jurisdiction

Method (executions, 1976-2004)	Jurisdictions
Lethal Injection (780)	Alabama, Arizona, Arkansas, California, Colorado, Connecticut, Delaware, Florida, Georgia, Idaho, Illinois, Indiana, Kansas, Kentucky, Louisiana, Maryland, Mississippi, Missouri, Montana, Nevada, New Hampshire, New Jersey, New Mexico, New York (state death penalty was declared unconstitutional on June 24, 2004), North Carolina, Ohio, Oklahoma, Oregon, Pennsylvania, South Carolina, South Dakota, Tennessee, Texas, Utah, Virginia, Washington, Wyoming, U.S. military, federal government
Electrocution (152)	Alabama, Arkansas, Florida, [Illinois], Kentucky, Nebraska (only state that mandates electrocution), [Oklahoma], South Carolina, Tennessee, Virginia
Gas chamber (11)	Arizona, California, Maryland, Missouri, [Wyoming]
Hanging (3)	New Hampshire, Washington
Firing squad (2)	Idaho, [Oklahoma], Utah (only for inmates who chose this method prior to its elimination as an option)

Source: Death Penalty Information Center, February 2005. States in brackets authorize the listed methods only if their current methods are found to be unconstitutional. All states that use the gas chamber, hanging, and firing squads offer lethal injections as an alternative.

century, they were more often carried out behind prison walls by a centralized and professional state bureaucracy. In 2004, hanging was an option in only three states, and only three state-sanctioned hangings were conducted from 1977 to 2004.

Death by shooting has played a minor role in American executions because of its inevitable disfigurement of the body and the significant possibility of botched executions. Only two state-sanctioned executions between 1977 and 2004 were by firing squad.

Twentieth Century Innovations

The possibility of botched executions and a growing public discomfort with capital punishment in general led states to seek more technologically advanced methods of execution that promised to be fast, painless, and reliable. They turned to electricity and chemistry.

New York carried out the first electrocution in 1890, and the electric chair was soon found throughout the United States. Prisoners were strapped to wooden chairs, and current was passed through their bodies in sufficient quantities to cause death by cardiac arrest. This tech-

nology was expensive and required expertise in the new science of electricity, resulting in the further centralization of executions. Later conducted indoors, usually at night, deep within state penitentiaries and at the hands of a professional bureaucracy, the public in whose name executions were carried out was by now insulated from the process. The few witnesses permitted by officials continued to report gruesome errors, however, and it became apparent that electrocutions did not guarantee a speedy and painless death as had been promised.

Nevada, in 1921, became the first state to employ lethal gas. The condemned was secured to a seat inside a small, airtight chamber. Pellets of sodium cyanide were dropped into a small container of sulfuric acid, producing cyanide gas. The gas blocked the ability of the body to absorb oxygen, producing unconsciousness followed by death from asphyxiation. Even when carried out properly, prisoners were frequently observed to struggle, sometimes violently, as they reacted to the gas. This method never spread beyond a small number of western and southern states. Eleven executions between 1977 and 2004 were by lethal gas.

The current mode of execution dates from 1982, when Texas carried out the first lethal injection. Its apparent effectiveness in delivering a humane execution resulted in its rapid spread, and lethal injection was in 2004 the sole method of capital punishment in most states and the preferred option in the rest, except for Nebraska. The condemned is strapped to a gurney, and deadly chemicals are injected intravenously. Sodium pentothol, a fast-acting sedative, is administered first, followed by pancuronium bromide, which paralyzes the muscles and causes the collapse of the lungs. Finally, potassium chloride is administered to stop the prisoner's heart. Death comes within minutes, and the convict does not struggle, whether because of the loss of consciousness or because of paralysis. The procedure is clinical, even to the point of applying alcohol to the prisoner's skin before inserting the needle, to avoid infection.

Whether death by injection is, in fact, painless is hotly contested, as observers have no way of knowing. Critics charge that the process is meant to cloak the killing of the prisoner in the trappings of medicine—to anesthetize a society no longer comfortable with state-sanctioned homicide—yet risks silent suffering by the condemned. It has not escaped their notice that several states that employ lethal injection to execute prisoners forbid the use of pancuronium bromide by veterinarians to euthanize pets. Whatever the merits of this debate, lethal injection is not likely to be replaced by any further innovation in the near future.

John C. Hughes

Further Reading

Banner, Stuart. *The Death Penalty.* Cambridge, Mass.: Harvard University Press, 2002. A comprehensive cultural history of American executions.

Bohm, Robert M. *Deathquest.* Cincinnati: Ander-

Table used for lethal injections in Mississippi in 2002. Witnesses to executions in this chamber watch from behind the two-way mirrored windows. (AP/Wide World Photos)

son Publishing, 2003. Introductory textbook on capital punishment.

Constanzo, Mark. *Just Revenge*. New York: St. Martin's Press, 1997. An overview of all aspects of capital punishment.

Johnson, Robert. *Deathwork*. Belmont, Calif.: Wadsworth, 1997. Examines death row and its effect on prisoners and personnel.

See also Capital punishment; Cruel and unusual punishment; Death-row attorneys; Punishment; *Stanford v. Kentucky*.

Execution of judgment

Definition: Process of carrying into effect the orders, judgments, or decrees of courts

Criminal justice issues: Convictions; courts; judges; sentencing

Significance: In criminal law, after defendants are convicted and sentenced, the execution of judgment is the crucial stage at which the court's decisions are actually implemented.

In civil law, the execution of judgment affords winning parties the benefit of the final judgments or decrees. For example, in a personal injury matter in which a plaintiff prevails, the execution of judgment includes payment of damages to cover costs or loss from injury.

In criminal matters, execution of judgment typically refers to the successful completion of court punishment orders. Execution of judgment in such cases may include payments of ordered fines, defendants reporting to prison to serve sentences, or in capital-punishment judgments, the actual execution of the defendants. In the broader sense, "execution" refers to the process required to carry forth the order of the court contained in the decree or judgment.

The execution of judgment may be deferred or suspended by a court. In each instance the actual completion of the sentence is delayed or in some way altered rather than carried forth. For example, defendants convicted of felony crimes may find their sentences to include set periods of incarceration in prison. Their sentences may also be suspended pending lawful conduct of the de-

fendants under specific rules or conditions of probation. In such instances, the execution of judgment is limited or in some cases completely postponed so that defendants may complete the conditions of their probation. Upon successful completion of probation, the sentences may then be permanently set aside with no formal execution of the original sentence.

Carl J. Franklin

Further Reading

Allen, Harry E., Clifford E. Simonsen, and Edward J. Latessa. *Corrections in America: An Introduction*. 10th ed. Upper Saddle River, N.J.: Pearson Education, 2004.

LaFave, Wayne R., Jerold H. Israel, and Nancy J. King. *Criminal Procedure*. 4th ed. St. Paul, Minn.: Thomson/West, 2004.

United States Sentencing Commission. *Federal Sentencing Guidelines Manual 2003*. St. Paul, Minn.: West Publishing, 2004.

See also Convictions; Probation, adult; Punishment; Restitution; Suspended sentences.

Expert witnesses

Definition: Qualified witnesses, considered experts in their fields, provide scientific, technical, medical, or other specialized testimony

Criminal justice issues: Technology; trial procedures; witnesses

Significance: Testimony by expert witnesses can aid jurors in comprehending complex evidence; however, there are also risks that jurors may overvalue such testimony because of the professional positions of the witnesses or will completely dismiss the testimony because of its complexity.

In the second half of the twentieth century, case complexity within criminal and civil trials dramatically increased. As a result, reliance on expert witnesses and their role in the court system has also greatly increased. Within the adversarial trial system, the objective of expert testimony is to explain or clarify scientific, technical,

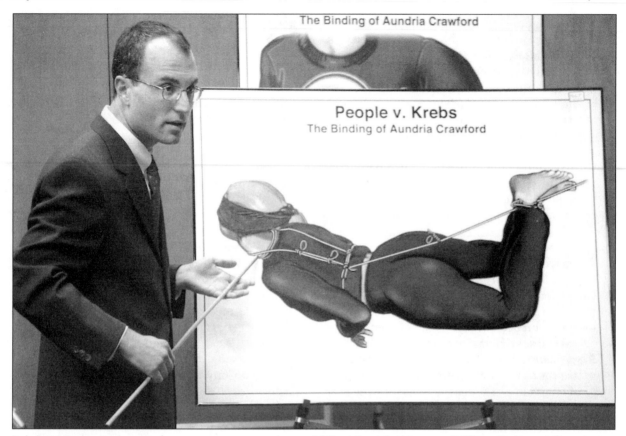

Pathologist George Sterbenz testifying as an expert witness during a 2001 murder trial in Monterey, California. Sterbenz performed an autopsy on the murder victim and used computer-aided drawings to explain how the victim had been bound. *(AP/Wide World Photos)*

or medical evidence for the benefit of the jury. Product liability, medical malpractice, antitrust, and many other issues arise in cases that require the testimony of an expert witness.

Rules and guidelines place limits on the types of witnesses who may be considered experts. It is the judge's responsibility to decide, first, if the testimony of the expert will assist the jury in understanding the evidence or in determining a fact that is at issue. Second, guidelines help judges ensure that any testimony heard is from a witness who is appropriately qualified to speak on the subject. As more expert witnesses are brought into courtrooms to comment on various complex subjects, concerns arise that experts are merely "hired guns."

Private Versus Court-Appointed Experts

One important issue to consider is how an expert witness is selected. Due to the adversarial nature of trials, each side may present an expert witness of its own choosing. Privately appointed experts have the potential of being biased in favor of the attorney who hired them. In addition, attorneys also have the opportunity to shop around until they find an expert who agrees to or is willing to present testimony in their favor. Privately appointed experts can be quite expensive, meaning that those with greater wealth may have an advantage in affording a helpful expert witness over those who lack financial resources.

An alternative to the privately appointed expert is the court-appointed expert. Although court-appointed experts are more common in other countries, some venues within the United States, such as family court in Texas, use them extensively. The benefit associated with using a court-appointed expert is that the witness is known to hold an objective position and is not perceived as having a hidden agenda.

Although approved of by judges and experts themselves, research has shown that attorneys are the least likely to favor using court-appointed experts. Not only do attorneys fear losing control over the trial process, there is also relatively less communication between court-appointed experts and attorneys. Court-appointed and privately retained experts both have their benefits and drawbacks; however, privately retained experts are most likely to be used in the U.S. justice system. The next important issue to consider is how jurors perceive and evaluate expert witnesses and their testimony.

The Influence of Expert Testimony on the Jury

Once the judge has ruled on the admissibility of expert witness testimony, it becomes the jury's responsibility to weigh and evaluate the testimony. An important issue that continues to arise is the potential confusion of jurors that may result from a "battle of the experts."

Many court actors express apprehension at how the jury may interpret expert witness testimony. Some claim the intellectual incompetence of jurors will interfere with their ability to understand most expert testimony. This juror incompetence is said to result in one of two outcomes. In the first, jurors may simply rely on the superficial characteristics or credentials of the expert, taking the testimony for fact and not critically evaluating the testimony. In the second, the expert testimony and evidence may be too complex for jurors, and they will simply disregard it. In other words, there is a perception that jurors will either undervalue or overvalue the expert testimony.

Research has been able to assuage many of the concerns regarding jurors' interpretations. Although studies have revealed that jurors do have difficulty understanding complex expert testimony, research has also shown that jurors not only critically evaluate the quality of an expert's testimony, but also critically evaluate the witness's credentials. In addition, difficulty in understanding and adequately evaluating expert testimony has been linked more often to the poor presentation of the evidence and testimony than to intellectual inadequacies among jurors.

Jurors themselves have revealed that they are not passive receptors, simply accepting expert testimony and complex evidence in an uncritical manner. To the contrary, jurors actively and critically evaluate and discuss complex evidence and testimony. Although there always stands a risk that jurors will misunderstand or undervalue complex expert testimony, it has been established that jurors take their responsibility quite seriously and adequately evaluate and integrate complex expert testimony. As science, medicine, and technology continue to advance, the role of the expert witness will continue to be relied upon to assist jurors in adequately comprehending important yet complex evidence.

Erin J. Farley

Further Reading

Anderson, Patrick R., and Thomas L. Winfree, Jr. *Expert Witnesses: Criminologists in the Courtroom*. Albany: State University of New York Press, 1987.

Billings, Paul R., ed. *DNA on Trial: Genetic Identification and Criminal Justice*. Plainville, N.Y.: Cold Spring Harbor Laboratory Press, 1992.

Freeman, Michael D. A., and Helen Reece. *Science in Court: Issues in Law and Society*. Brookfield, Vt.: Ashgate/Dartmouth, 1998.

Huber, Peter W. *Galileo's Revenge: Junk Science in the Courtroom*. New York: Basic Books, 1991.

Smith, Roger, and Brian Wynne. *Expert Evidence: Interpreting Science in the Law*. New York: Routledge, 1989.

See also Cross-examination; Evidence, rules of; Eyewitness testimony; False convictions; Forensic anthropology; Forensic entomology; Subpoena power; Testimony; Trials; Witnesses.

Extradition

Definition: Legal procedure requiring one jurisdiction to surrender persons charged with crimes to another jurisdiction

Criminal justice issues: International law; jurisdictions; terrorism

Significance: In a federal system such as that of the United States, extradition plays an important role in connections among different jurisdictions.

Article IV, section 2 of the U.S. Constitution

A Person charged in any State with Treason, Felony, or other Crime, who shall flee from Justice, and be found in another State, shall on Demand of the executive Authority of the State from which he fled, be delivered up, to be removed to the State having Jurisdiction of the Crime.

The fundamental principle defining the procedure of extradition is provided in the U.S. Constitution. In 1793, shortly after the Constitution was adopted, the U.S. Congress passed a law charging the governors of the states with the duty of delivering up fugitives from justice found in their states. This law also gives the governors of territories the same responsibilities.

There are certain exceptions to the requirement that fugitives be surrendered to the states from which they fled. For example, if suspects are imprisoned in the states to which they travel, if they face charges there, those charges take precedence. The fugitives must stand trial and serve sentences if necessary in the states in which they currently reside before being sent back. Sometimes an extradition will be delayed for months or years while the state in which an alleged offender is apprehended processes the person through its own criminal justice system.

In the 1861 case of *Kentucky v. Dennison* the U.S. Supreme Court stated that although the governor of the state to which the suspect fled had a "moral duty" to return the fugitive, the federal government or the federal courts could not require him to do so. Congress addressed this problem in 1934 by making it a crime for a person to escape from one state to another for the purpose of avoiding prosecution for certain crimes. In 1987 the Supreme Court overruled parts of *Kentucky v. Dennison* in a case involving a suspect who had fled from Puerto Rico to Iowa after being charged with a felony.

Extradition Within U.S. Territories

In *Puerto Rico v. Branstad* the Supreme Court justices reconsidered whether the federal courts had the power to order governors of states to fulfill their duties under the extradition clause of the U.S. Constitution. The case involved Ronald Calder, who worked in Puerto Rico. Calder was charged with first-degree murder and released on $5,000 bail after his arraignment. When the suspect failed to appear at two preliminary hearings, he was declared a fugitive from justice. The police in Puerto Rico believed that Calder had returned to his family in Iowa, and they notified the authorities there that he was wanted on murder charges. The suspect surrendered to local police in Iowa, posted bond, and was released.

The governor of Puerto Rico requested that the governor of Iowa extradite Calder. When an extradition hearing was held in Iowa, the suspect and his attorney testified that Calder could not receive a fair trial in Puerto Rico because he was white and because he feared that witnesses in Puerto Rican courts were often corrupt. Discussions about reducing the charges against Calder were held among the parties. When those negotiations broke down, the Iowa governor refused the request for extradition.

At that point the governor of Puerto Rico went to federal court, in which he filed a complaint that the refusal to return Calder violated the extradition clause of the U.S. Constitution and the 1793 Extradition Act. He asked that the federal court require the Iowa governor to comply with the request to return the fugitive. The U.S. Supreme Court agreed that the federal courts have the power to compel a governor to deliver a suspect. They found it one of many constitutional duties imposed on the states that must be enforceable in federal courts. Extradition is a duty imposed directly on the states by the Constitution. Governors do not have any discretion in determining whether to comply, and if they refuse to comply, they could by ordered to do so by federal courts.

The courts have considered the question of when an accused person who leaves the state in which a crime was committed becomes a fugitive from justice. They have determined that it is not necessary that an indictment be issued or that the accused leave for the purpose of escaping prosecution that is anticipated or has begun. The accused is considered eligible for extradition once the criminal justice process begins. The motive for fleeing is immaterial. The law mentions treason, felony, or other crimes as offenses for which a suspect may face extradition. This has been interpreted to mean any act prohibited in the original state, including misdemeanors.

Procedures for Extradition

Governors may demand the return of fugitives from justice only after the fugitives have been formally charged with crimes. Requisition warrants must be issued requesting the return of the accused. At that point, the governors of the asylum states may issue warrants for the arrest of the suspects until agents of the demanding states arrive to remove them. The accused, however, do not have the right in all states to hearings before the governors of the asylum states to determine whether the charges are valid. Also, suspects cannot prevent extradition by predicting what will happen at their trials. Suspects may not delay or prevent extradition by asking for investigations of the motives of either the governors of the states that demand their return or the governors of the asylum states.

After suspects have been informed of the charges and of their rights, including the right to counsel, they may sign waivers of extradition by which they voluntarily consent to be transported back to the demanding states. If the accused wish to raise questions such as whether the statute of limitations on the crimes in question has expired or whether incarceration in the prisons of the demanding states constitutes cruel and unusual punishment, they must wait until returning to the demanding states and then raise such questions in court. At that time, all parties may be heard, testimony may be given, and appropriate relief may be determined. If the accused can demonstrate that they were not in the states in which the crimes were committed at the times they occurred, it is possible to raise *habeas corpus* claims—that is, claims that their detention or incarceration would be illegal and thus not subject to extradition. If there is a dispute about the alibis of the accused, the suspects may not have the matters resolved through *habeas corpus*. Court proceedings after extradition would be the proper place to determine the validity of their alibis.

Even if accused persons are brought back by unlawful violence or by abuses of the legal processes to the states in which the alleged crimes have occurred, they are subject to trial and punishment. Once returned to the original states, the suspects may be tried for offenses other than, or in addition to, those for which they are extradited.

Fugitives to and from the United States

The United States has treaties with most nations providing for international extradition procedures. When foreign nationals charged with crimes flee to the United States, both state and federal judges may issue warrants to arrest them. The fugitives are then brought before the judges, who hear and consider the evidence against them. If the judges deem the evidence sufficient to meet the requirements of an appropriate treaty, they certify that fact to the U.S. secretary of state. The proper foreign authorities may then issue warrants of requisition to have the accused handed over to them. Meanwhile, until the suspects are formally surrendered, they must be properly incarcerated. If the suspects are believed to be in the United States but their whereabouts are unknown, or if it is believed that the suspects are in the process of fleeing to the United States, judges from the District of Columbia may issue the original arrest warrants.

Treaties also provide for the return to the United States by foreign governments of fugitives from justice who have left the United States. Procedures are included in bilateral treaties, which are negotiated country by country. Issues such as the international drug trade, terrorism, and opposition by many governments to the death penalty in the United States complicated extradition negotiations during the late twentieth century. For example, in 1997, drug-related crimes led to an agreement between the United States and Mexico providing that even persons who are sentenced and serving time in one of the countries may be extradited to the other for trial. The U.S. Justice Department estimates that there are hundreds of pending extradition warrants between the two countries at any time, because individuals often commit crimes on both sides of the border. Postponing extradition until suspects serve their sentences in one country may make prosecution in the other country difficult, as witnesses forget the facts of cases or become unavailable. After facing prosecution in the requesting country, prisoners are returned to complete their original sentences.

A notable extradition case occurred in 1997 when seventeen-year-old Samuel Sheinbein, who was accused of first-degree murder in Maryland and faced charges as an adult, fled to Israel. The Federal Bureau of Investigation (FBI) faxed a copy of a federal warrant for unlawful flight to avoid prosecution and asked that Sheinbein be extradited under a U.S.-Israeli treaty. However, Israel had a law prohibiting it from extraditing its own nationals. Sheinbein claimed Israeli citizenship because his father had been an Israeli citizen. The dispute lasted almost a year, while some members of the U.S. Congress threatened to cut off aid to Israel unless the young man was returned.

Although an Israeli court ultimately ordered that Sheinbein be sent back for trial, the case highlighted two questions about international extradition. The nationality defense (laws that prohibit a country from surrendering its citizens for trials abroad) may complicate and sometimes thwart prosecutions of criminals. Some treaties provide for the nationality defense while others do not. Also, international human rights provisions allow a requested state the right to deny extradition if the accused would be subject to the death penalty in the requesting state but not in the requested state. As the United States is among a minority of nations that continues to execute offenders and among an even smaller minority that permits the execution of juveniles, death-penalty issues may complicate extradition proceedings.

Mary Welek Atwell

Further Reading

Blakesley, Christopher L. *Terrorism, Drugs, International Law, and the Protection of Human Liberty*. Ardsley-on-Hudson, N.Y.: Transnational, 1992. Considers extradition in the context of contemporary issues.

Cassese, Antonio. *International Criminal Law*. New York: Oxford University Press, 2003. Introduction to international criminal law examining the substantive aspects of the law and the procedural dimensions of state practice, including extradition.

McDonald, W. F., ed. *Crime and Law Enforcement in the Global Village*. Cincinnati: Anderson Publishing, 1997. Collection of essays on issues of international law, including extradition.

Preston, William. *Aliens and Dissenters: Federal Suppression of Radicals, 1903-1933*. Cambridge, Mass.: Harvard University Press, 1964. Study of the federal government campaign against foreign radicals during the early twentieth century that considers the role of extradition.

Shearer, I. A. *Extradition in International Law*. Manchester, England: Manchester University Press, 1971. Older study that discusses principles of extradition across national borders.

See also *Alvarez-Machain, United States v.*; Arrest; Bounty hunters; Canadian justice system; Constitution, U.S.; Criminal justice system; Deportation; Diplomatic immunity; International law; International tribunals; Marshals, U.S.; Mexican justice system; Scottsboro cases.

Eyewitness testimony

Definition: Accounts given by persons who have directly observed crimes or actions related to crimes

Criminal justice issues: Evidence and forensics; witnesses

Significance: The description of criminal activities by an eyewitness has long been accepted by judges and juries as convincing. Psychological tests have repeatedly shown, however, that human perception and memory are flawed and that testimony is not always reliable. In this way, innocent people are sometimes incorrectly identified and convicted.

An eyewitness to an event is someone who has observed that event directly. Accounts by eyewitnesses are given special importance in criminal trials. Frequently, such testimony is the single largest determinant of a trial's outcome. Research by psychologists, however, suggests that testimony describing crimes and identifying perpetrators can be flawed by limitations in human perception and memory. Since psychologist Hugo Munsterberg began staging mock robberies in 1908, hundreds of crimes have been simulated for the purpose of psychological experiments. Such experiments have demonstrated that people, in remembering events they have witnessed, can unwittingly distort facts, resulting in mistaken testimony.

Eyewitness Testimony and False Convictions

The 1988 film *The Thin Blue Line* is a documentary about Randall Dale Adams, who was wrongly convicted of killing a police officer. As a result of public attention raised by the documentary, and the evidence developed in the course of making it, a Texas criminal court ordered Adams released pending a new trial. However, the state of Texas eventually decided not to retry the case. The film, made more powerful because it dramatizes a true story, meticulously documents evidence to suggest that Adams had been framed. Its depiction of why the key witnesses had reason to lie helped to free Adams and provides a useful counter to the popular conception that eyewitness testimony is the most reliable testimony in criminal cases.

Timothy L. Hall

Perceiving and Remembering

Perception of any event can be influenced by the perceiver's expectations. Many aspects of a street crime, for example, make accurate identification of the offender difficult: The crime occurs quickly, the offender has probably never before been seen by the witness, the witness is under great stress, and distracting stimuli (such as a gun) are often present. In addition, studies have shown that a witness is less likely to notice identifying features of an offender whose race is different from that of the witness.

Folk wisdom and the law both assume that memories are stored like photographs and that somewhere in the brain lie exact images of past events, which can be later retrieved. This assumption is inaccurate. Experimental work by psychologist Elizabeth Loftus has documented how easily incidents occurring after an event are incorporated into memories of that event. For example, she introduced to children totally fictitious stories of being lost in a supermarket. These stories are later accepted by some of the children as personal memories. She modified memories of a video-presented traffic accident by introducing into her inquiry vivid words like "crash" and found that damage from the accident is thereafter remembered as more severe. Loftus cautioned that people's memories of a real crime can easily be modified as media accounts, suggestions by police officials, or imagined distortions that slip into one's memories of the original event. Such effects can be magnified with the passage of time.

Retrieving One's Memory of the Crime

The retrieval task typically presented to witnesses after a crime is to try to identify the offender from a book of suspects' photographs or from a police lineup. An assumption common among witnesses is that the offender is among those in the lineup staged by the police. This subtly transforms the identification task into the multiple-choice quiz of selecting from the lineup whatever option is most similar to that stored in memory. If the police have erred by apprehending a suspect with superficial similarities to the real offender, the witness's choice will confirm the police error. Police officials may subtly, or sometimes explicitly, reinforce the witness's choice by their reaction. Even initially hesitant witnesses may become convinced of the accuracy of their memories and, by the time of the trial, exude confidence. Most studies have found little relationship between the accuracy of testifying witnesses and the confidence they project.

Special retrieval problems are presented by witnesses testifying about such activity as sexual abuse that occurred during their childhood. While children rarely concoct detailed descriptions of such abuse without a basis of fact, child witnesses are particularly susceptible to suggestive questioning by adults. Testimony by adults based upon repressed memories from their childhood and later "recovered" in therapy is particularly suspect of having been contaminated by suggestion.

Impact on the Justice System

Mistaken eyewitness identification by confident witnesses has been shown to be the primary source of wrongful conviction. Anecdotal accounts of such wrongful convictions have been cited by many observers. In 1996 the National Institute of Justice collected cases of people convicted of a crime who had later been conclusively exonerated by DNA evidence. Seventy-five percent of the hundred clearly wrongful convictions studied were based upon mistaken eyewitness identification, which offers systematic proof of the fallibility of eyewitness testimony.

Encouraged by recommendations from the institute, efforts were begun during the late 1990's to improve the gathering of eyewitness evidence by many police departments. These included the use of open-ended, nonsuggestive interview questions; better constructed lineups, with foils all generally similar to description of the offender; and presenting suspects to the witness in succession, thus avoiding the forced-choice implications of the common simultaneously presented lineup. Police officials were cautioned against reinforcing witness responses and of the importance of remaining noncommittal.

The American system of justice must necessarily rely upon the reports of eyewitnesses. This is not always a problem. In some crimes the offender is well known to the victim. Often major features of a crime are confirmed by concurring witnesses. Yet identification by those who experience a fleeting contact with a criminal-stranger or testimony by those whose memories have been contaminated with distorting suggestions must be viewed with caution. A mandate of forensic science is that of distinguishing valid from flawed eyewitness accounts and establishing procedures for collecting such accounts that ensure their reliability.

Thomas E. DeWolfe

Further Reading

Loftus, Elizabeth F. *Eyewitness Testimony*. 2d ed. Cambridge, Mass.: Harvard University Press, 1996. A psychologist discusses research upon conditions influencing the reliability of eyewitness testimony.

Wells, G. L., and Elizabeth F. Loftus. "Eyewitness for People and Events." In *Handbook of Psychology*, edited by A. M. Goldstein and I. B. Weiner. New York: John Wiley & Sons, 2003. Outlines factors that affect event memory and result in mistaken identification.

Wells, G. L., and Elizabeth A. Olson. "Eyewitness Testimony." *Annual Review of Psychology* 54 (2003): 277-295. This review discusses cases of convicts cleared by DNA evidence.

Wells, G. L., et al. "From the Lab to the Police Station: A Successful Application of Eyewitness Research." *American Psychologist* 55 (2000): 581-598. Account of the national guidelines for collecting and using eyewitness testimony.

Wrightsman, L. S., E. Greene, M. T. Nietzel, and W. H. Fortune. *Psychology and the Legal System*. Belmont, Calif.: Wadsworth, 2002. Chapter 7 of this textbook reviews the work on conditions that influence the reliability of eyewitness testimony.

See also Circumstantial evidence; Criminal prosecution; Cross-examination; DNA testing; Evidence, rules of; Expert witnesses; False convictions; Forensic psychology; National Institute of Justice; Perjury; Police lineups; Testimony; Trials; Witnesses.

F

False convictions

Definition: Occasions in which innocent persons are convicted of crimes that they have not committed

Criminal justice issues: Appeals; convictions; defendants; verdicts

Significance: In addition to being grossly unfair to defendants who are erroneously convicted, false convictions damage public confidence in the criminal justice system. Moreover, public safety becomes an issue when convictions of the wrong persons allow guilty criminals to remain at large.

The criminal justice system is designed to protect society by identifying and bringing to justice individuals who have violated the law. Determining guilt or innocence requires the services and expertise of police officials, prosecutors, defense attorneys, judges, and jurors. The system, therefore, contains numerous decision points involving human judgment and, because fallible human beings are involved in the process, errors can sometimes occur which produce a false conviction.

False convictions have long been a concern of responsible members of the criminal justice community. In the eighteenth century, British theorist and philosopher Jeremy Bentham, whose ideas influenced the U.S. Constitution and the American criminal justice system, called false convictions "mis-seated punishment." Modern research concerning the causes and frequency of false convictions did not begin until the early twentieth century, when Yale law professor Edwin Borchard published case studies of sixty-five false convictions that occurred in the United States between 1812 and 1930. Borchard's pioneering work was followed, from the 1950's through the early 1980's, by a small number of other publications identifying additional cases.

During the mid-1980's the topic of false convictions began receiving increased attention from both researchers and the popular media—primarily as a result of the unprecedented availability of DNA testing. Because each person's DNA is unique, it has become possible for some prisoners to have old evidence that was used to convict them—evidence such as specimens of blood, hair, tissue, semen, or other body fluids—reexamined in order to determine if the results of earlier, less accurate tests were misleading or faulty. Between 1989—when the first DNA exoneration occurred—and 2004, at least 145 falsely convicted individuals were cleared using DNA testing. Additionally, several hundred other cases of false conviction have come to light using other investigative techniques. Many of these cases have received widespread newspaper and television coverage.

Repercussions of False Convictions

False convictions in the criminal justice process carry high personal and social prices. First, they compromise public safety. When a falsely accused person is convicted of a crime, that individual is punished in place of the one who actually committed the offense. Therefore, for virtually every person falsely convicted of a crime, there is a corresponding guilty person who has not been brought to justice and who may be continuing to commit crimes in the community.

False convictions also undermine the public's confidence in the judicial system. Every year, stories are published in the media concerning individuals who have languished in prison for years and are later found to have been falsely convicted. Stories of this nature can shake citizens' faith in the ability of the criminal justice system to separate the innocent from the guilty and to do justice. False convictions can, therefore, damage the symbolic status of the criminal justice process—a process that symbolizes the United States' moral stance against crime and the desire to achieve justice. A loss of confidence in the criminal justice system can have serious and widespread negative consequences. For example, if jurors become skeptical of police testimony or prosecutorial judgment, they are more likely to

Dawayne Erby embraces his father upon his father's release from a Missouri prison after having served seventeen years for multiple rapes. He was released in August, 2003, after DNA testing proved that he was not guilty. *(AP/Wide World Photos)*

acquit a guilty individual. A loss of confidence in the criminal justice system can also lead to vigilante-style justice.

Additionally, when an innocent person is falsely convicted, several separate injustices occur. Primarily, the falsely convicted persons unjustly suffer. They are often subjected to the horrors of prison life, are denied freedom (often for several years), and possibly face execution. Death-penalty opponents are quick to point out that individuals falsely convicted of capital crimes may be executed before they can be exonerated. The average time between sentencing and exoneration in false-conviction cases is slightly more than ten years. By contrast, the average time between sentencing and execution

of death penalties is also approximately ten years.

The families of the falsely convicted also unjustly suffer when there are separations of husbands from wives, parents from children, and brothers from sisters, as well as possibly substantial losses in income and public shame. Moreover, family members typically exhaust all their available resources when attempting to correct their relatives' false convictions. Other participants in the criminal justice process may also suffer. Often jury members, witnesses, police officers, prosecutors, defense attorneys, and judges are distressed when they discover their actions have contributed to sending innocent persons to prison, or worse, to death row.

Dysfunctions in the Criminal Justice System

False convictions allow researchers opportunities to analyze system dysfunctions. Once victims of false conviction are identified, details of their cases can be examined from the moments when they enter the system until their convictions, in order to determine where the system has failed. For example, analysis of a false conviction case may reveal flawed procedures used by police in the handling of eyewitnesses. Evidence of police or prosecutorial overzealousness or corruption may be exposed. Errors by defense attorneys or forensic experts might be discovered. Knowledge of this kind can be used to improve the criminal justice process through implementation of better procedures and increased training, accountability, and funding. Ultimately, this information should lead to improvements in the criminal justice process that will reduce false convictions and advance the system of justice.

How frequently false convictions occur is unknown. The hidden nature of so many aspects of false convictions creates numerous challenges to researchers attempting to determine the true extent of the problem. In the past, criminal justice professionals tended to believe that false convictions only rarely occurred. Edwin Borchard's 1932 book *Convicting the Innocent* was written in response to a local district attorney who had commented, "Innocent men are never convicted. . . . It's a physical impossibility." Even as late as the mid-1980's, some members of the criminal justice system were stating that false convictions never occurred. However, such notions have now been largely dispelled because hundreds of individuals have been proved to be victims of false convictions since 1989.

Many researchers believe that the recently revealed cases represent only the "tip of the iceberg." Cases that have been discovered are often the result of modern DNA testing, which is only available in a small percentage of criminal cases in which evidence such as hair, tissue, or body fluids is present. Also, the great majority of false convictions exposed since 1989 have involved only two types of cases: rape—in which DNA testing has unique detection power—and death-penalty cases—in which intense appellate court review is most likely to occur. It is probable that many false convictions involving other types of offenses such as theft, assault, or drug crimes would be uncovered if similar appellate efforts were expended or if powerful tools similar to DNA testing could be used.

Why False Convictions Occur

Research has isolated many factors associated with false convictions. These factors generally fall into the categories of unintentional error or misconduct. Every major study of false convictions has concluded that unintentional eyewitness error is the primary factor associated with false convictions. Crime witnesses or victims are notoriously unable to provide precise accounts of what they see. Mistaken identification is particularly harmful to innocent defendants because judges and jurors tend to believe the veracity of eyewitnesses' claims over those of accused defendants.

Another type of unintentional error associated with false convictions is the presentation of evidence by prosecution "expert" witnesses that is later found to be misleading or erroneous. Unintentional errors by criminal justice officials often occur because of heavy caseloads. Judges, in order to move cases and relieve heavy dockets, encourage plea bargaining instead of full fact-finding trials. Police and prosecutors, without the time and financial resources necessary to properly process cases, can take part in rushes to judgment that ultimately result in false convictions.

False Convictions and Prison Populations

Estimates of the frequency of false convictions have ranged from as low as 0.5 percent to as high as 20 percent of all criminal convictions. More than two million convicts were incarcerated in U.S. jails and prisons in 2005. Given that number, a false-conviction rate of only 1 percent would mean that more than 20,000 people were incarcerated in 2005 for crimes they did not commit. A 5 percent error rate would mean that false convictions account for 100,000 prisoners, and a rate of 20 percent would mean that more than 400,000 people in jails and prisons did not belong there.

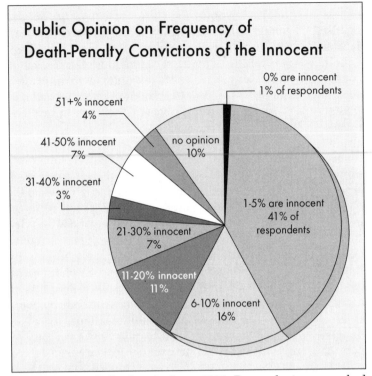

Public Opinion on Frequency of Death-Penalty Convictions of the Innocent

0% are innocent
1% of respondents

51+% innocent
4%

41-50% innocent
7%

31-40% innocent
3%

no opinion
10%

1-5% are innocent
41% of
respondents

21-30% innocent
7%

11-20% innocent
11%

6-10% innocent
16%

Source: Gallup Poll taken in June, 2000. Respondents were asked how often innocent people had been sentenced to death during the previous twenty years.

dices, and personal ambitions that may affect their judgment and decision making. Police, in order to bolster their cases, have been found to suppress exculpatory evidence or to make unduly suggestive comments to witnesses during pretrial identification procedures.

In some cases, police officers have been found to have planted evidence on innocent people in order to gain convictions. For example, between 1999 and 2000, the Rampart scandal in Los Angeles involved police officers who planted evidence or otherwise framed nearly one hundred suspects. In 2003, a dishonest undercover police officer from Tulia, Texas, was found to have framed thirty-nine innocent people during a drug-operation investigation.

False convictions involving prosecutorial misconduct most often entail the suppression of exculpatory evidence and knowingly using false testimony. When prosecutors have weak cases, they may also elicit testimony from so-called jailhouse snitches, who are willing to testify they overheard other inmates confess to crimes in return for reduced sentences. Several cases of false conviction have occurred because of the use of these snitches.

Although errors can be categorized as unintentional or intentional, the practice of listing cases by a single type of error can be misleading and can present an oversimplification of the dynamics of false conviction. In most cases of false conviction, multiple factors are simultaneously at work.

Robert J. Ramsey

Poorly trained or underprepared defense attorneys also contribute to the incidence of false conviction. Competent counsel can uncover police practices responsible for misidentifications, coerced or false confessions, and faulty forensic science. Because falsely convicted individuals are usually indigent, even competent attorneys may not have the necessary financial resources or time to investigate and defend their clients' claims of innocence properly. Of the false convictions uncovered by DNA testing, 25 percent have involved innocent people who confessed to crimes they did not commit—usually because they were overwhelmed by the criminal justice system. Young offenders and individuals with diminished mental capacity are especially vulnerable to system pressures.

Some of the more unsettling findings in cases of false convictions are incidents of intentional misconduct by police, prosecutors, defense attorneys, and judges. All members of the criminal justice profession are subject to biases, preju-

Further Reading

Christianson, Scott. *Innocent: Inside Wrongful Conviction Cases.* New York: New York University Press, 2004. Investigative reporter's account of forty-two wrongful conviction cases.

Connors, E., T. Lundregan, N. Miller, and T. McEwen. *Convicted by Juries, Exonerated by Science: Case Studies in the Use of DNA Evidence to Establish Innocence After Trial.* Alexandria,

Va.: National Institute of Justice, 1996. Close examination of some of the first cases of false convictions that were overturned by DNA evidence.

Gross, S., et al. *Exonerations in the United States: 1989-2003*. New York: Open Society Institute, 2004. Study of the first fourteen years of post-DNA exonerations of falsely convicted persons.

Huff, C. R., A. Rattner, and E. Sagarin. *Convicted but Innocent: Wrongful Conviction and Public Policy*. Thousand Oaks, Calif.: Sage Publications, 1996. Examination of the implications of false convictions on government policies and law enforcement generally.

Radelet, Michael L., Hugo A. Bedau, and Constance E. Putnam. *In Spite of Innocence: Erroneous Convictions in Capital Cases*. Boston: Northeastern University Press, 1992. Review of four hundred wrongful convictions in capital cases by dedicated opponents of capital punishment. An engaging book for both scholars and lay readers.

Scheck, Barry, Peter Neufeld, and Jim Dwyer. *Actual Innocence: Five Days to Execution, and Other Dispatches from the Wrongly Convicted*. New York: Random House, 2000. Case studies of the exoneration of wrongfully convicted defendants by the Innocence Project, which is dedicated to overturning convictions of innocent prisoners through DNA testing.

See also Appellate process; Confessions; Convictions; DNA testing; Double jeopardy; Expert witnesses; Eyewitness testimony; *Habeas corpus*; Justice; Miscarriage of justice; Pardons; Plea bargaining; Police corruption; Police lineups.

Faretta v. California

The Case: U.S. Supreme Court ruling on self-representation

Date: Decided on June 30, 1975

Criminal justice issues: Attorneys; constitutional protections; defendants

Significance: In this case, the Supreme Court ruled that the Sixth Amendment guarantees criminal defendants the right to conduct their own defense.

Charged with grand theft, Anthony Faretta was appointed a public defender at his arraignment. Worried that the public defender's heavy caseload would prevent him from giving his case adequate attention, Faretta asked to represent himself. He had previously represented himself in a case, but his trial judge in this case was hesitant to grant his request. Nevertheless, after cautioning Faretta of the ramifications of waiving counsel, the judge accepted his request. Before the trial began, the judge reviewed Faretta's ability to represent himself by questioning him on jury selection and on the hearsay rule. Not satisfied with Faretta's responses, the judge revoked his earlier decision and appointed a public defender for Faretta.

Faretta was tried and found guilty. Afterward, he appealed his conviction on the basis that he had been denied the right to conduct his own defense. An appellate court upheld the lower court's decision, noting that Faretta had no constitutional right to represent himself, and the Supreme Court of California refused to review the case. Faretta then appealed his case to the U.S. Supreme Court.

The Court decided in Faretta's favor, ruling that the Sixth Amendment's phrase "assistance of counsel" means that defendants are primarily responsible for their own defense. The Court added that counsel must be available to provide aid to receptive defendants. In essence, therefore, the Sixth Amendment confers a right to self-representation. The Court also noted that when defendants "knowingly and intelligently" give up right to counsel after being apprised of the dangers of self-representation, their choices should be noted in the court records. Therefore, in forcing Faretta to accept a state-appointed public defender against his will, the California court deprived him of his constitutional right to conduct his own defense.

The right to counsel is guaranteed in the Sixth Amendment to the U.S. Constitution. Criminal defendants are always reminded of this right when the Miranda warning is read to them. A corollary to this right to counsel, however, is that counsel must be effective. To be certain that lay persons unfamiliar with the intricacies of the law do not jeopardize their cases, even when they are innocent, defendants are encouraged to use the

Wording of the Sixth Amendment

In all criminal prosecutions, the accused shall enjoy the right to a speedy and public trial, by an impartial jury of the State and district wherein the crime shall have been committed; which district shall have been previously ascertained by law, and to be informed of the nature and cause of the accusation; to be confronted with the witnesses against him; to have compulsory process for obtaining witnesses in his favor, and to have the assistance of counsel for his defence.

Federal Bureau of Investigation

Identification: Primary investigative and enforcement arm of the federal government's Department of Justice

Date: Established in 1908; renamed the Federal Bureau of Investigation (FBI) in 1935

Criminal justice issues: Federal law; investigation; law-enforcement organization

Significance: As a division of the U.S. Department of Justice, the Federal Bureau of Investigation (FBI) has seen its investigative and other powers greatly expanded as Congress has gradually added one duty after another. The FBI has been engaged in combating many forms of interstate and international criminal activity. It has also strived to raise the standards of regional police units, which the FBI frequently assists in training.

knowledge and skills of professional counsel. Nevertheless, defendants may waive the assistance of counsel and represent themselves in court.

Judges have the responsibility to determine if defendants are capable of acting as their attorneys. They consider several matters in making this determination: Can the defendants communicate effectively in English? Have they enough basic legal knowledge to conduct their defenses without unnecessary interruptions, delays, or the possibility of mistrials or appeals? Defendants who choose to defend themselves cannot afterward complain that they lacked effective counsel.

Victoria M. Time

Further Reading

Acker, J. R., and D. C. Brody. *Criminal Procedure: A Contemporary Perspective*. 2d ed. Sudbury, Mass.: Jones and Bartlett, 2004.

Roberson, C. *Criminal Procedure Today: Issues and Cases*. 2d ed. Upper Saddle River, N.J.: Prentice-Hall, 2003.

Stuckey, G. B., C. Roberson, and H. Wallace. *Procedures in the Justice System*. 7th ed. Upper Saddle River, N.J.: Prentice-Hall, 2004.

Zalman, M. *Criminal Procedure: Constitution and Society*. 3d ed. Upper Saddle River, N.J.: Prentice-Hall, 2002.

See also Counsel, right to; Defendant self-representation; Supreme Court, U.S.

The forerunner of the Federal Bureau of Investigation (FBI) was established in 1908 by U.S. attorney general Charles J. Bonaparte, who hired nine former Secret Service agents on a permanent basis in the U.S. Department of Justice. This investigative division was first funded from "miscellaneous expenses" without specific mandate from Congress. Bonaparte actually opposed legislation to specify this new investigative division's authority, assuring congressmen that personal and political activities would not be investigated but that the new division's responsibilities would focus on interstate commerce and antitrust violations.

History

The period of the attorney general's direct supervision was rather short. By 1910 the unit's dictate was to enforce the new Mann (White Slave Traffic) Act, which made it a federal crime to transport women across state lines for illicit purposes. Now, as personal and commercial activities increasingly projected themselves across state lines with the creation of nationwide transportation systems and national markets—together with the crimes that go with them—the investigative arm of the Department of Justice acquired an expanded role mandated by Congress, together with aditional personnel and funds. Thus, in 1919, Congress passed the Dyer (Motor Vehicles Theft) Act to combat automobile theft, which the unit was assigned to investigate, while the Volstead Act, also of 1919, gave the "Feds" the power to investigate and prosecute violations of the Constitution's Eighteenth Amendment, prohibiting the manufacture, transportation, sale, import, and export of alcoholic beverages.

Even before that time, the early bureau was involved in internal security matters—at first because of the opposition to World War I, as well as possible espionage and sabotage. Thus, the agency had to investigate cases arising from the Espionage Act of 1917, the Selective Service Act (draft dodgers) of that same year, the Sedition Act of 1918, and the Immigration Act of 1918.

Simultaneously and thereafter, radicals of all kinds became the focus of the bureau's investigation: labor union leaders, members of the Socialist Party, those sympathetic to the Bolshevik (communist) Revolution in Russia in 1917, pro-Irish activists supporting the rebellion for independence from Britain (1916-1922), black militants such as Marcus Garvey, and others. The head of the antiradical alien enemy unit was J. Edgar Hoover, one of the architects of the 1920 Palmer raids against suspected radicals and leftists during the so-called Red Scare.

Following that period, often viewed as one involving abuse of power and scandal (including the Teapot Dome scandal of 1923-1924), the bureau witnessed a few years of administrative reform and retrenchment coinciding with the early years of Hoover's directorship (1924-1972). The New Deal era (1932-1939) was to see the naming of additional federal crimes, thus empowering the bureau. These included kidnappings—mostly involving Prohibition-connected gangsterism—and the use of the U.S. mail for extortion, the robbing of federally chartered banks, and, with the growth of fascism and Nazism, espionage. The bureau's detentive, wiretapping, and break-in powers were also extended.

By that time the bureau had become the FBI, and its agents were now authorized to carry

The FBI's Changing Names

Date	Official name
July, 26, 1908	(No official name)
March 16, 1909	Bureau of Investigation
July 1, 1932	U.S. Bureau of Investigation
August 10, 1933	Division of Investigation
March 22, 1935	Federal Bureau of Investigation (FBI)

weapons and to make arrests independently of state and local law enforcement. A broad surveillance program was instituted against subversives in 1936.

During World War II, curbing German espionage and communist activity became the FBI's major focus, and its internal security investigative powers grew even more. Especially with the passage of the McCarran (Internal Security) Act of 1950 and the Communist Control Act of 1954, during the Cold War period (1947-1991), the FBI sustained its emphasis on the containment of communism (especially during the witch-hunt orchestrated by Senator Joseph R. McCarthy of Wisconsin) and of various types of radical activism.

In the meantime, there was additional targeting of organized crime (and enlarged empowerment of the FBI) with the passage of such legislation as the Omnibus Crime Control and Safe Streets (OCCSS) Act of 1968 and the Racketeer Influenced and Corrupt Organizations (RICO) Acts of 1970 and 1986.

However, the Watergate scandal of 1972-1974 and legislative disclosure of abuse of power by several federal agencies, including the FBI, led to new guidelines, reorganization, and reform to make the agency more accountable to Congress and the general public. After the terrorist attacks of September 11, 2001, terrorism and counterterrorism have occupied center stage amid the concerns and activities of the FBI.

The dynamic nature of American society and its evolving views of crime—the new forms that it took, novel threats to internal security, and Congress's response to these—have, in part, accounted for the changing role and powers, even abuses of power, of the FBI. Another factor was the nature and character of the man with whom the agency had become so closely identified for much of its history: director J. Edgar Hoover. Hoover's obsession with "security" investigations helped to provide a particular bias to the agency's activities for much of his nearly fifty-year tenure.

To this day, the public is divided in its assessment of the FBI. Some recall the heroic role played by the "G-men," by "The Untouchables," immortalized by the media, while others dwell on the high-handed nature of some of the agency's operations and the autocratic nature and tactics of its best-known director.

Organization

The FBI is the principal investigative arm of the U.S. Department of Justice, headed by the attorney general, who is therefore the bureau's nominal head. It is a field-oriented organization in which eleven divisions and four offices at FBI Headquarters in Washington, D.C., provide program direction and support services to fifty-six field offices, some four hundred satellite offices known as resident agencies, four specialized field installations, and more than forty foreign liaison posts, each of which is headed by a legal attaché (legat) or legal liaison officer who works abroad with American and local authorities on criminal and civil matters within FBI jurisdiction—

that is, on cases not assigned by law to another federal agency. Accordingly, the FBI has priority in such matters as national security, counterintelligence, counterterrorism, cybercrime, international and national organized crime or drug matters, and financial crimes. To implement these functions, the FBI is primarily charged with gathering and reporting facts, locating witnesses and alleged perpetrators, and compiling evidence in federal cases.

Among the services the FBI provides are fingerprint identification; laboratory examinations; police training; the Law Enforcement Online communications, information services for use by the law-enforcement community; and administration of the National Crime Information Center and the National Center for the Analysis of Violent Crimes. Also, the bureau provides law-enforcement leadership and assistance to state and international law enforcement agencies.

The organization is headed by a director, now appointed by the U.S. president with the advice and consent of the U.S. Senate. The term is currently limited to ten years. There is a deputy director and thirteen assistant directors, who supervise deputy assistant directors. Each assistant is in charge of one of the eleven headquarters divisions, the Office of Congressional Affairs, and the Office of Professional Responsibility. The Office of the General Counsel is headed by the FBI's general counsel, while the Office of Equal Employment Opportunity is administered by the equal employment manager.

The FBI has about 11,400 special agents (diversified in every way but with a predominance of white males) and some 16,400 support employees, of whom about 10,000 are at FBI Headquarters. Nearly eighteen thousand are assigned to field installations. In 1911, the original bureau had eighty-one agents and thirty-three support staff members, with an appropriation of $329,984. During the early twenty-first century, the FBI had an annual budget of some $3.5 billion.

Heads of the FBI and Its Predecessor Agencies

Name	Title	Date appointed
Stanley W. Finch	chief	July 26, 1908
A. Bruce Bielaski	chief	April 30, 1912
William E. Allen	acting chief	February 10, 1919
William J. Flynn	chief	July 1, 1919
William J. Burns	director	August 22, 1921
J. Edgar Hoover	acting director	May 10, 1924
J. Edgar Hoover	director	December 10, 1924
Clyde Tolson	acting director	May 2, 1972
L. Patrick Gray III	acting director	May 3, 1972
William D. Ruckelshaus	acting director	April 27, 1973
Clarence M. Kelley	director	July 9, 1973
William H. Webster	director	February 23, 1978
John Otto	acting director	May 26, 1987
William S. Sessions	director	November 2, 1987
Floyd Clarke	acting director	July 19, 1993
Louis J. Freeh	director	September 1, 1993
Robert S. Mueller III	director	July 5, 2001

Programs

The FBI's programs include background checks on federal job applicants and appointees slated for sensitive federal agencies as well as those of presidential nominees to executive or judiciary positions. Other programs involve the investigation of civil rights violations, domestic terrorism, national foreign intelligence (foreign espionage and foreign counterintelligence within the United States), and drug trafficking by organized groups, as well as racketeering, violent crimes, kidnapping, sexual exploitation of children, extortion, bank robbery, consumer product tampering, crimes on Indian reservations, unlawful flight to avoid prosecution, and threats—or other harm to—the president, vice president, or members of Congress. Finally, the FBI's white-collar crimes program targets such criminal activity as money laundering, bank fraud and embezzlement, public corruption, environmental crimes, fraud against the government and health care, election law violations, and telemarketing fraud. The FBI's strategic plan prioritizes combating threats to national and economic security or to U.S. citizens and their property as well as criminal enterprises.

Notable FBI Cases

During the early years of the FBI's predecessors (1908-1924), high-profile cases involved violations of the Mann (White Slave Traffic) Act of 1910, focusing on the likes of Jack Johnson, a black heavyweight champion accused of eloping with and seducing a white woman, whom he later married. There was also the case of Edward Y. Clarke, at one time acting imperial wizard of the Klu Klux Klan. Under the authority of the Espionage and Sedition Acts of 1917 and 1918 during World War I, the bureau prosecuted the likes of William D. "Big Bill" Haywood of the Industrial Workers of the World (IWW, or Wobblies), Jacob Abrams, and Emma Goldman of the Union of Russian Workers, all held to be radicals, anarchists, or subversives.

The Hoover years opened with the tracking down of "bad guys," as the age of Prohibition-driven gangsterism and kidnappings, corruption, and rackets of all kinds had arrived. Cases involving the likes of Al "Scarface" Capone, John Dillinger, Clyde Barrow and Bonnie Parker (pop-ularly known as Bonnie and Clyde), George "Machine Gun" Kelly, Alvin "Creepy" Karpis, Charles "Pretty Boy" Floyd, Louis "Lepke" Buchalter, and Willie "the Eel" Sutton catapulted the FBI and its director to fame.

Two famous kidnapping cases in that era were those of the twenty-month-old child, eventually found dead, of hero-aviator Charles Lindbergh (for which Bruno Hauptmann was executed in 1936) and of wealthy Oklahoma City oilman Charles F. Urschel. Most of the perpetrators ended up in prison or were killed in shoot-outs with the G-men, as agents were now known. Even more important, the favorable publicity moved Congress to empower the bureau to intervene in additional crimes formerly considered to be regional, or where local law enforcement proved itself unable to cope.

Even before World War II's outbreak in Europe in 1939, the FBI became involved in German espionage cases such as that of Guenther Gustav Rumrich and Frederick ("Fritz") Joubert Duquesne and in sabotage cases such as that involving George John Dasch and the Long Island (Nazi) Saboteurs. The Smith Act of 1940, outlawing advocacy of the violent overthrow of the government, had given the "Feds" additional authority to pursue radicals. Even before the Japanese attack at Pearl Harbor in 1941, the FBI was again responsible for locating draft evaders and deserters.

Overlapping these mandates was the ferreting out of communists and other leftists, increasingly emphasized after the advent of the Cold War in 1947. Thus, there was the case of the *Amerasia* journal and the trials of William Remington, Alger Hiss, and Judith Coplon. With the surrender of the tripartite Axis powers, communist espionage and subversion became a major issue. Witness the 1957 trial of Colonel Rudolf I. Abel, a Soviet Committee for State Security (KGB) intelligence officer, and most notably of the American "atomic spies," Julius and Ethel Rosenberg, executed in 1953 for giving the Soviet Union classified information.

There was then a recurrence of targeting organized crime, with the trials of Joseph P. Valachi (1963), who later cooperated with the FBI, and the Mafia (La Cosa Nostra). This was to continue through the 1970's, 1980's, and 1990's, with the

Agents of the FBI and the federal Bureau of Alcohol, Tobacco and Firearms inspecting the damage to the Alfred P. Murrah Federal Building in Oklahoma City made by the April, 1995, bombing. *(AP/Wide World Photos)*

Pizza Connection case, the Commission case, the Patriarca case, and that of John Gotti. Notorious crime "families" such as the Profacis, Luccheses, Genoveses, Bonannos, Trafficantes, Magaddinos, and Zerillis were not neglected.

Neither were civil rights cases such as those of Medgar Evers and the three civil rights workers Michael Schwerner, Andrew Goodman, and James E. Chaney, all murdered in Mississippi; of Viola Liuzzo, murdered in Alabama; and of Martin Luther King, Jr., murdered in Tennessee. The post-World War II years also involved a new crop of radicals such as Patricia Hearst and others of the Symbionese Liberation Army, and of Leonard Peltier of the American Indian movement.

The FBI was also involved in the militia cases (Randall "Randy" Weaver's Christian white supremacists at Ruby Ridge, Idaho, in 1992, and the Freemen at Jordan, Montana, in 1996) and

cases involving religious groups (such as the Branch Davidians at Waco, Texas, in 1993). Last but not least was terrorism, whether by individuals such as Theodore J. Kaczynski, the Unabomber (1978-1996), or groups of Muslim fundamentalists at the World Trade Center in New York City (1993 and 2001).

Espionage cases also continued—not only those involving Soviet operatives but also U.S. government employees of agencies outside the FBI—for example, John A. Walker and Jonathan Jay Pollard, both of the U.S. Navy; Ronald Pelton of the National Security Agency; and Aldrich H. Ames of the Central Intelligence Agency. There were additional cases of double agents in the FBI itself.

Undoubtedly, with the advent of weapons of mass destruction—especially biological and chemical—the FBI will be involved, as it was in the anthrax scare on the East Coast in 2001. Since its origins, the FBI's investigations have intersected with major events and public issues in American life and have thus been equally controversial.

Moles and Double Agents

Even though there was considerable mumbling about director J. Edgar Hoover's supposed eccentricities and idiosyncrasies when it came to the behavior of his special agents—according to stories, true or apocryphal, he would not tolerate homosexuals or adulterers, mandated formal dress even before air-conditioning was available in district offices, had a phobia about overweight men or even those with sweaty palms—unquestionably, during his near half-century at the helm, there were extremely few cases of disloyalty, such as that of William G. Sebold in 1941. Things changed, however, after Hoover's death.

One of the most notable—indeed, notorious—cases of disloyalty within the agency was that of FBI special agent Robert Philip Hanssen. Hanssen's clearances allowed him to access classified information at the CIA, the National Security Agency, the White House, and the defense department. They also enabled Hanssen to check an FBI database that would show any possible investigation of himself by his employer. Hanssen, a computer whiz who had majored in chemistry, spoke Russian, had an M.B.A., and had helped the FBI create a database of Soviet intelligence officers, including their addresses, appearances, likes, and dislikes. He was also involved with anti-Soviet electronic bugs and video surveillance.

In 1979, Hanssen started working for the GRU (Soviet military intelligence), blowing the cover on Soviet double agent General Dmitri F. Polyakov. The latter, like several others who had worked undercover for the United States and were compromised by Hanssen, was executed in Russia. Back in New York in 1985 after a stint at FBI Headquarters, Hanssen returned to spying for the Soviets, this time for the more prestigious KGB. After that, he worked for the Russian SVR, the successor to the KGB's foreign intelligence unit, sporadically until 2001. But on February 18 of that year, Hanssen was arrested at a dead drop (a drop used for the clandestine exchange of intel-

ligence information) in Foxstone Park, Vienna, Virginia, close to where he lived with his wife and six children. Another team of agents at a second drop site found $50,000 in $100 bills left for him.

The damage Hanssen had caused was incalculable. Over twenty-one years of spying for the Soviets and then for the Russians, he transferred to them six thousand pages of classified documents, twenty-seven computer discs cataloging secret and top-secret programs, including one on how to ensure the survival of the U.S. government in the event of a nuclear attack. Instead of the death penalty, which Attorney General John Ashcroft had sought for him, in exchange for continuing debriefings about Russian undercover operations and FBI countermeasures, Hanssen got a life sentence in prison without parole in July, 2001, and his wife was allowed to collect some of his pension. He admitted getting a kick from outwitting the intelligence communities, both the FBI and the KGB, because it gave him a sense of power, of control.

Peter B. Heller

Further Reading

Churchill, Ward, and Jim Vander Wall. *The COINTELPRO Papers: Documents from the FBI's Secret Wars Against Dissent in the United States.* 2d ed. Cambridge, Mass.: South End Press, 2002. Purports to show through documentary evidence (including deletions) how the FBI in such case studies as that of the Puerto Rican Independence Movement was willing to sacrifice (according to the bureau's director) more than a small measure of American liberties in order to preserve the great bulk of them. Bibliography, index.

De Loach, Cartha "Deke." *Hoover's FBI: The Inside Story by Hoover's Trusted Lieutenant.* Washington, D.C.: Regnery, 1995. A sympathetic "insider" assessment by the bureau's number three man, including interesting reminiscences about the difficulties of trying to "terminate" Hoover's tenure. Bibliographical note, index.

Kessler, Ronald. *The Bureau: The Secret History of the FBI.* New York: St. Martin's Press, 2002. A critical assessment, especially during the "dirty years," of the FBI's abuse of power. Bibliography, index.

Mitgang, Herbert. *Dangerous Dossiers*. New York: Penguin/Primus, 1996. The FBI's secret war against prominent intellectuals, domestic and foreign, in all art forms. Bibliography, index.

Reebel, Patrick A., ed. *Federal Bureau of Investigation: Current Issues and Background*. New York: Nova Science, 2002. A series of essays to support the conclusion that the FBI is a "first-rate organization with a mission impossible." The case studies include those of the Oklahoma City bombing (1995), the Montana "Freemen" standoff (1996), and the Branch Davidian siege (1993). Exhaustive bibliography; author, title, and subject indexes.

Whitehead, Don. *The FBI Story: A Report to the People*. New York: Random House, 1956. A reporter refutes the frequent allegations that the FBI represented a shadowy menace to civil rights. Includes famous case histories, based on privileged access to selected FBI documents. Notes, chronology, index.

Whitnah, Donald R., ed. *Government Agencies*. Westport, Conn.: Greenwood Press, 1983. Includes a succinct history of the FBI. Chronology, genealogy, and other appendixes; index.

See also Attorney general of the United States; Bank robbery; Branch Davidian raid; Bureau of Justice Statistics; COINTELPRO; Crime Index; Drugs and law enforcement; Espionage; Gangsters of the Prohibition era; Hoover, J. Edgar; Justice Department, U.S.; Law enforcement; Motor vehicle theft; Organized crime; Royal Canadian Mounted Police; Ruby Ridge raid; Skyjacking; Ten-most-wanted lists; Treason; Unabomber.

Federal Crimes Act

The Law: First law to define federal crimes
Date: Became law on April 30, 1790
Criminal justice issues: Federal law; law codes
Significance: The Federal Crimes Act defined a variety of federal crimes and their corresponding penalties, thereby laying the foundation for the United States Criminal Code.

Enacted only one year after the ratification of the U.S. Constitution, the Federal Crimes Act of 1790 was intended to enumerate and establish penalties for federal offenses for which the Constitution had expressly granted jurisdiction to the federal government. Most notably, the act defined as federal crimes treason, counterfeiting, piracy, bribery and perjury in federal suits, and murder and manslaughter committed within federal enclaves—such as forts, arsenals, and dockyards. The act also mandated that defendants accused of capital federal crimes were entitled to attorneys. Penalties established for federal crimes under the act ranged from fines of three hundred dollars to death.

Although the Federal Crimes Act was intended only to define offenses that fell within the narrow jurisdiction granted to the federal government by the Constitution, its passage set a precedent for later expansion of federal jurisdiction to include a number of other crimes that led to the establishment of the United States Criminal Code. Subsequent federal legislation, including the Federal Crimes Acts of 1825 and 1970, altered some of the crimes and punishments defined in the 1790 act, while dramatically expanding the number of federal crimes and the authority of the federal government to prosecute and punish offenders.

The section of the act requiring the government to provide legal counsel for capital defendants set a precedent that bolstered subsequent interpretations of the Sixth Amendment right to counsel, which ultimately established that all criminal defendants have a right to legal representation.

Michael H. Burchett

Further Reading

Friedman, Lawrence M. *Crime and Punishment in American History*. Portland, Oreg.: Basic Books, 1994.

Marion, Nancy E. *A History of Federal Crime Control Initiatives, 1960-1993*. Westport, Conn.: Greenwood Press, 1994.

See also Arson; Attorneys, U.S.; Bill of Rights, U.S.; Bribery; Counsel, right to; Counterfeiting; Miranda rights; *Miranda v. Arizona*; Perjury; Treason.

Felon disfranchisement

Definition: Federal and state laws impose civil restrictions on persons convicted of felony crimes

Criminal justice issues: Convictions; political issues; punishment

Significance: In 2004, an estimated five million U.S. residents were denied civil participation or other constrainment of their liberties as a result of having been convicted of a crime punishable by imprisonment for more than one year in the United States.

Based on federal law, states have the ability to restrict the rights of formerly convicted felons. These restrictions may preclude offenders' abilities to vote; to possess a firearm; to serve on a federal jury; to hold certain federal offices, jobs, or licenses; to enlist in military service or receive certain military benefits; to serve in a range of capacities relating to labor organizations; to participate in or receive certain federal contracts; to participate in federal or designated state social service programs (such as Social Security, health, disability, public housing, and other benefits and services) based on the type of felony conviction; and to be issued a passport if their conviction is for a federal or state drug offense in which a passport was used or if the offender crossed an international boundary in the commission of the crime.

Persons attempting to enter the United States may be denied entry if they have been convicted of, or admit to committing, any crimes recognized by federal or state law as involving moral turpitude. Illegal aliens who are convicted of felonies may be deported and are ordinarily disqualified from naturalization.

Felony convictions for certain sex offenses typically require offenders to submit to sex offender registration. Minimum national standards, as set forth in the Wetterling Act, require all registered sex offenders who move to another state to notify the Federal Bureau of Investigation and the new state of residence.

Formerly, only Vermont, Maine, and the District of Columbia allowed prisoners to vote, but in 2004 thirty-eight states permitted those with fel-

ony records to do so. About a dozen states allow convicted felons to own or obtain special exceptions to allow them to possess firearms under certain conditions.

Laws affecting convicted felons have a disproportionate impact on racial and ethnic minorities, who are overrepresented in the criminal justice system.

Wayne J. Pitts

Further Reading

Behrens, Angela, Christopher Uggen, and Jeff Manza. "Ballot Manipulation and the 'Menace of Negro Domination': Racial Threat and Felon Disenfranchisement in the United States, 1850-2002." *American Journal of Sociology* 109 (2003): 559-605.

Uggen, Christopher, and Jeff Manza. "Democratic Contraction? Political Consequences of Felon Disenfranchisement in the United States." *American Sociological Review* 67 (December, 2002): 777-803.

_____. *Locking Up the Vote: Felon Disenfranchisement and American Democracy.* New York: Oxford University Press, 2004.

See also Felonies; Moral turpitude; Right to bear arms; Sex offender registries.

Felonies

Definition: Serious criminal offenses, such as murder, rape, kidnapping, arson, embezzlement, or armed robbery, that, according to federal guidelines, are punishable by imprisonment of a year or more or by death

Criminal justice issues: Law codes; legal terms and principles; violent crime

Significance: Federal and state definitions of felonies and misdemeanors vary somewhat, but in all jurisdictions the distinction is an important one.

Criminal offenses are often grouped into two major categories, felonies and misdemeanors, which indicate the seriousness of the crime. Misdemeanors are less serious offenses, such as disorderly conduct; felonies are more serious crimes, such as murder, rape, and armed robbery. Federal guidelines define a felony as any crime "punishable by death or by imprisonment for a term exceeding one year." Most states maintain similar definitions, although some states classify crimes according to the place of incarceration for offenders. If incarceration is to be in a state prison, the offense is a felony; if it is punishable by a term in a local jail, it is considered a misdemeanor. (There are further complications in some areas; in Michigan a few misdemeanors are deemed serious enough to warrant time in a state penitentiary.) In some jurisdictions an offense may be considered either a felony or a misdemeanor depending on a number of factors. Larceny (theft), for example, may be classified as a felony (grand larceny) if the value of the item or items stolen is sufficiently high or a misdemeanor (petty larceny) if their value is relatively small.

Most states maintain separate court systems for felonies and misdemeanors. Felonies are tried in county courts, or courts of general jurisdiction. Misdemeanors are handled by local courts with limited jurisdiction. By far, most criminal cases are handled by local (minor) courts, partly because so many charges are only misdemeanors and partly because felony charges are sometimes reduced to misdemeanor charges before a trial begins. Because the charges and punishments meted out to convicted felony offenders are significantly more serious, the handling of felony cases by the courts is much more complex than the handling of misdemeanors. Felony cases involve pretrial, trial, and post-trial proceedings, and they can take a year or more.

In 1963, in the landmark case *Gideon v. Wainwright*, the U.S. Supreme Court held that defendants charged with serious crimes must be provided with a state-appointed attorney if they cannot afford to hire their own attorney. At first this requirement was applied only to felony cases, but in *Argersinger v. Hamlin* (1973) the Court extended the protection to people accused of misdemeanors if the misdemeanor charge could result in imprisonment.

The exact origin of the term "felony" is unknown, but many scholars trace it to the Latin words *felonia* and *fallere*, meaning "to deceive." In England, a felony originally was a breach of

the feudal bond resulting in either the temporary or permanent forfeiture of the guilty party's assets. Gradually the definition expanded. In the twelfth century, Henry II attempted to codify the laws of the realm, and he established forfeiture as one of the penalties for murder, theft, forgery, arson, and other similar criminal acts. Soon all crimes punishable in England by forfeiture of property (eventually abolished in 1870), physical mutilation, burning, or death were considered felonies. In 1967, England replaced the former distinctions with the categories of arrestable and nonarrestable offenses, but the felony/misdemeanor distinction remains important in the United States.

Donald C. Simmons, Jr.

Further Reading

Dix, E. G., and M. M. Sharlot. *Criminal Law*. 4th ed. Belmont, Calif.: Wadsworth, 1998.
Dubber, Markus Dirk. *Criminal Law: Model Penal Code*. New York: Foundation Press, 2002.
Flemming, Roy B. *Punishment Before Trial: An Organizational Perspective of Felony Bail Processes*. New York: Longman, 1982.
Uggen, Christopher, and Jeff Manza. *Locking Up the Vote: Felon Disenfranchisement and American Democracy*. New York: Oxford University Press, 2004.

See also Common law; Crime; Crime Index; Criminal law; Criminal records; Felon disfranchisement; Information; Mandatory sentencing; Misdemeanors; Punishment; Three-strikes laws.

Fifth Amendment

The Law: Part of the Bill of Rights, an amendment to the U.S. Constitution providing protections relating to trials, punishment, and compensation for takings

Date: Ratified on December 15, 1791

Criminal justice issues: Constitutional protections; trial procedures

Significance: Over time, the U.S. Supreme Court has helped to define the Fifth Amendment and the protections that it affords all people in the United States.

Text of the Fifth Amendment

No person shall be held to answer for a capital, or otherwise infamous crime, unless on a presentment or indictment of a Grand Jury, except in cases arising in the land or naval forces, or in the Militia, when in actual service in time of War or public danger; nor shall any person be subject for the same offence to be twice put in jeopardy of life or limb, nor shall be compelled in any criminal case to be a witness against himself, nor be deprived of life, liberty, or property, without due process of law; nor shall private property be taken for public use without just compensation.

The Fifth Amendment affords citizens and residents of the United States a multitude of rights, including the protection from government coercion. However, thanks to many Hollywood films and television programs, most Americans have only a superficial understanding of the amendment. For example, most people know that the Fifth Amendment protects people from having to testify in court about anything that will make them appear to be guilty of crimes. While this is true, the Fifth Amendment offers many other important protections.

Throughout history, it has not been unusual for outcomes of trials to be based solely on testimonies of the persons accused of crimes. In the more remote past, it was common for defendants to threatened, beaten, and even tortured until they confessed to the crimes with which they were charged. One of the purposes of the Fifth Amendment was to make similar coercion impossible.

The Fifth Amendments's protections from self-incrimination are also afforded to persons who testify before grand juries. There are limits to the types of communication that are protected by this clause of the amendment. For example, while the protection applies to the spoken word, it does not apply to anything that is written. The written word can be considered documentary evidence.

Other Protections

In addition to guaranteeing people the protections from self-incrimation, the Fifth Amendment's due process clause guarantees that police cannot arrest people and hold them in jail without indictments from grand juries. Due process prevents government officials from imprisoning suspects on their own judgment. The Fifth Amendment requires government to act fairly and precisely. More specifically, government cannot rely on the personal judgments of individuals or their impulses when making decisions. Rather, government officials must stay within the scope of the law. The principle of due process ensures that defendants are informed of the criminal charges against them and that they have opportunities to explain themselves. Further, if arrestees choose to maintain their silence rather than speak on their own behalf, they cannot be automatically assumed to be guilty.

The due process guarantees of the Fifth Amendment are often compared to those of the Fourteenth Amendment. However, the two amendments differ. The Fifth Amendment has a number of express provisions shared by other Bill of Rights amendments that include fair and nonarbitrary jury trials and grand jury indictments, nonexcessive bail and fines, and fair compensation. Interpretations of the two amendments are substantially the same; however, the Fourteenth Amendment binds the individual states to standards of fairness and justness found within the Fifth Amendment's clause.

The Fifth Amendment does not guarantee trials by grand juries. According to the Supreme

Due Process and the Fourteenth Amendment

Ratified in 1868, the 433-word Fourteenth Amendment is the lengthiest amendment in the U.S. Constitution. It addressed a variety of important constitutional issues, but its central relevance to criminal justice is contained in this single sentence that concludes the amendment's first section:

No State shall make or enforce any law which shall abridge the privileges or immunities of citizens of the United States; nor shall any State deprive any person of life, liberty, or property, without due process of law; nor deny to any person within its jurisdiction the equal protection of the laws.

Court's 1884 *Hurtado v. California* decision, indictments by grand juries are not guaranteed. However, most states do allow for prosecution by indictments. In 1987, the Supreme Court ruled that active members of the armed services are not guaranteed grand jury hearings.

The Fifth Amendment also

The Supreme Court and the Fifth Amendment

The U.S. Supreme Court's 1966 *Miranda v. Arizona* ruling is a good example of how the Court has reinforced the self-incrimination clause of the Fifth Amendment. The *Miranda* decision requires police officers to tell suspects whom they arrest of their right to remain silent during police questioning.

---

includes a double jeopardy clause stating that a person cannot be tried twice for the same crime. Once defendants are found innocent of the crimes for which they are tried, the government cannot try them again, even if new evidence can be introduced. The double jeopardy clause also states that if the accused are found guilty and serve their punishments, they cannot be tried and punished again for the same crimes. However, the double jeopardy clause does not apply when criminal charges are brought by separate sovereign jurisdictions. The case of the Oklahoma City bomber Timothy McVeigh is an example. McVeigh was first found guilty of committing federal crimes in the 1995 bombing of the Alfred P. Murrah Federal Building and was also found guilty of committing Oklahoma state crimes because the explosion took place in Oklahoma. As the federal and state authorities were separate sovereigns, it was not considered to be double jeopardy for both levels of authorities to charge him.

The eminent domain clause of the Fifth Amendment states that the government cannot take private land and use it for public property without giving just compensation to the owners. This section of the amendment stems from the treatment of the colonists by the British during the American Revolution. During the Revolution, British soldiers often seized colonists' property, livestock, or belongings in the name of the king, without paying any compensation. Under the Fifth Amendment, the government may not take property without compensating the owners adequately.

Overall, the Fifth Amendment is an important part of the Bill of Rights established by the Framers of the Constitution. Designed to protect the rights of people accused of capital crimes or other high crimes, the amendment sums up many of the basic ideals established in the other nine amendments of the Bill of Rights. Many of the rights and guarantees spelled out, not only in the Fifth Amendment, but also in each of the first ten amendments, can be traced back to English common law. For example, the concepts of having grand juries and the expression "due process" are rooted in English common law. The Fifth Amendment thus affords people much more than the right not to testify in their own defense.

Karen L. Hayslett-McCall

Further Reading

Berger, Mark. *Taking the Fifth*. Lexington, Mass.: D.C. Heath, 1980. Study of the Fifth Amendment focusing on the protections against self-incrimination.

Fireside, Harvey. *The Fifth Amendment: The Right to Remain Silent*. Springfield, N.J.: Enslow, 1998. Useful general work on the Fifth Amendment.

Garcia, Alfredo. *The Fifth Amendment: A Comprehensive Approach*. Westport, Conn.: Greenwood Press, 2002. Part of the publisher's Contributions in Legal Studies series, this book examines the interconnections among the Fifth Amendment's three clauses relating to criminal justice: the privilege against self-incrimination, the right to a grand jury indictment, and protection against double jeopardy.

Holmes, Burnham. *The Fifth Amendment*. Englewood Cliffs, N.J.: Silver Burdett Press, 1991. Introductory survey of issues relating to the amendment.

Levy, Leonard W. *Origins of the Fifth Amendment*. 1968. Reprint. New York: Macmillan, 1986. Historical study tracing the legal principles contained in the amendment back to the Magna Carta in thirteenth century England.

Quick, Bruce D. *Law of Arrest, Search, and Seizure: An Examination of the Fourth, Fifth, and*

Sixth Amendments to the United States Constitution. Rev. ed. Bismarck, N.Dak.: Attorney General's Office, Criminal Justice Training and Statistics Division, 1987.

See also Bill of Rights, U.S.; Common law; Confessions; Double jeopardy; Due process of law; Grand juries; *Massiah v. United States*; Military justice; Miranda rights; *Miranda v. Arizona*; Pleas; Self-incrimination, privilege against; Supreme Court, U.S.

Films and criminal justice

Criminal justice issue: Media

Significance: Films with criminal justice themes system convey important ideas and information about the criminal justice system to the public; at the same time, however, they also frequently distort the realities of criminal justice in the United States.

Virtually as long as artists have attempted to depict life, they have found fruitful subjects in accounts of those accused of crimes and the law which undertakes to apprehend, try, and punish them. Modern filmmakers follow in a tradition at least as old as *Antigone*, a fifth century C.E. play by the Greek writer Sophocles. In that play, a woman is accused of defying the king's law to honor her dead brother. One need only scan the list of Academy Award-winning films to see the enduring presence of criminal law as a cinematic theme, from *Mutiny on the Bounty* (1935) and *The Life of Emile Zola* (1937) to *Unforgiven* (1992) and *Chicago* (2002). The cinema's fascination with criminal law extends even into the future, as witnessed by films such as *Robocop* (1987), *Demolition Man* (1993), *Judge Dredd* (1995), and *Minority Report* (2002) that speculate about forms that criminal justice system may take in the future.

By its very nature, criminal law is a complex technical subject. Accordingly, films only ninety minutes to two hours in length are poorly positioned to capture the details of criminal justice. In real life, the kinds of cases that find fictional counterparts in films typically consume weeks or months in their investigation and prosecution. Accordingly, it is the rare film that does not distort the real processes of criminal law in one way or another. Nevertheless, films about the criminal justice system can—in broad strokes at least—illuminate the law. They can fairly indict the law and, sometimes, they can honor it. So long as viewers understand the inherent limitations in simple treatments of what is often quite complex and understand the general bias of filmmakers for the sensational, then those who watch films can learn something useful about the real-life criminal justice system.

The Routines and Tedium of Criminal Justice

The eminent jurist Oliver Wendell Holmes, Jr., once observed that the "life of the law has not been logic, but experience." He might also have said that the "life of the law has not been logic, but long hours." Monotony, tedium, and routine characterize the lives of those involved with the criminal justice system. In contrast to film cops, real-life police spend far more time interviewing witnesses, cultivating and consulting informants, and running searches in computer databases than they do engaging in dramatic car chases and desperate gun battles. Indeed, they spend more time writing reports than they do in stark rooms with one-way mirrors interviewing witnesses.

In contrast to their film counterparts, real-life courtroom attorneys seldom wring tearful confessions out of lying witnesses—or not-so-tearful confessions, such as one that Jack Nicholson makes to Tom Cruise in *A Few Good Men* (1992). Instead, they spend most of their time out of court, methodically preparing cases. In fact, the vast majority of criminal cases never go to court. Prosecutors and defense attorneys engage in plea bargains that settle most criminal charges short of trials. When attorneys do appear in court, they are tamer than films suggest. Whereas film lawyers spend much of their courtroom time swaggering about, most real courts require lawyers to examine witnesses either while seated behind tables or while standing behind lecterns. Tedium makes for bad cinema, however, and filmmakers accordingly present more glamorous, or at least more exciting, versions of the criminal process.

This is not to say, however, that the law even

Jack Nicholson as the tough Marine colonel in *A Few Good Men.*
(Castle Rock Entertainment)

at its most mundane is not interesting. Television viewers who followed the coverage of the 1995 criminal trial of O. J. Simpson for the murders of Nicole Brown Simpson and Ronald Goldman, for example, received lessons in the monotony of real-life courtroom practice but nevertheless found the trial often fascinating. With its celebrity defendant and celebrity defense attorneys, the Simpson trial, and gruesome murders, was precisely the kind of sensational murder case that dominates film law. It is not, however, the kind of trial that dominates the everyday life of the criminal justice system. In real life, drugs, thefts, and more mundane versions of domestic violence occupy a far more prominent place than do former football players and bloody gloves.

Attorneys with Guilty Clients

Nowhere does film law stray further from reality than when it suggests that the abilities of criminal defense attorneys to do their jobs hinges on their confidence in the innocence of their clients. One often gains the impression from watching films about criminal justice that defense lawyers spend most of their time representing innocents falsely accused of crimes. Moreover, one might infer that it is improper for lawyers to represent clients whom they know—or strongly believe—to be guilty. Film lawyers who find themselves representing guilty defendants sometimes behave dramatically. In . . . *And Justice for All* (1979), for example, the lawyer whom Al Pacino portrays discovers that the judge whom he is defending is guilty of rape and feels compelled to announce that fact to the jury during his opening statement, rather represent a guilty client. In *Guilty as Sin* (1993), the lawyer whom Rebecca De Mornay plays plants evidence to incriminate her client after she discovers that he is guilty of murdering his wife. In *Criminal Law* (1988) the lawyer played by Gary Oldman continues to represent a guilty client (Kevin Bacon) after suspecting that his client is a serial killer, so that he can stop him from committing more murders.

The dilemmas that these film lawyers experience in discovering their clients' guilt are completely unrealistic. Criminal defense lawyers are ethically required to represent their clients diligently, without regard to their guilt or innocence. Knowing that a client is guilty does nothing to diminish this obligation of diligent representation. As the lawyer in *Before and After* (1996) explains to the parents of a son accused of murder: Many of his clients have been guilty of one thing or another since they were five years old, but they still deserve a good defense.

A lawyer who betrays a guilty client in real life is not likely to be allowed to remain a lawyer for long. In . . . *And Justice for All*, Pacino realistically faces the threat of disbarment for secretly informing the police that one of his clients has fantasized about committing a certain crime that is being perpetrated by an unknown assailant. However, the same film fails to address the possibility of Pacino's disbarment for denouncing his murder-case client in his opening statement.

A more realistic message permeates *Reversal of Fortune* (1990), a film based on a book written by Harvard law professor Alan Dershowitz. With the assistance of some of his law school students,

Dershowitz represented Claus von Bulow on appeal after Bulow was convicted of murdering his wife. For Dershowitz, it did not matter whether Bulow was innocent or guilty; he regarded the man as entitled to the best representation that he could afford (and Bulow could afford to pay for a prominent Harvard Law School professor). Similarly, in *Primal Fear* (1996), Richard Gere plays a criminal lawyer who rushes to represent a young client accused of murdering an archbishop, not because he believes the young man is innocent, but because he is eager to collect the publicity that the case promises to provide. Only gradually does he come to believe that his client is innocent.

In most American jurisdictions, lawyers who know that their clients are guilty may find themselves restrained in ways not experienced by lawyers without that knowledge. For example, most states prohibit lawyers from offering evidence they know is false during trials. Accordingly, if lawyers know their clients have committed certain crimes, they cannot sit silently and allow their clients to testify the contrary in court. Nevertheless, the lawyers remain free—and are, in fact, absolutely obligated—to challenge vigorously the prosecution's evidence and otherwise represent their clients zealously.

"Technicalities" and Criminal Justice

A common film critique of law is to suggest the injustice of a system that lets guilty criminal defendants escape punishment on the basis of so-called technicalities. One such technicality, known as the exclusionary rule, is a prominent feature of modern criminal justice proceedings. This rule generally requires that evidence unlawfully obtained cannot be used against criminal defendants in court. For instance, under the Fourth Amendment to the U.S. Constitution, which protects citizens against unreasonable search and seizure, if police illegally enter a home and discover therein evidence of a crime, the evidence they find is generally not admissible in court. The exclusionary rule is justified by the necessity of deterring the police from engaging in illegal behavior. The rule is based on the notion that the only effective way to deter police from engaging in unconstitutional behavior is to make them understand that the fruits of their illegal

conduct cannot be used to convict criminals.

Films sometimes treat the exclusionary rule as a merely arbitrary technicality that allows criminals to go free. Not uncommonly, the apparent unreasonableness of this rule inspires vigilante justice of one sort or another. A prominent example is the fiction San Francisco detective "Dirty Harry" Callahan (Clint Eastwood), who always finds ways to have bullets track down criminals who are unleashed on society by the exclusionary rule. In *The Star Chamber* (1983), renegade judges hire killers to execute the criminals that they have had to release by virtue of the exclusionary rule or other related constitutional doctrines. Films seldom dramatize the real justification for the exclusionary rule: to deter police misconduct.

Law-Enforcement Mayhem

Filmmakers—at least those of the action-film variety—love to blow things up. When police or other law-enforcement personnel are involved in action films, they can usually be counted on to cause, or at least contribute to, a variety of explosions, fiery collisions, and other forms of mayhem. Sergeant Martin Riggs (Mel Gibson) of the Lethal Weapon series, for example, pulls down a house in *Lethal Weapon 2* (1989) and sets off a bomb that destroys an office building and burns down a construction site in *Lethal Weapon 3* (1992). Although law-enforcement superiors in films sometimes express dismay at the property destruction accomplished by their officers, films tend to convey an all-in-a-day's-work attitude toward police mayhem.

In real life, law-enforcement officers do not have a blank check to destroy things (or injure people) in pursuit of their official duties. Legal doctrines on this issue are complicated and vary from state to state. Nevertheless, police departments and other law-enforcement agencies are often found liable for damages that occur in connection with their work.

In principle, governments at all levels—federal, state, and municipal—possess sovereign immunity, which means that they cannot generally be sued for damages unless they consent to the suits. In practice, however, governments at every level must consent to such suits—at least under certain defined circumstances—by statute. For example, the Federal Tort Claims Act of 1946 authorizes suits against the federal government when its agents or officials act negligently. Similar laws exist for state and local governments. Accordingly, law-enforcement officers who act negligently may generally be sued by citizens injured as a result of their negligence or recklessness.

One of the most famous chase scenes in film history occurs in *The French Connection* (1971), in which actor Gene Hackman plays the maniacal police detective Popeye Doyle. Midway through the film, Doyle commandeers a car from a civilian and then recklessly pursues a criminal fleeing in an out-of-control elevated train. The film's skilled editing makes the ground-level car's pursuit of the overhead train exceptionally exciting. Meanwhile, the chase scene itself shows Doyle hitting several other cars and narrowly missing several pedestrians, including a young woman pushing a baby buggy. In real life, if a New York police officer were actually to kill an innocent person in such a reckless chase, he or she could be named defendant—along with the city of New York and the New York Police Department—in wrongful death lawsuits.

Intimate Relationships

The criminal justice system aspires to an objectivity in which reason replaces emotion and law reigns in the place of passion. Objectivity, however, makes for dull films. Accordingly, one of the favorite plot devices of cinematic justice is to create sexual relationships among characters—between, for example, police officers and lawyers, detectives and suspects, and suspects and their attorneys. *Basic Instinct* (1992), for example, finds a police officer sexually involved not with one suspect, but with two, in a murder investigation.

Cinema lawyers are also not immune from inappropriate sexual attractions. Typically, these involve lawyers who have sexual relationships with their clients, as in *Physical Evidence* (1989), starring Theresa Russell as a lawyer who represents a former cop, played by Burt Reynolds, who is accused of murder. In *Jagged Edge* (1985), Glenn Close plays a lawyer who gets involved with her client, played by Jeff Bridges. Occasionally, however, lawyers form attachments with other players in the criminal justice system, such as the highly unlikely romantic relationship that an attorney played by Cher forms with a member of the jury in her case, played by Dennis Quaid in *Suspect* (1987), or the attachment that Al Pacino forms with lawyer Christine Lahti, a member of the state bar ethics committee, in . . . *And Justice for All*.

As these summaries suggest, a willingness to step across established professional boundaries tends to be attributed more often to women than to men in films about the law. There are exceptions, such as *Body of Evidence* (1993), in which Willem Dafoe plays a lawyer who rushes to bed his sexually adventurous client (Madonna), who is accused of murdering her husband, and *Body Heat* (1981), in which a lawyer actually conspires with his client/lover to murder the latter's husband. Nevertheless, films about the law seem especially prone to promoting stereotypical views of women, portraying them as emotionally more vulnerable and generally less competent than their male counterparts. Such stereotypes do not do justice to the many women who participate in the criminal justice system.

The frequency of sexual encounters involving police, lawyers, and others in criminal justice films is matched by the ambivalent attitude displayed toward such encounters by the law in real life. Police informants, for example, sometimes have sexual relationships with the targets of criminal investigations, but courts have generally been reluctant to punish these individuals, unless police deliberately set out to use sex to trap criminal targets.

Rules that govern the conduct of lawyers have generally refrained from containing explicit prohibitions against sexual relationships between lawyers and their clients. Nevertheless, when such relationships have been found to have affected attorneys' representation of their clients adversely or otherwise to have harmed clients, courts and ethics committees have not hesitated to punish the lawyers involved. These results reflect the broader principle that lawyers may not represent clients when some competing interest—including sexual or other kinds of personal attachments—might undermine their ability to serve their clients diligently. For example, most states explicitly prohibit lawyers who are married to each another from serving on opposite sides of the same case. The famous pairing of Spencer Tracy and Katharine Hepburn as opposing prosecutor and defense attorney in a sensational murder case in *Adam's Rib* (1949) would ordinarily be prohibited.

Maverick Justice

Ideally, the criminal justice system identifies and then punishes or rehabilitates those who fracture the social order. Films about criminal justice, however, regularly emphasize that either this system itself or the actors within it are themselves fractured and broken. When the justice system is broken, mavericks must act lawlessly to restore law.

Some mavericks do not choose this role but are assigned it by a system that is corrupt. Al Pacino, for example, plays an undercover cop in *Serpico* (1973) who is ostracized by his corrupt colleagues for testifying at a grand jury investigation about police extorting money from criminals. Equally common are mavericks who believe that the law is too soft on criminals and take it on themselves to mete out meatier justice. Harry Callahan is a prominent example of this kind of maverick. *Dirty Harry* (1971) and its sequels—*Magnum Force* (1973), *The Enforcer* (1976), *Sudden Impact* (1983), and *The Dead Pool* (1988)—followed in the wake of what has been called the "rights revolution" under the U.S. Supreme Court leadership of Chief Justice Earl Warren. The Warren court expanded the rights accorded to defendants in the criminal process. The most famous example of this expansion occurred in *Miranda v. Arizona* (1966), decided only five years before *Dirty Harry* was released. That decision required that defendants be advised of their rights before being questioned by police. In the minds of Dirty Harry and the audiences who cheered him, however, constitu-

tional developments such as *Miranda* distorted justice and impeded its pursuit.

Films are also prepared to remind the public of the dangers posed by lawless law. Thus, in *The Star Chamber*, judges tired of having to release criminals on technicalities choose to manufacture a shadow justice system, in which killers are contracted to kill other killers. As it happens, however, the system is not as badly broken as the vigilante judges imagine, and their lawless law turns out to be simply lawless after all. Sometimes one maverick must take on others, as Harry Callahan does in *Magnum Force*, the first sequel to *Dirty Harry*, when he confronts rogue cops who are dispensing their own brand of justice.

Maverick cops such as Harry Callahan are easier to portray than maverick lawyers. They wield the power of vigilante violence against criminals who manage to elude the power of the criminal justice system. Lawyers generally possess no power other than that which they derive through their professional competence as advo-

The definitive screen portrayal of a hard-boiled detective may be Humphrey Bogart's performance as Dashiell Hammett's Sam Spade in 1940's *The Maltese Falcon*. That classic film ends with Spade solving the tangled mystery of the falcon and proving that his new lover, the beautiful Brigid O'Shaughnessy (Mary Astor) is guilty of murder. Unmoved by Brigid's charms, he turns her in. *(Arkent Archives)*

cates within the justice system. At most, they can assume the role of maverick in more subtle ways than the maverick cop, by violating rules of the legal system as they remain planted firmly inside that system. A lawyer such as Al Pacino plays in . . . *And Justice for All*, who announces his client's guilt in open court, is a maverick, to be sure, but he ceases be a lawyer. In fact, as Pacino's character sits on the courthouse steps following the mistrial inevitably granted after his outburst, he should be planning a new career, for he will surely be disbarred. By contrast, a rogue cop such as Harry Callahan can continue to do good business in film sequels.

Innocents at the Mercy of Law

A recurring theme in films about criminal law is the possibility that innocent men and women may find themselves the victims of the criminal process. In Alfred Hitchcock's *The Wrong Man* (1956), for example, a musician played by Henry Fonda finds himself arrested for a crime he did not commit and only narrowly escapes going to jail, when the real criminal, who looks very much like him, is finally caught. *The Wrong Man* is harrowing, precisely because the process that mistakenly identifies Fonda otherwise proceeds competently and in an orderly way through every step.

Although the criminal justice system accords to those accused of crimes the presumption of innocence, this presumption does not prevent innocents from being wrongly convicted. It does not even mean, technically, that participants in the justice system suspend belief in the likelihood that individuals charged with having committed crimes actually committed them. Instead, the presumption of innocence means that the criminal justice system requires the state to prove the defendant's guilt beyond a reasonable doubt, and that, without such proof, a criminal defendant must be acquitted.

Films can be useful in prompting viewers to consider whether particular punishments are justified in the light of the reality that at least some innocents will inevitably be called upon to experience them. In *The Shawshank Redemption* (1994), for instance, the brutality of prison life takes on a sharper focus when this brutality is borne by an innocent man, wrongly convicted of

murdering his adulterous wife and her lover. In films such as *The Life of David Gale* (2003) and *True Crime* (1999), the possibility that innocent men may be executed is used to indict capital punishment.

Heroic Lawyers (and Clients)

At the conclusion of the trial of Tom Robinson in *To Kill a Mockingbird* (1962), Atticus Finch, famously played by Gregory Peck, silently gathers his things and prepares to leave the courtroom after the jury finds his client guilty. The black citizens of Macon, Alabama, who have watched the trial from the gallery, remain in the courtroom as Finch prepares to leave. One black gentleman finally prods Atticus's daughter, who has been watching from the gallery, to get up, saying, "Miss Jean Louise, stand up. Your father's passin'." That line of film dialogue sent an entire generation of students to law school. It suggested that the law was a profession that offered possibilities for heroism and honor, even if those qualities are accompanied by occasional defeats, such as the courtroom defeat Atticus Finch suffers.

Although more recent films continue to offer specimens of heroism among lawyers, modern films are less likely to present narratives in which heroic white lawyers represent powerless black defendants. Long before *To Kill a Mockingbird*, alternatives to the heroic lawyer story line existed. *Intruder in the Dust* (1949), for example, based on the novel of the same title by William Faulkner, presents a comparable legal setting—an African American man wrongly accused of a crime (killing a white man) who is defended by a white attorney. In *Intruder in the Dust*, however, the attorney assumes that his client is guilty and fails to represent him vigorously. Lucas Beauchamp, the accused murderer, must persuade a teenage boy—the lawyer's nephew Chick—to uncover the evidence that will exonerate him. The resulting expedition, in which an elderly secretary and a young black friend join Chick, involves digging up a grave.

More recently, in *A Time to Kill* (1996), a black man kills the men who rape his daughter as they are on their way to a courtroom to be arraigned. In this film, the father, however, is anything but a powerless victim; he is a determined and force-

In *To Kill a Mockingbird*, Gregory Peck (left) plays a white attorney assigned to defend an indigent black man (Brock Peters, right) charged with rape. *(Museum of Modern Art, Film Stills Archive)*

ful man who not only avenges his daughter's brutal rape but also participates actively in the preparation and presentation of his own subsequent defense. Similarly, in *Ghosts of Mississippi* (1996), based upon the real-life retrial of Byron de la Beckwith for the 1963 murder of civil rights leader Medgar Evers, Alex Baldwin plays the part of assistant district attorney Bobbie De-Laughter, the lawyer who brings Beckwith to trial long after his initial trial resulted in a hung jury. Although Baldwin plays a heroic character, the true hero of the film is Myrlie Evers, Medgar's wife, played by Whoopi Goldberg, who perseveres in a decades-long battle to see her husband's killer brought to justice.

Immoral Lawyers

In a culture in which nasty jokes about lawyers are popular ("How can you tell if a lawyer is

lying?" "His lips are moving."), films about criminal justice sometimes pose serious questions about the ethics of attorneys. The antilawyer spirit animating lawyer jokes often finds a comfortable ally in films that treat attorneys as having sold their souls, as in the case of the young lawyer played by Keanu Reeves who finds himself an apprentice to Satan (Al Pacino) in *The Devil's Advocate* (1997) or the even younger lawyer (Tom Cruise) hired by a Memphis law firm whose principal client is the mob in *The Firm* (1993). More often, however, films about the law dramatize less remarkable forms of immoral conduct by lawyers.

Greed and dereliction are sins sometimes laid at the doors of attorneys in films about the justice system. James Woods, for example, plays a burned-out civil rights lawyer who now spends his days counting the money he gets from drug dealers in *True Believer* (1989). In . . . *And Justice for All*, a lawyer shows up late for a court hearing. Then, he pays so little attention to the matter he is handling that his client is sentenced to jail and commits suicide. In real life, common ethical complaints lodged against lawyers include failure to attend adequately to the affairs of their clients and misappropriation of their clients' funds.

Prisons and Executions

Since the era of silent film, prison life has been a recurring film subject. Prison films, such as *The Hurricane* (1999), about Rubin "Hurricane" Carter, frequently claim to replicate—or at least be based on—real events. More often, however, prison films are simply vehicles for stock themes and plots as divorced from real prison life as cinema courtroom scenes are divorced from real-life trials. Real prison life is more about boredom and unpleasant companions than it is about escapes, such as those in *Mrs. Soffel* (1984) or *Escape from Alcatraz* (1979)—or riots, as in *The Last Castle* (2001). Sometimes, however, claims to tell a true story are well founded. *Brubaker* (1980), for example, credibly dramatizes the efforts of Arkansas prison warden Tom Merton to reform prison life in his state.

A subspecies of prison film—the execution film—frequently strives for a different kind of connection with reality, an impact on the institution of the death penalty as carried out in the United States. Not uncommonly, these films build cases against the death penalty by dramatizing executions, or near-executions, of defendants innocent of the crimes for which they are sentenced to die. *The Life of David Gale* (2003) and Clint Eastwood's *True Crime* (1999) are examples of this kind of execution film. The participants in the death-penalty debate understand that the innocent are sometimes executed, but these films help inform this debate by insisting that the innocent are not merely unnamed statistics but real individuals (or fictional characters made to stand in for real individuals).

Sometimes, though, filmmakers attempt to dramatize issues arising from the death-penalty debate without the use of innocent prisoners. Sharon Stone plays a vicious murderer whose imminent execution is the subject of *Last Dance* (1996). Although the character played by Sean Penn in *Dead Man Walking* (1995) claims not to have pulled the trigger in a murder, he is, nevertheless, a nasty piece of work. *Dead Man Walking*, the superior film, calls attention to an important reality in the death-penalty debate, when it notes that there are no rich defendants on death row. The films indict capital punishment not because it executes the innocent but because it executes only the guilty who cannot afford high-quality representation.

Timothy L. Hall

Further Reading

Bergman, Paul, and Michael Asimow. *Reel Justice: The Courtroom Goes to the Movies*. Kansas City, Mo.: Andrews and McMeel, 1996. Witty and informative summary of the plots of and legal issues raised by seventy films. The book covers both civil and criminal trials and includes sidebars covering significant legal issues raised in films about the law. The writing in the book is often more entertaining than the scripts of the films reviewed.

Black, David A. *Law in Film: Resonance and Representation*. Urbana: University of Illinois Press, 1999. This book, by a film scholar, is far more about film and film theory than it is about the law. Readers interested in modern critical theories about literature and film may find this text helpful.

Browne, Nick, ed. *Refiguring American Film Genres: History and Theory*. Berkeley: University of California Press, 1998. Covering a wide range of issues relating to various film genres, this book includes a chapter relevant to criminal justice and film, titled "God Bless Juries!," by Carol J. Clover. The chapter explores the treatment of juries in films about the law.

Chase, Anthony. *Movies on Trial: The Legal System on the Silver Screen*. New York: New Press, 2002. Although this text covers a wide variety of legally related films—including films about civil and international law—it contains a useful chapter on films relating to criminal law, including such films as *Dirty Harry* (1971) and *True Believer* (1988).

Clarens, Carlos, and Foster Hirsch. *Crime Movies*. New York: Da Capo Press, 1997. Originally published by Carlos Clarens in 1980, this book was reissued in 1997 with an afterward by Foster Hirsch covering more recent films, such as *The Untouchables* (1987) and *Pulp Fiction* (1994). As revised, the book now covers crime films made from the silent era through the last decade of the twentieth century.

Denver, John, ed. *Legal Realism: Movies as Legal Texts*. Urbana: University of Illinois Press, 1996. Collection of essays by an assortment of legal and humanities scholars. The films analyzed run the gamut from the *Godfather* trilogy to *Thelma and Louise* (1991) and *Basic Instinct* (1992).

Harris, Thomas J. *Courtroom's Finest Hour in American Cinema*. Metuchen, N.J.: Scarecrow Press, 1987. Focusing on the trial phase of the criminal justice process, this book highlights films containing memorable courtroom scenes. It contains discussions of films about civil as well as criminal trials, including films such as *Witness for the Prosecution* (1958), *Twelve Angry Men* (1957), *I Want to Live!* (1958), *Anatomy of a Murder* (1959), and *Inherit the Wind* (1960).

Leitch, Thomas. *Crime Films*. New York: Cambridge University Press, 2002. Serious treatment by a film scholar of cinematic portrayals of the criminal justice system, including discussions of films involving police and other law-enforcement personnel, lawyers and courts, and prisons.

Rafter, Nicole. *Shots in the Mirror: Crime Films and Society*. Oxford, England: Oxford University Press, 2000. This book includes a discussion of cop films, courtroom films, and prison and execution films. Although the book does not provide detailed summaries or commentaries on films, as are offered in Bergman and Asimow's *Reel Justice*, it explores broad themes about criminal justice by referring to a variety of crime films.

Sherwin, Richard K. *When Law Goes Pop: The Vanishing Line Between Law and Popular Culture*. Chicago: University of Chicago Press, 2002. This book, by a former-prosecutor-turned-law-professor, complains that the justice system is being corrupted by expectations people derive from television and film accounts of the law.

See also Attorney ethics; Bank robbery; Criminal justice system; Literature about criminal justice; Mafia; Plea bargaining; Print media; Television courtroom programs; Television crime dramas.

Fines

Definition: Monetary payments required of defendants that provide compensation to either the government or the victim

Criminal justice issues: Punishment; restorative justice; sentencing; white-collar crime

Significance: Fines are popular sanctions that have been used as alternatives to probation and prison. They are also imposed on defendants when restitution is to be made to the victims of the crimes. Fines are not as popular in the United States as in European countries but are commonly used in the United States as punishments for traffic violations and white-collar crimes.

Monetary punishments have a long history in criminal justice, dating back to before ancient Rome. Through succeeding centuries, their use decreased as prisons were used more frequently to punish criminals, and as the belief in the effectiveness of deterrence-based policies. While deterrence policies focus on decreasing the likelihood that convicted criminals will repeat their crimes, fines fulfill the goals of greater efficiency and restitution. Indeed, fines are currently becoming more popular again in the United States, through the expansion of restitution programs and increasingly critical concern about the budgets of criminal justice correctional programs.

Fines provide a number of cost-effective advantages for criminal justice, while also providing alternatives to overburdened correctional programs, such as incarceration and probation. The financial cost of prison and probation programs have been a source of controversy, and some claim that they can increase the criminal tendencies of nonviolent criminals. By contrast, fines can provide a sense of justice whereby victims and governments are repaid for the offenders' crimes, while sheltering nonviolent offenders themselves from more hardened criminals in the correctional system.

Fines are now most commonly used in the United States for minor offenses and for white-collar crime. This contrasts with their use in Europe, where fines are the preferred method of punishment for most offenses, particularly property crimes. The distinction between Europe and the United States may in part be due to the greater retributive desires of the American populace. Fines are viewed by many in the United States as too lenient to be assessed as punishments for most crimes, and ineffective as deterrents. The use of fines for punishment also generates much controversy because of the disproportionate punitive impact that they have on the rich and the poor.

Brion Sever

Further Reading

Burns, Ronald, and Michael Lynch. "Another Fine Mess . . . The Preliminary Examination of the Use of Fines by the National Highway Traffic Safety Administration." *Criminal Justice Review* 27 (2002): 1-25.

Raine, John, Eileen Dunstan, and Alan Makie. "Financial Penalties as a Sentence of the Court: Lessons of Policy and Practice from Research Magistrates Courts of England and Wales." *Criminal Justice* 3 (2003): 181-197.

Waldfogel, Joel. "Are Fines and Prison Terms Used Efficiently? Evidence on Federal Fraud Offenders." *Journal of Law and Economics* 38 (1995): 107-139.

Waring, Elin. "Incorporating Co-offending in Sentencing Models: An Analysis of Fines Imposed on Antitrust Offenders." *Journal of Quantitative Criminology* 14 (1996): 283-305.

See also Animal abuse; Color of law; Contempt of court; Drunk driving; Environmental crimes; Jaywalking; Misdemeanors; Punitive damages; Regulatory crime; Sentencing; Traffic fines; Traffic law; Trespass.

Fingerprint identification

Definition: Matching of fingerprint patterns found on surfaces to those of known persons

Criminal justice issues: Evidence and forensics; investigation; technology

Significance: Fingerprint identification is one of the longest-established and most certain methods of identifying criminal suspects and linking them to crime scenes.

Friction ridge characteristics are located on the fingers, palms, and feet of the human body. The raised ridges and furrows on tips and at the end of the first joint of the fingers have identified people for centuries. Fingerprint patterns are unique to individuals; even identical twins do not have identical fingerprints. Fingerprint patterns form in the third fetal month of human development and remain the same until death and advanced decomposition.

Ridges rise above furrows to form specific patterns that are unique to each person. Fingerprints fall into three basic patterns: arches,

---

Mark Twain and Fingerprints

Although Mark Twain never knew the word "biometrics," he might fairly be credited with introducing that science to fiction in *Pudd'nhead Wilson* (1894)—the first novel to use fingerprint evidence as a plot device. During the mid-nineteenth century, the novel's title character, attorney David Wilson, mystifies and amuses the simple people of Dawson's Landing, Missouri, by collecting their fingerprints on glass slides. For years, the villagers dismiss him as a "puddingheaded" fool—until the final chapter, when he displays his legal brilliance in a murder trial. Wilson creates a sensation by using his slides to prove the innocence of the murder suspect whom he is defending. However, that revelation is minor compared to his second use of fingerprint evidence at the trial. Drawing on glass slides he has collected over more than two decades, he proves that the culprit in the murder case is a man who was born a slave and somehow got switched with the infant son of his master in infancy. The theme of switched identities that are sorted out by fingerprint evidence gives the novel a strong claim to be called the first application of biometrics in fiction.

loops, and whorls. Subclassifications further divide the basic patterns. The pores in the skin secrete a residue that leaves traces of latent fingerprint impressions. After a person has touched a nonporous surface like glass, patent prints are visible to the eye. Plastic, or indentation, prints may be found on soft surfaces such as putty. Invisible latent prints require development with laser, powders, and chemical techniques.

Fingerprint pattern interpretation assists in the classification, searching, and suspect elimination processes. The analysis of fingerprint minutiae, such as ridge endings, dots, islands, bifurcations, and other features, allows for the specific identification of a person. Comparison of fingerprint minutiae to an individual fingerprint creates a means of personal identification.

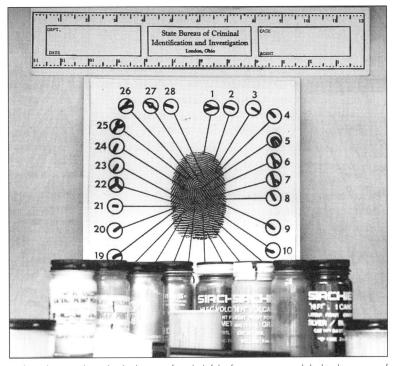

A chart showing the individual types of marks left by fingerprints stands behind an array of the various types of powders used to collect prints. *(AP/Wide World Photos)*

Elimination prints help identify family members and others who have legitimate access to the crime scene. Occasionally, witnesses or police officers will touch an object at the scene of a crime. Elimination prints help isolate those of the suspect.

Developing Fingerprints

Before beginning the collection process, examiners photograph fingerprints in place, whether the prints are visible, latent, or plastic. This procedure provides a permanent record and protects the fingerprints from any damage that may ensue as a result of the collection process. When searching for latent prints at a crime scene, examiners proceed in the least intrusive manner possible. They apply nondestructive resources to the print surface, such as lasers or a long-wave ultraviolet light source. Occasionally, a simple pen light with an oblique angle may reveal patent or latent prints. Physical and chemical methods may follow, depending on the surface.

The use of dusting powders, chemicals, and lifting applications presents a health hazard to investigators. Protective safety glasses are required for viewing prints with lasers and other light sources. Examiners wear respiratory masks and rubber gloves when applying fingerprint powder and other chemicals. When possible, this work is done in a well-ventilated area with a fume hood.

Fingerprint Computer Applications

The Federal Bureau of Investigation (FBI) maintains the national fingerprint database. State and municipal law-enforcement agencies maintain independent fingerprint record systems. Automated Fingerprint Identification System (AFIS) technology has the ability to search for individual fingerprints. This electronic database links suspects with their fingerprints. The FBI's Integrated Automated Fingerprint Identification System (IAFIS) permits state and local examiners to search other state fingerprint databases. These database files contain prints of known offenders and forensic files of unsolved cases, which contain unknown fingerprints. The purpose of these forensic files is to link offenders to unsolved cases.

Acid and Fingerprints

Criminals occasionally attempt to destroy the indentations on their fingertips with acid. However, all the minutiae down to the true dermis cannot be eliminated. Some ridge characteristics survive acid treatment, and the acid damage itself forms new fingerprint characteristics.

Formerly, searching record systems for single fingerprints could take years. The old Henry system and the former FBI extension system required all ten fingerprints for a successful search and match. As criminals rarely leave ten perfect prints at the scene of a crime, successful matches were an exceptional event in the absence of a known suspect.

Investigative Application

In one application, police were investigating serial burglary cases in a suburban community. The fingerprint expert dusted for traces of the burglar's prints. The search produced only footprints, and the same footprint patterns emerged at every case location. The preliminary and follow-up investigation centered on one known female burglar. She specialized in jewelry thefts, breaking and entering in the daytime. The offender lived less than three miles from all the crime scenes.

The fingerprint examiner obtained footprint impressions from the suspect and compared them to footprints taken from each burglary location. The expert matched twenty-four minutiae ridge characteristics from the burglar's feet to thirty other burglaries. The match involved basic minutiae ridges, such as ridge dots, endings, islands, and bifurcations. Comparisons provided a positive identification of the suspect as the one who committed the burglaries. During the subsequent interrogation process, the burglar revealed that she had worn gloves to avoid leaving fingerprint trace evidence. Furthermore, she had removed her shoes to avoid shoe impressions. Although wearing gloves did avoid a fingerprint match in the AFIS and IAFIS databases, the barefoot burglar overlooked the possibility that her foot impressions would exhibit the same points of identification as her fingers.

Thomas E. Baker

Further Reading

Becker, Ronald F. *Criminal Investigation*. Gaithersburg, Md.: Aspen Publications, 2000. Handbook for use by crime laboratory personnel.

Cole, Simon A. *Suspect Identities: A History of Fingerprinting and Criminal Identification*. Cambridge, Mass.: Harvard University Press, 2001. History of the development of human identification techniques since the seventeenth century.

Evans, Colin. *The Casebook of Forensic Detection: How Science Solved One Hundred of the World's Most Baffling Crimes*. New York: John Wiley & Sons, 1998. Fascinating and often entertaining histories of one hundred famous and not-so-famous crimes solved with forensics from 1751 to 1991. Fingerprinting is one of fifteen forensics fields covered.

Genge, Ngaire E. *The Forensic Casebook: The Science of Crime Scene Investigation*. New York: Ballantine, 2002. Clearly written explanations of all aspects of forensics; ideal for younger readers.

James, Stuart H., and Jon J. Nordby. *Forensic Science: An Introduction to Scientific and Investigative Techniques*. 2d ed. Boca Raton, Fla.: CRC Press, 2005. Well-illustrated, clearly written, and up-to-date guide to all fields of forensics.

Saferstein, Richard. *Criminalistics: An Introduction to Forensic Science*. 8th ed. Upper Saddle River, N.J.: Prentice-Hall, 2003. Comprehensive introductory textbook to forensic techniques.

See also Booking; Burglary; Chain of custody; Cold cases; Computer information systems; Crime labs; Crime scene investigation; Criminal history record information; Criminal records; DNA testing; Document analysis; Evidence, rules of; Forensics; Latent evidence; Shoe prints and tire-tracks; Trace evidence.